ALAN WHO?

My Life So Far:
Part Memoir/Part Journal (1939-2019)

Or how I left Boardman, Ohio for the big city

ALAN G. SPENCER

Alan Who ?
Copyright © 2021 by Alan G. Spencer

For information contact :
aspencer1616@gmail.com

ISBN : 9798713792503

First Edition : April 2021

DEDICATION

In memory of my father David and mother Esther, to my darling wife Penny and to the rest of my dear family.

CONTENTS

ACKNOWLEDGMENTS

This story would not have been possible without the assistance of many individuals. Thank you to David and Esther Shwartz, Linda Waldman, Penny Spencer, Bennett and Marni Spencer, Ronna and Ted Belinky, Alan Appelbaum, Jerry Aronson, Guy Guilbert, Bill DeCicco, Scott Meyer, Lois Camberg among many other individuals too numerous to mention. And finally, I'd liked to acknowledge Rich Aver for suggesting the main title of this book, *Alan Who?*

INTRODUCTION

I set out to write a history of my life. It is not just a memoir because I've included journal entries of day-to-day activities along the way. Not every day is included and the journal parts are mainly toward the end of this book. It is something I always wanted to do but didn't seem to create the time to actually sit down at my computer to make it happen until I started writing it on Friday, September 28, 2006. Since that time, whenever I get the urge, incidents and feelings about my life pop into my brain, I sit down at my computer and continue to create my story.

When grandson Danny was almost one and one-half years old, I thought it was important to start the process of writing about my life so my children, grandchildren and future generations would know about what my life was like growing up and into adulthood. Writing this book, forced me to remember things I had long forgotten and brought back a wonderful and interesting journey into my past. Although this book is written in chronological order, the reader does not have to be read it from the beginning to the end in sequence. I've created attention-grabbing chapters titles and bold headlines so the reader can jump around and read what seems interesting. It is also part journal, so day-to-day activities may not seem that interesting but I wanted to include as much as I could into this book.

Another reason I wanted to write this book was to be able to share my life with the love of my life, my darling wife, Penny. She is my best friend, has been the light of my world and a fantastic companion for over 52 years. Penny knows me like no other and this book will help her bring back some of the treasured memories we spent together. Although I am 79 years old at this writing, my story begins in 1939 when my mother met my father two years before I was born.

ROOTS STARTED IT ALL

After watching *Roots*, Alex Hailey's television mini-series in the fall of 1977, I became fascinated with genealogy and the tracing of my ancestors. I was very active in Jewish genealogy and was involved as a founding member of the Jewish Genealogical Society of Illinois. I was also one of the catalysts who sparked the founding of the International Jewish Genealogical Society. Later in this book, I cover more about my involvement in Jewish genealogy.

Even before *Roots*, I started collecting data about my family's history, first interviewing my father's mother and father (grandparents) Ben and Rose Shwartz, about stories of them growing up and what life was like in Poland. My grandmother lived in a large metropolitan city, Warsaw, and my grandfather was from a small town, Opatow, about 70 miles south of Warsaw. I also talked to my parents about what it was like growing up in Struthers, Ohio and Brooklyn, New York.

When genealogy software first made it easy to enter family data and keeping records of ancestors, I started to really get motivated to wanted to know more about my family. It would have been nice to be able to read all of the details of my grandparent's life. Oh, how I wish my grandparents had written about their life in Poland and Romania during the late 1800s and early 1900s.

WRITING THIS BOOK WAS A CHALLENGE

Writing this book has been a task since I never kept a real journal until recently. There were many sources I used to write this book. Fortunately, one of these sources was my mother who kept memorabilia from my childhood that helped me remember dates, places and times of certain life events.

Other sources included letters Penny and I wrote to my parents and the metal film cans of Super 8 movies I took that enabled me to recall many events of my life. A huge help were the detailed labels on the film cans with specific dates of events.

Another important source of valuable material was created in 2007 by the Boardman High School class of June 1959 of which I was a graduate. Dave Beede, one of my classmates, created a Google Group, two years before our 2009 50th high school class reunion. As a result of this on-line group, I was able to recall events in my grade school and high school life through emails as my classmates recalled events, names and happenings. My high school graduating class has been very close and Bill DeCicco, my best friend in high school, who is part of this on-line group, is able to remember details of his life and has shared them with all of our Google group. Another valuable source of material came when I started cleaning our garage and I found old personal bank checks that had key dates on them that provided additional information on various events in my life.

After my mother moved to Cleveland, I asked her to write her memoir and she did. Over a period of several years, I would enter her hand-written notes into my computer, print them, then each time I visited her in Cleveland, I would ask her to make corrections and additions. I now have a permanent record of her life. I interviewed my father and mother on audiocassette about their life and will have the tapes transcribed in the near future. Eventually, I want to write a history of our Czernikowski family that will be a real challenge.

My story starts on Saturday, July 29, 1939 when my mother met my father with Chapter One, Before the Beginning.

C H A P T E R   O N E
Before The Beginning

THE FOLLOWING EXCERPT WAS ADAPTED FROM MY MOTHER'S MEMOIR

SATURDAY, JULY 29, 1939: MOTHER & FATHER MEET

Here's the set-up: My father was home for the summer from teaching high school English in Puerto Rico and was working in his father's (Ben Shwartz) grocery store located at 124 Poland Avenue in Struthers, Ohio as he had done for the past three summers.

Margaret (Peggy) Weily, my father's first cousin, had been a student at Ohio University and was a sorority sister of my mother. In the early summer of 1939, Peggy invited her friend Esther Sohmer, my mother, and her sister, Elsie Sohmer, native New Yorkers from Brooklyn, to visit Struthers to see her new baby boy, Corky, who had been born on June 24.

Esther and her sister Elsie took the Pennsylvania Railroad to Youngstown to see Corky. Peg asked her first cousin, Dave Shwartz, to be nice to Esther, her invited guest and her sister Elsie. On Saturday, July 29, 1939, my mother was sitting in Peg Weily's living room writing a postcard to her New York family, when David (my father) came into the house and was formally introduced. They went out every night for one week during her visit. Elsie went out with Peg's younger brother, Ralph during the same week.

"I saw Dave every day except one. He had a teaching position through the United States Department of Insular Possessions in Puerto Rico for three years, as jobs were hard to find during the Depression. He taught high school English in Arecibo and Mayaguez. Luckily for me, his parents told him to settle down, just before I came."

"We hit it off right away. I stayed a week and when my sister, Elsie and I left, David gave me a letter telling me not to open it until the train passed Pittsburgh. Inside was a lovely letter plus his picture with this written on it in Spanish. "Always faithful."

The outside of the envelope said,
"A Senorita Esther Sohmer
de Senor David Shwartz"
Bien Viaje Muchachita Para Siempre
Inside he wrote:
Sunday 8:45 a.m. August 5, 1939
Dear Essie Sohmer:

"You know, I certainly am sitting here in a genuine pensive mood and for once I don't crave solitude. Well, I really don't feel lonely, because at this moment I have you on my mind and in my heart. Yes siree, I'm even enclosing a picture of myself which I hope will satisfactorily meet with your approval. Hmm-funny people like me seldom take good pictures.

1

Golly, I hate to think of you leaving this night...our lovely week together has flown like the night. Between singing, dancing, talking, worrying and loving--it all has been marvelous--almost too marvelous to show capability of expression. Es, I don't believe either of us will ever forget each other, because God Himself had thrown us together to the extent where perfect harmony has been fully enjoyed--and when that sort of thing occurs--it's needless for me to mention more.

Had a long talk with both Dad & Mother about you--in my sedate and reticent manner--you know. Without them knowing my interest in you--they have acclaimed you a very fine type. My parents and sisters are harsh judges and when they like a thing, it must be full of fine characteristics......that's you. My mother has always liked a quiet type of girl, sensible, and feminine. There again you shine...that's swell...actually so. Why?...I'll tell you when I come to N.Y.C.

Hoping that you'll arrive safely in New York City and be more contented with your findings than ever. Take good care of Elsie & give her a great big kiss for me."

Bye sweet Essie,

Lovingly,

Dave

"He wrote to me and I answered. I received a telegram later in August that he was coming to visit me at our family home at 1760 E. 10th Street in Brooklyn. I met him at Pennsylvania Station on 34th Street in Manhattan and was a little shocked and amused to see his luggage that consisted of a twenty-pound brown grocery bag. During the summer, he worked at his father's grocery store, Shwartz's Market in Struthers. His explanation about the luggage was that he was so excited about seeing me again that he took the first thing that came to his mind.

Even though his luggage wasn't first class, he made a great impression on my family. We decided to marry but he hesitated to give me his Masonic ring as a symbol. He hated to part with it. My family was delighted with the forthcoming marriage, as I was, too.

Although I had met his parents before, as well as his two sisters when I visited Peg in July, he and his dad came to look my family and me over in September. We went to the New York World's Fair in Flushing Meadow, New York. Evidently, we all passed the test because it became official."

A BROOKLYN, NEW YORK WEDDING

The wedding date was set for Sunday, October 29, 1939, exactly three months after we had met. The ceremony and reception were held at the Chateau D'Or in Brooklyn, a catering hall. It was a 2:30 p.m. wedding. David wasn't too happy about wearing a morning suit (a tuxedo with tails and a top hat) but he was handsome. He was willing to put it on if it made me happy. It was also the custom for a wedding at that time of day. David's parents, Ben and Rose Shwartz, his two sisters and their husbands, Dorothy and Morris Lockshin, Gert and Dr. Sam Epstein, his cousins, Peg and Fred Weily, Ida

Dorothy and Jay (Cohen) Hart all came from Struthers for the wedding. Elsie was my maid of honor and Morris Lockshin was David's best man.

For some reason, before the wedding, my nephew, Shelly Pressler, age 9, locked himself in the only bathroom before he came out after a few hours. We were leaving for Atlantic City on our honeymoon in the evening but Sylvia and Ben Brecher insisted that we attend a party she had for our out-of-town and Brooklyn friends. It was a reunion time and lovely."

"When David and I first decided to marry, he wrote to Puerto Rico to ask for a year's leave of absence. I had no desire to reside there when Dad told me of the vermin that were prevalent. Not for me since I had been to Havana, Cuba and saw that poverty was rampant and on a par with Puerto Rico."

On our honeymoon, we walked everywhere in Atlantic City and I caught a cold. When we returned, I had laryngitis. I had visited Struthers again before the wedding to find an apartment. In 1939, there weren't any apartments to rent in Struthers. The ex-mayor had lost his wife and he converted his three-bedroom house into a suitable place. We had to share the bathroom. We kept one bedroom—his furniture and turned one bedroom into a living room and one to a kitchen. The bathroom part bothered us, but we had no choice."

OUR FIRST HOME

"The apartment was only temporary, so we decided to build our own home at 152 Morrison Street in Struthers, Ohio. We looked at several before we chose a two-story Cape Cod with four rooms downstairs, one of which we turned into a den and then two bedrooms upstairs. The one bathroom was located upstairs.

In June 1940, we were traveling by car to New York to attend a cousin's wedding. That day I knew for sure that I was pregnant. We were both delighted as well as our families when we told them. This trip was before any turnpikes. I was feeling nauseous and asked David to stop at a service station. We were so excited talking about the expected baby that we missed our turn off and went 20 miles out of our way. We had to turn around and retrace our route. My morning sickness lasted for five months; all day and every day. David fixed most of his own meals, though we usually ate Sunday dinner with his parents in their home on Poland Avenue.

My sister Elsie was marrying Joe Davidson who lived three houses from ours at 1760 East 10th Street in Brooklyn. Their wedding was scheduled for September 15, 1940 and on doctor's orders, I could not go to the wedding because of my condition. I couldn't believe Elsie would get married without me being there."

CHAPTER TWO
The Early Years

STRUTHERS, OHIO

"My due date for Alan's birth was February 28, 1941. Our new house was to be ready for occupancy on February 15; however, the house wasn't actually in move-in condition until Saturday, March 15 as David told me when he came home for lunch that day. He was working full-time at his father's supermarket in Struthers. My labor was progressing when David came home for dinner. He asked me if I would object if he showered before he took me to the hospital that was on the north side of Youngstown and quite a distance from Struthers. He didn't know how long we would be there. Even today, I laugh when I think of his reason for delaying my trip to the hospital.

Alan was born in Youngstown's Northside Hospital about 4:00 a.m. on Sunday March 16, 1941. He weighed 6 lbs. 12 oz. The pregnancy was worse than the birth. I was asleep. Alan was delivered by Dr. McClenahan. I had packed all of our things to be moved to the new house before I went to the hospital, so David moved the day after, March 17 to 152 Morrison Street in Struthers, Ohio. "

(A side note: My mother told me that she liked Alan Ladd, the popular movie actor at the time, and so my parents decided to name me Alan. I was named after my mother's father, Abraham Sohmer. My middle name, Gerald, was chosen after my grandmother Rose Shwartz's father, Gabriel Turkus who died in Palestine and is buried on the Mount of Olives in Jerusalem).

"My sister Sadie and her husband Harry Dollinger and my mother, Luisa, came to Struthers for the bris held at our new home a week after Alan was born which was the following Sunday, March 23. We stayed at the hospital for eight days, the custom at that time. Then I was confined to the upstairs for several days. Norman Lockshin, Alan's first cousin, was born exactly three weeks before him. (My Chicago friend Ray Pershing made me laugh when he told me his bris was successful but he didn't walk for one year after it).

Alan was really a wonderful baby. When people visited our house, they remarked many times that you didn't know there was a baby in the house.

Looking out the window the second day home, I noticed smoke and fire coming from the back of our garage. The house was diagonally across from Struthers High School at the end of the street. Some students had been in the habit of using our lot as a short cut to and from school. They were smoking there and started a grass fire but it could have been worse. The fire department came and put it out. Excitement!

Dorothy and Morris had cousin Marilyn who was four years old when Norman, their second child was born. Alan and Norman became great friends and grew up like brothers. In the summer months, Dorothy and I would cool off the boys by putting them in our double kitchen sink."

4

(My side comment—I found a certificate in my mother's archives that said "I was successfully vaccinated by David Hauptman, M.D. on September 15, 1941"). We must have been visiting New York at the time since Dr. Hauptman was my mother's family physician in Brooklyn.

(I had a favorite monkey doll named *"Go Go."* It had a cloth and stuffed body and a hard head but I don't know what the head was made of. It could have been papier mache or some type of early plastic. I don't really remember the monkey but I've seen old photos of it. I also have no idea who named the monkey since I was an infant when I got it).

CHAPTER THREE
World War II and Living in Brooklyn

"Alan was ten months old on December 7, 1941 when Japan attacked Pearl Harbor. It was a Sunday afternoon and David and I were riding in the car listening to the car radio when we heard the news about the Japanese attack. We were at war with Japan and then a short time later with Germany and Italy.

Dave decided to work at the Ravenna Arsenal to help the war effort. He received great letters of recommendation and even though I was seven months pregnant with Linda, he was told he would be drafted. He decided to drive to Cleveland to plead his case in front of the regional Selective Service Board. The board ignored what the arsenal said of needing him."

THURSDAY, OCTOBER 21, 1943—DAVID WAS ASSIGNED AS A CHIEF PETTY OFFICER—U.S. NAVY—BASIC TRAINING

"Since David was a college graduate, the Cleveland Draft Board made him a Chief Petty Officer in the U.S. Navy and he was in the Seabees. He was scheduled to leave to go into basic training on Thursday, October 21, 1943, so he could go overseas for the war effort. The day before he left Youngstown, Alan and I boarded a New York bound Pennsylvania Railroad train to New York City to live with my mother's family at the house on 10th Street in Brooklyn.

We lived with my mother, Lizzie, my sister Fay, my brother-in-law, Murray Pressler and their son, Alan's first cousin, Shelly. Shelly was eleven years older than Alan. That was an awful time. [Side Note: As a young boy I can remember having to turn off the lights in the house just in case there would be an air raid by an enemy. I also remember ration stamps for food, as there were only certain items you could buy because of the war effort].

David entered into basic training at Camp Peary in Williamsburg, Virginia. The facility was "Home of the Seabees" and at that time, also a training camp for the U.S. Marines and the Navy trained who together. Basic training by the Marines was tough, but Dave got through it."

(Note: David's official rank was Chief Petty Officer, CSK, 858-18-83 29th Special Battalion, Platoon 379 Area E).

My mother kept seventeen of my father's post cards written to her from basic training and before he left for the Pacific. The post cards were addressed to Mrs. David Shwartz 1760 East 10th Street   Brooklyn, 23 New York.

The following are excerpts from some of those post cards I have in my possession and they are being included in this memoir.

MONDAY, OCTOBER 25, 1943

(Front of postcard had United States Naval Construction Battalions-WE BUILD AND FIGHT WITH ALL OUR MIGHT) With the flying bee and Seabees in a circle)

Dear Esther and Alan:

Thought I would be fitted up for my uniform this a.m. but have to wait until this p.m. Walked 2 miles in heavy downpour of rain and got soaked-but I guess I can take it-others do. All I know is I had a good home when I left right...left...right...left. All my love, Dave.

WEDNESDAY EVE, OCTOBER 28, 1943

(Front of post card had Seabee Commando Landing Practice, Camp Peary, Virginia.

Hi There Mom!

Before this is over, I'll be a climber. Had a fair today. All the boys are going over to the movies tonight just across the way. Would like to be going with you. Day after tomorrow is our anniversary—will be thinking of you all day. No mail yet. Maybe tomorrow. Love, Dave

FRIDAY NIGHT OCTOBER 30, 1943

(Front of postcard is a picture of a sign that has Camp Peary hanging from a wooden frame)

Honey: Received your sweet letter that I will try to answer tomorrow. Dear, please have Fay pick me up some band-aides. Enclose 4 or 5 in an envelope when you write me. Thanx dear. Hello to all from me. Dave

SUNDAY, NOVEMBER 1, 1943

11:30 a.m. (front of post card Seabees Unloading Supplies, Camp Peary, Virginia) Sent from Camp Peary, Virginia

Dear Esther:

I was going to surprise you by calling New York by phone, but there were too many fellows lined up. They only have one public telephone, I discovered and it's practically an impossibility to get at it.

Plan to study all afternoon. Tonight, I'm going to the movies. "Behind the Rising Sun" is playing.

Love to all, Dave

MONDAY, NOVEMBER 29, 1943

(Front of postcard photo of Raleigh Tavern and Colonial Coach, Williamsburg, Virginia) Sent from Camp Peary, Virginia

Dearest Esther: Dropped over to Williamsburg for a couple of hours-came back and was in bed by 10:30. A number of boys stayed out overnight but I couldn't see it. The town is very small & very quiet-typical southern aristocratic town much like Poland, Ohio. I'll write later. Dave

(Side Note: The earliest recollection of my mother reading me a story was back in Struthers when she took out a book from the Struthers Public Library. *The Five Chinese Brothers* is a children's book, purportedly based on an "old Chinese folktale" about five brothers who each have a remarkable talent and use their abilities to save the life of one of their siblings when he is convicted of a crime, he was not able to prevent committing. The book was written in 1938 by Claire Huchet Bishop and is still available in paperback form today. In hindsight this was not a good book to read to a very young person).

I also recall another book my mother read to me about the duck Flibbity Jibbit. Junket, a Danish dessert and its trademark Flibbity Jibbit have been a favorite of children since the 1940s. This unique dessert is based on Scandinavia's famous red pudding and is a light, easily prepared Rennet custard dessert which creates a tasty pudding, pie filling or glaze.]

TUESDAY, DECEMBER 21, 1943—SISTER LINDA IS BORN

"Linda was born on December 21, 1943 at Brooklyn Jewish Hospital. My sister Fay took me to the hospital and David was notified of Linda's birth by telegram, finding it on his cot the next morning when he returned from a hike.

"David got leave over New Year's 1943 and saw Linda when she was ten days old. After basic training, a few months later on May 10, 1944, he left for Port Hueneme, California before shipping out to the Pacific area via San Francisco.

Before he left for Port Hueneme, Alan and I went by train from Brooklyn, New York to Struthers, Ohio to visit Dave's parents. Fay and my mother took care of Linda while we were away.

"Before David left to go overseas, we decided how I would know where he was stationed. It was on Guam in the Mariana Islands. He was the supervisor of the docks there, working twelve hours on and twelve hours off. It was so hot the perspiration dropped on his letters and left blots. He was really a stevedore, in charge of loading and unloading ships that brought war supplies to Guam for our armed forces in the Pacific. We each wrote daily, sometimes days would go by with no mail and then I'd get many letters. That was the same for both of us. My mother, Louisa, was wonderful to us. Fay and Shelly lived with us and Murray came home several times a week from working as an attorney in Newark, New Jersey. My sister Elsie, her husband Joe and Arleen, their daughter, lived close by as did my sister Sadie and her husband, Harry Dollinger.

The following are excerpts from more post cards sent by my father.

(Apparently my father took a troupe train to Camp Rousseau, California through the southern part of the United States).

WEDNESDAY, MORNING MAY 11, 1944

(Front of postcard Fountain Square and Carew Tower at Night, Cincinnati, Ohio) 7:25 a.m. in Cincy eating breakfast in station. Love you always, Hello to Linda and Alan   Dave

WEDNESDAY, MAY 11, 1944

(Front of postcard photo of Brown and Williamson Tobacco Corporation, Louisville, Kentucky) Manufacturers of Raleigh. Wings and Kool Cigarettes and Sir Walter Raleigh Smoking Tobacco. 2:00 p.m. Best wishes, David Love to the kiddies. Post Marked Louisville, Kentucky.

WEDNESDAY, MAY 11, 1944

(Front of postcard photo of Brown and Williamson Tobacco Corporation, Louisville, Kentucky) 3:00 p.m. Dearest Essie: Just ate chow & had to say hello again. Will write a little later. Dave.

THURSDAY, MAY 12, 1944

Sent from Cincinnati, Ohio Hi Honey, Southern Indiana—first time in this section—beautiful. Going at swell clip. I know you're going with me every mile. Dave

THURSDAY, MAY 12, 1944

Sent from Little Rock, Arkansas

Hi Honey. Love, Dave

THURSDAY, MAY 12, 1944

Sent from Texarkana, Arkansas

Doing well Essie. Lovingly, Dave

SATURDAY MAY 14, 1944

Sent from Tucson, Arizona USO Troops in Transit Lounge

Honey, I'm finally on the edge of California State. Happy Mother's Day. Your husband, Dave. Kisses to Alan and Linda.

TUESDAY, JULY 18, 1944

(Front of postcard photo of United States Navy Landing, Long Beach, California) sent from Port Hueneme, California—Honey: Received a letter from Aunt Minnie. She liked the picture very much. She mentioned in her letter that Aunt Margaret just came back from the hospital. What was wrong with her? Dot also wrote & liked the picture too. I'm beginning to believe it must have been a good one. Wally is home from overseas. Love, Dave.

SATURDAY, JULY 22, 1944

(Front of postcard. Photo of the Hollywood Bowl entrance and Cahuenga Pass Freeway, Hollywood, California) sent from Port Hueneme (US Naval Base), California—Dearest: Just a little word mid-afternoon to say hello. I'll probably get a chance to write you later on. Waiting for a letter from you at 5 o'clock. Your loving husband, Dave

MONDAY, JULY 24, 1944

(Front of postcard is a photo of a Boeing B-17C Flying Fortress in flight over California) sent from Port Hueneme (US Naval Base), California

My Dearest: Just a little word of encouragement before going out on detail this morning. Rested well last night and feel like a million this morning. Hope to receive a letter from you to-day-haven't heard since Saturday morning. I'll be gone all day but I will write tonight. Happy thoughts, Dave. All my love to the folks.

MONDAY, JULY 31, 1944

(Front of postcard photo of Ventura County Court House, Ventura, California) sent from Port Hueneme (US Naval Base), California

7:00 a.m. Dearest; Spent entire weekend with Aunt Marie and Albert. Didn't have any time this morning to write to you—letter will follow. Had a nice quiet rest and wonderful meals. Aunt Marie says she is waiting to hear from you. Called Aaron's house, but they weren't at home. Your loving husband, Dave.

[My father is referring to his uncle Aaron Turkus, his Aunt Marie and my grandmother, Rose's brother Aaron who lived in California.]

THURSDAY, AUGUST 4, 1944

(Front of postcard photo of Ventura County Court House, Ventura, California) sent from Port Hueneme (US Naval Base), California

7:30 p.m. Dearest Es: Two and half full days and no letter from you—anything wrong at home? I take it that the mails must be held up. If I don't get a letter tomorrow, I'll be on the verge of real worry. Hope everything is all right. Write real soon, please honey. All my love to everyone at home. Love, Dave

THURSDAY, AUGUST 10, 1944

On this day, the United States armed forces captured the island of Guam from the Japanese. At this point, I am assuming my father left California for Guam sometime near the end of August 1944. Guam was a strategic location for the United States. Ships were now able to unload supplies and equipment to help defeat the Japanese in the Pacific.

FRIDAY, AUGUST 11, 1944

(Front of post card Lockheed P-38 Lightning Interceptor in Flight Over California

Dearest Esther: Received your card this afternoon. Glad you and Alan had a chance to go to the beach and get cooled off, even if the sun wasn't out. Am not sure whether I will get a chance to go to L.A. this weekend or not. I take every opportunity to get out of camp. Lots different than my terrific existence in Peary. Thank goodness. Loads of Love, Dave

(Back of post card: The Lockheed P-38 Lightning Interceptor has a speed in excess of 400 miles an hour. It is designed to fly at altitudes from 30,000 to 40,000 feet).

THE SUMMER OF 1945

"The summer of 1945, the Presslers, Davidsons, my mom, Luisa, Alan and Linda and I rented a bungalow in the Catskills on Loch Sheldrake, New York.

ALAN'S FIRST FISHING EXPERIENCCE

On one occasion, Shelly took Alan fishing in a rowboat on the lake. They were trolling for bass. Shelly told Alan to hold on to the fishing rod and not to let go no matter what. Shelly started rowing the boat with his back to Alan. He happened to look back to see Alan just about to go over the side of the boat. Alan's fishing line had hit a snag and his fishing line was stuck on the bottom of the lake, probably caught on a rock. The fishing rod was pulling Alan over the side of the boat but Shelly caught him before he fell in the water."

LIVING IN BROOKLYN, NEW YORK

As a young boy, while living in Brooklyn, I remember going to my first motion picture, the animated film *Pinocchio*, produced by Walt Disney. I had never been in a movie theater and as I remember, I loved the movie. I believe my cousin Shelly took me, but I can't recall. To this day, I have a fondness for the story and the film. During my 60th birthday party at our condo's clubhouse in Scottsdale, a DVD of *Pinocchio* was showing on a screen.

During the World War II, I can also remember going to Madison Square Garden to see the Ringling Bros. Barnum & Bailey Circus. I must have been around 5 years old but I can't remember who took me. I do remember the clowns and especially the ones who drove around the rings in a very small car. When the car stopped, many clowns got out. This was very funny to me because the car was so small it was hard to believe that so many clowns could get out of such a small car.

During our stay in Brooklyn, my uncle Joe Davidson took me to see the 1945 Macy's Thanksgiving Day Parade. I barely remember the event but as I recall the streets were very crowded with people. The giant balloons were very impressive for a little boy.

On many occasions, my Uncle Harry and Aunt Sadie Dollinger would take the family to dinner at Lundy's Restaurant in Brooklyn. The famous seafood restaurant was located on Sheepshead Bay very close to Coney Island and about three miles from our East 10th Street home. Throughout the late 1940s and into the 1950s, every time our family visited Brooklyn, we went to Lundy's and Uncle Harry would treat us. I can't remember exactly what I ate there because it was before I started eating fish but it might have been flounder, one of their signature dishes. I remember, all the waiters were African American, wore white gloves and served food like you were on a southern plantation. This restaurant made a deep impression on me.

EARLY LOVE OF CARS AND OUR BROOKLYN NEIGHBORS

During the war, there was a family living almost directly across the street from our home named Cardin. Mr. and Mrs. Cardin had a son, Sherman who was my cousin Shelly's friend and same age and a daughter named Bella, a little older than Sherman. Bella was a beautiful redhead with a body to match.

As a youngster, I loved cars and would sit on the front steps with Mr. Cardin and point out the makes and years of the cars as they drove up and down 10th Street. He was my substitute father when my own father was overseas stationed in Guam during World War II.

Next door to the East 10th Street house on the north side of us, lived the Lair's. Mr. Lair had a thick black handlebar mustache and drove a black 1939 four-door Packard sedan that was always parked in front of his house. He had two daughters Rea and Anita. Rea married my uncle Joe's brother, Ruby Davidson who happened to live several houses down the street from 1760 East 10th Street.

On the south side of our house, the Rosenzweigs lived. I used to play with Arnold, a little older than his sister Ann and me, who was my age. We kept in touch with them for a little while but lost contact with them when my aunt Elsie and uncle Joe Davidson sold the family house on East 10th Street and moved to Queens in Long Island.

A FUNNY STORY WITH MY COUSIN SHELLY

One time my cousin Shelly, already in high school at the time, decided to take me to a neighborhood Kings Highway bowling alley and pool hall. I think a friend of his might may have been working there as a pinsetter. In those days, there was no automatic pin setting bowling machines that put the pins back after a bowling ball was rolled down the alley and the pins were knocked down. Pin boys did the job. When asked by my Aunt Fay where we went, my cousin replied to his mother, *"to the Yeshiva."* For many years after that incident, I thought bowling alleys and pool halls were called *Yeshivas.*

BRIGHTON BEACH—A VERY MEMORABLE EXPERIENCE

One summer weekend day in 1948 when my mother, sister and I were visiting her family in Brooklyn, New York, I had a chance to go to Brighton Beach and swim in the Atlantic Ocean. Bella Cardin was a beautiful tall redhead living across the street from our family home and an older sister to Sherman, my cousin Shelly's friend. Bella who must have been in college at the time convinced my mother it would be a fine idea and fun for me if she could take only me to Coney Island and Brighton Beach to go swimming. My mother must have thought it would be fine, so she let me go with Bella. Bella had a boyfriend and his job was delivering to grocery stores around Brooklyn bagels in an old Chevrolet panel delivery truck. The panel truck had no windows on each side with two small windows in the back double door with no seats in the back part, just a driver and passenger seat. I'm not sure my mother knew how we would be going to the beach. Providing no specific details, Bella must have told my mother her boyfriend would drive us there. My mother probably wouldn't have allowed me to go with Bella if she knew how we would be going.

So off we drove to Brighton Beach with Bella sitting in the passenger seat next to her boyfriend and me in the back of a small panel delivery truck, sitting on the floor with bags of bagels all around me and very little to grab to steady myself. This situation was not very safe holding onto the side of the panel truck with no seat. So here I am bouncing down Coney Island Avenue toward Brighton Beach sitting on the floor of a bagel delivery truck with bagels everywhere with no seat and no seat belt. I believe Bella's boyfriend dropped us off at the beach because he had bagel deliveries to make. Once we got to Brighton Beach, Bella was responsible for me so she could not let me out of her sight.

After swimming in the Atlantic Ocean, I was taken into the women's locker room. For the first time, I saw naked women taking showers and walking around. The shower stalls were open so you could see everything. This was a revelation to me and it stuck in my memory for many years. I stood there in amazement taking in the sights as this left a lasting impression on a little boy and by the way, Bella was a true redhead.

SATURDAY, MAY 12, 1945—VE DAY

On May 12, 1945, the European part of World War II ended with VE Day (Victory in Europe). A few days before, President, Franklin Delano Roosevelt died and Harry Truman became President of the United States. The war in the Pacific ended with two atomic bombs dropped on Japan, the first on Hiroshima and a few days later, the second bomb on Nagasaki. It was August 14, 1945. There was wild rejoicing everywhere on the Allies side. General MacArthur signed a peace treaty on the battleship Missouri in September. My father came back to the states (California) on a Navy ship in December, 1945 and was officially honorably discharged on Tuesday, January 7, 1946, but did not get to Brooklyn to see us until after my mother's January 12th birthday.

(Side Note: My sister and I knew my dad because the entire family talked about him all the time he was away in Guam and we saw his pictures. As a five-year-old, the image is vivid in my mind and I can remember my father coming home from being overseas in the Pacific. I was sitting on the bench in front of our

Brooklyn home and saw him walking down East 10th Street coming from Kings Highway. I felt excited to see him and nervous too. Linda met him for the first time when she was two years old. He was as happy to be home as we were to have him).

"When David came home on a Friday, he said he had to visit his parents because he had a civilian Navy job in Long Beach, New York and was to start on Monday. While in Struthers, he was able to accomplish a lot. He bought a car and sold our home to a friend he met walking down the street, Lush Irwin by name. He never consulted me. He thought we'd be living in Brooklyn.

We stayed in Brooklyn for 8 months but the commute from Brooklyn to Long Beach Long Island was not a happy time for my husband who longed for life in a small town".

AUGUST 14, 1945—VJ DAY—VICTORY OVER JAPAN DAY

With the bombing of Hiroshima on Monday, August 6 and Nagasaki on Thursday, August 9, 1945, it was announced on this day that Japan had unconditionally surrendered to the Allied forces, effectively ending World War II. This was a joyous day in our household because we knew my father would be coming   home.

CHAPTER FOUR
Our Move Back To Ohio

OUR FAMILY MOVED BACK TO STRUTHERS, OHIO

After eight months of trying to live in Brooklyn, my parents decided to move back to Struthers, Ohio and our family stayed with my grandparents for a short time. While living in Struthers, I remember briefly attending kindergarten and my teacher's name was Mrs. Dunn. I don't think I went the entire year because we moved to Boardman in 1947. I was also sick a lot and probably missed many days of school.

The Sexton Street School was within walking distance of my grandparent's house at 168 Poland Avenue and I can remember walking to school with my mother and seeing a white Peking duck that was a pet to one of the neighbors near the school. I would look at this white pet duck in the front yard. I'm not sure if the duck was on some type of leach or rope so it wouldn't walk or fly away. It seemed to be always there every time my mother walked me to school and it stayed in my memory as a young child.

My parents bought a house in Boardman, a very small suburb on the south side of Youngstown. After World War II, the township of Boardman was rapidly expanding as veterans began buying houses for their family. In 1947, our four-member family moved to a small two-bedroom house at 89 Shadyside Drive in Boardman and I started first grade. There is more about my first-grade experience in a few pages.

OUR HOME ON SHADYSIDE DRIVE IN BOARDMAN

The Shadyside house had one big bedroom that seemed like an attic upstairs where Linda and I slept. Downstairs there was a kitchen, living room, dining room and one bedroom where my parents slept. There was only one bathroom. The single-car garage was detached. My cousin Shelly was attending Kent State University at the time and would periodically come to visit us during his breaks. I can't remember where he slept during his visit, probably in the living room.

There were trolley (streetcar) tracks at the end of our street going down Southern Boulevard to downtown Youngstown and because my mother did not drive, we used to take the trolley to the Uptown area where my father had the store or we'd go downtown too. Eventually the bus line came out our way with stops on Market Street about one block away and the trolley line disappeared. Freight trains would periodically use the trolley tracks that were still there and a cement company on route 224 and Southern Boulevard used the old trolley line for deliveries.

OUR SHADYSIDE DRIVE NEIGHBORS

Cecil Shryock and his family lived in the house to the right of us on Shadyside Drive. They had a daughter who used to baby-sit Linda and me. Across the street lived the Martinco family and they had a son named Terry who was a real troublemaker. I think he changed his name to Martin or his family did. Terry was a year or two older than me and many years later he married Tina Passarelli, our neighbor directly across the street on Stillson Place, our next house. The Martins had three children and eventually got divorced.

JACK AND JILL KIDDIE STORES AND OUR UNIQUE CARS

While my father was in the service, his dream upon returning home from his World War II Navy duties was to own and operate a clothing store for children. He accomplished that dream by opening a single storefront on March 1, 1947 at 2633 Market Street in Youngstown's uptown neighborhood just north of Indianola Avenue. He named the store *Jack and Jill Kiddie Stores* and its slogan was "We Major In Minors From Heaven to Seven." A few years later, the store was expanded to a second storefront that became vacant directly next door and the slogan changed to "We Major In Minors From Heaven to Eleven."

As a youngster growing up in Youngstown, we had two Crosley station wagons with Jack and Jill Kiddie Stores painted on each side of the car. A Crosley was a tiny two-door car made just prior to and after World War II. It stopped production in early 1952. My father named each car Alexander. So, we had Alexander I and Alexander II. People around Youngstown knew this car and it was also parked in front of the store as an advertising gimmick.

Crosley Motors Incorporated had its corporate headquarters and engineering facility in Cincinnati Ohio, with assembly plants in Richmond, Indiana (1939-1942) and Marion, Indiana (1946-1952). The Crosley automobile was the brainchild of Powell Crosley, who had already made his fortune as a radio and appliance manufacturer, owner of Cincinnati's radio WLW the "Nation's Station" and the Cincinnati Reds baseball team. We also owned a red Crosley radio.

One time when we were visiting the Davidsons in Brooklyn, New York, my father was pulled over by a New York City policeman for being in a lane of traffic for driving a vehicle with advertising that was forbidden. Any vehicle with advertising had to be in a separate lane that ran parallel to the street like an access road. At that time, my father had traded in the second Crosley and was driving a 1952 Nash Rambler station wagon with Jack and Jill Kiddie Stores painted on each side of the car. The Rambler was manufactured by American Motors and about twice as big as the Crosley. My father only got a warning, not a ticket because we had an Ohio license plate and he pleaded ignorance of the Brooklyn traffic law.

CHILDREN'S CLOTHING SHOWS IN CLEVELAND

About four times a year, on a Sunday when Jack and Jill was closed and when Linda and I were young, my father would drive our family to Cleveland to the children's clothing show where my father would buy merchandise and other store items for the next season. Since the Ohio Turnpike was not yet built, we would drive on route 422 which went through Warren, Parkman, Moreland Hills and Chagrin Falls to Cleveland. The children's clothing show was usually held at the Statler Hilton in downtown Cleveland. On our way home, we would usually stopped to eat dinner at Solomon's Restaurant located in a shopping center on Cedar Road near Warrensville Road in University Heights. There were a few times we drove to Pittsburgh for a children's clothing show which was about the same distance as Cleveland.

When I was in high school, I periodically helped my father in the store by sweeping the floors and cleaning up. We would drive to the store on a Sunday and my father would be busy with inventory or pricing items while I mopped the floor or straightened boxes.

Jack and Jill Kiddie Stores was open for seventeen years and closed in 1964 when Strouss Department Store opened up a children's clothing store across the street. The handwriting was on the wall because Jack and Jill could not compete with the buying power and the pricing of a department store. When the store closed, my father decided to go back to teaching and took refresher courses at Youngstown State University to update his teaching certificate, which had lapsed. With my father's assistance, my mother got a job selling lady's dresses at McKelvey's Department Store in downtown Youngstown. A little while later, my mother chose to return to Youngstown State University to get 24 hours for her elementary certification. She worked, went to school at night and in the summer received her Ohio elementary teacher certification.

My father went back to teaching freshman and senior English full-time at Woodrow Wilson High School on Youngstown's south side. He taught there until June 1982 when he officially retired at age 70. During that time, he held several part-time jobs by teaching the Rodef Sholem Temple Confirmation Class as well as teaching English to foreign doctors at Woodside Receiving Hospital in Youngstown. My mother taught fourth-fifth grade at Bennett Elementary School for thirteen years and retired on a teacher's pension with health benefits.

CHAPTER Five
Elementary School

MY ELEMENTARY SCHOOLS

When we first moved to Boardman, there was only one school building. It was a large brick multi-flour structure on Market Street, just south of route 224 and it comprised of grades kindergarten through high school. My first-grade teacher was Miss Thompson, my second-grade teacher was Mrs. Love and my third-grade teacher was Mrs. Velker. I don't remember any of their first names.

Our wooden and metal school desks were a design with an inkwell, pencil groove, bookshelf and a separate folding seat in back of the actual desk. The top of the desk and the seat were made of hardwood with cast iron scrollwork on the legs. The standard child's desk was 28" tall, 20" wide and 28" deep with the seat down. The desk and the folding seat were screwed to the floor, totally different from the school desks today that are self-contained and movable.

In third grade, I noticed that I could not see the blackboard where I was sitting, so my parents took me to an optometrist to have my eyes examined. In those days, teachers wrote with chalk on blackboards because computers and iPads hadn't been invented. Math problems and other means of communications were printed on blackboards. So, at age nine, I was fitted with my first pair of eyeglasses and was able to clearly see the blackboard. As I recall, over the course of my elementary years, I probably broke my glass frames a number of times since the frames were made of plastic.

PNEUMONIA AND MOTHER'S EYE OPERATION IN NEW YORK

Near the end of October 1947, a little more than one month after I started first grade, two very dramatic and traumatic events happened in my life: my mother had to have an eye operation in New York City and was away for what seemed like a long time. I also contracted pneumonia and had to be hospitalized. The hospital stay had a profound and emotional effect on my life and still affects me to this day. It is a phobia about spending time in a hospital both as a visitor and as a patient.

BACKGROUND OF BOTH INCIDENTS

First, my mother was diagnosed with a detached retina. While getting up one night to go to the bathroom, she bent down to put on her slippers and accidentally bumped her head on the nightstand next to the bed. After that incident, she started losing sight in her left eye. [Excerpt from my mother's memoir] "I soon had difficulty with all the numbers and seeing traffic because of my eyes. Dr. Keyes, a Youngstown ophthalmologist, checked me out and sent me for a complete physical exam. It showed I was otherwise healthy. He said, "You are going blind." David and I couldn't believe it. The doctor was not familiar with detached retinas.

"Again, luck was with me, my nephew Shelly Pressler wanted to go to Kent State University and David found him a room there. Because of returning Korean War veterans, he had to have a room before he was accepted to the university. Sadie, Shelly and his parents came to Ohio to get him settled.

Not satisfied with a Youngstown eye specialist, my mother saw another ophthalmologist in Sharon, Pennsylvania who recommended seeing Dr. John McLean, an eye specialist in New York City. "When the New York relatives heard about my problem, they called Dr. David Hauptman, our family doctor in Brooklyn. He said to bring me to New York. So, Linda and I left for New York with Sadie, Fay and Murray on Monday, September 19, 1947."

In the meantime, my grandparents moved into our house on Shadyside Drive to help my father take care of me. Louise Boyd, our cleaning woman, periodically came to the house to help. None of us knew what was ahead. My mother saw two eye specialists in a matter of days, instead of waiting for months in Youngstown. My mother was in New York Cornell Medical Hospital on Friday and was operated on for a detached retina on Monday, September 26, 1947. Dr. John McLean operated on her. She was flat on her back for three weeks, sandbags at her head and everything done for her, even feeding. The bed linen was not changed and she was on a rubber sheet. It was the hottest October ever. My Aunt Sadie visited her every day. Both eyes were covered. Nowadays, detached retinas are much more easily repaired by laser surgery and the recovery time is much quicker. No sand bags and no lying on your back for three weeks.

Linda was staying in New York where my Aunt Fay took care of her while my mother was in the hospital from her eye surgery. After the operation, my mother was recuperating in the Brooklyn home at 1760 East 10th Street. My father was only able to visit her in New York twice because of his obligations with the children's clothing store. As I remember, my father seemed to be having a rough time.

When my mother finally left the hospital, she had to wear a special insert inside her glasses in front of her left eye for three months to protect it and to help heal. In December, Aunt Sadie accompanied Linda by train back to Boardman.

MY HOSPITAL TRAUMA AT AGE SIX

During the very same time while my mother and sister were in New York, I developed a severe case of pneumonia. I had a horrible cough and developed a fever that broke after 24 hours. My case was so bad my Uncle Sam, who was our family physician, recommended I go to Southside Hospital to be treated with penicillin. My father and my first cousin Shelly Pressler, who was a student at Kent State University at the time and who happened to be visiting us, drove me to Southside Hospital and left me there. My father and cousin told me that I was going to see my cousin Norman that was totally not true. Because my mother was in New York and not present when all of this happened to me, I assume she would have explained my going to the hospital in a much different way. As I recall, it was the first real emotional upset in my life as I felt abandoned and to this day this event was extremely traumatic.

I was seven years old but the hospital placed me in a crib with high sides and I can distinctly remember standing up, holding onto the bars and crying as my father and cousin left my hospital room. I received many penicillin shots in my buttocks and had to miss several weeks of first grade because of my illness. As a result of this incident, I vowed never to spend another night in a hospital room and luckily it didn't happen until I was sixty-eight years old with valley fever. (You can read more about my case of valley fever in a Chapter Twenty-Six).

According to correspondence I found written by my father to Aunt Sadie and Uncle Harry, I was in the hospital for approximately eight days. I had to stay two extra days because the X-ray showed my lungs were still congested. While in the hospital, my father had a nose specialist check me because apparently my speech was nasally. My father wrote, "The nose specialist gave my Uncle Sam a report. Alan's nose was plugged with adenoids. Little wonder why he has spoken with a terrific nasal and holds his mouth open." My father picked me up at Southside Hospital at noon on Wednesday, November 5, 1947.

This time was the very start of my first-grade year and this episode set me behind the other children in my class as they were beginning to learn to read while I was out of school. It took me several years to catch up. My difficulty in learning how to read during this time might also have been diagnosed as Dyslexia if teachers knew about it at the time. Although I had difficulty with reading, my spelling was quite good. Finally, in third grade, my parents hired a reading tutor, Mrs. Baird, who helped me with my reading. I have a vivid memory of Mrs. Baird as she used to wear these apple earrings. These earrings were apples cut in half. I also remember she used to wear very distinctive perfume. Her son, Arthur, was a year ahead of me in school and I knew him.

MY PNEUMONIA NUMBERS 2, 3 AND 4

The next bout with pneumonia was when I was a junior in high school. I asked Carol Bender, a classmate of mine, to the Junior Prom but had to cancel at the last minute because of my illness. In 1965, while living in Mount Pleasant, Michigan and attending graduate school at Central Michigan University, I caught a mild case of pneumonia but was not hospitalized.

I developed my 4th case of pneumonia as a result of valley fever contracted while staying in Arizona. Requiring a hospital stay, this fourth stint with pneumonia was really bad. Chapter Twenty-Six of this book is devoted to my 2009 hospitalization with valley fever and pneumonia.

TEMPLE CONSECRATION IN FIRST GRADE

Our family was a member of Temple Rodef Sholem located on Youngstown's north side where I started Sunday school in first grade. Being in first grade, the temple held a consecration service near the beginning of the school year. Consecration is an invention of American Reform Judaism and is part of a service to mark the season when young children begin their formal Jewish education and receive miniature Torah scrolls. At the time, my grandparents were watching me due to my mother's eye operation in New York.

In Sunday school, each first-grade pupil received a piece of paper with a few lines to memorize for a small part to participate in the service. I cannot remember the exact circumstances of what happened or if I gave the small paper to my father or grandparents to help me learn my part, but I never memorized a word and never practiced. At the Friday night service, the entire class was on the bema ready to recite and the teacher was pointing to each child to say his or her part.

I remember spotting my father and grandparents sitting in the sanctuary and me waving to them. When it was my turn to recite my few lines, I didn't know it and so the teacher skipped me and went to the next child. There must have been a rehearsal to make sure each child knew his or her part but apparently there wasn't and somehow the fact that I didn't know my part completely missed the teacher. I can imagine it must have been an embarrassing moment for my father and grandparents.

MOTHER RETURNS AFTER HER NEW YORK EYE OPERATION

When my mother finally came back to Youngstown, she could not do a lot of things, like bending, lifting or picking up objects for almost a year. We hired a woman named Mrs. Valeski to take care of Linda and me. For some reason, Linda and I were very mean to her and she eventually quit because she couldn't stand us. After the operation, our cleaning woman, Louise Boyd, would come to our home more often to help my mother.

There weren't many children our age living on Shadyside Drive so I think that is why my parents decided to move to Stillson Place where new houses were being built and there were young families with children.

MOVE TO STILLSON PLACE IN BOARDMAN

In 1949, we moved to a larger two-story colonial-style three-bedroom house at 5951 Stillson Place. The house had one bathroom on the second floor and a half bath one the first floor near the back door. You entered the front door into a small hallway. On the right was a small guest closet and across from the closet was a tiny shelf with a drawer and a mirror. Above it was where my father kept his car and house keys.

On your immediate right was the living room and on the left was the dining room. The dining room had a mahogany dining room set with six upholstered chairs around the table and two matching chairs against two different walls. It had a matching corner cabinet on the northwest wall housing some crystal vases and wine glasses my parents had received as wedding presents. I can't ever remember actually using the wine glasses on any occasion as my parents did not drink or entertain very much. Another matching piece, a long buffet with four drawers rounded out the furniture that my parents had purchased from Youngstown's Penner's Furniture right after they were married in 1939. A front picture window faced west and onto Stillson Place.

The living room had a couch along the north wall, two end tables on each side of the couch with lamps on each and a hexagonal table with a lamp in front of the picture window facing the street. The front table had some shelves in it and my grandmother's tea set was on several of the shelves. A spinet piano was on the east side of the living room with a picture window behind it that faced the closed-in porch that was used as our family room. When the house was built, the family room did not exist. A year or two after we moved in, my parents added it over an existing outdoor concrete patio that came with the house.

From the kitchen, just before going to the family room, there was a half bathroom with a toilet and sink. With its knotty pine walls, the family room is where we had our television set, a hide-a-bed couch, two ranch-style wooden chairs and matching table with a lamp and a built-in storage area for a card table and chairs. To the left of the living room was a small but utilitarian kitchen with a stove, refrigerator, sink and an eat-in area for a kitchen table. After a few years of moving into the house, my parents added knotty pine to the walls inside the eat-in area. There was no dishwasher built into the kitchen so years later a portable dishwasher was purchased.

As you walked up the flight of stairs, the bathroom was an immediate left with a hall closet next to the bathroom. My parent's bedroom was right next to the bathroom and had matching mahogany furniture with a dresser, two nightstands and a comfortable easy chair. A linen closet was in the hallway in between the bathroom and the master bedroom. A walk-in closet was also in the master bedroom. The master bedroom was the largest bedroom room in the house with my sister's bedroom the next biggest. My room was across the hall from the bathroom and was the smallest bedroom. Each bedroom had two windows. The house came with a one-car garage. In the days after World War II, few families owned two cars. Most women were homemakers and did not work. Also, my mother did not drive, although she did have driving lessons at one time, but she never learned to actually drive a car.

Facing our house, the Pipolys lived to the right of us at the corner of Stillson Place and Withers Drive. Mrs. Margaret Pipoly was a single mom. Her husband had died and she shared the house with her twin daughters who were in high school at the time and her son, Bobby, who was a year younger than me.

To the left of our home was the Barrett family. Their son Dick was 2 years older than me. Their daughter Susan was Linda's age. Mr. Barrett worked for a Cadillac dealership located at 917 Wick Avenue on Youngstown's north side and eventually bought out the family when the owner passed away. Mr. Barrett would drive home the latest Cadillac and we would get to see them before most of the public as the car was parked right next door to us.

EARACHES DURING CHILDHOOD

During my years in elementary school, I would periodically get earaches. I must have been 8 or 9 years old when I would wake up in the middle of the night with an excruciating pain in my ear. My father would come into my room and put his finger in my ear to reduce the pain.

On several occasions, we would wake up my sister and drive to the doctor's office in the Home Federal and Loan building in the downtown Youngstown. The doctor would meet us there to lance my ear and drain it. Because the pain would have been unbearable, he would give me ether, which put me to sleep. A recurring dream I had under the anesthetic was a weird one and I can remember it to this day. Here's the dream: A train track with an elephant running on one leg along the track. After the doctor drained the puss from my ear, I would always wake up and throw up. Then I would feel better and we'd drive home. I think this happened several times during my childhood.

Skip ahead to Scottsdale, Arizona: Once, while I was driving to our Scottsdale condo on the 101 coming back from an evening activity, I told this dream story to Jan and Rich Aver who were sitting in the car's back seat. It made them laugh so much that we all started laughing so hard that tears welled up in my eyes almost preventing me from driving. I actually could hardly see the road and almost had to pull over from laughing so much. Penny, Jan, Rich and I were laughing hysterically and it's a story that frequently pops up in our conversations.

MARKET STREET ELEMENTARY SCHOOL

By the time I was going into fourth grade, the Market Street Elementary School had been built within walking distance of our home. My fourth-grade teacher was Mrs. Harrington and she was one of my favorite elementary school teachers. My mother was a room mother in my fourth-grade class and was very active in the school's PTA.

I started collecting stamps about this time and United States and world geography was my favorite subject. It's hard to believe but at the time, I memorized all of the major capitals of the world plus all the U.S. state capitals. I collected both United States and world stamps. I loved collecting stamps and my Aunt Sadie and Uncle Harry would save cancelled stamps from the Sohmer Press business letters they would receive and send them to me. My cousin Shelly also collected stamps and gave me some plate blocks from the 1940s and first day covers that I also collected. This hobby helped me tremendously with learning the different countries, their locations and capitals. Geography and maps became a fascination with me. I kept on collecting stamps into my 40s when my interest dropped off. I still have my stamp collection and Penny's father's collection on the shelves in my bedroom closet.

Fourth grade classmates of mine, Chris Horsch, David Garwood and myself decided to put on a little singing act for the class. We dressed up in our sister's dresses and sang the Gilbert and Sullivan song, *"Three Little Maids From School."* Don't ask me to remember why we did this but I guess it went over well. Many years later in August 2006 to be exact, Chris Horsch, who had been living in Chicago, reconnected. Chris was an attorney working for the South Shore Bank and he was able to get baseball tickets. With his wife, Patty, Penny and I attended a Chicago Cubs baseball game together. I also reminded Chris of the Gilbert and Sullivan song we performed.

In August 1951, I was ten years old and going into the 5th grade and Linda was eight years old and going into the 3rd grade. Linda developed a mild case of polio with no paralysis. Our family doctor, Uncle Sam Epstein, diagnosed the problem. As I recall, she was confined to the bedroom for quite a while but made a full recovery.

During this time but I can't remember the exact date, Youngstown's WKBN-TV, Channel 27, held a telethon to raise money for Cerebral Palsy. Helen O'Connell, a popular big band singer from the 1940s, was one of the celebrities who participated in this Youngstown televised event. I asked my father to drive me to the television station so I could meet Miss O'Connell. My father drove me to the station and I actually had a chance to shake her hand. My fifth-grade teacher was

Mrs. Rosalie Grauer and I was a class clown. One incident in fifth grade class stands out in my memory. Mrs. Grauer had enough of me horsing around so one day she picked me up and put me in the class waste paper basket. In those days you could touch a student without getting into trouble. This particular incident was resurrected in our high school class 10th year reunion when a history of the class was read at the event.

RADIO AND THE EARLY DAYS OF TELEVISION

As a young boy growing up in the 1940s, I can remember listening to various radio programs because there was no television. Youngstown's affiliated network radio stations were WKBN (CBS) and WFMJ (NBC). WBBW was an independent radio station affiliated with the Mutual Broadcasting Network headquartered in New York City.

This was a time before television became available to the general public. The Jack Benny Show, one of my favorite CBS radio programs, was broadcast at 7:00 every Sunday evening and my family and I were glued to the radio listening to his funny program. Jack's program consisted of vignettes of everyday life in Hollywood with various characters as part of Jack's life. Rochester, Jack's butler, played by Eddie Robinson, Don Wilson (Jack's announcer); Phil Harris (Jack's orchestra leader) and his wife Alice Fay, Mary Livingston (Jack's real-life wife) and Dennis Day were all part of his entourage. Other characters would periodically show up in the program and were a vital part of Jack's life. Sheldon Leonard (who later became a successful television producer/actor and Mel Blanc (voice of Bugs Bunny and many other cartoon characters) among others come to mind.

As a youngster, my other favorite radio programs were the *Lone Ranger*, Jack *Armstrong All American Boy, Our Miss Brooks, The Shadow* (What evil lurches in the hearts of man, only the Shadow knows) the *Green Hornet, Sky King and His niece Penny, Sergeant Preston of the Yukon* and his dog King, *Fibber McGee and Molly* and *Ozzie and Harriet*, to name a few Periodically, we would listen to *Edgar Bergen and Charlie McCarthy, Bing Crosby, Fred Allen* and *Bob Hope* who had 30-minute radio programs with different guests each week.

In 1949, our Stillson Place home was the first on our street to get a television set. Our first television was black and white and I believe was about 12 inches. It was placed on the west wall of our living room. At first, we would sit on the couch for hours watching this new invention. At that time programming was only broadcast in the late afternoon and evening. There were no programs during the daylight hours, just a test pattern on the screen. The first television program broadcast around 5:00 p.m. In the beginning stages of television, the DuPont Television Network, CBS and NBC were the only networks with programming.

After school, I would watch *Captain Video, Kukla, Fran and Ollie* that originated from Chicago and Mr. Wizard, which also was broadcast from Chicago. Most of the shows were broadcast from New York with a few exceptions from Chicago. Starting on Tuesday evening, June 8, 1948 at 8:00 p.m., comedian Milton Berle hosted his first variety show on the NBC Television Network and was a favorite of our family when we started watching his program in 1949. As the years went by, some of my famous radio programs became television shows and we would watch them. *Ozzie and Harriet, The Life of Riley, Our Miss Brooks, Amos and Andy* and *The Jack Benny Show* were a few of the old radio shows that went on to become huge television hits in the 1950s.

In the early days of television in the late 1940s and early 1950s, my father and I used to watch professional boxing and wrestling together. Wrestlers like Killer Kowalski, Gorgeous George and Yukon Eric were among our favorite wrestlers and the most famous at the time. Professional boxing matches were usually televised on Friday nights with Gillette razor blades sponsoring the bouts. To this day, boxing is one of my favorite sporting events to watch.

On Sunday mornings in the mid-1950s, my father and I would periodically tune in to Oral Roberts, a Tulsa, Oklahoma Christian televangelist preacher who would "heal" members of his audience. We would watch only a part of this program as it made us laugh. The audience in a large auditorium would come down to the front of the stage and Oral would say, "If you believe in Jesus, then "heal" this woman of her broken leg," We could not understand how people could believe this man but he had a television program for many years and made millions of dollars asking his dedicated audience to send in money. He was so popular that in 1965 he established Oral Roberts University, a private evangelical liberal arts university.

MY FAVORITE TELEVISION SHOWS WERE COWBOY MOVIES

In the early days of television, there was very few original programs, so the networks would broadcast many old western movies. I became a huge fan of cowboy and Indian films and used to watch them on a regular basis. Today, I still like to watch a good western. One of the cable channels broadcasts them on a regular basis. Some of the favorite cowboy movie stars I used to watch on early television and were such actors as Bob Steele, Johnny Mack Brown, Wild Bill Elliott, Tim Holt, Lash LaRue, Ken Maynard, Tom Mix, Hoot Gibson, Roy Rogers and his horse Trigger with his wife, Dale Evans, Gene Autry with his horse Champion, Hopalong Cassidy, and the Lone Ranger with Tonto, his faithful Indian companion. William Boyd played Hopalong Cassidy and Clayton Moore was the actor who was The Lone Ranger. Gabby Hayes, Andy Devine, Smiley Burnette and Fuzzy Knight usually played sidekicks of the cowboy stars. At that time, there were very few John Wayne movies on television.

In the mid-1950s, *The Mickey Mouse Club* was very popular among youngsters my age. This television program was a long-running American variety series that began in 1955 and was produced by Walt Disney Productions. The show featured a regular but ever-changing cast of teenage performers. The series has been revived and reformatted several times since its initial 1955-1959 run on the ABC network. Even the original series has been repackaged and rerun over the decades.

MY EDUCATED FATHER AND MOTHER

My father and mother were both college graduates, a rare occurrence during the depression. My father graduated with a B.A. degree from Ashland College (now Ashland University) in Ashland, Ohio and my mother graduated from Ohio

University in Athens, Ohio with a B.A. degree majoring in history and teaching. My father spent two years at Hiram College and transferred to Ashland College while my mother went to CCNY (City College of New York) for two year before transferring to Ohio University.

I had a great relationship and a fabulous childhood with both of my parents but it was my father to whom I felt especially close. It was a male bonding "thing" I guess. Whenever he wasn't working, we spent time together doing father and son things. We would go fishing at various lakes around the Youngstown area, usually with my cousin Norman. (You can read more about our fishing later in this book).

Both my parents always encouraged me in any endeavor I undertook. They were very supportive and proud of me. They always acknowledged my accomplishments and gave me positive feedback throughout all of my early life and during my high school days. Positive reinforcement and supporting each of my children as they were growing came naturally to me as it carried over from my parents. My father taught me many things about life. Shaking hands and tying a tie were two things I learned from him. He told me when meeting someone for the first time, when shaking hands with them, I should squeeze the other person's hand as hard as I could and look them in the eye and say glad to meet you or it is a pleasure to meet you. Every time you shake hands with anyone, do the same thing. He taught me to tie a necktie in a Windsor knot that was made popular and named after the way England's Duke of Windsor tied his neckties. He also wore lots of cologne that my Uncle Murray and Uncle Harry dubbed *"foo foo"* water. I would take on this ritual into my adulthood but after many years of Penny asking me to stop wearing the "stuff" so I finally gave up using it.

My father had a terrific sense of humor and made me laugh all the time. He made funny faces and he could also make me cry just by looking at me. He made up crazy sayings and pronounced phrases funny, like, *choo'n gum*, instead of chewing gum. He made up funny songs, like *ra-ta-ta-ta-ta-ta* and do a little dance along with it. He would provide body movements to go with the songs. He was very comical. A little song he made up was *"Horses, horses, crazy bout horses, making (fart sound), on the Shwartz's."* He also made-up lyrics to popular songs like *"Jimmy crack corn and I don't care, Jimmy crack corn and I don't care, Jimmy crack corn and I don't care, and Peanuts is my name."*

He also taught me some Spanish phrases that I remember to this day and a joke in Spanish that I have told to many Spanish-speaking people I've worked with at resort hotels.

THE SPANISH JOKE MY FATHER TAUGHT ME

My father told this joke in Spanish and translated it into English as he told it. Here is the joke in English. *"A man goes into a department store to buy a pair of socks. The clerk goes in the back storage room and brings out a pair of pants. The man says, no senior, I don't want a pair of pants (pantalones); I want a pair of socks. The clerk goes in the back storage room and brings out a shirt. No senior, says the man, I came in to buy a pair of socks. The clerk once again goes into the back storage room and brings out a belt. The man customer is very frustrated at this point and says to the clerk, pointing to his socks. The punch line is replying in*

Spanish, the man inadvertently spells out on a sheet of paper (S-O-C-K-S), because that is exactly what the Spanish words mean - eso sí que es (S-O-C-K-S) (that is what it is).

MY FATHER THE MUSICIAN

My father was a musician and pianist. He also played the Lowry organ and the vibraphone. The vibraphone is a subfamily of the percussion family and consists of tuned metal bars usually played by holding two or four soft mallets and striking the bars. When he worked at Strouss Hirshberg Department Store's music department, they had one of these instruments on display and I would see him play it. The music department also sold Lowry organs and he was able to demonstrate them to customers.

I used to get a kick out of listening to my father play the piano and sing. He started taking piano lessons at a young age, studying classical music. Since my grandparents were from Europe, classical music and opera were very important to them. I think they weren't too happy when he starting playing popular music and jazz. My father was quite a talented pianist. He played in a band in high school and college and later in life took up playing the Lowry organ as well. He played reminiscent in the style of Frankie Carl and Fats Waller, two famous piano players from the 1930s and 1940s. He bought sheet music of their arrangements and would frequently sit down at the piano and play. I grew up listening to this style of music and to this day enjoy listening to big bands from the 1930s, 1940s and early 1950s. Later, as I became more proficient with playing the trombone and we would play duets, with him accompanying me on the piano but I'm getting ahead of myself.

BASEBALL FAN

My mother was a huge baseball fan. Having grown up in Brooklyn, New York, she used to go with my Uncle Harry and Aunt Sadie to the old Ebbetts Field in Brooklyn to root for the Brooklyn Dodgers. In 1958, the Brooklyn Dodgers became the Los Angeles Dodgers moving to the West Coast. When the Dodgers moved to L.A. that was enough for my mother to stop being a Dodger fan.

After marrying my father and moving to Ohio, she slowly weaned herself away from the Dodgers and became a Cleveland Indians fan. While I was growing up, she would talk baseball with my friends. She knew the names of all of the Indian's baseball players plus their batting averages. Until my mother passed away in November 8, 2012, she followed the Indians on a daily basis and was a huge Indians fan. Since moving to Stone Gardens in Beachwood, my mother attended three Cleveland Indians baseball games at Jacobs Field that is now called Progressive Field.

SUNDAY WAS FAMILY DAY

Sunday was a ritual around our house because it was dedicated to visiting relatives. Most of the time we would go to my cousin Norman Lockshin's house on the north side of Youngstown and hang out there with the family. We would generally stay for dinner. Sometimes, we would drive to Newton Falls, a small community about thirty miles from Boardman to visit my father's Aunt Annie (my grandfather's younger sister by four years) and Gert and Marty Spritzer. The Spritzer's had four children, Hal (two years older than me) Ronnie (my age),

Marlene who now goes by Marnie (Linda's age) and Lori born two years before Marty died. Gert and Marty settled in this small Ohio town and Marty eventually became its mayor. They owned a small children's clothing store, similar to Jack and Jill Kiddie Stores. After Marty's untimely death of a heart attack in his forties, the entire family moved to Cincinnati.

Periodically, we would drive to Uhrichsville, Ohio, a small town south of Canton and close to New Philadelphia to visit Jack Shwartz and his family. Jack was my father's first cousin and one of the sons of Bernard Shwartz, the older brother of my grandfather. Jack was an optometrist there. Jack and Ruth Shwartz had three children; Francine, Susan and Mark. Francine was three years older than me; Susan was eight years younger than me and Mark was two years younger than Susan. Francine, an attorney, married Jerry Jacobs and two of their children actually live in Chicago. Julie Jacobs was a reporter for the Chicago Sun-Times and her younger brother Greg Jacobs is a producer with Siskel/Jacobs Productions. Julie no longer is living in Chicago.

When cousin Gert with her second husband Sid Phillips and Jack and Ruth Shwartz retired, they bought houses near each other and became full-time residents of Sun City, Arizona. I took the time to visit them in the mid 1980s when I was producing a conference in Scottsdale.

EATING OUT AND OTHER THINGS

While growing up and once a month on a Sunday when we weren't visiting relatives, our family would eat at various restaurants in Youngstown. Downtown's Mural Room was a favorite spot. It was a white table restaurant and upscale with terrific food. We only went to this restaurant on very special occasions because it was expensive. The Twentieth Century restaurant was also a popular north side restaurant that we would frequent. Many of the Jewish families on the north side would go to this restaurant. Ding Ho, a Chinese restaurant on Market Street was another favorite of our family. One of the first times we went to this restaurant, our waiter asked us after our meal, if we wanted "fudgy" cookies. We all looked at each other and realized with his thick accent, he meant fortune cookies. For many years after this incident, our family would joke about having a "fudgy" cookie.

A BOY SCOUT FOR NOT TOO LONG

When I was in fifth grade, I also briefly joined a local Boardman Boy Scout troop. My parents bought me the shirt to go with the Boy Scout uniform, but I never made it past the Tenderfoot rank which was the lowest level of being a Boy Scout. It wasn't long before I lost interest and after a few months I dropped out. I don't remember earning many merit badges.

One incident does stands out during this time. In one of our troop meeting, a local podiatrist visited and examined each boy's feet. He had us walk a straight line and he observed our walking. After my examination, he said I walked with my right foot turned in slightly and that is why the heel on my right shoe was wearing down from the inside. A meeting was set up with my parents and the podiatrist recommended I be fitted with an aluminum insert that would fit inside my shoe. Over time, this hard insert would straighten my foot so it wouldn't turn in anymore. They took a molding of my right foot to create the aluminum insert. At the time, I can remember it was rather embarrassing to take off my shoes in gym class and have this metal insert in my shoe visible to the other kids in my class. I would try to hide the insert by sliding it as far into the shoe as possible so it wasn't visible. I can't remember but I believe in sixth grade, I finally didn't have to wear the insert.

My sixth-grade teacher was Mrs. Shreve. About midway through the year, Mrs. Shreve left our class. I'm not sure if her husband was transferred or for another reason. Our teacher for the rest of the year was Mrs. Mumford and that year was the best one yet in my elementary school. My grades were really good and I especially enjoyed geography, my best subject. I actually corrected the teacher making a mistake about one of the countries we were studying. I can't remember exactly what it was but what she was telling the class some fact that wasn't correct. It had something to do with a geography question concerning a foreign country. Since I had been collecting stamps, I had gained knowledge about the world's countries and so suggested a different idea to her. I also remember writing a report on the Cape Verde Islands. The following year, I started Junior High School at the school building where I had originally started in first grade.

OUR DOG FLIP

While growing up in Struthers, dogs were always part of my father's childhood and he had several of them throughout his youth. One of his dogs was named Mike and was a wirehaired terrier. As a result of this love for dogs, periodically my family would drive to Coursin's farm, north of Youngstown, where Mr. Coursin raised English smooth hair fox terriers.

One Sunday morning either in April or May 1950 when I was 9 years old, my father decided to drive to Coursin's farm and buy a dog and we named her Flip. My cousin Shelly had a wirehaired terrier for a short time and he named it Flip, so Linda and I thought that was a neat name. The puppy was about four months old, so we figured the dog's birthday was on December 11 and used to celebrate Flip's birthday every year on that date. My mother really took care of Flip

Our pet dog died in the summer of 1963 when she about 13 years old. After I graduated college, one evening I had gone on a date. When I woke up the next morning, I looked in the corner of the kitchen, where Flip's bed usually was and asked my father what happened to her. The evening before, Flip had been outside running around with my father. Flip came in the house laid down on the floor in the den and my father said to my mother, I think she's dying and she passed away after I left for a date. My father took Flip to the veterinarian where she was cremated. At the same time, Linda had gone to Geneva-on-the-Lake with her friend Diane Calhoun and was away when Flip died. After returning from the lake, Linda came down to breakfast and asked what had happened to Flip. My mother burst out crying and relayed the story of what had happened.

THANKSGIVING WEEKEND 1950—A HUGE SNOW STORM

In my memory, northeastern Ohio and Youngstown in particular, had the largest snowstorm that paralyzed the Mahoning Valley over the 1950 Thanksgiving weekend. My first cousin, Shelly Pressler, was attending Kent State University at the time and drove to our house to spend the short Thanksgiving weekend with us. Officially, the storm dumped twenty-eight inches of snow in a period of seventy-one hours, by Saturday, November 25, 1950 with drifts eight to ten feet deep. My cousin Shelly helped my father dig out of the driveway and I remember my sister and I were not allowed to go outside until the driveway was cleared.

CHANUKAH 1950—AMERICAN FLYER ELECTRIC TRAIN SET

My cousin Shelly who was on winter break from Kent State University and my father surprised me with an American Flyer train layout that they set up in our basement while I was sleeping. Chanukah and Christmas coincided that same year, so when I came downstairs on Christmas morning, my father told me to go downstairs and look in the basement.

To my surprise, I saw a plywood sheet on top of two sawhorses and an American Flyer train layout all set up and running. I played with that set for many years and found out later, that when I went to college, my parents gave away the set. Many years later, when Penny and I were visiting Chicago's Museum of Science and Industry, to my astonishment, I saw my same American Flyer engine and tender in a museum case. I have also seen the American Flyer engine and tender in cases inside of antique malls we've frequented.

BABYSITTING WITH THE SLICKER SISTERS

When my parents went out for an evening and that was not very often, Lois or Jean Slicker were our babysitters. The sisters were in high school and Linda and I were in elementary school. The sisters lived on Brainard Drive around the corner from Stillson Place. Lois was mostly with us but when she couldn't sit, Jean was assigned. The only time I can actually remember one of them staying with us was when I about nine or ten. I got nauseous and threw up in my bed. There I was sitting in my bed with vomit all around me. I think Lois was staying with us at the time. She immediately called my parents and they came home early, cleaned me up and changed the sheets on my messy bed. I was in sixth grade when we no longer needed a sitter.

MY BASEBALL CARDS COLLECTION

As a youngster I collected baseball cards that came in bubble gum. I started collecting in the late 1940s and into the mid 1950s. I had many rookie baseball cards and a sizable collection with some duplicates that I traded with my neighborhood friends. I don't remember exactly how many cards I had but it was a very nice collection.

When I went to college, I discovered my parents went through my room and threw out all of my baseball card collection. In the mid-1990s when baseball card collecting was going through the roof in value and was very popular with collectors, I found out that if I had my childhood baseball card collection, it could be worth about $100,000. Also, another thing my parents gave away when I went to college was my trombone. After high school I never played a trombone again.

BICYCLES

As a youngster, I had several two-wheel bicycles. My first bike was a 24" high Schwinn. I did not have training wheels; I just learned to ride a bicycle by trial and error. I outgrew my original bike and my next was a 26" AMF Roadmaster. I believe this is the bike that got stolen at the Shady Run Swimming Pool. I rode my bike to the swimming pool but I didn't have a lock on the bike. When I came out of the pool at the end of the day, my bicycle was gone. In those days, kids didn't use locks because we didn't think people would steal bicycles. After that incident, I got another bicycle and bought a lock that I used anywhere I went. I can't remember what brand of bike my next one was.

By the way, my parents wouldn't let Linda or me ride our bikes in the street, only the sidewalks. My friends could ride their bicycles in the street, but not us. Finally, when I got older, we were allowed to ride in the street. We wore no helmets in those days because there weren't such things for children

JULY 1952—SUMMER AT OVERNIGHT CAMP FITCH

The July after turning 11 years old was the only time I went to a two-week overnight camp. I decided to go to Camp Fitch, a YMCA camp, located in Conneaut, Ohio about seventy-five miles north of Boardman. I was the only one in our tent from Boardman. The other boys were from the north side of Youngstown and attended Harding Elementary School across the street from my Cousin Norman's house on Cordova Avenue.

We slept in a twelve-person tent with side flaps and a concrete floor. We had to walk to the bathroom and showers. There were 3 sets of bunk beds on each side of the tent. In the middle of the tent, between the bunks, was a place to put out trunks and suit cases. I slept in a top bunk. One camp counselor was assigned to each tent. Our counselor was about 16 years old. I can't remember his name but he had blond hair. As I recall, our tent mates were my first cousin Norman, Lockshin, my second cousin, Bobby Weily, Ollie Drabkin along with Seth Kaufman and Bobby Chagrin (all friends of ours from Sunday school who lived on Youngstown's northside and were friends of my cousin Norman).

My parents drove me to the camp and as I recall, since this experience was the first time I had been away from home on my own, I was very home sick the first few days of being there. I quickly became adjusted however and thoroughly enjoyed my entire two-week stay. I had a chance to ride a horse for the first time and shoot a 22-caliber rifle. All of the normal activities took place at this camp. Parent's weekend was at the end of the first week. My parents and Linda drove to the camp to see me. It was a fun time but I never went to another overnight camp. I sent several 2-cent postcards to my family during my two-week stay. I can't believe my mother saved a few of my postcards and the following are what I wrote to my family during camp.

TUESDAY, JULY 15, 1952

Dear Mommy, Daddy & Linda. I am having a good time. I shot 15 bullets today. I lost my postcard and pencil. Will you bring me some Sunday, Love Alan

THURSDAY, JULY 17, 1952

Dear Mom, Dad & Linda, I am sorry but the mail has been slow. I have a surprise for you. How are you feeling? Is Linda missing me? My pencil just broke so I have to use a pen. Norman & I went horseback riding yesterday. It was lots of fun. Your son Alan

FRIDAY, JULY 18, 1952

Dear Mom, Dad & Linda. Can Linda swim yet? Norman had his keys in his trunk and somebody locked it. So, his mother is sending the keys in the mail. How is Grandma & Grandpa feeling? I hope daddy is making money. Your Love boy, Alan

MONDAY, JULY 21, 1952

Dear Mom, Dad & Linda, When you come Saturday to take me home, will you please bring me the pictures I took? When you come Sat. I hope Linda can swim. Mother kiss Daddy & Daddy kiss mother for me. Your son, Alan

TUESDAY, JULY 22, 1952

Dear Dad, How are you feeling? I got Linda's letter yesterday. Yesterday there were high waves. I hope Flip don't cry for me. So, what's a matter for you? Love Alan

CAMP FITCH COUNSELOR DURING COLLEGE

Camp Fitch played another role in my life so at this point I want to jump ahead to the summer of 1960. During this summer and in between my Freshman and Sophomore year at Ohio University, Bill DeCicco's cousin Bob Doyle (Boardman High School Class of 1956) who was an executive with the Youngstown YMCA and Camp Fitch for almost 50 years, invited Bill and me to serve as camp counselors for a six-week session in August. I think we were paid about $20.00 per week and provided all of the Sunbeam white bread (baked in nearby Erie) we could eat.

Bill DeCicco recently sent me an email about a letter he wrote to his parents from Camp Fitch on August 16, 1960. Bill's mother saved many of Bill's letters and the following is an excerpt from one: "Alan brought the *Vindicators* from last week up to camp. Thanks for sending them. I think Alan likes it up here. He has some of the youngest campers. He told them he is the judo champ of the world and they all think he really is." Bill recalls, my group of campers included a few from Girard, Ohio like the grandchildren of Joe Baglier who owned Baglier Ford. He also remembers me having "Girard" campers with the last name Boyd. I do remember having the Baglier grandson.

SUMMER VACATIONS THE CATSKILL MOUNTAINS

Each summer when my sister and I were in elementary school, our family vacation consisted of one week traveling east by car to New York's Catskill Mountains to visit our east coast relatives. In 1947, my Aunt Sadie and Uncle Harry Dollinger bought a small summer bungalow in High View, New York just off of Route 17 about ninety miles north of New York City. The house was located between Bloomingburg and Wurtsboro on the Shawanga Lodge Road. The house had two bedrooms downstairs and one large bedroom upstairs that was like an attic. When the New York cousins and their parents visited, three and four cots were placed upstairs for the nieces and nephews to sleep while the adults would sleep downstairs on the first floor and in two separate bedrooms. My Aunt Sadie was a pack rat because she stored many paper towels and toilet paper in this

31

upstairs bedroom.

There was a front porch that had three Adirondack chairs on it and stone steps led up to the porch where we would sit days and nights. The bungalow had one small bathroom, an eat-in kitchen, with a table and a small refrigerator. There was a huge freezer in the basement along with a shower and bathroom there. The basement seemed to be always damp and smelled musty. All of the prepared foods and pastries were kept in the basement freezer.

Before coming to the country house, my aunt and uncle always stopped to buy several cherry cheesecakes from Junior's Restaurant in Brooklyn. They knew how much I loved Junior's cherry cheesecake. World famous Juniors Restaurant started in 1950 by Harry Rosen and is still in business today. It's located at the corner of Flatbush Avenue and DeKalb in Downtown Brooklyn. The restaurant makes the best cherry cheesecake I have ever tasted. My aunt and uncle also stopped in Middletown, New York to buy staples at Sullivan's Food Market. I believe Middletown was about forty-five minutes from their summerhouse.

Each summer four families would drive to the Catskills and meet my Aunt Elsie and Uncle Joe Davidson and their two children, Arleen and Billy. On several occasions we would actually drive into New York City to visit and stay at my Aunt Elsie and Uncle Joe's apartment in Forest Hills, Queens. From there we would get in the car and meet my Aunt Sadie and Uncle Harry at the Sohmer Press at 480 Canal Street and we would all drive to the country house in a car caravan.

One time, around 1949, my father did not make the trip so my mother, sister and I must have taken a train to New York City and we drove to the Catskills in the same car with the Dollingers. We stopped at a place called the Big Apple, a restaurant and ice cream parlor. I must have been maybe 8 or 9 years old. We bought ice cream cones and it dripped on my hands that got sticky and messy. I made such a stink that Uncle Harry had to stop the car so I could wash my sticky hands. As a child, I used to wash my hands a lot because I hated dirty hands.

Periodically, my Aunt Fay, Uncle Murray and their son, my cousin Shelly, would also be in the summerhouse at the same time. My Uncle Murray and Uncle Harry were avid golfers and would play at The Concord Resort in Lake Kiamesha about thirty minutes north of the summerhouse. After my grandmother Luisa died in 1947, the Davidsons moved into the family's Brooklyn house at 1760 E. 10th Street. The Davidsons lived in the Brooklyn house until they sold it and moved to Forest Hills, Long Island in the mid 1950s.

One time during a summer vacation we drove to Atlantic City to visit my father's first cousin, Stanley Fink, his wife, Jenny and their son Lee. Stan was the morning editor of the Atlantic City daily newspaper. They actually lived in Margate, a suburb of Atlantic City. Stanley had been a war correspondent during World War II stationed in the Pacific and I believe my Dad told me he actually ran into Stan on Guam during the war. On the way to Atlantic City, we stopped in Newark and spent time with Aunt Fay, Uncle Murray and Shelly. They lived at 667 Irving Avenue at the time. Sometimes we would take long weekends and leave on a Thursday and come back to Youngstown on a Monday.

SCENIC ROUTE 6 THROUGH PENNSYLVANIA

On one summer occasion traveling back to Youngstown from the Catskills, we took scenic route 6 through the Alleghany Mountains National Forest by Kane and Warren, Pennsylvania. Linda was not a good car rider and would get carsick. There were miles and miles of beautiful mountains with ups and downs all the way across Pennsylvania. At one point, my father had to stop the car on a curve in the road because Linda had to vomit. She actually threw up several times on that trip back to Youngstown. My mother was also not thrilled with this route. This negative experience was the first and last time we took scenic route 6.

C H A P T E R Six
Junior High and High School

SEPTEMBER 4, 1953—SUMMER & LABOR DAY WEEKEND

In the summer of 1953 instead of driving to the Catskill Mountains, our family decided to visit New York City. I loved spending time with my father every chance I could. While in New York, my father and I went to the Brooklyn Paramount Theater located at 385 Flatbush Avenue Extension to see a brand-new movie *The House of Wax* starring Vincent Price. This 3-D film had been released in April and I was excited to see my first 3-D movie with my father. When watching a 3-D movie, you had to wear special glasses to see it. The film is about a horribly disfigured sculptor who opens up a house of wax museum in New York. Vincent Price kills his victims and then dumps their bodies into a vat of hot wax. The film follows this mad man as he sets his sights on his Marie Antoinette played by actress, Phyllis Kirk. This movie scared the hell out of me. As a twelve-year-old, I thought Vincent Price was the creepiest actor with a very scary voice and his presence on the screen made me shake. For many years after viewing this film, every time I saw Vincent Price in the movies or on television, my skin would crawl with fear.

In those days, New York theaters had stage shows after each feature film and before the repeat of the next showing. Singer Eddie Fisher, who had just been discharged from the Army and his Philadelphia pal, comedian Joey Foreman, were on the bill after the movie. Eddie Fisher would eventually have his own television show "Coke Time", marry actress Debbie Reynolds two years later and Elizabeth Taylor after a bitter divorce from Reynolds. My Dad and I had a great time together during our New York visit.

On the way back to Youngstown from our Labor Day trip to New York, our family stopped at the Pocono Animal Farm in East Stroudsburg, Pennsylvania. My father took pictures of my sister and me with various animals. There is a photo of me feeding a deer. Other animals at this farm were a donkey, kangaroo, camel and llamas.

(Skip ahead to 1961) During my sophomore year at Ohio University, I had the pleasure of seeing and hearing horror film actor Vincent Price who was also a Chinese gourmet cook and art collector. Price was part of an in-person lecture about art and was held in the university's Memorial Auditorium. He was a brilliant speaker and many years before my fear of him had disappeared.

RADIO CITY MUSICAL HALL AND NEW YORK CITY

Our family would periodically travel to New York to visit our relatives. On two separate occasions I can remember going to Radio City Music Hall at 1260 Avenue of the Americas, not too far from Rockefeller Center and Macy's Department Store. The venue would have a floorshow featuring the world-famous dancing women *The Rockettes*, and show a first run movie.

In 1948 our family saw *Easter Parade* with Judy Garland, Fred Astaire and Ann

Miller. In 1953, we saw *By The Light of the Silvery Moon* starring Doris Day and Gordon MacRae. Each time we would see the famous dancing *Rockettes.*

THE PARK THEATRE—BURLESQUE THEATER

One Saturday afternoon after religious school when my cousin Norman and I were in 8th grade, we decided to go the Park Burlesque Theater in downtown Youngstown. Obviously, we were both underage but my voice had already changed and was much lower than Norman. It was decided I would walk up to the ticket window and buy two tickets using my low voice. The woman behind the ticket counter did not hesitate to take our money, so Norman and I strolled inside the theater. We must have thought we were so cool.

Meanwhile, once inside the theater, Norman forgot his glasses and kept on borrowing mine throughout the show. We saw naked women dancing across the stage with a comedian in between acts doing some funny bits that we didn't think were all that funny. One of the funny lines one of the comedians would say, was, "if you know what I mean" after a punch line.

PIANO AND TROMBONE LESSONS

Sometime around 5th grade, my parents wanted my sister and me to take piano lessons. I was not thrilled about taking piano lessons. We took lessons at Yarling Rayner Studios on Market Street in the uptown neighborhood very close to Jack & Jill Kiddie Stores. I was not very good and didn't practice but Linda was much better. I hated to practice and eventually, after about a year of torture, I decided piano lessons were not for me. I don't remember my piano teacher.

I really wanted to play the trombone and eventually, in seventh grade, I was able to start taking trombone lessons once a week from Mr. McPherson in the Strauss' Music Store on Elm Street just north of downtown Youngstown. Every Saturday morning, with my trombone case in hand, I would take the Boardman bus by myself to my lesson. Religious school at Rodef Sholem Temple was on Sundays at the time but, when religious school switched to Saturdays, I stopped taking trombone lessons. My trombone experience in high school is coming up a little later in this book.

SLEEPOVERS WITH COUSIN NORMAN

When Norman and I were in elementary and junior high school, we would take turns sleeping at each other's house, usually over a weekend during the school year or anytime during summer vacations. We would sleep in the same bed and took baths together. If Norman slept at my house, we would get up early on Sunday and go fishing with my father. We would go to Lake Milton located west of Youngstown on route 224 or Berlin Lake, near Lake Milton or Pymatuning Reservoir about 40 or 50 miles north of Youngstown just off of route 7 in western Pennsylvania. We would usually rent a boat at these places. I remember one time catching green frogs in a minnow bucket and bringing them home as pets. They died shortly after bringing them home. One time, after a Norman sleepover at our house, while driving to one of the lakes, I think it was Lake Milton; my father got lost looking for Dog Track Road. Dog Track Road was a recurring joke for many years after that.

A VOMIT STORY FROM OUR CHILDHOOD

On one particular occasion during a sleepover at my house, and I can't remember exactly how old we were, possibly 10 years old, we had eaten dinner and were preparing to go to bed. Norman and I were in the bathtub and he was demonstrating his ability to create "hockers." For those of you who have never heard the term, let me describe what I am talking about. Coughing up phlegm from the bottom of your throat and spitting them out creates them. We also called them loogies.

Anyway, Norman would let this mass of phlegm escape from his lower lip, and then suck it back into his mouth. He kept on doing this several times. This act made me so sick that I started throwing up in the bathtub. When Norman saw me throw up, he also started throwing up. The bathtub was full of vomit. We tried to let the bathwater out of the bathtub but the washcloth we were using got stuck and the water wouldn't go down the drain. We were making such a commotion that my father came running upstairs to the bathroom to find the both of us sitting in the bathtub full of vomit. He finally found the washcloth that was stopping up the drain and got rid of the water in the bathtub. It was a mess.

MY PET HORNED TOAD

I also had a pet brown horned toad I named Poncho Francisco. A friend of my father's visited Texas and brought back the toad that I kept in an aquarium for quite a while but I don't remember how long. I fed it "live" ants and crickets.

SATURDAY AFTERNOON MOVIES--NEWPORT THEATER

During elementary school, I remember the Newport Theater and its 5-cent double features every Saturday afternoon that also included previews, serials, news of the day, five Loony Tunes cartoons and a couple of Three Stooges movies. According to my friend and classmate Bill DeCicco, today a Burger King occupies sit of the theater. The theater was located on Midlothian Blvd near Market Street on the south side of Youngstown. For 5-cents, you could spend entire Saturday afternoon watching a variety of movies just about all geared to kids. At one point, the theater raised the price to 10-cents. I can't remember if we took the bus there or were taken by a friend's parent. Since my mother didn't drive and my father worked all day Saturday, I suppose we got to the theater one way or the other.

COUSIN ARLEEN DAVIDSON AND THE HOUSE PIT

My grandfather and grandmother were visiting us at our Boardman home while New York cousins Arleen and Billy Davidson were staying with us. Arleen was around 10 or 11. Linda and Arleen decided to go for a walk in our neighborhood on Withers Drive for some reason without tying their shoelaces. The Thompsons were in the process of building a house at the corner of Withers Drive and Griswold. Arleen and Linda thought they would check out the construction site but were warned not to go but they went anyway.

Arleen was sitting on top of a dirt pile trying to tie her shoelaces, when she lost her balance and slid into the basement excavation. Linda immediately ran back home screaming, "Arleen fell in a hole." My grandfather ran to the construction site, put a ladder that was at the site down the embankment and got Arleen out of the hole. He was probably around sixty-five at the time. Linda was grounded because of the incident but Arleen got all the sympathy. My Uncle Sam came to our house to look at the deep cut Arleen got on her leg but it was nothing serious.

RELIGIOUS SCHOOL

Our family was a long-standing member of Rodef Sholem Temple on the north side of Youngstown. Although they lived in Struthers, my grandfather and grandmother joined during the second decade of the 20th century. The Lockshins and Epsteins were also members. Since I grew up in a southern suburb of Youngstown, every Sunday morning, my parents would drive my sister and me to attend Sunday school. In later grades, the religious school switched to Saturdays. We usually car-pooled with the two other Jewish families living in Boardman. Carol Bender, Carol Strassels, Linda and I would drive with a parent to Rodef Sholem Temple. Growing up, my cousin Norman Lockshin and I were very close. Up until college, I used to see Norman and his family about every Sunday, when we would drive to the north side of Youngstown for a visit and dinner at the Lockshins.

BOARDMAN JUNIOR HIGH SCHOOL

Boardman's junior and senior high school were in the same Market Street building and a little over one mile from my home. Linda and I took a school bus there and back every day. The bus dropped us off across the street from our house. For the first time in seventh grade all the classes were departmentalized, so I had a different teacher for each subject. There was no such thing as a middle school in those days. One of the most memorable teachers was John Harr who was my science teacher. He was 6 feet 4 inches tall and was the tallest person I had ever met up until that point in my life. But he was a very nice gentle giant and a wonderful teacher.

In August 2006, at my high school's 45th class reunion, Mr. and Mrs. John Harr were the guests of honor and I told him the story of how I thought he was the tallest person I had ever seen. He got a kick out of the story. Mr. Ed Lugibl was my seventh-grade geography teacher. At the time, the class wasn't called social studies and it was one of my best subjects. I had a great interest in geography that I gained from collecting stamps started in 4th grade. At one time I knew all of the state capitals and the capitals of each country in the world, even the small ones.

A very popular fashion statement among the junior high school boys was wearing clodhopper boots. These laced boots were big, oversized high-top boots that made clunky noises on the floor when you were walking. They came in black, were cut just above the ankle and resembled army combat boots. The idea was not to polish them so they looked dirty. Another popular article of clothing were replicas of civil war caps worn by the union army. These blue caps were all the rage while I was in seventh and eighth grade. They also came in gray and looked like the caps worn by the confederate army. I don't recall many of my classmates wearing confederate caps.

FRIDAY, MARCH 5.1954—MY BAR MITZVAH

In the beginning of the 7th grade, I started to study for my Bar Mitzvah with my cousin Norman. The momentous occasion happened on Friday, March 5, 1954 at 8:00 p.m. My cousin Norman Lockshin and I studied with Cantor Lawrence Ehrlich and had Rodef Sholem Temple's first double Bar Mitzvah. Although Norman turned 13 on February 23, I was 12 with my 13th birthday just 11 days away.

In honor of our special occasion, our parents bought tailor-made suits for each of us. Norman and I had one button Bar Mitzvah suits made at Shy Lockson Tailors located on the first floor of the Warner Theater Building. Upstairs from Shy Lockson Tailors were the studios of radio station WBBW where I would later work as a disc jockey, newscaster and announcer after college. Getting a tailor-made suit from Shy Lockson was a very popular thing to do and a big deal. Norman's suit was light gray and mine was a light blue. The belt loops were drop-down about a ½ inch from the top of the pants, a common thing back then. Also pegged pants were all the rage and so both of our trousers were pegged. The pants were full at the top and then tapered at the bottoms just over the shoe.

The flowers on the pulpit were given by Norman's parents, my Uncle Morris and Aunt Dorothy and my parents. Norman and I were short so we had to stand on a box behind the bimah in order to be seen. Following the service both of our parents hosted an informal reception downstairs in the Strouss Hall in honor of our Bar Mitzvah. Norman and I had been studying with Cantor Lawrence Ehrlich for many months preparing for this event into manhood. Dr. Sidney Berkowitz, the rabbi of our temple, addressed the congregation on "A New Review of an Old Book" *The Book of Exodus*.

BAR MITZVAH DINNER FOR FAMILY AND FRIENDS

At 7:00 p.m. on Saturday, March 6, 1954, my parents invited our cousins and their friends to a dinner at The Colonial House located at 2619 Market Street in Youngstown in honor of my Bar Mitzvah. My parents hired a photographer to take everyone's photo at the event. All of my New York and east coast relatives were there. For my Bar Mitzvah, my cousin Shelly gave me a Kodak Brownie Hawkeye box camera with a flash attachment. You had to use flash bulbs in the flash attachment because the camera was so simple there was no way to adjust the lens aperture. Rechargeable flash attachments had not yet been invented so even sophisticated 35mm and larger format cameras had to use flash bulbs. I took lots of photos with it, started to enjoy taking pictures and developed my love for photography by using this simple Kodak camera.

DON'T BE A LELAND

I'm not sure how this started but my father used to refer to someone who was not quite "with it" as a Leland, a name that signified being a dunce or a loser. He used to say, "don't be a Leland or wasn't that guy a Leland or didn't that guy act like a Leland." It is a saying from my father that has stuck with me over the years.

MY FIRST DATE

My first cousin once removed, Ralph Shwartz, my father's first cousin, lived on Centervale Avenue in Boardman about one mile south from our house. He had a brand new 1952 Dodge convertible with a continental spare tire kit on the back of the car. It had an orange paint job and was a really cool looking car. I wasn't old enough to have a driver's license so he volunteered to drive me to pick up my date, Sally Goodstein, who lived on the north side of Youngstown. I think we went to a Jewish dance but I don't remember. I believe I was in 8th grade and 14 years old. I can't remember much about the date but Sally was very good looking and a popular girl who was in junior high in the Rayen High School building. It was the same high school my cousin Norman attended. I believe Sally was about the same age as me.

A FAMILY INCIDENT WITH MY SISTER

As an ongoing incident, I used to taunt, provoke and harass my sister Linda. Psychologists call it sibling rivalry. I am not sure exactly when this incident happened but it was sometime in our youth.

I was walking behind my sister as she was going into the kitchen from the dining room. I don't know if I said something to her or poked her or what but Linda turned around with a pencil in her hand and stabbed me in the upper part of my chest. It wasn't a deep wound but it did leave a pencil mark in my chest. I don't think there was blood but we have talked about this incident for years.

GRANDMA AND GRANDPA'S HOME

After Saturday religious school, Linda, Norman and I would go to my grandparent's home (Ben and Rose) for lunch while we were in high school and if we happened to be home from college. My grandmother always made Cole slaw a certain way every time. She would grate cabbage and carrots, put a little paprika on top and mix it with a little mayonnaise. A favorite meal she would make for me was a stuffed veal breast with farfel, a dish like pasta. This is when I ate meat.

My grandfather, Ben, was a fantastic baker. He was known for his apple and cherry pies. He also made wonderful chocolate chip cookies and orange cookies. He had a separate bakery on the lower level of his grocery store on Poland Avenue and he learned to bake while watching his baker in the shop. He also used to make pizza with a deep crust, long before I discovered a deep-dish pizza after I moved to Chicago. On one occasion my grandfather made a cherry pie while my Aunt Elsie and Uncle Joe were visiting us in Youngstown. Uncle Joe said I never eat cherry pies because I always bit into a cherry pit. My grandfather said, I have made hundreds of cherry pies and nobody has ever bitten into a cherry pit. Well, guess what? Uncle Joe took a bite out of my grandfather's pie and bit into a pit. We all had a big laugh.

My grandfather always wore a tie and a dress shirt. I can only remember a handful of times he didn't wear one. Both of my grandparents had Polish accents and they were fantastic to be around. I thoroughly enjoyed talking to them. My grandfather would tell me stories when he was in the Russian army during the 1904-1905 Russo-Japanese war. He was stationed in freezing Irkutsk, Siberia. I wish I would have asked him more questions about his ancestors but I wasn't into genealogy at the time so questions I wished I had asked never got answered.

SEPTEMBER 1955 TO JUNE 1959—HIGH SCHOOL

I had an interesting four years at Boardman High School. There were very few Jewish classmates in my high school and only ten Jews in my graduation class. On the whole, I was not a good student in high school. It was mainly because I did not study very hard but I received a tremendous amount of encouragement from my parents. My focus was on the band and having a good time. After four years, however, my grades were good enough to get into Ohio University.

In high school, I took two years of Latin (my freshman and sophomore year) and two years of French (my junior and senior year). My favorite teacher was Miss Alma Klinger who taught both French and English in my junior year and senior year. French was a subject that needed studying and I did not put in the time to learn the different tenses of verbs. I was OK with the French vocabulary but trying to speak the language was not one of my strong points. In fact, Miss Klinger was our graduation classes' favorite teacher and we dedicated our senior yearbook to her. Miss Klinger always wore unusual looking shoes that she must have purchased in France. They resembled modern-day Mephisto shoes and were unlike any shoe I had ever seen. In 1969, Miss Klinger attended our tenth-year class reunion and I was excited to speak with her. I actually did better in freshman and sophomore Latin then French because it was memorization and you didn't have to speak it.

OILY SKIN

I had oily skin as a teenager that resulted in a common case of skin acne. I inherited this skin condition from my mother who had a bad case of acne as a teenager and had some facial scars to prove it. Our family physician, my Uncle Sam Epstein, recommended I avoid a list of foods and beverages as they were supposed to cause acne, most likely because of the sugar content. My case was not as severe as my mother because my face had no permanent scars. As a result of avoiding certain foods and beverages, I never developed a taste for carbonated soft drinks because Coca Cola and Pepsi Cola were on the list of beverages not to drink. I did not eat chocolate or candy for many years because these items were also on the no eat list. I also had to use a Fostex acne medicated cleansing bar instead of regular soap.   This special soap was formulated to dry and clear acne blemishes, blackheads, and whiteheads as it cleaned deep to remove dirt and oil from my face and body. Some of the acne blemishes were on my shoulders too and I had to use a special shampoo version to wash my hair. It was very embarrassing but the acne disappeared my freshman year of college.

YOUNGSTOWN'S WHOT RADIO AND DICK BIONDI

In 1955, when I was 14 years old and just beginning my freshman year of high school, Youngstown radio station WHOT AM 1330 on the dial went on the air and became a very popular station of Youngstown teenagers. The station played the most up-to-date rock n' roll music and disc jockey Dick Biondi and Boots Bell became legendary local celebrities. You'll read more about Dick Biondi later in this book.

Also, as a teenager, *American Bandstand* was an ABC Network Television show my sister and I watched after school each day. Dick Clark, a Philadelphia disc jockey, brought the idea of teenagers dancing to current popular music from the studios of Philadelphia's WFIL-TV to network television. The program was originally a local show but was broadcast for the first time nationwide on August 5, 1957. Teenagers from the Philadelphia area appeared on the show. The latest music was played and popular singers and singing groups appeared lip-synching to their own record. The teenagers would be interviewed and periodically would rate the music. This show was a powerful force for the record industry as it influenced the sale of records. Teenage singers such as Frankie Avalon, Fabian, Bobby Rydell, Connie Francis and Bobby Darin along with many African American performers would appear on the show.

Many Philadelphia teenage couples became household names during the running of the show. Two popular teenage celebrity dancers were Justine Carrelli and Bob Clayton. 13-year-old Justine was the blond dancer when she started dancing on the show and her counterpart, Bob was 16 years old. The couple danced on the show for three years before they parted ways, but in 1992 they saw each other and danced at the show's 40th reunion. When she started dancing with Bob, the couple became America's sweethearts for a long time and teenagers watched the show each day just to see them blissfully dance together.

THE BOARDMAN HIGH SCHOOL MARCHING BAND

By the time I entered ninth grade, I was a good enough trombone player to join the Boardman High School Marching Band led by our high school band conductor, Richard Bame. Mr. Bame graduated from Ohio State University and played the sousaphone. At the time, the Ohio State Marching band was the best college marching band in the country. The university band spelled out script Ohio on the field and it was a great honor to dot the "I" in Ohio by the top-ranked sousaphone player and Mr. Bame had that honor. Everything our high school marching band did was a direct copy of the Ohio State University Marching Band. Our signature formation on the field was spelling out the word **band** in script form at every football game for the next four years.

Among my classmates in the band were Bill DeCicco Myron Mondora, Bill Hinely, David Pitts, Roy Fowles, Chris Horsch, Donna Bayless, Ron Meikle and a many others I can't remember. Upper classmates included Ken Reinhardt, Carol Sue Clark, Tom Dowling and Howard Bradley who were trombone players. Carol Sue Clark was two years ahead of me and a talented trombone player. I believe she went on to play the trombone professionally. I was mostly friendly with members of the marching and concert bands. Each year in the fall, we were a marching band performing at every high school football game. During the winter months and in the spring, we were a concert band, playing concerts in the school and giving concerts at other high schools in the area and in two other Ohio cities.

BAND CAMP

The last week of August and just before my high school freshman year, the Boardman High School Marching Band went to Camp Lambec in North Springfield, Pennsylvania on the southern shore of Lake Erie. The camp was operated by the Reformed Presbyterian Church and had a strong affiliation with Geneva College in Beaver Falls, Pennsylvania. Cliff Altmann was the head basketball coach at Geneva College and the director of the camp. He later became Geneva College's athletic director. Coach Cliff's son, Biff Altmann, was a counselor at the camp.

The camp was located a few miles down the road from Youngstown's YMCA camp, Camp Fitch, where I was a camper one summer when I was eleven years old. Also, while in college one summer, I was a camp counselor there.

During the summers of 1955 thru 1958 about ninety BHS band members and faculty combined a week of intensified musical and marching band rehearsals with recreation activities offered at the camp. As I recall, most of the camp's buildings were painted green. The band camp prepared us to perform over each Labor Day weekend in front of the main grand stand at the Canfield Fair.

The Canfield Fair was a big deal in those days as it rivaled the Ohio State Fair held in Columbus. I can remember the camp's recreation hall, where we practiced music daily, the field where we marched daily and the mess hall where we ate three meals a day.

BILL DECICCO, MY BEST HIGH SCHOOL FRIEND

My best friend in high school was Bill DeCicco. Bill was over 6 feet tall and when we were together, we were quite a pair---like the cartoon characters *Mutt and Jeff*. Bill played the bass drum in the marching band and the bass clarinet in the concert band and orchestra. During summers and the school year, we would spend time at each other's house. His father was a respected medical doctor in Youngstown and his mother a retired nurse.

One night during our senior year, at band camp, Biff Altmann, Coach Cliff's son, lent his car to Bill DeCicco and me and we sneaked out of Camp Lambec headed to the town of Conneaut a few miles away to have a couple of beers. We got no further than the *White Turkey*; a famous open-air drive-in restaurant that I understand still exists on Conneaut's east side. After guzzling down nothing stronger than a root beer float, and afraid we might get caught AWOL, Bill and I immediately drove back to camp and no one found out about our camp absence.

I FELL BACKWARDS INTO A BASS DRUM

During the school year, the band would take school busses to the different area away football games. One such time, I happened to be fooling around on the band bus when I went flying backward into the bass drum and my fall broke the skin of the drum. My parents weren't too happy about my antics as they ending up paying to replace the new bass drum skin. I also played trombone in the high school orchestra for two years during my junior and senior year. We took many trips during the four years I was in the band. My most memorable was my first trip to Washington, D.C. to play and march in annual Cherry Blossom Festival Parade.

SUMMER 1956—LAKE GEORGE, NEW YORK
FISHING WITH THE PRESSLERS

My Uncle Murray and his son Shelly were avid fishermen. They owned a 1940s Johnson outboard motor and would rent a rowboat to go salt water fishing off of Brooklyn's Sheepshead Bay. They would leave early in the morning and usually caught flounder, bringing them back to the house on East 10th Street, cleaning them outside on the driveway and my family would have them for dinner that evening.

In July 1956, in between my freshman and sophomore year of high school, my uncle and cousin invited my father and me to join them on a one-week fishing trip to the beautiful Adirondack Mountains and Lake George, New York. Since I was 15 and did not yet have a driver's license, my father drove the entire four-hundred plus mile trip from Boardman.

We left very early one July morning, traveling north on route 7 to Conneaut, Ohio. Then we headed east to Erie, Pennsylvania toward Buffalo, New York on the New York Thruway. We passed by Jamestown to Troy, then headed north through Glen Falls, Saratoga Springs arriving in Bolton Landing in time for a late lunch where we met my Uncle Murray and Shelly. We parked our car and ate lunch in a diner-type restaurant in the small town.

After lunch, we parked our car then purchased some food supplies, got our suitcases and took a small launch to a secluded tiny island that would be our home for the next week. Each of us had our own rowboat with an outboard engine. Our sleeping quarters consisted of a four-person tent with four individual cots. Uncle Murray and Shelly slept in their own tent not far from ours.

My uncle caught about a six-pound smallmouth bass and cooked it over an open fire. In fact, a picture was taken with me hold the bass. I can't remember how many fish we caught but I took a drink of water right out of the lake because Lake George's water was crystal clear and the land around the lake was pristine.

MAY 1957—MARCHING BAND TRIP TO WASHINGTON, D.C.

Around the beginning of May 1957, our high school band was invited to march down our Capital's Constitution Avenue in the famous Washington D.C. Cherry Blossom Festival held every year. Operation Band-Wash Manual was a ten-page document prepared by our band director, Richard S. Bame and included congratulatory notes from Superintendent of the Boardman Schools, I. J. Nisonger and the Principal of Boardman High School, J. W. Tidd.

At the invitation of the Washington D.C. Cherry Blossom Festival, the Boardman High School Band marched approximately a mile and one half down our Capital's Constitution Avenue from just west of the United States Capitol Building to a few yards east of the Lincoln Memorial. To practice for this special event, our band marched several times on Glenwood Avenue behind the Boardman Plaza when the roadway ended in a field just south of Stadium Drive. We traveled both ways from Boardman to Washington, DC on three Greyhound buses via the Pennsylvania Turnpike.

Roy Fowles and Bill DeCicco sat directly behind the driver of Bus #2, Fred Smith, and convinced him to see how fast he could make the bus go down a steep hill on US 40 (this was before Interstate 70) in Maryland. I think Bill told me they hit about 80 mph before the "governor" kicked in on the bus. On second thought, this probably was a bad idea as we could have been a national headline prior to our arrival at the nation's capital.

The Carlyle Hotel was our home from Thursday evening May 2nd until Sunday morning May 5, 1957. This was likely a one-star (two at the most) hotel located on Capitol Hill between Union Station and the U.S. Capitol Building. The majority of our meals for our group, for approximately 100 including chaperones, were in the hotel dining room. Each person was limited to one suitcase and one overnight case. Segregation was rampant as all boys were housed on the 3rd and 4th floors while the girls occupied the 6th floor penthouse. Someone smuggled in several cigars and band director Richard Bame was really ticked when he caught Tom Lance sitting on the commode smoking a huge stogie. Most of us were housed three and four to a room and some of us had the distinction of serving as room captains.

One page of the manual was a list of ten rules (commandments). These included: move as a group, follow the schedule, be punctual, and dress appropriately, no shouting out of bus windows. Also, there was a nightly curfew and everyone was reminded they were "guests of the hotel" so I guess this meant no tossing water balloons out of the hotel windows. Finally, be courteous and considerate. A summary of the schedule of events follows:

THURSDAY, MAY 2, 1957—BOARDMAN TO WASHINGTON

Our marching band left Boardman High School during the afternoon with a stop for dinner on the Pennsylvania Turnpike at Breezewood Interchange. We arrived at the Carlyle Hotel around 11:30 p.m. with lights out one hour later.

FRIDAY, MAY 3—TOUR OF NAVAL ACADEMY

We toured the U.S. Naval Academy in Annapolis, Maryland and ate lunch on our own in the town. The U.S. Naval Academy left an impression on me because many years later I have been lucky enough to take other tours of the Naval Academy campus on two different occasions during fishing trips to Annapolis. Breakfast and dinner are scheduled at the Carlyle Hotel and a tour of the Smithsonian Institution.

SATURDAY, MAY 4—PHOTO & OTHER SIGHTSEEING

Parade begins at 9:30 a.m. Group Photo in front of U. S. Capitol Building with our Youngstown district United States Congressman Mike Kirwan. Sightseeing including: Alexandria, Virginia, Mount Vernon (George Washington's Home), Arlington National Cemetery, Tomb of Unknown Soldier (now known as the Tomb of the Unknown), Lincoln Memorial, Jefferson Memorial and the White House. We will cruise down the Potomac River to an amusement park and return to the hotel.

SUNDAY, MAY 5—RETURN TO BOARDMAN

We returned to Boardman with a stop for lunch at the Breezewood Interchange on the Pennsylvania Turnpike. Our group's photograph in front of the Capitol Building actually appeared in the May 19, 1957 Rotogravure Section of the *Youngstown Vindicator*, our local newspaper. The Youngstown safety patrol boys and girls also were among the 30,000 youngsters who visited at the same time.

SATURDAY, APRIL 18, 1958 — FAIRBORN ORCHESTRA TRIP

I played trombone in the Boardman High School Orchestra during my junior and senior year. The high school orchestra was invited to perform an exchange concert in Trotwood, Ohio that is located in the northeast corner of Dayton, Ohio. On Saturday, April 18, the Boardman High School Orchestra traveled by school bus to Madison High School in Trotwood. Their high school orchestra had previously played a concert at our high school. We left at 7:47 in the morning and had a concert at their high school that night at 7:30. The entire trip was highly organized with committees of students in charge of various duties like checking uniforms, loading instruments, music stands, etc.

Before our trip, each orchestra member received a small pamphlet entitled Operation Orch-Mad that listed everything we would need to know about the trip. We stayed with families of a Madison High School orchestra member. Each BHS orchestra member roomed with a fellow member. My roommate was Ken Aguilar, a trumpet player. We left on Sunday morning, April 19 and arrived in Boardman around 6:00 that evening.

HIGH SCHOOL SOCIAL CLUBS

There were clubs or fraternities during my high school years and I belonged to two of them; the "Minute Men" at Boardman High School and a Jewish club, "Rodans," on the north side of Youngstown. Most all of the "Rodans" members went to the north side Rayen High School, my cousin Norman's high school. In either late 1957 or early 1958 the Minute Men held a meeting at Dave Allen's house on Brookfield Avenue. Dave's father, whose nickname was Rib, took a professional photograph of the club members in their family room. It was taken during our junior year as Bill DeCicco recalls Howard Bradley, Dave Erickson, Ron Anderson, Dave and me were in the photo.

Minute Men members from the class of 1959 included Frank Billet, Myron Mondora, the late Jim Plummer, Bill DeCicco and myself. I know that I am forgetting many others including possibly the Stillson twins. Hopefully Bill DeCicco can locate this photo somewhere. The "hell" night initiation for our class was held in Southwoods about the time the roadway was being built by old man DeBartolo. Each of our BHS high school fraternities had fraternity jackets. All had white lettering except for the Hermits. The colors were: Minute Men - Black; Cavaliers - Red; Alywins - Blue and Ivyites - Green. As Bill DeCicco recalls, "the Hermits jackets may have been two tone (was it brown and gold with orange letters?) But his memory is fading."

The Boardman High School girls had only two sororities. Chi (the Greek X) and Rho (the Greek P). They wore pins. The Minute Men pin was in the shape of the current interstate highway sign with a gold "mm" encased in black.

Several years after my high school graduation, it was perhaps a good idea that the Boardman Board of Education totally eliminated fraternities and sororities. In the mid 1960's Bill DeCicco recalls driving through the Cyclone car wash on Ridge Avenue at the top of the Market Street bridge and witnessing a couple of the car washers wearing Boardman Minute Men jackets. For the Rodans on the north side of Youngstown, in order to be initiated into the club I had to memorize a short and stupid paragraph.

The paragraph went something like the following: "Oh, most noble and humble benefactor of my destiny, this humble misconception of humanity desires to open your oral cavity. Thank you, sir, sir you thank." My cousin Norman Lockshin was in another Jewish fraternity on Youngstown's northside called CBA.

RELIGIOUS SCHOOL CONFIRMATION

After my Bar Mitzvah, I continued my Jewish education at Congregation Rodef Sholem until 7:30 p.m. on Tuesday, June 4, 1957 when I was confirmed. Each member of the confirmation class had a part or parts in the service. My cousin Norman Lockshin read the blessing after the Torah reading and Mark Tessler and I returned the Torah to the Ark. I also had a reading from "A Kingdom of Priests."

There were twenty-eight students in my confirmation class with most of them living on the north side of Youngstown and going to Rayen High School. Carol Bender, Carol Strassels and I were the only confirmands from Boardman High School. Three out-of-town confirmands were David Hoodin from Niles and Robert Schaffer and Susan Lebow from Warren, Ohio. Although Norman Shaw was officially in our confirmation class, he was absent from the ceremony away at a Pennsylvania boarding school and was confirmed in the fall of 1957. Following our religious school confirmation, a reception honoring the confirmands and their families was held on the lower level of Rodef Sholem temple in Strouss Hall.

ROCK N'ROLL MUSIC

Rock N'Roll music was the music of my teenage years. It became popular with Bill Haley and The Comets' *Rock Around The Clock*. Adults thought the music and the beat were vulgar and obscene but teenagers thought the music was fantastic. This new music was quite a departure from the pre and post-World War II music of the big band era. My father on the other hand, loved rock n'roll music and couldn't understand what the adult fuss was all about.

AMERICAN BANDSTAND AND ROCK N'ROLL MUSIC

As a teenager, one of the most popular daytime television shows was broadcast after school on the ABC television network. Dick Clark and *American Bandstand* went on national television for the first time in August 1957 and the teenage nation was hooked on the latest music and dance craze. Every day after school, the show was broadcast from the Philadelphia studios of WFIL-TV. Dick Clark introduced the most popular records in the country while the Philadelphia teenage audience danced to the music. Popular recording artists of the day would appear on the show and lip-sync their record in front of the camera while the teenagers danced.

It was a favorite show and we got a chance to know the dance couples by name. Bob Clayton and Justine Carrelli and Kent Rossi and Arlene Sullivan were the most popular couples. Many other couples were seen together and we were fascinated by these kids, watching them dance each day after school. My sister and I tuned in to learn the latest gossip about the couples" romances. The show also featured dance contests and other promotions to keep our interest. The show was so popular we would sometimes talk about what happened on the show at school the next day.

1957 —JUNIOR YEAR—MY DRIVER'S LICENSE

I couldn't wait to get my driver's license so I crossed off every day on the calendar until my 16th birthday. I didn't take a driver's training course in school because that meant I wouldn't be able to get my driver's license until the end of the semester, almost 2 1/2 months after my 16th birthday. So, my father taught me how to drive. At that time, driver's training was not mandatory in Ohio high schools. Parallel parking was part of the driver's license test and I had no problem passing.

HIGH SCHOOL ACTIVITIES

Starting with my sophomore year, I was a reporter for three years on the *Boardman Bugle*, our high school newspaper. I joined the Photo Arts Club my junior and senior year and was the secretary for the group. I learned to develop and print film as well as take photos with a 4" X 5" Graphflex press camera. 4 X 5 Graphflex press camera were large and bulky cameras used by newspaper photographers at the time. In the 1930s, 40s and 50s you would always see photographers with these huge Graphflex cameras. They took 4" X 5" black and white sheet film. You had to load film into holders inside a changing bag or dark room that was a real pain. Boardman High School had a very professional darkroom and I learned how to mix chemicals use a photo enlarger to make custom black and white prints. At this time, 35mm single-lens reflex cameras were not used to take newspapers photographs.

During my high school years, I designed my own darkroom in the basement of our house using the fruit cellar and the existing wooden shelves. I lined the shelves with glossy contact paper and used glass Pyrex containers for developing chemicals. My Grandfather Ben gave me an old 5" X 7" wooden box camera with an 1896 Cook lens that he brought with him from Poland. The camera came with a wooden tripod and wooden film holders and took 5" by 7" black and white sheet film. I had to load the sheet film into the holders in total darkness and it required some practice. I took many photos with this antique camera and developed the film and made prints in my downstairs darkroom.

Later, as 35mm single-lens reflex cameras became more popular, newspaper photographers started using them for their assignments and 4" X 5" Graphflex cameras became obsolete. You periodically see these old 4" X 5" Graphflex press cameras for sale at antique malls or at antique fairs.

NORMAN AND HIS FATHER'S 1955 FORD STATION WAGON

My cousin Norman's father, Uncle Morris, owned Shwartz's Market, a small grocery store in Struthers, Ohio. My grandfather started the Struthers, Ohio grocery store around 1912 and built the building on which it was housed on Poland Avenue.

The store had a two-door 1955 Ford station wagon that was used as a grocery delivery vehicle with a three-speed manual transmission. This car was really fast. Norman, unbeknownst to his father took the car to a Youngstown drag strip and entered it in some drag races. I wasn't with him at the time. He won his first race, then blew a piston on the second race and had to slowly drive home. He was afraid to tell his father what he had done and the car had to be fixed.

One day, when Norman and I were riding on Mahoning Avenue, he took the station wagon up to 110 miles an hour. I thought the police would catch us and give Norman a speeding ticket or worse but luckily, no cops were around.

A 1946 HUDSON—MY FIRST CAR

In my junior year of high school, my parents let me buy a car from our next-door neighbor, Donald Pletcher. The car was a 1946 Hudson Super 6 four-door sedan with standard transmission. Most cars before and immediately after World War II had manual transmission. I paid Mr. Pletcher $80.00 for the car. I owned the car for about two years and sold it in 1959 to a used car dealer for $60.00. The metal fenders around the headlights started rusting and the bearings in the engine started to make funny noises so I sold the car before the entire car fell apart. I think the car had about 75,000 miles on the odometer. In those days, cars did not last very long. New car models would be introduced each year and the public was encouraged to buy a new car.

DRIVING TO WARREN IN MY 1946 HUDSON

In high school, some north side friends would periodically take turns driving to Warren, Ohio to see girls. Warren was about 30 minutes from the north side of Youngstown. One time it was my turn to drive so we took my 1946 Hudson. The car would only go about 60 miles an hour but on this occasion, I was going faster. It turns out I burned out the bearings on the car and had to sell it after the trip. Anyway, during the Warren trip, my cousin Norman was sitting in the front passenger seat and our friend Jimmy Newman, who later was a fraternity brother of mine at Ohio University, was in the back seat. I was casually driving when I was about to approach a railroad crossing and I came to a stop just before the tracks but in front of the crossing gates. The railroad lights started flashing and the crossing gates started to come down, as a train was about to approach. In my excitement and being a standard transmission car, the Hudson stalled as the cross gates started coming down. As the gate was about to crash into the hood of my 1946 Hudson, I was able to get the car started and back up slightly to avoid being hit by the gate. Luckily no other car was behind me. Norman and Jimmy were laughing hysterically. There was no danger in getting hit by the train because we weren't on the tracks, just under the crossing gates.

My parents wouldn't let me drive my car to school, so I took the school bus everyday with my sister and our other neighbors.

MY NEXT TWO CARS

My next car was a 1953 Ford two-door hardtop with standard transmission. The car was two-tone, beige on the bottom and the hard top was maroon. I loved this car. My next car was a robin egg blue two-door sedan 1956 Ford with a manual transmission.

OUR FAMILY CAR WAS REALLY FAST

In 1957, I convinced my father to buy a great looking family car. It was a tri-color 1955 Dodge Custom Royal Lancer two-door hardtop V8 with a four-barrel carburetor, dual chrome exhausts and white-wall tires. It had a black body, red in the middle and a white top. Even though this car had an automatic transmission, it was extremely fast and I wanted to test just how fast it was.

A RACE WITH NORMAN SHAW'S FATHER'S PONTIAC

Norman Shaw's father owned a 1956 Pontiac two-door sedan with a three-speed manual transmission. Norman claimed his father's car was really fast. So, one evening with my cousin Norman and me in our family's 1955 Dodge and Norman Shaw in his father's 1956 Pontiac, we drag-raced down Belmont Avenue. It was a fairly close race but I think the Pontiac beat our Dodge by a nose. I believe we only got up to 80 miles an hour but I can't remember any of the specific details.

RECORD HOPS AND WHOT DISC JOCKEY DICK BIONDI

Norman Lockshin and I along with a few of our friends would go to the Elms Ballroom located on Elm Street on Youngstown's north side and attend a "record hop" as they were called in those days. The Elms Ballroom was an old-fashioned dance hall with a wood floor and a small stage with a marquee in front. Dick Biondi, a popular Youngstown disc jockey and local celebrity, was heard on WHOT radio, a rock n roll format station, would be the host of these "hops." Dick, who was in his mid 20s at the time, sported a full beard and each week, he would dye one-half of his beard the colors of a local high school. We would mainly go to the Elms to try to meet girls. Teenagers from all of Youngstown area high schools would go there. The hops were usually held on a Friday night and Dick Biondi would promote them on his radio show. Dick Biondi would eventually end up on Chicago's WLS radio and became famous for getting fired by making an off-color remark while on the air.

FAST FORWARD TO BENNETT IN HIGH SCHOOL & DICK BIONDI

Jumping ahead of my story, as a project, our son Bennett while a student at Glenbrook North High School, had a chance to interview Dick Biondi who was then working at WJMK radio, Magic 101, the oldies station in Chicago. Bennett and I drove to the station's broadcasting studios in the old Union Carbide Building on North Michigan Avenue where he interviewed Dick for his high school project. I told Dick as a teenager; I attended his Youngstown "record hops" that brought back a lot of memories to both of us.

The Elms Ballroom was also the home of many African American artists and gospel groups. James Brown, the Godfather of Soul, often appeared there. At the time, he was totally unknown to mainstream America but the black community embraced him and attended by his many Youngstown appearances.

YOUNGSTOWN'S UPTOWN AREA

In the early 1950s, prior to the construction of the Boardman Plaza, Youngstown's Uptown area was the second largest commercial district in Mahoning County after downtown Youngstown. Some prominent Uptown businesses included: Bermann Electric, Sears and Roebuck, Fannie Farmer Candies, F. W. Woolworth, Nichol's 5 and Dime, the Donut Shop, Mr. Wheelers, Stambaugh-Thompsons hardware store, Jack and Jill Kiddie Stores (owned by my father), Spratt Photography Studio, the Colonial House, Ciceros, Smith Boot Shop, Western Auto, Strouss-Hirschberg, Isaly Dairy, G. C. Murphy, Jones Drug, the Dinner Bell, Uptown Theater, Mickey's Bar, Molnar Motors, Mahoning Bank, Union National Bank and a Sohio Station where Market Street split into Southern Boulevard. I include these businesses in my memoir strictly for historical purposes and to remember these places while growing up in Youngstown.

BAKER'S SHOE STORE—A WOMEN'S SHOE SALESMAN

When I was 16 years old and a junior in high school, I got a Saturday job selling women's shoes at Baker's Shoe Store in downtown Youngstown. Bakers was part of a chain of retail shoe stores under several brand names owned by Edison Brothers from St. Louis, Missouri. My cousin Norman Lockshin started working there first and told me about the possibility of working at this store. Many of his friends from Rayen High School and Rodef Sholem Religious School also worked there. Les Abramovitz, Marty Ardman, Bobby Shagrin and Seth Kaufman were coworkers but Bobby and Marty were not working there when I started. Each Saturday, before the store opened, the guys would meet for coffee at a restaurant across the street from the shoe store. This was my first introduction to coffee. At the time, I drank it with cream and sugar. Now it's only black. We had some crazy times at that store. A salesman would never drop a metal shoehorn. Shoehorns had a curve at one end where you could wrap around your finger and were able to grip it. If you dropped it on the floor and if one of the salesmen was around, they would step on it and flatten it. As a salesman you had to be aware of this silly practice.

While I worked at the store, Bill Vanek was the store manager and Frank Muntz was the assistant manager. Other salesmen I worked with were Paul Brittain, Joe Bayus, a short nervous guy with shifty eyes, Dan Stanislaw, and Joe Dohar. I remember Joe saying, "I am the Do-Har."

One Saturday morning before the store opened, we almost caused quite a commotion when a couple of the guys started a minor fire in the basement stock room. I don't remember why it happened but they were playing with matches. It was only a small fire and quickly put out before either manager knew about it.

On one very unusual occasion, I decided to sell a pair of shoes without saying one word. Norman who happened to be working with me that Saturday, told my customer I was deaf. I only whistled. I did end up selling a pair to that woman. I usually worked all day on Saturday, during the busy holiday season and on school vacations when they needed me.

As I recall, every week an Edison Brothers company newsletter, *The Whirlwind News*, would be handed out to each salesmen. The newsletter listed the various shoe stores under our District Manager. Ode Winkler, and his name appeared at the bottom of the first page. Mr. Winkler's territory included the following shoe stores: Coles and Chandler's shoe stores in Cleveland, the Bakers store in Rochester, New York, the Burt's shoe stores in Toledo, Ohio and Erie, Pennsylvania, Chandlers and Bakers stores in Buffalo, Bakers in Youngstown, Coles in Akron and Bakers in Syracuse, New York. Names of the top sales people in each store would be highlighted. The newsletter would salute the outstanding store of the week. Since all of us were part-time employees, none of our names ever appeared in the newsletter.

PRACTICAL AND HARMLESS JOKES

In those days, Norman and I used to do practical joking, not destructive or anything that was malicious, just fun and sometimes dumb things. I can't remember all of the silly things we did but on one occasion, Norman and I had been fishing on Lake Milton or at least driving by the lake. We decided it would be fun to steal a road sign that said Lake Milton. The next day we felt so guilty, we drove back to Lake Milton and put the sign back in the same place where he had stolen it.

1958—JUNIOR ACHIEVEMENT DURING MY JUNIOR YEAR

In my junior year of high school, I was in Junior Achievement. JA is still in existence and uses hands-on experiences to help students understand the economics of life. Local businesses and teachers partner with Junior Achievement and bring the real world to students with hands-on programs. The organization teaches how students can impact the world around them as individuals, workers and consumers. JA programs continue through the middle grades and high school, focusing on the key content areas of entrepreneurship, work readiness, and financial literacy. Volunteers who are part of the local business community work with elementary and high school students on various projects some of which are the making and selling of practical products created by the groups.

I was involved with the Junior Achievement bank. We were in charge of the money that was generated by each group. Every group manufactured items to sell and our job was to collect their money and keep track of it in their business account. On one occasion I remember taking a field trip to a Youngstown bank where we saw a $10,000.00 bill. Our group picture made it into the *Youngstown Vindicator*.

A NOTORIOUS NICKNAME DURING MY JUNIOR YEAR

For some unknown and stupid reason and I can't figure out why, one day, I decided to bring a pair of dice to school and started playing with them during my physical education class. The teacher, Jerry Thorpe, who was also our high school's head football coach, caught me playing with them and nicknamed me Capone after the Chicago gangster, Al Capone. The nickname stuck with me for the rest of my high school days and in my senior yearbook, the caption under my picture read, *"Capone, life of the party."* At the same time, a very popular network television program starring Hollywood actor Robert Stack as Chicago lawman Elliot Ness was being broadcast. Ness was out to get Al Capone so the Capone nickname stuck with me until the end of my senior year.

SEPTEMBER 20 & OCTOBER 25, 1958—BEGINNING OF YEAR

My senior year was an exciting one for me and for the Boardman High School Marching Band. On September 20 our band marched during the half-time show at a Cleveland Browns football game at the old Cleveland Municipal Stadium and the game was televised.

On October 25 the marching band members boarded school busses and traveled to Columbus, Ohio to watch the Ohio State University versus the University of Wisconsin football game and to see the Ohio State Marching Band in action. I distinctly remember Don Flowers, a former Boardman High School band member and Ohio State Marching Band member, greet our members after the game. I wrote a news story about this band trip in my high school newspaper, the *Boardman Bugle*. I also took typing class in high school from Miss Parker. I often said that the two major things I got out of high school was learning how to type and getting along with people, having been a member of the band.

MARCH 15, 1959—BAY VILLIAGE, OHIO BAND CONCERT

On a very snowy and blustery day on March 15 in my senior year of high school the concert band performed in Bay Village, Ohio. Dr. Sam Shepard, who made national headlines for being convicted of killing his wife, was from Bay Village and we played at their high school several years after his notoriety.

Our high school concert band was also involved in regional band competitions and would go to Warren, Ohio and other cities to compete. At the time, we believed we had one of the best marching and concert bands in the state.

ANNUAL BAND AWARDS BANQUETS

Toward the end of each of my high school years and usually in the middle of May, the band would hold its annual awards banquet in honor of the concert band and orchestra. I attended every one of these award banquets. The evening event was sponsored by the Boardman Band-Orchestra Mothers' Club and was held in the banquet hall of a local church.

The evening consisted of an invocation and a welcome by a parent. A band member served as a Master of Ceremonies before the catered dinner was served. After dinner there would be a group sing and music played by one of the ensembles (string or woodwind quintet or brass sextet). Our bandleader/teacher, Richard S. Bame, handed out the awards toward the end of the evening. I received some awards but I can't remember the details. Each senior received an award.

MY FATHER'S CAREER CHANGED

During my senior year of high school, my father's business at Jack & Jill Kiddie Stores was dealt a major blow when Strouss Hirshberg's, one of the two major Youngstown department stores, opened a children's clothing store directly across the street from Jack & Jill. When this happened, my father thought seriously of closing the store and going back to teaching.

(I found a postcard written to my Aunt Sadie and Uncle Harry by my father on October 28, 1958. It said the following): Dear Sadie and Harry:

"Today, I had a thrill that lasted from morning till night. Early this morning, just as I was getting up, the phone rang and the Department of Education requested I report to East High School to teach for the day. Naturally, it was a tremendous excitement because years have gone by since I have stood before a high school class. They were pleased with my work and asked me to come out tomorrow at $20.00 a day and only work for 6 ½ hours. Two months ago, I applied for substitute teaching, after many months struggling to get back my teaching certificate, which I let expire 12 years ago. I'm trying everything to keep the home fires burning. Business reverses due to the drastic work lay-offs during 1958 had its share of lethal blows. Love, Dave"

My father had to go back to college in order to get his Ohio teaching certificate. So, on June 20, 1959, he completed his first week of post-graduate study at Youngstown University. Besides working in the store, his study schedule was no less than seven hours per day that was grueling. I think he always wanted to teach at the university level but that dream evaded him. Meanwhile, my father's grades from his course work at Youngstown University were outstanding. In the summer of 1959, he was offered a teaching position at Woodrow Wilson High School, on Youngstown's south side. He taught English and the administration put him in charge of the fast-learning groups. He had to take 18 hours of additional courses in order to obtain tenure. My father saw the writing of the wall and so Jack & Jill Kiddie Stores closed its doors when the lease was up on July 31, 1959. Early October 1959, my father was appointed to the Public Relations Committee of Woodrow Wilson High School. He was chosen to represent the school to the public. He taught freshman and senior English at this high school for 23 years until he retired from teaching in 1982 at age 70. Meanwhile in 1962, my mother decided to go back to college to re-instate her teaching certificate by taking additional courses at Youngstown University.

I DID THE FAMILY GROCERY SHOPPING

Sparkle Market located at 6315 Market Street in Boardman was one of my first memories of living on Stillson Place. Next to the supermarket was Bertrando's barbershop and Sill's Tailor. While in high school, I would often do the family grocery shopping at the Sparkle Market. I got to be a pretty good shopper, knowing the store's aisles, the prices of items and watching for ads in the newspaper. Since both of my parents worked, I took it upon myself to do the family grocery shopping.

For the two years after I graduated from college, I lived at home and did most of my family's grocery shopping. Sparkle Market was opened in 1946 and was locally owned and operated by the Anzevino family. The Sparkle Market had been serving the Boardman area for nearly six decades. I received an email from one of my high school classmates saying the Anzivino family sold the supermarket to a young couple, but they could not make it go. The store closed in November 2013.

MY HIGH SCHOOL GUIDANCE COUNSELOR

During the early part of my senior year, all of the graduating class had to meet with a college counselor and take achievement and dexterity tests to see what would be the best options after graduation. After taking a series of tests and after analyzing its results, my guidance counselor told me that I shouldn't go to college because I had amazing dexterity. Instead, I should consider studying to become an apprentice plumber. He said I could make a good living eventually as a master plumber. Of course, I laughed and decided to apply to Ohio University and was accepted in January 1959.

For some reason, Goshen College in Goshen, Indiana recruited me to attend and I received unsolicited information from Goshen. I have no idea how they got my name or why they would ever ask a Jew to go to a Mennonite college. Mennonites are members of an evangelical Protestant sect originating in 16th century Holland and were characterized by simplicity of living, plain dress and rejection of military service, among other things. My best friend in high school, Bill DeCicco, kept on joking about me accepting to go to the "Land of Goshen." For many years, it was a standing joke in our friendship. Joanne Yoder one of my senior classmates, and a Mennonite, actually ending up going graduating from Indiana's Goshen College.

THE SENIOR PLAY

I always had an interest in theater and I really wanted to audition for a part in our senior play that was *The Man Who Came To Dinner*. It was a comedy in three acts written by George S. Kaufman and Moss Hart. I couldn't try-out because our family had planned a trip to New York City as a graduation present to me. The auditions to the play took place over the winter break of my senior year so no senior play for me. I did make an appearance with my friend Bill DeCicco in our senior assembly that took place a little later in the year.

SENIOR ASSEMBLY

Each year the senior class put on a variety show that was called the senior assembly. A number of students with talent performed for the entire student body. Classmate Gene Roncone who had a band during high school played rock n'roll music and a few people played musical instruments. Bill DeCicco and I decided to put on a ventriloquist act whereby I would sit on Bill's knee and Bill would talk and I would respond. We used some old Jack Benny radio material, e.g., Bill would ask me, "What's your name?" And I would say, Sy. Bill would say Sy and I would say Si. Bill would say, what do you do Sy? And I would say, sew. Bill would say sew and I would say, Si. Do you have a sister? I would say Si. What is her name? I would say Sue. He would say Sue and I would say Si. You get the idea. When we got on stage, I was sitting on Bill's knee, just like a ventriloquist dummy. Bill was so nervous his legs were shaking and I was bouncing up and down. I don't think the audience saw it but we finally got through the act.

MY HIGH SCHOOL DANCE BAND

During my senior year, a few of the high school band members decided to form a dance band using big band music charts. Myron Mondora, a clarinet player, reminded me that my parents allowed us to practice in our living room. We actually performed at a Sweetheart Ball but I can't remember if we performed any other place. I think it was more for our own enjoyment than anything else. Myron recently told me our old high school now has a big band, part of its current music program

SENIOR PROM

My senior prom was a memorable one. On Saturday, May 16, 1959, my date was Ann Brandmiller, who happened to be one of the most popular girls in the entire high school. The theme for the party was *An Evening In Paris*. Frank Ambrose and His Orchestra provided music for dancing. Ann was the homecoming queen in the fall of our senior year and a class secretary officer. I was friendly with her and found out from one of her friends that she didn't have a date, so I asked her to go with me. I double-dated with my best friend, Bill DeCicco who took Eva Massaro. Eva was up for Senior Prom Queen and was the daughter of one of my father's college friends, John Massaro. Mr. Massaro was a science teacher at our high school. I rented tuxedo pants with a white dinner jacket, cumber bun and shoes and bought Ann a corsage. I was on the senior prom decorating committee and the high school gymnasium was decorated with streamers hanging down from the ceiling. Following the prom, everyone journeyed to the Foster Theater to see the movie "Gidget" sponsored by the senior class. And then the juniors ate breakfast while the seniors were treated at the Four-Square Club.

FRIDAY, JUNE 5, 1959—HIGH SCHOOL GRADUATION

At 8:15 p.m. on Friday, June 5, 1959, I graduated from Boardman High School. We were the first class to graduate in a new auditorium. There were 435 in my graduation class but only ten were Jewish; besides me, there was Sue Harshman, Charlene Rogavin, Arnie Nashbar, Clarence Nachbar, Ron Mostov, Carol Bender, Carol Strassels, Barbara Zeigler and Ron Rappaport (one-half Jewish).

SEVERAL SUMMER JOBS

I had different summer jobs during my high school years and immediately upon my June 1959 graduation. The summer before my freshman year at Ohio University I worked for the traffic department of the Mahoning County engineers where Youngstown and Boardman were located. I was first assigned cutting grass along the side of roads with a sickle that I absolutely hated. While cutting the grass I was bitten by some insect because for one month, I itched like crazy and I couldn't stop scratching. After that job I worked on a crew painting lines down the middle of the highway. Sometimes I drove the truck that followed the men lining the road. After that job, I was assigned to work in the kitchen of the Mahoning County's employee restaurant that I actually enjoyed. I made simple sandwiches. Periodically I also sold shoes on Saturdays at Baker Brothers Shoe Store in downtown Youngstown or whenever they needed me. Selling women's shoes was a job I first started in May 1958 while a junior in high school.

DELIVERYING ARTIFICIAL FLOWERS

A summer job after my freshman year was driving a Volkswagen Microbus with standard transmission to deliver artificial flowers for Hazel Kirschbaum Florist in Boardman. The well-known local florist had a store on Market Street close to my house, supplied decorative flowers to a variety of clients in northeastern Ohio and western Pennsylvania. My job was to deliver orders to her clients. I used to travel to various locations in and around Pittsburgh and as far east as the small towns of Greensburg, Tarentum, Aliquippa and Ambridge, Pennsylvania. *Bubbles and Sherman* was a famous Jewish deli located in the Squirrel Hill section of Pittsburgh where I would periodically stop during my runs to Pittsburgh. I loved this job and I got to see a lot of western Pennsylvania.

One time but I can't remember the exact Pennsylvania location, got pulled over by a local policeman and issued a speeding ticket. My Ohio driver's license was taken away and replaced by a slip of paper that permitted me to drive. I told my mother about the traffic ticket but I was afraid to mention it to my father. I paid a nominal fine through the mail and they sent back my Ohio's driver's license. Because I pleaded guilty and paid the fine, I don't think I had any marks put against my driver's license. Many years later, I told my father about the traffic ticket.

JULY 1959—COLLEGE ORIENTATION AND PLACEMENT TESTING

Before the beginning of my first year of college, for a few days in July 1959, I drove to Ohio University with Sam Roth and Sam Birnbaum, two Youngstown friends of mine. We attended orientation sessions and were tested for placement in our freshman courses. I think Sam Roth drove. Sam Birnbaum was one of the few Jewish families living on the south side of Youngstown. I knew Sam since sixth grade when we picked him up at his Pyet Street home and drove him and me to the Jewish Center on Bryson Street on Youngstown north side. Sam Birnbaum and Sam Roth became my Phi Sigma Delta fraternity brothers at Ohio University.

SANDY SUPER—MY FIRST GIRLFRIEND

During the summer before my freshman year at Ohio University, I had a romantic relationship with my first real girlfriend named Sandy Super who was the same age as me. Her family moved to Youngstown a short time before and we started going out together. She lived on the north side of Youngstown. Sandy was starting her freshman year that fall at Ohio State University in Columbus. We dated the entire summer and both of us went off to our separate colleges. I invited Sandy to Ohio University for a weekend and I took her to see Alfred Hitchcock's movie *Psycho*. Sandy was a sweet girl, a wonderful friend and we had lots of laughs together but that was about it, nothing serious.

Our long-distance relationship didn't even make it past the first semester of our freshman year. I would periodically see Sandy at the Jewish Center during college years breaks. After graduating from Ohio State with a degree in teaching, Sandy married Southsider Bill Copperman and settled in Youngstown. Bill was a close friend of my cousin Bobby Weily. Sandy had two children with Bill, a boy and a girl. Unfortunately, Bill had a heart attack and passed away unexpectedly at a young age and I totally lost contact with Sandy.

JUMP AHEAD TO EARLY 2011—SANDY RE-CONNECTION

While in Scottsdale, Arizona during Penny and my trip there, I ran into Larry Cohen from Youngstown. (Side Note: How I met Larry after a current events class is an entirely different story that I will get into later in this book). Natalie Kane, a member of a current events class and her boyfriend, my cousin Corky Weily, had met Larry Cohen several weeks before at a restaurant.

On Thursday, January 20, 2011, Larry, and his wife Renee Yarov, also from Youngstown, Corky, Natalie, Penny and I went out to dinner at Scottsdale's Village Tavern and Sandy Super's name came up during the conversation. Larry Cohen, Bob Weily, Bill Copperman and Jimmy Newman were close friends in Youngstown and so they knew Sandy and her husband Bill Copperman. I asked Renee for Sandy's phone number and decided to call her when I returned to Chicago. I had not spoken to Sandy is about fifty years. Sandy was absolutely surprised to hear from me and we traded email addresses, photos and would stay in touch. After Bill's death, she married Samuel Zians who had two children of his own. She is currently living in Florida. It turns out Bobby and Jim Pazol from Youngstown and Scottsdale also know Sandy and her husband.

CHAPTER SEVEN
College

AUGUST 1959—OHIO UNIVERSITY

My parents along with my sister, Linda, drove me to Ohio University in late August 1959. When asked to relieve my father at the wheel, I was so nervous about starting college I couldn't drive the car. All of my belongings fit in the trunk of our car unlike when Penny and I drove Ronna to the University of Wisconsin before her freshman year.

My freshman dormitory was Johnson Hall located at the bottom of Jefferson Hill in the east green. The hill was very steep and in order to get to class, you had to walk up the hill. In the winter, the ice and snow made it slippery and difficult to walk. The cafeteria where I ate all of my meals was located in Jefferson Hall across the street from Johnson Hall. A semester meal ticket was purchased and you had to show the cashier the ticket when you went through the cafeteria line. My freshman roommates were both sophomore, Alan Appelbaum from Canton, Ohio and Alfred Frankel from Cleveland. Al Frankel was the manager of the university baseball team and Alan Appelbaum wrote sports columns for the *Ohio University Post*, our university newspaper. I couldn't believe three Al's were assigned to the same dormitory room. Alan Appelbaum told me that one time he visited Al Frankel's Cleveland house. Al's parents were German and had escaped Hitler, immigrating to the United States right before the start of World War II.

Our second-floor dormitory room was simply furnished and not very large. There was one bunk bed and a single bed, plus three desks with three chairs, three reading lamps and three dressers. Each week, clean sheets and pillowcases could be picked up from a closet on our floor. Since neither of the roommates wanted to sleep permanently in the upper bunk, each week one of us alternated between the single bed, the lower bunk bed and the upper bunk bed. No dormitory room had individual telephones and you had to go outside of your room to make a call. To earn spending money during my first college year, I worked at the dormitory switchboard patching phone calls to telephones located in each hallway. When you had a phone call, people would either yell in the hallway that you had a call or came to your room to let you know.

FRESHMAN ENGLISH

I was having some difficulty with my freshman English class as we had to write papers on various topics. My roommate, Alan Appelbaum, was working on a major in journalism so I told him I was having difficulty with writing assignments and getting poor marks on my papers. Alan volunteered to write my next paper. When I got my paper back, it was an F. You can imagine Alan's surprise when I showed him the mark on the paper. By the end of my first semester, my writing had improved and I managed to get a C in the class. This story keeps on resurfacing itself by Alan who lives in Wilmette, Illinois about 15 minutes away from us. Alan pledged out fraternity and became the Sports Editor of the *Ohio University Post* and spent many long hours at the newspaper's offices in the Baker Center. After Alan graduated in 1962, he stayed one more year at Ohio University completing a Master's degree.

Dennis Shere, another fellow classmate of mine, also worked at the *Post* and eventually moved to Chicago after being the editor of the Dayton, Ohio daily newspaper and after his marriage ended. Dennis worked for the Moody Bible Institute for many years and decided at age sixty to go to law school to become an attorney. He was one of the attorneys who worked on Chicago's famous Browns Chicken murder case representing Juan Luna who was convicted of the murder and sentenced to life in prison. Dennis wrote a book about the famous case and he sighed a copy for me.

During my freshman year, I became very friendly with David Levin and Arnie Sukenik both from Painesville, Ohio and Jack Cohen from Beaver Falls, Pennsylvania. They lived in another dormitory and I met them eating my meals at Jefferson Hall. We became very close friends and hung around together for most of the first semester. I studied hard and made grades so I could pledge Phi Sigma Delta fraternity, one of two Jewish fraternities on campus during my freshman spring semester.

Rob Heller was also a freshman from Long Island, New York and lived in Johnson Hall down the hall from me. He didn't study much and played the drums most of the time. By the end of our freshman year, he flunked out of school.

A HOLLYWOOD TALENT AGENT STORY

Skip Ahead to 1993: I was thinking of female singers to suggest to my International Foodservice Manufacturers Association (IFMA) client for its upcoming November Presidents Conference. I thought of recommending singer Helen Reddy, so I called the Williams Morris Talent Agency in Los Angeles and was told her agent was Rob Heller. I thought to myself, could this person be the same Rob Heller that lived down the hall from me in Johnson Hall during my freshman year at Ohio University?

I decided to call Rob to see if Helen Reddy would be available for a particular November date. Rob answered the phone and I spoke. I'm Alan Spencer from Williams/Gerard in Chicago and I'm thinking of suggesting Helen Reddy to one of my clients for a possible November singing date. By the way, "Are you from Long Island?" Rob said, Yes. I said, "Do you play the drums?" Rob said, Yes. "Did you go to Ohio University in 1959 and live in Johnson Hall?" Rob said emphatically, "Yes, Who is this?" Then I told him how I knew him and who I was.

Apparently, Helen Reddy was not available or too expensive, I can't remember. I found out some information about Rob. After flunking out of Ohio University, Rob went back to Long Island and graduated from Hofstra University, moved to Hollywood and became a talent agent in 1964. I eventually booked singer Julie Budd for IFMA's Presidents Conference that November.

I ALMOST BOOKED JERRY SEINFELD

During the early to late 1980s, well before Jerry Seinfeld's NBC television show, Williams/Gerard's Washington office used to hire Jerry to perform his standup act for many convention dates. He usually charged $2,500 per engagement. During this time, I once suggested Jerry to perform for IFMA's November Presidents Conference but my client's president rejected my idea, so I never had a chance to hire Jerry Seinfeld. In 2012 our Chicago office hired Jerry to perform for Northwestern Mutual Insurance Company annual agents conference held in Milwaukee. By this time, Jerry was a very popular and expensive act. Penny and I went to the show and Jerry was absolutely hysterical and performed a terrific show. After the success of his NBC television show, his entertainment fee escalated for an unbelievable figure. He told the audience during his Milwaukee performance "you agents must be doing very well to be able to afford me."

AN EMBARRASSING COLLEGE FRESHMAN MOMENT

During the first semester of my freshman year, my cousin Fred Weily had a 50th birthday party and I was home for the weekend to celebrate. My mother, father and sister were at the party. Everyone was drinking liquor. My second cousin Bobby Weily, Fred's younger son, was filling my glass with doubles and triples of either bourbon or scotch, I can't remember. I got very drunk and it was very obvious to everyone at the party. My parents were extremely upset with me and I was totally embarrassed.

When I got back to our home, I went straight to bed. I can remember the ceiling was spinning and I immediately went to sleep. In hindsight, I drank so much; I could have had alcoholic poisoning.

The next morning, it seemed like I was just as drunk as the night before. When I awakened, I was so sick but I didn't throw up. I got a ride back to Ohio University and as I shaved the next day, my face was still numb. It took a few days before my face got back to normal and I never got that drunk again.

PHI SIGMA DELTA FRATERNITY

At the beginning of the second semester of my freshman year, I rushed a fraternity. There were only two Jewish fraternities on campus, Phi Epsilon Pi and Phi Sigma Delta. Dave Levin, Jack Cohen and Sam Roth all chose to go Phi Sigma Delta and I was asked to pledge. Each pledge was assigned to a "big brother" who was an active member of the fraternity. Chuck O'Koon, from Louisville, Kentucky was my big brother. The address of our fraternity house was 95 University Terrace, across from a women's dormitory, Scott Quadrangle and next door to Hillel Foundation on one side and the natatorium (swimming pool) on the other.

A HELL WEEK TO REMEMBER WITH PORK LIVER

It was a tradition in our fraternity that pledges going through hell week had to have all of their hair cut off. However, just before my pledge class was to be initiated in the fall of 1960, the university said that the cutting of a pledge's hair was considered *hazing* and the practice was banned from campus. I was very happy to hear this news because I can remember the beginning of my freshman year; the pledges one year ahead of me had their hair cut off and were essentially bald.

The fall semester of my sophomore year, our fraternity pledge class came back to campus a week ahead of time to what was called "Hell Week." As part of the tradition of Hell Week, all of our fraternity pledges had to wear beef liver in our underpants for an entire week before school officially started. Part of our duties as pledges was to assist coeds with moving their luggage into dorm rooms. Our pledge master, Ralph Marrinson, was supposed to buy beef liver that the pledges had to wear in their underwear as part of the initiation into the fraternity. The local butcher only had pork liver, so Ralph bought pork liver instead. No previous pledge master had ever bought pork liver.

As part of the initiation process, all pledges slept on the first floor of our fraternity house and on the morning of the third day, when we all awaken, flies were swarming all around our crotches. The stench from the rotting pork liver was overwhelming. The upper-class fraternity brothers who had already moved into the house ahead of time told our pledge master Ralph to immediately get rid of those stinking pork liver underpants. All of the pledges were ordered to take off their smelly underpants and Ralph had a pledge detail assigned to bury our underwear in the backyard of the fraternity house. After that incident, I decided not to eat liver ever again and I've kept that promise.

During my freshman year, my father went to Youngstown University taking refresher courses to become certified as an English teacher and began teaching at Woodrow Wilson High School on the Southside of Youngstown.

Our fraternity was involved with J-Prom (Junior Prom) skits that were part of springtime activities at the university. Fraternities teamed up with sororities so each could put up a king and queen candidate to be chosen as the overall J-Prom king and queen. Each fraternity and sorority put on skits in fierce competition. We had to rehearse singing and dancing after classes. Each skit had to have an overall theme. Elaborate costumes were made and scenery constructed. We took popular songs and wrote parodies to them to fit into our theme.

My sophomore year, Al Goldstein, a fraternity brother of mine from Baltimore, was crowned J-Prom king. Al was a huge baseball fan and wanted to be the voice of the Baltimore Orioles baseball team upon graduation. I don't know if his dream ever happened. During my freshman or sophomore years I owned a 1955 Ford two-door sedan but was not permitted to drive it to college.

SUNDAY, JUNE 19, 1960—MARILYN & LARRY'S WEDDING

Between my college freshman and sophomore year, my first cousin Marilyn Lockshin and Larry Levy got married. Marilyn graduated from Northwestern University a year earlier and met Larry who was from Cleveland Heights, Ohio. Their wedding took place at Rodef Sholem Temple in Youngstown. The couple settled in an apartment on West Jarvis Street in Chicago's East Rogers Park.

WOUB RADIO IN ATHENS, OHIO

I had always been interested in radio and worked part-time at the university radio station WOUB-FM from my sophomore year in 1961 to my senior year in 1963. I had my own music program and was an all-around radio announcer/newscaster.

ROGER AILES, WOUB'S STATION MANAGER

Roger Ailes was the station manager during my sophomore and junior years.

Roger was a year ahead of me and right before Roger's graduation in 1962, I asked him what he was going to do after graduation. He told me he was going to move to Cleveland to become one of the production assistants on the *Mike Douglas Show* that at the time was broadcast nationally from studios in Cleveland.

Roger later made an international name for himself as a political consultant for the Republican Party and helped to get Richard Nixon elected president of the United States. Then he later assisted Ronald Reagan, George W. Bush and Donald Trump get elected president. He became a major force in broadcast television news. After leaving CNBC, he created 24-hour Fox News and was chairman and CEO of Fox News and Fox Television Stations, working for entrepreneur Rupert Murdoch. Roger resigned his position in July 2016 after many accusations of sexual harassment and died on May 18, 2017 after hitting his head in a fall in his Palm Beach, Florida home. Several motion pictures including a documentary were produced about Roger showing him as a nasty and ruthless person with a terrible reputation who gained tremendous power in television news and national politics.

CAN'T STAY UP LATE

As a young child, during elementary and high school, I always went to bed early and woke up early. My human clock is on this kind of timer. During all of this time, I rarely stayed up late and usually was ready to conk out around 9:00 p.m. While in college, I could not study beyond 9:00 or 9:15 p.m. and never pulled an all-nighter studying for an exam except one time. One particular night during my junior year, I stayed up all night cramming for a final exam. I believe it was a history course. I walked to the final exam and I could not keep my eyes open. During the exam I actually dozed off a few times because I was so tired and totally exhausted. This was the first and only time I stayed up all night studying for an exam. I don't remember how I did on the test but immediately following taking it; I walked back to the fraternity house, got into bed and fell into a deep sleep. I slept for all most twenty-four hours straight. My roommates tried to wake me up and they thought something was wrong with me because I couldn't get up.

Jump Ahead: As an adult and senior citizen, I still can't stay up late and usually start getting ready for bed around 9:30 p.m. or thereabouts. The bedroom television is usually turned on to the news and I'm usually sound asleep before the end of the news by 10:35 p.m.

JANUARY 1962—MY MOTHER GOES BACK TO COLLEGE

At the beginning of the second semester, my mother started taking courses at Youngstown University to get her Ohio elementary school teaching certificate. In the summer of 1963, she took 6 more hours of classes the first six weeks of summer school. She was required by the state of Ohio board of certification to take four subjects over a four-year period in order to get her provisional teaching certificate fully accredited because she switched to elementary education from high school. She eventually earned enough credits to get an elementary teaching certificate and started a job teaching 5th grade at Bennett School in Youngstown in the fall of 1963.

1962—SUMMER SCHOOL & PAYING JOB ON WOUB RADIO

The summer of 1962 between my junior and senior year, I went to summer school in Athens. I had a paying job at WOUB, the student radio station. The money helped to pay for some of my expenses. I was involved with radio remote broadcasts from the Baker Center, did newscasts and had my own music program. I went to summer school to take two classes prior to my student teaching in Cleveland in the fall. That summer, I remember working with Bill Van Horn, a fellow worker at WOUB. After graduation, I believe Bill became a newscaster for a Columbus, Ohio radio station.

TUESDAY, FEBRUARY 6, 1962—ALAN MEETS PENNY CAMBERG

At the beginning of my second semester junior year and the first week of February 1962, I went to what was called a mixer/dance sponsored by Hillel Foundation. As I mentioned, the Hillel Foundation was located next to the Phi Sigma Delta fraternity house but the mixer was in another location and I believe held in a dormitory. At this mixer I met a first-semester freshman, Penny Camberg, who had just graduated a few weeks earlier in the January 1962 mid-year class from Cleveland Heights High School.

I was immediately attracted to Penny the minute I saw her and started talking to her. She had a very unusual hairstyle; a pageboy fluff and I hadn't seen one exactly like hers before. We talked a lot and we danced the jitterbug. I noticed she placed her arms and hands in a certain way when she danced. We quickly became friends that evening and I invited Penny to attend an *Artists and Models* Costume Party at my fraternity house. I believe it was the next weekend after meeting her. For the party, I dressed as a half man, half woman. The top half of me was a man and the bottom half was a woman. As a woman, I borrowed a skort, panty hose and high heel shoes from Bonny Bern, a friend of mine from the girl's dormitory Scott Quadrangle, across from our fraternity house. On the top half of my body, I wore a man's vest without a shirt and a black beret I owned. There was an immediate attraction to Penny from the first moment we met but I did not want to get involved in a relationship with any woman during college. I wanted to have a good time and graduate college with no attachments.

Although I had a great time with Penny at our party, we did not have another date. Penny and I remained friends and periodically I would see her on campus throughout the second half of my junior year.

DRIVE TO CLEVELAND TO SEE PENNY CAMBERG

During the summer of 1962, between my junior and senior year, I kept thinking of Penny so I called, invited her to go on a date and I drove to Cleveland to see her. She told me she had another date but broke it to go out with me. When I drove to her house in University Heights, I met her mother, Dorothy, her sister, Lois and Sam Zipp, a man her mother had been dating for many years. When I entered the home, Lois, age thirteen at the time, was sitting on the steps leading up to the second floor and she was wearing pajamas. I can't remember where we went on our date but we had a great time together. Penny's home had a finished basement and after our date we came back to her house and talked.

Driving back to Youngstown I kept thinking about our wonderful evening together but can't remember the details. At this point, we were just friends as no serious relationship was about to happen.

JUMP AHEAD TO MEMORIAL DAY WEEKEND IN 1967

It wasn't until I re-connected with Penny on this Memorial Day weekend that my relationship with her took on a whole new meaning and I started to have strong feelings for her after briefly seeing her again during my sister's party. There is much more about what happened and our love story later in this book.

STUDENT TEACHING IN BEACHWOOD, OHIO

Ohio University students majoring in education were given a choice of where to student teach. They could choose Athens or a surrounding area near Athens or in the Cleveland metropolitan area. I thought it would be a great experience to live in a large city and be on my own, so I chose to go to Cleveland and student teach.

September 1962, the first semester of my senior year of college, was spent off-campus when I moved to a tiny 3rd floor apartment in a single-family house on Daleford Road in Shaker Hts., Ohio. I was assigned to student teach sixth grade at Beachwood's Fairmont School with Mr. Rico Palatta as my supervising teacher. The house was owned by a couple having previously moved from Lake Forest, Illinois. All they talked about was Chicago, Lake Forest and Trader Vic's, their favorite restaurant next to the Sheraton Chicago on North Michigan Avenue.

University housing listed places to rent for student teachers living in Cleveland so that is how I was able to find the Shaker Heights apartment. The sparsely decorated one bedroom apartment was a tiny space on the third floor of a large single-family house on a corner lot. It had its own entrance. Each night, I ate dinner with the older couple that owned the house. The toilet and the kitchen were in the same room. The rent was extremely reasonable. One memorable event during my Cleveland stay involved an evening in October 1962 when the family and I were glued to the television set to watch President Kennedy's speech to America about the Cuban missile crisis.

My father sold me his 1960 four-door robin's egg blue, Ford Fairlane 500 that I drove to Cleveland for my student teaching. A friend of mine from Youngstown, Seth Kaufman, had dropped out of college and was taking a break. He was living in Shaker Hts. with the Wortschafter family and working as a lab technician at Cleveland's University Hospital. During that semester we would get together on the weekends looking for girls at various nightspots around Cleveland. The two dances that were very popular at the time were the "Twist" and the Bossa Nova. I happened to be a good dancer at the time and we had no trouble meeting girls.

CHICAGO ON MY MIND

The first time I really paid attention to Chicago was when my father was friendly with Vince DeNiro, an infamous Youngstown gangster, who used to buy clothes for his children at Jack & Jill Kiddie Stores. Youngstown was known as "Little Chicago" because of the gangsters that operated there in the 1930s, 1940s and into the 1950s. Vince DeNiro owned the Colonial House restaurant a few doors north of Jack & Jill Kiddie Stores. After Jack & Jill closed for the day, Vince would come into the store and buy clothes for his children. One day in the early 1960s, when Vince's car was parked in front of Murphy's Department Store directly across the street from Jack & Jill Kiddie Stores, he was killed gangland-style when his car blew up as he started it.

In the fall of 1955, Chicago came to mind again, when my first cousin Marilyn Lockshin started classes at Northwestern University in Evanston, Illinois. My Aunt Dorothy, Uncle Morris and their son Norman would periodically drive to Chicago to visit Marilyn at college. In 1958, my junior year of high school, Kent Ross, a fellow Boardman High School band member and Jewish, who graduated a year ahead of me, was accepted to the University of Chicago. Miriam McClure, one of my 1959 classmates was accepted to Northwestern University in Evanston, Illinois. All of these connections made me think of Chicago. So, Chicago was in the back of my mind as a possible city in which to move after I would leave Youngstown that I had every intention of doing in the future. The true love for Chicago did not take shape until my 1962 Thanksgiving vacation.

NOVEMBER 1962—THANKSGIVING AND CHICAGO

During my Thanksgiving break from student teaching, I drove home to Boardman from Cleveland. My cousin Norman Lockshin, his parents, my Aunt Dorothy and Uncle Morris, invited me to join them for a weekend trip to Chicago to visit Norman's sister, Marilyn and her husband, Larry Levy. Marilyn attended Northwestern University in Evanston, Illinois, graduating in June 1959. She met Larry, a native of Cleveland Heights, at Northwestern, got married on June 9, 1960 and were living in an apartment on W. Jarvis Street in the Rogers Park neighborhood on Chicago's north side.

Norman and I stayed in Larry's Northwestern University fraternity house during our trip. We had most of the house to ourselves, as the house was vacant because of the Thanksgiving holiday break. We had such a great time that I decided I would like to move to Chicago sometime in the future. We went to the Cairo Club two nights in a row on N. Clark Street and saw a hypnotist. Marilyn and Larry suggested we go to *Second City* the second night but the hypnotist was so entertaining, we went back to see him on the second night. The hypnotist wasn't that good the second night and we should have taken Marilyn and Larry's advice and gone to Second City. We would have seen many of the original members. The second half of my senior year was an easy one and I couldn't wait to graduate.

MY FATHER TAKES TWO JOBS

At the beginning of the school year, my father started teaching three Saturday religious classes at Rodef Sholom Temple on the north side of Youngstown. Then he departed for his second Saturday job, namely, McKelvey's Department Store where he sold pianos and organs. At the same time, my father, who had been a heavy smoker for thirty-five years, finally quit. Before he quit; however, my sister and I would torment him by taking the cigarettes out of his pack and rolling up white paper and writing cancer sticks on each rolled up piece. Even in those days, we knew cigarette smoking caused cancer.

Rabbi Berkowitz at Rodef Sholom Temple asked my father to become the teacher of the confirmation class that he taught until he retired from teaching at age 70. He also taught English to foreign doctors at Youngstown's Woodside Receiving Hospital. The hospital treated people in the early stages of mental illness that might respond to early and intensive treatment. Many of the doctors were from eastern European countries and the hospital provided English classes for them.

MARCH 1963—SPRING BREAK SENIOR YEAR OF COLLEGE

Just before my 1963 college spring break, there was a huge rainstorm in Athens and the Hocking River flooded. I called Youngstown's WBBW radio collect and they recorded my voice with a thirty-second news story I had prepared about the flood and they used it immediately on the air. I used the name of Alan Stewart WBBW's special correspondent on the scene in Athens, Ohio.

My senior year, I was able have a car on campus. I paid my father for his 1960 Ford Fairlane 500 4-door, light blue, V-8 automatic transmission. It was not a very cool car. While I was planning on going to Miami Beach for my senior year spring break, my sister Linda drove my car home to Boardman and returned back with it after spring break.

MIAMI BEACH TRIP—1963—MY SENIOR YEAR

Three of my Phi Sigma Delta fraternity brothers and I drove to Miami Beach, Florida for our spring break. We drove in Jimmy Newman's brother's car, a 1962 four-door Ford Falcon with Ken Silver and Jimmy Berns and we all took turns driving. As we entered southern states such as West Virginia, Tennessee, and Georgia, we were amazed that white and colored bathrooms and drinking fountains still existed. Segregation was quite prevalent in these states and it wasn't until President B. Lyndon Johnson signed the Civil Rights Act of 1964 forbidding segregation of public facilities that the white and colored bathrooms and drinking fountains started to slowly disappear in these states.

While Jimmy Newman was driving, a Georgia state highway patrolman stopped our car for speeding. We all thought the patrolman was going to feed us to the alligators. We heard rumors and stories of motorists being stopped and never being heard from again but nothing happened to us. I'm not sure if Jimmy got a warning or a traffic ticket.

Before arriving in Miami Beach, we stopped in several Fort Lauderdale places. One of them was the Elbow Room to see where the movie, *Where the Boys Are*, was filmed and we also stopped at the Cast-A-Ways Motel located in North Miami Beach, a very popular hangout for college students.

Once in Miami Beach, we stayed at the Shoreham Hotel directly in front of the Atlantic Ocean on Collins Avenue. The hotel was torn down many years ago and high-rise condominiums were constructed. The Shoreham Hotel was north of the famous Fontainebleau Hotel that is located at 44th Street and Collins Avenue. I don't remember specific details of the Florida trip but I do remember going to Junior's Restaurant for breakfast and ordering cherry cheesecake. Two famous Miami Beach restaurants frequented by Jews were Wolfie's and Pumpernik's. After graduation, I loaded my 1960 Ford with Linda and our belongings and drove home.

CHAPTER EIGHT
After College and Graduate School

THE SUMMER OF 1963

I graduated from Ohio University at 1:45 p.m. on Sunday June 9, 1963. My parents and Linda attended the commencement ceremony that took place outside on the college green. I had five tickets so my parents invited my Aunt Sadie and Uncle Harry to join us but they couldn't break away from their New York printing business. After graduation, I lived for two years at home on Stillson Place with my parents in Boardman, Ohio.

During my first summer living at home, I went out on a date with a girl who told me she was a xerographer in a law office. Since I had never heard of that profession or term before, I asked her what a xerographer did. She told me that a company named Xerox had invented a new machine that made photocopies of documents and her job was to copy documents. Her title was a Xerographer and all she did all day was make photocopies on this new machine. At that time, her job seemed very important but by today's standards it is rather silly, non-challenging and a totally insignificant job.

SUMMER 1963—TORONTO, ONTARIO AND YOGURT

During the early summer of 1963, my grandfather Ben wanted to visit his wife's cousin who lived in Toronto, Ontario Canada. So, I volunteered to drive my grandfather there. My grandmother Rose's first cousin Dorothy Askenzy and her family were living there at the time. Isadore and Dorothy (Turkus) Askenzy escaped Poland and moved to Israel in the late 1940s, then moved to Toronto with their two daughters, Nelly and Anita. We stayed in their apartment.

Isadore made homemade plain yogurt and offered it to me. It was the first time I had ever eaten yogurt and I thought it was delicious. At that time, yogurt was not popular in the United States and was not offered in any grocery store.

JUMP AHEAD TO 1985 IN BRITISH COLUMBIA

In February 1985, I was doing a site survey for a May meeting I would be producing in Vancouver, British Columbia. After the site survey, I had some time off, so I took a ferryboat to Victoria Island and had a chance to visit with Isadore and Dorothy Askenzy who were living in Victoria Island, British Columbia. I brought a tape recorder and interviewed Isadore about his life, how they escaped Europe and eventually got to Canada. Isadore was 89 years old at the time and lived to be 100 years old. I was able to re-connect with their daughter Anita Carroll who lives in Beaux Arts, a suburb of Seattle, Washington with her family. I also emailed Anita the recording of her father.

GRANDPA, GIN RUMMY AND ME

From time to time my grandfather and I used to play gin rummy. He was a terrific card player and used to beat me all the time. He would knock with picking up just a few cards and I would be left with many points in my hand. My father used to tell me that when he was a small boy, the entire family with aunts, uncles and cousins would gather every Sunday. The adults would play cards and there would be lots of laughter while all of the young cousins played together.

COUSIN NORMAN'S BOAT

After college, my cousin Norman bought a small motorboat and we used to go water skiing but I don't remember doing much fishing from it. He named the boat *Verboten* (for boatin), a German word, and his water skiis, (for ski-in). He stored the boat in the backyard of his house on Cordova Avenue. I remember his future wife Sheila periodically riding in it with us.

A FUNNY BUT EMBARASSING DATING INCIDENT

During the 1963 summer, I went out with Darla Goldberg a few times. Darla lived on the south side of Youngstown and was a few years younger than me. On one occasion while back at her house, we were horsing around in her living room while on the couch when I accidentally kicked the 20-gallon fish tank with my shoe. The glass on the fish tank shattered and water from the fish tank and the fish flew everywhere. It made such a crashing noise her parents came running into the room to see what had happened. Fish were flopping all over the wet carpeted floor and I was so embarrassed. Most of the fish died and the floor was a mess. It could have been a great hysterical scene from a Hollywood movie.

TEACHING IN YOUNGSTOWN, OHIO

Before I graduated from college, I applied for a Youngstown Public Schools teaching position and was looking forward to be hired for the start of the 1963 school year. On July 16, 1963, I received a letter from the Board of Education and accepted a job teaching in the Youngstown Public School System but had not been assigned a school or a grade level. Youngstown school started in September 1963. My beginning salary was $4,400.00 a year but jumped up to $5,000.00 a year during the school year.

In August, I found out that I would be teaching sixth grade at Paul C. Bunn Elementary School. The school was named after a former Youngstown school superintendent who served from 1944 to 1956. Although the school is physically located in Boardman Township, it is part of the Youngstown Public School District. The school building was on 12 acres and had 22 classrooms, a multi-purpose room with a stage, a learning center and the usual offices, teacher's lounge and clinic. The staff served an enrollment of between 650 and 700 children. Full-time personnel included 23 classroom teachers, a principal, a secretary, three custodial persons and three cafeteria workers. Half-time personnel included a speech and hearing therapist, an instrumental music teacher and two additional custodial workers. On call were a psychologist, supervisors, a visiting teacher, a doctor and a dental hygienist.

The school's principal, Clay Folsom had been a principal at other Youngstown public schools but it was his first year as principal at Paul C. Bunn. I had 36 children in my first class and my year of teaching was a real challenge. One of the demanding students in particular, Dennis McMillan, had been held back and was repeating sixth grade. Dennis was six feet tall, towered over me and with a low I.Q. It was difficult to keep his attention. Thirty-six students are a lot to handle for a first-year teacher.

I car-pooled to school with another classroom teacher, Isabel Ortega, who lived on Cadillac Drive around the corner from our Stillson Place home. Isabel graduated Boardman High School one year before me so I knew her because we rode to high school on the same school bus. During our first Paul C. Bunn, teacher orientation, I was happy to see someone I knew. Isabel was great company on our way to school each day and we talked about everything. We were both single although as I remember Isabel was seriously dating someone.

At the end of my first year of teaching, the principal asked every teacher to do a self-evaluation. I listed eighty-eight activities I had done to enrich the curriculum. I taught chess, started a chess club and giving up part of my lunch period for it, started a classroom newspaper that expanded into a school newspaper and many more things too numerous to mention.

Meanwhile, my mother was teaching fifth grade at Bennett School, another Youngstown Public School, and my father was teaching senior English at Woodrow Wilson High School. The children in my sixth-grade class would eventually go to Wilson High School and have my father as their English teacher. Three of my members of our family were teaching in the same school system at the same time. It might have been a first in the Youngstown Public School System.

During the second semester of my first year of teaching, on Sunday, February 9, 1964, the Beatles made their first "live" American television appearance on *The Ed Sullivan Show*. I remember one of my students, Gary Hungerford, came to school the next day with his hair combed just like the Beatles. For that time, long hair was not in fashion. When I look back at the Beatle's hair, it really wasn't that long, just cut in a different way.

YOUNGSTOWN'S WBBW AM RADIO 1240 ON YOUR DIAL

During the summer after graduation from Ohio University and before my fall 1963 teaching job started, I was a part-time disc jockey and newscaster on Youngstown's WBBW radio. My radio name was Alan Gerald and I called myself the "Night Watchman" because I was on the air all night, from 11:00 p.m. to 6:00 a.m. At the time, the station was a top-40 rock n'roll radio music station but in the fall of 1963, the station management decided to play "Beautiful Music." It is hard to believe I made 75 cents an hour as a disc jockey and newscaster.

I learned how to work the console board because there was no engineer on duty during my "on air" shift. I was responsible to spinning my own records, reading commercials "live" and all of the things associated with being a disc jockey and newscaster. The radio station was on the second floor of the Warner Theater Building at 260 West Federal Street in downtown Youngstown. The Warner Theater was named after the Warner Brothers of Hollywood fame, originally from Youngstown and started their careers in New Castle, Pennsylvania by owning and operating a motion picture theater in that small town.

(As a side note, my grandparents, Ben and Rose Shwartz were married in the Warner Brothers' parents' house on Elm Street on New Year's Eve, December 31, 1911. I had wondered if any of the Warner Brothers actually attended my grandparent's wedding. I read Harry Warner's autobiography and found out all of the brothers had already moved to Hollywood by that time).

I used to get fan mail from listeners. One amusing letter I received from a listener wrote to Dick James, my station manager, who writing a congratulation on the front of the letter using his initials.

" Dear Sir, as a long-time listener to WBBW, I wish to send in my many thanks for putting

Alan Gerald, on earlier. This D.J. is Mr. Personality himself, with a capital P. When a gal puts on the radio, she wants to hear someone that sounds like the guy who lives next door, not someone that just says, "A word about this product and the next record is so and so." Youngstown has finally had something good happen to it. A Disc Jockey that is refreshing, witty and full of life, that's Alan Gerald. Thank you very much for taking time out to read this letter."

A satisfied listener, Miss Barbara Flaker

During my first school year, I worked the all-night Saturday to Sunday morning shift. Some programming for Sunday mornings were broadcasts from American churches and as a public service, I also played radio transcriptions of programs produced by Armed Forces radio broadcast overseas. One of the programs was called *"Command Performance"* and was originally broadcast by Armed Forces Radio in Europe. These were the days before talk radio. There was a phone in the studio and I used to get calls from friends and girls who were my fans. I have a scrapbook with some of the fan letters I received.

My second cousin Bob Weily and my friend, Seth Kaufman, would come to the studio and keep me company especially over a Saturday night. In those days, there were no computers, no Internet so WBBW received its up-to-the-minutes news from a wire service that came over a Teletype machine from a service bureau located in the newsroom. For my hourly newscasts, I would rewrite the news, shortening stories to fit into a local newscast that I broadcast.

MUTUAL BROADCAST SYSTEM (MBS)

WBBW was an affiliate of the Mutual Broadcasting Network. This network no longer exists but during my shift time, the network had hourly national newscasts from its studios in New York City and the station would tie into the network to broadcast the news on the hour and on the half-hour. Among the famous Mutual Broadcasting System (MBS) newscasters was Westbrook Van Voorhis, who used to announce all of the *"March of Times"* radio and theatrical newsreels series during World War II. He had a very distinctive, very deep and recognizable voice.

Time Magazine began a series of news broadcasts on CBS radio and theatrical newsreels with the *March of Times* title from 1931-1945. It was one of the first big media cross-promotion ideas and was a smashing success. The newsreels were seen on early TV as "shorts" and later in episodes that were longer, but they didn't become a staple of network TV.

Westbrook Van Voorhis was famous for his dramatic delivery, *"Time Marches On!"* heard on both radio and on the theatrical newsreels. Van Voorhis was a classic newsreel announcer known for a melodramatic "voice of doom" style imitated by others. Although he was not the first narrator on the series, he was the one most people associated with the series.

The radio series was a dramatization of news events in a format similar to radio drama, interspersed with the facts of the newsworthy story read by Van Voorhis. The newsreels shown on TV were more like theatrical newsreels seen regularly through the 1940s. In a moment you'll see why I am mentioning this particular announcer.

WBBW SHIFT CHANGE

In the fall of 1963, my WBBW radio shift was switched from 11:00 to 6:00 a.m. to early Sunday morning. I used to wake up very early to arrive at the station by 5:00 a.m. on Sundays. On the way to the radio station, I would turn on my car radio and listened to radio 720 on the dial, Chicago's WGN radio. I would listen to Franklin McCormick who had an all-night radio program. WGN was a 50,000-watt radio station and could be heard clearly in Youngstown during the night and just before sunrise. Also, during my time living at home with my parents, around 11:00 p.m. at night, I used to listen to The Jack Eigen Show that was broadcast on Chicago's WMAQ radio 670 on the dial, another 50,000-watt radio station. Jack used to broadcast from a local restaurant and interviewed celebrities who happened to be in town at the time for a show or concert. Some of the interviews took place from the famous Pump Room located in the Ambassador East Hotel. Booth 1 was the most popular with Frank Sinatra and other frequent famous visitors.

MY TWO MUTUAL "NETWORK" BROADCASTS

On two separate occasions during my WBBW Sunday morning shift, I received a telephone call from the Mutual Broadcasting System network office in New York City asking me to prepare a news story for broadcast on their hourly national news. I had to write the story within an hour in between doing my regular announcing duties and as a result, I was heard coast-to-coast on a Mutual Broadcasting System newscast on two separate stories.

DOUBLE MURDER IN YOUNGSTOWN

The first radio news story I prepared was about a double-murder that took place in Youngstown the day before. This was very exciting and I got paid for it. On October 3, 1963, for my network story, I received a check from the Mutual Broadcasting System, Inc. 1440 Broadway in New York City for $10.00. It is hard to believe that the fee for appearing on a network radio newscast was only $10.00.

My name also appeared in Esther Hamilton's *Around Town* column in the *Youngstown Vindicator*. For many years, Esther, a local Youngstown celebrity, had a *Vindicator* column that appeared daily and focused on events and people making news in the Youngstown metropolitan area, much like what Irv Kupcinet wrote in his daily column for the Chicago Sun-Times.

YOUNGSTOWN NEWSPAPER STRIKE

The second radio network news story I wrote that appeared coast-to-coast was about an extended newspaper strike at the *Youngstown Vindicator* that had finally been settled after one of the longest major metropolitan newspaper strikes in

United States history. So, on April 22, 1965, I received another check from the Mutual Broadcasting System for another $10.00. I audiotaped the broadcast and have it as a sample of my Youngstown radio days on network radio.

During my WBBW radio days, I made some blunders and bloopers while on the *"air."* One time during a newscast, I messed up the title of Drew Pearson, a well-known syndicated newspaper columnist at the time. During the actual newscast I said, *"Drew Pearson well known Communist"* instead of columnist. As a radio announcer I was taught never to say excuse me on the "air." Always use the word *"rather."* So, I corrected myself by saying, "rather a well-known columnist."

I was taught to say the station's call letters were Double-U, BB, Double-U, instead of Dub-e-ya, BB, Dub-e-ya.

WBBW RADIO STUDIO AND A MINIATURE GOLF CONTEST

One of my father's colleagues from Woodrow Wilson High School, Leonard whose last name I do not remember, came to WBBW's studio one Sunday morning and took a variety of black and white photographs of me at the control board and at the entrance door to the radio station.

During the early part of my second summer, the city of Youngstown sponsored the 1st Annual Putt Putt miniature golf tournament. Area radio personalities participated in this tournament. It took place at a Boardman miniature golf course on route 224. I entered the press/radio contest and won second prize with 18 over par. Joe DeCola from the *Youngstown Vindicator* won $50.00 with 11 over par.

The Twist was a very popular dance craze during this time. I was a good dancer and entered a twist contest at a local Youngstown nightspot, the name of which escapes me. I won the contest and was awarded ten free dance lessons at Youngstown's Arthur Murray Dance Studios. I took the lessons and learned how to mambo, samba, rumba and cha cha.

HISTORIC NATIONAL EVENTS WORKING ON WBBW RADIO

There were key events in one's history that standout and make an indelible mark on your life. Three such historical events happened to me while I was working on my shift at Youngstown's WBBW radio. I had first-hand knowledge and was able to broadcast these stories to my hometown.

The aftermath of President Kennedy's 1963 assassination was one such event when the assassination took place on Friday, November 22, 1963, I was teaching sixth grade Youngstown's at Paul C. Bunn School. While the president was in Dallas, Texas, that afternoon, following lunch, I walked my class to the school's stage in the auditorium and we started watching a 16mm educational film. It was the perfect place to watch a film because you could get the stage dark for better viewing. Toward the last few minutes of the film, the principal's voice came over a load speaker on the stage. I immediately stopped the projector and heard him announcing to the school that the president had been shot while driving in an open-top convertible, part of his motorcade in Dallas. The class and I were stunned. We returned to our classroom and turned on the class television to watch Walter Cronkite and the CBS network news of the tragic event. Everyone was shocked, saddened and numb by the tragic news. In the beginning, we did not know if the president was alive or dead. The class and I just sat in our seats and watched as "live" coverage continued.

It was rare for the First Lady Jacqueline Kennedy to accompany her husband on political trips, but she happened to be beside him, along with Texas Governor John Connally and his wife, for a 10-mile motorcade through the Dallas' downtown streets. Large and excited crowds gathering along the parade route and sitting in the back seat of a Lincoln convertible, the Kennedys and Connallys were waving to the people. As their car passed the Texas School Book Depository Building at 12:30 p.m., shots were fired from the sixth floor gravely wounding President Kennedy and seriously injuring Governor Connally. The President was pronounced dead about 30 minutes later at Dallas' Parkland Hospital. He was only 46 years old. Lee Harvey Oswald allegedly fired the shots and was arrested a few hours later.

Vice President Lyndon Johnson, who was traveling in the motorcade only three cars behind the President was sworn in as the 36th president of the United States at 2:39 p.m. Johnson took the presidential oath of office aboard *Air Force One* as it sat on the runway at Dallas Love Field airport. Mrs. Kennedy, who was wearing the bloodstained clothes with her husband's blood and about thirty people, witnessed the swearing in ceremony. Seven minutes later, the presidential jet took off for Washington.

The next day, November 23, President Johnson issued his first official proclamation, declaring Monday, November 25 to be a day of national mourning for the slain president. On that day, hundreds of thousands of people lined the streets of Washington, D.C. to watch a horse-drawn caisson bearing Kennedy's body from the Capitol Rotunda to St. Matthew's Catholic Cathedral for a requiem Mass. The solemn procession then continued on to Arlington National Cemetery, where leaders of ninety-nine nations gathered for the state funeral. The event was also broadcast on network television and no one went to work that day. Kennedy was buried with full military honors on a slope below Arlington House, where Kennedy's widow lit an eternal flame to forever mark the grave.

SUNDAY, NOVEMBER 24, 1963—MORE HISTORIC RADIO EVENTS

Two days after the Dallas tragedy, on November 24, I was working my usual WBBW Sunday morning shift. The station interrupted its music format to play solemn music since the President's death on Friday when I read the printout from the news wire Teletype machine that Lee Harvey Oswald had been shot. My responsibility was to broadcast the latest news as it was happening that I did when it was time for the hourly local broadcast.

Two other important events that took place when I was working during my WBBW Sunday shift were the follow-up to the assassination of Civil Rights leader Medgar Evers on Wednesday June 12, 1963. On Friday, June 21 Byron De La Beckwith, a fertilizer salesman and member of the White Citizens' Council (and later of the Ku Klux Klan), was arrested for Evers' murder. There were follow-up stories about the assassination and I was able broadcast these news stories to a

Youngstown radio audience.

Another horrible story took place on Sunday, August 15, 1963 during my shift at the radio station. It was the sad story of the bombing of the16th Street Baptist Church in Birmingham, Alabama when four black girls were killed. Members of the Klu Klux Klan set off the bomb and I broadcast these two stories to my audience.

JUDGE AT A HIGH SCHOOL DEBATE

I can't remember how or why I was chosen to be a judge at a high school debate. On one Saturday during my second year of teaching, I drove to Warren G. Harding High School in Warren, Ohio and was a judge in a high school debate between area debate teams. The overall topic was Non-Proliferation of Nuclear Weapons. Two teams were squared off, one was pro and one was con. Throughout the day, there were several teams I judged. It was the first and only time I ever judged a high school debate. It was quite interesting and I was impressed with high school students and their detailed preparation.

1963 TO 1965—THE YOUNGSTOWN PLAYHOUSE AND ME

During the time I was living at home and working in Youngstown, I became involved with three different plays at the Youngstown Playhouse. For a community theater building, the Youngstown Playhouse was quite elaborate with an excellent lighting, sound system and orchestra pit. At the time, it was highly regarded as a top regional theater company in the country.

My first play was Herb Gardner's *A Thousand Clowns*. I worked backstage as a prop master and helped to build and paint the scenery for this show. My second play was *Desperate Hours* and I had a small speaking part. The play was about a family terrorized by an escaped convict who invades a suburban house. Actors Humphrey Bogart and Frederick March starred in the movie version of this play. I played a policeman, *Dutch*, who only spoke over on a police station desk intercom but I did not actually appear on stage.

My third play, *Wonderful Town*, was a musical, about two sisters from Ohio who live in Greenwich Village New York and meet all of these crazy characters. Adolph Green and Betty Comden wrote the play and I had three different onstage roles. Ella Gerber, a theatrical director from New York City, directed the play. Ella had accepted a temporary guest director's position for the 1964-65 theater season.

In one scene, I played a sixty-five-year-old garbage man with grey hair; in another scene, a person on an African safari and an expanded onstage role as Speedy Valenti, a hip cat who had girls following me all across the stage. My character owned a nightclub in New York's Greenwich Village and I wore a Zoot Suit as a costume. I really enjoyed working in the theater and on one-occasion I invited my 6th grade class to come to the play to see their teacher perform. One evening many of them showed up to cheer me on during the curtain call. They were sitting in the first row. Before opening night, I developed laryngitis and went to a Youngstown ear, nose and throat doctor recommended by the Playhouse staff. Dr. Tarnapolski coated my throat so I could speak. After leaving his office, I was able to talk and my voice was good enough to go on stage.

A NAME CHANGE

In April 1965, while living in Youngstown, I legally changed my name from Shwartz to Spencer. My first cousin once removed (my father's first cousin), Ralph Shwartz, a Youngstown attorney, provided all of the legal work associated with the name change. As a result, I had to write letters to the Social Security Administration and the Internal Revenue Service and changed my Ohio driver's license to reflect my new name. My father was all for the name change.

I changed my name for a variety of reasons. Our original family name was Czernikowski and the family lived in a small village about 70 miles south of Warsaw called Opatow, Poland. My great-uncle Max Czernikowski was the first brother to move to the United States. My theory is that when my great-uncle Max came to the U.S. in 1909, he did not want to be known as a Polish Jew so he changed his name to Shwartz and spelled the name without the "c." Schwartz in German means black and czerny in Polish means black, so I believe that's how he decided to call himself Shwartz. When all of the other brothers immigrated to the U.S. each of them changed their name from Czernikowski to Shwartz, all except one brother, Jacob, who spelled his name Schwartz and settled in Pittsburgh, Pennsylvania.

No one ever spelled our name correctly. Most added a "c" in the name and I was forever correcting people with the spelling. Also, I was on the radio at the time and did not want to use my last name so I chose to call myself Alan Gerald. I thought that maybe I would eventually make a career in radio and I would like to have a name that sounded more English so I chose Spencer. I knew a Bill Spencer at Ohio University and I thought Spencer was a cool sounding name, so I chose it. Bill Spencer actually married Patty McMurray, a girl from my class at Boardman High School. Patty's brother, Dean, two years ahead of me in school, was a drummer in our high school band. Dean married one of our band's majorettes, Elaine Kubrin, a 1959 high school classmate. At a future Boardman High School reunion, Dean asked me if I picked the name Spencer after having known Bill Spencer and I told him yes.

MY PURPLE 1963 FORD

In 1964, I bought a pre-driven purple 1963 Ford Fairlane four-door hardtop sedan owned by the wife of Youngstown's Donnell Ford's President. I think my father knew the car dealership's owner and found out the owner's wife was selling the car for a great price, so I bought it. I owned the car for several years until a Chicago Police car slid into my left rear passenger door on a rainy day in the fall of 1967. I'm getting ahead of myself. (You can read more about this accident a little later in this book).

1963 TO 1965—SKIING IN WESTERN PENNSYLVANIA

My friend, Seth Kaufman, and I would drive an hour east of Pittsburgh to go skiing at Seven Springs Resort in Ligonier, Pennsylvania in the Laurel Mountains along US route 30 east of Greensburg. My first time, I took a ski lesson because I didn't want to break any bones or dislocate any appendages. After going a few times, I eventually became an intermediate skier. I was on the verge of mastering a stem Christie turn, when I moved to Chicago and gave up skiing.

In the Midwest, any ski area worthwhile was located too far away e.g., Boyne Mountain and Boyne Highlands near Cadillac, Michigan and I didn't feel I wanted to spend the money for these trips so I decided not to continue skiing. To meet people, for a short time, I joined a Chicago ski club. Helmut Teichner was the leader of the club and he also started and led the Wilmot Mountain Ski School located just over the Illinois border in southern Wisconsin. He was an uncle to Martha Teichner, the *CBS Sunday Morning* reporter. At one of the ski club meetings, I met a stockbroker and, in the fall of 1966, I bought my first two mutual funds from this guy. Although I was not married, nor did I have any children, I bought the two mutual funds for the sole purpose of eventually cashing them in for two children's college education.

I did go skiing one other time with Bennett and Ronna at Wisconsin's Wilmot Mountain but that place was a little hill compared to the Laurel Mountains of Pennsylvania.

FRIDAY, AUGUST 14, 1964—NORMAN'S BACHELOR EVENT

On this Friday evening before Norman got married, Jimmy Newman, Bob Weily, Seth Kaufman and I went to an all-African American bar in Youngstown to celebrate the big event. We were the only white people in the place. At that time, it was very safe to go to such bars in an all-black area of Youngstown. We had such a good time there. I started dancing with a black woman and the boys were hysterically laughing. It was one crazy time.

SATURDAY, AUGUST 23, 1964—NORMAN'S WEDDING

My cousin Norman Lockshin married Sheila Nathanson from Shaker Heights, Ohio at Wade Park Manor in Cleveland. I served as Norman's Best Man. Norman met Sheila at the University of Pittsburgh while he was attending W & J (Washington & Jefferson College) in Washington, Pennsylvania. As a little background, W & J was an all-men's college and mixed social events were held with the University of Pittsburgh. At that time, Norman was in medical school at Ohio State University and I went visit the couple in Columbus after they were married. Their first son, Steven, was born on April 27, 1966.

CENTRAL MICHIGAN UNIVERSITY

In 1963, during my first year of teaching, I decided to apply to graduate school to pursue a Master's degree in education. I considered several universities and had to take the Graduate Record Exam. Central Michigan University in Mount Pleasant, Michigan had a fantastic reputation for its school of education. They had a lab school that was well known in Michigan and supposedly better for teacher education than the University of Michigan or Michigan State University. Central Michigan was founded as a state teacher's college in the late 1800s. Part of the application process was to give personal references so I asked my friend, Bill DeCicco if it would be O.K. to give his father's name as a reference. After speaking with his father, Dr. Gabriel DeCicco, a Youngstown family doctor practicing medicine, he said it would be fine to give his name as one of my references. I never told Dr. DeCicco that I changed my name so when Central Michigan University sent him a reference letter asking about me, he wrote back to the university saying he never heard of me. Despite this faux pas, I got accepted to the university to begin studying for my Master's Degree.

On a beautiful spring day in April 1964, I took the weekend to drive to Mount Pleasant to look over the campus and to choose housing for the summer's session. In June 1964, immediately following the end of my first year of teaching, I started graduate school at Central Michigan University. I lived off campus in a Mount Pleasant house and was away from Youngstown the entire summer, so I did not work at WBBW for the following two summers.

In the fall of 1965, and after teaching in Youngstown for two years, I decided to move to Mount Pleasant, Michigan full-time to complete my Master's Degree on a part-time basis. I needed to take only a few hours each semester to complete my Master's Degree so I decided to look for a teaching job. I landed a sixth-grade teaching job in Coleman, Michigan, a small rural farm community about 20 miles east and north of Mount Pleasant.

CONCORD MANOR APARTMENTS

During the two summers I spent in Mount Pleasant, I lived with two different families in a small upstairs apartment. Longing to live in a "real" apartment, I was able to find a great place at the end of the 1965 summer session. In August, a newly constructed private Mount Pleasant apartment building had just opened and I was the first person to move into the entire complex. The brand-new Concord Manor Apartments was located at 1100 Vernon Street, very close to the CMU campus and C-8 was the apartment number. My apartment had two-bedrooms and two bathrooms. My three roommates were arbitrarily assigned to my apartment by the university: Earl J. Band and Tom Fleming, both graduate students from Detroit were in one bedroom.

MY GRADUATE SCHOOL ROOMATE, STEVE KLEIN

Steve Klein, a graduate student from Southfield, Michigan and I shared the other bedroom. Earl Band left after a semester to get married and Rene Travis joined our foursome rooming with Tom.

I introduced my roommate Tom Fleming to his future wife, a girl I had been briefly dating. Tom was attracted to Pam Peterson, a tall blond and asked me if I had any objections of him going out with her. Of course, I had no commitment to her whatsoever and I gladly gave him my blessing to go out with Pam. They ended up getting married a year or so later. Tom was a great guy who had night blindness and couldn't drive a car. He had to be led around during the night. It was the first time I ever met anyone with night blindness.

Steve Klein and I used to shoot pool at *The Bird*; a local bar frequented by students and local Mount Pleasant folks. In the back of the bar, there was one pool table that cost a quarter to play. Steve and I would put in a quarter in the pool table at the beginning of the evening, took on all comers and kept on winning games throughout the evening. Steve was a much better pool player than me but I held my own.

We had lots of fun in our apartment, throwing many parties during the school year. While at Central I went out with many different girls. Some of the time, I dated a Detroit girl, Melanie Vanderlist whose friend, Rita Small, lived in Huntington Woods, another Detroit suburb. I was older than many of the girls so it was great fun going out with them. Steve didn't study much and as a result, the university asked him to leave at the end of the school year. He eventually got his act together and earned a Master's Degree in Elementary Education from Wayne State University. For twenty-five years, Steve taught fifth grade in Royal Oak, Michigan and retired to Tucson, Arizona with his wife Cindy and their three-year old daughter, Melissa.

STEVE KLEIN AND I RECONNECT IN 1990

In November 1990, Steve Klein, my graduate school roommate at Central Michigan University in 1965-1966 and I reconnected when I wrote a letter to Wayne State University to try and find Steve. The letter was forwarded to Steve's mother and he contacted me from his house in Tucson. I produced a client conference for the International Foodservice Manufacturers Association (IFMA) at the Loews Ventana Canyon Resort in Tucson, right down the road from Steve's house and was able to spend some time with Steve, his wife Cindy and their 4-year-old daughter, Melissa. Steve is still a close friend and we try to see each other in Tucson every winter when Penny and I are in Scottsdale, Arizona.

MELISSA KLEIN AND MATTHEW LANDAU'S TUCSON WEDDING

On Sunday, March 23, 2014, Penny and I attended Melissa Klein's wedding to Matthew Landau at The Buttes at Reflections 9800 N Oracle Rd in Tucson. Steve Klein was a very proud father of the bride, A happy occasion happened on July 13, 2019, when Melissa and Matt Landau celebrated the birth of their son Jeremy.

A TRIP TO NEW YORK

One summer when I was still living in Youngstown and after attending summer school, at Central Michigan University, my family drove to New York on one of our yearly trips. On this particular trip, through my contacts at WBBW, I arranged to go with my father to the New York radio studios of the Mutual Broadcasting System. While there, we saw Jim Ameche, the younger brother of Hollywood film actor, Don Ameche who was also in the studio broadcasting. As an aside, the brothers grew up in Racine, Wisconsin and we also saw Westbrook Van Voorhis there as well. I also met and spoke briefly with Mr. Van Voorhis.

On the same day, I can't remember how I obtained permission, but I was able to go in the NBC studios in Rockefeller Center and sat in on a rehearsal of the *Tonight Show* starring Johnny Carson. In those days, the *Tonight Show* was doing the nightly show from New York City before moving to Los Angeles.

Johnny's guest performer that night was singer Jane Morgan who was married to her manager, Jerry Weintraub. The time was well before Jerry Weintraub became a big-time Hollywood producer. One of his biggest film hits was *The Karate Kid*. During his wife's rehearsal, Jerry was sitting a few rows in front of my father.

AUGUST 1965 TO JUNE 1966—TEACHING IN COLEMAN

During Central Michigan's summer school at Central Michigan University, I applied for a full-time teaching sixth grade job in the Coleman Community School

System located in Coleman, Michigan, a small farm community located 20 miles northeast of Mount Pleasant. I was hired and signed a one-year contract on August 17, 1965 for a salary of $5,200.00.

Driving to Coleman from CMU's Mount Pleasant campus, you had to go 10 miles east on route 20, a two-lane highway toward the city of Midland, then head north 10 miles on another two-lane highway to Coleman. The community was extremely poor and one of my pupils actually did not have running water in his house. Mind you, this is 1965-66.

Each day, I car-pooled twenty miles to Coleman with four teachers who were Mount Pleasant residents; Brad and Nancy Raby (a married couple), Eleanor Thurston and John Wiley. The five of us took turns driving. Brad and Nancy invited me to their apartment for dinner one evening and they served tacos. It was the first time I had eaten Mexican food because Mexican restaurants were virtually non-existent at the time or at least I had not been to one. Brad was part Mexican and for them, the dinner was routine. We had some fun rides to Coleman and became fast friends during the year we drove together.

Harry Brugger, President of the Coleman School Board, once came to see me complaining that his daughter wasn't being taught reading, writing and arithmetic. My class was doing many interesting and creative projects in class and his daughter was telling her parents about these creative activities not specifically related to strictly academics. Mr. Brugger wanted me to tone down the creative activities but since my students loved them, I kept it up in spite of Mr. Brugger's demands. While teaching in Coleman, I wanted to continue my education, so early in the 1965-66 school year; I applied to several universities including Northwestern University, Michigan State University, Indiana University and Penn State University to start working on my (EdD) Doctorate in Education degree. In each of my applications, I asked for financial aid. I did not hear back from any of these universities in a timely manner, so I decided to apply for a teaching position in the Chicago area.

TEACHING JOB INTERVIEWS IN THE CHICAGO AREA

Since I hadn't heard a reply from any university about getting into their doctoral program, in April 1966, during my spring break from Central Michigan University and my teaching job in Coleman, I decided to drive to Chicago to interview at several Chicago area elementary school districts. I set up interviews in Evanston, Lincolnwood and Winnetka and I was offered a job in each of these school systems.

TUESDAY, MAY 24, 1966—JOB OFFER IN WINNETKA

Right before receiving my Master's Degree, on May 24, 1966, I received a letter from the Winnetka Public Schools. It read in part, you are hereby notified of your election to the faculty of the Winnetka Public Schools for the year beginning September 1, 1966, your salary to be in accordance with the regularly adopted salary schedule of the Board of Education. A copy of the current schedule is enclosed herewith and made a part hereof. This contract is subject to the School Code of Illinois and the lawful regulations of this Board. Paul J. Avery, Superintendent of Schools signed the contract.

I decided to accept a teaching position in Winnetka. The next letter said I would be teaching 5th grade at Skokie School but when I got home from Europe in August, I found a letter dated July 8, 1966 that read:

Dear Mr. Spencer:

As we finalize the building assignments of teachers for the fall it develops that our greatest need at the moment is for a male 4th grade teacher in the Crow Island School. Mr. Willis Mortensen, principal of Crow Island, has examined your papers and has requested that you be assigned to him as replacement for Mr. Gerald Wilkins, recently transferred by the Board of Education to supervise the learning laboratory at Skokie School. Crow Island is a school with an international reputation, noted for its physical facilities and for the innovations in elementary education that have emerged from the faculty. We hope that this change in assignment will be agreeable with you.

In reviewing your personnel portfolio today, we note that confirming transcript has arrived, indicating that your Master's degree was awarded in June 1966. Your salary placement is therefore revised to Column III, Step 3, on the new schedule, an increase from $6,100 to $6,650. Enclosed is a copy of the new schedule. Cordially, Paul J. Avery, Superintendent.

So, the above letter is how I found out I would be a 4th grade teacher at Winnetka's Crow Island School.

SUNDAY, JUNE 11, 1966—MASTER'S DEGREE GRADUATION

My parents and sister drove to Mount Pleasant, Michigan to see me receive a Master of Arts in Education with a major in Elementary Education from Central Michigan University. The commencement was held in the Ronald W. Finch Building at 10:30 a.m.

CHAPTER NINE
Move To Chicago

JUNE 1966, MOUNT PLEASANT AND DRIVE TO CHICAGO

I stayed in Mount Pleasant until the end of June, packed up my belongings, loaded my 1963 four-door hardtop purple Ford Fairlane and drove to Chicago. When I got to the city and was in East Rogers Park, I accidentally drove down a one-way street, going the wrong way and a Chicago policeman in a squad car happened to see me and pulled me over.

My car trunk was loaded with all of my belongings from Michigan and the back seat was filled to capacity with clothes and an old refinished chair. The officer must have thought I had stolen goods in the car. He was about to write me a traffic ticket when I said to him "isn't there another way to settle this incident without giving me a ticket?" The police put out his hand and I slipped a $10.00 bill in it and drove away. This was my introduction to Chicago Police. I could have been arrested for bribery but in those days, this practice seemed to be the norm.

The next day, as I was driving on Western Avenue, about ready to turn onto Devon, I saw Ralph Marrinson, my Ohio University fraternity brother, walking across the street. I pressed my car horn and pulled over to talk to Ralph. He had moved to Chicago a year or two before me and was an assistant hospital administrator at Chicago's Weiss Memorial Hospital on the outer drive near Montrose. Ralph met a Catholic girl and was engaged to her at the time. I attended Ralph's wedding a few months later that took place in a Catholic Church on Irving Park Road, but I can't remember where the reception was held.

I always wanted to go to Europe and I was able to take an extended vacation by myself before my teaching position in Winnetka started in September. Before leaving for Europe, I stayed with Marilyn and Larry Levy and they kept my belongings in their basement.

EUROPEAN SUMMER TRIP—JULY 6 TO AUGUST 16, 1966

Each summer, the National Education Association offered discounted chartered flights to Europe for teachers, so I was able to take advantage of the inexpensive flights. The flight was non-stop on a Capital Airways DC 8 chartered jet from Chicago O'Hare to Amsterdam's Airport Schiphol. [The following was taken from a journal I kept during my first European trip].

WEDNESDAY, JULY 6, 1966—FLIGHT TO EUROPE

I arrived at Chicago's O'Hare Airport at 7:30 p.m., bought flight insurance for $4.00, talked to a girl at the insurance counter for a half-hour and checked my 33 lbs. of luggage (one large suitcase) at 8:28 p.m. In those days, suitcases did not have wheels, nor did I have a backpack, so you can imagine me schlepping around a large suitcase all over Europe.

I saw Linda Lehman, an Ohio University alumnus who I took out once or twice. She was in Alpha Zeta Delta and lived in Detroit and was a 6th grade teacher in one of the Detroit suburbs. There were many young teachers from Warren and Farmington, Michigan. It was a lively group "cute" and wonderful. Our departure was delayed for about one-hour because of refueling. I spoke to Linda Lehman for several hours and having been at the airport for 4 ½ hours, Linda, including almost everyone else, was getting a little punchy. Just before takeoff, it started to drizzle. My seat was on the aisle and over the wing.

THURSDAY, JULY 7, 1966—ARRIVAL IN AMSTERDAM

The Capital Airways DC 8 finally took off at 1:36 a.m. and it took 15 minutes just to taxi. They served a snack at 2:15 a.m., turkey, cheese & ham sandwiches plus cake. The plane was chilly and I used a blanket and pillow to sleep. Captain Leeds made an announcement and gave the passengers a variety of statistics about the flight. We were flying at 33,000 feet. The jet was fully loaded with fuel weighting 115,000 lbs. and 294,000 lbs. of total weight. There were six stewardesses aboard [now they are called flight attendants]. The flight took 6 hours and 45 minutes and we were cruising at 580 and 590 miles per hour. The temperature outside of the aircraft was 43 degrees below zero.

A woman and her daughter seated to my right were from Washington, D.C. I slept for a few hours until about 4:00 a.m. as it started to get light outside. Breakfast was served one and one-half hours before landing. I had waffles, applesauce, a sweet roll, coffee and sausage that was lousy.

At 7:07 a.m. we passed over Dublin, Ireland and started to approach Amsterdam at 7:50 a.m. eastern time. At 8:00 a.m., I saw beautiful countryside with patches on the fields. The weather was cloudy. Everything looked green and we landed at 8:05 a.m. New York time that was 12:05 in the afternoon Amsterdam time. It was 65 degrees in Amsterdam and drizzling.

Upon arrival, I got $20.00 in Dutch Guilders and will see how long it lasts.

At 1:45 p.m. I missed a bus to the Central Station but took a KLM shuttle to the main terminal where I went through customs without any trouble as they didn't even open up my suitcase. On the shuttle bus, I met a French paratrooper. It cost 1.5 Guilders for the bus ride. I called a youth hostel for 10 Dutch cents where I planned on staying for the first night. Then I took a $.40 tram ride to the city center and arrived around 2:45 p.m.

I checked into the Anne Frank Youth Hostel at 3:45 p.m. While checking in, I met two girls from Akron, Ohio. The cost of the hostel was 8.50 Guilders or $2.35 that included breakfast. Two people were assigned to a room and my roommate was Fred Weinstock from Allentown, Pennsylvania. At 5:00 p.m., I stopped at a snack shop (Automatiek "Rudy" Rozengracht 90 Amsterdam Telephone 244174) for tomato soup. The soup cost 70 Guilders or about 20 cents US, 10 Dutch cents=$.03 US cents and 25 Dutch cents=$.07 US cents

All retail stores close at 6:00 p.m. It cost 25 Dutch cents to send airmail to the United States. I ate spaghetti at a sidewalk café about $.75US. It was one of the oldest sidewalk cafes in Holland, about 100 years old. All of the Amsterdam newspaper people come here.

Flowers are sold everywhere. I am meeting many people. Resa from E.

Patterson, New Jersey wanted to hitchhike to Copenhagen with me. Too bad, I'm headed to London. 11:00 p.m. What an education I got this evening. I walked around Amsterdam's red-light district, chatted with some of the girls but did not indulge. The usual price to participate is 15 Guilders or about $4.20US. I walked back to my youth hostel and went to sleep.

POST CARD TO MY PARENTS—DATED JULY 7, 1966

Dear Folks,

What a place! Just like you read about—bicycles galore. Am staying in the Anne Frank youth hostel for $2.35 a night including breakfast. Have Jewish roommate from Allentown. Trip smooth. Took 5 hrs. 45 min. after 1 hr. delay before takeoff. Met OU girl at the airport who I took out. She's going to tour Europe too. The people are great & speak English. Money system strange. Can't believe I'm here at last. Love, Alan

FRIDAY, JULY 8—AMSTERDAM

Got up at 8:00 a.m. It was chilly in the room. I ate breakfast and went shopping. It cost 15 Dutch cents to use of a public toilet. I found a hotel with a small room. At 12:00 noon, I placed a call to Brussels, Belgium to Henry Askenazy. You give the operator the number of your coin box, you give her the number you want and hang up. She calls you back and connects you.

Henry Askenazy is Isadore Askenazy's son from his first marriage. Isadore is married to my grandmother Rose's first cousin, Dorothy Turkus. When they emigrated to Canada, their name was changed to Askenzy and they moved to Toronto, Ontario. Isadore wrote to his son to tell him I would be in Europe for the summer and I would call him. Henry was very happy to talk to me. I told him I would be in Brussels on Monday afternoon.

I met more people from Michigan. I am planning on hitchhiking to The Hague tomorrow, then on to Rotterdam for a night. Just walking around enjoying the people and sights until my 2:00 p.m. tour of the city. Herring stands are open for breakfast only. People love them over here. I ate lunch for 1.45 Guilders, about 42 cents US that consisted of potato salad & roll and butter and 7-UP. In a snack bar, I met 2 men from Goteborg, Sweden. At 2:00 p.m. I went on a Cebuto tour at 34 Damrak. Dam Square is the main square in Amsterdam. I met two Israelis, a husband and wife who spoke perfect English. Very nice. They had just completed their master's degrees at Columbia University in New York.

The houses are so narrow that they have hooks on the roof so they can get furniture in the upper floor rooms. The stairs are also so steep that it is impossible to move furniture in and out of houses. Many roads and streets have separate routes for bicycles. Hunger, flood and illness are the symbols of Old Amsterdam. *A herring a day, keeps the doctor away. Too many herrings a day, keeps everybody away.*

Found a cheese cutter and paid $.75US each for 3 cheese cutters to take back as presents. Had supper with a Canadian fellow who goes to a Technical School in Toronto, Ontario. Ate at a Chinese/Indonesian restaurant that cost 2.25 Guilders or 85 cents US. I had fried rice with egg and meat. Yummy. King-Do Oude Doelenstraat. I did a silly thing. I left my loafers at the Anne Frank Youth Hostel.

Here I am and no one is in the office.

Met three Jewish girls from Adelphi College on a tour and study group. We hoofed it to the Student Lanz (student center) about ¾ miles away from the Anne Frank Hotel. We got lost but finally found the spot. Big party going on with plenty of New York Jews here plus foreigners. Paid 75 Guilders for a draft beer (21 cents US). So many American tourists, it's hard to believe. A band is playing plus they have Dutch records. Hearing rock 'n roll in Dutch is unique; however, I have heard many American and English songs too. Heard Frank Sinatra's "Strangers In The Night" many times in the past two days. At 10:45 p.m. this place is jammed and I haven't really met anybody, just observing.

SATURDAY, JULY 9—AMSTERDAM, THEN TO BRUSSELS

Woke up at 7:30 a.m. by the bells of a church, got dressed and ate a hard-boiled egg, two pieces of bread (white and whole wheat), jam and coffee, as much as you can eat. The room cost 11.50 Guilders (about $3.10US). I finished breakfast and walked with my suitcase to the Anne Frank House to pick up the loafers I left there. It's 9:00 a.m. I am waiting for the two Israelis who finally show up at 9:45. They have rented a car and will take me to Rotterdam. At 10:15 we are all going to see Rembrandt's Museum for 50 Dutch cents, went to a Dutch flea market, to a flower market, then to the Portuguese Synagogue in the old Jewish section of Amsterdam.

It's 12:00 noon. It is a hot day. I stopped at Wimpy's to eat on Leisenstraat. I went to the Rijksmuseum and left at 3:30 p.m. for Rotterdam. Saw Rembrandt's paintings.

Stopped at a Shell station to change oil and bought a Sprite as I was very thirsty. Now on my way to The Hague which took about 15 minutes. The center of the highway is lined with trimmed bushes. We stopped in The Hague, bought food for sandwiches. Also stopped in Miniature City and Court of the International Justice and Parliament Houses, then left for Rotterdam.

ARRIVAL IN ROTTERDAM

At 7:45 p.m., we arrived in Rotterdam. We got mixed up all the time and didn't know where we were going so we had to ask 15-20 people for directions. No one knows anything. Rotterdam is a modern city compared to Amsterdam. There are modern apartment houses. We also saw the world's largest man-made harbor in Rotterdam. (As a side note, my grandmother Rose, age 22 (my father's mother), (Rosa Schwartz as listed in the ship manifest) arrived in the United States on November 20, 1911 on the ship Volturno which left Rotterdam in the Netherlands. Although she was not married to my grandfather at the time, her name is listed as Schwartz. She traveled with my grandfather Ben's father, Israel Schwartz, age 50).

We finally stopped the Politie about 15 kilometers out of the way. We again stopped to ask directions, about 9:00 p.m. Still lost. A man at a Shell service station helped us. We're going back to Rotterdam to stay. David and Lilli Moses are the couple with whom I have been riding. We decided to go to Breda, The Netherlands at 9:40 p.m.

Everyone I talk to thinks I'm Italian. A fellow at a gas station and a lady at the desk at the hotel thought I was Italian. At 10:15 p.m. we stopped at a nice hotel (Hotel Brabant Zevenbergschenhoek at Oude Rijksweg 20) in Breda. The room cost 11.50 Guilders or $3.10US for the night.

SUNDAY, JULY 10—BREDA, NETHERLANDS & BRUSSELS

Got up at 7:10, had breakfast and left Breda at 8:40 on the way to Brussels, Belgium. The weather is damp and chilly. Interesting note: soft-boiled eggs are served with plastic spoons because stainless steel spoons give off a funny odor to the eggs. The Israeli couple taught me how to eat European-style. We arrived in Belgium at 9:10 a.m. and went through the border and forgot to stop. We arrived in Antwerp at 9:45 a.m. Antwerpen (as it is called in Belgium) is a modern city with large apartment buildings. We arrived in Brussels at 10:15 and stopped at the site of the 1958 World's Fair buildings and took slides of the Atomium, a magnificent structure. Brussels—Place de Brouckere—people are very friendly and speak French. I cashed $20.00 and we stopped at the Manneken Pis, ate lunch across from the Royal Palace. David and Lilli Moses dropped me off at the Tourist Center. I checked my suitcase at the railway station. The restaurants in Belgium are expensive. The coffee stinks and the menus are impossible to read. Met a fellow from Ohio University and a Sigma Chi. His friend helped me take my baggage to the Hotel Du Blod overlooking Place Rogier. I walked around, got cleaned up and washed my hair. At 7:15 p.m. I'm off to see Brussels nightlife. I went to a French movie. The woman at the ticket window thought that I was Italian. She said that I look like a typical Italian. After the movie, I went to Caprice d'Eve and met a Spanish girl living in Brussels who spoke only Spanish and French. With her was another Spanish girl who was with a German fellow who did speak English. I had an enjoyable evening with laughter and dancing.

POST CARD TO MY PARENTS—DATED JULY 10, 1966
(PICTURE OF HOTEL BRABANT IN THE NETHERLANDS)

Dear folks, Stayed here last night on way to Bruxelles. Called Henry Askenazy long distance from Amsterdam. Will meet him on Monday. Love this place! Got a ride with Israeli couple free! Met them on bus tour. What an education this trip is. Tell Grandma, Amsterdam is magnificent. Going to London next, then Paris.
Love, Alan

POST CARD AUNT SADIE & UNCLE HARRY—DATED JULY 10, 1966
(PICTURE OF BRUXELLES-BRUSSEL)

Dear Aunt Sadie and Uncle Harry.
Got a ride here with Israeli couple from Amsterdam. Feel great lost some weight. Got chilly but now warm. So far very inexpensive. Also went to The Hague, Rotterdam & Antwerp. Tuesday, leave for London, then Paris & southern France. Great trip. A must for you and Uncle Harry. Great people-friendly. Love, Alan

MONDAY, JULY 11—BRUSSELS, BELGIUM

I awakened at 9:20 a.m. and ate a fair breakfast. I went to Au Bon Marche but couldn't find an adapter for my electric razor but mailed postcards. At 11:30, I checked out of the hotel and called Henry Askenazy. I plan to meet him for lunch at the Hotel Palace. He reserved a very nice expensive lunch at La Maison du

Cyzne-"The House of the Store." for $10.00US.

I had an excellent meal, meat (fillet), French fries and wine (Beaujolais). It was supposed to be Brussel's best restaurant. At the end of the meal, they brought Henry a cigar and lit it for him. After lunch, we went to his office. He works for the information service. It was raining so I took a tram back to my hotel. I went to Bon Marche to have my raincoat shortened for $2.00. I sat in a restaurant waiting for my raincoat to be shortened.

At 7:30 p.m. I ran into the Dean of Central Michigan University's Business Administration in the lobby of my hotel and shot the breeze. At 8:30 p.m. I ate a snack at La Grande Place and met a French woman from Le Havre. At 10:00, I met some guys from the U.S. and walked for one hour, went back to my hotel and went to sleep.

TUESDAY, JULY 12—BRUSSELS, BRUGGE TO ENGLAND

Got up at 8:30, had breakfast at 9:15 and finally tried to leave Brussels hitchhiking at 11:20. After no ride for 45 minutes, I got a ride to Ghent. Five minutes later a Congolese Army Sargent going to Ostend picked me up. He was very kind and took me to Brugge instead of Ghent. We ate in a snack bar and toured the city. He spoke English beautifully and was originally from East Belgium where they speak Flemish. This language (similar to Dutch) is usually spoken in the north of Belgium and French is spoken in the south of Belgium. At 2:00 we arrived in Ostend and at 2:40 p.m. I got a ride to Niewpoort with an English-speaking man whose daughter lives in California.

We arrived in Niewpoort/Baden at 3:05 in front of a police station. At 3:15 p.m., the same fellow picked me up again. At 3:40 we were almost at Dunkirk about 20 kilometers away. After a one-hour wait, I finally got a ride on a motorcycle to the French border where I asked a French couple for a lift. They drove me to Dunkirk and we arrived at 5:30 p.m. The French couple took me 20 kilometers out of their way to get me to the Calais Airport where I arrived at 6:00 p.m. I bought a ticket on a British United flight to England. At 7:45 I arrived at the British United Airport in Southend-On-Sea, England, a resort town on the Thames River Estuary in Essex. The airfare cost $11.50US. Can you believe how cheap things are at this time? The world's longest pier is 1½ mile long in Southend-On-Sea. This is the town where the Thames River goes into the ocean. I took a one-hour train ride to London and started looking for a room. They love the movie "Peyton Place."

At 9:05 p.m. I found a room in a boarding house at Rochford, England in a very nice bed and breakfast. At 10:00 p.m. I went to a local pub across the street from the rooming house. In England, a saloon is a better class bar and a public bar is second-class. Clubs close at 10:30 p.m. and a bell is rung at closing time.

WEDNESDAY, JULY 13—TO LONDON

Awakened at 7:15. Breakfast at 7:45. Caught a train to London. My room and breakfast cost 1 Pound 6 pence ($3.64US). What a beautiful day, the sun is shining and I arrived in London in one-hour. I looked for a hotel and found one for $6.16US. It is expensive but hard to find because of the World Cup competition that I had no idea was going on at the same time.

At 2:00 p.m. I caught a bus tour of London then ate lunch-steak pie, roll and tea for $.70US. I walked around London and ate supper at several restaurants, just snacks. I bought tickets to the play *Oliver* for $3.50US and sat in the 14th row. *The Prime of Miss Jean Brodie* was playing in an adjoining theater and I inadvertently walked into that theater thinking it was *Oliver* and came in 5 minutes late to see *Oliver*. The play was terrific. At 10:15 p.m. I walked to the Empire Room at Leister Square where I met a very nice Jewish girl, Barbara Hirsh. We're going to Soho tomorrow night. Later, Barbara and I walked through Soho. A man fell in front of us as we were walking on the sidewalk. He apparently had an epileptic seizure. Barbara and I said goodnight. She went home and I went back to my hotel.

THURSDAY, JULY 14—LONDON

I awakened at 9:00 a.m. and made reservations on a bus/plane to Paris. I went to the British Museum and saw the original Magna Charta, Rosetta stone and Egyptian statues. This place was a real thrill. In the late afternoon, I headed to the Zoological Gardens when it started to rain. The zoo was terrific. I also checked out Madame Thousand's Wax Museum. Supper cost 5 shillings. I went to Barbara Hirsch's house to pick her up for a date at 8:00 p.m. The English have a term for necking. It's snogging.

Barbara and I had coffee and cookies until 9:15, then walked to the bus and took the Tube (subway) to Leister Square. We walked hand-in-hand all over London for three hours crossing the Thames River, to Big Ben, Westminster Abbey and Buckingham Palace. I dropped Barbara at her house, said goodbye and took a taxi back to my hotel by 1:00 a.m.

POST CARD TO MY PARENTS—DATED JULY 14, 1966
(PICTURE OF THE MONUMENT—LONDON, ENGLAND)

Dear Folks, Am Seeing The Sights Of London, Buckingham Palace & the rest. Went to the top of this monument, took many pictures. Saw the musical "Oliver" last night. Met Jewish girl-Londoner at dance hall. Have date with her for tonight. Going to Soho, miniskirts plentiful. Now in National Gallery. Having a wonderful time. Tonight Palladium-London laughs. Love, Alan

SATURDAY, JULY 16—LONDON TO PARIS

I woke up at 7:30, got dressed and stuffed down my breakfast. I arrived late and missed my bus to Paris. I left at 10:22. [It is not clear in my diary but I must have taken a later bus to the airport because at 1:45 p.m. I was in the air heading toward the English Channel and arrived in Beauvais, France at 2:20 p.m.]

I arrived in Paris at 4:15 p.m. and by 5:00 I was in the Hotel Saint Severin for 15 francs a night ($3.09US). This hotel is a real dump and will look for something better in the morning. For dinner, I had spaghetti Bolognese, a salade, rolls and a glass of Beaujolais wine. I am getting along with my French. The dinner cost about $2.00US. I walked around the area to get my bearings and at 9:00 p.m. I found myself at the Lido on the Champs Elysée and went inside. I walked outside again as the bar was too far away. I walked around Pigalle, went back to my hotel and fell asleep around 12:30 a.m.

SUNDAY, JULY 17—PARIS

Slept until 11:15 a.m. I must have been exhausted. I washed some clothes and was off to the Louvre. I spent two-hours there and was out by 3:15. The Mona Lisa was awesome. I ate lunch in the museum's cafeteria that was expensive $1.35US. I went back to my hotel for my camera. At 4:15 p.m. I was snapping shots of Paris. At 5:20, I was waiting to get to the top of the Eiffel Tower that cost $1.44US. It took me 45 minutes of waiting to get to the 3rd level. At 6:35 p.m., I finally made it to the top of the tower. What a great view of Paris. I took a bus to the Luxembourg Palace, then walked to St Michel where I met a French girl who spoke some English. The food is expensive but the hotel rooms are cheap ($3.04US) per night. Tired, I went to bed at 11:15 p.m.

POST CARD TO MY PARENTS—DATED JULY 17, 1966
(VARIOUS PICTURES OF PARIS, FRANCE)

Dear Folks, Went to top of Eiffel Tower today. Also saw the Louvre-both magnificent. Weather chilly, damp & rainy. Next stop Switzerland or southern France-haven't decided yet. Can't tell boys from girls-long hair. Mixed couples-white/black, etc. Staying in Latin Quarter-Left Bank. Love, Alan

MONDAY, JULY 18—PARIS

I awakened at 9:00 and went to the Gare de Lyon to get a train ticket to Cannes. I changed $20.00US. I can't understand why I have to wait so long to get a reservation. At 12:45 p.m. I'm still waiting and finally at 1:50 p.m. I got a train reservation to Cannes. After leaving the railroad station, I bought some bread and had lunch. I stopped at an antique shop on the way to the Bastille. I walked for miles and at 4:25 p.m. came to the Cathedral Notre Dame. This is a beautiful church and I don't see how they built it so many years ago. I met many people along the street.

I ran into the girl I met in Amsterdam, Resa from East Patterson, New Jersey. We decided to eat supper together for $.80US in La Source near my hotel and then journeyed to the Arc de Triumph, then walked to the Eiffel Tower at 7:45 p.m. Resa works with an electron microscope in geology (oceanography). We both decided to go to Versailles manana. It started to rain but we didn't care. At 9:00 p.m. we had coffee ole at a sidewalk café. (Coffee olé has plenty of milk). We toured Pigalle and Momartre together and were back at my hotel by 11:15 p.m.

TUESDAY, JULY 19—PARIS

7:45 a.m. I awakened to rain again. The weather stinks. I had breakfast that consisted of coffee olé, two crescent rolls about $.50US expensive. I met Resa and we left St Michel about 9:20 on the way to Versailles and got there about 10:25 a.m. We stayed until about 12:00 noon. We toured the beautiful gardens, ate lunch (horrible cheese), wine in a sidewalk café near Versailles. At 2:30, we went to visit a porcelain factory but it was closed. They had a museum there, so Resa and I saw that. At 3:00 p.m. Resa and I were exhausted so we went back to my hotel room to take a nap. We woke up at 5:30. I left Resa and went shopping for some bread and cheese and bottled mineral water. Met a Jewish girl, Herta Friedman from Zurich, Switzerland who spoke English and who helped me buy items. I went to her apartment and she gave me a plastic shopping bag. I brought the food back to my hotel room and Resa and I ate it. Resa went back to her hotel room and I went to sleep by 10:30 p.m.

WEDNESDAY, JULY 20—PARIS TO CANNES, FRANCE

I awakened at 7:05 a.m. and went to the railroad station (Gare de Lyon) for my train departure to Cannes at 9:15. I reserved a seat for 2 francs. The train left 3 minutes late. I sat in a compartment with seven other people. I met a couple with a little boy who lives Algeria, a Flemish drama student going to the Avignon Drama Festival and three other French girls.

At 12:04 p.m. we arrived in Dijon and at 2:00 p.m. we were in Lyon, Valence at 3:00 p.m., Orange at 4:00, Avignon at 4:15, Marseille at 5:31, Toulon at 7:15, Frijus at 7:37 and St. Raphael at 7:46. We have been passing sections of the Mediterranean Sea. Beautiful mountains with houses on cliffs. It is dusk now and a beautiful sight to behold. We have gone through numerous tunnels (almost as bad as the Pennsylvania Turnpike). We finally arrived in Cannes. I am staying in a real "rat trap", the L'Isle de France Restaurant and Hotel. I couldn't find anything else available. I am paying 16 francs with breakfast for about $3.30US. The weather here is beautiful. I met a fella from Luxembourg. I am meeting him at 9:00 a.m. for the beach. He spoke some English.

POST CARD TO MY PARENTS—DATED JULY 20, 1966
(TWO PICTURES OF CANNES AT NIGHT, FRANCE)

Dear Folks,

Hard to believe but I got here today by train from Paris. Saw harbor at Marseilles-will beach manana. Then to Juan-le-Pin and Nice-Monte Carlo, then to Italy. What a vacation. Mediterranean magnificent. Many mountains. Love, Alan

THURSDAY, JULY 21—CANNES TO NICE

Awakened at 7:15 a.m. "Rain, rain go away, please come again when I'm not here." Bought a black beret for $3.00US and met three guys from the U.S.A. in a Cannes parking lot. They were going to Nice, so I hitched a ride with them.

In Nice, I checked my suitcase and looked for a hotel room that only took 15 minutes. I checked into the Hotel Franck Zurich for 14 francs a night. I ate lunch that was crummy for 5 francs, $1.00US. I had a steak, French fries (Pommes Frites), and a salade. I rented a Vespa motor scooter for 12 francs (about $2.50US) and drove on a highway to Monaco, Monte Carlo. What a view. I have never seen such beautiful scenery. Pictures galore. I saw the Palace and Casino at Monte Carlo. I drove back to Nice that is tremendous, got cleaned up and went to the municipal casino where I played roulette for one hour. I lost $.40US all toll. I saw a show at night in the club casino. There were nude girls dancing, nothing extra ordinary and went to sleep at 1:30 a.m.

FRIDAY, JULY 22—NICE

Ill fait tres beau aujourd oui. I bought a beach towel for $1.00US, and then went to the beach. What a beautiful day and such a suntan you wouldn't believe. At 1:00 p.m. I headed west on my Vespa on the highway for a ride in the hills overlooking Nice. I rode in my bathing suit to catch the rays. I ate supper for 6 francs and 50 centimes ($1.20US). I had a three-course meal and bought a railroad ticket to Pisa, Italy. Tomorrow morning, I leave for Pisa.

SATURDAY, JULY 23—NICE TO PISA, ITALY

I left Nice at 9:32 a.m. and met a girl, Karen Jensen, originally from Youngstown who lived on Brookfield Street in Boardman. The trip to Pisa would be an all-day affair. We lost an hour going to Italy. This is a beautiful country. The Italian Riviera is indescribable as the train traveled along the northern coast of Italy. I saw many trailers and tents on the way to Genoa arriving at 3:28 p.m. I arrived in Pisa at 6:40 p.m. Upon arrival in Pisa, I found a cheap hotel, Hotel Astor for $2.59US that included breakfast. I ate dinner for $.49US that was spaghetti, bread and wine at the railroad station restaurant. I met a fella from Long Island and his French friend who were on their way to Rome. We visited the Leaning Tower at night.

SUNDAY, JULY 24—PISA TO ROME

Before I left Pisa, I decided to walk to the top of the Leaning Tower. It is now 10:21 a.m. and I am hitching a ride to Rome (I hope) via the Mediterranean Sea route. I started hitchhiking at 10:31 a.m. to Livorno, Italy and at 10:56 got a ride with an Italian man with his son. At 11:21 a.m. I was dropped off just south of Livorno. It is 11:41 and I am now waiting for another ride. At 12:29 p.m. I got a ride for 10 kilometers and two minutes later; I got another ride for another 10 kilometers. I am now eating lunch in a small resort town in the middle of nowhere. It is 12:50 p.m.

At 1:30 p.m. I am in Rosignano. 2:50 p.m. Another town 4 kilometers away. Oh, well, it's time to go back to Rosignano because I am having a difficult time getting a ride to Rome. Back at the Rosignano train station, I bought a ticket to Rome that cost 2,500 Lire (about $4.05US). The train doesn't leave until 5:21 p.m. and I must change trains at Cecina. The connecting train leaves there at 7:30 p.m. and arrives in Rome at midnight. Meanwhile, I caught some sun on the beach at Rosignano and got on the train to Cecina to wait for an express train at 7:30 p.m. In Cecina, I ate lasagna, a roll and mineral water for 400 Lire ($.65US). I chatted with five middle-aged fat women in broken Italian. I met an Italian army officer who spoke English and saw a funeral procession. The Italian army officer gave me the name of an Embassy man who would help me in Rome.

The train arrived 20 minutes late. At 7:35 p.m. I am finally on my way to Rome. I met an English girl on the train who works as a governess for an American family in Rome. She gave me her telephone number in case I needed anything. I arrived in Rome at 11:15 p.m. ahead of schedule and called the YMCA for a quick room that was available. The cost of the room was 1,550 Lire plus an additional 280 Lire for breakfast, less than $2.40US.

MONDAY, JULY 25—ROME

After breakfast, I went to the American Express office to get a letter from the girl I met on the train. Waited for one hour and no letter. I ate lunch for $.97US. It was a big lunch consisting of minestrone soup, ravioli, bread and a glass of milk.

After lunch, I visited the Coliseum, Forum and the Roman Baths. I came back to the YMCA exhausted and fell asleep until I awakened at 6:00 p.m. I ate dinner and went browsing. I met two Texas girls and saw *Sound and Lights of Rome* from a nearby hill overlooking the Forum. I came back to the "Y" by bus.

TUESDAY, JULY 26—ROME

I went to explore Rome on foot and walked all morning and afternoon. I saw the Trevi Fountain, Pantheon, St. Peter's Cathedral, Piazza Navonna and Castel Sant Angelo. When I returned to the YMCA, I found out I had a new roommate, Mario Quattrone, who was Italian and had a Triumph Spitfire sports car. I was lucky to have met Mario because in the evening, while driving around Rome, we picked up two American college girls and took a driving tour of Rome at night. It was a wild ride as I sat in the crunched-up back seat with one of the girls.

WEDNESDAY, JULY 27—ROME TO FLORENCE

9:00 a.m. Mario and I were off to the Sistine Chapel until 12:15 p.m. We met two girls and drove them around to the Catacombs and the Appian Way. Outside of Rome was modern with contemporary buildings. I decided to leave Rome at 8:25 p.m. on a train to Florence. Got to Florence at 12:00 midnight and met a fella from Ohio University who remembered me. I took a nice room in a pensione near the railroad station for $2.00US.

THURSDAY, JULY 28—FLORENCE

At 10:30 a.m. I saw *David* by Michelangelo in the Piazza d'San Marco-Academia. Then bought some leather gloves for 900 Lire or $1.45 US. I met some girls who showed me the way and toured a straw market. I then went to the National Galleries. My student card from Central Michigan University entitled me free admission to the Galleries. I met Bill Schoenberg's girlfriend in the Gallery. Bill was my cousin Norman's friend from Washington and Jefferson College.

After going through the Galleries, I decided to go shopping on the Ponte Vecchio and bought another pair of leather gloves as a gift. I actually bought seven pairs of leather gloves for $12.00US. I then visited the Palace Pitti and other landmarks and bought myself a pair of leather gloves for $2.95US. It is definitely fun to bargain with the local vendors. At 7:00 p.m. I decided to take a walk until 10:30 when I met two New Jersey Jewish girls in a café. We talked until 11:30 and then I walked back to my pensione.

FRIDAY, JULY 29—FLORENCE

I shopped all morning and bought a beautiful leather briefcase for $5.40US. It's beautiful. I took a pair of shoes into a shoemaker to get heels and soles put on. It cost $2.10US. After picking up the shoes, I walked to the Medici Chapel in the afternoon. I tried to get opera tickets for tonight but can't, so I walked back to the pensione and went to sleep at 11:00 p.m. relaxed.

SATURDAY, JULY 30—FLORENCE TO MILAN

I got up early and took the 9:18 a.m. train to Milan. I left Florence at 9:45 and got to Bologna at 11:00. Parma at 11:50 and at 12:31 p.m. Arriving in Milan. I found a room at Albergo Calypso via Petrella, angle via Gaffurio for 1600 Lire or $2.59US for one night. After washing up, about 2:00 p.m. I headed for the Duomo, a very famous Roman Catholic Church. Then I went to the Santa Maria delle

Grazie and saw the *Last Supper* by Leonardo DaVinci. After seeing this unbelievable painting, I was off to LA Scala Opera House Museum which cost 250 Lire or $.40US.

I wondered through the amazing opera house, then walked to a large park erected by Napoleon and saw Arco della Pace and Castello Sforzesco, a 14th century castle and residence of the Lords of Milan. I took an elevator in the park near the Arco Della Pace for a fantastic view of Milan for 250 Lire. The elevator was in the Tower in the Park (Parco) near Piazza Sempione where I walked around and ate dinner at 8:00 p.m. at a small Pizzeria for $.47US. I had spaghetti, wine and bread, what a deal!

SUNDAY, JULY 31—MILAN TO INNSBRUCK, AUSTRIA

I left Milan at 7:23 a.m. after much confusion at the railroad station. I boarded the train and at 8:40 we had arrived at Brescia; Verona at 9:30; Trento at 11:01; Bolzano at 11:50 and Brenner at 1:15 p.m. (change in time). I gained one-hour at the Austrian border. I arrived in Innsbruck at 2:05 p.m., checked my baggage and got information about trains leaving to Munich. One leaves tomorrow at 9:50 a.m. to Garmisch. I will visit Garmisch and leave for Munich at 3:48 p.m. I found an inexpensive room in a large university dormitory. Two Frenchmen are in my room plus two Americans and three Englishmen. Also staying in the dormitory was a girl I had met in Cannes, Pat Block from Flushing, New York.

I went to Hungerburg, 2,800 feet above the city of Innsbruck. For lunch, I ate goulash soup with bread for $.28US. At 6:00 p.m., I am still on the mountain and what a beautiful view of the valley below. I ate supper and had a hot dog with bread on a street stand for $.24US and goulash soup again for $.20US. I bought a one-way ticket to Garmisch, then to Munich for $3.36US and went to bed at 9:00.

MONDAY, AUGUST 1—FROM INNSBRUCK TO MUNICH

I met two Jewish guys from Illinois who took me to Garmisch free. We left Innsbruck at 10:00 a.m. and arrived at 11:30 at Garmisch and went to a small Bavarian village and saw the Linderhof, an old Palace built on the mountain slopes near Garmisch. The castle served as the home of King Ludwig II of Bavaria 1869-1878. It was Bavarian Baroque architecture.

I paid $1.25US for gasoline that was worth it. We then drove off to Munich where we stopped on the way to see Dachau, a famous concentration camp during World War II. We arrived just as it closed. Tomorrow, we will return. I ate supper for about $.65US, two German hot dogs, French fries, rolls and soda.

I found a hotel near Dachau (Hotel Ruprecht 8 München Lochhausen Kreuzkapellenstrabe 68 (Telephone 0811-876524) after almost all hotels were filled in Munich for about $1.75US or 7 Deutsche Marks (DM) without breakfast. We paid 7.40 DM for the room or about $1.85US plus 3 DM for breakfast ($.76US) After getting cleaned up, we all went to the famous beer hall, Holfbrauhous and for $.32US you got a large 16 oz. stein of beer. Singing and shouting and a German band wearing the traditional Bavarian costumes were playing.

TUESDAY, AUGUST 2—DACHAU CONCENTRATION CAMP

We toured Dachau Concentration Camp and the museum that was extremely depressing but very interesting. The photographs of what life was like during World War II were detailed in the museum. At wartime, the conditions were deplorable and it was a sad situation. It is hard to believe that humans could treat their own kind in such a horrific way.

As a little background, Dachau Concentration Camp was built in 1933 and was the first concentration camp and a training ground for camp commandants who studied crowd control and torture. The camp was originally built to hold 5,000 inmates but when the Americans liberated the camp in 1945, they found 30,000 packed inside the walls. Some inmates were so sick, they died after being liberated. We visited the gas chambers, crematorium and graves. The tour was one-hour and forty-five minutes.

TUESDAY MORNING, AUGUST 2—BACK IN MUNICH

At 11:45 a.m. I said good-by to my two Illinois friends who were driving to another city and was dropped off at the Munich railroad station where I bought a railroad ticket to Heidelberg for 31 DM or $7.83US. I went to the Deutsches Museum for $.12 ½ US admission and got a student reduction. The Deutsches Museum is the world's largest museum of science and technology with about 28,000 exhibited objects from 50 fields of science and technology. The museum was founded in 1903 at a meeting of the Association of German Engineers_(VDI) as an initiative of Oskar von Miller. I found out it is also the largest museum in Munich._

TUESDAY, AUGUST 2—MUNICH TO HEIDELBERG

I returned to the railroad station to catch the 4:32 p.m. train to Heidelberg. Before I got on the train, I bought a roll of film at a large department store for $2.35US and left Munich on the 4:32 p.m. train. We were in Augsburg at 5:08 p.m., Gunzburg at 5:55, Ulan at 6:14, Stuttgart at 7:20 and arrived on time in Heidelberg at 8:56 p.m. The weather was chilly, damp and rainy all day.

Arriving at the Heidelberg railroad station, I started talking to two girls I met from Montreal, Quebec, Canada. An American man overheard me speaking English and joined the conversation. Chris Cohen, who was a senior law student at Ann Arbor's University of Michigan, was working for an insurance company during the summer in Ghent, Belgium. Chris spoke fluent French. He was on a short vacation trip and happened to over hear me speaking to the two girls. The girls went their separate way but Chris and I instantly became friends and decided to find a place to stay for the night. After much searching in the rain, we finally found one room. The hotel room was $4.00US a night a cost that we split.

WEDNESDAY, AUGUST 3—HEIDELBERG & CHRIS COHEN

The next morning Chris and I toured the campus of Heidelberg University. The weather was lousy, raining. We decided to take a train to Mainz. On the way, we discussed taking a Rhine River boat, sailing north from Mainz to Koblenz. I hoped the weather would clear up for our trip on the Rhine. We boarded the train and we arrived in Mannheim at 11:20 a.m. and we crossed the Rhine and arrived in Mainz at 12:10 p.m. The weather turned nice. Sunshine at last. We got on the Rhine River boat and left Mainz at 2:00 p.m.

At 2:16, we sailed by Wiesbaden and arrived in Koblenz at 7:25 p.m. The 5-hour Rhine River cruise was interesting as we passed many old castles along the way. Once in Koblenz, we hiked to the railroad station where we boarded a train at 8:59 p.m. for an all- night journey to Berlin. The train pulled into Bonn at 9:38 p.m., Cologne at 10:00 p.m. where we had to change trains for Berlin. We arrived in Dusseldorf at 10:48 p.m., Duisberg at 11:00 and finally found a couchette for 9 DM or $2.25US. We slept until 4:30 a.m.

THURSDAY, AUGUST 4—BERLIN

After World War II ended with Germany's surrender, the country was divided into four sectors, controlled by the United States, France, Russia and the British. At this time, the communists were in control of one-half of Berlin and of East Germany. Berlin was actually located in East Germany and in order to get to Berlin, you had to pass through Potsdam. This suburb was about 16 miles southwest of Berlin and after the communists built the Berlin wall, it separated East Germany from West Germany. Potsdam was the gateway to West Berlin.

Our train arrived at the Potsdam border at 7:00 a.m. and the train stopped. Several young East German soldiers dressed in full military uniforms entered the train with rifles on their shoulders and searched each car. The East German military were looking for illegal people or contraband or who knows what. They checked everyone's passport, looked underneath seats, above the seats in the overhead compartments and scared the hell out of Chris and me. It was very intimidating to see these young soldiers standing by the side of the train, and then entering each car during the stop. We had to pay 10 DM ($2.50US) for a Visa to transport to Berlin. Once everything was clear, the train started moving and we entered West Berlin. I believe it was in the Berlin train station that Chris and I met Ann-Marie Schlosser, a young and single French woman who was traveling by herself. Chris has kept in touch with her after his return to the United States and for many years later. She lived in Nantes, and then moved to Paris where she got married.

(As a side note: About ten years after we met her, Chris got a telephone call from Ann-Marie. She was attending a marketing convention in Ohio and came to visit Chris and his wife Judy at their Glencoe home. Chris and Judy have also visited Ann-Marie and her two children, Line and Tristen in France. She's now divorced. Chris found out she received the French Legend of Honor Award from the President of France. She taught marketing in Vietnam as well as Croatia or Slovenia and she speaks excellent English).

While in West Berlin, Chris and I found a place to stay at the Fasanenhaus Pension on Fasanenstrasse 73. The price was 20 DM plus 15% service charge or about 11 DM each ($2.75US without breakfast). A Jewish woman runs the pension. We paid for two-nights that was 30.47 DM ($7.60US). At 4:05 p.m. Chris and I decided to take a tour of West Berlin and after the tour, at 6:15 p.m., we went to eat dinner at a bargain restaurant where we ate goulash, potatoes and bread for $1.25US. We tried to get into Resi; a famous Berlin dance hall but couldn't because the rule was you had to wear a tie and jacket. At 9:15 p.m. we were mighty tired.

The weather was raining again, lousy weather and had rained all day. Chris and I decided to tour East Berlin the next day.

FRIDAY, AUGUST 5—WEST AND EAST BERLIN

At 9:00 a.m. Chris and I left for East Berlin on the U-bahn (subway) and got off at Checkpoint Charlie. On August 13, 1961, the German Democratic Republic closed the border by erecting the Berlin Wal. Tourists from abroad, diplomats and the military personnel of the Western Powers were only allowed to enter East Berlin via the crossing point at Berlin Friedrichstrasse.

Soon the United States military police opened a third checkpoint at Friedrichstrasse. The other two checkpoints were Helmstedt at the West German-East German border and Dreilinden at the West Berlin and East Germany border. Based on the phonetic alphabet the Helmstedt checkpoint was called Alpha, Dreilinden Checkpoint Bravo and the checkpoint at Friedrichstrasse got the name Charlie or Checkpoint Charlie. The main function of each checkpoint was to register and inform members of the Western Military Forces before entering East Berlin. Foreign tourists were also informed but not checked in the West.

CHECKPOINT CHARLIE

As an American, Chris and I were able to go into East Berlin through Checkpoint Charlie. At 9:45 a.m. it took 18 minutes until 10:03 to get checked in. You would hear stories of Americans going into East Berlin and not coming back so both of us registered at Checkpoint Charlie and told the guard that if we were not back by 7:00 p.m., to come look for us. This was a scary thing to do.

We went through a large Soviet Union-style long bar that came down as a gate. It was about as wide as one lane of traffic. The checkpoint was actually in the American sector of West Berlin and was housed in a blockhouse. The small house was about 2 feet higher than a soldier and could hold about six or seven people inside. Only one American GI was inside the blockhouse with a weapon. We didn't know if his weapon was loaded.

EAST BERLIN

While in East Berlin, Chris and I walked around to several stores and took public transportation usually trolleys and busses. We passed very large and monolith buildings with virtually no color appearing very drab, dreary and grey. The storefronts had no signs, no words on the buildings designating what was inside the stores unless they were chiseled into the building. So, it was hard to find where the stores were and what they sold.

East Berlin had many damaged buildings from World War II, still standing and very few automobiles and people in the downtown area. Many of the buildings still had bullet holes left over from the war. Chris and I went to a museum of German history showing World War II photographs of concentration camps. We spent two hours there and took a tram ride to the suburbs. I also sent a souvenir postcard to myself. You are compelled to change 5 West German Marks for 5 East German Marks. I should have taken my camera but left it back in the pension.

While riding on a trolley toward the late afternoon, I started having stomach cramps and I really had an urge to go find a toilet. It must have been something I ate the night before because I was feeling very uncomfortable. I walked up to the trolley driver who of course did not speak any English. I was excitingly raising my hands and pointing toward myself saying "toiletten" "toilletten." According to Chris, in order to try to explain this to the driver without words, I crossed my knees and crossed my hands so my palms were toward myself with my wrists crossed saying "toiletten" "toilletten." I opened my eyes real wide and my eyebrows wide. The driver, if we were in the United States would have thought I was on candid camera. In any event, he probably thought I was crazy.

I had an emergency urge to go to the bathroom and I was in agony. I told Chris I had to leave him on the trolley and would meet him back at Checkpoint Charlie at 7:00 p.m. I jumped off the trolley at the next stop and ran helter skelter trying to find a public toilet. I kept asking people I saw on the sidewalk for "toiletten," "toiletten," that means toilet in German. I finally found a public toilet close to the trolley stop and barely made it in time where I dropped my pants as fast as I could and let go with explosive diarrhea. At 7:00 p.m. I met Chris at Checkpoint Charlie and we went back to our hotel room. Our day had been quite interesting.

SATURDAY, AUGUST 6—EAST BERLIN TO COPENHAGEN

I met two girls at the pension who graduated from Ohio University and who knew Linda Lehman. They were surprised to hear she was in Europe. My next city is Copenhagen, Denmark so I decided to take an East German train to Copenhagen. It is a shorter distance and cost less to travel via East German railroad rather than another route through West Germany. I went to a travel agency to buy my ticket to Copenhagen. The ticket cost 55.10 DM. I reserved a couchette and seat for Saturday evening, August 6. The overnight train will leave at 7:00 p.m. and arrive in Copenhagen at 6:00 a.m.

Before leaving West Berlin, Chris and I visited the zoo and then went to the Dahlem Museum and saw the colored sculpture of Queen Nefretete and paintings by Rubens and Rembrandt. We grabbed a bite to eat (soup with wieners and apple cider for $.35US). Chris had to go back to his office job in Ghent and I would be taking an East German train to Copenhagen so we exchanged addresses and phone numbers, said goodbye and agreed to keep in touch with one another as Chris said he would be moving to Chicago after law school the following summer.

I went to a West Berlin subway station to go to East Berlin to catch the train to Copenhagen. While at the station I met a Danish guide, who was taking a tour group going to Copenhagen. The guide spoke English so I decided to hang with his group. I followed his group onto the subway that took about 15 minutes to go to East Berlin. The East German train was scheduled to leave at 8:04 p.m. for the overnight trip to Copenhagen and scheduled to arrive there at 6:30 a.m. The train finally left at 8:25 p.m. My compartment is full of Danes who were "bombed out of their minds." I went to sleep in my couchette at 9:00 p.m. but was awakened about 12:30 a.m. for a passport check in Warmemunde, East Germany. The train stopped there as the locomotives were switched from an electric locomotive to an old-fashioned steam locomotive. When we stopped, armed and uniformed East

German border guards entered the train looking for illegal people and searching each railroad car.

SUNDAY, AUGUST 7—COPENHAGEN, DENMARK

The train arrived in Copenhagen at 6:32 a.m. and I had to wait to change my money at 7:00 a.m. I was told rooms were difficult to find. I didn't feel like waiting for the tourist office to open at 9:00 a.m. so I phoned some hotels listed in Arthur Frommer's book *Europe On $5 A Day*. I found a hotel room at the Absalon Helgolandsgade 19 Ve 3618 for only one night, and then phoned another place (a private house) for one more night. At 8:30 a.m., I checked into the hotel but my room was not ready so I and ate some Danish pastry and coffee ($.28US)

After eating, I walked around Copenhagen's downtown area, and then I walked back to the Hotel Absalon. The Hotel Absalon cost 23 Kroners with breakfast $3.60US. My room was ready so I took a hot shower, shaved and felt much better. I went to visit the Ny Carlsberg Glyptotek Museum that had the best collection of Degas's sculptures and paintings I have ever seen plus many contemporary artists. It is free on Sundays, so I didn't have to pay. I had dinner at a student place for 4.75 Kroners about $.70US, then went to Tivoli Gardens and saw a stage show and met a German fellow too.

MONDAY, AUGUST 8—COPENHAGEN

I transferred hotels and am now staying at the Anderson family residence. The room cost $2.50US a night without breakfast. I decided to rent a bicycle and rode out to the famous Little Mermaid statue and other sites in Copenhagen. It started raining and I got wet. I visited the largest department store in Scandinavia. I rode my rented bicycle around Copenhagen and went to bed early because I was exhausted.

TUESDAY, AUGUST 9—STOCKHOLM, SWEDEN

Got up at 6:45 a.m. carted my baggage to the railroad station, ate breakfast and caught a 9:50 a.m. train to Stockholm. I am sharing a compartment with four eighteen-year-old Swedish girl students who are very pleasant and fun loving.

The train went from Copenhagen to Helsingor, Denmark and reached the ferryboat to Sweden at 10:50 a.m. The ferry from Helsingor, Denmark to Helsingborg, Sweden took 20 minutes. After landing in Sweden, I took a train to Stockholm. The train arrived in Almhult at 1:45; Alvesta at 2:10, Vaxjo [Nassajo] at 3:15, Linkoping at 4:35, Norrkoping at 5:07, Katrineholm at 5:45 and Stockholm at 7:12 p.m.

Upon my arrival in Stockholm, I checked my baggage at the railroad station and tried to find a hotel at the tourist bureau. I called many hotels myself. Every place was full. I finally got a youth hostel for 6.50 Kroner a night about $1.25US for a clean bed in a school classroom K.F.U.M. 23 Ragvaldsgatan at about 9:15 p.m. I checked into my room, got cleaned up, made my bed and went out to see Gruna Lund, a famous night spot, like Tivoli Gardens in Copenhagen. I met a Norwegian and his friend there. The youth hostel closes at 12:00 so I had to leave a little early.

WEDNESDAY, AUGUST 10—STOCKHOLM

At 8:00 a.m. I was ready to see Stockholm. I went to the Wasa, a 17th century wooden ship that was sunk on its maiden voyage in 1628. It was housed in a gigantic building with mist spraying all over the ship to keep it moist. If the ship wasn't kept sprayed with mist, the wood would rot and fall apart.

By 12:00 noon, I was at the Milles Garden and waited 25 minutes for a bus back to Stockholm and another 5 minutes for a tram. Next stop, Farsta. At 3:15 p.m. I was in Farsta, a very modern mall plaza with apartment houses. I saw the Katarina Elevator, went to the top and took some photos of Stockholm. I went back to the hostel to shave and "freshen up." [Without a shower and hot water, can one really be clean?] I left the hostel at 5:15 p.m.

At 7:21 p.m. I am waiting for Tram #7 on the way to Gruna Land. Went to the Dans In for 6 Kroners [$1.25US] and met two Swedish guys who spoke perfect English. I danced with many girls and had a great time. I also went to a casino and lost $1.00US. After the casino, I went back to the hostel and went to sleep.

THURSDAY, AUGUST 11—STOCKHOLM TO OSLO, NORWAY

Awakened at 8:00 a.m. I packed my suitcase and left for the train station where I checked my luggage, packed briefcase with shaving equipment, etc. for a sauna bath later in the day. Went to Skanson Park but it rained before I could see anything. Left for the Museum of Modern Art and arrived at 12:45 p.m. Many pieces are by Pablo Picasso, Paul Klee, Jackson Pollack and Max Ernst. There was also one by Francis Bacon. At 3:00 p.m. I was having a sauna bath and massage. The massage was great and relaxing. I had a masseuse give me a rub down, scrubbed me with a brush and then a sauna that was very hot, then a little hotter. It felt great and very clean.

At 7:15 p.m. I went to the National Museum to see the Christina exhibit, a former Queen of Sweden, born in 1626 and reined from 1648 to 1689 during the Thirty Years War. A gigantic collection of art by her contemporaries was on display. I decided to take an English-speaking tour at 8:00 p.m. Very good tour. By 9:31 p.m. I was at the railroad station for my 10:01 p.m. all-night train to Oslo.

FRIDAY, AUGUST 12—OSLO, NORWAY

The train arrived in Oslo at 8:01 a.m. after a very pleasant night on a beautiful sleeper car for $3.50US or 18 Kroners. Upon arrival at the railroad station, I went to a room finding service and got a very nice room close to the center of Oslo for 15 Kroners ($2.10US). The name is Studenterhjemmnet 13 Underhaugveien. All of the following are on a peninsula, called Bygdoy that is southwest of the city proper and I saw the Viking Ships Museum, the Kon Tiki, The Fram and the Norsk Sjofartsmuseum of old Norge boats. I saw a girl get hit by a small truck while I was trying to find the #30 bus waiting to go to Kon Tiki; however, she wasn't hurt.

At 1:40 p.m. I was at the Folksmuseum. The weather is warm and sunny. I bought my lunch in a small delicatessen (3 small sandwiches with salami and cheese for $.37US) plus some pastry for $.21US that I fed to some ducks and swans. Next, I journeyed to Vigelandsanlegget, a magnificent park dedicated to Oslo by Gustav Vigeland, a famous sculptor (1869 to 1943). Frogner Park, then to Holmenkollen, home of the World Ski Jumping Championship and the world's oldest Ski Museum. It was fascinating and I got a free ride down the mountain with a German family. Otherwise, the subway cost 1.50 Kroners or $.21US.and is an eighteen-minute ride.

At 7:15 p.m. I went back to the hostel after walking in the downtown area and had a bite to eat (2 hot dogs and a glass of milk for $.45US). I finally got out of the hotel at 9:00 p.m. and the lights wouldn't work. I visited a student nightspot called the Dovrehallen on Storgatan Street. It was swinging but not too crowded and met a very friendly Norwegian and a Frenchman who hated to live in Paris and despised Charles DeGaulle and his actions. Going back to the hostel, I ran into two Americans from California. I missed my stop on the subway and had to travel and wait for another at 12:25 a.m.

SATURDAY, AUGUST 13—OSLO

I went shopping after a whopping breakfast of bread, meat, cheese, coffee and milk. Bought an original etching by Ric, a Swiss artist for 70 Kroners ($9.75US). I then went to the Edvard Munch Museum. I liked his woodcuts, etchings and engravings but I didn't care for most of his paintings. At 4:00 p.m. I walked around Oslo. All of the retail stores close at 3:00 p.m. on Saturday. So, I went back to my hostel to shave and shower.

Afterwards, I went strolling and saw a billiard parlor and went inside. I started playing pool [American pocket pool] with two Norwegians and taught them 8 ball. They were drunk. A girlfriend of one of the guys was very good looking and "stacked." I proceeded walking up the street where many people seemed to be drunk. I have never seen so many people "smashed." It seems like public drunkenness is common in Oslo on the weekend. I then met a Norwegian man who plays jazz trombone in an orchestra during the winter. We wondered around Oslo and talked to all the girls. He's going to live in Seattle, Washington next October. In Oslo, if you want to talk to a girl on the street, you grab her arm and squeeze.

SUNDAY, AUGUST 14—OLSO AND BACK TO COPENHAGEN

Got up one hour late. I set my alarm for 6:15 a.m. and got up at 7:15. It left me one hour to get to the train station to catch my train back to Copenhagen. At 8:00 a.m. I found a taxi and made it to the train on time. The taxi ride cost 6.10 Kroners or $.85US. The train left Oslo at 8:25 a.m. I met four Canadian nurses from London, Ontario on the train. We arrived at Fredrickstad at 9:44, Goteborg at 10:05, Sarpsborg at 1:36 and the ferryboat to Copenhagen at 5:16 p.m. We arrived in Copenhagen at 7:00 p.m. Unfortunately, it's raining again. Glad to be dry on a comfortable train. The sun started to shine as we pulled into the Copenhagen station. I proceeded to find a room. After several unsuccessful calls (meanwhile I was buying my ticket to Amsterdam), I met a very nice good looking (believe it or not) a New York Jewish girl named Marsha Glassman. I went to the room finding agency at the railroad station and they found me a bed in a bathhouse for 20 Kroners or $2.85US. A sauna bath and shower were included in the price. Marsha and I went to Tivoli Gardens and had a very good time. We saw a marching band, a ballet that was comical and we danced to a terrible sounding orchestra.

MONDAY, AUGUST 15—COPENHAGEN, DENMARK

I got up at 6:30 a.m. and took a shower and sauna for one hour fifteen minutes. I left my room at 8:00 a.m. and headed for the railroad station to change my shirt and check my briefcase. I found out all ticket couchettes were filled to Amsterdam. I walked around for two hours trying to find an antique shop where I saw a marble desk set that I wanted but couldn't locate it. I was supposed to meet Marsha at the information center at 11:00 a.m. I bought some rolls, cheese and salami and had lunch. I then visited The Frihedsmuseum (Museum of the Danish Resistance Movement during World War II). The museum was very impressive. I then walked to the Christainsborg Palace that was closed. It was next to the National Museum that began its collection with Old Stone Age items up to the 1800s.

I walked around town until 6:00 p.m., and then met two girls from Oregon, Sharon and Diane who were great to talk to and they treated me to a beer. I went back to the railroad station and my train left for Amsterdam at 8:55 p.m. I found a vacant car and slept until 6:30 a.m.

TUESDAY, AUGUST 16—BACK TO AMSTERDAM

This is it!! Homeward bound. My train arrived in Amsterdam at 10:27 a.m. It is a great feeling to be going home to America but I'll miss all the wonderful things I saw and the people I've met. I took a bus to the Amsterdam airport and our chartered Capital Airways plane took off at 3:20 p.m. We are cruising at 33,000 feet and arrived in Goose Bay, Labrador at 5:15 p.m. and arrived in New York at 11:00 p.m. that was 6:00 p.m. New York time.

WEDNESDAY, AUGUST 17, 1966—ARRIVAL IN NEW YORK

My Aunt Sadie and Uncle Harry met me at JFK International Airport. I had grown a mustache and goatee; hadn't had a haircut and they didn't recognize me. I stayed with my aunt and uncle in New York for a day. My Aunt Sadie got me a ticket to see Barbra Streisand in *Funny Girl* on Broadway, then I flew to Chicago.

RETURN TO CHICAGO

While teaching in Coleman, I wanted to continue my education, so early in the 1965-66 school year; I applied to Northwestern University, Michigan State University, Indiana University and Penn State University to start working on my (EdD) Doctorate in Education. Each of my applications, asked for financial aid.

NORTHWESTERN UNVERSITY

On March 23, 1966, I received a letter from Northwestern and in part it said, "that they were unable to offer financial assistance for my graduate study for the academic year 1966-67. There were simply far more requests for such assistance than could be granted and I regret that many meritorious applications could not be funded." William R. Hazard, Assistant to the Dean.

INDIANA UNVERSITY

While I was in Europe, a July 25, 1966 letter from Indiana University was sent to my Mt. Pleasant, Michigan apartment address, then forwarded to my Boardman address. In part it read: I am happy to inform you that your application for a student appointment has been approved. You have been assigned as a graduate assistant in the Elementary Education Department to assist Dr. James Walden. In return for your work, you will receive a salary of $1,900 beginning September 12 and ending June 5, 1967. This amount will be payable in ten monthly installments of $190 each. We are also glad to point out that graduate assistants, research assistants and teaching associates, if non-residents of Indiana, are exempt from out-of-state fees but are required to pay fees on an in-state basis. This will represent a savings of approximately $600 for one academic year for non-residents of Indiana. Will you please inform me as soon as possible of your decision to accept or reject this appointment? If you accept this appointment, you should complete and return the enclosed Pay Advice Form to Dr. Ray Butler, Director of Administrative Services, School of Education, Indiana University, and Bloomington, Indiana 47401 Sincerely yours, Howard T. Batchelder, Associate Dean and Director of Graduate Studies

As soon as I returned from Europe and found the Indiana letter, I immediately wrote to Indiana University saying I had already accepted a teaching job in Winnetka, Illinois. An August 25, 1966 letter was sent back to me that read:

"Dear Mr. Spencer, Thank you for your letter of August 22 addressed to Dean Howard T. Batchelder. Since Dr. Batchelder is out of town, I am taking the liberty of responding to your letter. We appreciate the position you find yourself and are sorry that acknowledgement of your appointment did not precede the offering at Winnetka. We regret that you will be unable to be with us this year, and we assure you we have placed your application on file for the school year 1967-68. Thank you again for your letter of explanation. Best wishes.

Yours very truly, William T. Voorhies, Assistant Director Graduate Studies

PENNSYLVANIA STATE UNIVERSITY

Upon my return from Europe, there was also a letter waiting for me from Pennsylvania State University, accepting me into their doctoral program in education and offering me a small stipend. I wrote back saying that I had already accepted a job in Winnetka but to hold a space for me in the program for the following year. Well, my working on a doctorate degree never happened because I moved to Chicago in August 1966 and rest is history.

CHICAGO APARTMENT SEARCHING

Upon returning from Europe, I stayed with Marilyn and Larry Levy while looking for an apartment to rent. After a few days in the Windy City, I found a one-bedroom apartment on Chicago's East Rogers Park neighborhood at the corner of Greenleaf and Sheridan Road (7025 N. Sheridan Road). The monthly rent on the apartment was a little more than I wanted to spend but I took the apartment anyway. It cost $125.00 per month plus utilities. I was only making $6,650.00 per year at the time. I signed the lease on August 31, 1966 so my lease was from September 1 to September 20, 1967.

I bought a bed and went to local house sales to buy some inexpensive furniture, some of which I still have today. A small wooden table I bought for $3.00, Bennett put tile on the top and it is currently in our Northbrook living room.

MET DENTIST JORDON BLOCK AT LINDA'S APARTMENT

Before I actually moved to Chicago, my sister Linda was friendly with a native Chicagoan, Jordan Block, an Army dentist who was stationed in Cleveland at the time. I met Jordan on several occasions and he told me to look up a friend of his when I moved to Chicago by the name of Raymond Pershing. He said Ray is a great guy and he thought we would get along.

AUGUST 1966—RAYMOND PERSHING

The first person I called when I moved to Chicago was Raymond Pershing. Ray was living at 2950 N. Commonwealth Avenue just south of Diversey Harbor at the time and about a fifteen-minute drive from my East Rogers Park apartment. When I first introduced myself to Ray, I acted as if Jordan Block and I were buddies, when in fact we had only met a few times in Cleveland. Ray and I have been friends since and we periodically see each other

WINNETKA TEACHNG AT CROW ISLAND SCHOOL

I started teaching fourth grade at Crow Island School in Winnetka, Illinois, a north shore suburb about twenty miles of Chicago. Classes started after Labor Day 1966. I had a terrific class my first year. I taught in the classroom at this school from September 1966 until June 1972 and was the director of Crow Island's Resource Center from September 1972 until June 1974 when I left teaching.

The year before I retired from Crow Island School, myself along with a group of current teachers and some administrators, traveled to Stamford, Connecticut and visited an elementary school whose modular structures were designed by Curtis and Smith Associates of Massachusetts. Many of the designs were incorporated into Crow Island's new Resource Center being constructed during the summer of 1974. I am very proud of the fact that in 1975, the Resource Center was awarded a citation for excellence in design by both the Illinois School Board Association and the American Association of School Administrations. It was featured in a display at the AASA Convention in Dallas that year.

Crow Island School is an architecturally famous elementary school. Betty Williams Carbol, wrote *The Making of A Special Place*: *A History of Crow Island School*. The following is an excerpt from her booklet.

"Carleton Washburne, Superintendent of the Winnetka Schools and the Board of Education found an architect, Larry Perkins to design Crow Island School. At the time, Perkins, Wheeler and Will (now Perkins and Will) was a young enthusiastic firm begun in 1936. Eliel and Eero Saarinen were approached by Larry Perkins whose family had been friends of the Saarinens. The famous father and son architect team worked on the design of Crow Island School. They also designed Rockefeller Center in New York and the TWA terminal at LaGuardia Airport.

The October 24, 1990 issue of *Education Week* is quoted as saying, "The school, opened in 1940, is considered to be the most architecturally significant school building in the United States. The one story, flat roofed brick building resembles thousands of others scattered across the national landscape and would not be out of place in any American neighborhood." In 1956, *Architecture Record* poll rated Crow Island School as 12th among all buildings and first among all schools as the most significant in the previous 100 years of American architecture.

CONNECTION TO MY BOARDMAN ELEMENTARY SCHOOL

After moving to Chicago and teaching at Crow Island School, I periodically went back to visit my mother and father who continued to live in Boardman. On one occasion, during my first winter break from teaching in 1966, I happened to be at Bertrando's Barbershop, my hometown barber on Market Street when the retired Superintendent of Boardman Schools was also there getting his haircut. Since the Boardman school system was small, I.J. Nisonger knew many students. He knew I had graduated from Boardman High School and asked me what I was doing. I told him I was living in Chicago and teaching fourth grade at Crow Island School in Winnetka, Illinois.

To my surprise, he mentioned that Market Street School, I attended from fourth to sixth grade, was patterned after Crow Island School in Winnetka. I was astounded when he mentioned this. He told me that a group of Boardman Board of Education members traveled to Winnetka in the late 1940's to visit the famous school. They were very impressed with the school's design and decided to build their new elementary school, the first one in Boardman, after Crow Island School in Winnetka. After my haircut, I drove to the Market Street School and a custodian who was cleaning the building during the winter break let me inside the building. I wanted to take a look for myself after I mentioned who I was. Sure enough, the school looked very similar to Crow Island School and I was amazed. It never occurred to me when I started teaching in Winnetka that my own elementary school had this connection.

During my tenure at Crow Island School, I began making 16mm educational children's films and documentaries that were distributed to schools throughout the U.S. and English-speaking countries. You can read more about my filmmaking later.

OCTOBER 1966—PART-TIME TEACHING JOBS SEARCH

In October 1966, I started writing letters to various Chicago area colleges and universities to see if I could get a part-time job teaching elementary education courses in the evenings or on Saturdays. I wrote to the education departments at University of Chicago at Chicago Circle, Illinois Teachers College-Chicago North, Pestalozzi Froebel Teachers College, Loyola University, DePaul University, Northeastern Illinois State College, National College of Education and Roosevelt University. For the next several months, I received very nice rejection letters to each of my letters. I had great credentials, but I really needed a doctorate degree or at least 36 hours toward a doctorate in order to teach at the university level. So, my plans to teach at a higher level never came to be.

THURSDAY, JANUARY 27, 1967—CHICAGO BLIZZARD

Chicago was paralyzed with the biggest blizzard in its recent history. Everything was shut down and schools were cancelled for several days. Two other significant events happened on the same day; a huge fire at McCormick Place that destroyed most of the building and three astronauts died in a horrific fire in their space capsule before they even took off.

At 5:02 a.m. on this date, it began to snow. Nothing remarkable about that as it was January in Chicago, and, besides, 4 inches of snow had been predicted and that was no big deal. But it kept snowing, all through this miserable Thursday and into early Friday morning, until it finally stopped at 10:10 a.m. By the end, 23 inches covered Chicago and the suburbs, the largest single snowfall in the city's history. Thousands of people were stranded in offices, in schools and in buses. About 50,000 abandoned cars and 800 Chicago Transit Authority buses littered the streets and expressways. Most people just wanted to get home. According to the *Chicago Tribune,* one woman who worked downtown and lived on the city's North Side, normally a 35-minute commute, spent four hours making the trip.

In south suburban Markham, six hundred fifty students in four schools camped out in libraries and gymnasiums because school buses were stranded. Looting was rampant in the city. Long lines formed at grocery stores, and shelves were emptied in moments. According to the *Chicago Tribune,* as a result of the record snow, 26 people died, including a 10-year-old girl who was accidentally caught in the crossfire between police and looters and a minister who was run over by a snowplow. Several others died of heart attacks from shoveling snow.

The Blizzard of '67 proved the wisdom behind Chicago weather saying, "If you don't like the Chicago weather, just wait a minute." Only two days before, the temperature had reached a record 65 degrees.

MARCH 1967—SPRING BREAK IN MIAMI BEACH

Raymond Pershing and I became fast friends. In March 1967, I convinced Ray to go to Miami Beach with me during my first spring break from teaching. We stayed at The Shoreham Hotel on Collins Avenue, where I had stayed during my Ohio University senior year spring break. It wasn't the greatest hotel, but it was reasonably priced. We rented a car and drove around Miami Beach. Our main goal was to find girls. It rained for most of our stay so we decided to spend a great deal of time drinking in a variety of local bars. On one particular occasion, we were at The Castaways, a motel in North Miami with a famous bar where lots of girls hung out. We were seated at the bar talking to two girls and I had to go to the men's room. Upon returning to my bar stool, there was a rather tall and muscular man sitting next to the same girl I was talking to before leaving for the men's room.

Ray had been intently talking to another girl and apparently didn't notice that the tall guy had taken my seat when I was gone. I astounded Ray by walking up to the bar stool, looked up into the eye of the tall guy and said to him, *"Hey buddy, that's my girl,"* whereupon the tall and muscular guy jumped off the stool and looked down on me. He was probably about 6 foot 2 or taller and stood head and shoulders over me. In a very apologetic way, saying (tongue in cheek) he was very sorry and promptly left. The tall guy knew I was kidding but Ray just stood there in amazement and was completely dumbfounded at my brash display of masculinity. Obviously, the guy knew he could have taken his thumb and crushed me with no effort so he was being funny with his comment.

While in Miami Beach, Ray and I saw his cousin Dave and his wife. Dave drove us to various places in the area and we both got nauseous sitting in the back seat because of the way Dave was driving. He drove in a jerky manner speeding up and slowing down. Ray and I were looking at each other and couldn't wait to get out of his car. It was quite an experience we will never forget.

COUSINS MARILYN AND LARRY LEVY

When I moved to Chicago, Marilyn and Larry Levy were living in an apartment on N. Bosworth near Howard Street. I frequently was at their apartment babysitting for their daughter Lisa who was two and one-half at the time. Marilyn had been trying to potty train Lisa but Lisa wanted no part of it. One time when Marilyn and Larry were out for the evening, I was babysitting Lisa and she told me she had to go to the bathroom. When Marilyn and Larry came home to the apartment, they were amazed to hear that Lisa went to the bathroom on her own. By the time the Levys moved into their Dewey Street house, Samantha was born on March 21, 1967 and I was her first baby sitter at about 2 months of age.

GOSPEL SINGER MAHALIA JACKSON AND ME

On one of my round-trip travels from Chicago to Youngstown to visit my parents, I was having lunch at a restaurant counter on the Ohio Turnpike. Mahalia Jackson, the famous gospel singer, and her entourage were on their way back to Chicago, having appeared at a concert somewhere in the east. I immediately recognized her as we were sitting directly across from one another. She kept on staring at me. After a short while, she motioned for me to come to her. As I approached, she said, "You look very familiar. Weren't you my drummer at one time?" I was very surprised to say the least and introduced myself. I smiled and said that I wasn't a musician but I was flattered she asked me to over to say hello.

ART INSTITUTE OF CHICAGO

After moving to Chicago, one of the first museums I visited was The Art Institute. The first Ohio University semester of my freshman year, I took a fine arts course. We studied art, dance and music. The course book had photos of paintings and we were asked to identify famous paintings and artists by their style.

Chicago's Art Institute has a fine collection of impressionist's paintings. Georges Seurat most famous work filled me with emotion when I first saw the actual oil painting of *An Afternoon on the Island of La Grande Jatte*. I remembered this particular painting because of studying it in college. I was totally mesmerized by this painting as I stood in front of it for a long time soaking up those Seurat's pointillism brush strokes. The museum also houses many of the other impressionists I studied in my college fine arts book including Renoir, Van Gogh, Degas, Gaugin and Monet. I was in awe of seeing these actual paintings for the first time.

CHAPTER TEN
Penny Camberg—A Positive Turning Point

APRIL 1967—PENNY IS MOVING TO CHICAGO

My sister Linda attended a party at Judy Shermer's apartment at the Cliffview Apartment complex in Cleveland. She saw Penny Camberg there and found out Penny and a teacher friend, Francine Lombardo, were planning on moving to Chicago in August. Penny had signed a contract for a kindergarten teaching position in Arlington Heights, Illinois and would be starting teaching at North School in the fall of 1967. Linda told me she saw Penny and the news about her moving to Chicago.

In late May 1967, during the Memorial Day weekend, I was invited to visit and stay in Southfield, Michigan with my Central Michigan roommate Steve Klein. As the weekend approached, Steve wasn't feeling well so my trip to his house was cancelled. I spoke to Linda who invited me to drive to Cleveland instead and stay with her for the holiday weekend. She was having a party that weekend and lived at Ellicott Apartments in Warrensville Hts. I decided to invite Penny to Linda's party so I could talk to her about Chicago. Upon my arrival in Cleveland, I called Penny's house and her mother answered the phone saying Penny was on her way back from Cedar Point with her sister, Sandi and I left my sister's phone number. After Penny returned back from Cedar Point, she returned my call and said she would come to the party at Linda's apartment. As the party was about to start, Linda asked me to go to a store for soda because she thought she might not have enough for the party. So off I went to a store.

When I returned from the store with the soda, Penny had already arrived. When I entered the living room, Penny came up to me and planted a kiss on my cheek and gave me a big hug. I had no idea who she was since I hadn't seen her in over 3 years. She was wearing contact lenses and had a new nose. She looked fantastic. We spoke about Chicago and other interesting things all evening, and then Penny drove me to a restaurant in her new 1966 Chevrolet Super Sport convertible where we drank coffee and talked until midnight. During that wonderful evening, there was something going on between the two of us. As a result of our seeing each other, I started to have strong feelings for Penny and couldn't wait until she moved.

A 1967 CHICAGO SUMMER JOB

Another fourth-grade teacher at Crow Island, Sondra Cooney, whose husband was an executive with the American Hospital Association, offered me a summer job working in the department that sorted IBM cards from a large machine. This was before computers. The IBM punch cards had holes in them and I would run them through a machine and give them to another person who did something with them. Another part of my job was to enter data into the machine. I took a bus from my East Roger's Park apartment to the American Hospital Association headquarters located in the Furniture Mart at 680 North Lake Shore Drive near

Ontario Street. The job only lasted one summer but it gave me some extra income from teaching.

PENNY AND FRAN VISIT CHICAGO BEFORE THEIR MOVE

Penny and friend Francine Lombardo visited Chicago during the summer to look for an apartment and found a 13th floor one-bedroom, one-bath apartment at 441 E. Oakdale Avenue. The moved was scheduled for August 1967. I believe the rental of their apartment was an astronomical price of $178.00 per month but split two ways, wasn't such a bad deal.

AUGUST 1967—PENNY CAMBERG MOVES TO CHICAGO

I had Penny's new Chicago telephone number and I asked her for our first formal date almost immediately after she moved to Chicago. Ray Pershing and I double-dated and took our dates to Jimmy Wong's famous Chicago restaurant for delicious Chinese food located in Lincolnwood on Peterson Avenue. It was a very pleasant evening with much conversation. Penny didn't eat much food and as I found out afterwards, she didn't particularly like Chinese food.

After our first date, I saw Penny a few times and I started having serious feelings for her. I couldn't stop thinking about her; however, this didn't stop either one of us from dating others. I always wanted to believe that falling in love would be just like its portrayed in the movies and my love for Penny happened exactly that way. When Penny and I were apart all I could think of was she. Since I had never been in love, nor had I ever experienced any kind of a serious relationship, the love I developed for Penny was absolutely amazing. My roommate, Chris Cohen used to tell me I appeared to be walking around in a fog. My feeling of love for Penny was "magic."

In fact, many years later when Penny and I both saw the film *Sleepless In Seattle* in a Lincolnshire movie theater, just when Meg Ryan's mother said it was like magic when she met her husband, I sucked in and exhaled a great big yelp and started bawling with tears running down my face. It was contagious because Penny started crying too. I could not stop crying because it reminded me of the stung feeling I first had for Penny. As we left the movie theater I was still crying and couldn't stop. As I started to drive the car out of the parking lot, I had to stop because the tears were still rolling down my cheek and I couldn't see where to drive. In August 1967, my sister Linda graduated Kent State University with her Master's Degree and Penny sent her a graduation card. Linda related to me that she told our parents this must be serious because why would Penny send her a graduation card?

My apartment lease ended on September 30, 1967. My friend Ray Pershing was living in a garden apartment at 516 W. Oakdale but was planning on moving to another apartment on N. Orchard. I decided to sub-lease his apartment and moved in by myself before Chris Cohen moved to Chicago. Toward the end of September before my move to Oakdale, I invited Penny to dinner at my North Sheridan apartment. I had a small round charcoal grille on my tiny back porch, originally purchased while living in Michigan and I decided to make hamburgers on the grill for Penny. During that date I realized that if I let Penny go, it would be the biggest mistake in my life. I had fallen deeply in love with Penny.

SUNDAY, OCTOBER 1, 1967—MY MOVE TO OAKDALE AVENUE

I moved from my apartment at 7025 North Sheridan Road to Ray Pershing's old apartment at 516 W. Oakdale Avenue. In the early part of October, I was in bed with the flu and Penny came to my apartment to cheer me up and give me chicken soup. At this point, I was absolutely deeply and madly in love with Penny but was afraid to tell her I loved her and was apprehensive to even mention marriage. At this point I didn't know how she felt or if she loved me too. From August 1967 to the middle of October I saw Penny a total of ten times, not on ten dates, just ten times. I absolutely knew she was the one for me.

OCTOBER 1967—CHRIS COHEN MOVES TO CHICAGO

In June 1967, Chris Cohen graduated from the University of Michigan Law School and moved to Chicago soon afterwards. We had kept in touch since meeting each other in Heidelberg, Germany and briefly traveled together, a year earlier. Chris and I became roommates on Sunday, October 1, 1967. Bernie and Bonnie Wilson lived on the first floor of our apartment building. They had a Dalmatian dog named Seaton. Bernie was from Detroit, Bonnie was from Columbus, Ohio and we quickly became friends.

One day in early October, Chris was stripping a chest of drawers in front of our apartment. He had newspapers on the sidewalk and was dressed in old clothes. He said I was walking back from seeing Penny who lived down the street from our apartment. Chris said "my face looked ashen, I looked stricken, like I had lost my best friend and his dog." "I said, Alan what is it?" "His eye brows peaked and he looked at me like, oh my goodness. And then he took the heel of his hand and hit the top of his forehead and said, I'm in love." Chris also told me I was walking into walls, dazed and confused, mumbling to myself, obviously smitten with Penny and madly in love with her.

When Chris moved to Chicago, he had taken a job working in a legal aid office in a rough Chicago neighborhood. Several years after I got married, he ran for Alderman in Chicago's 46th ward and won the election and served in the Chicago city council for four years. I worked on his campaign and helped him get elected. Chris and I continued to periodically see each other on the Metra train after we both moved to the suburbs. He moved to Glencoe, got married to Judy Calder and has two daughters, Katherine and Christina.

THE PROPOSAL

On a Friday night in mid-October, I got up enough courage to tell Penny I loved her. Penny responded by saying she loved me too. I immediately called my sister and told her that I loved Penny and that Penny loved me back. The thought of buying an engagement ring did not even enter my mind. I was so crazy in love to marry Penny and since I had never told any female I loved her or ever thought of getting married, I was totally oblivious to buying an engagement ring. What was I thinking?

One week later, in my apartment, as Penny was sitting on my sofa and after I knew Penny loved me, I got down on one knee and asked Penny to marry me. I told her how much I loved her and we would have a very interesting life together.

She accepted my proposal without hesitation and we were engaged with no ring or symbol to signify it. I guess it didn't matter to either of us at the time because we were deeply in love. After Penny accepted my proposal of marriage, we called our parents. Her parents must have been astonished because they had just sent their daughter to live in Chicago and three months after moving to the city, she got engaged.

In late October, Penny's mother, Dorothy, came to Chicago to visit her daughter and to check me out. She treated us to dinner at the London House, a famous restaurant/jazz club. Famous trumpet player, Dizzy Gillespie was the featured performer that evening and he was fantastic. After meeting me, her mother approved and we decided to announce our engagement during the 1967 Thanksgiving weekend. As a courtesy, when I saw Penny's stepfather, Sam in Cleveland, I asked him for Penny's hand in marriage. I can't believe it did not occur to me to buy an engagement ring or another symbol of my love for Penny. It wasn't until we got to Youngstown at Thanksgiving that I went with my father to a jeweler friend of his and bought Penny a diamond heart necklace.

NORMAN & SHEILA IN CHICAGO AND THE CHICAGO POLICE

From July 1, 1967 to June 30, 1968 Norman and Sheila Lockshin were living in Chicago's Prairie Shores Apartments because Norman was an intern at Michael Reese Hospital. Periodically, I would visit them. On Saturday December 2, 1967 at 3:30 p.m. without Penny accompanying me, it had been raining and the road was slippery. After visiting Norman and Sheila, I was driving out of their apartment complex when a Chicago Police car was coming around a corner, driving too fast for conditions. The police car driven by Vice Officer Raymond J. Galto of District 21 skidded and crashed into the passenger side back door of my 1963 purple Ford Fairlane four-door hardtop XL on 26th Street near Ellis (next to Michael Reese Hospital). The accident happened so fast and the impact caused the police car's siren to go off. I almost jumped out of my seat as the crash scared me. I was going about 5 miles an hour and the police car was going a little faster. The accident was not my fault. Within ten minutes a police photographer arrived at the scene to take photos of the accident. At the accident scene, the officers assured me that the city of Chicago would definitely pay for the damages to my car.

I tried to get the Chicago Police Department to pay for the repair of the damaged door but the only money I could get was $160.00 from the city of Chicago's Committee on Finance that finally came in the mail on March 19, 1968. The check would not cover the cost of the repair that was about $750.00. The note that came with the check stated: In accordance with the Council order of March 6, 1968, shown on Page 2340 of the council proceedings of that date...one hundred and sixty and no/100 dollars.

On February 18, 1968, I wrote to my Chicago alderman, Thomas Rosenberg, to complain about the payment but had no luck in getting any more money. On February 26, 1968, I received a very nice letter from Thomas Rosenberg, the alderman of the 44th Ward saying how disappointed he was in the treatment I received with reference to the accident in which I was involved through no fault of my own. According to the letter, "I have all the information that you forwarded to me and I intend to follow through on your particular case, no. 3310. In my opinion, there is no reason why you should not be entitled to the full amount of money due you. I will use this office to see to the satisfaction to which you are entitled. I will merely state that I am sorry that you did not contact me immediately and let me handle this claim for you thereby eliminating all this red tape." Yours Very Truly, Thomas Rosenberg. A copy was sent to Edward J. Barrett, Ward Committeeman, Democratic Headquarters on Clark Street in Chicago. The damage to the car was never repaired and eventually I sold the car to a Glenview Volvo dealership on Waukegan Road with the smashed-in rear passenger door.

1968—HAIRCUTS AT COLIN OF LONDON

In 1968 I started to get my haircut at Colin of London, a hairstyling barbershop located in a building downstairs on the south side of Chicago's Oak Street. I believe Michael Berman who was a medical intern in Chicago recommended this barbershop to me. Michael was married to Nancy Berman, the art teacher at Crow Island School and we became friendly with them. Otto Bodner was the hairstylist who worked at this shop and would cut my hair on a regular basis. Otto grew up in Germany near Nuremberg and immigrated to Chicago in 1965. The barbershop catered to celebrities, including movie stars when they were in town. Arthur Rubloff and radio personality Paul Harvey were regular customers.

Otto subsequently left Colin of London and opened his own shop on the lower level at 51 West Huron. After many years of operating his hairstyling shop, the Huron building was sold and his lease was terminated. Following the shop closing, Otto rented a chair at a barbershop in the basement of a hotel on East Superior Street. Then, after five years, he moved his barbershop to its current location in the lower level of the Hyatt Regency Chicago. Maria, who works with Otto, makes men's hairpieces and wigs by hand. Maria has worked for Otto for many years.

For the past several years, when Penny has her haircut at J Gordon Designs, I try to coordinate my haircut with hers. In the past, we have two variations on how this is organized. I will drive Penny to J Gordon for a 10:00 a.m. appointment with Cheryl and I will make an appointment for 10:30 a.m. with Otto. Or Penny will drop me off at the Hyatt Regency Chicago and drive to J Gordon and park the car. After my haircut, I'll walk to the number 22 Clark Street bus and take it to Deming where there is a Starbucks. I'll wait for Penny to be done, and then I'll walk to J Gordon and meet Penny.

CHAPTER ELEVEN
Engagement, Wedding, Honeymoon, Chicago

1967—OUR ENGAGEMENT AND THANKSGIVING

Penny and I drove to Cleveland on our Thanksgiving break from teaching. We celebrated our engagement by going out to eat at a Westside restaurant in Cleveland with Penny's relatives and my parents who drove to Cleveland for the event. Penny's stepfather, Sam Zipp and her mother Dorothy lived on Severn Road in Cleveland Heights. After their 1965 marriage, Dorothy moved into Sam's house.

On my first trip to meet the family, I slept in Lois' room over the garage that didn't have much heat, as it was a very cold room. I was shivering even though I had covers. The next morning, as I recall, they laughed when I told them I froze the previous night. They joked that it was a test and if I survived, I would be welcomed into the family.

The following evening, the Cleveland relatives drove to Youngstown for a dinner at the Colonial House on Market Street with my New York and Youngstown relatives. Penny had a chance to meet both of my grandparents at that party. My father was close to his first cousin Ralph Shwartz who was an attorney in Youngstown. Ralph and his wife Lillian were furious because their daughter was not invited to our engagement dinner. After this incident, it created a rift in their relationship. While in Youngstown, during Thanksgiving vacation, my father and I went to a jeweler and I bought Penny a diamond heart as a symbol of our engagement.

TUESDAY, FEBRUARY 6, 1968—MY GRANDFATHER DIES

My grandfather was in the North Side Hospital with a heart condition. He passed away one month before his 85th birthday. Penny and I drove into Cleveland for the funeral that was held at Youngstown's Shriver-Allison North Side Funeral Home. He is buried in Todd Cemetery on Youngstown's north side. I had a great relationship with my grandfather. We used to have talks about his life in the Russian army during the Russo-Japanese war and we played gin rummy and he would always beat me. I was happy that Penny had a chance to meet both of my grandparents.

TUESDAY, AUGUST 22, 1972—MY GRANDMOTHER DIES

After my grandfather died, my grandmother Rose lived on her own in the house for a short time before she went to Heritage Manor on Youngstown's Gypsy Lane, a home for the Jewish elderly. She died on August 22, 1972 at age 84 but had a chance to see and hold her great-grandson, Bennett. The funeral was held at 3:00 p.m. on Wednesday, August 23, 1972 at Shriver-Allison Northside Chapel and she is buried next to my grandfather in Todd Cemetery in Youngstown. My grandmother was an amazing cook and used to make a favorite dish of mine, stuffed veal breast [when I ate meat]. As a youngster, I would also watch her make Cole slaw from scratch was also delicious

THURSDAY, MAY 2, 1968—PENNY'S THYROID OPERATION

Before our wedding, Penny went for a routine physical exam by Dr. Leon Carrow, Penny's gynecologist. Dr. Carrow felt a small bump on Penny's thyroid gland on the left side of her neck. She made an appointment to have it checked out. On Thursday, February 22, 1968, Penny went to Chicago Wesley Memorial Hospital for a CAT scan of her thyroid. As a result of the scan, Penny was diagnosed with a small nodule on her left lobe of her thyroid gland. The charge for the radiologist was $14.00.

On Thursday, May 2, 1968, about one month before our scheduled Cleveland wedding, Dr. James Hine performed the one-hour and fifty-five-minute thyroidectomy that removed the left lobe of Penny's thyroid gland. Penny's mother flew from Cleveland to Chicago for the operation that was conducted at Chicago Wesley Memorial Hospital. While Penny was in the hospital, one of the nurses came into her room and told her another patient might want to talk to her because the nurse thought she was Penny's age. It turned out the girl was in high school and only 16. It goes to show you that Penny looked young and continues to look young and beautiful to this day.

While visiting Penny, I was close to a window and a window blind fell on my head. It didn't hurt much and scared me more than anything, but just to be cautious, I got an x-ray at the hospital. Everything turned out O.K. and Penny's operation was a success. On May 5, Penny received a bill from the surgeon for $400.00 for the operation and the bill from anesthesiologist Dr. John Fitzler was $80.00. Penny was covered with Fireman's Fund American Insurance Company through Arlington Heights Public School District #25. The total bill came to $1,000.35. The insurance company paid the entire bill except for a $100.00 deductible that Penny had to pay.

A EUROPEAN HONEYMOON WAS IN MY PLANS

Since both of us were teaching and our summers were free from school, I decided that a nearly two-month honeymoon would be perfect in Europe. I was planning the entire trip and much of it was based on the countries I had visited during my 1966 summer.

The first step was to buy a car to be picked up in Europe so on January 28, 1968, through Winnetka Import Motors, Inc. located at 666 Green Bay Road in Winnetka, Illinois, I ordered a Type 3, two-door, light blue Volkswagen fastback with standard transmission to be delivered to a Paris, France VW dealership by June 26. The car was built to United States specifications as far as emission controls and the total cost was $1,979.30 delivered to Unimotor, a Volkswagen dealership located at 42 Avenue De Saxe in Paris where we would arrive on June 27th. Before our trip, the car was paid in full at the Winnetka Volkswagen dealership. If we could have picked up the car in Wolfsburg, Germany, where the VW factory was located, it would have been $76.00 less. At the time, the car would have retailed in the U.S. for about $2,750.00. When I bought the car, I also ordered an International Driver's license and International license plates.

Then, in the early part of February I wrote to the National Education Association, Division of Educational Travel in Washington, D.C. for a list of charter flights to Europe for teachers. I received a letter on February 26, 1968 stating that we were confirmed on a flight to Paris NEA/CW-1/91 & 92. The flights usually depart in the evening for a next morning arrival in Paris. The return flights usually leave in the early afternoon for a late afternoon arrival in Chicago.

The cost of the round-trip charter flight from Chicago to Paris was $337.00 per person with a departure on June 26, returning to Chicago on August 19, 1968. Since Penny and I were not yet married, her reservation was made under her maiden name and her passport reflected the same. I had to send in a deposit of $125.00 to hold both of our airline reservations.

On Monday, April 22, 1968, I closed my bank account at the Upper Avenue National Bank of Chicago located at 923 N. Michigan Avenue and received two cashier's checks for $1,879.30 and $64.69 that was the balance in my savings account. I used the money toward our honeymoon.

The only reservation we had on our entire European honeymoon trip was a ticket on the Bergen Line, a ship across the North Sea from Newcastle, England to Bergen, Norway. You drive your car onto the ship and it sails across the North Sea overnight to Norway.

The following is a letter I received from the Bergen Steamship Line 505 Fifth Avenue New York, NY 10017 (212) 986-2711

> Dear Mr. Spencer
>
> Thank you for your card dated April 8, 1968 and we are pleased to enclose herewith our sailing schedule on the England/Norway Service.
>
> You will note that on the LEDA ship, the cheapest accommodations are tourist minimum at $28 per person, on the JUPITER; the cheapest accommodations are Sleepettes at $22 each.
>
> The cost of the Volkswagen is in addition to the passenger fare and is $23. We do not sell any space for "sitting up" on the ship.
>
> For your information, these sailings are very heavily booked during May, June, July and August and especially if you expect to take a car, we would suggest that you make your reservation just as soon as you have a definite date. We will be pleased to make the reservation for you. Sincerely yours, Ann Masterson (After reading this letter, we decided to immediately book a room on the ship with bunk beds).

SATURDAY APRIL 27, 1968—WEDDING RING SHOPPING

Penny and I went wedding ring shopping and decided on a simple but elegant gold filigree wedding band for her at Holland's Jewelers at 119 N. Wabash Avenue in Chicago. They took a measurement of Penny's finger and I put down a $15.00 deposit. The ring was promised for be picked up on Friday May 10, 1968 and the total cost was $57.75.

SUNDAY, JUNE 16, 1968—OUR FATHER'S DAY WEDDING

Penny did not want a big wedding and would have been content to get married in the rabbi's study. Since Penny and I were the first to get married in our family, I guess Penny's parents and my parents wanted a little bigger wedding so we ended up with a larger wedding.

We were married by Rabbi Philip Friedman at Temple Brit Emeth on E. Shaker Blvd in Pepper Pike, Ohio on Father's Day. The catered reception and dinner were in the downstairs social hall. We took family pictures before the ceremony and Penny looked beautiful in her white mini dress. I wore a black two-piece suit. The reception and dinner were well planned by Penny's mother. We basically showed up with little input and that was totally fine with us.

Rabbi Friedman did not believe in the tradition of breaking the glass, so I did not break a glass at the ceremony. My cousin Shelly told me after the wedding that because I didn't break a glass, we weren't officially married. Brit Emeth is no longer a synagogue but a religious school and we pass it whenever we visit Cleveland.

Immediately following the wedding ceremony and dinner, we bid goodbye to our guests and family and took a taxi to the Sheraton Hotel that is located at Cleveland Hopkins International Airport. After we got settled in our room, Penny and I were on the bed counting the checks we received during the evening and to our amazement, written in the memo portion of my Uncle Murray's check was the following: "Quit counting your money and go to bed." Penny and I had a good laugh. Our wedding gifts were left in Cleveland in the trunk of Penny's 1966 Chevy convertible. After our honeymoon, our plan was to return to Cleveland and drive the Chevy back to Chicago with the wedding gifts.

FLY BACK TO CHICAGO AFTER OUR WEDDING

The following day, on Monday, June 17, Linda took cousin Arleen to the Cleveland Airport to fly back to New York and they ran into Penny and me as we were waiting to fly back to Chicago. They got a huge laugh because we were boarding the plane with a brown grocery bag. Apparently, we hadn't brought enough suitcases, so our carry-on was a brown paper bag. It reminded us of my father arriving in New York for the first time to meet my mother's relatives and he was carrying a grocery bag with his clothes. We flew to back to Chicago and a few days later, on Wednesday June 26, 1968, we left for Europe on our extended honeymoon.

OUR EUROPEAN HONEYMOON AND JOURNAL

(The following is an excerpt from the journal kept by Penny on our almost two-month European honeymoon).

WEDNESDAY, JUNE 26, 1968—OFF TO EUROPE

Bernie and Bonnie Wilson drove us to O'Hare Airport. Along the way, we opened individually wrapped gifts they packed for us in a little flight bag. On one side of the bag it said, Spencers and on the other side Europa 1968. We checked into O'Hare Airport by 8:15 p.m. There was a delay in our World Airways chartered flight because of air traffic at Kennedy International Airport in New York. We left Chicago at 11:50 p.m. It took 7 hours and 40 minutes to reach Paris. The air speed was 625 mph. It is 4,700 miles from Chicago to Paris. The air route taken was from Chicago over Cleveland, New York, Nantucket, the North Atlantic Ocean, over Shannon Ireland, to the coast of France near Brest, to Le Bourget

Airport in France. (Le Bourget was the airport where Charles Lindbergh landed after his historic flight at 10:22 p.m. on Saturday May 21, 1927).

ALPINE MOTORING CONTEST

Before leaving for our honeymoon, I read about an Alpine Motoring Contest that we could enter. I thought, why not, so I wrote away to the Alpine Tourist Commission in New York to get the marketing materials. The contest was for the years 1968-69 and was a great campaign to encourage tourists to visit seven European alpine countries. The countries were Austria, France, Germany, Italy, Monaco, Switzerland, and Yugoslavia. Each participant in the program was sent contest rules, regulations, and an invitation to the Alps (playground of Europe) brochure outlining each country. Other materials included in the packet were a control book that had to be stamped in each country plus marketing materials and a panoramic highlights brochure hyping each country.

The object of the contest was to get the control book stamped when you were in each Alpine country. There were certain cities and checkpoints in each country and when you had all of the countries listed on the card stamped, you would get a gold medal sent to you in the mail. We went to each of the seven countries and got our control book stamped. In October 16, 1968, we received a gold medal and a letter congratulating us for completing the seven countries tour. It is the only gold medal I've ever received for all of my athletic accomplishments.

THURSDAY, JUNE 27, 1968—ARRIVAL IN PARIS

We arrived at Le Bourget Airport in Paris at 1:15 p.m., one hour late. After clearing customs, we took an Air France bus to the city terminal, then a taxicab to Unimotor, 42 Avenue de Saxe to pick up our Volkswagen Fastback Type 3.

We met two couples on our flight that were also waiting for their car. One of the guys graduated from Central Michigan University and is a theology student in Holland, Michigan. We both took off at the same time. We bought the basic VW liability insurance policy for $31.00 and a 2-month full coverage collision policy for $48.00. We finally left Unimotor at 6:15 p.m. after waiting for a customs clearance since 3:00 p.m. We decided to leave Paris to eat and find a hotel outside the city. Paris was one traffic jam and it took an hour to get out of the city. [Alan drove the car while Penny did the navigating]

By this time, we were both pretty tired and ornery. We found a café with food in Paissy where we finally decided on beefsteak with potatoes, salad and wine. The T.V. was on with the news and men were sitting or standing around watching. The name of the café was Chez Mazius 21 Rue du General de Gaulle. Poissy (Yvelines). The dinner cost 1675 francs ($3.35US)

After driving up and down one-way streets, the wrong way, we found all the hotels filled so we drove toward Rouen, stopping in Les Mureaux. We got a room for 20 francs ($4.05US), not including breakfast for 5 francs ($1.01US). The faucet dripped all night and the douche made sucking noises. (The room was over a bar and across from railroad tracks).

114

FRIDAY, JUNE 28—LEAVING FRANCE FOR ENGLAND

Per usual, we woke up at dawn, 5:00 a.m. We were dressed by 6:00, got organized, took some pictures and ate breakfast, coffee with warm milk and four croissants. After scraping off our new car stickers on the window, we set off for Dieppe at 8:00 a.m. We stopped at Rouen for a drink of orange juice and arrived at Dieppe at 11:15 a.m. The ferry ticket to England ticket cost 161.50 francs or $32.23.

Luckily, we got to the ferry in time for the 12:45 p.m. trip across the English Channel. We drove the car onto the ferry, parked it, and went upstairs where we ate in an ugly cafeteria. Then Alan got seasick, as the channel crossing was a little rough. We met an older couple from Lincolnshire, Illinois. The lady gave us some tablets that we saved since Alan already took two Excedrin.

Amazingly, as soon as the boat slowed down, Alan snapped out of it and felt fine. We arrived at Newhaven, England at 4:30 p.m. and prayed we'd get used to driving on the left side of the road. It was scary but we're doing O.K. At 7:00 p.m. we stopped for dinner in Redfield. It was so much easier ordering food in English. The waitress recommended a great motel like the U.S. with a bath and pool.

SATURDAY, JUNE 29—OFF TO LONDON

Breakfast woke us up at 8:00 a.m. We were still in bed when the waiter brought in rolls and coffee. After taking some pictures, we left for London at 10:00 a.m. Alan followed the directions perfectly, not one mistake. He even remembered the way once we were in London where we arrived at 11:10 a.m.

Then we began searching for a room. Some of the hotels were too expensive, some full, and some had no double beds. It wasn't too long before we found a room at St Athans Hotel near Russell Square and the University of London. Room number 37 was on the third floor with a toilet across the hall and a shower the floor below. The owners are extremely nice. Breakfast is included in the 2 £ 15 shillings or $6.60 per night.

After getting settled in the room, we ate around the corner in a quaint Italian restaurant where the Spanish waiter had to take our order twice. It cost 1£ 10 shillings and 10 pence ({$2.64) for minestrone, spaghetti, a salad, roll and 1/2 carafe of wine. The restaurant said Continental and English Cuisine Ristorante.

The underground (subway) is just around the corner, so we took it from Russell Square to Piccadilly. As one of the hippies got on, he said, it really was like a cattle car being all packed in. While running to catch the train, I lost a valuable book on London. It was a mad rush to get off at Piccadilly. The underground is so far down, we had to take two escalators, one of which was broken and we had to walk it. Alan took some great movies at Trafalgar Square to open up the series on London. We bought a magazine on what's happening in London to decide on a play. After walking and asking directions everywhere, we decided on the musical *Cabaret*. It was already 4:00 p.m. so we decided on the matinee knowing we'd be pooped by 8:30 p.m. We sat in the Upper Circle for 1£ or $2.60 a seat. Before the show, we stopped for strawberry cake and coffee at the Hollywood Restaurant where Alan took his obnoxious cough medicine from the chemists.

Another disaster occurred when Alan dropped the tripod on my foot and I really cracked up. The play was fantastic. After leaving The Palace Theater, we walked to Soho and ate a delicious pizza at Trattoria del Buox Vivatoire. We each had an individual pizza. They're made with garlic, anchovies and olives. We couldn't find our bus line so we took the underground back to our hotel.

SUNDAY, JUNE 30—LONDON

We woke up at 7:30 a.m. and had breakfast at 8:45. Alan took some movies of the hotel. Then we walked to The Post Office Building, the tallest structure in Great Britain. It is 620 feet high and opened in 1965. There are exhibits of the history of the telephone and the function of the tower for communication and television. We went up to the 34th floor, took some movies, and then went down to the 33rd floor where there were no windows but bars.

It only took 15 minutes to walk back to the hotel where we called The Royal Albert Hall to reserve tickets for the London Symphony Orchestra. Then we decided to drive to the hall to pick up the tickets. On the way, we stopped at Hyde Park to take pictures. Alan was posing me in crazy shots and everyone thought we were "someone." After picking up the symphony tickets, we drove near Trafalgar Square to find a hamburger stand for a quick snack. Instead, we ate in The Trafalgar Room, one of four restaurants in a corner building. We each had steak and kidney pie.

In the late afternoon, we drove to Big Ben, The Houses of Parliament and Westminster Abbey. Alan took pictures and I fell asleep in the car. After an hour and a half nap, we dressed for the concert. We had excellent seats, $3.00 a piece in the stalls, 4 rows from the front. The concert consisted of *Scheherazade*, *Paganini Variations* and Ravel's *Bolero*. By this time 9:40, we were starved so we drove to Soho. Per usual we got lost and at 10:56 p.m. we found it. We ate in Bianchi's Restaurant. Alan had lasagna and I had spaghetti. The salad was served with tuna fish (very interesting). We drank Beaujolais wine. It all cost $4.92. The hotel's dishes for breakfast were Johnson's Athena pattern, our same plates in Chicago.

MONDAY, JULY 1—LONDON

Alan had to go out early before 8:30 to put 2 shillings or 24 cents in the meter to park 4 hours. We ate breakfast and spent a while washing our clothes. Our first mistake was taking the car. We drove to Buckingham Palace parking on The Mall arriving at 11:10 a.m. for the 11:30 changing of the guards. It was extremely hot and crowded and difficult to take pictures. A band marched and played not only typical marching songs as well as some jazz.

We parked at the Whitcomb Street Car Park and walked to find a hair dryer but got way laid by Carnaby Street. We walked in a couple shops and found exactly what we wanted at Irvine Sellars Mates. Alan found a wool navy pin stripe suit and a yellow shirt. I found a camel suit really different and a light dress.

Since the alternations would take until 5:30, we searched in all the department stores for a hair dryer. There was only one that runs on all currents and everyone was out so we took the double decker bus to The Strand. At the Ronson Store, they told us any chemist carries the model we wanted. We bought it and then found out it is not a hood model but it was our only choice. It cost $3.60.

We took the bus back to Carnaby Street to pick up our clothes. The sales people went out of their way to please. Our last mistake was taking the bus to the Car Park instead of walking. We got completely lost and at 6:00 p.m. finally found our car. Alan took a shower and I lay down. About 8:30 p.m. I washed my hair in the shower. It is so hot I couldn't bear using the hair dryer very long. Alan got four different pastries at the corner shop and we packed to leave tomorrow.

TUESDAY, JULY 2—LEFT LONDON FOR THE NORTH

We got up about 8:00 and left London at 10:15. It was quite easy finding our way out of the city onto the road to Windsor. We arrived there at about 11:15, parked the car in a Car Park and walked through the city to Windsor Castle. We caught the Palace Guards and took some film.

Then we bought tickets for the Doll House and Masters Drawings. The Doll House itself was magnificent, furnished like a real castle. In glass cases were all the accessories for it, from miniature dishes to knives. The drawings were by Leonardo Da Vinci and Ghirlandaio, etc. Some were sketches, some plans for murals. We took a hike up 125 stairs to the Round Tower. Were we bushed? We got some great movies. For lunch, we stayed in Windsor and ate at The Anchor House for $4.11. Penny had scampi's and Alan had mixed grille.

At 1:45 p.m. we left for Oxford that only took 45 minutes. Alan stopped to take pictures. In Oxford, we parked on the street and then stopped at a snack shop so I could take something for a headache. There, Alan asked a young guy directions and we went to Christ Church. Alan thought he lost his contact lens, disaster, but it was in his eye. We saw choirboys on their way to practice before Christ Church. Then we went inside the cathedral. It was free but a sign asked for money for the church. We bought a post card. You just put the money in a box.

After the church, we were quite tired so we left for Chipping Norton. On the way, we stopped for dinner at a cafeteria for $2.30. Alan had tomato soup and beef and curry. Penny had spaghetti. We decided to call a Trust House to make sure we had a room before evening. It was a good thing because there is an agriculture exhibition and most hotels are full. This place is great. You are served tea before breakfast and you get a newspaper. The room is very nice and they have an actual bathtub. We should really be rested by tomorrow.

LETTER I WROTE TO MY MOM AND DAD FROM THE WHITE HART HOTEL IN CHIPPING NORTON, ENGLAND

Tuesday, July 2, 1968—8:00 p.m.

Dear Mom & Dad, Penny and I are in Chipping Norton as you can see from the letterhead. This small "typically English town" is located about 20 miles from Oxford (site of the famous Oxford University) and about 35 miles from Stratford-On-Avon (Shakespeare's home). This country is beautiful. Tomorrow we'll drove around this section—The Cotswolds (Midland Hills) and drive to Stratford, then north to Glasgow and Edinburgh.

Penny and I splurged on Carnaby Street in London. That's the famous mod clothes street. I bought a tailored coat, bellbottom trousers navy wool pin striped suit-double breasted for $40.00 plus a yellow shirt to go with it for $5.00. Penny bought a camel wool mini suit for $40.00 & a cotton dress—mini of course. I always wanted a mod suit. I will be able to wear it in the evenings (Saturdays) when I take Penny out in Chicago. The suit sounds "way out" but really it is conservative. I would never buy something that I wouldn't wear in the U.S. Alterations cost ½ as much as they would in U.S. & they were done the same day. The stores really cater to you.

Our food choices have mainly been Italian restaurants although we did eat steak & kidney pie---something like beef pot pie---very good. We left London today at 10:15 a.m. & headed for Windsor to see the residence of the queen at Windsor Castle. We took some terrific movies. Penny and I also climbed to the top of the round tower and saw the changing of the guard, recorded it on film. Then we drove to Oxford to see the university.

The car handles like a dream with terrific gas economy, good acceleration and roomy for both of us. The place we're staying tonight is the cleanest place so far. (A very large bedroom with sink and they serve you tea in bed before breakfast. The price of the room includes breakfast and is standard throughout most of Europe. We're paying $7.65 for a double but in London we only paid $6.20 a day. The English money is easier for me to understand this time around, mainly because we'll be in England for a much longer time. Please read this to grandma and tell her that Penny and I are thinking of her and also mail this to Linda. P.S. I forgot to tell you we heard the London Symphony Orchestra on Sunday evening. Love Penny and Alan

WEDNESDAY, JULY 3—THE COTSWOLDS

Today was a great day! We got up early by 7:30 when tea was served with the newspaper. We were charged, we later found out. Breakfast was really big, juice, cereal, eggs, toast, and coffee although we were still starved by 11:30.

Alan took another movie of me coming out of our hotel yawning and I ripped my coat, pulling off a button. We left Chipping Norton at 10:00 and drove to the Rollright Stones. They are stones arranged in a circle at the top of a hill. Legend is that the stones were once people. Then we drove through Morton in Marsh and Broadway, where we bought a note pad and bubble bath and hose. After this, we drove through Mickleton to Stratford-On-Avon. We satisfied Alan's hunger for Chinese food at the Hong Kong. It cost $4.45 for four dishes.

We bought a group of five tickets to different places of importance in Shakespeare's life. The house where Shakespeare's was born, the house he bought, the foundation of which only stands, his daughter's house, the gardens, Guild Hall, the grammar school, Klopton Bridge, Trinity Church where Shakespeare was born and Harvard House where the mother of John Harvard, founder of Harvard University, lived were all part of the 5-ticket package.

From Stratford, we drove to Warwick Castle. The guide was great. He asked where we were from and knew the "Windy City." We saw defense weapons, armor, beautiful tapestries, paintings, chandeliers and other adornments. Originally there were no windows because of attacks. For more modern living, ten feet of drilling was necessary to get through the wall. This gives an idea why the castle was never taken. The Earl of Warwick still lives in the castle. Toward the end of the afternoon, we drove to Kenilworth Castle; however, we were tired and so drove as far as we could. We drove to the outskirts of Birmingham on M6 and ate at a service plaza restaurant like in the U.S.A. over the highway. It cost $2.80.

Quite tired at 8:45, we turned off the next exit for a bed and breakfast. There was nothing so we took another road to Audley, stopping at a hotel. No vacancy there, but a man called a new hotel and we followed him there. It is a Trust House, Staffordshire Post Hotel running along M6 and the nicest place so far. Overnight cost was $9.60 plus 8 shillings for breakfast.

THURSDAY, JULY 4—OFF TO SCOTLAND

Happy 4th of July! We even saw a couple with Texas license plates on their car. For breakfast, we decided on the continental; getting juice, one roll, and coffee. Starved, we left at our usual time of 10:00 a.m. for a day of driving.

We stopped at Carnforth for cheese at a grocer and bread in a little bakery. The two women were so nice. We talked for a while bought some chocolate cakes and got back on the road to Carlisle since we had made a wrong turn. We also cashed $70.00 worth of traveler's checks. In Carlisle, we stopped again for orange quash and cheese cake at $.48. We also bought six stamps at the Post Office. At about 3:30, we crossed into Scotland. All along the way stone hedges or walls divided the hills dotted with sheep. At one point two sheep jumped over a stone wall onto the green.

We arrived in Glasgow about 5:30 p.m. with no map of the city. No gas stations had any. A man in one gas station on his way home from work took us to a couple of hotels. Alan couldn't understand him. One place had no room. We took the next hotel and wrote the man a note that we were leaving to drive on. It was so bad. We don't know how we took it. It smelled and was cold-Ugh!! The man's wife had relatives in Long Island. After speeding out of there, we went to another Shell station. They had no map but a man there called a hotel he stays at and got us a room. It is The Brabloch, old and very nice and clean with breakfast for $8.40. We splurged for fried potatoes, salad and wine. For dessert, we split pear sponge. The dinner cost $5.65. It's amazing how light it is here even at 9:30 p.m.

FRIDAY, JULY 5—GLASGOW —WE ACTUALLY SAW THE QUEEN

Today, we woke up at 6:45 a.m. because Alan yelled out that we overslept and it was past 10:00. We were also awakened for tea at 7:30 when all we wanted was to be woken up. Breakfast was pretty blah. The scrambled eggs were icky and the toast cold and stale.

Alan called a Volkswagen dealer (Finlay's of Paisley) for our first car service at 779 miles on the odometer. We brought the car in at 10:00 right in Paisley where we stayed. It was to take until 3:30 p.m. or 4:00, so we took the red bus into Glasgow (passing our almost hotel). At the information bureau at George Square, we found out Queen Elizabeth was coming to Glasgow that afternoon. The tours didn't return until 8:00 so that was out. We decided to have a snack at the railroad station cafeteria (very good) and wait for the Queen since she was coming right to the square. At 12:30, she came walking down the street wearing a yellow suit and hat that really showed up great. She wore hose with seams and heels with pointed toes. She just glowed and waved to the people. We were standing right by the gates as she walked down the path. Alan took a movie of her as she walked. After lunch at Sloane's in Argyle Arcade, we took the bus back to the car dealer. It was only 2:30 but luckily our car was ready and they had washed it.

LOCH LOMOND AND STIRLIING CASTLE

Loch Lomond was our next stop. Then we drove on to Stirling, the highlight of our trip so far. The castle had fantastic vaults, turrets and the greatest view of the city of Stirling, the statue of Robert the Bruce who with Wallace, helped unify the clans of Scotland and the body of water that runs into the Firth of Forth.

As we were leaving Stirling, we decided to get ice cream at a truck outside the castle. The owner, Mr. Toppalano described all the ice creams recommending the nougat because when people leave Scotland, they always remember how gooey it is. It was an ice cream sandwich, wafer and around the outside there was white cream covered with chocolate. Mr. Toppalano took our picture and then Alan took me with him. He told us some of the history of Scotland and where he came from. Ninety-five per cent of the ice cream owners were Italian when he came to Scotland. It's probably a little less now. He also told us a scenic way to go to Edinburgh over the Kincardin Bridge and then the bridge (Forth) about 2 miles, new and very nice. He had a very thick Scottish accent and was difficult understanding everything he said even though he was speaking English.

EDINBURGH, SCOTLAND

As soon as we entered Edinburgh, we called some of Arthur Frommer's places and were told to call a place down the street from one we called. The woman was very nice at Lairg so we stayed. The room was in the basement with heater and shower. There was no hot water and we both washed our hair.

After getting settled, we ate at the Honeydew Café. Alan got chicken salad, a piece of chicken that he didn't want. I got icky Welsh rarebit. But we made up for it with a banana split for dessert.

SATURDAY, JULY 6—EDINBURGH, SCOTLAND

Breakfast at 8:30 was kind of icky. The toast was soggy from sitting and the bacon and eggs were greasy. That didn't stop us from keeping to our 10:00 schedule. After switching to an upstairs room (not as nice), no heater but at least the bathroom is right outside the room), we went to see Edinburgh Castle. We are staying about 10 minutes from the center of town.

We wanted to start at the Mound but missed it and walked up the hill through the footpaths, a very long walk with no access to the castle. We walked around not too much out of the way taking the tour because we were already tired. We did walk around the grounds and toured the museum of Robert Burns, Sir Walter Scott and Robert Louis Stevenson. It was really interesting. A sign said to watch for the eleventh step. In old houses some of the steps were made of different sizes to trip intruders or people who were trespassing.

We had lunch ($3.70) at a very nice restaurant on famous Princes Street, then conked out from 2 to 4:00 at the hotel. Alan took some clothes to the dry cleaner and we picked them up at 5:00. We were both in the mood for pizza, so we went to a place we'd seen driving in for the first time ($1.70). It wasn't too hot. Holyrood Castle was closed but we walked around the grounds and then drove up to the top of the hill. It was a mess of litter from all day.

Then we drove all along the Firth of Forth through resort towns, past castles and a motor museum with an old fire engine in front. In North Berwick, we heard bagpipes so we parked and watched for a little while. The men were dressed in kilts and stood in a circle playing while the people stood all around them.
A little further on, there was a small carnival with rides including Dodgem and games of chance. Alan had a hot dog with onions and I had a candy apple. We got back to the hotel at 9:45 p.m.

SUNDAY, JULY 7—LEAVING EDINBURGH, SCOTLAND

After talking it over, we decided to leave Edinburgh for Newcastle, instead of waiting until Monday. It turned out to be a very good choice. It was raining when we left Edinburgh at 9:30, a little before our usual time. For two nights it cost $11.40. We tried out the defroster for the first time and used both heaters for a while. At Alnwick, we stopped for something to eat at a little café. We each had a cheese sandwich, potato chips, and coffee, and split a piece of pastry, all for about $.64. After eating, we toured Alnwick Castle that was one of the best. A different man was in each room to answer questions. From there, we went into the castle where there were paintings of the Dukes of Northumberland. The present Duke just arrived as we were there. There were also marble tables, china, silver, etc.

One of the dungeons is open and when we were looking at it, one man went down there to the shock of his younger daughter. The guide turned off the light to show what it was like to be imprisoned there. This was one of six death dungeons because once thrown down there, there was no way up and the prisoner was not fed. In the tower were relics of the Stone Age, the Bronze Age and Roman relics. A tombstone was just recovered a month ago and soon they will determine how old it is. Below the tower was a sand box where the duke's children play.

We left the Alnwick Castle after about an hour at 2:15 and arrived in Newcastle at 3:10. I fell asleep and woke up to Alan saying there was a circus, Billy Smart's, the largest circus in the world. Alan got out to find out about tickets but it opens tomorrow at 5:00 and by that time, we'll be on the ship to Norway.

Per usual, we drove around trying to find a place to stay. We went up to see one room in The Grand Hotel but it was awfully gloomy, so we drove to South Shields. The first bed and breakfast we tried had a real sweet room, so we took it. $2.60 a piece. Dinner across the street was obnoxious. We came back to the hotel and figured out the ship instructions at about 6:20 p.m.

MONDAY, JULY 8—NEWCASTLE TO BERGEN, NORWAY

Breakfast in this little boarding house was the best the whole trip so far: fried egg, tomatoes, mushrooms, bread, toast, corn flakes, tea or coffee and the lady was so nice. We had a lot of time to waste so we asked her if she knew any places of interest. She just moved from Brighton so she didn't know the area but gave us a little booklet. We had seen a sign to the Roman fort and museum and it was well-worth seeing. The foundations of the fort, all labeled were in the back of a museum with Roman relics from tombstones to button fasteners, skulls and sculptures.

After this, we rode around in the dreariest weather. We stopped at a coffee shop for apple tarts and coffee and bought some pastry. Finally, we went down to the Tysie Commission Quay where our ship to Norway was waiting. We were one of the first cars in line, leaving the car and going inside the waiting room. It was 2:30 p.m. At 3:30, they started loading the cars onto the ship. We had a hard time finding our room. It had bunk beds and a lavatory.

In one of the lounges, we had Bloody Marys'. They were strong and we began to feel sick so we went to the cafeteria for dinner. We had fish sticks (three each), French fries, green beans, a roll, a huge piece of vanilla cream cake and coffee for $2.92. Then we really began to feel sick, so we tried to locate the purser for motion sickness tablets. Finally, we were told to ring the bell from our cabin. A lady gave us two packages. We each took one and slept on and off until 3:00 a.m.

LETTER TO MY PARENTS
ON BERGEN LINE SHIP STATIONERY

Monday July 8, 1968 at 4:45 p.m.

"Dear Mom and Dad,

Well, here we are---aboard ship—ready to leave for Bergen, Norway and the third country of our European honeymoon. While in Edinburgh, Penny and I drove along the Firth of Forth toward the North Sea on Saturday evening. We saw some beautiful countryside villages and to our surprise we came upon a Scottish bagpipe band playing Scotch songs in a car park (parking lot). After we left the music, we drove by a carnival and decided to spend some time there. It was a spontaneous and enjoyable evening.

Last night we spent in South Shields near Newcastle-on-the-Thyne. We decided to leave a day ahead of time from Edinburgh so we wouldn't have a long drive to catch the ship today. This proved to be a smart idea! We were going to stay in Sunderland which is about eight miles from South Shields but after driving around there for about 45 minutes, we discovered no hotels to our liking.

Our ship's cabin is very nice! It has an upper and lower berth, private bathroom-toilet-no tub or shower. We had our VW fastback serviced in Paisley, a suburb of Glasgow on Thursday. We stayed in Paisley the night before so it was no trick going to the car dealer. Since the first service (600 miles) is a complete car physical and charged to the VW factory, the car had to be in the garage from 10:00 to 2:30 p.m. Penny and I took a bus into Glasgow and spent the day there, then returned to pick up the car. The ride took approximately 30 minutes.

In the afternoon, we left for Loch Lomond and the city of Stirling (the strategic center of Scotland) and then on to Edinburgh where we arrived at 9:00 p.m. We found a hotel recommended in *Europe on $5 A Day*, about $6.20 for both of us including breakfast "clean as a pin."

It gets dark in England rather late. The sun starts to set around 9:45-10:00 p.m. We haven't used our car lights yet because of it. We now have 1,145 miles on the car. I'm surprised that I got a chance to write you another letter. The only time I have is when the stationery is provided. Please send this letter to Linda. Tell grandma we love her & think of her often." Love Alan and Penny

TUESDAY, JULY 9—ARRIVAL IN BERGEN, NORWAY

At 8:30 a.m. we got up for breakfast on the ship and had eggs, toast, bacon and coffee. Still a little woozy from the trip across the North Sea, we took another pill. Alan conked out downstairs and I kept conking off and on in the lounge.

A girl began talking to me and the girl across from me. The later was Norwegian and I could tell she could speak English faintly but I think we were talking too fast for her. The former was one of a four girls and a four boys group traveling by bicycle from American Youth Hostels. She was from New York.

At 11:30, I woke Alan to get ready for the Bergen docking. We went through showing our passports in the cafeteria and were the first car to leave the ship.

In Bergen, Norway, Alan asked about a restaurant for lunch. It was very nice with English translations on the menu. We both got a sort of beef stew with whipped potatoes, peas and carrots. It was absolutely freezing. Alan asked directions to the top of the hills so we could see the city. Finally, we found a correct road. The way it twisted was unbelievable, but it was worth the trouble to see the spectacular view below. We saw the cable car that goes up the side of the mountain. The city of Bergen was very quaint but we didn't spend much time there. We were anxious to get to Oslo so we drove to a ferryboat to take us across a fjord to the road to Oslo.

Luckily, we got to the ferry that would take us across the Hardangfjord in time for the 7:30 p.m. trip. I was really sick from everything. The view of the fiord was beautiful being surrounded by mountains. Once we got to the other side, we asked at Information about a place to stay for the night. A guy called ahead and said we were lucky to get a place. It was the Maurseth Hotel in Voringfoss over one-hour away. The roads were just unbelievable with twists, hairpin turns, no guardrails, gravel part of the way and hardly room for 2 lanes. But we made it.

The room wasn't half-bad, a great heater where we dried all our clothes practically. And a shower bath that was really welcome. When we finally went to bed at 11:30 p.m. it wasn't even dark. One thing really shocked me was when we walked in our room. The blanket was rolled under the bedspread looking like a body. The clerk said I wasn't the only one to be shocked.

WEDNESDAY, JULY 10—OSLO, NORWAY, HERE WE COME

Again, breakfast was unbelievable-smorgasbord from fish to cheese, corn flakes and boiled egg. We began again on our way to Oslo at 10:00 after buying postcards and gas. The cards were expensive over $1.00 for 7 and a booklet of cards. At about 12:00 noon, we stopped for an orange drink in a kafeteria. Then about 2:00 p.m. we stopped at a grocery store for rolls, cheese, chips, apples and our favorite chocolate chip cookies. It was about $2.00 (and a candy bar too). We stopped at the side of the road looking over a fjord. Earlier when we were still high in the mountains, it snowed. What a crazy feeling in the middle of July. I took movies of Alan making a snowball and took some slate for the rock garden.

A little later there was a bulldozer pushing a boulder off the road. They're really blasting away the rocks to improve the roads but meanwhile-Yoik!! All along the roads children stood with either strawberries or reindeer antlers in their hands outstretched. Poor Alan-the drive was really nerve wracking. We finally reached Oslo at 5:00 p.m. We tried one hotel from the book but it was filled, so we are staying in a place that's a hotel during the summer and a university dormitory during the rest of the year. It is called the Studentbyog Sommerhotel and cost $10.50 a night including breakfast.

THURSDAY, JULY 11—OSLO, NORWAY

Breakfast, just like dinner, was a madhouse. We were up at 8:15 and out by our usual time. Breakfast didn't really fill us up, a boiled egg, bread, coffee, and sweet roll. After this lusciousness, we checked out deciding any place would be better. We drove to Bydoy to see Fram and the Kon-Tiki. There was a man from Akron who spoke to us. We went to see The Vigeland Sculptures at Frogner Park. We fed the ducks and took 10 frame pictures of the sculptures on the movie camera. After all this, we called a hotel listed in Arthur Frommer and were lucky enough to get a room at Hotel Pension Hall, where member of the Norwegian Parliament stays during the winter. It's a first-class hotel but still smells.

We checked-in and went into town looking for Kleenex, etc. However, Alan had to do the shopping because I was conking. We took Frommer's advice again for our restaurant eating at Tivoli garden in The Continental. I had scampi and Alan had sirloin steak with Béarnaise sauce. For dessert, we each had walnut layer cake. Excitedly, we went across the street to see an American movie, "Where Were You When The Lights Went Out." Darling. Then I got a memorable driving lesson. We were so tired, we conked out without even washing at 11:00 p.m. Whoops. Forgot something else. After the boats, we went to the Folks Museum. We walked all around the village. In one house, the lady asked us in to hear her music on the longleik. It is a string instrument placed on a table. Attached to the plucker were strings tied to a Norwegian boy and girl, and as she stroked, they danced. In another house, a girl was making clay dishes on a potter's wheel.

FRIDAY, JULY 12—OSLO, NORWAY

Breakfast was a real splurge today at The Continental Breakfast Room. Our hotel was lousy, so we walked out and the same restaurant we went to last night was serving breakfast. We had smorgasbord for $4.20 but it was worth it. From there, we went to a Norsk Design Shop-O.K. Then onto The Vigeland Museum that didn't open until 1:00. Disappointment.

By 1:00, we were at Akershus Castle for a tour. The girl spoke English very well and was so sweet. We were a bit disappointed by the castle because almost everything was reconstructed, very plain. Above the altar of the Church there was written Jehovah in Hebrew. The guide didn't know the significance. Also, a Jewish star is above the Vigeland Museum. Naturally, it rained all the time we were in the castle. A German woman who we helped with her umbrella took me to a shelter and let me go get Alan (my man as she calls him). She thought we were Italian.

Halfway down the hill, Alan ran in the pouring rain, got the car, drove it through the castle gates and picked me up. We got ice cream already packaged cones and orange drink in town and then drove back to the hotel. Taking Frommer's advice again, we went to see the Non-Stop Show at Le Chat Noir. It was really great.

Before the show, we grabbed two hot dogs, chips and a Coke by the dock and ate them at the City Hall Park. After the show in the Ladies Room, I got a ticket and nearly cracked up. I just gave the woman $.50. Hungry again, we found a snack shop next to the show and got hamburgers and a Pepsi. We saw the piano player from the Deep River Boys walk by.

SATURDAY, JULY 13—OFF TO GOTEBORG, SWEDEN

Our plans to leave Oslo early today were somewhat foiled by a very nice but talkative couple from America. We were down for smorgasbord breakfast by 8:30 but this couple began talking to us. This year is their fourth trip overseas. The guy is a physical chemistry professor in Istanbul, Turkey. The girl is originally from the Southeast side of Cleveland and the guy from Shaker Heights. He went to the University of Chicago and loves the city.

At 9:30 a.m. we finally left, cashed a traveler's check and decided to wait until Copenhagen for china. It was a long ride until we reach Goteborg, Sweden at 3:30 p.m. Alan was cracking up. We found the information center and a hotel quickly. It is the Orgyte Hotel near everything.

Alan took a sauna bath not too far away and I slept. Then we went to Liseberg, the second largest amusement park. We had great shish kabobs and French fries and, on the way, out got vanilla and strawberry glass cones. Really different! Our hotel is one of the nicest we've stayed at.

SUNDAY, JULY 14—ON TO COPENHAGEN, DENMARK

Breakfast was smorgasbord and again exceptionally good, especially the pastry. We left at our usual 10:00 a.m. The guy at the hotel desk said it would take 5 hours to reach Helsingborg but it only took 2 1/2. We were lucky again waiting only 10 minutes for the ferry to Denmark. That only took 25 minutes and then less than an hour's drive to Copenhagen.

The great motel I read about had no receptionist and looked closed. Two Danish guys were waiting too and told us of another hotel even giving us directions. It had no bath so we vetoed that. Alan called some more places and found a fantastic place, a tourist apartment with bath and toilet, a bedroom and a sitting room. It's right across the bridge from the center of Copenhagen.

Since we hadn't eaten since breakfast, we decided to eat lunch at Tivoli Gardens. We had our most fantastic meal since London (says Penny), Italian, of course. Delicious spaghetti cooked in garlic, mixed salad with wine and lasagna.

Three guys from New York, really vulgar were sitting behind us. Smashed, we left the restaurant, our most expensive $8.00 and walked and walked. Eartha Kitt was the main attraction. We saw an outdoor trapeze act, very well.

Of course, we got chocolate candy, popcorn, chocolate soda and orange drink along the way. While drinking, we met two girls. One is from San Francisco and the girl she was with was from Malmo, Sweden. She takes care of the American girl's sister and so both came to visit her family.

MONDAY, JULY 15—COPENHAGEN, DENMARK

Because of the rain, our plans were curtailed but we still saw some great things. Breakfast was simple compared to what we've been used to but good. We were out again by 10:00 and went to the Ny Carlsberg Glyptotek Museum. We loved the Egyptian ruins, Roman ruins and Renaissance art.

After this, we went to the largest department store in Scandinavia, Le Magasin du Nord. The displays were fantastic as were most stores. We bought a serving fork for our dinnerware and two spoons at a Dansk shop since the other store was sold out. We also ate in the store's cafeteria. It was so hard getting a seat and I hated the egg salad sandwiches. We tried seeing Rosenberg Castle but it was closed by then so we got something to eat at Westphalia. I was starved so, got a delicious platter with creamed mushrooms on top of spinach.

The highlight of the day was the Schumann Circus in an intimate auditorium in the round. The acts were fantastic. We got to bed late because we both had clothes to wash and I washed my hair at 12:30 a.m.

TUESDAY, JULY 16—COPENHAGEN

It was another day of rain. Blich! After breakfast we went to the Carlsberg Breweries. We parked on the street and the entrance for the tours was quite a walk in the rain. By mistake, we got in a regular tour group and had beer after in a special hall. The tour wasn't so hot since we were hardly allowed to see anything. It was interesting that all the net proceeds go toward art and science as the founder willed. We came back to the hotel to change to dry clothes and left for the Rosenberg Castle. We couldn't find the entrance so decided it really wasn't worth it, got hot dogs and went to a very interesting museum, The Bymuseum. It is Danish history depicted in paintings and antiques.

Alan went for a steam bath and massage at 3:30 p.m. and came back at 6:30. I slept for over an hour. We both were in the mood for Italian food, so we went back to the same restaurant at Tivoli Gardens. Afterwards, it was too early to see the park lit up and so after a delicious ice cream cone, we searched for the oldest house in Nytorv and the building in which Hans Christian Anderson lives. We finally found it in the sailor's hangout area. Since we wanted to get up early the next morning, we went back to our hotel after that and got to bed around 9:30.

WEDNESDAY, JULY 17—COPENHAGEN TO AMSTERDAM

By 8:15 a.m. we were eating breakfast and by 9:00, paid the $29.00 hotel bill. We went looking for the shopping where you can walk and no cars are allowed, after Alan got the correct money. We parked by a square with a fountain, benches, and pigeons all around.

At first, we walked on the wrong side of the area, going into a few antique shops. After looking up the name of a good china shop, we asked directions and found The Stroget. The shop recommended was the Royal Copenhagen Shop. It has the most beautiful china. On the second floor are the seconds. There was a loud woman from The South who we noticed right away. For us, we decided on a large cup with a lacy-sided saucer and a smaller set for my mother. Altogether it cost $11.90 to shop and everything. In some shop in New York, the sales woman said it would cost $28-$30 a set. It was too good to be true and the sun was gone by the time we came out at 11:00 and it began to rain. We just made it getting an orange drink, two apples and a banana, pastry, and hot dogs before it really came down, harder than ever.

We left Copenhagen at about 11:30, got to the ferry near 2:00 p.m. and got on the 2:30 ferry ($10.56) to Germany. We almost didn't because we were short a small amount of money but the guy took it in German money. The ferryboat took an hour and wasn't bad at all. We drove until about 6:00 p.m., had dinner at a restaurant right off the expressway ($3.01) for hamburgers, French fries, salad and drove until we needed gas. There, the man suggested we go a different way than we planned. It was very nice of him. He didn't speak English but drew it on the map. From there, we drove to Cloppenburg, Germany and got the first hotel we tried with a bathtub. Cloppenburg is in Lower Saxony and between Bremen and the Dutch border.

THURSDAY, JULY 18—AMSTERDAM, THE NETHERLANDS

Alan got up at 6:00 a.m. thinking it was 7:00. He got dressed and at 7:30, I got up and we were down for breakfast by 8:15. It was delicious-cheese, bologna, delicious rolls and white and dark bread. None of the girls spoke English but though we wanted one to carry our luggage. Alan nearly went into hysterics trying to get her out of the room.

We arrived in Amsterdam a little after 1:00 p.m. parked the car and went to a restaurant to have lunch and call hotels. Naturally, the phone didn't work so the office let him in. There were no vacancies so the owner got us a hotel. We were to be there at 2:30, so we rushed to get the car only to find the hotel was right around the corner. What a place! It might rate second to France. After checking in, we went walking in the Rembrandtsplin Section. We bought quite a few gifts at one store, a spoon for Lois, scissors for Uncle Murray, a cheese board & knife for mom and dad

Hungry, we decided to go to an Italian restaurant we had seen. It also was around the corner from our hotel as is the whole shopping section. The pizza and salad were very interesting, the artichokes, delicious. On the way walking to the car, we stopped at an Italian ice truck at the Dam Square and got different colored scoops of ice cream between wafers. We drove to see a good section for jazz but I was too tired so we came back. Tomorrow, we'll need a lot of energy.

FRIDAY, JULY 19—AMSTERDAM

What a way to start a day going to Van Moppes, the largest diamond cutting and polishing factory in the world. After a delicious breakfast of cooked egg, soft bread, jelly, cheese, and coffee, we went on the tour. The hotel man said to take the tram but after they ruined our luggage with Clorox, we decided to drive ourselves. It was so easy and quick.

After that, we drove to The Waterlooplein or flea market—amazing the junk they have. Alan took some great pictures of people eating. Then we walked to Rembrandt's house and the Portuguese Synagogue that was closed, as when Alan was there last. To end our touring, we took a canal boat ride. The woman guide spoke Dutch, German and English. What better way to end the afternoon than having a delicious Italian dinner, escargots and spaghetti for me and lasagna for Alan. The smell was fantastic.

As soon as we got back to our hotel, we got ready for our big evening. The Netherlands National Ballet's *Romeo and Juliet*. We loved it even if Alan missed the stabbing at the end by falling asleep. The only restaurant was closing but we had cake and delicious coffee. Alan was correct about the stairs in the hotels, once were houses. They go straight up and down. It takes me so long to climb them.

SATURDAY, JULY 20—AMSTERDAM

Today, our main destination was the Begijnhof. It is right off the main shopping street, the Kalverstraate and consists of brick houses built around a green lawn with a statue in the middle. Its purpose is housing for the elderly and looks like a page out of the 1800s. A Catholic Church there is very pretty. Leave it to Alan. He found the purse and the store I had originally seen it in. It cost $4.00.

After this, we had "The Works" at a Bali restaurant, Indonesian food. There is one specialty. They give you two kinds of rice that you put in the center of your plate and then choose from twenty side dishes and surround the rice with them. We had beer to drink. What a meal! To top it off, we naturally had ice cream at Wimpy's. We also found out how to shop for shoes. I saw a pair we both just loved, seeing the same ones in different stores for 24, 35 and 40. At the cheapest shop, we looked on the racks but they didn't have my size. Not tired yet, Alan remembered the miniature city, Madurodam, in The Hague. It was 45 minutes away and really worth it. Alan tried to find the Peace Palace where he had lunch one day during his 1966 European trip, but the one on the map wasn't the one he had been to. He may have been to the Governor's Palace. We were so tired when we got back to the hotel at about 7:30, we went right to sleep.

SUNDAY, JULY 21—OFF TO GERMANY

Since we got to bed so early last night, we were up by 6:30. As we were getting up, we heard the bells of two different churches bong the time. We were the first down to breakfast and left before 9:00. We drove straight through until about noon stopping at a rest place for lunch. Alan had roast beef but I had nothing because of a stomachache.

We drove on stopping a couple more times before Freiburg, Germany, where we're staying in a beautiful Esso Motor Hotel. We have what they call an apartment with a couch. It's extremely nice. We had dinner for $6.00. I had steak, French fries and salad and Coke and Alan had sauerbraten, dumpling, salad, Coke and a caramel-like pudding that came with it and soup for an appetizer. Upstairs, we washed, all the clothes, washed our hair and are pooped at 9:00 p.m. On the way, we saw signs to Camberg, Germany. It was really creepy to see my name up there.

MONDAY, JULY 22—ON THE WAY TO CHAMONIX, FRANCE

Getting the 3,000-mile lubrication and check-up on the car and all that junk took all morning. We were up early, had a good breakfast and easily got to the VW dealer by 10:00. The car was ready in an hour but we had to go to the bank, post office and then had a little bit of trouble getting back to the hotel. There, we had the car washed and gassed and left at 1:00 p.m.

The scenery was great and we ended up in Chamonix, France. We're staying at The Savoy, our biggest splurge at $20.00 per night. It's really nice but the sheets are rough. We had dinner at a restaurant off the main street. The French fries were great as was the salad but the steak was tough.

TUESDAY, JULY 23—CHAMONIX TO NICE, FRANCE

We were the first down to breakfast and found out the hotel overcharged us $4.00 for a total bill of $24.00. When we left, I accidentally kicked a mop and it fell into Alan. Today, we reached our peak of insanity, thinking the drive from Chamonix to Nice would be shorter than it was. Leaving at 10:00 a.m. we arrived in Nice about 7:30 p.m. The tunnel under Mount Blanc was eleven kilometers and really long and creepy. We stopped in Torino, the filthiest city we've hit yet at about 12:00 noon, thinking it was the place to have our Alpine contest booklet stamped. The place was 80 kilometers away so we ate in the train station (spaghetti) and continued.

The city of Cuneo was very interesting; however, we were unable to find any information about it. The road to Nice goes through all these narrow streets of small villages. At the gas station, a little boy and girl wanted to know where we were from. They were really cute. The roads consisted of up to eight lanes. They just kept coming and it seemed like we'd never reach the Mediterranean. Once in Nice, the traffic jam was amazing. We're staying at The Royal on the Promenade for $12.50 a night. We had dinner at an Italian place catering to tourists. The pizza was very good and filling.

WEDNESDAY, JULY 24—NICE, MONTE CARLO & ITALY

What a busy and eventful day. We began with a continental breakfast on the hotel veranda, went to American Express, where there was a letter from Lois, then we started for Monaco. It only took about a half hour and was absolutely beautiful. Each home was a brighter, different shad than the one before. We went inside the Monte Carlo Casino and walked up to the Prince's castle. The guards were changing and it was a beautiful view. We stopped for something to drink on our way to the northern part of Italy. We drove toward a small town on the Italian Riviera that we hadn't decided on yet, stopping for membership in the automobile club of Italy. This was about 1:00 p.m. We were on the main highway from Ventimiglia to San Remo, Italy. Ventimiglia is the first town in the Italian Riviera after leaving the French border.

It wasn't long before, in a small city, Ospedaletti, Italy about six kilometers from San Remo, the car in the back of us driven by a young kid named Francesco

Cassai didn't watch and at a sudden stop, hit our car, breaking the lens of one of the back lights, denting the fender a tiny bit and pushing the license plate in. The kid driving was very nice trying to explain his name, etc. Alan filled out an accident report but it was very difficult getting the insurance straightened out. We found out we were not fully insured for collision on the green paper we received from the Paris dealership. What a shock!!

We went directly to the VW dealer in San Remo (Autorigambi Bruzzone Corso O. Raimondo 89) and they replaced the bumper that was really not necessary. Thank goodness it was only a little dent. We had only driven the car 3,340 miles at this point. The owner of the dealership called the kid and he paid there. We had eaten before the accident (spaghetti) so continued until about 6:30, looking up towns and hotels. When it began to rain, we weren't too pleased but hoped it would stop by tomorrow.

We decided to stop in Loano using the AAA book for hotels. The second hotel had room. We ate in the hotel. For dinner, we had delicious roast beef, potatoes, beans, vegetable soup and ice cream over fruit salad and wine, so they save it for the next meal. The name of our hotel is Hotel Moderno.

THURSDAY, JULY 25—LOANO, ITALY

Today, we finally got the sun! We were out in the morning from a little after 10:00 until noon. The beach was just packed, so many little kids. A girl interpreted the man at Piccolo Marina, our beach. We had to pay at our hotel, however; he said we could pay in the afternoon. We got deck chairs. Lunch was something else, noodles with meat sauce, veal rolls, potatoes and squash. For dessert, we had the most delicious fresh fruit served in ice water.

We rolled out at 2:00 and went back to the beach until 4:00. Alan went out in a rowboat for about 45 minutes and nearly cracked it up bringing it in. Dinner was delicious too, cream of mushroom soup, roast chicken, salad and baked apple. The appetizer for lunch was your choice of about six dishes, peppers, artichokes, olives, tuna fish, and onions. At 4:00 p.m., we came back from the beach and ate dinner after a walk-through town. We took the car and got gelato after dinner.

FRIDAY, JULY 26—LOANO, ITALY

Today, we were out on the beach at 10:00 a.m. There was a market consisting of fruits and vegetables, leather goods, woodcarvings and clothes all along the walk to the beach. It wasn't as crowded today and seemed hotter.

We came in for lunch at 12:00, tomato juice, veal stew or assorted fish (eels, octopus), cheese or fruit. This time we didn't roll out to the beach. We decided to set on the rocks instead of in the sand to get wet. It was much better. Clouds covered the sun at 4:00, so we walked back getting gelato cones on the way. Alan went to the bank that was closed and the post office where he got beautiful stamps. Dinner consisted of veal scaloppini, potatoes, a vegetable we don't know, and ice cream. We got our favorite wine again. I just couldn't take the cold so we went into the siting room to write post cards. Everyone spoke French. They began to leave and soon after to our surprise, the lights went out. We transferred to the bar and finished writing and then sat outside.

When Alan went to get something to drink, he began talking to the sister of the girl who helped us on the beach. The sister speaks Flemish, French, Italian and English. The entire family came outside and we all were talking to one of the clerks. A travel company recommended the family to Loano. The boy was really funny. It was a late night from here at 10:30 p.m. The family was from Belgium.

SATURDAY, JULY 27—MONTEROSSO & ITALIAN RIVIERA

We made a smart move today, going to the beach by 9:45 with our car and staying out until 12:00, eating lunch after showering and checking out for Monterosso. The clerks were very nice saying they hoped we would return. It was beginning to cloud over so we didn't feel too bad about leaving. At about 2:15 p.m. we started driving for Genoa. We should have gotten off the Autostrada at Sestri Levante but went further so we paid our toll and turned around.

The Autostrada ended at Rapallo. We decided that instead of going straight to La Spezia, we would take a look at Portofino. We saw the port but cars were backed up going so slowly to the city we turned around. To pep us up from the wine we finished at lunch, we got gelato cones in Rapallo.

After leaving Sestri Levante, we saw mountains, the same twisting to Nice. At about one-fourth of the way to La Spezia on the mountain road, there was a sign to Levanto and Monterosso. We arrived in Levanto at about 7:00 p.m. I had a headache probably from the sun. We decided to go to Monterosso. This road was even less of a road, dirt and gravel. We arrived at 8:00. The first Spiaggio hotel we tried had one room left at the top. The clerk spoke English and when Alan asked for the room, told him in Italian. He also ran the restaurant where we had dinner— pizza, salad and delicious wine like Lancers, spaghetti and minestrone soup. Our room is over the kitchen and the garlic smell was fantastic. About 9:00 the jukebox was blasted and they must have been dancing. What noise. They played *Judy in Disguise* in Italian. Earlier in the car, we had heard *Simple Simon Says* in Italian. Everything costs $9.60.

SUNDAY, JULY 28—ON THE ROAD TO PISA

We got off to a pretty early start and were taking pictures by 9:00. The breakfast rolls were so hard, Alan had to break them and even then, they were hard to chew on the outside. The movies we took were of the statue of a man carved out of a cliff on the beach. Alan climbed up trying to reach him but there just weren't enough places to climb. On the way down he scraped himself on a rock and almost fell. Cars weren't allowed up to another ruin so we didn't take any movies there.

We bought some post cards at the hotel but since they didn't have stamps, a young guy with a girl took Alan to get stamps. He also explained how much the cards were because the old lady was practically unintelligible. He said we spoke too fast. When Alan went in again to ask directions to La Spezia, it turned out the two young girls sitting across from us in the hotel restaurant were English and spoke Italian. They're from outside London. Their directions didn't help much because we still took the "scenic" route but it was worth it and we hated to leave.

We left Monterosso at 10:15 a.m. stopping all along the way to take movies and get something to drink in La Spezia. It took us about 3 hours to get to Pisa.

There was a group of six American girls, trying to order, but not too successfully. In Pisa, we ate spaghetti, salad, rolls and Coke at a hotel restaurant. There were two groups of American Army guys there. A U.S. Army base is nearby. The Leaning Tower of Pisa is amazing as are the other buildings. While waiting for Alan to take movies, I sat at the base of one of the buildings and a creepy Italian guy sat down next to me. We couldn't communicate too well and luckily Alan came soon. In a nick knack store where we bought postcards, there was a couple from St. Louis. They were really impressed by Alan's knowledge of Italian.

At 4:00 p.m., we left and arrived in Florence by the Autostrada at 5:00. Right away Alan called hotels and got us one with a swimming pool. Getting there was a different story. We must have asked 25 people for directions. Finally, we got to Villa Belvedere. It is beautiful and we're staying in the guesthouse. The funniest thing was the taxi driver we asked directions called up here and asked if we had shown up yet. Naturally, we hadn't. At night, the fountain is lit up. Dinner was delicious, barbecued chicken with lemon-roasted potatoes, green beans and salad.

MONDAY, JULY 29—FLORENCE, ITALY

Did we get up late! 8:40 a.m. but did we get dressed quickly! By 9:00, we were on our way to breakfast served outside on the patio. The rolls and jelly were delicious. We had no trouble finding our way to parking at the Pitti Palace. We went first to the museum of more modern painting. It must have been five flights up. In back, was a grotto that interested us. A guide lets in a few people at a time. We went in alone. It was a refrigeration room with running water all over. Even without it, it was cold. The sculptures were of coral and absolutely amazing. On one wall was happiness, in the corners were statues of morning, noon, evening and on the ceiling was the animal kingdom. There was also a statue of Helen of Troy and Venus.

From there, we went to the Duomo by the Ponte de Vecchio trying not to look in the stores. We got our signals crossed and found that the Academia with David is closed on Monday so we saw the Piazza de San Lorenzo and San Marco and then went to the San Lorenzo Market. Amazing, Alan bought sun glasses and we bought a leather covered liquor bottle. I got pins for Claire and Alan got me a tray for my dresser. Lunch was delicious, cantaloupe with ham or rigatoni, chicken or veal steak, delicious peas and carrots and three flavors of ice cream.

The pool was terrific. We were outside from 2:30 to 5:00. Alan turned red. Dinner was something else too, tomato soup with croutons, cheese mixed in with ravioli, veal, pizzaiola or beef, French fried potatoes, zucchini, salad and ice cream. After dinner, we went for a drive around Florence, first to the Piazza del Michelangelo built about five years ago. The view of Florence was beautiful.

TUESDAY, JULY 30—FLORENCE

Although we were up at 7:45 and out by 9:15, it didn't help much because we got lost trying to park closer to where we were going today. We did park by the Duomo and walked to the Accademia to see Michelangelo's *David*. The line extended outside if you want to call it a line. It was really a jumble. But it didn't take long to get inside. Having bought your ticket, you had to cross over the ticket line jumble to get through the gate. The wait and confusion were worth it because *David* is the most amazing sculpture we've ever seen. There were also a couple of Michelangelo's unfinished works too.

Back at the Duomo, we couldn't go in the Cathedral because there were dress regulations but we did go in the Baptistry with its pictures of Hell and horned monsters eating the little people. In the Museum del Opera, we saw works by Pisano, Donatello and Giotto. A church with St. John the Baptist was made out of silver and very intricate. Finally, we went crazy shopping and, on the way, back took movies from the Piazza Michelangelo. Lunch consisted of melon or spaghetti, delicious beef with Parmesan sauce, tomato with breadcrumbs, garlic and parsley. More people were swimming today. Grandpa (little Cornel Morton), Grandma (beatnik with pigtail) and the three kids. Then a young married couple. Around dinner, several more couples went in the pool. For dinner, we had minestrone soup, steak or turkey with sauce, salad, potatoes, string beans and cake. Alan got so full; he could hardly make it. We sat on a swing for a while but he conked.

WEDNESDAY, JULY 31—FLORENCE TO NAPLES

It wasn't so horrible leaving one of our favorite places because the weather wasn't so hot. It sure got there near Rome though. We left Florence at 9:15 a.m. and stopped for a drink, then for lunch at an extremely nice Pavensi. We had spaghetti.

We arrived in Naples at 3:30. Alan went straight to information and got some literature and then called hotels getting the Ambassadors Palace right away. It is a high rise right near everything. We see the Maschioangili Castle, the Bay of Naples, and Mt. Vesuvius from our room, 2711. The room cost $13.00. The lobby is something else; marble, tapestry chairs with gold edging.

After getting settled, we walked to find out about ferries for the Isle of Capri, then went inside the Castle that is used for meeting rooms for military and naval, and had dinner at a pizza restaurant. Finally, we got our carriage ride around Naples. It cost $4.00 plus $1.60 for a photograph a guy took (unexpectedly from nowhere). The ride was a lot of fun. We saw the domed enclosed building housing the opera, theater and cinema, the port where I got a beautiful red rose, the National Museum and other Naples sights. We were delivered right to our hotel.

THURSDAY, AUGUST 1—ISLE OF CAPRI

What an absolutely fantastic day! We began by getting up at 7:15, eating breakfast with a treat of orange juice for extra (we had to wait for the man to bring in the oranges), and taking the ferry to Capri. The boat was packed and the ride very pleasant. We took the 9:15 and arrived in Capri at 10:25.

When we got to the island, we asked at the tourist building about the tour we had chosen from a guide. He said outside on the dock, the guides would tell us. It seemed that everyone went to the Blue Grotto and back but we wanted to see the Green and White Grottos plus other sights, so we went all alone with our own guide all around the island for $12.00. Was it cool!

We began at 11:00 a.m. We saw the Palace at the Sea and the baths of Tiberius, then the Blue Grotto. We transferred into a rowboat and even had to sit on the floor of the boat when entering the grotto. The water was a milky powder blue. At the end by the cliff, it was translucent and you could see far below. It was 60 feet deep. Back in our rowboat, we saw the Marina Piccolor, the villa of Gerber (baby food) as of three years ago, the Fargniloa Rocks, three rocks in the sea, one of which has blue lizards, rocks forming donkey ears, others forming a yawning lion at one angle, and the Natural Arch. We also saw the highest point of the island. The Green Grotto was translucent too, and the White Grotto was a white cliff with formations. The stalagmites, they call them spaghetti.

It was a fantastic ride on the Santa Lucia!! We had lunch at the Grotto Verde, very clean and good. I had spaghetti with mussels and Alan had macaroni. We had an antipasto and wine, all for $2.75. I bought a navy pullover for $3.00 and we bought a Capri book, two big post cards to send home and I bought a lipstick. We took the 3:00 p.m. ferry from Capri and drove back to Naples, stopping for ice cream and aqua minerale at a bar on our street.

After a load of wash, we went to dinner at a place called Ciro. We had passed it on the ride last night. I had cantaloupe, veal with lemon, salad and a Coke. Alan had veal scaloppini, French fries, minestrone with rice and orange soda. It cost $4.96. The waiters stood there smiling and thanking us for another tip besides the service charge. Alan gave them the usual 32 cents. We cracked up when guys playing the violin and accordion off-key and a guy singing came around to our table for money. On the way back to our hotel, a dirty little boy was begging for money. We finally gave him some. And he said prego, thank you. Our movies are a riot!

FRIDAY, AUGUST 2—POMPEII

Up early again, we had breakfast, paid our hotel bill and were out by 9:00. Alan cashed traveler checks at a bank around the corner; we picked up mail from both our families and started out for Pompeii. The funniest thing happened. A guy on a motorcycle passing by asked if we were on our way to Pompeii. We said we were and he said to follow him because he works at a cameo factory near there. Out a little further he said we could buy some cameos for our family.

So, there we went. It's amazing how they make cameos out of shells (and how this guy brings in the customers). Alan gave him a gas coupon he asked for. He also said he knew about all engines and asked if we were bringing the car back to the U.S. He said to use super gasoline and even that's no good in Italy. Inside the cameo factory, this guy introduced us to a guide who showed us how they carve the cameos and showed them in the display cases. There was a young boy, age fourteen, under apprenticeship. He will be an apprentice for five years. I bought a pair of earrings and a broach.

After this tour about 11:00 a.m., we left for Pompeii about five minutes away. The heat was so unbearable I couldn't stand it so we just went to a couple places. We took the Amalfi Drive to Sorrento. It was mountainous like Monterosso but the flowers and flowering trees plus the villas were brighter and reflected a wealthier people. We drove down to the sea where boats take off for Capri, got something to drink and drove back to Rome. It took us from 4:30 p.m. to 8:30 to get to Rome. We called the AGIP Motel that is right outside the city but it was filled. Later we called the Michelangelo Hotel right outside Rome, got a room and directions, and followed them great. The motel is very nice. We did have to call for a plumber for a leak on the bathroom floor but the air conditioner is the coldest ever. Starved and exhausted, we walked around the corner for delicious pizza.

SATURDAY, AUGUST 3—ROME

We decided to sleep as late as we felt because of the long ride yesterday. We were out by our old 10:00 a.m. Breakfast was a little different, twisty rolls, plain dark toast, and a little plain cake. The information man advised us to drive to The Sistine Chapel since it closes at 1:00 p.m. and we'd have to walk a half hour. It took us 15 minutes considering getting lost a couple times. We found a great parking space in front and only stood in line a short time.

The Vatican Museum and Library were filled with luscious things. The marble was too much. In the library, their largest Hebrew bible (Old Testament) book and smallest are displayed. The Sistine Chapel was fantastically beautiful and crowded. After trying many times, Alan throw a coin that touched the basin at the bottom of the winding stairs to the rooms. We were quite amazed when we were through to see it pouring. We left when we thought it had stopped but it started raining again. We got pretty wet even though we were parked close by but by the time we went the short distance to St. Peters Basilica, the rain had stopped and the sun was shining brightly. Hungry, we went to the first restaurant we saw. I had veal masala and Alan had veal funghi. For fried potatoes, they served us canned potato sticks.

At St. Peter's Basilica, we got the tape-recorded explanation, finally got used to walking together, and had a great time. It was one of our most enjoyable tours. After this, we took the elevator up and looked down from one of the domes done in mosaic. Then we walked up to the top of the Cupola. What a hike, especially with winding stairs and no breaks in the steps plus the curving in of the Cupola wall. The view was magnificent. Back to our hotel and an hour sleep before eating near the Castle Saint Angelo. I had veal a la Bolognese and Alan had lasagna.

We had bought tickets from the hotel for *Sound and Lights*. This included a bus tour of the city. It was really worthwhile. We were picked up first at 8:45 p.m. and dropped off first at 12:00 midnight. The tour helped us today. (ha!) And the production was very moving (especially the two characters in front of us who were making out through the whole show.

SUNDAY, AUGUST 4—ROME

We were off for the Borghese Villa at 10:15, passing many things we saw during last night's tour. There were cameras watching you everywhere. The cameras were pretty obnoxious but the sculptures by Bernini were great. The gardens by the Villa surprisingly weren't kept as well as we thought they would. A mixed-up in directions caused a slight delay in getting to The Pantheon. What a place! We listened to a tape afterwards. The sculpture "Madonna and Child" by Raphael was there and he is buried underneath.

We had lunch across the street, spaghetti and drove to The Coliseum. We walked up the stairs and I stayed there while Alan walked to the top. He was to wave when ready to take movies of me. But while waiting for him to signal me, two

Italian Army guys asked if I'd take their picture. I said I would as soon as Alan took mine. This was all in sign language. It seemed Alan wasn't ready so I took their picture. Then they wanted mine but I said no.

Meanwhile, Alan was taking mine all the time. As he left to walk down to me, four other Army guys came by for the same. They took my picture when I was just sitting and waiting. When Alan told me what he did I cracked up. After recovering, he took movies of the Arch of Constantine and then we took crazy movies in ruins you didn't have to pay to get in.

We stopped for ice cream and at a Laundromat near us but it was closed. At about 7:00 p.m., we went to Ricci's, recommended by Frommer as the best pizza in Rome. I liked it O.K. We then walked up the Via Nazionale because Ricci's is right off it at Via Genova. Then we drove to The Piazza Navona where we really saw some sights.

Originally, we went to get Tartuffes. First, we looked at the three fountains. We sat at a table in front of the bar-gelateria and ate the most heavenly dish I've ever tasted. All of a sudden, we saw fire as a man in an undershirt and Levis with long white hair, swallowing fire, and then a sword. A circle of people surrounded him and gave him money. Then a guy in a serape was making silver pendants so we bought one for both of us for $1.60.

LETTER TO ALAN'S PARENTS—SUNDAY AFTERNOON, AUGUST 4, 1968 ON HOTEL MICHAELANGELO STATIONERY (VIA STAZIONE S. PIETRO 14)

"Dear Mom and Dad, Penny and I like Rome so much we've decided to stay here two extra days. We'll be leaving here on Wednesday morning, August 7th for Venice-Trieste and Vienna. We hope to drop our car off in Bremen, Germany on August 15 or 16th--take a train to Paris and spend only two days there. We have already made reservations at the Belmont Hotel, 30 Rue de Bassano, Paris for August 17th & 18th. (We called before we left Paris after our arrival on June 27).

Your letters have really been great. We got three pieces of mail in Naples & some in Nice. The Michelangelo is a few blocks from St. Peter's Bascilica & Vatican City. We arrived in Rome late Friday night after a full day in Naples & vicinity. Funniest thing happened—some guy on a motorcycle passed us in Naples and asked if we were going on our way to Pompeii. We said we were and he told us to follow him because he worked at a cameo factory near there. We toured the factory. It's fascinating to see how they carve cameos out of seashells. There was a young boy, fourteen, under apprenticeship there for five years. Penny bought a broach & earrings.

We hit Pompeii, then drove on the Autostrada south to Salerno—then north to Amalfi & the "Drive" to Sorrento—then off to Rome. It was quite an exhausting day but well worth it. Yesterday, we visited the Vatican first, with stops at the Sistine Chapel (ceiling by Michelangelo), the Vatican Museum & Library & then went for lunch. We returned to St. Peter's Basilica & walked to the top of the dome. What a magnificent view of Rome & the Vatican gardens. Needless to say, I got some great pictures. To end up the day, we took a one-hour night tour of the city & also saw the *Sound & Lights* performance next to the Coliseum that lasted 45 minutes. (*Sound & Lights* tells the story of Rome with voices & lights up the Roman forum while the story is told).

We've been seeing things I missed the first time on my European trip plus some other "musts." Later 10:45 p.m. Today was really fun! We started out at the Villa Borghese Gallery in a large park on a hill. Famous paintings & sculptures are everywhere. Then we went to the Pantheon (the best-preserved monument of ancient Rome). It's a mausoleum of Raphael & some members of the old kings of Italy. After that we ate lunch & visited the Coliseum and took some crazy pictures across the street at some ruins. Then Penny took a picture of me throwing a coin into the Trevi Fountain. Tomorrow night, Penny & I are going to the opera to see *Aida*. It's presented outside at the Baths of Caracalla. We are very healthy, a little less wealthy & a lot wiser. Love, Alan and Penny"

MONDAY, AUGUST 5—ROME

Most of the morning was spent changing hotels since the Michelangelo Hotel only had room for three nights. They called the Leonardo da Vinci Hotel for supposedly the same rates. Were we surprised to find it is $22.00 for one night? The man at the desk was a real snot. He wouldn't give Alan directions here and said we should call a taxi and follow it. Dumb! The guy at information helped us.

Once settled at the Leonardo da Vinci Hotel, we took our laundry to a Laundromat. It took from 11:30 a.m. to 1:00 p.m. We met two guys in the service stationed in Crete on a thirty-day leave. We brought the stuff back and found we were hungry. We saw a gelateria pasticeirra so we stopped and it was really worth it. We had the most delicious gelato cantaloupe, pistachio, vanilla, and chocolate and a piece of pastry. We had quite a conversation with the owner even though he only spoke Italian. On the same street, Via Covour Vincola, was St. Peter in Chains. His chains were there. We had bought a great book on Rome describing all the churches, museums, etc. including works of art and the rooms in which they could be found. We wish we had bought it earlier.

In this book, we read about the Jewish ghetto and the large synagogue. We parked near Capitoline Hill, walking to the Teatro di Marcellus and around the corner of the Tiber River was the synagogue. A bus of New York Jewish girls just left so we were the only ones in there. A young boy handed Alan a yarmulke as we walked in and a guy our age took us on a tour. The synagogue was very pretty but nothing spectacular. The interesting thing was that it was built in 1904 and was spared from the bombing in World War II because it was considered part of the Vatican area. The guy had more questions to ask us than we could get in to ask him. There are 13,000 Jews living in Rome.

Alan found a place that sold contact solution. It was a camera, lens and optic store. Earlier, we asked the guy at the hotel desk for an eye doctor in the phone book since we didn't know how to look it up. The receptionist was a young girl who only spoke Italian. She called in a sister who spoke French so I asked for the doctor. It seemed that the building was being repaired and the doctors weren't there so she gave us his phone number. We didn't do anything about it but it was fun. Because we were in a rush to get the bus to the outdoor opera, *Aida*, we ate at a sidewalk restaurant right near our hotel where only three other customers were. The minestrone soup was delicious and the spaghetti good. (So was the wine).

We waited with some chattering old ladies in the lounge until we couldn't stand it anymore. They were complaining they didn't have time to put on any jewelry and felt so underdressed for the opera. The man we had spoken to at the desk about the opera and his wife were on the bus. They're from Brooklyn, New York and she has a cousin in Cleveland Heights. They had arrived in Rome at 3:30. The opera was really spectacular and I fell asleep during each act. It ended at 12:45.

TUESDAY, AUGUST 6—ROME

So, beat from the opera last night, we slept until 9:00 a.m. Breakfast was pretty bad. It was about 11:00 by the time we left for the Baths of Diocletian. The Church of Santa Maria dela Angeli was built using one wall of the original baths. Next to it is the Terme Museum that is the best-preserved part of the baths. The Rome book really helped explain all the interesting mosaics, statues and sarcophagus. Part of the swimming pool is still intact. This took about an hour since we only viewed what was in the book. It was enough. The Capitoline Museum was next with some huge statues.

We finally decided we were hungry, so we ate at the train station since I'd never seen it. Bombed from the war, we went back to the hotel and completely conked for two-hours, being awakened by the maid walking in without knocking. While Alan was downstairs getting stamps, he surprised me by ordering a snack since I had washed my hair. We decided to bring in all the maps for the rest of the trip. We decided we might not go to Venice.

WEDNESDAY, AUGUST 7—TRIESTE HERE WE COME

After stealing all the ashtrays and eating their lousy breakfast, we checked out of the Leonardo da Vinci Hotel heading for Bologna, Venezia and Trieste. Thanks to me, leaving at 9:00 didn't do much good because I read the directions wrong and we were heading for the Napoli Autostrada. By 10:00, we were where we were supposed to be. We stopped at a Pavensi Tourist Market buying Camembert cheese, chips, crackers, cake, popcorn and Coke in cups without tops. I was sure there were lots of parcheggios (rest stops) so we drove with me holding onto the cups. Five restaurants later and twenty miles we came to one. The cheese was icky, the crackers sweet, and the Coke warm. Alan thanked me for the nice lunch.

We reached Firenze about 1:30 p.m., Bologna about 3:00 and Venice about 5:00. We drove all the way to the last place you could go with your car and asked at information what you do next. You take the waterbus at the station about a five-minute walk. We decided to forget Venice, too much trouble so we continued toward Trieste. Since we were passing by the airport, we stopped at the restaurant but it wasn't open yet so we drove a little further. Alan spotted a pizzeria and really hit the jackpot. It was jammed and no wonder. The pizza was delicious, cooked in a fire oven. As we walked in a completely drunk man sitting at the first table mumbled something to us. Was he scary, especially when he got up and walked toward us?

We reached Trieste about 8:15 p.m. searched for hotels listed in AAA and finally after almost leaving the city, we asked a man and The Jolly Hotel was right around the corner. We got a great apartment and took baths. Considering everything, we didn't even get aggravated. We have 5,000 miles on the clean car from the floody rains off and on all day.

THURSDAY, AUGUST 8—LJUBLJANA, YUGOSLAVIA

Today we left Italy-Wah!! We got our Alpine contest book stamped in Trieste in a castle on top of a mountain and left for Yugoslavia and Austria at 10:00 a.m. We got to Ljubljana, the capital of Slovenia, at about 12:15 and got our contest card stamped again and then went into a self-serve restaurant. Alan could eat but I couldn't so outside, I just got some pommes frites. Sitting in the car, eating all of a sudden, we heard someone say where are you from? It was a couple from Philadelphia. They had stayed overnight at a new hotel and were on their way to Innsbruck. The way of living in Yugoslavia is amazing. The country people were dressed in black with boots and were all covered up. They farm with oxen and travel by horse and wagon.

(Sidebar: We were thinking of going to Czechoslovakia however, at that very time, the Soviet Union invaded the country and ousted Alexander Dubcheck, the Czech leader, who was getting too liberal for the Russian government. That idea went out the window).

LETTER TO ALAN'S PARENTS FROM TRIESTE

"Thursday, August 8, 1968

Dear Mom and Dad, Just had to write to you on this "Jolly" paper even though we're no longer here. Yesterday, Penny and I left Rome driving toward Vienna, Austria. We arrived here about 8:15 p.m. after a long but not tiring day.

I forgot to tell you that we're in an Alpine Motoring Contest. It lasts for two years & in that time you must have traveled to key cities in certain countries and get a booklet stamped in these cities. If you visit five different countries one receives a gold medal. Well today we got three different stamps & we now have enough for a gold medal. We've gotten our booklet stamped in Chamonix, France, Monaco, Trieste Italy, Ljubljana, Yugoslavia and Graz, Austria, where we are now. We left Trieste about 10:15 a.m. & arrived in Graz about 5:30 p.m. Italy time but we forgot to change our watches & it was really 4:30 p.m. I'm waiting to eat supper, we're starved.

We passed through Yugoslavia briefly. The language barrier was a little difficult to break. We stopped in Ljubljana. I mailed a card to Linda & I ate lunch. Penny didn't like the place I chose, so she only had French fries. Later, after dinner, Penny and I are "stuffed." It's only 8:30 p.m. but we want to get up early so we can be in Vienna before noon. As of this writing, we'll spend about three or four days in Vienna, then possibly visit Salzburg-Berchtesgaden, Germany (where Hitler made his hideaway), then Bremen. We'll be waiting to tell you all about our trip. Love, Penny and Alan. Give grandma our love."

ARRIVAL IN GRAZ, AUSTRIA

At about 5:30, we arrived in Graz, Austria, forgetting it was really 4:30 because of the time change. We decided to wait until we were fresh to go to Vienna and stopped at the first hotel listed in AAA we saw—Park Hotel. It is a first-class hotel. Starved, we had to wait until 6:30 (7:30 our time) to eat. Needless to say, we didn't feel so hot. Dinner was delicious. I had a shrimp cocktail; Alan had a thin corned beef like meat and we split Chateaubriand. For dessert, we had strawberry cake and delicious instant coffee.

FRIDAY, AUGUST 9—VIENNA, AUSTRIA

Today, we broke all records getting up at 7:00 a.m. and leaving at 8:30. We arrived in Vienna at 12:00 noon. In pouring rain, Alan had to call about five different places before he found Hotel Tyrol with vacancies. It was listed in the *Europe on $5.00 A Day* as an expensive place that discounts carriers of *$5.00 A Day* during the winter. The room is very nice with pieces of cut glass in front of the light bulbs in front of mirrors giving a very bright and rich look. All the tabletops are mirrored. We ate in a restaurant across from St. Peter's Church. It had great food but they took too long. After this we searched for a book for Uncle Harry of which there is none to suite him. Then we went inside the Cathedral. It's absolutely amazing, chandeliers hanging from high-beamed ceilings and beautiful arches.

Next came shopping. We got Aunt Sadie, a petit point compact and lipstick, Aunt Marie a compact and atomizer, Sandi, a sugar spoon, and us a corkscrew. Pooped, we went back to our hotel and soon left in the rain to find a restaurant. First, we passed a place next to a miniature Ferris wheel but I didn't know if it was a restaurant so we went in the restaurant at the bus station. My right contact lens popped on the floor but we found it. Alan didn't like the restaurant so we left and went back to my place. Alan had goulash and I had toasted cheese. Their coffee is just delicious! The Ferris wheels I had seen were only two of the many mechanical toys on exhibit. There was a bowling game with three men, a robot working a machine, levers and hammers.

SATURDAY, AUGUST 10—VIENNA

Today, we were up at 7:15 and down to breakfast by 8:00. An old lady fainted and really shook us up. Alan saw her later and she seemed O.K. First, we got my dad a copper plate. We tried Geingross Department Store but theirs just didn't strike me so we went to a copper shop near us. They had gorgeous stuff.

At 10:30, we went to the Kunsthistoric Museum that really has a collection of Rembrandts, Breughels, Reubens, Van Dycks, Tintorettos, Titians, and Caravaggio plus great Flemish and Dutch painters like Frans Hals and Holbein. We had lunch at their buffet. I had tuna fish and Alan had hot dogs. We got the 1:00 p.m. tour of the famous Schoenbrunn Palace. One guide takes the German speaking group and then the English. It wasn't bad at all. The palace, of which we saw forty-five rooms, is magnificent. At 3:00, we came back to the hotel and then got cake and coffee at a café, not so hot. After resting, we left for dinner at about 6:30. It only took us two trips around the block to find the Greek restaurant we were looking for-Haydn Stuben on Barnbitestrasse near Geingross. The meal was excellent—shish ka bobs with Greek salad. Alan stole a candy bar and pretzels on the table and I had eaten the bag of almonds. We decided to return to the hotel to wash our hair and rest.

SUNDAY, AUGUST 11—VIENNA

We had a very interesting day. Very diversified. Since we were up at 7:30 and have been getting ready faster and faster, we were at The Hofburg for a tour about 9:00. We only missed two rooms because the tour had already started but it was no great loss. The Girl Guide was so blah and rushed through so fast, it wasn't fun—quite different from the guide at Shonbrunn Palace. The only time she smiled was at the end when she got tipped.

Next, we went to see the Lipizzaner horses and The Spanish Riding School. All they did was let you in the performance hall and played a recording about it. It was all pretty disappointing. So was getting back to our car because we got lost.

At about 1:15, we drove up to Kahlenberg to see the view of Vienna. It was hazy but very pretty. Jean had also recommended Grinding, a little village outside of Vienna. It was very interesting. We had lunch at Kahunburg. I had delicious liver and salad. Alan had his usual favorite hot dogs. After lunch about 2:15, we drove to see the Blue Danube River. It's not blue. Then we went to our third amusement park, The Prater, a famous one. The Ferris wheel is great and they have such different rides; an airplane with propeller that you fly, go carts, and Alan's favorite, the Fun House that is on the second floor. We had the most delicious kind of waffles, langos. They're made in garlic butter and fried. Then we walked all around and Alan got a bratwurst and I got a chocolate ice cream cone that tastes like a fudgesicle. Tired to pieces, we came back to the hotel at 5:30 p.m.

MONDAY, AUGUST 12—VIENNA

We were up early again and began the day by going to the pipe factory across the street from the hotel. You go through a hallway where there is a statue of Mary and Jesus then up three flights of stairs. We rang the bell and a little middle-aged man came to the door and welcomed us in putting out two chairs right away. We bought two Vienna gold pipes for our fathers and then went back to where the man makes the pipes using lathes. He was so kind, typical of all the Austrian people.

After this, we walked a couple blocks up to an art gallery, Rudolf Otto, Original-Oil paintings by contemporary artists and old masters and bought Uncle Harry two paintings, one of flowers and one of a clown. As we were leaving, Alan saw an original Bernard Buffet lithograph print that he bought. We paid about $100US including airmail charges. It took him another fifteen minutes to finish the transaction. Anyway, we love it. The print will be sent to our Oakdale apartment in Chicago. The Albertina Museum was quite a disappointment. All the rooms seemed closed off. Hungry again, we ate at the Coq d'Or, went to see the Opera House and got Grandma three petit point doilies. We took Arthur Frommer's *Europe On $5.00 A Day* book again going to the Hotel Graben for dinner. The vegetable soup was delicious as was the veal. The waitress was just great. Afterwards, we went to The Stadtspark to hear a concert. It was "Eh". We sat on the benches with the old folks for a while, saw the statue of Johann Strauss, then went back to our hotel.

TUESDAY, AUGUST 13—OFF TO NUREMBERG, GERMANY

Up early for a change, we took movies of City Hall, Johann Strauss' statue, and the sign to Budapest. By 10:00 a.m. we were on our way to Nuremberg, Germany. We arrived here at 5:15 p.m. three hundred fifty miles after leaving Vienna. We only stopped once, for lunch, wieners.

As we got off the Autobahn, there was our favorite, The Esso Motor Hotel. They had room so here we are. It only took us two hours to get through with dinner. Our waiter deserted us going to the other side of the restaurant. Alan's shish ka bob was pork—ugh—fat. My filet was very good. We sat at a table next to a German couple and their friend from India. It seemed they had met on business a couple years ago. Very interesting.

WEDNESDAY, AUGUST 14—ON TO BREMEN, GERMANY

Today was one of Alan's happiest days. He bought a Hohner harmonica and a melodica. It was pouring when we left Nuremberg and rained on and off from 9:30 until 4:30 p.m. when we arrived in Bremen. We only stopped twice. The first time we tried for lunch but it was so crowded we only got cookies, cheesecake, and apples. The second time we got ice cream sandwiches. Alan found the Columbus Hotel listed in the AAA right away. We got a room and Alan bought our train tickets to Paris and made arrangements to ship our car back to the United States and Chicago. Dinner was half delicious. Our soup was great, tomato for Alan and onion for me. The spaghetti and steak weren't so hot. It sure was great listening to the Armed Services Radio Network all day, even the hillbilly part.

THURSDAY, AUGUST 15—BREMEN, GERMANY

Everything went as planned. We were up at 5:30 and got our wakeup call at 6:30. Breakfast was served in the brightest room with white chairs trimmed in blue and we each had our own basket of delicious rolls. We left our hotel at 7:30 a.m. and had no trouble finding the shipping terminal for the car. We dropped off our light blue Volkswagen Fastback at the Transoceanic Terminal located at Kap-Horn-Strasse Autoumschlagsanlage in Bremen, Germany where it would be loaded onto a Volkswagen ship, the MS Wilfred would depart to America through the Saint Lawrence Seaway. The cargo ship loaded new and used Volkswagen automobiles to be delivered to dealerships in the Midwest. Alan paid for marine insurance from Gradmann & Holler to cover any damages to the car in shipment to the United States. The man took care of us very quickly and I read a real good article in *Newsweek* about Wilkie. All of the paperwork was arranged through the TASP Deugro Tourist Automobile Shipping Program and a Chicago customs broker, Schenkers International, Inc. located at 327 S. LaSalle Street.

Our car was considered used, so the tax on it was considerably less when Alan went to get an Illinois license plate. The cost of shipping our car to Chicago was $154.67. After dropping off the car, we took a train from Bremen to Paris where our plane would leave to fly back to Chicago.

A taxi was called for us to take back to our hotel and by 8:30 we were ready to leave for the train station across the street. We put our luggage in a locker, bought magazines and waited. The train to Cologne came at 10:07 a.m. and it was fun. We had hot dogs and read. There was only one other person, a lady in our train car and she got off about halfway to Paris. Then two men got on.

We had to take two different trains to get to Paris. When we got to our first destination, Cologne, at 2:00 p.m. we checked our luggage again in the train station and spent practically the whole time getting through to Paris on the telephone to reserve our room for two more nights. Finally, the guy got the Paris operator for us because it was so busy. Alan had an interesting talk with a guy in Cologne who was on business from Nottingham, England.

At 3:40 p.m., we got on our second train for Paris. We were all alone the entire time until we arrived in Paris at 10:00 p.m. A guy with sandwiches and soft drinks came around ringing a bell and we bought stale cheese sandwiches. We were disappointed, no dining car. We played Bonnie Wilson's games, read and slept.

FRIDAY, AUGUST 16—PARIS, FRANCE

At 4:30 a.m. and again at 7:00 a.m. we were awakened by someone trying to get into our smelly hotel room. Dumb! Breakfast was obnoxious served in a dirty room by waiters wearing dirty jackets. It nauseated me so much we're eating out.

At about 9:30, we left for our longest walking day. First, we went to the Arc de Triumph right near our hotel. Alan took movies from on top and some guy pestered me in French. Then we took the long walk to L'Hotel de Invalides. By the time we got there, there was only a half hour before it closed so we ate lunch, cheese omelets and salads. At about 12:45, we went to see Napoleon's tomb and other Frenchman such a Marechal Foch's tomb in the Church of the Dome. At 1:30, we toured part of La Musee d'Armee. We had never seen such fantastic armor or guns. We went in the Church of Heryor but couldn't find Napoleon's death mask. Needing a rest, we took a 3:00 p.m. boat tour down the Seine River. It was freezing but we saw a lot. A little after 4:00 p.m. we walked back the Champs Elysée and decided we were hungry so we got hamburgers, French fries and a banana split at Wimpy's. Remembering that Waterhole #3 was playing across the street, Alan went to find out what time the next feature started. He came back unnoticed by me and stood next to me for quite a while before I noticed and cracked up.

In the movie, if you want to sit closer than the middle, you have to tip the lady. Dumb!! Two young American guys told us. They thought the movie was great and Alan cracked up the whole time. After the movie, we had coffee at a sidewalk café.

SATURDAY, AUGUST 17—PARIS

For breakfast, we had delicious rolls and croissants in one of the sidewalk cafes on the Champs Elysée and took a cab to the Left Bank. The hippies or bums are something else. The shops have some real tough stuff. We ate at Wimpy's after sitting in the Luxemburg Gardens until a lady came collecting money for sitting.

After lunch, we took a cab to The Bastille and walked to The Victor Hugo Museum. The square around which this complex of houses was built is beautiful. It's a little park with fountains and a sand box. The museum was great. Hungry again, we split a huge hot dog with cheese. Then we got a cab back to our hotel, rested up and went to Pizza Pino for dinner.

SUNDAY, AUGUST 18—PARIS

Because we wanted to get to The Louvre for the 10:30 a.m. tour (that isn't given on Sunday), we ate breakfast at our hotel. At about 9:15, we got a cab and waited around outside The Louvre until 10:00. We spoke awhile to a family of three who also wanted to know where the main entrance was. The father and mother both had accents and the daughter about fourteen had a little. They're from California and had torn out the same AAA pages as we had. Then a guy heard us talking and came over. He was also from California and wanted to change his charter flight to get back two days ahead for his sister's wedding.

We got a guidebook that wasn't much help so we just wandered in the paintings. At 11:30, we were through, so in the rain, we walked to the Left Bank stopping in an entranceway to an apartment building to get out of the rain. A little before 1:00, we ended up at Wimpy's for hamburgers, French fries and sundaes. After Wimpy's, we took the subway to see a movie with Sidney Poitier, *To Sir With Love*. It was even better this time. The movie was in English with French subtitles.

On our way to find The Drugstore, we saw a crowd. They were looking at the filming of what seemed to be a commercial, very unorganized. The Drugstore was something else. We decided to eat so we went upstairs and had shrimp bowls. It seemed like we were inside a lantern. Hands held up the columns of the building and they had six fingers.

MONDAY, AUGUST 19—PARIS AND HEADING HOME

Today is our final day in Paris. We left from Le Bourget Airport flying over London, Belfast, Ireland, Goose Bay Labrador, Quebec City and Toronto before arriving in Chicago on our 4,300-mile chartered flight.158 passengers were on our flight. A partial list of the purchases and gift we made during our European honeymoon included: a man's suit in London-$40.00; woman's suit in London-$40.00; woman's dress-$17.0; three Dansk serving pieces-$10.00; petit point doilies-$3.00; Hohner harmonica-$8.54; Hohner Melodica-$12.31; silver spoon-$5.00; liquor bottle with leather top in Italy-$4.00; cameos in Italy-$45.00; plate-$1.40; pipes-$4.00; bathmat-$.75, Bernard Buffet original lithograph-$100.00 shipped home, among some other smaller items, less than $300.00 for all items and gifts.

TUESDAY, AUGUST 20, 1968—BACK IN CHICAGO

After our arrival in Chicago from our fabulous honeymoon, we bought two one-way plane tickets to Cleveland to see Penny's parents and to bring our wedding presents back to Chicago. I had moved into Penny's apartment at 441 W. Oakdale, a high-rise apartment building that Penny shared with Francie Lombardo for the past year. The 13th floor apartment faced south and from our outside balcony, we could see the downtown skyscrapers. In fact, the John Hancock Building was still under construction and we watched the giant cranes working on the structure. Roter Management managed our building and our monthly rent was $193.00. When Francie and Penny first moved into the apartment, the rent was $178.00 per month, a sum I could not afford by myself.

SUNDAY, AUGUST 25, 1968—DRIVE TO CLEVELAND

We arrived in Cleveland in time to see the Chicago riots during the 1968 Democratic Convention happening in Grant Park. All three-television networks broadcast the disturbing events. The incident made worldwide headlines with Mayor Richard J. Daley's outrageous and disturbing order to shoot to kill. After a few days staying in Cleveland, we loaded Penny's yellow/black top 1966 Chevrolet Super Sport convertible with all our wedding gifts and drove back to Chicago.

OUR EVERYDAY LIVING ROUTINE IN CHICAGO

We shopped for groceries at the local Kroger and A & P near Wellington and Treasure Island by Roscoe. All three grocery stores were on Broadway. We took our dry cleaning to Barry Regent Cleaners, paid our telephone bill to Illinois Bell Telephone and I bought my clothes at Winsbergs, a men's clothing store in Lincolnwood. We bought our gasoline at the Standard Oil gas station on Diversey, shopped at Marshall Fields & Co., Carson, Pirie Scott & Company, Charles A. Stevens and Weiboldt's Department Stores. We bought the Chicago Tribune newspaper from the Surf News Agency and had it delivered. Penny had her hair cut at Studio Coiffures on Surf Street.

Other aspects of our everyday life included Penny's gynecologist, Leon Carrow, Dr. Morris Kaplan for allergies, Dr. George Allen, for Ear, Nose and Throat and our primary care physician Dr. Guy Hollifield at Northwestern Memorial Hospital. Our dentist was Dr. Arnold Gorchow.

When I first moved to Chicago, Marilyn and Larry Levy lived in the same apartment building as Dr. Gorchow and his wife Marsha, so I started going to him after my Chicago move in August 1966. Our bank was North Shore National Bank at 1737 W. Howard Street and our insurance company was Sol Holland Company. Larry Levy recommended Sol Holland to me and I have been using this company for homeowners and automobile insurance since moving to Chicago. We purchased furniture from Maurice R. Mandel & Sons on South Michigan Avenue. The place was a discount furniture store operated by a Jewish family. When our ninety-six-inch beige corduroy sofa was delivered, the company could not get it into our apartment through the building's elevators or the narrow hallway, so they decided to haul it up from the balcony. I shot film of the move.

SEPTEMBER 1968—OUR VOLKSWAGEN ARRIVES IN CHICAGO

In mid-September, I received a written notice that our Volkswagen fastback had arrived in Chicago via the Volkswagen ship, MS. Winfred, was unloaded and sitting on the dock at Calumet Harbor, Illinois waiting for me to pick it up. I took public transportation to Calumet Harbor and arrived at the dock. When I opened the car door, I discovered to my surprise our Blaupunkt radio had been stolen by dockworkers, either in Germany or the United States. The mileage on the car's odometer was 6,173 miles. Penny and I traveled to eleven European countries and had a honeymoon of a "lifetime." The total cost of our honeymoon was approximately $3,800.00 including the price of the Volkswagen Fastback. To duplicate this adventure for the amount of time we spent and to the places we saw, would probably cost at least $100,000 or more today.

On Tuesday, September 24, I drove to Winnetka Import Motors at 666 Green Bay Road to get a quote for a replacement radio. A new AM/FM radio would cost me $149.73 including tax. I immediately sent a letter to Gradmann & Holler with the quote that they received on October 7. They wrote me back saying a replacement price for a radio "Emden" is about $110.00US. On October 21, I received a letter from Gradmann & Holler and a check for $124.05 for a new radio. It wasn't a Blaupunkt, however. What a deal!

On Tuesday, October 22, 1968, I drove to Nugent Volkswagen at 301 Waukegan Road in Glenview to have the new radio installed. The new Montreal radio cost $99.50 and the dealer charged me $12.75 to install it for a total of $117.23 with tax. I loved this car. It had a rear air-cooled engine, an all-round torsion bar suspension, heater and air-conditioning, three-speed manual transmission, a clock and the trunk was in the front of the car. One of the problems I had was it wouldn't always start when it rained and it would backfire on occasion. The few years I drove the car in Chicago, I had to replace a distributor cap, voltage regulator, spark plugs, gaskets, points, gas filters and fuses, among other things that periodically went wrong with the car. Once I replaced the distributor cap, it started in the rain.

To see a type 3 Volkswagen Fastback as they were called is very rare today. They were produced from 1961 to 1973. The car came in three body styles: two-door Notchback, Fastback and Squareback. They were called Type 3 because the first type was the Beetle, the second was the microbus and the third was our car, the Volkswagen Fastback sedan. The concept of the Type 3 was to be more of a family car than the Beetle with a larger engine and more luggage space. It was a very comfortable riding car with terrific gas mileage.

PENNY STARTS TEACHING AT SCHILLER SCHOOL

Penny started her new position as a kindergarten teacher at Schiller School located in the heart of the Cabrini Green, a low-income housing complex located on Chicago's near north side. The brick school building, built in the late 1800s, was part of the Chicago Board of Education.

There were some really great teachers at the school including future Illinois Secretary of State Jesse White, Judy Sigale, Rhoda Schlesinger and Jerry Aronson, among others. Jerry, who had recently graduated with a Master's Degree from the Illinois Institute of Technology was teaching sixth-grade and had just completed working on *Options*, a film produced for Chicago's Museum of Contemporary Art featuring an art collection at the museum. We became good friends and it was Jerry who helped me produce my first 16mm film two years later.

THANKSGIVING 1968

As teachers, both Penny and I had pretty much the same vacation time from school. Whenever we could, we traveled back to Cleveland and Youngstown to visit our parents but on this particular Thanksgiving, our first, as newlyweds, we decided to invite both sets of parents to spend Thanksgiving with us in our Chicago apartment. It was a Thanksgiving to remember. Penny made a beautiful Thanksgiving feast in our tiny high-rise apartment kitchen. As Penny was taking the turkey out of the oven, it slipped and fell on the floor. She just picked it up, dusted it off and we ate it. It was delicious and no one got sick.

DECEMBER 1968—NEW ORLEANS WINTER VACATION

On our first winter break as a married couple, Penny and I decided to fly to New Orleans to visit my cousin Norman Lockshin, his wife Sheila and their two-year old son, Steven. Norman and his family were living in Metarie, Louisiana, a suburb of New Orleans, at the time. The year before, Norman completed his medical internship at Chicago's Michael Reese Hospital and was now serving in a New Orleans public health hospital to fulfill his military obligation as a physician.

It was a great vacation and was the first time Penny and I had been in a warm climate during winter. Seeing Christmas decorations in a warm weather climate was awesome. Norman and Sheila gave us a fascinating driving tour in the French Quarter around Bourbon Street as well as other parts of New Orleans. We saw the Mississippi River Bridge, Tulane University, Sophie Newcomb College, Charles Avenue with the trolley line running up and down the street, the International Trade Mart, lots of mansions and Lake Pontchartrain. We also went to Jackson Square, St. Louis Church and the Public Health Hospital where Norman worked.

We walked by the Pontalba Buildings that form on two sides of Jackson Square in the French Quarter. The matching red brick buildings are block-long four story structures built in the 1840s by the Baroness Micaela Almonester Pontalba who was responsible for their design and construction. The Baroness (November 6, 1795- April 20, 1874) was a wealthy New Orleans businesswoman and one of the most vibrant personalities of that city's history. An opera and many novels have been written about her dramatic life. In Truman Capote's short story *Hidden Garden,* he describes the Pontalba Buildings as "...the oldest, in some ways most somberly elegant, apartment houses in America, the Pontalba Buildings." These buildings were declared a National Historic Landmark in 1974.

FISHING IN LEEVILLE, LOUISIANA

While visiting New Orleans, Norman and I drove near the fishing town of Leeville where we went fishing. Leeville is about 2 hours southwest of New Orleans and almost to Grand Isle, deep in the heart of bijou country. The water is brackish, meaning part freshwater and part salt water. We fished on shore and caught many red drum (redfish) and crabs. The redfish we gave to some men fishing near us and the crabs we brought back to Norman's apartment where we cooked them. They were delicious.

I got a big kick out of the unusual name of their daily newspaper for the greater New Orleans area, *The Times Picayune.* It was fun reading local and world news, classifieds, and subscription information with a Cajun twist.

WEDNESDAY APRIL 2, 1969—SCHILLER SCHOOL

I was on Spring Break from teaching at Crow Island School so I took my Super 8 movie camera to Schiller School where Penny taught Kindergarten. I also went there on April 1, 1970 to take Super 8 movies of her class. In June 1971, Schiller School was demolished and a new school, Sojourner Truth School was built to accommodate children from the Cabrini Green housing projects. Penny moved into the new building and was teaching there until March 1972, just before Bennett was born on May 22, 1972.

ARVIND SINGH MEWAR (A PRINCE OF A GUY)

Penny and I met Arvind Singh when I was living at 516 W. Oakdale. At the time, Arvind was in Chicago studying a hotel management course because his family owned the Taj Lake Palace Hotel in Udaipur, India. Arvind explained that he was a prince back in India and showed us slides of Jacqueline Kennedy visiting his father's lake hotel and also slides of his sister's wedding with elephants, etc. I also took a short Super 8mm movie of Arvind's birthday that took place at our 502 W. Briar Place apartment.

While writing this book, I found a postcard from Rome, Italy dated July 16, 1969, written by Arvind to Penny and me on his way back to Bombay, India. Being curious I decided to go on-line to see what became of Arvind and to my amazement, he was listed in Wikipedia. "Arvind is the second son of Bhagwat Singh Mewar and the younger brother of Maharana Mahendra Singh Mewar. Upon the death of his father in 1984, Arvind became the head of his branch of the family as his elder brother voluntarily split from the family, but retained the title of Maharana. He is the 76th custodian of the Mewar dynasty.

According to Wikipedia, Arvind married Princess Vijayaraj of Kutch, Gujarat and has three children. Princess Bhargavi Mewar, Princess Padmaja Mewar and Prince Lakshyaraj Singh Mewar.

Arvind has been rather successful in his business ventures as he is the Managing Trustee for the Maharana Mewar Charitable Foundation and the Chairman and Managing Director of the HRH Group of Hotels. His father established both of these organizations. As a side note, after India became independent from Britain in 1947, his father started focusing on the preservation of palaces, a tradition of the House of Mewar and earning money through these palaces by converting them to Heritage Hotels."

Arvind's son, Prince Lakshyaraj, is listed on Linked-In and I was able to write him but received no reply. We have a photo of Arvind and the Wilsons that I am currently trying to locate in our home.

JULY 1969—A CALIFORNIA ONE-YEAR ANNIVERSARY TRIP

For our first summer trip and to celebrate our one-year anniversary, Penny and I decided to drive to Los Angeles, California, and then fly back to Chicago from San Francisco. In those days there were companies that specialized in transporting cars to various destinations around the country. I found an ad in the newspaper and I signed a contract to deliver a new car to a Los Angeles dealership in seven days. We drove a "Drive-A-Way" 1968 Buick Riviera two-door car following Route 66 that winds from Chicago to Los Angeles. We took our time driving, seeing many sights along the way and had a terrific time on the road.

We left Chicago on Friday, July 18 driving for a night's stop west of St. Louis, Missouri past the Gateway Arch that had been completed only three years earlier. The second day, we drove to central Missouri where we stopped by Meramec Caverns and took a guided tour down into Fisher Cave. Meramec State Park is located along the Meramec River that is a favorite for canoeists and fishermen. There are more than forty caves in the park that's located about three miles south of Sullivan on Missouri Route 185. The last stop on the tour is what they call The Amphitheatre, a large room curved in a semicircular shape, with flat rocks forming rows for seats and a "stage" area made out of rock. It was amazing. What is more amazing is that Penny went on the tour that by the way did not freak her out.

CHINESE FOOD AND THE MAN ON THE MOON

On Sunday, July 20, 1969 we were stopped in Oklahoma City for the night. I asked Penny what type of food she would like to eat. She said, Chinese food. "You don't like Chinese food," I said. Penny decided she wanted to try it again, so we did. From that day on, Penny liked Chinese food.

This day was a very historic day for the United States of America because after dinner when we got back to the motel, we turned on the television to see Neil Armstrong land on the moon. Armstrong's second and last spaceflight was as mission commander of the *Apollo 11* moon-landing mission. On this famous "giant leap for mankind", Armstrong and Buzz Aldrin descended to the lunar surface ("The Eagle has landed") and spent two and one-half hours exploring the moon while Michael Collins orbited above the moon. This event was a very exciting thing to watch on television, yet a strange time to be an American since the war in Southeast Asia was going full blast and people were protesting against it.

After leaving Oklahoma City, we drove to Albuquerque, New Mexico and visited my cousin Paul Shwartz and his wife Clara who moved there in the 1950s. From there, we drove to Gallup, New Mexico for the next night. Driving west from Gallup and east of Holbrook, Arizona, Route 66 passed through a portion of the Painted Desert and Petrified Forest National Park where we paid a short-term entrance fee of $1.00. We also drove through Winslow, Arizona to Flagstaff.

FLAGSTAFF, ARIZONA TO THE GRAND CANYON

On Friday, July 25, we stayed at a Holiday Inn on U.S. Highway 66 in Flagstaff, Arizona. The room itself was $19.50 with tax of $.78 for a grand total of $20.28. From Flagstaff we drove to Williams, traveling north on Route 64 to the Grand Canyon where we spent a few hours. Our short-term entrance permit cost $1.00. In those days, gasoline averaged anywhere from 32.9 to 39.9 cents per gallon so you could fill up a car with gas from $5.00 to $7.50 depending on your location. After leaving the Grand Canyon, we arrived in Las Vegas on Saturday, July 26 where we stayed at the famous Sands Hotel. Our bill for the night was $24.15. Steve Lawrence and Edi Gorme were the headliners at the Sands, so we saw the show that night and left for Los Angeles the following morning. We arrived in Los Angeles on Sunday, July 27, dropped off the car at the designated dealership and rented a car for the next phase of our west coast trip.

LOS ANGELES, SAN DIEGO AND SAN FRANCISCO

We spent several days in the Los Angeles area, visited Universal Studios in Burbank, Disneyland, the Watts Tower, the Hollywood Bowl, then drove to San Diego. We saw many of the sites there and especially their world-famous San Diego Zoo. We ended our vacation by driving our rental car north on California route 101 along the ocean, stopping off at San Simeon, San Juan Capistrano, took a tour of the Hearst Castle, Big Sur and spent some time in Carmel before driving into San Francisco. We took in all of the San Francisco sites, including Fisherman's Wharf and riding cable cars. We flew back to Chicago on United Airlines on Sunday, August 10, 1969. It was a fantastic twenty-four-day trip.

WEDNESDAY, OCTOBER 1, 1969—LARGER APARTMENT

Penny and I decided to look for a larger apartment and on April 19, 1969, we found a beautiful third floor walk-up at 502 W. Briar Place that became available on July 1, 1969. We gave a $50.00 deposit to Ernest Rott, the owner. The three-bedroom, two-bath apartment was huge. It had a very large living room about 20 feet by 30 feet, a good-sized dining room and two large bedrooms with a small bedroom off the kitchen that was originally used as a maid's bedroom. The second bedroom had a gigantic walk-in closet with built-in drawers. The apartment came with a single-car garage located in the alley directly behind the apartment building.

Ernie and Trudie Rott, a couple originally from Europe (he was Czech and she was from Vienna, Austria) owned the apartment building they had bought for about $60,000.00 many years before. They lived across the street from the apartment with their two sons who were in high school at the time. The rent was very reasonable, $245.00 per month and it stayed that way for many years, going up slightly to $375.00 at the end of our nine-year stay. Federal Storage & Moving Company gave us a written quote to move us from W. Oakdale Avenue to W. Briar Place. It was a bargain considering we had a ninety-six-inch couch that had to be lowered from 441 W. Oakdale Apartment 13 D to the parking lot below. The total cost of the move was $145.00. Allied Van Lines represented the moving company. It took about two and one-half hours to move with a van and three men.

We became very close to both of our downstairs neighbors. Chuck and Sharon Goodman lived on the second floor and Harriett and Mickey Cholden were on the first-floor apartment. Neither of us had any children when we moved into the apartment. The Choldens never had children but Chuck and Sharon had Naomi who was born in 1971. The Goodmans had a cute Yorkshire terrier named Cupid and they called it Cuppie. Mickey used to walk Cuppie every evening. I got Sharon interested in photography and she became a professional photographer a few years later. In 1973, after their son, Joshua was born, the Goodmans were the first to leave the apartment building for a home in Highland Park. Bob Epstein, a Chicago attorney, moved into their second-floor apartment. We totally lost contact with the Choldens and Goodmans until 40 years later.

JUMP AHEAD FORTY YEARS

Penny had been friends with Chuck Goodman's brother's wife, Adrienne. When Penny and I were in Arizona producing an IFMA meeting, Adrienne told Penny had Chuck Goodman passed away from throat cancer on November 4, 2009. Jump ahead to January 2014. While Penny and I were in Scottsdale, Sharon Goodman called and left a message. Penny called her back, talked to a long time and vowed to keep in touch. Meanwhile in August 2014 we ran into Harriett and Mickey Cholden at the Chicago Art Institute at the Magrette show. We made a date to have dinner on Thursday, October 16 and to invite Sharon Goodman to join us. So, on Thursday, October 16, 2014, Harriett, Mickey Cholden, Sharon Goodman and Penny and I met at Bonefish Grill in Skokie for dinner. What a great reunion, full of laughter and remembrances but we forgot to take a photo.

FRIDAY, DECEMBER 19, 1969— FLORIDA VACATION
RENTED A MOTORHOME AND DROVE TO FLORIDA

Penny and I felt adventurous and decided to rent a sixteen-foot Winnebago motor home and drive to Florida for our two-week winter break from teaching. We found a recreational vehicle (RV) rental company in a Chicago suburb, drove there to get instructions on how to operate the RV, then drove the motor home back to our apartment to load up supplies and leave on our Florida adventure.

RAN INTO A BLIZZARD

We left Friday afternoon following Interstate 55 south through St. Louis. While driving near Cape Girardeau, Missouri, we ran into a severe snow and ice storm. The snow was coming down fast and the ice build-up on the road made driving extremely slippery and dangerous. We both saw a car plow into a guardrail on the opposite side of a bridge over which we were passing. After the very moment we saw another car smash into the guardrail, then our RV proceeded into a 360-degree spin that scared the hell out of us. We immediately made a decision to pull off the road at the next exit, park overnight at a nearby gas station and wait until morning to start again.

Around 6:00 a.m., on Saturday, December 20, we continued our journey south because the blizzard had subsided. We continued driving south on I-55 through Memphis, Tennessee, Jackson, Mississippi ending up in New Orleans where we paid Norman, Sheila and Steven another visit. Penny drove the motorhome and I took super 8mm movies of her driving. From New Orleans we drove along the gulf coast passing through Biloxi, Mississippi through Mobile, Alabama south to Pensacola, Florida, Panama City, Destin ending up in St. Petersburg and Sarasota, Florida.

On the way back to Chicago, we decided to take another route and followed I-75 north through Macon, Atlanta, Chattanooga and Knoxville, Tennessee north to Lexington, Kentucky where we drove west on I-64 to Louisville, Kentucky, then, north on Interstate 65 to Indianapolis, Indiana and back to Chicago.

It was really too long of a trip to make in two short weeks and we were both exhausted when we returned to Chicago. We had a few issues with the motorhome as the instructions for doing certain things escaped our memory. Penny was not too happy about taking the motorhome in the first place. There were some unhappy moments during this trip but our marriage persevered in spite of a few moments of yelling, screaming and swearing.

FLORIDA TRIP HIGHLIGHTS

Memorable highlights of interest were the state of Georgia and the estate of one of the founders of the Coca-Cola Company, Asa Griggs Candler. Candler did not invent Coca Cola but made his fortune selling it through his company. The mansion is located at the northeast corner of Elizabeth Street and Euclid Street in the Inman Park section of Atlanta. The mansion's Miocene pottery collection was especially intriguing described by a woman with a thick southern accent. We also went to beautiful Myakka River State Park very close to Sarasota, Florida. We both went fishing one afternoon off a pier near Sarasota and we each caught a few Puffer fish.

OCTOBER 1970—SPOON RIVER TRIP WITH THE WILSONS

There was an article in the *Chicago Tribune* about a Spoon River Scenic Drive in Fulton County southwest of Peoria, Illinois. Over a weekend in October, Penny and I decided to drive there with Bernie, Bonnie and their infant son, Marc. The Spoon River became nationally known from the work of Edgar Lee Masters, author of the noted *Spoon River Anthology.*

Much of Fulton County is farm and timberland. The town of Canton, is located in the heart of Spoon River Country and the natural wonders of the Spoon River Valley were beautiful during the fall of the year. Spoon River carved a wide scenic valley through Fulton County as it flows from London Mills to the south and east where it joins the Illinois River near the southeastern corner of the county.

CHICAGO POLITICS—OUR INVOLVEMENT

Penny and I became active in independent Chicago politics in the early stages of our marriage. In 1969, Bill Singer was running for alderman in the 43rd ward and we were part of an independent group through grass roots campaigning to get Bill Singer elected. We got involved with the Independent Voters of Illinois. Dick Simpson, a professor at the University of Illinois' Chicago campus, was also an outspoken advocate of independent politics.

"Singer won over the Democratic machine candidate by 427 votes in a closely contested election, but won his second aldermanic term with seventy per cent of the vote in the ward, thus clearly establishing himself as a solid local vote getter." The above was printed in the February 8, 1978 issue of *Illinois Issues.* In the Chicago City Council, Singer was a key member of the small but active minority bloc and opposed the machine on matters he considered to be crucial to the city's interest. But he voted with the majority ninety per cent of the time on routine matters, like appropriations for street cleaning, snow removal and sidewalks.

A group of independent voters were also opposed to 4 Plus Ones. These were four-story apartment buildings that were being constructed in our neighborhood. Developers were destroying old neighborhoods by tearing down three-flat apartment buildings and building these 4 Plus Ones over several lots. We held meetings in our apartment to bring up this to Chicago's City Council meetings. One-time, famous Chicago author and television personality Studs Turkel's wife, Ida, attended one of our apartment meetings. Studs and Ida lived in an apartment on N. Pine Grove immediately behind our apartment building and we could actually see directly into their window. We had no intention of looking but periodically, from time to time; we would see Studs through the window.

Penny and I wrote many letters to the Illinois House of Representatives, Illinois Senate and the United States Congress to support legislation to extend Medicare and social security benefits to individuals who receive a pension under a retirement system and to their dependents and survivors. We received letters from our Illinois state General Assembly representatives Arthur Telcser and John Merlo from the 11th District, Robert Cherry, Illinois State Senator, from the 11th District, Paul Simon, Illinois Lieutenant Governor, Sidney Yates our 9th Congressional district congressman and United States Senator, Charles Percy. All the individuals acknowledged receiving our correspondence and would consider voting for a law.

HIGH SCHOOL AND FRATERNITY COLLEGE REUNIONS

I've attended six high school class reunions, starting with our first one being our tenth-year reunion held in Boardman, Ohio at the Leffingwell Hills Country Club. The ten-year reunion was held on Saturday evening July 5, 1969. Other reunions were our twentieth held in the summer of 1979 at the Tippecanoe Country Club and our 25th was held at Boardman, Ohio's Mr. Anthony's Restaurant on Saturday evening, August 25, 1984. On Saturday, August 12, 2000 our forty-first high school reunion was held.

I also attended our forty-fifth Boardman High School reunion dinner held on Saturday, August 14, 2004 at the Tippecanoe Country Club. Penny and I drove to Cleveland to attend the event in Boardman. Classes from 1958, 1959, 1960 and 1961 were invited to this reunion. Linda, Penny and I drove into Boardman from Cleveland and then back to Linda's house after the event. I missed our fiftieth high school reunion that took place on the weekend of August 14-16, 2009 because nephew Todd Waldman married Rachel Jacobs in Cleveland that very same weekend. However, on July 19 and 20, 2011, Penny and I attended a seventieth birthday party for the entire class. The two-day event was held in at The Lodge At Geneva-on-the-Lake, Ohio. We had a great time at this event.

During Labor Day weekend in 2014, our Boardman Class of 1959 had a fifty-fifth reunion starting in Sandusky, Ohio and ending in Boardman with a high school football game and a dinner at the Tippecanoe Country Club on Saturday evening, August 30, 2014. A detailed description of this reunion is later on in this book.

On October 24 to 26, 1986, the Ohio University chapter of Phi Sigma Delta fraternity, of which I was a member, held a reunion of our fraternity brothers at the Marriott East Beachwood. Unfortunately, I was disappointed I could not attend as I was producing a client convention at the New York Hilton Hotel. However, I received the brochure that was put together for the event.

I was lucky to attend another fraternity reunion held in July 2006 of our Phi Sigma Delta fraternity. The event was held at the Beachwood Hilton Hotel and I stayed at Linda's house. Penny was not interested in attending, because most of the guys did not bring their wives.

FRATERNITY BROTHERS MOVE TO CHICAGO

Unbeknownst to me, four Phi Sigma Delta fraternity brothers moved to the Chicago area. The brothers were Jack Cohen, Paul Mesnick, Alan Appelbaum and Merrill Greenstein. I'm not sure how I found out they lived in the Chicago area but several times into the early 1980s we got together. There was Merrill Greenstein, a self-employed handyman who lived in Northbrook with his wife Roberta, Jack

Cohen, who was working for Sealy mattress company, lived in Skokie with his wife Bobbi, Paul Mesnick, an anesthesiologist, was single and living in the city on Dearborn Street and Alan Appelbaum and his wife Marilyn, who worked as a writer for a public relations firm lived on Romona Road in Wilmette.

One other fraternity brother, Don Goode, living in Hobart, Indiana, was part of the group. At the very beginning of our freshman year, I actually went out with his wife, Jill Colt, originally from Cleveland, before Don met her. They were married after Don graduated. Unfortunately, Don died of a heart attack at age 52.

Penny and I started getting together with Alan and Marilyn Appelbaum on a semi-regular basis around 2004. In the recent past, Alan and I attend Chicago Cubs baseball games along with three other men, Al Freeman, Lou Bluestein and Joel Probisky. When individual Cubs tickets go on sale, Alan used to buy selected tickets at Chicago's Wrigley Field and Milwaukee's Miller Park. I usually attend three Chicago Cubs baseball games a year; one game is always at Miller Park.

I'm can't predict the number of Wrigley Field Cubs baseball games I'll attend in the future; however, while living in Scottsdale during the winter months, I usually go to one or two spring training games. Alan Appelbaum and I keep in contact with Paul Mesnick and we have all gone out to dinner on several occasions.

CHAPTER TWELVE
Filmmaking and Leaving Teaching

THE SUMMER OF 1970—*TURN OFF POLLUTION*

When I started teaching, 16mm film was the preferred medium for classroom use. Videotape was in its infancy and only used in broadcast television. Too often, educational films had been adult-narrated lectures that tell a child what he is seeing on the screen. Rarely had these films been concerned with children's feelings about a given subject. When I started teaching, youngsters had grown more visually oriented having been brought up with television. At times they related better to film than to books. Good motion pictures, followed by spontaneous classroom discussions, in many cases are better learning tools than teacher prepared lessons, especially if they truly involve their young audiences and approach them as more than passive viewers.

To test my convictions, I wanted to make a 16mm film of my own on a subject that would be of concern to the urban as well as rural or suburban children. Pollution and the environment were hot topics and seemed to fit into that category. Using a positive approach and involving juveniles in solving ecology problems, my film encouraged boys and girls to start in their own neighborhoods, their own schools and to help stop the destruction of the environment. I also decided that if I were going to make an effective film about children, I would have to let them in on it. The result was *Turn Off Pollution*; an 11-minute film made for children starring children and narrated by children.

RHODIE MYERS AND KEVIN WHITE THE FILM'S STARS

The Winnetka School district 36 gave me a $250.00 grant from the Winnetka Centennial Teacher's Fellowship Fund to make the 16mm film. The fund was originally organized in 1960 to encourage teachers in the district to develop new ideas and materials. The grant was used to pay for the film processing and the rest of the cost was absorbed by my savings account. I always wanted to shoot a film and I applied for this grant during the school year. Rhodie Myers, age 10 and Kevin White, age 10, were the two children I used as actors in my first 16mm film. Rhodie was a fourth-grade pupil of mine at Crow Island School and Kevin was the stepson of our current Illinois Secretary of State, Jesse White. At the time, Jesse was the physical education teacher at Schiller School where Penny taught for four years before Bennett was born. Jesse was an inspiring teacher and mentor to his community.

Jerry Aronson, a sixth-grade teacher at Schiller School, part-time cinema instructor at Chicago's Columbia College and an "underground" filmmaker, helped me shoot a sync-sound interview portion of the film and assisted me with editing tips as well as serving as the film's technical advisor. His name is listed in the credits. Soon after the school year ended in June 1970, I started shooting scenes. During that summer, I spent long hours with students filming in the metropolitan Chicago area. The nature shots were photographed in sections of northern suburban forest preserves, Berkeley Prairie and Skokie Lagoons, to be exact and in Chicago's Lincoln Park. Other scenes were filmed at the Lincoln Park Zoo and along busy streets. Children making posters and writing letters to industrial firms were photographed at Oscar Meyer School on Chicago's mid-north side with the cooperation of Project Wingspread, a government sponsored program that brings together suburban and city children.

Rhodie Myer's father had a 16mm Bolex camera that I borrowed to shoot most of the film. I rented a 16mm Arriflex S camera and a Nagra tape recorder to shoot the sync-sound children interviews at a Chicago school playground. Jerry Aronson did the camera work on the interviews and I ran the Nagra tape recorder. Penny was at the video shoot. The entire production took two and one-half months. Some 1,800 feet of film was edited down to 400 feet. Dick Girvin, a sound specialist and technician from Zenith Cinema Service composed original music for the film. The audio studio was located on Chicago's West Foster Avenue. By the way, *Mutual of Omaha's Wild Kingdom*, a television series in the 1960s and 70s hosted by Lincoln Park Zoo Director, Marlon Perkins, was edited and sound mixed at Zenith Cinema Service. When working at Zenith to finish my film, I would see photos of Producer Richard "Dick" Reinauer, Director Don Meier and on location scenes taken all over the world.

(As a side note: Years later I would actually meet *Wild Kingdom* series producer Dick Reinauer who was a patient of Arnie Grauer. Dick appeared on-camera in a documentary, *War Dogs of the Pacific*, about his World War II experience as a Marine dog handler. As a war dog handler his interview is filled with vibrant recollections of historical facts and fascinating stories of his world travels).

Our friend, Carter Ross, was cast and played the part of an official from the Department of Environmental Services. I was able to obtain permission to use one of the department's vehicles as a prop. The idea of a written script was too limiting, even if the children were to create it. I wanted a certain kind of spontaneity in the narration. My plan was to interview kids about pollution problems and add their unrehearsed comments into the soundtrack, communicating children's impressions complete with their unedited mistakes. The editing process was begun in July with the film completed in August.

ENCYCLOPEDIA BRITANNICA BUYS FILM RIGHTS

In September 1970, just after the school year started, I telephoned Encyclopedia Britannica Films, a company that distributed educational films to schools and told them I made a 16mm children's pollution film. The timing was perfect because the head of production had just received a memo from his boss that they needed a children's film about pollution.

Upon hearing what I had just completed, the head of production invited me to screen my film in their office in the Equitable Building at 401 N. Michigan Avenue. After I showed my film, they offered me a distribution contract to put it into Encyclopedia Britannica's 1971-72 film catalogue. I had an attorney friend look over the contract and I signed a distribution deal for a $2,500.00 advance against 12½% royalties, but I retained all television rights. The film cost about $1,000.00 to make. That meant that once the costs of duplicating the film was recouped by the company, I would get 12½% royalty on every sale. I was getting quarterly royalty statements until 1993.

In the fall of 1970, we had a world premiere showing in our 502 W. Briar Street apartment and invited all of our friends along with the Levys to see it. Bonnie and Bernie Wilson gave me a director's chair with my name on it. The principal of Crow Island School gave me permission to have an old RCA 16mm film projector that was ready to be thrown out. I showed the film on that projector and an eight-foot by eight-foot tripod screen I purchased. There was nothing wrong with the projector except its age. I still have the projector to this day but unfortunately it needs some maintenance to get it to work properly.

FILM'S PUBLICITY AND TELEVISION APPEARANCES

There was lots of positive publicity about my film. On November 30, 1970, I appeared on *Kennedy and Company*, a local Chicago morning talk and news show on WLS-TV, Channel 7 with hosts Bob Kennedy and Jenny Crim to talk about my film. Several clips from *Turn Off Pollution* were shown on the program and I was interviewed about my involvement in making the film. The popular Chicago morning talk show was the predecessor to the *Oprah Winfrey Show*.

On December 4, 1970, two minutes of *Turn Off Pollution* was seen on "Come On People" a television program on Chicago's public broadcasting station, WTTW, Channel 11. The program was sponsored by the Church Federation of Greater Chicago and dealt with our environment.

On December 23, 1970, I appeared on WGN-TV's *Jim Conway Show* with Rhodie Myers and Kevin White. The television station sent me a reel-to-reel audio recording of the television show. Years later Bennett copied and transferred the audio interview onto a CD. I also have an MP3 file of the audio.

In March 1971, the entire *Turn Off Pollution* film was shown on Director's Choice on WTTW, channel 11. An article about the film and me was printed in the panorama section of the *Chicago Daily News* on January 30-31, 1971. A photograph of the two boys fishing in Skokie Lagoon that I took during the making of the film was featured. My hometown newspaper, *The Youngstown Vindicator*, ran an article about my film and me. I also wrote an article about the making of the film that was published in the April 1972 issue of the *Official Journal of the Illinois Education Association*.

A kid's review of the film appeared in the nationally distributed March-April 1972 issue of *K-eight* Learning Through Media magazine. I also wrote a one-page article titled "Teacher turns students loose on Film on Pollution" that was published in the April 1972 issue of the *Illinois Education*, the official Journal of the Illinois Education Association. The film was also listed in the February 1972 issue of *Film News*, the international review of AV materials and equipment under the New Films section. *Turn Off Pollution* was also purchased and used by Chicago's "Open Lands Project" that aimed to change the physical environment of the city through skilled planning of urban land areas.

OCTOBER 1974—LECTURE AT UNIVERSITY OF KENTUCKY

In October, I was invited to be a guest lecturer on filmmaking at the University of Kentucky in Lexington, Kentucky. My Ohio University and Phil Sigma Delta fraternity brother and one-time college roommate, Jerry Ferstman, was a professor in the art department. He asked me to come to Lexington and show my *Turn Off Pollution* film and give a presentation to one of his classes. The University paid me a small stipend, but I don't remember how much.

FROM 1968 TO 1974 —JERRY ARONSON & ORGANIC FOOD

Jerry Aronson, originally from Detroit, Michigan got Penny and me into eating organic food. The Bread Shop, a small and funky North Halsted Avenue grocery store located a few blocks north of Belmont Avenue, sold organic flour, breads and other health foods. A healthy restaurant, The Bread Shop Kitchen, located directly across the street from the health food store, was a frequent and favorite place of ours to eat.

Jerry also introduced Penny and me to Japanese food at *Nanewa* restaurant in the 900 block of W. Belmont Avenue and next to Ann Sather's restaurant. Penny and I ate miso soup, sunumonu and teriyaki dishes for the first time. It was years before Sushi became popular. Jerry would come over to our apartment to edit and just visit and invariably fall asleep on our beige/yellow corduroy living room couch. Jerry's famous naps on our couch were a highlight of his many visits. I also have a few photos of Jerry holding Bennett on the famous couch. Jerry was a fantastic photographer and took several black and white publicity headshots of me.

UNCLE HARRY LOANS ME MONEY

During this time period, my New York uncle Harry Dollinger loaned me $13,500.00 to buy a KEM 16mm film-editing machine. It took six of my male friends including our downstairs neighbors Mickey Cholden and Chuck Goodman to lift and move this heavy editing machine up the back stairs of our apartment at 502 W. Briar Place and into the back room of our rental apartment. It was quite a site as it took several hours to move it since it was so heavy and bulky.

The German-built flatbed film editing system became very popular and was imported into the United States after the multi-screen film *Woodstock* that was released in 1970. This documentary was edited on a KEM. Up until that time, a single-screen Moviola was the standard way to edit motion pictures. I was one of the first people in Chicago to buy the KEM editing machine. The modular system that could have three different picture screens, could edit 16mm or 35mm motion picture film but my machine only had 16mm modules and two picture screens.

From April 8, 1972 until March 17, 1975, I made payments to Uncle Harry trying to payback the full amount of his generous loan. I whittled the loan down to $5,000. On October 25, 1975, Uncle Harry forgave the loan to even the final gift to $5,000.00. After many year of editing 16mm film on it, I had the machine moved to a small office on the 15th floor at 520 N. Michigan Avenue where Guy Guilbert and I had two rooms in Suite 1502. The Spot Shop was at this location until 1980.

Our office was next to an advertising agency, Rosenthal and Company. I struck up a friendship with Dale Irvin, a copyrighter for the agency who told me he wanted to be a standup comedian. Dale eventually left the agency and went on to fulfill his dream by appearing in various comedy clubs around the country. Later Dale appeared on national television as the announcer on a talk show hosted by Clint Holmes, a popular singer and entertainer. The television show originated from a studio in New Jersey. By the way, Clint and Dale have worked for me on several occasions as a banquet entertainment and as a corporate speaker while I was a producer at Williams/Gerard Productions. I'm going to skip ahead a few paragraphs in this memoir because Clint Holmes' name was mentioned.

AN ALMOST CLIENT DISASTER STORY

Let me tell you an amazing story of how a show I was producing almost didn't happen. The client was the Power Transmission Distributors Association, a meeting held at the Sheraton Centre Hotel in Toronto, Ontario on Saturday November 5, 1988. I hired Clint Holmes and two of his backup musicians to entertain at this meeting's closing banquet. I told Clint, his drummer and his accompanist, not to say they were working in Canada because if you were working, a "work" permit was required. To get around the permit, my instructions were to say they were on vacation and to absolutely not mention they were working.

Well, Clint made it through customs without an incident and so did his accompanist; however, when the drummer came through, he told the customs agent he was working. Upon that comment, the custom agents asked for his work papers. Of course, the drummer had no work papers. The customs agents were going to send the drummer back to the United States but the problem was, the drummer had Clint's sheet music and band arrangements. This is before cell phones.

Clint's drummer called me at the hotel. He was at the airport saying he had Clint's music and I should talk to a Canadian customs agent who was standing next to him. I got on the phone and pleaded with the agent to let me come to the airport and get the music from the drummer. After a few minutes of telling the agent I would not only loose a client but probably be fired from my job, I should be allowed to come to the airport and get the music from the drummer before Canadian officials sent him back to the United States.

After a long conversation, the agent agreed, so I immediately in a panic, hired a limousine to take me directly to the airport. I arrived at the Toronto International Airport, got the music from the drummer and immediately headed back to the hotel for a 4:00 p.m. rehearsal with Clint and the band. In the meantime, I was able to get a backup drummer for the gig. We started to rehearse and about 5 minutes before the doors opened for the dinner to begin, we completed the rehearsal. In the end, Clint Holmes was a success and my client was happy, not knowing what I went through but I had been a nervous wreck.

OLD GLORY MARCHING SOCIETY (A DOCUMENTARY)

Jerry Aronson, who received his Master's Degree in Photography from Illinois Institute of Technology, also taught filmmaking at Columbia College had access to free editing equipment. During summers, he also taught an advanced photography class at South Shore High School. His class published a magazine titled *Visions* that contained photographs taken by his students. One summer I took Jerry's photography class at South Shore High School. It brought back memories of my high school days when I was a member of the photography club, used the school's darkroom and also the darkroom I had in my house in Boardman.

Jerry and I collaborated on several films. On Memorial Day 1971, we produced a documentary on the *Wellington Oakdale Old Glory Marching Society*. I rented an Éclair 16mm camera from Helix that Jerry used and we had seven Columbia College students assisting in the filming. Jerry, Robin Rutledge and Ron Bell were the three cameramen while other Columbia students including Markus Kruesi, Richard Schmiechen, Christopher Swider, Marc Leif and Marvin McNeil handled the audio and other tasks. Jerry and I used Columbia College's editing facilities to edit the 16mm film on a Steenbeck film-editing machine.

On Thursday, May 27, 1971, Jerry Aronson and my name appeared in Irv Kupcinet's *Chicago Sun-Times* column. The following is what was in the newspaper. "The Memorial Day parade of the pint-sized patriots of the Wellington-Oakdale Old Glory Marching Society will be captured on film by Alan Spencer and Jeff Aronson (should have been Jerry). The film will be distributed to schools and educational TV stations as an example of an ideal neighborhood project."

The following year, on Monday, May 29, 1973, the film had its world premiere at the end of the parade at 1:00 p.m. outside Saint Joseph Hospital at 2900 N. Lake Shore Drive. The mention of the film's showing appeared in the Irv Kupcinet *Chicago Sun-Times* column and Joe Cappo's *Chicago Daily News* column.

I appeared on *Sunday In Chicago*, a local NBC television program, with Al Weisman and host Bob Hale to talk about the *Old Glory Marching Society* film. Being a film teacher at Columbia College, Jerry had connections at Cinema Processors, a film laboratory at 611 East Grand Avenue that processed 16mm film for the television stations and for Columbia College students. Jerry used to get favors from one of the processors, Dennis Shapiro, who usually worked the night shift. Dennis would get our film processed, either for free or at a reduced rate.

RE-CONNECTING WITH DENNIS SHAPIRO

Skip ahead to Ronna at the University of Wisconsin and a coincidence with one of the parents of her sorority sister. It turns out Ronna's Chi Omega sorority sister was Dennis Shapiro's daughter Tracy. What a surprise when Penny and I attended a Chi Omega parent's weekend and I recognized Dennis at the Chi Omega house. We got reacquainted with Dennis after twenty years and met his wife.

One of the owners of the Cinema Processor's film lab was Morrie Bleckman, the older brother of Izzy Bleckman. Izzy was Charles Kuralt's cameraman for many years. Kuralt hosted "On the Road" with Charles Kuralt seen on CBS television and was the first anchor for *CBS Sunday Morning* that started in the fall of 1979. Joe Palese was the other owner and Fred (can't remember his last name) was also the man with whom we would become friendly during our production days. It turns out Joe's daughter, Liz Palese-Sweeney, is the President of Global Video Chicago, a video duplication company I did business with at Williams/Gerard.

During this time, Jerry Aronson was hired by Coronet Films to produce a film called *"Lines Are Fun."* Marshall Ragir, a friend of Jerry, brought Guy Guilbert to score the film with an original music track. Guy was suggested to Marshall by Robin Rutledge who was a tenant in Guy's mother's apartment building in Old Town and a former student of Jerry at Columbia College. He brought Guy, a Chicago musician, to our West Briar Street apartment to watch the film on my KEM editing machine. Guy composed an original music track and underscored the film. Guy and I eventually became business partners and this story is a little later in this memoir.

ELLA JENKINS AND *THE JUMPING WITH RHYTHMS* FILM

On April 17, 1972, Jerry Aronson and I teamed up again with children's entertainer Ella Jenkins to shoot a film about *Jumping*. We filmed Ella working with children but during the editing process we realized that the film would go nowhere so nothing ever happened with it. I still have the film in our family room inside a film can. Many years later, Tim Ferrin, an independent producer/director, was trying to create a documentary about Ella Jenkins. With Jerry Aronson's permission, I gave Tim a DVD copy of *Jumping* and told Tim he could use it in his documentary. We only asked for credit when the documentary is released.

SUNDAY, AUGUST 14, 2016—ELLA JENKIN'S 90TH BIRTHDAY

Penny and I attended Ella Jenkins' 90th birthday reception held at the Ida Noyes Hall at the University of Chicago. I turned over the 16mm *Jumping* DVD copy of the film to Tim Ferrin who is producing an Ella Jenkins documentary for possible inclusion into his film. Guy Guilbert, my former business partner, flew to Chicago from Los Angeles to be at the reception because he played the bass and guitar on several of Ella's record albums. Penny and I had a very nice reunion with Guy and Ella. A few days later, we received a photo of us taken speaking with Ella.

THE DIVIDED TRAIL: A NATIVE AMERICAN ODYSSEY

During the summer of 1972, I accompanied Jerry Aronson with his film camera to an abandoned Nike site on Belmont Harbor where three Chippewa Native Americans were camped out. Jerry started filming Betty Chosa Jack, her brother Michael Chosa and a young Susan Powers.

Eventually Jerry followed the trials and tribulations of these individuals and over an eight-year period from 1970 to 1978 created a film documentary titled *The Divided Trail: A Native American Odyssey*. To complete the film, Jerry needed a shot of Wrigley Field, so I went to Wrigley Field and shot some 16mm footage of the outside sign and got the footage to Jerry. My name is listed in the credits. In 1978, the film was nominated for an Academy Award for best documentary short subject. Although Jerry's film did not win an Academy Award, Jerry did attend the awards celebration in Hollywood. In 1994, the film was released as a VHS tape by Picture Start along with *Walk in Balance:* Return to The Divided Trail that featured a re-edited version of The Divided Trail plus new footage of the participants. A DVD of the film was later released and I have a copy.

After leaving Chicago in 1974, Jerry created the film department at the University of Colorado at Boulder where he retired in December 2006. Two of his students became famous for creating the animated television show *South Park* and the Broadway hit musical *The Book of Mormon*

In 2005, Jerry also released a DVD version of his documentary *The Life and Times of Allen Ginsburg,* who was a renowned poet, radical and visionary from the 1960s. Jerry worked on the film for twenty-five years. His latest endeavor is *Chasing Ice,* a documentary he co-produced with Paula DuPre' Pesmen about global warming and our planet. It is a story about National Geographic photographer, James Balog. It was chosen to be show at the 2012 Sundance Film Festival on January 15 and was on the short list, fifteen documentaries considered for the 2013 Academy Awards. Unfortunately, only five documentaries are nominated and *Chasing Ice* missed the final cut of five films. The song at the end of the documentary and during the credits was nominated for 2013 Academy Award. "Before My Time" composed by J. Ralph, and sung by actress and singer Scarlet Johansson and Joshua Bell for best original song.

JULY 16 TO AUGUST 22, 1971—NEW ENGLAND VACATION

What an amazing trip! Before leaving on a five-week vacation to the East Coast and Canada, Penny and I drove her 1966 Chevrolet Super Sport convertible from Chicago to Cleveland, then Youngstown to visit our parents. After leaving Youngstown, we motored across Pennsylvania taking state and county roads instead of interstate highways. We traveled through small towns and stopped at interesting places along the way. I had always wanted to go to State College, Pennsylvania, the home of Penn State University, so one of our stops was there. We drove around Penn State's campus and continued across eastern Pennsylvania making a stop in the Catskill Mountains in Highview, New York to see my Aunt Sadie and Uncle Harry.

CATSKILL MOUNTAINS

After staying overnight at my aunt and uncle's summer home, we drove through Bridgeport, New Haven and New London, Connecticut and headed south to Newport, Rhode Island. Newport was a city with an unusual and old setting. Newport had some of the finest examples of Colonial architecture in New England. We toured the old Vanderbilt mansion and other Newport historic places including the Touro Synagogue, the oldest synagogue building still standing in the United States and built in 1763. It is the home of Congregation Jeshuat Israel.

BOSTON, MASSACHUSETTS

From Newport, Rhode Island, we headed north to Boston, Massachusetts to see Penny's sister, Lois and her husband, Roy Cramer. We spent several days visiting Lois and Roy taking tours of Boston's historic places. We divided our time between Cape Cod, Plymouth, Old Sturbridge Village and Gloucester-Rockport where I caught my first flounder. One of the days was spent with Lois who took us to Martha's Vineyard on a boat. We also went to Salem, Marblehead, Cambridge, Waltham, Concord, Lexington, Walden Pond and walked the Boston Freedom Trail.

BAR HARBOR, MAINE

After leaving Lois and Roy in Boston, we traveled north to Maine, driving through Portland and Booth Bay Harbor, continuing north and spending the night in Bar Harbor and Acadia National Park. After Bar Harbor, Maine, we continued driving north to Bangor on U.S. 201 into Canada, ending in Quebec City, Quebec was about 241 miles from Bangor. Penny and I were so impressed with this city that we thought we were in France as most of the signs were in French and English. Many of the people preferred to speak French instead of English. Being a walled city, Quebec has the charm of Paris.

MONTREAL AND QUEBEC, CANADA

We spent a few days in Quebec, then drove west to Montreal, Quebec and spent a few days there. Quebec and Montreal were not to be believed. I had always heard about these two cities and wanted to see them. Montreal is a metropolis with "Man and His World" on the site of Expo '67. From Montreal we headed back to the United States driving south to New Hampshire, passing over Lake Champlain along route 2 through Montpelier, Barre to Mount Washington where we drove to its summit that is 6,253 above sea level. The drive down the mountain was very steep and as a result, the brakes on the 1966 Chevy heated up because of the steep decline and from the constant pressure being applied to them. Penny and I stopped at Barre and saw Rock of Ages where granite is mined and used in monuments and tombstones. I filmed how the granite is mined and showed it to my class when we studied rocks and minerals.

VERMONT AND MEETING AUTHOR, PEARL S. BUCK

From New Hampshire we drove west to Vermont where we stopped in the small village of Danby with a population of nine hundred fifty people. The small town is located halfway between Rutland and Bennington just off route 7. One quarter of a mile off a main highway, this village had almost been forgotten until Pearl S. Buck bought the town and began restoring it to its early 1800's appearance.

Before our trip east, Penny and was watching a television talk show where famous author Pearl S. Buck was talking about where she was living in a small Vermont town called Danby. Ms. Buck told the talk show host that she usually walked into the town center around noon with her caregiver. We decided to stop in Danby to see if we could meet famous author Pearl Buck.

DANBY, VERMONT

When Penny and I arrived in Danby, I proceeded to find out where Pearl lived. The woman on the second floor of the Village Square Country Store told me that too many people were bothering the author and she refused to tell me where she lived. She mentioned, however, that Ms. Buck usually took a walk around noon and perhaps we could get a glimpse of her walking with her Chinese houseboy. At that moment, the woman glanced out of the window and in amazement replied, "Here she comes now." I ran downstairs to get my telephoto lens on my camera and proceeded to take a few candid shots of her walking. As she approached in her Chinese dress holding fresh picked flowers, I walked toward her holding my camera low in my right hand so she would see I had no intention of taking her picture.

I introduced myself and told her we discovered Danby and asked if she minded if I took her picture. She told me "as long as you came all the way from Chicago, you may take my picture." After several photographs of Ms. Buck, Penny and I talked to her for a few minutes. Pearl Buck was warm, friendly and exactly how we had imagined.

We purchased a few of her books that she autographed including a children's book call "Welcome Child" that I read to my class. I finally found out where she lived and photographed the entire village. Unfortunately, I should have had my picture taken with her but I didn't. Meeting Pearl Buck turned out to be one of the many highlights of this trip.

STOP IN YOUNGSTOWN, THEN ON TO CHICAGO

From Danby we drove south passing through Pittsfield, Massachusetts and back to Chicago through Pennsylvania along Interstate 80, stopping in Youngstown and Cleveland. Over the course of the trip, I took two hundred fifty color slides and four hundred feet of color super-8 film that took us through six New England states and 4,600 miles plus Quebec City and Montreal, Canada.

PENNY FINDS OUT SHE'S PREGNANT

After we returned from our trip, Penny wasn't feeling too well and went to the doctor for a check-up. We had a feeling she was pregnant but the visit confirmed it. We were so excited to be welcoming a baby into our home. On March 10, 1972 Penny received a Notice of Maternity Leave Granted by the Chicago Public Schools and left teaching soon afterwards.

FRIDAY, MARCH 17, 1972—REMEY AND JULIE'S WEDDING

Bernie Wilson's first cousin, Remey Rubin, was divorced from his wife, Del and was dating Julie Danzker. We became friendly with Remey and Julie and they asked Penny and me to stand up at their simple wedding ceremony that took place on Friday, March 17, 1972. They were married in the rabbi's study and we were the only people who attended. Penny was seven months pregnant at the time.

MONDAY, MAY 22, 1972—BENNETT IS BORN

Penny had a fairly easy pregnancy. Penny and I chose to attend natural childbirth classes at a storefront conducted by Margaret Gompers, a nurse from Swedish Covenant Hospital. She was using the Dr. Dick Reed Method of natural childbirth delivery. The book on this method was written in 1959 and another way of natural childbirth and similar to Lamaze with breathing exercises.

Penny went into labor Sunday evening May 21. We had already packed a suitcase with Penny's nightgown and other essentials, so we were ready to go to Chicago's Wesley Pavilion of Northwestern University Hospital at a moment's notice. As the contractions got closer together, we arrived at the hospital around 11:00 p.m. We had been thinking of different names starting with a "B" for our new baby. Our new buddle of joy would be named for Penny's father, Bernard (who was also known as Ben) and my father's father (my grandfather, Ben).

At that time, fathers were not allowed in the delivery room, a rule changed for Ronna's birth so I was confined to the father's waiting room. I waited impatiently until Dr. Leon Carrow came out of the delivery room to tell me we had a baby boy. Bennett was born at 2:14 a.m. on Monday, May 22, 1972. I immediately called my parents on the waiting room pay phone and told them the great news, and then I called Penny's parents.

We decided not to have a bris, so Bennett was circumcised in the hospital. Friends recommended Mrs. Horn and we tried to hire her to be with Penny upon her hospital release but she had been already booked. Instead, we had another woman who helped Penny with Bennett.

Penny came home from the hospital on Friday, May 26. The helper woman arrived on the same day. When she arrived, she said she only ate pears and would not eat very much. She basically ate so much food plus she broke the Sylvania color television my parents had given us as our wedding present. The circuit breaker had popped out signaling that something was wrong with the circuit. Unbeknownst to us, she taped the circuit breaker shut so it wouldn't pop out. After she left, the television was not working properly and I discovered what she had done. I can't remember the cost of the repair but it was expensive to have the television fixed.

PLENTY OF SUPER-EIGHT MOVIES AND PHOTOS

On Monday May 29, 1972, when Bennett was one week old, he had his first bath. Bennett was a great baby. I took Super-8 movies of Bennett taking a bath at 3 months old, at a Chicago flea market outside of Chicago with Mike and Nancy Berman, at home at seven and nine months old and in January 1973 at the Levy's house in Evanston. I also have film of his first haircut at a local Chicago barbershop on West Belmont Avenue.

After college graduation and while living at home in Boardman, my father encouraged me at age 22, to take out an Equitable $15,000 adjustable whole life insurance policy from his friend, Ray Garea. My total annual premium was $256.35.

After Bennett's birth, I decided it was time to increase my life insurance policy by getting a $25,000 adjustable whole life insurance policy. Once again, I spoke to my dad and on January 10, 1973, I took out a $25,000 Equitable whole life insurance policy through Ray Garea. It was an Equitable Economatic life policy that meant cash dividends were built up over time and part of the policy was term insurance. The cash value of these two policies helped to finance the down payment for our Northbrook house in February 1979.

When Bennett was about 3 years old, we took him to the Illinois Railway Museum in Union, Illinois near Marengo, Illinois. He had such a good time riding on a trolley and I had just as much fun. As a child I rode trolley cars in Boardman to downtown Youngstown, so it brought back many memories.

DR. HOWARD TRAISMAN

After Bennett's birth, our pediatrician was Dr. Howard Traisman. Sharon Goodman, our second-floor neighbor recommended him. Dr. Traisman's office was first located on N. Broadway in Chicago, then his office moved to W. Howard Street on the northern border of Chicago and the southern border of Evanston.

We continued to use Dr. Traisman after Ronna was born. In going through old checks, I found two $38.00 checks, both written to Dr. Traisman by Penny, one on January 28, 1986 and the other $38.00 check written on February 5, 1986. A child's name was not written on either check. Since it was winter, I assume both visits must have been for colds or flu.

FORD STATION WAGON AND THE SEARS ROEBUCK COMPANY

In 1973, I was able to afford to purchase a new 1973 Ford Gran Torino station wagon that I bought at Wilmette's North Shore Ford on Green Bay Road that we drove for about eight years until 1981. The car was rusty by the doors but it needed a front wheel alignment, four new shock absorbers, and two rear springs installed. On Wednesday, April 8, 1981, I brought my car to Sears Automotive Center in Northbrook Court for the repairs. They told me the car would be ready at the end of the day.

When I went to pick up the car, I noticed a car parked that looked very much like my own but the front-end was severely damaged on the driver's side. At a closer look, I discovered the car was my car and I couldn't believe my eyes. I asked the service man what happened after the repairs were made and he told me when James Ramsay, the service man, was test driving my car, a woman, Mika Hessie from Deerfield, ran into the car in the parking lot with her 1976 Chevrolet Monte Carlo. Sears said they were not responsible for the damage and I was furious. A motorist's report of Illinois motor vehicle accident was filled out by the Northbrook Police and submitted to the woman's insurance company, Country Mutual Insurance. I had to rent a car from Snappy Car Rental.

I was very angry with Sears. I followed the procedure advised by Mr. Pat Gallo, head of Sears Security and by Mr. Allan Thellefson, manager of the Sears Northbrook Court Automotive Center store and waited for a call from Country Mutual Insurance, the woman's insurance agent. When that did not happen, I called Country Mutual Insurance and they estimated our car had over $1,200 in damages, was a total loss and not worth repairing. I was offered $650.00 for the car. After hearing this news, I wrote letters to Sears President, Edward Brennan, and copied James Urove, Director, Sears National Customer Relations Department, Michael Foort, Assistant to the President, All State Insurance and Allan Thellefson, manager, Sears Northbrook Court Store. There was no response or an apology or any acknowledgement from any Sears's person. According to Mr. Thellefson, Sears is self-insured through All State Insurance Company with a commercial garage liability policy for cars under its care. Since another party caused the accident and not a Sears's mechanic, he told me Sears was not responsible for the damage even though my car was under the care, custody, and control of Sears. I also spoke to Mr. Michael Foort, Assistant to the President of All State Insurance who reiterated this policy.

On Monday, June 15, 1981, I followed up with another letter to Sears President, Edward Brennan saying "I have waited more than one month for a response to my April 30, 1981 letter concerning the Northbrook Court Automotive Center and feel this is more than adequate time to formulate a reply. I cannot believe that a company of your stature would not have the courtesy to respond to my letter. I never got a response of anyone at Sears."

After this incident, I cancelled my Sears credit card and decided to boycott Sears for the rest of my life and to tell every person I encountered about this incident. To this day, I refuse to buy anything at a Sears store although I keep getting mail soliciting their business.

At the time I could not afford to buy another car, so my in-laws gave Penny and me $3,200.00 and I bought a pre-driven yellow 1977 Oldsmobile Cutlass two-door at the Ford and Mercury Dealership in Highland Park located at the corner of Lake Cook Road and Skokie Highway. I drove the 1977 Oldsmobile until 1984 when on Monday, March 19, 1984 I purchased a new 1984 grey Buick Century 4-door station wagon from Grant Dean Buick for $14,516.00. I traded in the 1977 Oldsmobile Cutlass 2-door sedan and the dealer gave me $1,856.00 for the Olds toward the purchase of the Buick.

SUNDAY, APRIL 1, 1973—MY SISTER LINDA GETS MARRIED

Bruce Waldman proposed to Linda in December 1972. On Saturday evening, March 31, 1973, Linda's mother-in-law and father-in-law had a rehearsal dinner for our New York relatives and for their relatives in an Eastwood Mall restaurant located in Niles, Ohio.

On Sunday morning, April 1, my parents sponsored a brunch for the out-of-towners at Youngstown's Twentieth Century restaurant on Belmont Avenue. In the meantime, Penny and I were up all night vomiting our guts out. My sister took care of Bennett, feeding and playing with him because we were as sick as a dog and weren't sure we would make the wedding. We got to the Rodef Sholem Temple at 3:30 in the afternoon. Our across the street neighbor, Carol Passarelli, had two family babysitters watching both Bennett and David Gomshay. Linda got dressed in the Temple and the photographer came.

That morning, Linda called Bruce in New Castle to see what was going on with him and no one answered. So, she called Edith Waldman, Bruce's mother, who said Bruce was in the hospital. He got the same stomach flu and was up all-night vomiting. Bruce did make it to the Temple but right before he walked down the aisle, Dr. Graul, gave him a shot of Compazine for the vomiting and the ceremony was started with Penny and I looking "green." In fact, Penny was wearing a green top and a flowered print dress on the bottom and her face matched the color of the dress.

Cousin Arleen Gomshay was my sister's only attendant. I walked my mother down the aisle and my father walked Linda down the aisle. As the rabbi and cantor are in the middle of the service, they see Bruce starting to weave and they sped up the ceremony. After the ceremony, Bruce went to the Rabbi's study and fell asleep while Linda went to the reception downstairs in Strouss Hall without Bruce until about 7:30 p.m. Bruce finally woke up about 7:30 p.m. Linda and Bruce danced a little bit and they left around 9:30 or 10:00 p.m. They were going to drive part of the way to Pittsburgh, then go on to Washington, D.C. for a few days because their honeymoon trip to South America did not leave for one week. They barely made it to a hotel outside of Youngstown as Bruce was still vomiting. The next day, Bruce felt better and they drove to Washington, D.C. before their honeymoon.

Linda and Bruce were married until January 1984 when Bruce decided to move out of the house claiming he had to get his act together. His father, Marty, had died in October 1984. Little did Linda know, Bruce was having an affair with his office assistant, Elizabeth. It took several years before they were actually divorced. According to Linda, Bruce kept on saying he wanted to be married, please don't do this, then Linda found out that he was still messing around with Elizabeth. At the end of May 1988, right before Ronna's Bat Mitzvah, Linda got the notice of the divorce.

In June 1988, Linda bought a house on Edgehill Road in Beachwood, Ohio and moved to Beachwood in November 1988. Bruce filed for custody of Todd and Andrew the end of July. According to Linda, he said, I'll show you, you can't take those kids. Hearings were held back and forth for almost a year and the judge ruled that Todd was old enough to say where he wanted to go. Todd wanted to stay in New Castle. Andrew was too young to make a decision.

The children spent the entire school week in New Castle and Linda had custody on the weekends, all summer and all vacations. Financial matters finally got settled many years later. Linda made a life for herself in Cleveland and taught fifth grade in the inner city since January 1994. In November 1988 to 1989, she substituted, and then she got a job as a teacher's aide teaching deaf preschoolers in the fall of 1989.

In the fall of 1990, she was moved to the Beachwood middle school as a tutor. She worked there until December of 1993 when she got a full-time position in the city schools of Cleveland where she started in January 1994. Her first semester she was working in Bolton and then she was transferred to Louis Pasteur Elementary School. In August 2007, she moved across the street to a newly renovated air-conditioned building called Franklin Delano Roosevelt Elementary School and retired in June 2012 having taught for thirty years.

IF (THE MOVIE)

During the summer of 1972, Chicago's Journal Films, Inc. commissioned me to produce an eight-minute 16mm film, targeted to preschool and primary age children. Its premise was to teach about making decisions on their own. The film showed there are choices and alternatives of action from which to pick. Several different scenarios were chosen. The teacher's guide suggested to stop the projector after each scenario and have a discussion about the choices made in the film. "You have to make your mind up, what would you do?"

I used children as talent from my previous class and others from Chicago's Oscar Mayer School as well as a "real" classroom teacher in one segment. The film was shot at different locations around Chicago including the Lincoln Park Zoo and Oscar Mayer School. Guy Guilbert composed the music, wrote the lyrics to the song and sung on the film's soundtrack as well as creating and playing several instruments on the film's music score.

Guy and I worked together editing the film on the KEM in my apartment. The music was recorded in the studio at Columbia College. According to Guy, "the engineer said, after we finished, that the recording session was the best thing ever recorded there. In Guy's words, he showed the engineer some technical tricks he didn't know: dropping in and out-stuff like that." Gilbert Aultschul, owner of Journal Films was happy with the results and Journal Films released *IF* for distribution in 1973. A complementary article about my film and me appeared in the *Winnetka Talk* newspaper on Thursday, May 17, 1973 along with my photograph.

A CROW ISLAND RESOURCE CENTER FILM (ALMOST)

In September 1972, I became the director of the Crow Island Resource Center. In April 1972, Crow Island principal, Don Crowe, Ray Ovresat from the architecture film Perkins and Will, Paulette Condos, third grade teacher and myself flew to Stamford, Connecticut to visit Margaret Skutch's Early Learning Center and Our Mother of God Academy to get some ideas for the school's soon to be constructed revamped resource center. Paul Curtis and Roger Smith, partners in Curtis-Smith Associates of Boston designed and created The Stamford Early Learning Center. Paul Curtis was a young English-born teacher with experience in British primary schools. The partnership designed and built interiors for elementary school learning centers. The most innovative ideas included flexible multi-level structures with book storage underneath scattered throughout the center.

After our Stamford visit, it was decided to hire Curtis-Smith Associates to design Crow Island's Resource Center in an existing space in the lower level of the building, previously occupied by the art room. I got the idea of trying to raise funds to create a 16mm color documentary film to show the innovative new resource center and how it was developed. I wrote a proposal with an estimated budget and applied to twelve different non-profit organizations to try to get funding for the project but had no success.

A TRIP TO SPRINGFIELD, ILLINOIS

I even travelled to Springfield seeking funding and met with Dr. Michael Stramaglia, Illinois Associate State Superintendent of Public Instruction in charge of media services. Also at the meeting were Al Binford, Director of Media Services production unit, Larry Broquet, State ITV, Mrs. Barbara Cole, Director of Program Coordination and Levi Lathen. From a letter I found in an old filing cabinet, the Springfield meeting was rather disappointing in several ways. "Since I was asking the state of Illinois for funds to produce a 16mm motion picture, I thought my talents as a filmmaker should be demonstrated. After showing *IF*, my latest 16mm color, sound motion picture, I produced for Chicago's Journal Films, Just two questions were asked by the committee members, "Did I use professional actors?" and "Did I do the singing in the film?" No other comments were made. From a group of professional educators, these two comments seemed ridiculous.

JUNE 1974—DECISION TO LEAVE TEACHING

I always knew I did not want to be a teacher for my entire working life. For several years before I decided to leave teaching, my mind was fixated on trying to figure out what I wanted to do with a new career. For the last several years, one of the main reasons I stayed in teaching was the Vietnam War. I did not want to be drafted and was able to get a teaching deferment from the Winnetka School Board. Thinking back, there was no way I was going to be drafted to fight a war that made no sense to me. I probably would have left for Canada if I hadn't received a draft deferment and many American men did exactly that. I was totally against the war in Southeast Asia, thought it was senseless and I wanted no part of fighting in a far-off land.

During my elementary school days, I collected stamps from French Indochina as Vietnam was once called. The French gave up fighting the North Vietnam communists' years before and my reasoning was why do we care what happens if the country is taken over by communism and why should the United States get involved with fighting in this far away land?

In March 1974, Larry Levy, my first cousin Marilyn's husband, approached me with a proposition and I decided to leave teaching to start working for him. I sent a letter to the Winnetka Board of Education stating I was leaving as of June 1974. The construction of the Crow Island Resource Center was completed in time for the beginning of the fall 1974 school year. The faculty and children were sad I was leaving and made bound books for me with letters, drawings and notes as a Crow Island School remembrance. I still have these books in our family room closet.

MONDAY, JULY 1, 1974—WORKING FOR LARRY LEVY

Larry Levy offered me a job representing him and trying to get film work in the Chicago area. I started working for Larry July 1, 1974 in a tiny office located in the basement of his Maple Avenue Evanston home. He had converted his garage into a neat studio but I was working in their dark basement sitting at a small table. Larry made his first film, *Funeral*, in 1969 and he wanted new business to expand his graphic design business and film business. Larry paid me one-half of what I was making when I left teaching, that was about $7,000. Penny and I struggled financially and our business relationship lasted for approximately one year.

LARRY AND I DRIVE TO FRED NILES STUDIOS FOR A SALE

On Saturday morning, July 12, 1974, Larry and I drove to Chicago's Fred Niles Studios located at 1058 W. Washington Street for a sale of equipment because the studio was going out of business. Fred Niles was one of largest producers of industrial and educational films. We did not buy anything but it was fun looking at this famous studio and the items that were for sale. The production studio was eventually taken over by Opry Winfrey's Harpo Studios. Originally the Niles Studio was Chicago's Second Regiment Armory. After Harpo Studios left Chicago, the building was torn down and the corporate headquarters of McDonald's was built on this location.

MULTIPICATION FILM

While working for Larry, I had a really great experience being the associate producer of a 16mm educational film called *Multiplication*. The film was my idea and Larry put up the money on spec. I worked very closely with Anna Keating on the stop-motion animated film. Anna had a complete stop-motion animation set-up in her Evanston apartment with an Arriflex camera and all the appropriate lenses.

To give legitimacy to our project and at my suggestion, we hired Winnetka Schools Consultant, Dr. Lola May, a highly respected mathematics educator to be our consultant on the film. I also suggested hiring Dick Orkin Creative Services to produce the soundtrack that we recorded before the animation actually started. Dick's company produced humorous radio commercials and I thought his voice and some of the ensemble of voice-over talent he employed for his commercials including voice-over-narrator Patti Wilkus would be perfect for the film's soundtrack. We wrote the script, had it reviewed by Lola May and Dick interspersed comedy into it. We recorded the soundtrack in Dick's Chicago studio.

It took many months to create all of the stop-motion animation movement. We used multi-colored socks, an egg carton with eggs and sixteen orange colored toy model Volkswagen Beetle cars to demonstrate the simple principles of multiplication. After it's completion, Larry entered the film in the 1975 Chicago Film Festival and it won a gold plaque award as best physical science film. I have a black Plexiglas plaque naming me the associate producer. After I left working with Larry, he sold the distribution rights to Paramount's education division and created *Addition, Subtraction* and *Division* to accompany *Multiplication*. The films were in distribution to schools for many years.

DICK ORKIN AND ME

I became friends with Dick Orkin and ran into him three different times after he moved his company to Los Angeles in 1978. He was the guest speaker at my first International Foodservice Manufacturers Association's COEX Conference. It was produced in February 1983 at the Fontainebleau Hotel in Miami Beach. At one of the hotel's restaurants, Dick and I had dinner together the night before his speech.

The second time we met was at the July 1990 Ninth Annual Seminar on Jewish Genealogy held in Los Angeles. On the seminar's opening night, Dick and legendary comedian Shelly Berman spoke. Dick was very much into Jewish genealogy and was an active member of the Jewish Genealogical Society of Los Angeles.

The third time we saw each other was at the Museum of Broadcast Communications on Saturday, June 27, 2015 after his interview with Chicago radio and television personality, Bob Sirott. I was sad to read of Dick's passing on December 24, 2017 at the age of 84.

EDUCATIONAL TOOL AND DIE COMPANY

While working with Larry, I didn't have success selling his filmmaking services so we tried to come up with ideas to make money. One of the ideas was to create a corporation that would produce and distribute educational filmstrips and other learning materials geared toward the basic curriculum areas for grades kindergarten through high school. We found two freelance writers, Rennie McKay and Daniel Quinn and Larry formed a partnership with them, naming the company Educational Tool and Die Company with Daniel Quinn as President.

Our first project was *Friday Afternoon Miscellany*. This booklet was intended to be a pre-printed spirit master program. With creating three idea pages and without printing a single spirit master booklet, it was decided to test the concept and place an ad in Scholastic's *Instructor* magazine. The ad read: It's Friday afternoon and your kids are squirrely. Right? Let us send you our book of 32 curriculum-based activities on spirit-duplicating masters, one for each Friday of the school year. The *Friday Afternoon Miscellany* engrossing activities and games in reading, math, science, social studies and language arts. Conceived and written by teachers who know what Friday afternoons can be like $4.95 each from the Educational Tool and Die Company, P.O. Box 367 Centerville, Ohio 45459.

In the ad, you could choose booklets for grade 2, grade 3, grade 4 or grade 5. The ad was so successful we received checks for over $12,000.00 in orders but the entire project never got off the ground and we returned all of the money.

Daniel Quinn wrote a letter thanking people for their interest in *Friday Afternoon Miscellany* and continued that he was sorry to say delays in production of these spirit masters have forced us to postpone fulfillment of orders at this time. Therefore, we are enclosing a check for the full amount of your order. We hope to be able to offer the miscellany in the fall, and if this is the case, we will inform you by letter. Sincerely yours, Daniel Quinn

WEDNESDAY, JULY 9, 1975—RONNA IS BORN

Six weeks before Ronna was born, Penny and I attended weekly Lamaze classes at Louis A. Weiss Memorial Hospital not far from our apartment. This method stressed breathing techniques to counteract the contractions and was different that the Reed Method we implemented before Bennett's birth. As I previously mentioned with Bennett's birth, Northwestern Memorial Hospital did not allow fathers to be in the delivery room but this time I was able to go into the delivery room and saw Ronna being born. Seeing that little girl for the first time gave me goose pumps. What an amazing experience witnessing Ronna being born. During the birth, I felt all kinds of emotions and excitement running through my mind and body. I wanted to take movies of the entire experience but Penny was against it.

MY HAIRCUT ON THE SAME MORNING RONNA WAS BORN

The morning Ronna was born, I had an 8:00 a.m. haircut appointment with my hair stylist, Otto Bodner. I had been up all night and came to my appointment directly from the hospital. It was a beautiful and sunny day and I had my movie camera with me, so after my haircut, I went to Lake Michigan and took movies of the sun rise over Lake Michigan. What an amazing day I will never forget.

SUNDAY MAY 16, 1976—LOIS AND ROY'S WEDDING

Penny, Bennett, Ronna and I flew to Boston to attend Lois and Roy's wedding. Getting out of Logan International Airport was a real challenge in those days. At that time, there was only one tunnel under Boston Bay into the airport and one tunnel going out and each tunnel was frequently backed-up with traffic. It wasn't until the 10-year-long "Big Dig" project finally got completed in 2006 that the traffic into and out of Boston International Airport finally became much easier. The wedding was held at The Castle on the campus of Boston University. Penny and I were in Sam Zipp's car driving to the wedding ceremony but we got lost because of a turn that Roy inadvertently left off of the directions. Larry, Sandy, Doug and Mara Fishman were following us in a rental car. We eventually got to the ceremony. Less than one-year old Ronna stayed with a babysitter and did not attend the wedding. We stayed a several days after the wedding to visit some friends in the area.

On May 19, Penny and I drove to New Haven, Connecticut to visit Nancy and Mike Berman. Mike was a gynecologist at Yale University Hospital in New Haven and his wife Nancy had been an art teacher at Crow Island School. On May 23, we drove to Dale City, Virginia to see Yvette and Frank Zgonc. Frank was stationed there with the United States Air Force.

CONGRATION KOL AMI

Penny and I joined Chicago's Congregation Kol Ami after our children were born. The temple was located on the second floor of the old Chez Paree nightclub at the corner of Ohio and Michigan Avenue. Rabbi Arnold Kaiman was the rabbi and he was a real character. Around 2000, I was walking on Michigan Avenue and ran into his second ex-wife, Dorie, who was not Jewish and told me she had not been in touch with Arnie in many years. Bennett and Ronna were named at this congregation. It did not make sense to continue driving into Chicago to go to temple services, so after moving to Northbrook in February 1979, we joined Temple Jeremiah on August 24, 1980 with a partial membership.

CHAPTER THIRTEEN
The Spot Shop

JANUARY 1976 TO SEPTEMBER 1981—THE SPOT SHOP

My teaching career had to change. Leaving teaching and working for Larry Levy was a risk I was initially willing to take. I had been working with Larry for almost one year and I wasn't very successful selling Larry's film production service plus there was a drain on my family's finances. So, we mutually decided that I would not be continuing working for Larry.

PRODUCING MY FIRST MUSICAL COMMERCIAL

In the middle of January 1976 Guy Guilbert received a phone call from a desperate Peter Postelnak, President of Bentley, Barnes and Lynn, a Chicago advertising agency, who needed Guy to produce music tracks for an upcoming radio commercial. Guy had been producing commercials with partner Mike Melford and the agency liked Guy's old demo reel. They needed a melody for new radio spots. The agency was freaking out trying to find him because the agency normally didn't create or produce broadcast music or television commercials and didn't know to whom to turn.

Guy was starving, doing nothing since his former partner in a music production company, Mike Melford, left to go to law school and I wasn't doing much either. According to Guy, "he knew the music production would be about $5,000 in his pocket. Also, it was his chance to launch a new commercial music production company because he would have something on the "air" and would be legit. He thought, 'BINGO! I'll call Alan. He isn't doing much. "I called and said these very words to Alan: "Congratulations, you're going into business!" Guy Guilbert asked me to join him in forming a production company.

Guy and I went to a meeting with Bentley, Barnes & Lynn advertising agency to learn about the project. After the meeting, Guy and I went to a Burger King in Old Town to celebrate and he thought up a name: Spot Shop Chicago.

A few days later, on Penny's birthday, Friday, January 30, 1976, we went into the south side studios of PS Studios, a recording company owned by musician Paul Serrano, to record a musical radio commercial for the *Chicago Sun Times* and *Chicago Daily News*, "*Chicagoland Job Mart*" featuring The Arbors, a local singing group comprising of two sets of brothers, one set being identical twins. The Arbors became nationally known after appearing on *The Arthur Godfrey Television and Radio Show*. The group originally met while students at the University of Michigan. Dave Antler was the audio engineer on this first session.

Guy generously allowed me to share in the profits of that first music job as a friendly incentive to join up with him, although I had no previous experience producing music. The radio commercials were a huge success and Guy and I went into business together, producing radio and TV musical commercials at first, and branching into film commercials as Spot Shop Chicago. After a while, we simplified the name by changing our company The Spot Shop. The first billing for the *Chicago*

Sun Times and *Chicago Daily News,* *"Chicagoland Job Mart"* was $5,960.90 and was invoiced on February 17, 1976. Guy did the composing, orchestrations, arranging, instrumental charts, played bass and sometimes piano on each recording as well as directing the musicians.

GREG SERGO OUR DRUMMER

On the original musical commercials we produced, our only drummer was Greg Sergo. Guy had worked with Greg for many years before I got involved. We used Chicago-based studio musicians Bobby Lewis on trumpet, Cy Touff on trombone and Rich Fedoli on saxophone/flute. On occasion, we also used Bob Hoban who played the mandolin and guitar, but later Bob moved to Nashville to try his luck in the country music business.

RECORDED IN MANY CHICAGO STUDIOS

During our five and one-half years in business, we recorded music in a variety of Chicago recording studios. Paragon Recording Studio run by Marty Feldman was a popular studio. Chicago Recording Company, Acme Recording, PS Studios on the south side and for voice-over work we used Kurt Johnson's Studio One at 645 N. Michigan Avenue. We also worked with engineer Mike King in his studio. Mike was a favorite engineer who had worked with Dick Orkin during his WCFL radio days and I believe was the audio engineer on Dick's famous *Chickenman* and *Tooth Fairy* syndicated radio programs. In the meantime, I was learning how to produce original musical commercials, because Guy was a good teacher.

On April 12, 1976 we produced a National Pride Car Wash musical jingle for Jack Badofsky, a partner in Marvin H. Frank Advertising. The billing was $1,618.17. On April 15, 1976 singer Paul Simon had a huge hit with *"50 Ways To Leave Your Lover."* Guy and Jeff Doucette, who later went to Hollywood and appeared in many motion pictures and television shows, wrote a comical parody, *"50 Ways To Beat Your Lover."* We recorded the song at PS Studios with Dave Antler as the audio engineer, Guy singing, Jeff Doucette laughing and me with metal nails in a bag for the pulleys, chains and whips sound effect. We released the record under the Pop Shop Record label. The audio for our film work was done at Universal Studios at the corner of Rush Street and Walton.

Guy was designing a promotional package that included a menu of our services with a photo of a place setting on the cover with a dinner plate, knife and fork and napkin. The cover design used an antique plate that we rented and had photographed in a studio. Our company logo was put in the center of the plate and was a very cool.

CHICAGOLAND JOB MART FILMED COMMERCIALS

On June 1, 1977 after the success of the musical *"Chicagoland Job Mart"* radio commercials advertising the *Chicago Sun-Times* and the *Chicago Daily News,* Bentley, Barnes and Lynn Advertising Agency and Paul Oleff, President, awarded Spot Shop Chicago our first filmed television commercial. The two television spots would be shot in Chicago. We auditioned a male, Scott Russell and female, Terri Kreeger who would appear in the two television commercials.

Our friend Remey Rubin, let us film the interiors in his Bonded Collection

Corporation office at 221 N. LaSalle Street at Wacker Drive and we got permission from the MidAmerica Bank in the United Insurance Building on the corner of State Street and Wacker Drive to film our actors going into their building. We used Larry Bloodworth as our cameraman with Guy directing and me producing.

Over the next five and one-half years, Guy and I created and filmed a variety of other television commercials, some appearing nationally over the three networks at the time. On February 22, 1977, we produced a commercial for Spring Air Postur Center Mattresses that was our first nationally televised commercial appearing on *The Tonight Show* and other nationally televised shows. The Alex T. Franz Advertising Agency gave us the project.

We hired Linda Sandberg, a Chicago model and actress, to be our female subject being lifted off of the Spring Air mattress by our magician, played by Guy. We dressed Guy in a high hat and red cape with a black wand. *Sleeping on a Spring Air Mattress is like sleeping on air* was the theme of the commercial. Robin Rutledge, Jerry Aronson's former Columbia College student, provided the 16mm film equipment, provided the lighting and camerawork on this commercial.

We became a regular production arm of Chase Erenberg and President Merrell Erenberg, was a big supporter of Guy and me. This agency had very limited experience in broadcast and our production company served as a great resource for them. We created many radio and television commercials for Sportmart, a Chicago-based retail sporting goods company since purchased by The Sports Authority, The Toy Chest in St. Louis and Union Hall, a discount department store located in Rockford, Illinois.

On July 6, 1977 we videotaped Channel 44's *Good Time Bunch Club* promo in Lincoln Park. It was 96 degrees that day. A Chicago actor, Brian Vanden Brouke, with whom I would hire many years later in 1988 on Outboard Marine's OMC Today Meeting, served as the talent on this shoot. Mike Torchio was the cameraman and Curt Mendelsohn was the assistant. Guy directed and I produced.

In June 1978, we produced a TV commercial for the *Lovable Livables*, cute stuffed animals another Chase Erenberg account. On September 16, 1978, we produced a TV commercial for Sportmart and after that we moved the KEM to our new office at 520 N. Michigan Avenue.

In October of 1978, we filmed the *Tarco Toys Bank-O-Matic Gumball* TV spot for Chase Erenberg and also produced a slide show for the Bank of Ravenswood. We worked with a Chicago animator and created a television commercial for the St. Louis, Missouri *The Toy Chest*. The music was recorded with Chicago actor, Rob Riley and Guy singing. We recorded the soundtrack at Acme Recording Studios on Chicago's N. Southport Avenue.

For the Union Hall commercial, Guy wrote the music for the tag line and we employed an animation studio from South Bend, Indiana, to create a computer-generated animated opening and closing which was very new at the time. The tag line, for the commercials was *Union Hall, Where You Pocket The Difference*. Jack Badofsky worked as a freelance creative director/writer on this project.

Jack Badofsky, a Creative Director for Advertising Agency Marvin H. Frank,

Inc., had worked with Guy on many occasions before we became The Spot Shop. Jack gave us several musical projects; National Pride Auto Wash with The Arbors and Balm Barr Cocoa Butter Crème with jingle singers Vicki Hubly, Donna Kime and Kitty Haywood, were two that I can recall.

Chase Erenberg also gave us an assignment with singers Ron Hawking and Josey Falbo, two Chicago famous jingle singers. Ron Hawking has since done several one-man singing shows in Chicago.

Haddon Advertising, Inc. gave us a musical commercial for M. Hyman & Sons. We used The Arbors again for this commercial and recorded it at CRC (Chicago Recording Company).

On December 19, 1978, one of our best locally broadcast television spots was created for WMAQ radio. We worked with Becker Studios in Chicago who made two custom wooden radios built with a cuckoo bird coming out of the top and money "pouring" out of the bottom. The theme was *"WMAQ Is Going To Make Me Rich"* and we cast Chicago actor Gil Pearson as the talent on the shoot filmed at Freese & Friends, 141 West Ohio Street. Al Landis, Creative Director at Campbell Mithun/Chicago gave us the project. As Guy reminded me, we hired David Hall, Ann Ryerson's husband, to be a grip on the shoot. It was the first and last time David ever worked as he inherited a lot of money and didn't have to work again.

We also produced industrial videos, one in particular was created as a promotional video for the Garfield-Linn Advertising Agency. It was for Brunswick's *"The Great and Greatest Bowling Tournament"* to be held in Las Vegas. We used Fred Winston, a local Chicago radio personality, as our narrator and bowling celebrity commentator "Whispering" Joe Wilson for part of the video narration.

In January 1979, we filmed an Italian U-Boat TV commercial featuring Rob Riley and Mary Gross as voice-over talent. It was the first time Mary Gross had ever been in an audio studio. Mary went on to fame as a repertory cast member on *Saturday Night "Live"* from 1981 to 1985 where she appeared with Julia Louis Dreyfuss, Christopher Guest, Jim Belushi, Martin Short and Billy Crystal, among others. Before leaving for *Saturday Night "Live"* and New York, I saw Mary in my bank and congratulated her on becoming a cast member. Rob Riley also wrote for *Saturday Night "Live"* for a few years.

In February, 1979, we produced a Serv-It-Hot TV catalog television commercial and in June of this year, a *Land of Lincoln Savings Bank* television commercial. On October 4, 1979 Guy directed a television commercial at Grignon Studios for the *Stratolounger Loback chair*. The spot was produced for Brodsky Advertising, Inc.

Merrell Erenberg and John Rosene became partners and formed Chase Erenberg & Rosene and they gave us an assignment to shoot a new toy commercial. On February 4, 1980, we filmed a television commercial for *Headlite*, a snap-together hobby kit from Monogram Models, a division of Mattel Toys on location in an Evanston house. We cast a young actor, twelve-year-old John Cusack who later became a huge Hollywood movie star. Other cast members included Jennifer Ursitti and Ted Spathies as the child actors in the commercial. Andy

177

Costikyan, a cinematographer famous for shooting Woody Allen's *Bananas* movie, was our cameraman on this project. I don't think the commercial ever aired on television or the hobby kit even got manufactured.

In May 1981 Guy and I produced a filmed TV commercial for Sportmart *The Edge* that was rotoscoped and animated. Actor Darrell Warren was hired to swing a golf club. Rotoscoping is taking "live" action footage and going frame-by-frame and using the footage to create animation.

Our business was O.K. for several years but it was a continuing struggle not knowing when our next project would come along. I did all of our company's repping, mainly contacting advertising agencies for business.

THE REIFICATION COMPANY

Late in 1976, my partner Guy, started playing the piano for the Reification Company, an improvisational group that performed every Wednesday night and the last weekend of every month at Sylvester's Pub located at 2700 N. Lincoln Avenue in Chicago. The group was composed of Ann Ryerson, Bernadette Birkett, Rob Riley, Bill Nigut, Nonie Newton, Tom Tully, Beth Jacoby, Norman Mark and Danny Breen. The group started working together in the winter of 1975. They were all members of Del Close's improvisional classes at Chicago's *Second City*. These individuals decided to start their own improvisational group and called themselves, *The Reification Company*.

I became involved with the group, attending their performances and for a while was their booking agent while Guy and I were partners in our music and film production business. From January 1977 to June 1977, I booked the Reification Company into various venues and got paid a 15% commission.

Some of the venues and money collected were as follows: New Trier East High School ($30); Loyola University ($35); Triton College ($80); DePaul University ($32.50); Northwestern University ($42.50); New Trier West High School ($90). Rob Riley was in charge of the group and for paying me my commission.

The most successful appearance that I booked for the group was in the *Wild Onion* room at the Hyatt Regency Chicago Hotel on East Wacker Drive. The room had entertainment and no longer exists as it was turned into a meeting room at the hotel. On April 3, 1978 I received a $393.90 check from Rob Riley for booking the Wild Onion at the Hyatt Regency Chicago. Guy, Danny Breen and I periodically used to play tennis together. Neither of us was any kind of athlete but it was always fun playing with Danny and Guy.

THE CAST WENT THEIR SEPARATE WAYS AND TO HOLLYWOOD

The Reification Company eventually broke up with its talented performers going their separate ways. Ann Ryerson appeared on the main stage of *Second City*, got married to David Hall, a local Lake Villa resident, moved to Hollywood and appeared in the film *Caddyshack* and several Robert Altman films, including *A Wedding* and many television shows, appearing occasionally on *Curb Your Enthusiasm* created by Larry David.

Danny Breen married Nonie Newton, had a son named Spencer, moved to

Hollywood and got divorced. Danny was a comedy writer appearing on many television shows; most notably HBO's *Not Necessarily The News, Seinfeld* and *Curb Your Enthusiasm* among others and was a comedy writer for many years. When his son Spencer was born, Danny told me I had nothing to do with naming his son Spencer. Following a seven-year battle with cancer, Danny died on December 29, 2017 at age 67.

Norman Mark was an Emmy Award winning film critic and entertainment reporter and also a multi-media journalist. He was upbeat, boundlessly positive and incredibly smart. He wrote for the *Chicago Tribune,* appeared on Chicago television and was a writer. Norman moved to California and became an entertainment writer for *Palm Springs Entertainment.* He died at Eisenhower Hospital in Palm Springs, California from complications of multiple myeloma on Monday, March 19, 2012 at the age of 72.

Bernadette Birkett married George Wendt, her second husband, a famous actor who appeared as the character Norm for ten years on the television sit-com *Cheers.* Bernadette appeared in several motion pictures and on many television shows, notably The Gary Shandling Show and others.

Bill Nigut eventually became a political reporter and television news anchor for twenty years on WSB-TV, an Atlanta television station. He was the Executive Director of the Atlanta Regional Arts and Culture Leadership Alliance. He also served as the Southeast Regional Director of the Anti-Defamation League, an international organization dedicated to fighting the fighting bigotry toward the Jewish people and to securing justice and fair treatment for all. In January 2007, he joined ADL. Since 2013, Bill has been a program host and senior producer for Atlanta's Georgia Public Broadcasting.

Tom Tully moved to Los Angeles and was involved in improv and other acting jobs. In 1998, I ran into Tom at Marriott's Desert Springs Resort in Palm Desert, California while producing a meeting there. Tom was hired by a destination management company as an actor for part of the convention's entertainment. What a surprise to see him over twenty years later.

Rob Riley and Beth Jacoby both stayed in Chicago. Rob was a writer for NBC's *Saturday Night Live* from 1984 to 1985, appeared on the *Second City* stage for several years, performed in Chicago area plays and writes for a living. In fact, Penny and I saw Rob perform on Sunday, November 13, 2011 at Skokie, Illinois' Northlight Theater production of *Seasons Greetings.* Rob moved to Los Angeles and married Danny Breen's ex-wife, Nonie Newton.

Beth Jacoby did voice-over work and for many years appeared as Beth Shalom on a Chicago Sunday morning Jewish television show. Beth married Ron Deitch and I ran into Beth many years ago walking in front of our office building.

Unfortunately, Beth died of a cancerous brain tumor on Thursday, May 5, 2016. On Friday, May 6, 2016 at 12:00 p.m. I attended Beth's funeral sitting alongside Rob Riley at Jewish Reconstructionist Congregation in Evanston, Illinois. Rob told me he was going to move to California that he did soon after the funeral. At Beth's funeral I also ran into Chicago voice-over actor Joel Cory and Penny

Lane, a former radio disc jockey and actress, friends from years many ago when I was producing commercials.

VALUCHA DE CASTRO

Guy introduced me to a Brazilian-born singer, songwriter and artist, Valucha de Castro, who lived in an apartment near Logan Square. Valucha, as she was called, played the guitar and was divorced. She was one of the first students of Chicago's *Old Town School of Folk Music* and later a teacher of Brazilian folk music there. Guy met her when she was associated with the school.

When Bennett was about three-years old, I took him to Valucha's house for a visit. Valucha played the guitar and sang the song *Guan Tana Mera* for us. When Bennett and I came back to our Briar Street apartment, he told his mother he heard the song *One Tomato* at a lady's house.

Guy and I created different business ventures under the name of Pop Shop Records, Spotlight Chicago and The Spot Shop. Under *Spotlight Chicago*, at one point, I actually thought I could book Valucha as an act for colleges. I ending book Valucha six times around the Chicago area and received a commission for my endeavors.

SPOTLIGHT CHICAGO (OUR TALENT AGENCY)

On October 19, 1978 I booked Valucha into Northeastern Illinois University for $200 and made $40 commission; on October 24 and 25, 1978, she appeared in Des Plaines District 62 for a total of $500 and I received $100; On November 14, 1978, Valucha appeared at Juliette Low School in school district 59 for $275 and I got $55; on November 15, 1978 she appeared in Mark Hopkins School district 59 for $150; on November 21, 1978 Valucha performed at the Ridge School District 25 for $150 and I got $30; and on December 14, 1978, Valucha appeared in Alliance Francaise for $220 and I received a commission of $40.

VALUCHA SINGS COMMERCIALS AND OUR WINNING LAWSUIT

Guy and I also used Valucha de Castro as a singing talent in a series of radio commercials for Chicago's chain of Café Margarita restaurants. This series of radio commercials was the first and only time Guy and I brought a lawsuit against one of our clients. Cesar Dovalina, the owner of Chicago's Café Margarita, a small Chicago restaurant on N. Wabash Avenue, also owned *La Raza*, the Spanish language newspaper. He had at one time five Café Margarita restaurants in the Chicago area. Cesar commissioned The Spot Shop to produce a series of musical radio commercials for his restaurant. We used Valucha de Castro as the talent as she sang various radio commercials that Guy composed and we recorded in a studio.

We gave a copy of the final commercials to Mr. Dovalina. Although we got approval at each stage of production, Mr. Dovalina said he didn't like the completed commercials and refused to pay us. Guy and I said "OK, if you won't pay us, then, you cannot use these radio commercials on the air."

About six months later, I started to hear the exact LaMargarita commercials on Chicago radio stations. I immediately called Michael Schlesinger, our attorney, and we filed a lawsuit against LaMargarita restaurant and Caesar Dovalina. Penny taught with Michael's wife at Schiller School so that's how I knew of Michael. Guy and I had an open and shut case and won the judgment in a short trial decided by a judge. Although we won, the client still refused to pay so we had to garnish his bank account and after many months, we finally got paid the entire amount plus our attorney fees. I found out later that in 1984, Mr. Dovalina pleaded guilty to evading about $250,000 in Illinois taxes at his restaurants and was sentenced to four year of probation. The judge was lenient because of Dovalina's work in the Mexican community.

VALUCHA LEAVES CHICAGO FOR MOSCOW AND WASHINGTON

A little after this time, Valucha started living with Jill Dougherty, a veteran television reporter for Chicago's WMAQ-TV Channel 5. I met Jill through Valucha. The two women eventually moved to Washington, D.C. and Jill became an on-air television correspondent for CNN. She served as White House Correspondent for a while, and then moved with Valucha to Moscow where she worked as CNN's Moscow Bureau Chief. Jill is considered an expert on Russia and the former Soviet Union. Several years later, Jill Dougherty was a guest presenter at one of my Palm Springs, California IFMA conferences and I was able to reacquaint myself with her. Penny was at this conference and she met Jill. In 2014, Jill became a Centennial Fellow and instructor at Georgetown University's Walsh School of Foreign Service. Valucha died of liver disease on February 12, 2007 in Washington.

POP SHOP RECORDS (OUR RECORD COMPANY)

Guy and I established Pop Shop Records, and recorded *"The Ballad of Resurrection Mary"* and *"50 Ways To Beat Your Lover"*, a parody of Paul Simon's song, *"50 Ways to Leave Your Lover."* We pressed 45-RPM records and actually sold a few. Guy wrote the lyrics and produced the music track that we recorded in Paul Serrano's south side recording studio. We also pressed a record with The Casualaires, a Chicago singing group. *"Rum and Coca Cola"* on the "A" side and *"Endless Love"* was on the flip side of the 45 RPM record. Nothing ever happened with the recordings. I think it might have been played on a few radio stations at the time but I can't remember.

THE TREE—(MOVIE)—OXFORD FILMS DISTRIBUTES IT

For several years, I had been shooting 16mm film of one particular tree near to the Lincoln Park Zoo. I had footage of the tree over several seasons. Guy and I edited the footage into a seven-minute film titled *The Tree* and I sold the distribution rights to Oxford Films, a subsidiary of Paramount Pictures Corporation for a 20% royalty fee. *The Tree* was distributed to elementary schools for use in language arts, science and ecology. I found a Paramount Communications sheet where I made $1,248 in royalties from this film in 1982. In 1983, Paramount must have sold its educational film holdings to Aims Media based at the same address location because I received a letter explaining about their computer reporting system.

The description in the Oxford Films catalog said, *"The Tree* presents a stimulating look at the seasonal changes of a mature tree during one year's time. The film visually captures and musically expresses the mood and splendor that surround a tree during each season. No narration is necessary. Lines, colors, shapes, patterns and special effects tell the entire story."

ORIGINAL MUSIC RECORDED IN KEN NORDINE'S ATTIC

Guy composed original music for the film with help from Gerry Smith and Brian Cook of *Smooch* (Guy's band). We recorded the soundtrack in Ken Nordine's attic recording studio on Chicago's N. Kenmore Avenue. Ken's son, Kevin, was the engineer on the project. Ken Nordine was a famous Chicago radio announcer and nationally known for a very distinctive style whose voice could be heard on Chicago's WFMT-FM radio. Ken created *"Word Jazz"* albums. He died in Chicago on February 16, 2019 at age 98.

520 N. MICHIGAN AVENUE OFFICE AND A BANK LOAN

Guy and I worked out of our 502 W. Briar Street apartment for most of the years we were in business, then for the last two years of our partnership in anticipation of getting more business, we rented a small office on the 13th floor of the 520 N. Michigan Avenue office building where we moved my KEM film editing machine. The building is now the location of Nordstrom.

In 1979, Guy and I took out a $10,000.00 loan at the Lake Shore National Bank to buy office furniture and had a custom-built credenza constructed to store books, films and tapes but after a year or so, Guy and I abandoned the office because of a lack of business. I was left with paying off the remainder of our loan that was about $7,000.00. I had the KEM moved to another Chicago editing studio and rented it to film editor John Fistler. On August 31, 1983, I sold the KEM to Gary Grand Pre for $7,500.00. Over the years I paid back Uncle Harry $8,500.00 of the $13,500.00 what he loaned me as he forgave the rest of my loan and a debt of $5,000.00 when he knew I was financially struggling.

SEPTEMBER 1981—ENDING A BUSINESS PARTNERSHIP

Working with advertising agencies was a frustrating experience in the first place. We could not meet with the client directly but had to go through advertising agency account executives or creative directors instead of the actual end client. I wanted to work directly with decision-makers and after five and one-half years of struggling to make a living, I had to earn a living to support my family, I decided to look for a real job! I began a job search after telling Guy I wanted to end our business relationship. Guy and I ended our business relationship in July 1981 and The Spot Shop was no more. Guy continued to produce a few projects on his own as Guy Guilbert Films. He was involved with creating a trilogy of production videos several animated short features that appeared on ABC's *America's Funniest Home Videos*; Jockey Bob, Bungy Bob and Ballerina Bob. Guy also composed, recorded and sang the music for the videos.

In March 1999, Guy permanently moved to Los Angeles and for a time was playing the piano for an improv group, *Off The Wall*. He continues with his painting that he started in 1995 while still living in Chicago.

CHAPTER FOURTEEN
Move To Northbrook

SATURDAY, FEBRUARY 3, 1979— SNOWSTORM MOVE

Penny and I thought it was time to move to Chicago's northern suburbs. Bennett's experience with Mrs. Baskin's kindergarten class at Chicago's Nettelhorst Public School was a positive one but we wanted our children to have a better education. Nettelhorst Public School was located at Broadway and Melrose about 4 blocks from our apartment. We didn't believe in private schools, nor did we have the money for one, so it was time to move to Chicago's northern suburbs.

In October 1978, we found a northern suburbs real estate agent, Mrs. Joyce Rubin and started looking for a house. I really wanted to live in Wilmette but didn't think we could afford a house there. The houses were close to $100,000 and our budget would not allow us to move into a house that expensive.

In the middle of December 1978, we looked in Northbrook at two houses on Midway Road and one house in the 800 block of Dell Road. We fell in love with the small house on Dell Road. The Wise family, who owned the house had just purchased a Northbrook condo and wanted to sell the house.

WE BOUGHT A NORTHBROOK HOUSE

On December 24, 1978, the day before Christmas, we put in an offer for the Dell Road house. It was originally listed for $88,000.00 but lowered to $84,000.00. Mrs. Rubin suggested offering $75,000.00 and we finally settled on $78,000.00. The Wises' had two mortgages and even wanted to throw in their old four-door Pontiac just to sell the house. Bell Federal Savings was our mortgage lender and after putting down $12,000 as a down payment, our mortgage payment was $411.00 a month. For the down payment, I had to borrow $7,000 from my sister's husband, Bruce Waldman. I signed a gift affidavit for a loan on January 2, 1979 and on May 2, 1986; the total loan was paid back to Bruce Waldman. I received a letter from Bruce dated May 5, 1986 thanking me for the last payment of $3,000 and stating that this amount repays in full the loan he made to me in January 1979.

The house is a tri-level with three small bedrooms and a bathroom up six stairs on the top level, a combination living room/dining room and kitchen on the middle level and a finished family room on the lower level with a bathroom, laundry room about half-way below ground with a crawl space and a door that is off the hallway near the entrance to the family room.

Our $78,000 offer was accepted on Christmas Day 1978 and we closed the end of January 1979. We hired Jack Raffe & Sons located at 4757 N. Harding Avenue in Chicago to move us into our new home. The moving van pulled up to our 502 West Briar Street apartment on Saturday, February 3, 1979. There had been a huge snowstorm a few days before our move, so our moving truck was parked in the middle of W. Briar Place for several hours loading our furniture, etc. and blocking our street to all traffic.

According to a Jack Raffe contract letter dated January 21, 1979, the initial estimate for the move was $314.00. The alley behind our apartment and our garage was completely blocked with snow and I hired two neighborhood boys to help me dig out the car from our garage. Since there was snow on the ground when we moved into the Northbrook house, we had no idea what was underneath the lawn or garden until the spring. It was a surprise to find a variety of flowers popping up in the front of the house when spring rolled around.

MARKET FACTS, INC. PART-TIME JOB

Our finances were very tight in 1979 as Guy and I weren't doing very well and extra funds were needed to pay our bills, so I decided to find a part-time job. I was hired at Market Facts, a research company located at 100 South Wacker Drive in Chicago. The company conducted telephone interviews on a variety of subjects; e.g., introduction of new products, public awareness of products, introduction of new packaging designs, building up store traffic, studying readership habits, political opinions and testing new products, to mention a few. I worked at the Market Facts office at 960 Grove in Evanston. Hope Kell was my Market Facts supervisor and the personnel director. There were two shifts: 8:00 a.m. to 3:30 p.m. and 4:00 to 10:00 p.m. I usually worked in the evenings. I wore a headset and was provided with a list of people to call and sheets of paper with standard interviewing rules, listing what to say and a list of daily responsibilities. This time was before computers so I had to write the answers on the questionnaire. I started on Monday evening August 13, 1979. I got my first paycheck on August 19 and after taxes I took home a total of $59.42. I was chosen for the training and development pool of editor/monitor. This promotion was awarded to me on the basis of my past interviewing record. The time of the training was Wednesday, December 5, 1979 at 5:30 p.m.

On February 18, 1980, I sent Hope Kell a letter requesting an indefinite leave of absence from Market Facts, Inc. because I would be starting teaching at Columbia College. I found the last pay stubs I found were from February 17, 1980.

SUMMER 1980—RONNA GOES TO MONTESSORI DAY CAMP

During the summer of 1980, Ronna went to Countryside Montessori day camp with Mika and Amy Onishi who were about Ronna's age. The cost of the day camp was $175.00. Hiro and Meoshi Onishi were living in Northbrook because Mr. Onishi worked at a Tokyo bank. One night they invited our family for a traditional Japanese dinner that was very interesting. The Onishi family lived two houses south of our home. Several years went by and the Onishis moved back to Japan and got divorced. For many years Penny kept up with Meoshi through letters and cards.

1980 TO 1981—COLUMBIA COLLEGE PART-TIME TEACHING

On August 6, 1979, I wrote a letter along with my resume to Tony Loeb, chairman of Columbia College's film department, asking for an interview for a part-time position teaching film in his department. I heard from Tony and a meeting was held with him on November 15, 1979. Another meeting with two film department faculty members, Jim Martin and Michael Rabinger was held on November 19, 1979. I was offered a job on a part-time basis to start the second semester of 1980 until the college found a full-time instructor.

I taught a Techniques II film course at Chicago's Columbia College for two semesters. The spring semester started on Saturday February 16, 1980 and ended on Saturday, June 7, 1980. The fall semester was from September 1980 and ended February 1981. The college was located in a twelve-story building at 600 South Michigan Avenue. The six credits description of the course was a continuation of Film Techniques I. Film Techniques II introduced sound to 16mm filmmaking. Students learned how to interview, how to shoot and edit sound, how to make a non-sync film with multiple tracks and how to use lighting equipment.

The fifteen-week class was held on Thursday evenings from 6:30 to 10:00 p.m. and on Saturdays from 11:00 a.m. to 5:00 p.m. with several breaks during the class. The textbook used in the course was *Cinematography* by Malkiewicz. I created pre-tests and study guides and tests and a 100-point grading system with various points based on attendance, attitude, effort and class participation, a group project, study guide and reading assignment, reports and written assignments and the individual film project. I made $1,800.00 a semester while teaching at Columbia College. The student tuition for the class was $235.00.

Michael Goi, an advanced film student, was hired to assist me with the class. Michael was extremely knowledgeable with the technical aspects of cameras, lenses, lighting and filmmaking. I on the other hand was most familiar with producing and editing. I basically left the technical parts for Michael to handle.

Michael graduated from Columbia and moved to Hollywood. He became a successful cinematographer, television and film director. He has written and directed two feature films during his career. Several years after I left teaching, one of my students, Diego Trejo, Jr. ending up running Columbia College's audio department.

CHAPTER FIFTEEN
Genealogy

(In 1980, I was a founding member of the Jewish Genealogical Society of Illinois)

In 1977, a mini-series was broadcast on network television, called *Roots*, written by African-American Alex Haley. It was an amazing series based on Haley's discovery of his African ancestors and the series inspired me to pursue my own Jewish roots. I started doing family research until February 1980 when I heard about a man named Stu Feiler who was giving a talk at the Morton Grove Public Library on Jewish genealogy. Stu was a teacher for Chicago's Board of Jewish Education and the first person to teach Jewish genealogy in high school. There was a dozen of us in attendance at that gathering.

Those who attended that genealogy meeting decided to meet the next week at Freya Maslov's house in Skokie, Illinois. At Freya's house, it was decided to form a Jewish genealogy group calling itself the Jewish Genealogical Society of Illinois of which I was a founding member and in charge of special projects. At the time, I believe the only two other Jewish genealogical societies were located in New York City and Washington, D.C.

GENEALOGICAL RESEARCH AT THE LDS LIBRARY

I started doing serious research by going to the Wilmette, Illinois Branch of the Church of Latter-Day Saints Library (LDS) or as it is most commonly known, the Mormon Church. The LDS library has microfilms available with specific records and I was able to find an index of microfilms that had records from Opatow, Poland. I ordered several of these microfilms from the main LDS library located in Salt Lake City and after several weeks the microfilms arrived at the Wilmette LDS branch. These microfilms listed my ancestors and I was able to make copies and translate the Polish civil records into English. The original microfilms are kept in a cave deep inside a mountain in Utah.

Over the years, the Mormon Church has painstakingly microfilmed hundreds of thousands of civil and church records from archives around the world. Among others, these microfilms contain Polish civil records. Now, many of these records have been cataloged and are available on-line. Part of the Mormon Church religion is to know who your relatives are so they can be *sealed* for eternity. Since the Mormon religion started around 1826 by Joseph Smith, genealogy is a large part of their religion.

INTERNATIONAL JOURNAL OF JEWISH GENEALOGY

During the summer of 1981, I created and became the first and only editor of *Search, International Journal of Jewish Genealogy* published by the Jewish Genealogical Society of Illinois and financially supported by membership dues. The journal was distributed around the world for eleven years from 1981 to 1992. The first issue came out in the fall of 1981. The journal published original research articles on how to successfully trace your Jewish ancestors.

I asked Scott Meyer, a fellow family researcher and one of the early members of the Jewish Genealogical Society of Illinois to by my Associate Editor. This was strictly a voluntary effort with the only reward of providing our subscribers with original material to help them find their Jewish roots. The front page of the first issue proclaimed that *Search is Born* and began with the realization that the Jewish genealogist was in need of a basic guide and research tool to trace their roots. It provided real access to proven research techniques, was a place to share practical ideas and acted as a reservoir of helpful tips that had been refined by others in their search for their Jewish descendants.

Scott and I published original articles that dealt with various aspects of tracing your Jewish roots. Our circulation grew over the years and we were quite successful having distributed the publication to various subscribers and libraries around the world, among them Harvard University Library in Cambridge, Massachusetts. When *Search* was started there were approximately thirteen Jewish Genealogical Societies in the world. As of this writing, I heard there are over seventy-five such worldwide Jewish genealogical societies.

1984 NATIONAL SEMINAR ON JEWISH GENEALOGY

From July 22 to July 25, 1984, Scott and I were deeply involved in the planning of the 1984 National Seminar on Jewish Genealogy held at the Holiday Inn on Sherman Avenue in Evanston, Illinois. The seminar was co-hosted by the Jewish Genealogical Society of Illinois and the Chicago Jewish Historical Society. Our steering committee came up with the name *Routes to Roots* of which I was a member. Seventeen Jewish genealogical societies participated in this event.

SEARCH ENDS PUBLICATION IN 1992

The burden and time-consuming elements of putting out an original research journal four times a year was too much and Scott and I agreed to stop publishing *Search* in 1992. The eleven-year run was a rewarding one and we received a great amount of recognition for our original work in the Jewish genealogy community.

INTERNATIONAL ASSOCIATION
OF JEWISH GENEALOGICAL SOCIETIES

I asked Scott Meyer, *Search's* Associate Editor, to recall the origins of how the International Association of Jewish Genealogical Societies was formed. During this time, Scott and I were instrumental with the formation of this organization that exists today and is bigger than either of us could imagine. The following is our recollection of the events leading up to the formation of this international group.

In 1986, Scott and I attended the Sixth National Seminar on Jewish Genealogy held in Salt Lake City, Utah and we became the catalyst in the formation of this international group. The following is Scott's take on the subject.

"Each year since the early 1980s, a conference on Jewish genealogy was held in a host city and was sponsored by the local Jewish genealogical society. The exception was when the conference was held in Salt Lake City, mostly because that city seldom had a strong local Jewish society. On those occasions, the conferences were run by a committee including members of large Jewish genealogical societies (Washington, D.C., New York and Los Angeles, etc.)

Usually offered at some point during each conference was a series of meetings for the presidents of the various Jewish societies in attendance. At that time, they could often discuss common concerns and share successes. Inevitably, someone would express the desire to form a more official organization made up of the presidents so that they could have a yearlong vehicle to express their concerns and help each other with ideas. In spite of the general acceptance of the concept, the annual presidents' meetings ended with no resolution of the issue.

It was also at these conferences that the editors of the various societies' periodicals met for similar reasons. Frustrated that the presidents had not been able to create an official yearlong mechanism to foster communication among the groups, the editors decided to act. With the late David Kleiman of the Washington, D.C. Jewish genealogical society at the helm and Alan Spencer of the Jewish Genealogical Society of Illinois as a second in command, they facilitated the discussions that led to a consensus: they would form an association of Jewish genealogical periodical editors! A document was drafted, and David and Alan requested time to speak before the presidents during one of their meetings, and the manifesto was read aloud.

The reading was not met with wild enthusiasm. "Shock" would be a better way of describing the reaction. In response, someone piped up, "Are you asking for our permission for that? "No," Alan said, "but we'd like your blessing!"

The fire had been lit under the outraged group and, shortly thereafter, they approved their own document, creating the Association of Jewish Genealogical Societies, AJGS for short (and several years later to be known as the International Association of Jewish Genealogical Societies).

And whatever came to be of the association of periodical editors? They continued to meet at annual conferences, but the organization mentioned in their radical manifesto never came to light, since it was no longer needed in light of the creation of the AJGS."

Today, The International Association of Jewish Genealogical Societies is an independent non-profit umbrella organization officially formed in 1988 to coordinate the activities and annual conference of nearly ninety national and local Jewish Genealogical Societies (JGS) around the world. The IAJGS as it is known, has held summer conferences in several international cities, Jerusalem having hosted two international conferences and Paris and London having hosted one conference each. The organization provides a common voice for issues of significance to its members, to advance our genealogical avocation and to coordinate items such as the annual International Jewish Genealogy Conference.

RABBI MALCOLM STERN

Scott and I became very friendly with Rabbi Malcolm H. Stern, widely considered to be the dean of American Jewish genealogy. His best-known book, *Americans of Jewish Descent: 600 Genealogies (1654-1988)* documents the genealogies of Jewish families that arrived during the American colonial and federal periods (1654-1838) tracing many families to the present. The third edition, published in 1991, lists some 50,000 individuals. This work was the basis for much of Stephen

Birmingham's best-selling book, *The Grandees*. Rabbi Stern wrote many articles for genealogical and historical publications. We were happy to have had a chance to meet and know Rabbi Stern who was 78 when he died in New York City on January 5, 1994.

ENCYCLOPEDIA OF JEWISH GENEALOGY, VOLUME I

Miriam Weiner is a noted Jewish genealogical researcher and Jewish genealogist. She is the first Jewish person to be certified by the Board for Certification of Genealogists. She along with Arthur Kurzweil, author of *From Generation to Generation: How to Trace Your Jewish Genealogy and Personal History*, was editing a new book. In developing the concept for this new book, Miriam and Arthur asked Scott Meyer and me to author and edit one chapter in *The Encyclopedia of Jewish Genealogy, Volume I: Sources in the United States and Canada*. Jason Aronson, Inc. published this new book in 1991.

In our capacity as editors of *Search*, Scott and I spent countless hours, long weekends and short deadlines compiling, updating and editing United States and Canada Jewish genealogical sources first published in *Search*. We wrote the introduction to Chapter 2 describing how to use the guide and chapters 2 and 3.

Dina Abramowicz, from New York City's YIVO Institute for Jewish Research wrote a review of the book that reads as follows: "*The Encyclopedia of Jewish Genealogy* is an extremely welcome addition to the growing field of Jewish genealogical research. It surveys the field in a very useful arrangement: by geographical areas and by topics, revealing unexpected but very important sources of Jewish genealogical information. The editors are pioneers and ardent promoters of genealogical research and their continuous involvement in the field assures the quality and reliability of their work. Also impressive is the selection of contributors. The publication will be an indispensable tool for all reference librarians."

By the way, YIVO was founded in 1925 in Vilna, Poland (Wilno, Poland, now Vilnius, Lithuania), as the Yiddish Scientific Institute. The YIVO Institute for Jewish Research is dedicated to the history and culture of Ashkenazi Jewry and to its influence in the Americas. Since 1940, the Institute is headquartered in New York City and today YIVO is the world's preeminent resource center for East European Jewish Studies.

THE INTERNET CHANGED RESEARCHING ANCESTORS

Today, tracing your Jewish roots is much easier because the Internet has provided some amazing sources of information. www.jewishgen.org is an amazing website specifically geared to tracing Jewish roots. This site has Jewish records from all over the world. Volunteers have spent many hours translating gravestones in Hebrew from various Jewish cemeteries in a variety of countries into English. These records are available on www.jewishgen.org and also myheritage.com

www.ancestry.com, another website, is also used but doesn't have specific Jewish information unless your Jewish ancestors have a long history in the United States. In recent years, ancestry.com has partnered with jewishgen.org and some of the information on the Jewish website is now available on ancestry.com. Other genealogical websites are also available but not specific to Jewish roots.

Genealogy is a wonderful hobby and I am still pursuing my Jewish ancestors and plan to one day publish my family's history on my father's side.

23 AND ME—DNA TEST

In 2016 I sent away for the 23andMe saliva collection genetic DNA test kit. I also paid extra to check out my medical part of the test. I first registered my 23andMe account online and waited for the analysis of my DNA test results and report. Several weeks went by and my email revealed my DNA report was online and ready to see. I found out I am 98.5% Ashkenazi Jewish with ancestry from 3 other populations. It showed that my DNA suggests that 0.1% of my ancestry is Eastern European as well as 0.1% Sardinian and 0.1% Filipino & Austronesian ancestry.

In 2017, I found out from Bonnie Minsky, my nutritionist, that the raw data that was initially collected from my DNA sample could be downloaded to Bonnie's office. Bonnie's son Steve Minsky was able to insert my raw data into a computer program that further analyzed my results and let me know what areas of my DNA could use improvements. The eleven-page color printout listed in a detailed analysis every Gene of my DNA, What it means, Clinical Priority, Scientific rating, Assessment Recommendations, Diet and Lifestyle Recommendations and Supplement Recommendations. Also, people related to me through DNA started to be listed and I was able to contact several cousins. I did find a third cousin, Shelly Mesznik, who is related to me through my two-times great-grandfather on my father's side of the family. First, I emailed Shelly, and then we actually spoke on the phone. I spoke to her mother about twenty-five years ago but lost contact with her side of the family.

ANCESTRY.COM—DNA TEST

About the same time, I took a DNA test from 23andMe, I also ordered a saliva kit from ancestry.com. The results were about the same saying I was 100% Eastern European Jewish, primarily located in Poland, Romania, Belarus, Ukraine, Russia, Hungary and Israel. No medical information was given. People who are related to me through DNA were listed and I contacted a few but could not find a connection.

DNA RAW DATA RESULTS UPDATED IN NOVEMBER 2019

On November 19, 2019 I had my annual Bonnie Minsky nutritional consultation and found out that the raw data from my initial DNA test had a new updated twenty-three-page analysis. While I was still in a session with Bonnie, her son Steve printed a copy for me. Bonnie went over each of the updated pages and made written comments and notes in the margins.

AN AMAZING GENEALOGICAL DISCOVERY STORY

As the self-appointed family historian and family genealogist, I have been tracing both Penny's family and my side of the family since 1977. Over the years, several individuals have contacted me trying to connect with my family. They found me by going on jewishgen.org where I have listed many of our ancestor's family surnames. The website maintains old birth, marriage and death records from a variety of European countries. These records usually list the father and mother's names and many times the ages at marriages and deaths, many with specific dates. Some of the Warsaw Jewish cemetery records have been translated by volunteers and that information is available on the jewishgen.org website. This is how I have been able to trace the Turkus and Czernikowski families. For instance, I did not know grandma Rose's mother's name (great-grandma Turkus) is actually Perla Ryfka. She went by Pearl in America. Also, Norman and I used to tease her.

In early October 2019, a woman found my name on jewishgen.org and emailed me saying she was looking for the Turkus family from Warsaw. She was a descendant of a Turkus and wondered if we might be related. She also told me her daughter had gone on *23 and Me* and was listed as Amy B. Since I did the *23 and Me* and the ancestry.com DNA tests, I saw her daughter's name on my list as sharing 1.13 % DNA, so I knew we were related but I didn't know how.

After much back and forth over several days, sharing family charts and names, it turns out we have a new 5th cousin. Her name is Elaine Farran and we share the very same TURKUS 5th great-grandparents who are Eljasz TURKUS born in 1735 in Warsaw and his wife Frymet (LAST NAME?) born?

Elaine lives in New York near JFK Airport, is 75 years old and has 3 children and spends the winter in Boca Raton, Florida with her husband Bill. Her children are our 5th cousins, once removed. After all of these years, this is a very exciting discovery for our Turkus family and me.

Also, through 23 and Me, I connected with a 3rd cousin, Shelly Mesznik. Shelly is a descendant of our Czernikowski three-times great-grandparents. I had actually spoken with Shelly's mother about twenty-five years ago but never followed up with Shelly. I called Shelly in the fall of 2019 and hopefully we might be able to meet because her daughter and grandchild live in Chicago's Lakeview neighborhood.

OUR TURKUS FAMILY FROM WARSAW RE-CONNECTS

Although this book stops with my life in 2019, I must add this amazing happening in February 2021 before this book is published. My second cousin, Anita Carroll, who lives in a Seattle, Washington suburb, gave me the email and phone number of Dan Spiro, my second cousin, once removed who lives in London, England and is eighty-eight years old. Dan is my oldest living relative and is a Turkus descendant whose mother was my grandma Rose's first cousin. Dan has a daughter Suzanne who lives in Milan, Italy with her husband Elio Galante and their two daughters, Naomi and Sarah.

I emailed Dan and we started to correspond. Dan also called me several times at our Scottsdale condo and he sent me many family photos that I already had from my great aunt Marie's photo album. I decided it would be a great idea to reunite the Turkus family by creating a Zoom meeting with the family.

I called Elaine Farran, my fifth cousin and told her about our newly discovered Turkus family from London and Milan. Elaine was very excited and created a simple side-by-side chart that explained her part of the Turkus family and our relationship. Elaine sent the chart to each of the Zoom participants before our Zoom meeting.

TURKUS FAMILY ZOOM

On Saturday, February 13, 2021 at 10:30 a.m. Scottsdale time, 12:30 p.m. eastern time, 5:30 p.m. London time and 6:30 p.m. Milan time, the Turkus family had fourteen family members on a Zoom meeting. The Turkus family participants were Cousin Dan Spiro from London, his daughter Suzanne and her daughters Naomi and Sarah from Milan, Italy, Anita Carroll from Beaux Arts, Washington, Marilyn Levy from Santa Monica, California, Bruce and Suzyn Epstein from Youngstown, Ohio, Linda Waldman from Beachwood, Ohio, Norman and Sheila Lockshin from Rockville, Maryland and Elaine and her husband Bill Farran from Boca Raton, Florida. The Zoom meeting was an amazing experience and hopefully we will do it again in the near future.

It was wonderful to re-connect with distant relatives and my genealogical hobby had been extremely rewarding over the years. I've been able to keep in touch with many of our relatives and my genealogical computer program, Reunion, has helped me keep track of many of my ancestors and current family members from both Penny and my family.

CHAPTER SIXTEEN
Williams/Gerard Productions, Inc.

OCTOBER 1981 TO APRIL 2017—MY THIRD CAREER

During the summer of 1981, I told my business partner Guy Guilbert, I wanted to leave our production company because of a variety of reasons. Besides having little business, I became frustrated working with advertising agencies. Guy and I could never speak directly to the end client or the decision makers. Advertising agency producers would award us an assignment and spend time giving us input on each project. On some occasions, what we produced, the agency liked but the end client did not like, so changes had to be made to what the agency approved.

So, at age forty and one-half, I wanted to find a company I could join where I would use the skills I learned as a producer at The Spot Shop and work directly with decision-makers as well as provide me with a steady income for my growing family. In August 1981 I scheduled an interview with Creative Director Jim Finger at Chicago's Jack Morton Productions. The company produced corporate sales meetings, association conventions and banquet entertainment. On occasion films or videos were also produced. Jim told me that Jack Morton did not have any job openings but he suggested I call Williams/Gerard Productions.

In the middle of September 1981, I made a cold-call to Williams/Gerard's Chicago office in the Time-Life building and spoke to company president Bill Walsh. Bill told me he wasn't looking for anyone at this time but he transferred my call to partner Bud Melto. I told Bud my qualifications and he also said the company wasn't looking for anyone. He also told me they were always interested in speaking with someone who knows how to produce. So, I was invited to come to the office for an interview with Bud.

During my interview with Bud, I told him the following: "I have never been to a convention or sales meeting and I have no clients in your industry. I know how to produce; I know how to sell and I will make your company a lot of money and I want to retire from Williams/Gerard." Bud said I convinced him but he wanted me to meet his two other Chicago partners.

A few days later I was invited for a second interview to meet Chicago partners, Bill Walsh, the President and Bill Phebus, the Secretary/Treasurer. The morning interview in their conference room went very well and immediately afterwards I took a train home to Northbrook. Around 6:00 p.m., later that day I received a call from Bud asking me to join the company. Since they did not have an office for me, Bud suggested I start right after New Years on Monday January 4, 1982. I told them I didn't need an office and would use the telephone in the conference room as my temporary office but preferred to start on Thursday, October 1 and Bud agreed. So, I began working at Williams/Gerard as a producer on Thursday October 1, 1981 with no office. Instead, I used the conference room as my office for the first few days. It wasn't long before I had my own office and became successful selling new clients on our services and producing shows.

MY FIRST SHOW AT WILLIAMS/GERARD

In the beginning of November 1981, just a few weeks after I started working at Williams/Gerard, audiovisual technician and programmer Steve Dennison and I traveled to San Francisco where we set up a show. The client was the Data Processing Management Association (DPMA) Annual Convention held at the Civic Center in San Francisco. My client was John Venator, Deputy Director of DPMA. Another producer, Paul Fagen, who was fired just before I started working at WG, had originally had DPMA as his client. When I started working, the DPMA project was turned over to me and I had to jump right in without any experience. Steve Dennison programmed 35mm slides with twelve slide projectors in Chicago and supervised the equipment set-up using a San Francisco-based union crew. Onsite client rehearsals were held and Steve operated the backstage slide projectors during the meeting, Steve was a good teacher and I quickly learned when to have him run the pre-produced slide modules.

A BRIEF HISTORY OF WILLIAMS/GERARD

Started in business on February 1, 1976, Williams/Gerard Productions, Inc. was a privately held business communications and special events production company based in Chicago and located on the thirtieth floor in the Time-Life Building at 303 E. Ohio Avenue. The company also produces entertainment for banquets held during the conventions and film and videotapes whenever the opportunity exists. The company was formed by three partners, William Walsh, William Phebus and Gerard (Bud) Melto; hence, Williams/Gerard. Each of the men had worked as producers for Jack Morton Productions specializing in entertainment and audiovisual productions for associations and corporations.

There was a separate satellite office of Williams/Gerard in Arlington, Virginia owned by Dan Cullather and Doug DeRosa. They had also worked as producers for Jack Morton's Washington office and eventually merged their operations and accounting into W/G's Chicago office so there were five original partners.

In 1984, Williams/Gerard Productions, Inc. moved its production office to the fifth floor of an old brick building behind the Wrigley Building at 420 N. Wabash Avenue. Chicago's famous Shaw's Crabhouse had not yet moved into their space on the lower level of our building. Over the years, WG became one of the country's largest independent production companies specializing in business communications, special events, entertainment, videos/DVD productions, trade shows and marketing productions. For over 36 years, I produced conventions, sales meetings, special events, awards programs, video productions and entertainment for corporations and associations. I traveled around the United States and Toronto, Ontario producing these shows at resort hotel locations in Florida, California and Arizona cities. Penny eventually retired as a pre-school teacher and traveled with me to many of my produced conferences.

FIRST ANNUAL DINNER/DANCE/AWARDS PROGRAM

On Saturday evening, December 6, 1996, Williams/Gerard celebrated its twentieth anniversary in business with a dinner party and entertainment held at Chicago's Shedd Aquarium. The company brought together the three office staffs (Chicago, Washington, D.C. and New Jersey) for the event. Family members joined the party for the first time. The weather was absolutely freezing the night of the party and was one of the coldest days that winter with temperatures in single digits. Penny and I had to park away from the Shedd Aquarium and we were frozen solid by the time we walked to the party. Singer and impressionist Gordy Brown provided the entertainment along with a small band. There was plenty of catered food and lots of fun seeing everyone.

At one time, Williams/Gerard operated a 20,000 square foot Scene Shop facility in Broadview, Illinois. It was a valuable asset that provided our clients with a unique capability to assure superior quality, creativity control and cost effectiveness from the initial concept development through the completion of a show. The scene shop produced custom-designed scenery for some sixty-five to seventy shows a year. Phil Huber headed the shop and his associate, Rick Arnold, and I used the scene shop many times over the years. The shop eventually closed and moved into a smaller facility located on Chicago's Kingsbury Street. WG eventually closed the scene shop when the economy fell apart after September 11, 2001. The Broadview scene shop was also the location of our WG Sound Division. The company owned a full theatrical sound system. Glenn Churan was the manager of the Sound Division with his right-hand man, Robert "Bear" Davidson. Bear was a true craftsman who designed and built some of the most acoustically perfect sound systems available anywhere. On larger shows, this equipment was trucked around the country with Glenn as the audio engineer.

In late 1996, WG added a recording studio and CD/DVD production capabilities on the fifth floor. We went to digital recording instead of analog recording that had used audiotape. Digital recording allowed for a tremendous savings through time reduction with a superior audio output. In 1997, responding to increased business and the ongoing commitment to provide clients with the latest technology and innovative services. WG also expanded its Chicago headquarters by 33% with our computer graphics department taking additional space on the seventh floor. A New York City office was opened at 11 Penn Avenue and later moved to an office on Broadway.

AUDIOVISUAL INDUSTRY—1981 UNTIL EARLY 1990s

When I first started working at Williams/Gerard, we produced 35mm slides for our clients and showed them on multi-image 35mm Kodak carousel slide projectors. The standard number of projectors was twelve run by a simple computer program. The company owned all of the slide projectors and traveled them in road cases to every show we produced. Sometimes there would be twenty cases that would travel on airplanes as excess baggage. Airport skycaps would love seeing us when we pulled up to the curb because they would make enormous tips when they saw us with all of our cases.

In the 1970s, 80s and 90s, Audio Visual Laboratories (AVL for short) built a line of computerized multi-image slide show programmers that were the standard machines used in the "A/V business." The AVL Show Pro III and an AVL Dove Multi-Image AV computer were small units that made 35mm slide projectors show different slides to make panoramic images on a rear-projection screen. WG had technicians on our staff that made their living by programming 35mm slide projectors into multi-image shows.

Today multi-images with slide projectors are dead, 35mm slides have disappeared and all the people who were involved in producing and staging these shows are now working with other technologies, mainly digital slides, programmed in Microsoft PowerPoint or Apple's Keynote and shown to large audiences on sophisticated and powerful video projectors.

During the heyday of 35mm multi-image slide shows, Williams/Gerard produced shows with various themes and we sold them as customized modules. Sometimes the themes had a narration track with music and others with music only. These modules, as we called them, had original music tracks that could be customized with client supplied photos or on-site candid photos. Clients would rent these modules and show them at their conventions or sales meetings.

A few titles of these modules were as follows: *The Good Life*, *America* by Neil Diamond, *The Mobius Strip*, *The Future is Now*, *We're Building the Best*, *The National Anthem*, *The Decade*, *God Bless the USA* by Lee Greewood, *The Peak Performers*, etc.

During this time, WG staff members shot 35mm slides using a Marron Carrel animation stand and our company had our own 35mm darkroom set-up on the west side of the office to process all of the slides we produced. We also moved to an additional 2,288 square foot space on the fourth floor in early 1988. The space was used for a shooting stage, library and technician offices for Eric Root and Jim Gross. At one time WG had a LaGrange warehouse that stored all of our audio and audiovisual equipment as well as a scene shop on Chicago's Kingsbury Street.

The industry started to change and in 1987 WG invested in a Dicomed Producer XP design station for the creation and production of 35mm slides. It was the first computer-generated system automating the production of 35mm slides. Also, around this time, we produced our first all video meeting with no 35mm slides. In the late 1980s, video projection and digital slides created on a computer started to replace 35mm slides and multi-media slide projectors disappeared from shows. Digital images were now used instead of 35mm slides. Video projectors also became brighter and more powerful. In the beginning, light valve video projectors such as the GE 5055 became the standard in the industry and were used for many years. These video projectors only had 1300 lumens brightness with new lamps that are not very bright compared to the video projectors used today.

In 1988, I produced the Outboard Marine Corporation dealer meeting *OMC TODAY* at the Chicago Hilton and Towers. I had to bring in an Eidophor video projector in order to have a bright image on the screen. This monster projector weighted hundreds of pounds, required a highly trained technician and provided a very bright picture on the front projection screen from a long distance. Today, video projectors are smaller, less expensive and are much brighter than the Eidophor of yesteryear.

Up until May 1999, we used a Vista computer system to create digital slides. The system was based on using personal computers (PCs) instead of Apple's Macintosh computers. The decision to use a TVL Director 4 system over by our Vista system was driven by the desire to produce shows in a 16 by 9 format instead of the standard 4 x 3 video aspect ratio. The new TVL system had a resolution of 1024 X 768. Another reason we abandoned the Vista system is because this system is no longer being manufactured or repaired.

THURSDAY, FEBRUARY 3, 1983—MY FIRST PHOENIX TRIP

This morning was the first time flying to Phoenix and exploring Scottsdale, Arizona. Phoenix's Sky Harbor Airport's Terminal 2 was located in one small building at the west end of the airport. It was the only terminal in the airport. The car rentals were located directly outside on the east side of Terminal 2, just steps from baggage claim and the exit doors. For a large metropolitan city, I couldn't believe the airport terminal was so small. My first impressions of Phoenix and Scottsdale were absolutely awesome. So, on a warm February day in 1983, I flew into Phoenix, rented a car and was on my way to producing my first Scottsdale meeting at Marriott's Camelback Inn on Lincoln Avenue. The client was General Life Insurance Company of Milwaukee, Wisconsin. Little did I realize that my first trip to Phoenix/Scottsdale would turn into a love affair with the desert and the southwestern United States.

From the airport, driving north on 44th Street, it curved around to McDonald Drive. As soon as I turned the corner, for the very first time I came upon Camelback Mountain on the right side of the road. WOW! What an unbelievable view and feeling came over me! Camelback Mountain was breathtaking and I immediately thought of Penny and how I wished she were here with me at that very moment to share this amazing experience. At this point McDonald turned into North Tatum Boulevard and I kept driving north a short distance when I turned right on Lincoln Drive. I arrived almost immediately at Marriott's Camelback Inn on the north side of Lincoln Drive. I later found out the Camelback Inn was built in 1936 and was the first luxury resort built in Scottsdale, Arizona. When it was built, there was nothing around it but wide-open space.

During this first trip to Phoenix, there were no expressways and lots of patches of open land yet to be developed for a variety of uses. Houses were relatively inexpensive and the influx of people moving into the Valley of the Sun was just starting to really happen.

A few years later Penny was able to join me for a meeting I was producing in Scottsdale at the Camelback Inn and since that time, we have spent a great deal of days vacationing and relaxing in this desert paradise. (There is more to follow later in this book).

MARTY WAITZMAN, WILLIAMS/GERARD AND EXERCISES

Soon after moving to 420 N. Wabash from the Time-Life Building, Marty Waitzman was hired to be the Comptroller of Williams/Gerard. Marty was a former suburban policeman and a part-time law student who worked for the Certified Public Accounting firm of Blackman Kallick. One of Marty's assignments was to look over WG's accounting books. At the time, Jeanne Anderson was a one-person accounting department. Marty decided to leave Blackman Kallick and started working full-time for WG as its comptroller. He lived in a Wheeling, Illinois townhouse in the Inverness neighborhood off of Milwaukee Avenue, just south of Deerfield Parkway and drove to the office each day. He had to pass by my house on the way, so we decided to carpool and he picked me up each morning.

Marty convinced me to start doing some exercises and we both joined the Downtown health club directly across the street from our office. We would get up early and use the exercise machines but it was nothing strenuous. There was a track around the perimeter of the club and I started walking for exercise.

A WILLIAMS/GERARD HOLIDAY PARTY

Williams/Gerard used to hold our winter holiday parties in our office and in December 1983 I can remember one particular one Marty and I attended. WG hired a bartender who was mixing a variety of cocktails for the attendees. The drink of the night was a "Screaming Organism" that consisted of vodka, amaretto and Bailey's Irish Cream. The Bailey camouflaged the taste of the drink. I started sipping this cocktail and before I knew what was happening, I became very quiet and I was propping up the wall. I could hardly move. No one knew I was drunk and I asked Marty very quietly if he was ready to leave the party.

When I arrived home, Ronna said to Penny, "what's wrong with Daddy?" I was so drunk; I went immediately to bed and didn't wake up until the next day when I had such a hangover and my head was spinning. The only other time I had consumed as much alcohol was at my Cousin Fred Weily's fiftieth birthday party in Youngstown when I was a freshman at Ohio University. This family incident was in a previous chapter.

Around 1986, Marty finished law school and decided to leave Williams/Gerard for a private law practice, so WG was looking for a replacement. I recommended Paul Hurder, a Dell Road neighbor, who worked in the accounting office of the *Chicago Sun-Times* newspaper. It took a while, but Paul finally got an interview with the Chicago partners and was hired as WG's comptroller in 1986. Paul and his wife Betty had two children, Adam and Jordan at the time and we would spend New Year's at their house each year. Penny knew Betty Hurder from a neighborhood Mom's playgroup. Jan Aver was also a member of this playgroup with her son Aaron who was Ronna's age.

MONDAY, FEBRUARY 20, 1984— FLORIDA FISHING

I was producing an IFMA meeting at the Fontainebleau Hilton Hotel and Steve Dennison was my technician on the show. We had an afternoon off, so I invited Steve to go deep-sea fishing with me on a charter off of Miami Beach. We had success and caught Amberjack averaging about twenty pounds each.

BENNETT AND RONNA GROWING UP

As a matter of course, our bedtime ritual was to read stories to the children before they went to bed. We never had any difficulty with either Bennett or Ronna wanting to go to bed. It was a peaceful and relaxing time for them and us.

When Bennett was very young, Penny and I would have to go through a variety of songs before he would go to sleep. We even made-up songs. One of them was *Raggedy Ann and Raggedy Andy Are You Sleeping?* In the summer of 1982, when Bennett was ten years old and Ronna was seven, they both went to Decoma Day Camp and took the bus there.

On one particular bedtime occasion, when Ronna was in second grade, I was really tired and I asked Ronna to read me a bedtime story and she did. I was fast asleep in a matter of minutes and Ronna talked about this experience for many years. Ronna also liked to walk on my back because it felt good. In elementary school, she started gymnastics lessons and really liked it. She competed on the Glenbrook High School girl's gymnastics team, as did Bennett on the boys' team.

JULY 1984—A FAMILY TRIP TO THE CONCORD RESORT

Pa Sam treated our family to a weekend at the famous Concord Resort in Lake Kiamesha, New York about thirty minutes north of Aunt Sadie and Uncle Harry's summer home in Highview. I can't remember the details of this trip but I think our family drove to Cleveland, spent the night with Pa Sam and Grandma Deah, and then drove in separate cars to The Concord. Sandi, Larry, Doug and Mara drove there as well as Lois, Roy, Aaron and Leah drove from Boston and all of us met at the hotel. There was a game room where all of the children hung out. The Saturday evening entertainment was comedian Buddy Hackett.

SATURDAY AUGUST 25, 1984—HIGH SCHOOL REUNION

The Boardman High School class of 1959 had not had a reunion since 1969. I decided I wanted to attend the 1984 reunion so Penny and I to drove to Cleveland on Friday, August 24 and stayed overnight with Linda in Beachwood. Linda graduated Boardman High School in 1961 and she also decided to attend since multiple classes were invited to this reunion. On Saturday, August 25 the three of us drove to Boardman for the reunion that included a formal buffet dinner, the *Just the Two of Us* band, a program and a class photograph (cost $7.00) arranged and planned by our class president, Don Samuels. Linda, Penny and I had a good time. The dinner was held at Mr. Anthony's, a popular Boardman restaurant. The cost of the dinner was fifty dollars per couple with an open bar. After the reunion, we drove back to Cleveland. At the time, Bennett was twelve years old and Ronna was nine. Since we were away for only the evening, we left Bennett and Ronna at Linda's home while we were at the reunion. On Sunday, we drove to Northbrook.

OCTOBER 1984—FIRST VIDEOCAMERA/RECORDER

My first videotape camera came in two-parts. The RCA camera was separate from the RCA video recorder. I bought it from Highland Park's Columbia Audiovisual and it was shipped directly from RCA Consumer Electronics in Indianapolis, Indiana to our house. It was cumbersome to operate because the recorder went over your shoulder while you held the bulky camera and both the camera and recorder were heavy.

A MILD CASE OF CROHN'S DISEASE

In April 1984, I was losing weight and my appetite was non-existent. I went to see our internist, Dr. Arnold Grauer, who examined me and suspected I might have Crohn's disease. Dr. Grauer sent me to see a specialist, Dr. Howard Schacter, a gastroenterologist, at Northwestern Memorial Hospital.

On June 28, 1984, I had a colon barium enema and a series of tests, an MRI and a physical examination by Dr. Schacter. I was diagnosed with a very mild form of Crohn's disease. I was put on a very small dose of Prednisone and took the drug for four years. The drug makes you very hungry and I gained a little weight especially showing in my face that became a little puffy. Penny was the only one in our family who knew I had the disease, as I didn't tell anyone.

In the early summer of 1988, my disease and all of my symptoms totally disappeared. I actually became very thin while being weaned off of Prednisone and the drug was doing weird things to my body. I was actually taken off the drug too quickly because every muscle and bone in my body ached. For several months I was very sensitive and walked like an old man. I wasn't feeling like I had to eat. After this incident I never took Prednisone again.

Since 1988, I have had no signs of the disease except once in a while I have a full feeling on the lower right side of my abdomen near my stomach. Other than that, I am very healthy. In 1996, when I turned 55, I had a colonoscopy given by Dr. Schacter. The test showed my bowel was clear of any Crohns disease and my colon was given a clean bill of health. Since then, I've had several colonoscopies and all were normal. My last colonoscopy was on Monday, May 20, 2019 performed by Dr. David Shapiro at Lake Forest Northwestern University Hospital and my colon was clear with no signs of polyps.

CHAPTER SEVENTEEN
My Dad Gets Sick

(The following is adapted from my mother's autobiography.)

"David retired from teaching in June 1982 at age 70 and we drove to Denver for his check-up that was fine. In 1983, the following winter, we rented an apartment in Satellite Beach, Florida near Melbourne and his friend Mike chose it for us. It did not have a phone or TV and was not in the best shape. We, ourselves, would not have chosen it.

THURSDAY, FEBRUARY 24, 1983

While staying there, David began to hemorrhage from the mouth. Luckily Alan had just arrived from Miami Beach where he had finished producing, COEX 83 at the Fontainebleau Hotel for the International Foodservice Manufacturers (IFMA). He just happened to be staying with us on his way from Miami Beach to produce a meeting for Travenol Laboratories at Saddlebrook Hotel north of Tampa.

My next-door neighbor called 911 and Dr. Gardner, a specialist who was on duty at the Melbourne Regional Hospital that night, saved his life. He went into a hepatic coma for five days and was in the hospital a total of eighteen days all together. Linda, along with Todd and Andrew, were in Ft. Lauderdale, Florida visiting her mother-in-law, Edith Waldman. She and the Dorothy and Morris Lockshin were living in Pompano, Florida and came the next day. David recuperated at the apartment and Dr. Gardner said to go to the Cleveland Clinic on our return to Ohio. We came home on April 7 by plane and Mike drove our car back to Youngstown. My children, as usual, were wonderful and still are. At the Clinic, they said the bleeding was from his liver. He had sclerotherapy in his throat to seal off the bleeding. He appeared to recover but for the next two years, he was in and out of the Cleveland Clinic and St. Elizabeth Hospital in Youngstown.

It was Valentine's Day and I went to a luncheon at the temple. David was home sick. It was a lovely day. I was standing outside the temple building talking to a few women. The next thing I knew, I was lying on the ground. One of the women was a nurse, Pinky Ehrlich. She saw my left wrist and decided to take me to the hospital. Four x-rays found out I fractured it. I don't remember what was done then exactly. I made Pinky go back to the luncheon. I finally returned there. Pinky wanted to take me home, but I was worried about Dad seeing me so early so I stayed until the luncheon was over. It took months to heal. I had to used paraffin baths to help lessen the pain.

On one occasion, the Cleveland Clinic sent Dad home with a thrombosis in his arm on May 13,1984 that required three months of doctoring before it healed. His condition worsened in April 1985. David lost weight and looked bad but he didn't give up. His stomach was very extended and itched. After months of badgering by Alan who kept on saying we should get another doctor's opinion, Dr. Larry Wolkoff suggested we take him to Metropolitan General Hospital in

Cleveland and set up an appointment with Dr. Anthony Tavel, a Jewish doctor from London, who was practicing at the hospital.

Dr. Tavel immediately admitted David into the hospital for tests and his condition rapidly deteriorated. Since David was in the hospital and Bennett's Bar Mitzvah was rapidly approaching, Bruce Waldman asked for a divorce. Linda and I told Dad. If I had known he would not live to go to Bennett's Bar Mitzvah, I would not have told him. David was in the Metropolitan General Hospital for eighteen days when he died on Saturday May 18, 1985, one week before Bennett's Bar Mitzvah. Most of his hospital stays were for eight days or had the number eight in them.

The Youngstown gravediggers had a union and did not work on Sundays so the funeral was held on Monday, May 20. Dave's sister, Gert, was in Italy with her third husband, Phil Weiner. She asked me before she went if she should go. I told her to make her own decision. Norman, Dorothy and Morris, Arleen and Joe came from all the family. I was hurt for Dad."

TUESDAY, MARCH 5, 1985 (from a letter I wrote to my parents)

This week and next are a real bear! I am making four major presentations and am jammed up with work. Two of the pitches will be on the East Coast. I'll be in Manhattan next Tuesday to talk to the Telephone Pioneers and MacGregor/Riddell in East Rutherford, New Jersey on Wednesday. In January, MacGregor purchased Riddell and I'll be producing their show in Chicago in September.

TUESDAY, MAY 7, 1985 (from a letter I wrote to my parents)

I'm finally getting around to mailing the picture of myself in the red dinner jacket. Hope the enclosed cheers both of you up a bit. I leave for Vancouver on Saturday afternoon, returning on Thursday evening, May 16. Our family spent the entire weekend preparing for Bennett's Bar Mitzvah, working around the house and attending to last minute details.

SATURDAY, MAY 25, 1985—BENNETT'S BAR MITZVAH

Bennett's Bar Mitzvah was on Saturday morning, May 25 at Northfield's Temple Jeremiah. Bennett shared the bimah with Jonathan Carson. Bennett did a terrific job and made us all proud. My mother went to Bennett's Bar Mitzvah alone, a week after my Dad died with my sister Linda and her two sons, Todd and Andrew. It was both a sad and happy occasion.

Bennett's Bar Mitzvah reception and dinner were held in the Chaparral Room at the Marriott's Lincolnshire Resort about twenty minutes northwest of our Northbrook home. Rich Coffey, a man I worked with at Williams/Gerard, set up a six foot by nine-foot rear-projection screen and a four-tier set up of Kodak slide projectors with three-inch lenses. The hotel stacked three twelve-inch risers on top of each other and a thirty-inch-high banquet table on top of the risers so the stack of four projectors would be high enough to show on the rear-projection screen. Two sets of carry-off black drapes masked off the screen. This professional looking set up was for a slide show with music I put produced showing Bennett from birth to recent times. I also sent the hotel a detailed diagram showing how I wanted the room arranged.

Our Cleveland, Youngstown and New York relatives attended. We hired the six-piece Michael Lerich Orchestra for the reception but we requested that there would be no dancing because of my father's recent passing.

TUESDAY, JUNE 18, 1985 (from a letter I wrote to my mother)

Dear Mom, My show in New Orleans was a huge success. I was there for such a short time; I didn't see anything and never left the hotel. I wrote to Isadore Askenzy about Dad. I am enclosing a check toward the permanent light in the Temple for Dad. The meeting I am referring to was from June 20 to 23 for the Credit Union Executive Society of Madison, Wisconsin's Marketing Conference and Annual Convention at the New Orleans Hilton in New Orleans, Louisiana. My client is Jeanne Klemm, Vice President.

SATURDAY, JULY 29, 1985 (from a letter sent to my mother)

Bennett and I played golf at Northbrook's Sportsman's Golf Course. He's getting better and out drives me on many occasions.

MONDAY, OCTOBER 3, 1985 (from a post card I sent to my mother)

I'm sitting in the General Session of the Power Transmission Distributor's Association at the Hyatt Regency San Francisco. I will be producing their 1986 convention at the New York Hilton Hotel from October 26 to 29, 1986. I'm an observer here to see how their New York meeting can be upgraded. From all indication, it will be very easy to upgrade. They need lots of help. I saw Seth Kaufman and his family yesterday.

On July 8, 1985 my mother signed over the title to my father's 1982 Buick Century Limited two-door coupe to me. The car had 28,100 miles on it. I drove the car for three years until Bennett turned 16, then I gave the car to him when he was a sophomore in high school.

CHAPTER EIGHTEEN
Family, Children, Life and Arizona

JANUARY 1986—RONNA TAKES GYMNASTICS LESSONS

When Ronna was age eleven, was taking gymnastic lessons at Northbrook Gymnastics on Techny Road. She eventually was on the Glenbrook North gymnastics team and Penny and I would go to every meet to see her compete. Bennett was also on the Glenbrook North boys gymnastics team and we went to every meet to see him complete.

SATURDAY, AUGUST 23, 1986—GOLF LESSONS FOR TWO

I signed up for golf lessons with golf professional, Bev Miller. I think it was through Sportsman Golf Course but not sure. I might have taken two lessons but can't remember. Bennett was 14 years old and I introduced Bennett to golf when he was 10 years old. I started playing golf as a teenager at the Mill Creek Golf Course in Boardman, Ohio. At Sportsman's, Rich Aver and I used to play as well as Bennett and me.

MONDAY, JUNE 9, 1986—ORIGINAL TRUSTS CREATED

I hired attorney Bob Brookman, from the law firm of Goldberg, Kohn, Bell, Black, Rosenbloom & Moritz to create trust documents, wills and living wills for Penny and me. All the documents were signed in Bob's office on Monday, June 9, 1986. A Living Will Declaration was also created and signed on Thursday, June 12, 1986. Bob also created an irrevocable insurance trust for Penny. Penny is listed as the trustee of my Northwestern Mutual life insurance policy. That trust was drawn up and signed in Bob's office on Thursday, June 26, 1997. On the same day, Penny and I signed a Restatement of the Trust originally signed on Monday, June 9, 1986.

On Friday, November 25, 2016, Penny and I signed an Illinois Statutory Short Form Power of Attorney for Health Care. Attorney Richard W. Mortell, Jr. reviewed our original trust documents and created the new document that we both signed in his Northbrook office.

SEPTEMBER 1986—BENNETT, B'NAI BRITH & HAIRCUTS

Bennett was age 14 and joined B'Nai Brith where he met many friends, some lasting into his adulthood. He also got his haircuts at Tom & Rich for $7.50. Tom & Rich was located on Northbrook's Shermer Road. During this time, Penny also attended Northbrook Symphony concerts.

FEBRUARY 1987—MET ALLAN LAMAGNA IN TUCSON

While producing a Keebler Foodservice Conference at the Loews Ventana Canyon Resort in Tucson, Arizona, I met Allan LaMagna, a project manager, working for a Phoenix-based audiovisual company. Allan supplied the equipment and labor for the meeting and we became fast friends. I introduced Allan to Williams/Gerard and continued using him every time I had a client meeting in Arizona. Allan was originally from Chicago and in his former life, was the road manager for the Bee Gees, a famous singing group during their heyday in the late 1960s, 1970s and 1980s.

Soon after meeting Allan, and on one occasion, while I was producing a show in Scottsdale, Arizona Steve Dennison, a Williams/Gerard computer programmer/technician, and I were invited for a barbecue at Allan and his wife, Julie's house in Scottsdale. Their house was located on a corner lot at 96th Street and Cactus Road that seemed like it was in the middle of nowhere because it took about twenty minutes to get there from where we were staying. There were no expressways and the only means of getting to Allan's house was by driving north on two-lane Scottsdale Road. Now, the property is located in the center of Scottsdale. Allan eventually sold the house when he moved to Pine, Arizona, about ninety miles north. A fire station was built on this property and is around the corner from our condo.

SUNDAY NOVEMBER 17, 1991—441 E. BLUEBELL LANE HOUSE

In November 1991, I was producing IFMA's Presidents Conference at the Hyatt Regency Scottsdale Resort. Penny's Uncle Hy and Aunt Helen had moved from Cleveland to Scottsdale years before and we used to periodically see them while I was producing shows in Scottsdale. After my shows end, we usually stayed a few days at the Marriott Suites Hotel in Old Scottsdale. Aunt Helen invited Penny to go shopping with her on the Saturday before we left to go back to Chicago. I told Penny that while she was shopping with her aunt, I was going to buy a house.

My goal was to find an affordable and suitable house that I could buy as an investment and rent it. Not knowing any Phoenix real estate agents, I walked into a Prudential Real Estate Company office near Lincoln Drive on North Scottsdale Road and found a broker to take me to look at some potential houses. He drove me to several houses in Tempe, a suburb located about three blocks south of Scottsdale.

One house in particular at 441 E. Bluebell Lane in the Marlborough Park Estates caught my eye. It was a clean three-bedroom, two and one-half baths, 2,107 square foot with a two-car attached garage. The house was built in 1984 and the family who owned it, Jay and Cheryl Jean Elston, bought it new for $117,000.00. This little community is just west of Scottsdale Road off of McKellips Road and close to Papago Park and Sky Harbor International Airport. The Elston's and their three children wanted to sell it because their family had outgrown the house. The price of the house was originally listed at $135,000, reduced to $133,500, then at $127,000.00. I told the real estate broker that I wanted to put in a bid but wanted Penny to see it first. We were leaving Phoenix on Sunday, the next day, to fly back to Chicago.

On Sunday, November 17, just before we went to the airport, Penny and I met the broker at the Bluebell house and we took a quick inside and outside tour. Penny gave her approval to put in our offer of $125,000.00. The contract was drawn before we left by Sylvia Waters, the real estate broker for the seller and I gave Sylvia a check to hold the offer.

TUESDAY, DECEMBER 31, 1991—CLOSED ON BLUEBELL HOUSE

When we returned to Chicago, our broker called to say our offer was accepted and we closed on the house on Tuesday, December 31, 1991. I put down

$75,000.00and financed the rest. In Arizona, you don't need the services of an attorney to buy property so all of the correspondence was done through the mail without attorney legal fees. As a result of the purchase, we became close friends with Sylvia Waters, the real estate broker for the seller.

Upon closing, Sylvia gave me the phone number of a house painter and we had the interior of the house painted, the carpets cleaned and a service cleaned the house in preparation for renting. Sylvia, employed by Dan Schwartz Real Estate, acted as our rental broker and put the house on the rental market. Sylvia advertised the house and put up a rental sign in the front yard.

A HOME WARRANTY PROGRAM

Immediately after we closed, I bought a home warranty through First American Home Buyers Protection Corporation that made it easy for me in case something went wrong with the house. All a tenant had to do was call an 800 number and for $35.00, a repairman would come to the house and fix whatever was not working. If something could not be fixed, then a replacement would be covered by the home warranty insurance policy. Because of this home warranty, I did not need a company to manage the property. Sylvia Waters interviewed our first tenant who was Gary Langerfeld. He rented the house with his girlfriend from August 7, 1992 to May 30, 1994. We have been very lucky because there have only been nine tenants since 1992 and all of them have been very good by taking care of the house.

NINTH TENANT AND LAST TENANT—TEMPE HOUSE SOLD

One of my former tenants and real estate broker, Bob Lafferty, found me a new tenant. Robert Webb, a forty-year-old single attorney signed a one-year lease and moved into the Bluebell Lane house on July 12, 2012. After almost 3 years of renting, Rob asked me if I would consider selling the house. I actually said no at first. Around October 2015, Rob let me know he was looking to purchase a house but really didn't want to move because he loved the Bluebell house. Rob begged me to sell him the house and I finally gave in and said yes.

Rob had a friend who was a real estate broker so I hired Bob Lafferty to represent me in the deal. There were a few demands made for minor repairs before the house was sold but, in the end, we closed on the E. Bluebell Lane house on Wednesday, December 9, 2015 with a very nice profit. With all of the rent, house expenses and depreciation I was able to deduct from my income taxes over the 24 years I owned the house, I did rather well on the deal as an investment and was happy Rob convinced me to sell the house.

1984 TO 1986—BENNETT AT NORTHBROOK JUNIOR HIGH

Bennett developed a knack for creating videos at a young age. On one particular occasion, for a junior high school Spanish class, he dressed up as a girl using Penny fall hairpiece and in Spanish narrated a fashion show all in Spanish. It was absolutely hysterical and he got a good grade to boot.

He also created and produced videos using his friends as actors. One, shot in our backyard was a kungfu movie starring Jeff Kim and Eric Sandstrom. Bennett had his friends jumping off the roof and doing other crazy stunts and moves.

Bennett also played baseball and soccer and Penny and I would go to each of his games.

SATURDAY, MAY 28, 1988—RONNA'S BAT MITZVAH

Penny called the Sheraton NorthShore Inn and reserved a room block from Mary 27 to 29, 1988 for Ronna's Bat Mitzvah. Ronna shared her Bat Mitzvah with Julie Carson at Temple Jeremiah on Saturday morning, May 28, 1988. After the service, there was a reception at the Temple followed by a luncheon at Marriott's Lincolnshire Resort from 1:30 to 5:00 p.m. Michael Lerich and his orchestra played music. The cost of the seven-piece orchestra was $2,080.00.

On Sunday evening, May 29, 1988, Kenny Verne and Ronna had a combined kid's party at Northbrook's Caravelle Restaurant located on Waukegan Road, just southeast of Willow Road. Arlington Height's Paul Drake Productions provided the DJ for the event from 7:00 to 10:00 p.m. The cost of the DJ was $350.00 and included lights, bubbles and games.

Contests were the Limbo, Twist, Hula Hoop, Spot Dance, Freeze Dance, Silly Dance and most romantic dance. Prizes were cassette tapes supplied by us. Some of the fast dances included *Celebration* by Kool and the Gang, *Mony, Mony* by Billy Idol, *Twist and Shout* by the Isley Brothers *and Man In the Mirror* by Michael Jackson. The Sunday evening dinner buffet at the Caravelle Restaurant was for eighty-four people.

1986 TO 1990—BENNETT AT GLENBROOK NORTH HIGH

After my father passed away, we drove my father's car back to Chicago and Bennett inherited it at age 16. He drove it for a few years and then bought a white, two-door 1977 Oldsmobile Cutlass Supreme with T-tops. Bennett has been directing and producing videos since seventh grade. He was involved in Glenbrook North High School's video studio for three years and also appeared on various high school radio shows on WMWA 88.5 FM. Bennett developed a knack for creating some very clever videos. One of them mimicked a girl in his class, and he got in trouble with the video teacher; however, the video was funny. Bennett was on the Glenbrook North High School boys' gymnastics team for three years. He competed on the parallel bars, the Palma horse, the rings and the vault. Penny and I went to every one of his gymnastic meets and were very proud of him.

Penny and I volunteered to be on the parent's planning committee for the first GBN Grad Night. Bennett graduated from Glenbrook North High School on Sunday, June 3, 1990. Grad Night took place in the high school gymnasium and was conceived as a place for the class to go after graduation. The all-night party was filled with games and activities so that the seniors would not be getting into trouble after the ceremony. It was the first one held during Bennett's senior year. The parents totally organized the event. I hired mentalist Ross Johnson to perform at the breakfast as part of the event.

1987 AND 1988—RONNA AND YMCA OVERNIGHT CAMP

For two weeks, two years in a row, from the middle of July-August 1987 and 1988, Ronna went to Camp Echo on Long Lake in Fremont, Michigan. She went to camp with Cindy Templer, Amy Scott and Carrie Barris. The first year, the bus ride to Michigan was not air-conditioned but it was the second year.

FRIDAY, MARCH 24, 1989—BON JOVI CONCERT

Ronna was thirteen years old and a huge fan of the American rock band Bon Jovi. She really wanted to go to a concert so I volunteered to take Ronna and her friend Amy Scott to the concert held at the Rosemont Horizon. I ordered tickets in an upper level and we had a good view of the stage. I wore earplugs because the music was very loud. For an encore, the band played several songs but I stood up in my seat and yelled play *Bad Medicine* and the band did as their second to last encore song. After the concert, Ronna bought a shirt with a photo of Bon Jovi on the front and the names of the tour cities and dates on the back. I must admit it was quite an experience. I don't think too many fathers were there with their children but it was a fun time and Ronna and Amy enjoyed it.

1990—BECOMING A PESCATARIAN

Sometime in 1990 and I can't remember the exact date, I decided to give up eating any type of red meat, chicken or turkey but I loved fish and dairy. This idea was something I had been thinking about for some time and the reason I did it was in my mind for health reasons. The word pescatarian as defined by Webster's Dictionary is "one whose diet includes fish but no other meat." According to the dictionary, the term's first known use was in 1991. I guess I was ahead of my time.

I started to eat food that would give me protein, like beans, tofu, tempeh, lentil, barbecue seitan (a flavored wheat gluten often used as a meat substitute) hummus made from chickpeas or garbanzo beans, nuts, and other forms of plant protein. My idea became a challenge for Penny who was able to figure out lunch and dinner options for us. Penny still liked to eat meat especially when we would go out to restaurants. Later on, we started eating edamame.

Earlier in this book I mentioned our friend Jerry Aronson who taught sixth grade at Chicago's Schiller School with Penny and got us into eating organic food in 1968. The Bread Shop, a small and funky North Halsted Avenue grocery store located a few blocks north of Belmont Avenue, sold organic flour, breads and other health foods. A restaurant, The Bread Shop Kitchen, located directly across the street from the health food store, was a frequent and favorite place of ours to eat. At the same time, we bought a book written by American nutrition author Adelle Davis who was an advocate of improved health through better nutrition. Although we used this book as our food bible, some of her ideas were not accepted by scientific literature. She preached the benefits of whole grains and breads; fresh vegetables and vitamin supplements, limiting sugar and not eating packaged and processed foods. Jerry also introduced Penny and me to Japanese food at *Nanewa* Restaurant in the 900 block of W. Belmont Avenue and next to Ann Sather's Restaurant. Penny and I ate miso soup, sunumonu and teriyaki dishes for the first time. It was years before Sushi became popular. In 1999 I started going to nutritionist Bonnie Minsky as a consultant. Bonnie would analyze my annual blood test and advise me on what vitamin supplements to take.

FRIDAY, JUNE 3, 1990—BENNETT AND COLUMBIA COLLEGE

After graduating from Glenbrook North High School, Bennett enrolled in Chicago's Columbia College for the fall semester to study filmmaking. He lived at home for all four years, commuted on the Metra train to school and graduated from Columbia College on Friday, June 3, 1994 with a B.A. degree majoring in film. While Bennett was a high school student, he got some practical production experience because I was able to hire him while working on some Williams/Gerard's video projects. He was a grip and helped out the crew on a variety of projects over the years. After graduating, he was also a cameraman and a sound engineer and set up lighting on multiple video shoots.

While going to Columbia College, Bennett used my 16mm film editing equipment. He had my editing table with rewinds, Moviola screen, a five-gang synchronizer and split reels set-up in his room and was able to do many of his film assignments at home without having to work at Columbia College. It was definitely an advantage and convenience to be able to work on film projects at home. After graduation, his first professional paying job was on an independent feature film, *Strawberry Fields*. Bennett was second grip on the project that was on location in Chicago the entire month of October. He pushed the camera dolly on some scenes.

Bennett continues to work as a freelance videographer, audio engineer and lighting person in the Chicago video industry. He bought audio, camera and lighting gear and rents them on assignments whenever he can. On some video productions, he is a cameraman while on others, he is involved with only audio or lighting or both. Sometimes he is a videographer, lighting and audio engineer on the same video production. It all depends on the assignment and budget.

SATURDAY MARCH 16, 1991—MY 50TH BIRTHDAY PARTY

An invitation was sent to our family and friends to celebrate my 50th birthday. The front of the invitation was my cousin Shelly's photograph of me wearing his large shirt taken on the front lawn of our home. I was about 10 years old. Inside the invitation read, Alan Spencer is celebrating his 50th birthday and wants to celebrate with you at our Dell Road home in Northbrook, IL. RSVP. Please bring a memory (photograph or anecdote to include in a memory book.

My mother, sister Linda with Todd and Andrew came in from Cleveland. Other attendees were Sandy and Larry Fishman, Remey and Julie Rubin, Jan and Rich Aver, Jack and Bobby Cohen, Bonnie and Bernie Wilson, Paul and Betty Hurder, Chris Cohen and Cathy and Van Morris.

Sharon Goodman gave me a very special note card memory of me. On the outside of the card was a black and white photograph of me taking a picture in the snow. On the inside of the card was the following note: "Winter 1972 With Alan's guidance and encouragement, I had just purchased my first camera. Alan then took me out into the snow-covered neighborhood around Briar Place and taught me how to take pictures. Today, I am a professional photographer working out of my own 1,200 square foot studio. Thank you, Alan. Sharon"

Jan and Rich Aver provided another written memory during the party. The following is what they wrote. "Where's the Beef" We spend every New Year's Eve with the Spencers. One year was exceptionally cold. We decided not to go out but to order Chinese food and stay in. Alan and Rich went to Yu Lin's in Highland Park to pick up the dinner. They returned with mouths watering. We began dishing out dinner. Much to our disappointment, our beef Genghis Kahn was sans beef. Alan called the restaurant and of course spoke to someone who could barely speak English. Alan did a very good job of explaining the situation. Out they went to retrieve the missing beef.

Upon return, we discovered they gave us an entire dinner, not just beef. We began to dish out dinner a second time and again—no beef. We gave up. We'll eat what we have. Well guess what we found when we served up the Styrofoam noodles? Beef! Under the noodles!" We wound up with double Genghis Kahn and a very memorable New Year's Eve." Happy 50th. Jan and Rich Aver."

AUGUST 1991—NEWPORT, RHODE ISLAND FAMILY TRIP

To celebrate Grandma Deah's 80th birthday [she was actually 79 years old], Pa Sam treated the family to a trip to Newport, Rhode Island. The details of the trip are sketchy but Lois remembers the Fishmans went on their own, visiting some of the mansions there. At dusk one evening, Sandi was walking and all of a sudden, she disappeared having fallen into a hole. Luckily, she wasn't hurt.

After the trip, we drove back to Cleveland.

AUGUST 1991—BENNETT BUYS A 1966 PONTIAC GTO

After our Newport trip, the family was staying in Cleveland for a few days when Larry or Doug Fishman mentioned he knew of a 1966 Pontiac GTO that was for sale at a garage near their house. Doug, Larry, Bennett and I went to look at the car. Bennett decided to buy it but I don't remember how much he originally paid for it. On Saturday, August 10, 1991, we picked up a U-Hall box truck with an auto transport trailer at 3211 Mayfield Road in Cleveland Hts. and loaded the Pontiac onto the auto transport trailer. I drove the box truck and trailer and Bennett drove the car back to Northbrook. Bennett and I returned the box truck and trailer to a W. Fullerton U-Haul location on Monday morning, August 12, 1991.

Bennett found someone who partially restore the car. We built a garage in the back of our home so the GTO could be safely stored. After the GTO was restored, Bennett was able to park his car in the newly built garage. After driving the GTO for several years, Bennett decided to take the car to Volo Auto Museum to sell on consignment. While at Volo, there was a fire in one of the storage barns and water damaged the GTO beyond repair so the insurance company sent Bennett a check for $12,000.00 for the car.

MARCH 1992—REMODELED NORTHBROOK KITCHEN

In March 1992, we decided to remodel our home's kitchen. We hired the company that had done work for Marcy and David Levinson's kitchen. Although the Levinsons recommended this company, the father and daughter were a bad choice. The father turned over the remodeling project to his daughter, who did not know what she was doing. The daughter did not make our kitchen remodeling an easy or pleasant experience and I was constantly questioning decisions she made. On April 2, 1992, we ordered our kitchen appliances from Abt Appliances. At the time, Abt were located in Morton Grove, Illinois. The kitchen remodel was finally completed but not without angst.

AUGUST 1989 TO JUNE 1993—RONNA IN HIGH SCHOOL

Ronna did very well academically at Glenbrook North High School and was in several honors classes during her senior year. She was also on the Glenbrook girl's gymnastic team. We went to every match to see her perform. She was on the uneven parallel bars, floor exercises and jumped over the vault. Ronna also worked on the school newspaper and was co-editor during her senior year. Ronna had thoughts about going to college and applied to several.

DECEMBER 1992—UNIVERSITY OF WISCONSIN TOUR

On a bitter cold day in December 1992, Ronna, Penny and I along with Steve, Nancy and Amy Scott drove to Madison to take an outdoor tour to look over the University of Wisconsin campus. It was so cold that day but we endured and each girl decided to attend the university. In June 1993, Ronna graduated from Glenbrook North High School.

JUNE 1993—RONNA GRADUATES FROM HIGH SCHOOL

Ronna's high school graduation took place at the Sheely Center for the Performing Arts located at Glenbrook North High School on Shermer Road.

AUGUST 1993—RONNA GOES TO UW MADISON

During the summer we drove to Madison for a parent and student orientation program called Soar. Ronna started as a freshman in the fall of 1993. In the middle of August, we drove to Madison with a carload of Ronna's belongings and moved her into The Statesider, a private dormitory located just off State Street. It was raining that day but it didn't matter because Ronna was very excited to start her new adventure. After choosing the University of Wisconsin, one of the first things I told Ronna was she didn't have to worry about the football team going to the Rose Bowl because they usually lost many games. The last time the football team had been in a Rose Ball was 1963. In 1990, Barry Alvarez had been named head football coach of the Wisconsin Badgers and his first few seasons had been another losing record. Barry had inherited a football program that had not had a winning season since 1984, and had only won seven games in Big Ten Conference in that time. But Ronna's freshman year looked like a more promising football season.

As Ronna's first semester progressed, Wisconsin kept winning football games. Ronna purchased football tickets for us on the opposite side of the field from the student section during parent's weekend. The game would be nationally televised.at Camp Randall Stadium, so we received a postcard sent by the UW Ticket Office saying the game between the Wisconsin Badgers and the Michigan Wolverines had been changed to 11:30 a.m.

FRIDAY, OCTOBER 29, 1993—UW PARENTS WEEKEND

After breakfast, Penny and I drove to Madison for parent's weekend and were excited to attend our first Wisconsin football game. On Saturday, October 30, 1993, Penny and I walked to the game with Ronna and decided to meet back at the Statesider dorm after the game. Wisconsin had not beaten the University of Michigan in the past forty years when Wisconsin last went to the Rose Bowl. Coach

ALAN G. SPENCER

Barry Alvarez had put together a great football team. The game was extremely exciting and Wisconsin won.

At the end of the game, a mass of students rushed the field and many got hurt in the celebration. Fortunately for Ronna, she and her friends were not a part of the pushing and shoving and were not hurt but a few students she knew were not as fortunate. When it was announced that Wisconsin would be playing in the Rose Bowl, I told Ronna I wanted to go. Penny was not interested but Ronna and I started making plans to attend.

SATURDAY, JANUARY 1, 1994—ROSE BOWL GAME

Ronna and I were going to the 1994 Rose Bowl. She bought tickets from the Wisconsin Alumni Association and from Madison's Airport; we flew to LAX in a chartered Boeing 747. Our Wisconsin group stayed at the Hyatt Hotel in downtown Los Angeles. I rented a car and drove Ronna all over Los Angeles to various sites. We went to Hollywood and saw the Hollywood Bowl, Sunset Boulevard and a variety of other sites.

On Saturday, January 1, 1994, Ronna and I went to the Rose Bowl parade in Pasadena and had grandstand seats along Colorado Boulevard. The game was very exciting with Wisconsin beating UCLA 21 to 16. Running back Brent Moss was named Rose Bowl Player of the Game. What a great and memorable trip!

THEY DON'T HAVE ANY CONES

One time, when Penny and I were in Madison and we were picking up Ronna to bring her home for a break, we decided to stop at Big Mike's for a frozen yogurt. As Ronna left the car, Penny asked me to get her a chocolate cone.

Ronna and I came out to the car with an ice cream cone for each of us but I got Penny chocolate yogurt in a dish, instead of a cone. When Penny asked me why I didn't get her a cone, I said, "They didn't have cones." Ronna did not hear her mother ask me for a cone or she would have not let me get her yogurt in a dish. "They didn't have cones" has been a family joke for many years. I guess you had to be there to appreciate the humor in this comment.

JANUARY 1996—RONNA GOES TO SPAIN HER JUNIOR YEAR

Ronna decided to spend the first semester of her junior year in Seville, Spain. As she was about to leave for Spain, a huge winter snowstorm came into Chicago the end of January 1996 and many flights were cancelled. Ronna wasn't sure she was able to leave Chicago but at the last minute her flight took off from O'Hare Airport and arrived in Madrid the next day.

During Ronna's winter break and before she left for Spain in January 1996, she had an interview with *Siskel and Ebert At The Movies* to be their 1996 summer intern. The television show was a weekly Chicago produced program syndicated throughout the United States. Ronna sold herself to Associate Producer, Stuart Cleland, and upon her return to Chicago from Spain, became the show's summer intern. Ronna had previously been a summer intern with a Madison video production company and a TV station, while attending summer school in her junior year.

1996 SUMMER INTERN—*SISKEL & EBERT AT THE MOVIES*

For the summer when Ronna was an intern, she and I took the commuter train together to Chicago. The last day of shooting the program, I convinced Ronna to take her camera to the set and ask Gene Siskel and Roger Ebert if she could take their photo with her. She thought they wouldn't do it but I told her they would be happy to take a photo with her. On the set, Ronna stood between both of them giving Ronna two thumbs up. I had the photograph blown up, framed and put the photo on the second page of her resume.

FRIDAY, FEBRUARY 16, 1996—PENNY'S MOTHER DIES

In March 1995 Penny's mother Dorothy called Larry Fishman saying she wasn't feeling well. She went into the University Hospital with an apparent heart attack but was later diagnosed by Dr. Todd Locke with iron deficiency anemia. In December 1995, when Penny and I were in visiting Cleveland, Dorothy was in the hospital with an unknown illness. It was eventually diagnosed she had cancer. Dorothy had been feeling weak for some time and her condition was originally diagnosed as iron deficiency anemia. She was treated for this condition in January 1996 when she went into University Hospital (Lakeside) for a blood transfusion. After the transfusion, fluid began to develop in her abdomen and the hospital ran tests to determine what was causing the problem, they discovered cancer cells in the fluid. She left the hospital on Sunday, February 11, 1996 and was brought home by an ambulance, as her condition had gotten worse. Round the clock nurses' aides took shifts to watch her and make her comfortable.

Penny's sister, Lois Camberg had been in Cleveland since Penny left on Monday, February 12. Penny flew back to Cleveland on Friday afternoon, February 16 to see her mother. On Friday evening at 10:30 on February 16, 1996, Penny's mother, Dorothy Camberg Zipp died after a short illness. Between December 1995 and when she passed away, Penny flew back and forth to Cleveland to be with her mother. Lois was also there. Penny, Bennett and I flew there together on February 17 and we all flew home on Sunday, February 20. The entire family came in to Cleveland for the funeral except for Ronna who was studying in Spain and could not go to the funeral.

APRIL 1996—OUR VISIT TO SPAIN TO SEE RONNA

Penny and I decided to fly to Madrid to see Ronna during the first semester of her junior year. United Airlines had just cancelled their non-stop flights from Chicago to Madrid, so we had to fly to Paris and take an Iberia Airlines plane to Madrid. Our itinerary is listed below:

WEDNESDAY, MARCH 20, 1996—PARIS, FRANCE

We flew to Paris, France on a United Airlines flight. At 5:14 p.m. Penny and I left Chicago O'Hare-non-stop Connoisseur Class and arrived in Paris at 8:10 a.m. on Thursday March 21 at Charles DeGaulle Airport. We sat in seats 6 C & D. The flight served dinner and a snack. I ordered a vegetarian meal.

THURSDAY, MARCH 21, 1996—PARIS, THEN MADRID,

When we landed in Paris, Penny and I boarded Iberia Airlines flight that left at 11:45 a.m. It was a non-stop flight and arrived in Madrid, Spain at 1:45 p.m. Ronna took the Ava, Spain's version of the bullet train, to meet us in Madrid. At 2:30 p.m. Ronna met us at the airport where I rented a car. At 3:00 p.m. we drove to a hotel and parked the car. We spent several days in Madrid and drove to Toledo on our way to Seville.

THURSDAY, MARCH 21, MADRID

We stayed two nights at the Hotel Aramo PO Santa Maria de la Cabeza 28045 Madrid, Spain.

FRIDAY, MARCH 22, 1996—MADRID

We spent the better part of Friday visiting the world-famous Prado Museum. Their collection of art was amazing. When we came out of the museum, we ran into Jonathan Horn from Ronna's high school and Temple confirmation class. Jonathan was in Spain for the summer and just happened to be going into the museum when we walked out. What a coincident.

SATURDAY, MARCH 23—TOLEDO AND CORDOBA

At 7:30 a.m. we drove to Toledo and saw some sights there. From Toledo we drove and stayed overnight at the Hotel Melia in Cordoba that was a very nice place, then drove to Sevilla for a few days of sightseeing.

SUNDAY, MARCH 24—SEVILLA

After breakfast at the hotel, we left at 8:00 a.m. and drove to Sevilla arriving at 7:00 p.m. We stayed close to Ronna's apartment at the Hotel Baco, a quaint hotel. We met Ronna's housemother, Marilo, a retired nurse and her friend Packy.

MONDAY, MARCH 25—SEVILLA

We ate dinner at the Bar El Barailo, a small restaurant, and ate the most delicious seafood paella. It was one of Ronna's favorite places to dine.

WEDNESDAY, MARCH 27—SEVILLA TO MADRID, SPAIN

We left Sevilla and drove our Ford Escort rental car back to Madrid. At 4:30 p.m. Penny and I boarded our flight on Iberia Airlines Flight #3444 and flew to Paris, arriving in Paris at Charles DeGaulle Airport at 6:30 p.m. We took a taxi to the hotel and at 7:30 p.m. we arrived at Hotel des Marronniers, a very small hotel.

THURSDAY, MARCH 28—PARIS, FRANCE

The hotel room was almost big enough to turn around and the bathroom was like a broom closet. We met Sally Levine for dinner at 8:30 p.m. at the Brasserie Saint Benoit restaurant. Sally is Lynn Reer and Claire Levine's first cousin and was teaching a class in Paris for the semester.

FRIDAY, MARCH 29, 1996—RETURN TO CHICAGO

At 9:00 a.m. Penny and I left the Hotel des Marronniers for Charles DeGaulle Airport. We boarded a United Airlines flight that took off at 11:25 a.m. We were seated in Connoisseur Class and arrived in Chicago at 1:55 p.m. on the same day.

MAY 1996—RONNA RETURNS FROM SPAIN

Ronna returned from Spain and became a summer intern at *Siskel and Ebert At The Movies* before she started her senior year at University of Wisconsin at Madison in the fall of 1996. Each weekday, Ronna and I took the Metra train to Chicago. I went to my office and she walked to *Siskel and Ebert At The Movies*.

1996 TO 1997—THE MAXI PAD—RONNA'S SENIOR YEAR

Ronna's senior year was spent living with four great girls in a run-down house in Madison, just off of State Street. The house, nicknamed by the girls, "the Maxi Pad", was later condemned by the Madison Bureau of Health and leveled immediately after Ronna graduated. Alison Hayes, Katie Kennedy, Sarah Melies and Ronna were great friends who have remained close to this day. Ronna graduated from the University of Wisconsin in May 1996 and my mother and Bennett joined us for her graduation. The four women hold "Maxi Pad" reunions with now husbands and children.

Ronna had expressed an interest in pursuing a career in television. Following graduation, I suggested she move immediately to Los Angeles; however, Ronna did not take my fatherly advice and decided not to make the move to Los Angeles right away. She wanted to spend the summer of 1996 in Madison having fun. My reasoning for having her travel to Los Angeles immediately after graduation was, I thought that most of the television production jobs would be filled in June and July, as shows geared up for the 1996 fall television season that usually started production in August. Ronna decided that after spending most of the summer in Madison, it was time to move to Los Angeles.

Before leaving for Los Angeles, I helped Ronna with her resume and told her she had to stand out from all the other applicants who were trying to get a job in Hollywood. I suggested we put her photograph with Siskel and Ebert on the back of her resume along with two quotes. The quotes were: "Ronna—the best intern ever. Two thumbs up!" —SISKEL & EBERT. The other quote was "She made us laugh, she made us cry. We'd hire her in a minute!" —RONNA'S PARENTS

AUGUST, 1996—ALAN AND RONNA DRIVE TO LOS ANGELES

Our plan was for Ronna accompanied by me to drive my 1989 black Honda Accord to Los Angles while Penny took an airplane to Ontario Airport and was picked up by Ted and Linda Jass. Penny stayed at the Jass house while Ronna and I were on our way to meet her in Brea, California.

Before we left for Los Angeles, I laminated a map of the Los Angeles freeway system for Ronna to keep in her car while driving around Los Angeles. We had a small Budget U-Haul trailer put on the back of the Honda and packed Ronna's belongings into it. Emily Steinberg, Ronna's sorority sister and friend from college gave Ronna *The Horse Whisperer* on audiocassette, so we listened to it the entire way.

THURSDAY, AUGUST 15—ST. LOUIS AND OKLAHOMA CITY

At 5:00 a.m., Ronna and I left our home in Northbrook and arrived in St. Louis at 10:30. We were invited to have breakfast with Alison Hayes and her father Dan at his apartment. We had a wonderful breakfast and left for California at 11:50 a.m. Our first overnight stop was Oklahoma City arriving around dusk at 8:15 p.m. It was a very long first day and 850 miles from Northbrook. After arriving in Oklahoma City, we drove around the bombed-out site of the Alfred P. Murrah Building. There was a fence around the government building that had been blown up by twenty-seven-year-old Timothy James McVeigh on April 19, 1995. After viewing the bombed-out building, Ronna and I stayed at a Courtyard by Marriott and very quickly fell asleep after an exhausting long first day on the road.

FRIDAY, AUGUST 16, 1996—GALLUP VIA SANTA FE, NEW MEXICO

At 7:30 a.m. Ronna and I were on our way to Gallup, New Mexico, our next overnight stop. We were in Amarillo, Texas at 11:30 a.m. and decided to drive 75 miles north of Albuquerque to see Santa Fe, before stopping in Gallup at 8:45 p.m. for the night. We drove around Santa Fe and headed to Gallup. While there, we ate at a Mexican restaurant that had the best tortilla chips, so we bought some to take along on the rest of our trip. Periodically, we would try to find the old Route 66 and travel on it for a short time, before it went back to Interstate 40.

SATURDAY, AUGUST 17, 1996—GRAND CANYON TO SCOTTSDALE

We left Gallup and drove on Interstate 40 to Williams, then headed north to the Grand Canyon. After looking at the south rim of the Canyon for a short time, we headed to Scottsdale on Interstate 17 arriving at 5:00 p.m. Alison Hayes had flown to Scottsdale from St. Louis to see her mother, Margie. We stayed the night in Margie Hayes' apartment and after a restful night sleeping, I left early to get the muffler replaced at a Midas Muffler Shop located on N. Scottsdale Road. The day before, the muffler developed a hole in it and was too loud to tolerate, so I replaced it before continuing to Los Angeles.

SUNDAY, AUGUST 18, 1996—SCOTTSDALE TO CALIFORNIA

After getting the muffler replaced, Ronna and I bid farewell to Alison and Margie and left Scottsdale around 12:00 noon headed to Brea, California, about a six-hour drive. We arrived at 6:00 p.m. at Ted and Lind Jass' house where Penny was waiting and very happy to see us.

Once in California, Penny and I drove Ronna all around Los Angeles to show her the different freeways and how to get around. On Friday, August 23, we went to see Liz Dickler, a friend of Bennett, who was working at NBC Studios as an assistant to the head of production at NBC Television. We gave Liz Ronna's resume and asked her to keep her eyes open for possible production assistant jobs on TV sitcoms. Just as I suspected, production assistant's jobs were filled because production had already begun on the fall 1996 television season shows.

SUNDAY, AUGUST 25, 1996—PENNY AND I FLY TO CHICAGO

Penny and I left Los Angeles on Sunday, August 25. The next day, Monday, August 26, we got a call from Ronna saying she had an interview on Tuesday morning, August 27 as a production assistant on a new NBC television sit-com *Union Square*. A production assistant quit a few weeks into production and they needed an immediate replacement. Ronna brought in her resume to the interview and was offered a job to start the next day, on Wednesday, August 28. It was exciting for Ronna and for us as she was able to get a production job so quickly.

After staying with the Jass family for several weeks, in early September 1996, Ronna was able to find an apartment on Riverside Drive near Studio City and signed a one-year lease with Lisa Jass as her roommate. On September 13, I went to Pro-Pak and shipped a television set, a VCR, a stereo and books to Ted Jass' business, Equipment Direct, for Ronna's apartment.

After working on several one season NBC TV sit-com shows and pilots as a Production Assistant, Ronna became the Production Coordinator on NBC's *Will & Grace* for three years (1999-2002) and ended her L.A. television career as the Production Coordinator for two years on *Good Morning Miami*, (2002-2003) an NBC TV sit-com created by the same executive producers, Max Mutchnick and David Kohan, as *Will & Grace*.

FRIDAY, SEPTEMBER 26, 1997—FRANK LLOYD WRIGHT TOUR

For several years in a row, Penny and I drove to Oak Park, Illinois and toured various Frank Lloyd Wright designed houses. Each May, the Frank Lloyd Wright Foundation held tours of different Oak Park houses. When the Chicago Botanic Gardens announced a weekend trip to visit Frank Lloyd Wright's Taliesin in Spring Green Wisconsin, Penny and I decided to sign up. It was the first time we had been on a bus tour to any place.

FRIDAY, SEPTEMBER 26, 1997—SPRING GREEN, WISCONSIN

Penny and I drove to the Chicago Botanic Garden and parked our car. The tour group gathered in the Education Building's Linnaeus Room at 1:00 p.m. to meet our weekend guide, Mary Ann McKenna. After a preview of the exhibit, "The Midwest Landscape Influences on Frank Lloyd Wright," tea was served. After tea, we transferred our luggage from the car to the motor coach. Around 2:30, we boarded a luxury motor coach for the drive to Spring Green.

I wanted to have a birds-eye view of where we were going, so Penny and I sat in the front of the bus in the first seat directly opposite the driver. About fifteen minutes into the trip, I whispered to Penny that I thought the driver made a wrong turn. Penny said to me in a soft voice, "Alan, you're not producing this show." This was an expression she used to say whenever I was not in charge. About five minutes after I mentioned my comment to Penny, the driver made an announcement over the intercom that he made a wrong turn and had to go back to a previous exit. So, Penny's comment, "Alan, you're not producing this show" is a standard joke in our home, whenever I'm not involved with planning an event, outing with friends or when I'm not in charge. We arrived at The Springs Golf Club Resort, one of the most luxurious and best-known resorts in the Midwest. After arriving and unpacking, we ate dinner at one of the resort's restaurants but I can't remember which one of the two at the resort.

SATURDAY MORNING, SEPTEMBER 27—TOUR & THEATER

We ate breakfast at 7:30, had a briefing of the day's activities, and boarded the bus at 8:30 for a short drive to Wright's 800-acre estate at Taliesin. Wright built the first structure in 1897 and continued to design and build there throughout his 70-year career. In 1976, the property was named a National Historic Landmark. Our tour divided into small groups and was guided on a half-day private tour that included an extensive walk through the grounds, a visit to the Hillside School and a tour of Taliesin House. We ate lunch at the Riverview Terrace located in the visitor's center.

After lunch we returned to the hotel and had free time. After dinner, we departed in the motor coach for an evening at the beautiful natural outdoor amphitheater of the American Players Theatre. We lucked out with the weather because it was a beautiful evening and a clear sky. Shakespeare's *Comedy of Errors* was the play and we enjoyed it, returning to the resort for a good night's sleep.

SUNDAY, SEPTEMBER 28, 1997—BUS RIDE BACK

I can't remember what we did on Sunday morning, but after lunch at the resort, we boarded the bus for our home trip, stopping in Madison, Wisconsin at Monona Terrace to view the new conference center on Lake Monona. This new facility was originally proposed by Wright in the 1930s and was scheduled for completion in July 1998. We arrived back at the Chicago Botanic Garden around 6:00 p.m. The pre-paid package price of the entire three-day weekend trip for both of us was $465 including Friday tea at the Chicago Botanic Garden. All the meals and beverages were extra.

1985 TO 2002—CHICAGO BEARS FOOTBALL GAMES

Since 1975, Rich Aver owned season tickets to the Chicago Bears football games. For several years in the mid 1980s, Rich invited me to go with him to see the Chicago Bears play football. One of years was the amazing season when the 1985 Bears won the Super Bowl against the New England Patriots. Their only loss that season was to the Miami Dolphins. Rich and I drove to the Monroe Street parking garage and took a shuttle to Soldier Field.

In October 1995, when Rich moved to Fort Worth, he kept his Bears season tickets and I shared them with Larry Rosenthal, a friend of his from Prospect Heights, Illinois until the beginning of the 2003 season. Soldier Field was renovated during the 2002 football season. Before the start of the 2003 season, the Chicago Bears and the Chicago Park District decided to charge a one-time licensing fee for each seat in the stadium. This charge was on top of the cost of each ticket. When this policy was announced, that's when Rich decided paying a license fee for a permanent seat was no longer economical, so he gave up his two season tickets. The Bears played their first game in the newly renovated stadium on September 29, 2003 and with that, was the end of my attending Chicago Bears football games. There was also a time when Remey Rubin and I went to the Bears game. He had two season tickets so periodically Remey would invite me to go to a game with him.

AUGUST 1998—PORTLAND VISIT—PENNY'S COUSINS
TUESDAY, AUGUST 4, 1998—PORTLAND, OREGON

Penny and I decided to visit Penny's first cousins Lynn Reer, Claire Levine and Tom Bryson, Claire's husband at the time, in Portland.

WEDNESDAY, AUGUST 5—PORTLAND, OREGON

We ate breakfast at the Cadillac Café at 1801 NE Broadway Street in Portland. The café is a diner decorated with memorabilia from the 1950s. Our server made fun of me but I can't remember why.

THURSDAY, AUGUST 6—MOUNT HOOD

We drove to Timberline Lodge, a famous mountain lodge on the south side of Oregon's Mount Hood, about 60 miles east of Portland. The lodge was constructed between 1936 and 1938 as a Works Progress Administration (WPA) project during the Great Depression. Workers used large timbers and local stone, and placed intricately carved decorative elements throughout the building. President Franklin D. Roosevelt dedicated the Lodge on September 28, 1937.

The National Historic Landmark lodge sits at an elevation of 5,960 feet above sea level, within the Mount Hood National Forest and is accessible through the Mount Hood Scenic Byway. It is a popular tourist attraction, drawing more than a million visitors annually and quite impressive. The lodge was where they filmed, *The Shining*, the scary movie starring Jack Nicholson.

COLUMBIA RIVER GORGE

From Mount Hood, we drove to the Columbia River Gorge that begins just east of Portland. The Columbia River Gorge National Scenic Area stretches approximately 80 miles long and up to 4,000 feet deep encompassing both Northern Oregon and Southern Washington States. We saw wind surfers on the river and ended at Klamath Falls, a famous waterfalls in the area. We drove into the southern tip of Washington and had dinner at a restaurant just over the border.

FRIDAY, AUGUST 7, 1998—FLY TO LOS ANGELES

After leaving Portland, we flew to Los Angeles to see Ronna. Actor Stuart Whitman was on our flight to Los Angeles. After landing at the Burbank Airport, we took a taxi to the CBS studios to meet Ronna who was working as a production assistant on *Conrad Bloom*, an NBC television sitcom that lasted for one year. After arriving in L.A. that afternoon we went to the filming of *Conrad Bloom*.

MONDAY, AUGUST 10, 1998—PHOENIX, ARIZONA

Penny and I flew from Los Angeles to Phoenix to spend time in Arizona, staying at our favorite hotel, the Marriott Suites in Old Scottsdale on North Scottsdale and Indian School Road. We hadn't been to Jerome in a while so we decided to drive there the next day.

TUESDAY, AUGUST 11, 1998—JEROME, ARIZONA

When staying at the Marriott Suites, we order oatmeal crème Brule for breakfast. They made it in a special way with bananas and a glaze on top. It was delicious. After breakfast, Penny and I drove to Jerome and spent one night at the Surgeon's House. The next day, we drove to Prescott on the windy and twisty route 89A.

WEDNESDAY, AUGUST 12, 1998—PRESCOTT, ARIZONA

Penny and I spent the day in Prescott and drove back to Phoenix.

FRIDAY, AUGUST 14, 1998—LOOKED AT A SCOTTSDALE CONDO

Our friend, Allan LaMagna, told us that some rental apartments around the corner from his house were being converted back into condos. Allan and his wife Julie lived at the corner of Cactus Road and 96th Street in Scottsdale. The Mission de los Arroyos condominiums, located at 11333 North 92nd Street were so inexpensive he bought three units, including the model apartment he rented back to the condo developers until all of the units were renovated and sold. Allan suggested we check out the condos. This complex was originally built in 1984 as condominiums but because of the poor housing market, were turned into rental units. In 1998, as the Phoenix housing market started to turnaround, the 236 units in this development were being converted back to condos for sale. Once a condo unit was sold, it would be repainted, new carpet installed along with all new appliances.

I told Allan LaMagna Penny and I were not interested in buying a condo but agreed to take a look at a unit. We looked at a unit on the first floor that the developers had converted on speculation. The condo was located near the tennis court and because of its location the developers were asking a little higher premium but still a bargain especially because the condominiums located directly across the street at the Scottsdale Mission were selling for many more dollars. Allan was right, the price of the condos was too good to pass up. The unit had new beige carpeting and was recently repainted but no new appliances were installed. Since the condo was completed on spec, the developers did not want to install new appliances until the unit was sold. We decided to buy the condo as is and not purchase new appliances.

FRIDAY, AUGUST 14—SIGNED A CONDO CONTRACT

Penny and I decided to buy the unit for $113,400.00. Penny and I signed a contract for the purchase of a Plan B, The Sequoia, a 1,294 square foot two-bedroom, two-bath condo on the first floor. The complex was in a perfect location at 92nd Street at Cholla, just north of Shea Boulevard and in the heart of Scottsdale. When the 101 expressway was to be constructed, the condo would be close for easy access to any part of the valley. With closing costs including proration on taxes for 12 months, a charge for title, recording fees, escrow and new loan fees, the actual bottom-line cost was $115,982.69. We took out a fifteen-year mortgage for $75,000.00 from Norwest Mortgage, Inc. with our monthly mortgage payment of $663.69 but it did not include a twice a year Maricopa County property taxes. I would pay the Maricopa County property tax each year, the beginning of November and the beginning of March. Our unit was number 114 to be sold out of 236 total units. At the time of our purchase, the condo's monthly assessments were reasonable at $120.00 but as of this writing are $275 per month, still a bargain compared to gated communities.

SUNDAY, AUGUST 16, 1998—FLIGHT BACK TO CHICAGO

Penny and I flew back to Chicago feeling pretty good about purchasing the condo.

TUESDAY, SEPTEMBER 22, 1998—CLOSED ON THE CONDO

We had no intention of immediately occupying the condo, as our original idea was to rent it for income. Since our friend and realtor, Sylvia Waters did not get involved with renting condos, I found Southwest Accommodations, owned by Ken and Mari Welsh who would advertise the condo, rent it, collect the rent and manage the property. Upon buying the condo, I subscribed to a home warranty service with Home Buyers Resale Warranty Corp. The policy covers all appliances, including refrigerator, washer, dryer, dishwasher, water heater and air conditioner. If something is not working, call an 800 number and a $35.00 service fee is paid at the time when a repairperson arrives at the condo. If an item cannot be fixed, then it is replaced.

Our first tenant moved into the unfurnished condo on Wednesday, January 20, 1999. Michelle Rich, a real estate broker who rented her Scottsdale house for the extra income moved in with her son Mark for a monthly rent of $925.00. After Michelle moved out on July 19, 1999, Mark continued to rent the condo until January 19, 2000. After Mark's departure, Penny and I decided to start furnishing the place so in August 2000, we flew to Phoenix and started the process.

SEPTEMBER 1998—RONNA MOVES IN WITH LIZ DICKLER

Ronna moved into Liz Dickler's condo until October 2000.

CHAPTER NINETEEN
Bennett and Marni And Other Events

AUGUST 1998—BENNETT MEETS MARNI MILLER
Since childhood, Jill Birnbaum was a friend of Bennett and that friendship continued when Jill moved to Chicago. Jill's father, Sam and I have been friends since sixth grade in Youngstown, when we used to give Sam a ride to the Jewish Center on Youngstown's north side of Youngstown.

Jill Birnbaum and Marni Miller worked together at Gettys Design. After graduating from Cornell College in Ithaca, New York, Marni, originally from Philadelphia, moved to Chicago in 1994. One afternoon, Jill and Marni decided to see what was happening at a Bucktown yard sale Bennett and his roommates were having. At the time, Bennett was dating a girl but broke up with her. Bennett and Marni started dating on Sunday, November 8, 1998 and their first date, was at the Chicago Botanic Gardens. On one of their dates, Bennett gave Marni a bottle of car polish. Jump ahead to January 29, 2000.

SATURDAY, JANUARY 29, 2000—THE ENGAGEMENT
Bennett and Marni were visiting Manalapan, on the east coast of Florida, staying at Marni's family home on the ocean when Bennett asked Alan Miller for his daughter's hand in marriage. Little did the family realize Bennett had an engagement ring with him. On Saturday morning January 29, 2000, as the sun was rising over the Atlantic Ocean, Bennett proposed to Marni and she accepted.

SUNDAY JANUARY 30, 2000—ENGAGEMENT ANNOUNCED
The couple, now engaged, flew back to Chicago on Penny's birthday. Bennett, Marni, Penny and I were celebrating Penny's fifty-sixth birthday at the Red Star restaurant on Chicago's West Randolph Street when they told us they were engaged. Penny and I were surprised and excited to hear the great news and to hear the story of how Bennett popped the question.

MONDAY APRIL 16, 2000—SHARI HOFFMAN PASSES AWAY
Today was a very difficult day for Penny because her long-time friend Shari Hoffman died of breast cancer. At 1:00 p.m. on Friday, April 20 at Congregation Sol 1301 Clavey Road in Highland Park, a memorial service was held for Shari. Penny first met Shari when Ronna and Danielle, Shari's youngest daughter, were in elementary school. Shari and Penny used to go antiquing together and the four of us including Mickey, her husband, would periodically go to dinner together.

FRIDAY, JUNE 9, 2000—WEDDING—RYEBROOK, NEW YORK
Penny and I flew to New York's LaGuardia Airport to attend Lauri Pressler and Michael Herman's wedding on Saturday. We rented a car at the airport and drove to Ryebrook in Westchester County about one-hour north of the airport. All of the guests were staying at the Ryebrook Hilton.

SATURDAY, JUNE 10, 2000—LAURI PRESSLER WEDDING
The late afternoon-early evening wedding was in Lyndhurst-Tarrytown, New York. The weather was a scorcher tipping in around 96 to 100 degrees during the

outside ceremony. Right before the ceremony started, my first cousin Shelly, his wife Carol and the bride, Lauri, drove up in a horse-drawn white carriage. The wedding ceremony was held in a garden with chairs set up on a lawn in between the flowers. When guests arrived, we were given small white boxes and told to open them at the conclusion of the ceremony. When the ceremony ended, all the boxes were opened and hundreds of butterflies flew into the sky. It was an awesome sight and not expected. The dinner was held outside in a large non-air-conditioned tent. The wedding was a black-tie affair and everyone was sweating profusely.

SUNDAY, JUNE 11, 2000—FLY BACK TO CHICAGO

Penny and I drove to New York's LaGuardia Airport, dropped off our rental car at the airport and flew back to Chicago.

JULY, 2000—EXECUTIVE CONFERENCE
SATURDAY MORNING, JULY 29, 2000—TO CALIFORNIA

Penny and I left Chicago's O'Hare Airport at 9:15 a.m. on a non-stop United Airlines flight to Orange County, California's John Wayne Airport because I was producing *Chain Leader* magazine at the Ritz-Carlton Laguna Nigel Resort in Dana Point, California. We arrived at John Wayne Airport and I rented a mini-van and drove to the hotel. Williams/Gerard's Chris Mardorf was my computer programmer/technician was also on our flight. Our entire crew including Penny and me stayed at the Newport Beach Marriott Suites because my client didn't want to spend the money for us to stay at the Ritz-Carlton Laguna Nigel Resort. Ronna drove south from Los Angeles to meet us for lunch in the hotel's restaurant. At 5:30 p.m., we drove to Brea and Buca D'Beppo, where Frank and Carol Harrell and Ted and Ronna joined us for dinner.

SUNDAY, JULY 30—LAJOLLA & CLIENT MEETING SET UP

While I was involved with setting up the conference at the Ritz-Carlton and speaker rehearsals, Ted, Ronna and Penny drove to LaJolla for brunch at the Brockton Villa.

MONDAY, JULY 31—EXECUTIVE CONFERENCE

Chicago restaurateur Rich Melman spoke at this Executive Conference. His wife also attended and Penny sat next to the Melmans in the back of the ballroom before his speech.

TUESDAY, AUGUST 1, 2000—EXECUTIVE CONFERENCE

The conference was from 8:00 a.m. to 11:00 a.m. and the equipment was struck at 11:30 a.m. At 12:30 p.m., Penny and I drove Chris Mardorf, my computer programmer/technician, to the John Wayne Airport, then we drove into Los Angeles and met Ronna at her office. We got her car and returned the mini-van to the Burbank Airport. After returning the van, we went back to Ronna's office at the CBS Studios at 4024 Radford Avenue, Bungalow 3 in Studio City where she was working as the production coordinator on *Will & Grace*. Later, we checked into the Courtyard by Marriott at 13480 Maxella Avenue in Marina del Rey. We had three free nights at the hotel from Marriott Rewards. We spent the evening with Ronna and Ted.

THURSDAY, AUGUST 3—JERRY'S, THEN GETTY MUSEUM
Penny and I took Ronna to work again and ate breakfast at Jerry's Deli on Ventura Boulevard before going to the Getty Museum where we had reservations for 11:30. Afterwards we picked up Ronna from work.

FRIDAY, AUGUST 4—*WILL AND GRACE* AND THE BELINKYS
We picked up Ronna at her apartment and took her to the studio. We went to Huntington Gardens near Pasadena and returned to CBS Studios at 1:00 p.m. to see a run-through of *Will and Grace*. We had dinner with Herb and Lynda Belinky in the evening.

SATURDAY, AUGUST 5—BREA TRIP TO SEE LINDA AND TED
We drove to Brea the entire day with Ronna to visit with Ted and Linda Jass.

SUNDAY, AUGUST 6—THE LEVYS
At 11:00 a.m. to 1:00 p.m., Penny and I met Marilyn and Larry Levy and their kids. In the evening we spent time with Ronna and Ted.

MONDAY, AUGUST 7, 2000—FLIGHT TO PHOENIX
Ronna drove us to LAX where we took a United Airlines flight to Phoenix Sky Harbor Airport and we rented a car at the airport.

MONDAY, AUGUST 7, 2000—BEGAN FURNISHING THE CONDO
After our tenant moved out of our condo, Penny and I made a decision to spend as much time in Scottsdale as possible, so we began furnishing the place. Before leaving Los Angeles, I spoke to Dan and Roseanne Murphy, our Chicago friends who moved to Scottsdale in April, about a good place to buy a bed. They suggested Mattress Firm, so I called and arranged to meet at the store, buy mattresses and bed frames and them delivered the same day as our arrival on August 7.

After we picked up our rental car at the airport, we headed to the Mattress Firm at 542 W. Baseline Road in Mesa for a 2:00 p.m. meeting with store manager, Jennifer Thornton. We bought two-queen size mattresses (one for the master bedroom and one for the guest bedroom), plus multiple pillows and mattress pads and two frames. Delivery was arranged for a few hours after our arrival at the condo. The timing was perfect because our mattresses and all the extras arrived as scheduled. The two beds were set-up late in the afternoon so all of my pre-arranging worked out well. After buying the mattresses, we stopped to stock up on paper goods, tissue, toilet paper, paper plates, plastic cups and plastic silverware because the condo was totally unfurnished. I even had a contingency plan just in case the mattresses were not delivered upon our arrival. I made reservations at the Scottsdale Courtyard hotel and was able to cancel the reservation without a penalty.

WEDNESDAY, AUGUST 9—DAN AND ROSEANNE MURPHY
In the early evening, Penny and I met Dan and Roseanne Murphy at the Pointe Hilton at Tapatio Cliffs at 1111 N. 7th Street in Phoenix for a drink at their upper-level bar. The bar and patio overlook Phoenix and the view is spectacular especially at dusk. After drinking a glass of wine, we drove to an inexpensive Mexican Food and Lounge restaurant, Via Del O Santos at 9120 N. Central Avenue, a few blocks from the hotel where they serve $1.00 Margaritas.

THURSDAY, AUGUST 10, 2000—FLIGHT BACK TO CHICAGO
Penny and I flew back to Chicago on a United Airlines flight that left Phoenix at 2:37 p.m. and arrived in Chicago at 8:05 p.m.

FRIDAY, AUGUST 11, 2000—CLEVELAND, OHIO TRIP
Penny and I drove to Midway Airport and flew to Cleveland on a Southwest Airlines flight for a short visit to see my mother. Linda picked us up at the Cleveland Hopkins Airport and we drove to her home in Beachwood.

MONDAY, AUGUST 14, 2000—FLY BACK TO CHICAGO
Linda drove Penny and me to Cleveland Hopkins Airport and we flew back to Chicago on a Southwest flight and arrived at Midway Airport.

BENNETT AND MARNI GET MARRIED IN PHILADELPHIA
THURSDAY, OCTOBER 19, 2000—PHILADELPHIA
Penny and I were thrilled about Bennett's upcoming wedding to Marni Miller. We invited our friends and relatives to attend. What a great time and here's the sequence of events for a fantastic weekend. Penny and I left Chicago's O'Hare Airport at 10:00 a.m. on a United Airlines flight to Philadelphia. We arrived at 12:50 p.m. and took a taxi to the Four Seasons the site of the wedding ceremony.

FRIDAY, OCTOBER 20, 2000—THE REHEARSAL DINNER
The wedding rehearsal was at the Four Seasons Hotel. After the rehearsal, Penny and I hosted the rehearsal dinner in the wine cellar of the Panorama Ristorante at Penn's View Hotel on Front and Market Streets in Philadelphia. The event was scheduled from 5:30 p.m. to 7:00 p.m. I hired a Philadelphia trolley bus to take everyone to and from the Four Seasons to the restaurant. Jason King, Abby Miller's fiancé, videotaped the event. We only invited the immediate family. This way, the dinner was much more intimate.

SATURDAY, OCTOBER 21, 2000—DAY OF THE WEDDING
The weather was warm and sunny for an October day in Philadelphia. Photographs of the wedding party were taken outside of the Four Seasons Hotel. Rabbi Max Weiss officiated at the beautiful ceremony. At the time, Marni was working at the Gettys Group, a hotel design and consulting firm, as sales and marketing manager. Bennett was working as a freelance lighting technician for film and video productions.

SUNDAY, OCTOBER 22, 2000—BRUNCH & FLY TO CHICAGO
The Millers and we co-hosted a Sunday morning brunch at the Four Seasons Hotel. Penny and I left for the airport at 3:00 p.m. for a 5:30 flight back to Chicago, arriving at 6:51 p.m. Bennett and Marni went to Bali on their honeymoon. They had purchased a house at 1248 W. Superior Street in Chicago's Smith Park neighborhood. Before they moved into the house, it was rehabbed and after their honeymoon, they moved in. They turned a three-bedroom, two-bath house into a two-bedroom three-bath house. The rehab turned out great.

CHAPTER TWENTY
Ronna & Ted Belinky And Other Events

JULY 1998—RONNA GOES TO LAS VEGAS

Ronna and Kim Harrell were Production Assistants on the *Union Square* show and Ronna became very friendly with her. Jonathan, Kim's brother-in-law, had worked with Ted Belinky. Ted was part of Kim's older sister, Tammy, and Jonathan's wedding.

At the end of July in 1998, Ronna went on a trip to Las Vegas with Kim Harrell's mother and father and Tammy and Jonathan. They asked Ronna about herself and got around to asking her what actor she thought was cute. Ronna said she liked Matthew Broderick and they found out Ronna was a vegetarian. You're Jewish so we have to introduce you to our friend Ted Belinky.

The Harrells were going to have a barbecue so Ronna could meet Ted but it never ended up happening. At the beginning of October, Ronna received a telephone call from Ted. They were talking on the phone for a few hours. Ted was traveling a lot for work, so they started emailing each other for a couple weeks.

FRIDAY, OCTOBER 23, 1998—RONNA MEETS TED BELINKY

Ronna and Ted finally went on a date. Ronna said they had a good date and she liked him but there weren't sparks the first time. On Sunday, October 25, Ronna and Ted went on another date and that's when Ronna told me she really liked him. They dated for three and one-half years, when she relocated into an apartment at 1715 Camden Avenue Apartment 204 in West Los Angeles (Westwood) with Ted Belinky.

NEW YEARS 1999 TO 2000 IN PHOENIX

Jan and Rich Aver and Susan and Jeffrey Schesnol, friends of ours from Chicago, decided to spend the Millennium in Phoenix. Over the years, the Schesnols had periodically stayed at Two Bunch Palms Resort in Desert Hot Springs, California. During the 1930s, the resort was built as a simply furnished getaway for Hollywood movie stars. We checked out what Two Bunch Palms would charge for a weekend stay at the resort during this holiday season and it was absolutely outrageous. At the time, we had a tenant in our condo, so we couldn't stay there. Eventually we all decided to make reservations at The Pointe South Mountain Resort that was close to Jacqui Schesnol's townhouse so we could celebrate the new year of 2000 there. The Pointe is an all-suites hotel and we got rooms on the same floor. While there, Jan Aver got sick with a bad case of the flu and the weather was very chilly during our stay in Phoenix. Nevertheless, the stay was fun with our friends.

TUESDAY, DECEMBER 21, 1999—FLY TO PHOENIX

Penny and I flew to Phoenix on a non-stop United Airlines flight leaving Chicago O'Hare at 9:35 a.m. and arriving at 12:16 p.m. We rented a Budget Rent A Car located immediately outside of Terminal 2 and checked into the Scottsdale Marriott Suites located at 7325 E. 3rd Avenue.

WEDNESDAY, DECEMBER 22, 1999—ROOSEVELT DAM

We drove to Tortilla Flats and Roosevelt Dam and ate in Tortilla Flats. Part of the road is unpaved and very scenic.

TUESDAY, DECEMBER 28, 1999—JAN AND RICH—PHOENIX

At 3:45 p.m. we picked up Jan and Rich Aver at Sky Harbor Airport on an American Airlines flight from Dallas Fort Worth. They were living in Fort Worth, Texas at the time.

WEDNESDAY, DECEMBER 29, 1999—THE POINTE HILTON

Penny and I checked out of the Scottsdale Marriott Suites and checked into Hilton's The Pointe at South Mountain Hilton for four nights. The Pointe is an all-suites hotel and we got rooms on the same floor. We met up with Jeffrey and Susan Schesnol and Joyce and Joel Vagrin. After checking into The Pointe, I returned the rental car to Sky Harbor Airport and took a taxi back to the hotel. A large 8-passenger van was delivered to the hotel for the next few days.

We had 7:00 p.m. dinner reservations at Eddie Matney's restaurant at 2308 E. Camelback Road in Phoenix. After dinner, our rental van had a flat tire so I called our car rental company and a tow truck came and changed the tire. While in Phoenix, Jan Aver got sick with a bad case of the flu and the weather was very chilly during our stay in Phoenix. Nevertheless, the visit was fun with our friends.

THURSDAY, DECEMBER 30, 1999—JEROME AND SEDONA

All of us drove in a rented van to Sedona and Jerome. While in Jerome we showed the Avers and Schesnols the Surgeon's House where we had stayed overnight on several occasions. We saw Andrea Prince, its owner, and introduced our friends to her.

FRIDAY, DECEMBER 31, 1999— NEW YEAR'S CELEBRATION

We had 8:30 p.m. dinner reservations at Pasta Brioni. The food was great but we decided not to eat at this restaurant on the next New Year's Eve.

SATURDAY, JANUARY 1, 2000—ROSE BOWL

Rich Aver and I watched the University of Wisconsin Badgers defeat the Stanford University Cardinals in the Rose Bowl game, 17 to 9. Ron Dayne, Wisconsin's running back was named the Rose Bowl Player of the Game for the second consecutive year.

SUNDAY, JANUARY 2, 2000—DRIVE TO LOS ANGELES

At 8:00 a.m. Penny and I picked up a car and drove to Los Angeles to visit Ronna. We stayed at Ronna's apartment at 11755 Montana Avenue in Los Angeles. She shared the apartment with Liz Dickler.

MONDAY, JANUARY 3, 2000—LOS ANGELES

Penny and I stayed with Ted and Linda Jass at 689 Oakhaven in Brea, California and all of us had dinner at Bucca de Beppo in Brea.

TUESDAY, JANUARY 4, 2000—FLY BACK TO CHICAGO

Penny and I dropped off our two-day rental car at Ontario Airport and flew back to Chicago on a United Airlines flight to O'Hare Airport.

LOS ANGELES AND SAN DIEGO TRIP
SATURDAY, OCTOBER 28, 2000—FLYING J RECEPTION

Since I was producing the Flying J Reception on Sunday, October 29 in San Diego, Penny and I flew to Los Angeles to spend time with Ronna and Ted. We arrived in LAX at 10:35 a.m. and picked up our car from National Car Rental.

SUNDAY, OCTOBER 29—DRIVE TO SAN DIEGO

This morning we left Ronna, drove to San Diego and checked into the San Diego Marriott Hotel and Marina. The equipment set-up for the reception started at 2:00 p.m. in the Marina Ballroom. The reception was from 6:00 to 8:00 p.m. After the reception, I joined Penny in our hotel room.

MONDAY, OCTOBER 30—NANCY SCHUBERT STEVENS

Penny and I went to breakfast at Panikin on 1235 Coast Boulevard in LaJolla. We stayed around LaJolla and drove to see Nancy Shubert Stevens and her husband Tom at their house in Escondido. Nancy fixed lunch for us and we had a great time. Nancy, Janna and Angela lived a few houses south of us on Dell Road. Ronna was friends with Janna and kept in touch with Nancy after she and Tom moved to Escondido. After lunch, we toured the animal park near their house.

MONDAY, OCTOBER 30—BILLY JOEL CONCERT

In the evening, Gene Lundgren, a Williams/Gerard producer from our Washington office, invited Penny and me to attend a private Billy Joel performance for Freightliner Trucks. The concert was held in the San Diego Old Civic Center that is now called the Concourse in Golden Hall. It was within walking distance to the Marriott. Billy Joel was fantastic and the audience of about three hundred gave him a standing ovation at the end of his concert.

TUESDAY, OCTOBER 31, 2000—FLY BACK TO CHICAGO

We flew back to Chicago from San Diego and arrived in Chicago at 7:48 p.m.

SATURDAY, DECEMBER 16, 2000—FLY TO PHOENIX

Penny and I left Chicago for Phoenix and arrived at 10:53 a.m. We picked up our National Car Rental at Phoenix Sky Harbor Airport and drove to our condo.

MONDAY, DECEMBER 18—DINING SET DELIVERY

At 7:00 a.m. I had called the Scottsdale Mechanical Heating & Air Conditioning Company to come to the condo to tune-up our heat pump and air conditioner. They cleaned it, put in a new filter and declared it healthy. Our dining room set from the Stool & Dinette Factory was delivered. In the afternoon, Instant Blinds and Blind Ideas & Interiors came and measured for new vertical blinds throughout our condo. At 7:30 p.m. we actually attended a condo Board of Directors Meeting at Mission de los Arroyos Clubhouse. This was a rare moment because we happened to be in Scottsdale at the time of the meeting.

WEDNESDAY, DECEMBER 20—DESERT BOTANICAL GARDEN

In the morning, Penny and I went to the Phoenix Botanical Garden. At 12:45, we met Jeffrey, Susan and Jacqui Schesnol for lunch at Arcadia Farms. At 5:30 p.m. Penny and I met Margie Hayes for dinner at Flo's Chinese Restaurant at 94th Street and Frank Lloyd Wright Blvd. Flo's was a new restaurant to us. Marge is the mother of one of Ronna's University of Wisconsin roommates and a sorority sister.

THURSDAY, DECEMBER 21—CONDO BLINDS INSTALLED

From 12:00 to 2:00 p.m., Instant Blinds and Blind Ideas Interiors, Inc. delivered and installed all new blinds in our condo. We didn't like the ones that were already there. At 5:30 p.m. we met Rosanne and Dan Murphy at Malee's Thai Restaurant in Old Scottsdale. After dinner from 7:00 to 9:00 p.m., we enjoyed the weekly Thursday evening Scottsdale Gallery Art Walk.

FRIDAY, DECEMBER 22, 2000—TRIP TO PINE, ARIZONA

In the morning, Penny and I drove to Chompie's Restaurant and Deli to buy food to bring to visit Allan and Julie LaMagna in Pine in time for lunch. The trip to Pine usually takes about one and one-half hours on beautiful route 87, a scenic four-lane highway. As usual we had a terrific visit with Allan and Julie and left around 4:30 p.m. After returning from Pine, around 7:30 p.m., Penny and I met Jeffrey and Susan for dinner at Eddie Matney's Restaurant at 24th Street and Camelback Road.

SATURDAY, DECEMBER 23, 2000—DRIVE TO TUCSON

Penny and I drove to Tucson to visit Steve and Cindy Klein. Rather than stay at their house, we chose to stay at the Courtyard by Marriott on 201 South Williams Blvd. in Tucson. We had lunch with them at a restaurant I don't remember.

The reason we stayed overnight was to see Mark and Pat Tessler who lived not too far from Steve and Cindy. Mark was a Rayen High School friend and a fellow Rodef Sholom confirmand. Mark and Pat were both professors at Tucson's University of Arizona. Mark taught Middle Eastern courses and was an expert in Middle East affairs and Pat was a chemistry professor. Their daughter and future son-in-law happened to be in Tucson so we had a chance to meet them.

Located at the foot of a mountain, the Tessler house was spectacular. The interior was covered with artifacts and room décor from their many trips to the Middle East. Mark lived in Tunisia for a brief time. After our visit with the Tesslers, we drove back to Scottsdale.

TUESDAY, DECEMBER 26, 2000—JEROME AND SEDONA

In the morning we drove to Jerome and Sedona for the day and returned to Scottsdale in the evening.

THURSDAY, DECEMBER 28, 2000—HARVEY HART FURNITURE

In the morning, we left for Harvey Hart's house in Butcher's Hook, Arizona. We met Harvey at Jake's Corners off of route 87 at route 288 on the way to Roosevelt Lake. We ate breakfast at a restaurant in Jake's Corner and Harvey took us in his truck to his house. We had to drive over a shallow river to Harvey's house.

There are woods behind Harvey's house. He would go into the woods, pick up dead branches and bring them to his house so he could make furniture from them. Penny and I picked out different pieces of juniper pinewood from piles of wood he accumulated and Harvey made several pieces of furniture for us. Out of wood collected from the forest, Harvey made a hat tree, a square table, a large bench for the foot of our bed (this bench didn't fit into our bedroom so it's now in our living room), a magazine rack, a lamp and an end table next to our couch. After going to Harvey's house, Penny and I went to Thomasville Home Furnishings store on N.

Scottsdale Road to buy a new sofa. We found a Seabrook sofa with a fabric we liked. The sofa was not in stock and had to be ordered. The sofa arrived on Thursday, March 15, 2001, just before my sixtieth birthday party celebrated in our condo.

FRIDAY, DECEMBER 29, 2000—TEXAS NEW YEAR'S STAY

Around 9:00 a.m., we returned our rental car to the Phoenix Sky Harbor Airport and boarded an America West flight to Dallas/Fort Worth to visit Jan and Rich Aver. We arrived at the Dallas Fort Worth Airport at 1:40 p.m. and Jan and Rich picked us up there. We are staying with the Avers whose address in 7313 Lemonwood Lane in Fort Worth. The Schesnols arrive on Saturday.

SATURDAY, DECEMBER 30, 2000—SCHESNOLS ARRIVE

In the morning, Jeffrey and Susan Schesnol arrived from Phoenix and the Avers picked them up at the Dallas/Fort Worth Airport.

SUNDAY, DECEMBER 31, 2000—FORT WORTH, TEXAS

Jan and Rich entertain the Schesnols and Spencers over New Year's weekend.

MONDAY, JANUARY 1, 2001—NEW YEAR'S DAY

Rich, Jeffrey and I watched lots of college football games all day.

TUESDAY, JANUARY 2—FLIGHT BACK TO PHOENIX

At 6:30 a.m. Rich took Penny and me to the Dallas/Fort Worth airport for an 8:01 a.m. America West non-stop flight back to Phoenix. We arrived at 9:29 a.m. in Phoenix and picked up a National Car Rental at Phoenix Sky Harbor Airport.

WEDNESDAY, JANUARY 3—GUEST BEDROOM FURNITURE

After breakfast, Terri's Consignment store delivered a bookcase and dresser for the guest bedroom.

SUNDAY, JANUARY 7, 2001—FLIGHT TO CHICAGO

At 6:30 a.m. Penny and I returned our rental car to the Phoenix Sky Harbor Airport for our return flight to Chicago. We left Phoenix at 7:50 a.m. and arrived at Chicago O'Hare at 12:06 p.m.

SATURDAY, JANUARY 13, 2001—MOM'S 89TH BIRTHDAY

Almost immediately following our return from Phoenix, Penny and I turned around the following weekend and flew to Cleveland on Southwest Airlines from Midway Airport to be with my mother, a day after her 89th birthday. It was a short one-day trip returning on Sunday, January 14, 2001.

SATURDAY, MARCH 16, 2001—MY 60TH BIRTHDAY IN ARIZONA

While growing up, I didn't have any parties to celebrate my birthday with kids my own age, because my childhood birthdays were spent with my family or relatives. I decided when I turned sixty, I would throw myself a big birthday party in Scottsdale, Arizona. On my computer I designed and sent a clever invitation that included a six-year-old photo of myself on the front cover. My first cousin Shelly took my photograph in front of our family home in Brooklyn, New York. I invited my family and friends and reserved our condo's Mission de los Arroyos clubhouse for the party. On November 1, 2000, I sent a letter to the condo's management company to reserve the clubhouse for Saturday, March 17, 2001.

On January 29, 2001, I signed a contract with Santa Barbara Catering Company at 1090 West Fifth Avenue in Tempe, Arizona to provide the catering for my birthday party. Penny and I worked with Amie Dignan, the company's account executive and event planner, on the menu. The birthday cake that was one-half sheet was ordered from Scottsdale's Cakes Unlimited/Sweet Inspirations located at 5818 E. Shea Blvd. The cake was made to serve forty-five to fifty people. The evening included the food, service staff, rentals, florals and a service charge. The Santa Barbara Catering Company did an outstanding job and there were lots of positive complements about the food and the party.

MY 60TH BIRTHDAY PARTY ATTENDEES

Many relatives and friends attended my birthday party including my Aunt Dorothy Lockshin, Aunt Gert Epstein Weiner, Gail Epstein Silverman, Norman Lockshin, Arleen and Michael Gomshay from New York. Also, Sandi and Larry Fishman from Cleveland, Lois Camberg and Roy Cramer from Boston, Lynn Reer from Portland, Oregon, my sister Linda Waldman and mother from Cleveland, son Bennett and his wife Marni from Chicago and daughter Ronna and Ted Belinky from Los Angeles, all flew into Phoenix for the celebration.

Among our friends who also attended were Remey and Julie Rubin from South Haven, Michigan, Jeffrey and Susan Schesnol from Greensboro, North Carolina, Jan and Rich Aver from Fort Worth, Texas and Seth and Sharon Kaufman from San Francisco. Our Arizona friends who attended were Allan and Julie LaMagna and Lee Nelson and his wife. Allan supplied video projection and audio equipment so we could see one of my favorite movies, *Pinocchio*. Ronna, as a huge surprise, had produced a video of me from "still" photos Penny supplied to her. Nick Watters, an editor and writer and Ronna's friend and one-time writing partner, edited the video as a favor to Ronna. Ronna who was not married and still living in Los Angeles and had been dating Ted Belinky since October 1998.

Our guests stayed at the LaQuinta Inns & Suites located at 8888 E. Shea Blvd in Scottsdale. I made arrangements on December 5, 2000 for a reservation block of rooms and a special rate for the guests.

SUNDAY MORNING, MARCH 17, 2001
TED BELINKY INVITES PENNY AND ME TO BREAKFAST

The morning following my sixtieth birthday party, Ted Belinky invited Penny and me to have breakfast with him at Chompie's restaurant around the corner from our condo. He gave Ronna a lame excuse to be with us. During breakfast, he told us how much he loved Ronna and asked for Ronna's hand in marriage. We love Ted and of course, Penny and I were thrilled with having a new son-in-law.

FRIDAY, APRIL 6, 2001—TED PROPOSES TO RONNA

Ronna was working on a television pilot and when she got home late, there was a rose in the apartment door handle and she thought it was kind of weird. She walked into the apartment and there were rose pedals all over the floor and bouquets of red, orange and yellow roses, Ronna's favorite colors, spread all over the apartment. Ted came out from behind the door wearing a suit and had two glasses of red wine. Ronna started freaking out. Ted brought Ronna over to the couch and read this long poem. It was like forever, and Ronna said to Ted, "Get to the point." Ted had changed some of the poem to relate to their relationship. Ted finally asked Ronna to marry him and she said yes.

SATURDAY, APRIL 28, 2001—SOUTH HAVEN & ALLEGAN

Remey and Julie Rubin invited Penny and me to spend two days in South Haven and go to the antique market in Allegan, Michigan on Sunday. After breakfast, Penny and I drove to South Haven in time for lunch. After lunch we took a tour of the old pool house that was being converted into a place where Remey could store his many antique collections. The sheet rock had been put on all the walls and it needed to be painted. The floor was plywood.

Later we went in town. Remey and I sat on a bench in front of Yog's Grill while Julie and Penny must have gone into a store. Then we walked along the channel that goes into Lake Michigan. We saw boats coming from the lake. Afterwards we went to Sherman's Dairy for ice cream. We went back to the harbor and walked. We met a boy who was working on the topsail schooner Pierius Magnus boat that was docked. Near the schooner was a tug boat so I was able to talk to the captain and go inside to see the engine. While doing that, Remey, Penny and Julie sat on a bench next to the tugboat.

Later in the afternoon we went to the beach where Remey decided to fly a kite. Meanwhile, Penny relaxed on a bench. After kite flying, I took a photo of Remey and Julie sitting on the bench, then they took a picture of Penny and me on the bench. We walked to the parking lot and drove back to the Rubin's home.

SUNDAY, APRIL 29, 2001—ALLEGAN ANTIQUE MARKET

After an early breakfast, we drove to Allegan to the Allegan County Antique Market and arrived before 9:00 a.m. We were there for several hours, and then drove back to South Haven for some Sherman's ice cream. Remey took a photo of Penny and me in front of a Sherman's Dairy Ice Cream truck. After ice cream, we headed downtown South Haven and hung out, sitting on a bench, people watching.

THE REST OF 2001—MANY TRAVELS & MANY WEDDINGS

During 2001, Penny and I traveled extensively and attended many weddings of family and friends. All of the weddings we attended are listed in the addendum at the end of this book. The weddings all started with Mara Fishman and Chris Centanni's June wedding in Sanibel Island, Florida, a description and details are coming up in a few pages.

FRIDAY, MAY 11, 2001—FISHMAN-CENTANNI WEDDING

Ted Belinky flew into Chicago from Los Angeles separately from Ronna and we met him at O'Hare Airport. His flight arrived at 5:17 a.m. on Friday, May 11. Ronna was in Chicago, so that morning, Ted, Ronna, Penny and I flew together on the same plane to Ft. Myers, Florida for Mara's wedding. We arrived in Ft. Myers at 10:55 a.m. and picked up our rental car. All of us drove to the wedding hotel, the Sanibel Harbor Island Resort & Spa on Sanibel Island, Florida. We had a two-bedroom condo that overlooked a bay on the Gulf of Mexico.

Later in the day, Bennett and Marni arrived on another flight, rented a car and drove to the hotel. The rehearsal dinner took place in a party room at a nice restaurant on Sanibel Island. After dinner, Larry Fishman and Chris Centanni's father were throwing barbs at each other that were hilarious.

SATURDAY, MAY 12, 2001—MARA & CHRIS WEDDING

It was an outdoor wedding and the weather was a little windy. The reception and dinner took place in an inside ballroom where I had previously produced a Boston Whaler Business Meeting several years before. Actually, Doug and Mara came to that event because both were living in Florida at the time.

SUNDAY, MAY 13—BRUNCH AND FLIGHT BACK TO CHICAGO

There was a lovely brunch in the morning before our plane left Ft. Myers Airport. Ted, Ronna, Penny and I flew back to Chicago on the same plane and arrived at 2:22 p.m.

SUNDAY, JUNE 3, 2001—FAITH & MATT BEALL'S WEDDING

Penny and I flew into LAX on Saturday, June 2. Ronna was a bridesmaid in in the wedding party. At 4:00 p.m., Penny and I arrived at the Embassy Suites Hotel Brea-North Orange County. The rehearsal dinner started at 6:30 p.m.

FRIDAY, JUNE 22, 2001—TODD ZGONC FLORIDA WEDDING

There was another wedding and this time it was in Melbourne, Florida. Penny's best friend from high school and college, Yvette Zgonc and her husband Frank's son, Todd was getting married. So, it was back to Florida for another wedding. Penny and I flew to Orlando arriving at 11:50 a.m. We rented an Avis car and drove to Melbourne about forty-five minutes away. We checked into the Hilton Melbourne Beach Hotel around 3:00 p.m. At 6:30 p.m. the rehearsal dinner was held at the Quality Suites Oceanfront Hotel in Indialantic, Florida.

SATURDAY, JUNE 23, 2001—WEDDING IN MELBOURNE, FL

The wedding was held at the Holy Name of Jesus Catholic Church and the reception took place at the Hilton Melbourne Beach Hotel. It was fun to see Yvette and Frank and their grown children. We flew back to Chicago on a 4:40 p.m. non-stop United Airlines flight.

FRIDAY, JULY 13, 2001— McDERMOTT NEW JERSEY WEDDING

Penny and I, Harriet and Jay Weintraub and Dan and Roseanne Murphy were all invited to the McDermott-Welsh wedding in Red Bank, New Jersey. Penny taught with Donna McDermott at Little Explorers along with Roseanne Murphy and Harriet Weintraub. The Murphys were friends with Jerry and Donna McDermott and so as a group, the Weintraubs, Murphys, McDermotts and Spencers would periodically go to different restaurants for dinner. We always had a fun time with lots of laughs at these dinners. This morning we left Chicago's O'Hare Airport at 10:30 and flew on a non-stop United Airlines flight arriving at 1:34 p.m. at Newark International Airport. We rented a car and drove to Red Bank, New Jersey. We checked into the Molly Pitcher Inn at 88 Riverside Avenue in Red Bank and walked around the downtown area. The rehearsal dinner was held that night at the hotel.

SATURDAY, JULY 14, 2001—McDERMOTT/WELSH WEDDING

In the morning, Danielle McDermott and Brian John Welsh were married in a ceremony held at the Saint James Roman Catholic Church in Red Bank, New

Jersey. The reception immediately following the ceremony was held at Shadowbrook in Shrewsbury, New Jersey. Dan and Roseanne Murphy, Jay and Harriet Weintraub and the Spencers attended. In the evening, we were back at the hotel and took a group photo with Jerry, Donna, Danielle, the Murphys, Weintraubs and the Spencers. All of us had a great time at the wedding

SUNDAY, JULY 15, 2001—FLIGHT BACK TO CHICAGO

After breakfast we went to by the Red Bank Public Library at 84 W. Front Street, then stopped at the Red Bank Antique Center located at 226 W. Front Street and looked inside before driving to the Newark Airport for our 5:15 p.m. trip to Chicago on United Airlines non-stop flight arriving in Chicago at 6:53 p.m.

OCTOBER 2001—BAT MITZVAH AND WEDDING IN SAME DAY
FRIDAY, OCTOBER 5, 2001—LINDA'S BAT MITZVAH

This was a crazy trip because my sister Linda was having her Bat Mitzvah on Saturday morning, October 6 and Marni's sister, Abbey Miller, was getting married to Jason King at the Westin Philadelphia that same evening.

Penny and I decided to go to both events. We started in Chicago, drove to Midway Airport and flew into Cleveland on Southwest Airlines arriving at 1:25 p.m. We picked up an Avis rental car at Cleveland Airport and drove to Linda's house.

SATURDAY, OCTOBER 6—CLEVELAND AND PHILADELPHIA

In the morning, Linda had her Bat Mitzvah and a reception at the temple. Penny and I stayed until 1:30 when we had to leave to catch US Airways Flight #466 leaving at 3:28 to Philadelphia arriving at 5:05 p.m. Upon arrival in Philadelphia, we took a taxi to The Westin Philadelphia, 17th and Chestnut at Liberty Place, the site of the Abbey Miller and Jason King's wedding that took place that evening. Upon arrival at the hotel and hurriedly got dressed for the Miller/King wedding. It was a lovely affair.

SUNDAY, OCTOBER 7—PHILADELPHIA, THEN CLEVELAND

In the morning, it was back to Cleveland on US Airways flight that left Philadelphia at 7:45 p.m. arriving in Cleveland at 9:18 p.m. We rented a car and went to Linda's house to stay overnight.

MONDAY, OCTOBER 8—FLIGHT BACK TO CHICAGO

At 12:05 p.m., Penny and I flew back to Chicago on Southwest Airlines flight and arrived at Chicago's Midway Airport about one-hour later where we picked up our car and drove home. It was a whirlwind and crazy weekend. We were exhausted when we got back to Northbrook but we were glad we made the trips.

SATURDAY, OCTOBER 27, 2001—NASHVILLE TRIP

I wanted Penny to see Nashville so we took a short trip there because I produced a reception and theme party for one on my clients, Flying J during the American Trucking Association convention. We flew to Nashville on a non-stop United Airlines Express flight that left O'Hare Airport and arrived in Nashville at 12:36 p.m. I rented an Avis car at the Nashville Airport and drove to the Opryland Hotel.

SUNDAY, OCTOBER 28, 2001—FLYING J RECEPTION

Penny and I had breakfast, and then I went to the Suwanee Ballroom to set up the Flying J Theme party reception at the Opryland Hotel. Penny had a chance to see the decorations but did not come to the reception. Each year I would produce a theme party and entertainment during the American Trucking Associations Annual Convention. This year's theme was a Southern Garden with white columns and ferns around the columns. This year the entertainment was low key and sophisticated with a baby grand piano and violin duo.

MONDAY, OCTOBER 29, 2001—FLIGHT BACK TO CHICAGO

We dropped off our rental car at Nashville Airport and had breakfast at the airport. Our United Airlines Express flight departed for Chicago on 9:24 a.m. and arrived at Chicago O'Hare Airport at 10: 59 a.m.

SATURDAY, DECEMBER 22, 2001—MOM'S 90TH BIRTHDAY

I rented an Enterprise mini-van to drive Ted and Ronna and Penny and me to Cleveland to celebrate my mother's 90th birthday that wasn't until January 12. Bennett and Marni drove separately to Cleveland. We stayed at the Cleveland East/Beachwood Hilton Hotel. Linda and I planned the party at Ward's Inn, a restaurant inside an old house on Chagrin Boulevard east of Cleveland on route 422 in Moreland Hills, Ohio. Suzyn and Bruce Epstein and my Aunt Gert drove from Youngstown for the dinner.

SUNDAY, DECEMBER 23, 2001—DRIVE BACK TO CHICAGO

We drove back to Chicago and I returned the mini-van to Enterprise Rent-A-Car on Monday, December 24tH. Linda and I told our mother that we were planning her 100th birthday and she shouldn't disappoint us. My mother celebrated her 100th birthday on January 12, 2012 and our family helped her celebrate her century birthday with a luncheon on Saturday, February 4, 2012 at Mitchell's Fishhouse in Woodmere, Ohio. (More details about this event later in this book)

FRIDAY, DECEMBER 28, 2001—FLIGHT TO PHOENIX

At 7:30 a.m. Penny and I left Northbrook for O'Hare Airport and our flight to Phoenix on our non-stop United Airlines flight. The plane left Chicago O'Hare Airport: at 10:20 a.m. and arrived in Phoenix at 1:01 p.m. Phoenix Sky Harbor Airport: We picked up our four-door, full-size Dollar Rent A Car at Phoenix Sky Harbor Airport for a seventeen-day rental.

SATURDAY, DECEMBER 29, 2001—PICK UP AVERS

At 10:54 a.m. Penny and I picked up Jan and Rich at Phoenix Sky Harbor Airport on a non-stop American Airlines flight from Dallas/Ft. Worth. At 12:45 p.m. we ate lunch at Scottsdale's Arcadia Farms. After lunch we went to the Desert Botanical Garden and walked around for a few hours. At 7:00 p.m. The Avers and Spencers had dinner at Z'Tejas restaurant on N. Tatum at E. Shea Blvd.

SUNDAY, DECEMBER 30, 2001—CHANDLER AND AZ 88

The Avers and Spencers ate breakfast at Marriott's Suites. In the afternoon, The Schesnols, Avers and Spencers drove to Chandler and had lunch at the Kokopelli Winery & Bistro. After lunch the group walked around the area near the restaurant and stood in front of The Country Clipper, Chandler's oldest barbershop established in 1912. In the evening Penny and I had dinner at the restaurant AZ 88 with Jeffrey and Susan Schesnol, Jan and Rich Aver, and Jacqui Schesnol and her boyfriend, Scott.

MONDAY, DECEMBER 31, 2001—NEW YEAR'S EVE PARTY

The Avers and Spencers ate breakfast at U.S. Egg in Tempe. At 6:00 p.m. the Avers drove with us to Jacqui Schesnol's Phoenix townhouse. We had a great time at the New Year's party. Phil Voyce, Jacqui's friend, joined us at the party.

TUESDAY, JANUARY 1, 2002— JACQUI'S OPEN HOUSE

From 1:00 to 4:00 p.m. Jacqui Schesnol hosted an Open House.

WEDNESDAY, JANUARY 2, 2002—THE AVERS FLY BACK TO TEXAS

Penny and I drove Jan and Rich Aver to Sky Harbor Airport for their American Airlines flight back to Fort Worth, Texas.

THURSDAY, JANUARY 3, 2002—PINE TO SEE ALLAN AND JULIE

After breakfast, Penny and I drove to Pine, Arizona to visit Allan and Julie LaMagna. We spent the afternoon in Pine and drove home later in the day. On the way back to Scottsdale on route 87, there was an amazing sunset so I stopped on the side of the road to take fantastic pictures. I made five prints of these amazing sunset photos and they hang in our Northbrook kitchen.

FRIDAY, JANUARY 4, 2002—DRIVE TO TOMBSTONE, ARIZONA

After breakfast, Penny and I drove to Tombstone, Arizona. When we arrived, our first stop was the Boot Hill Graveyard and the Jewish memorial section of the cemetery. There was a plaque dedicated in 1984 to the Jewish pioneers and their Indian friends erected by the Jewish Friendship Club of Green Valley. We walked around the cemetery and saw many graves with interesting descriptions of how they died. After the cemetery, we drove into Tombstone and went to the Original Bird Cage Theater. Inside, there were many display cases of artifacts from the 1880s. A collection of rifles, pots, pans, organs and furniture from that era were on exhibition. We also stopped at the O.K. Corral and saw a reenactment of the Gunfight at O.K. Corral. The reenactment was a little hokey but fun to watch. We then drove by the Tombstone Library and headed south to Bisbee.

SATURDAY, JANUARY 5, 2002—BISBEE AND TUCSON, ARIZONA

Penny and I made reservations to stay at the Schoolhouse Inn, a former school converted to a hotel. Each hotel room had a name and upon check-in, we were assigned to the geography room. There was an old fashion pull-down world map on one wall and a globe on a stand underneath a big picture window that overlooked the road leading into the town of Bisbee. Before dinner we walked in Bisbee, passing the famous Victoria era Copper Queen Hotel and ate dinner at Café Roka, a fine dining restaurant located at historic 35 Main Street. The meal was amazing for such a small town.

The next morning after breakfast and before leaving for Tucson, we drove around Bisbee. We saw the U.S. Post Office and took a photo. We also drove by some copper mines that closed in the 1970s. The city was once known as the Queen of the Copper Camps. There is a Bisbee museum that preserves some of the history of the region but we didn't have a chance to tour it. Penny and I arrived at

Steve & Cindy Klein's house at 5726 N. Via Umbrosa in Tucson in time for lunch with their daughter Melissa. We visited for a while, and then went to lunch. I can't remember where we ate. After lunch, we drove to Scottsdale.

SUNDAY, JANUARY 6, 2002—VISIT WITH THE MURPHYS

After breakfast, Penny and I drove to see Dan, Roseanne and Karry Murphy at their house in Winfield a few miles south of Carefree. I took a photo on their patio. Penny accidently stepped twisted her ankle when she stepped down a step on a tour of their garage. She got an ice pack and Penny rested her foot on the sofa.

FRIDAY, JANUARY 11, 2002—TO L.A. FROM PHOENIX

Penny and I left Phoenix Sky Harbor Airport at 3:00 p.m. on a short Southwest Airlines flight to Burbank Airport. We arrived in Burbank at 3:25 p.m. Ronna met us at the airport and we drove to her apartment on Camden.

SATURDAY, JANUARY 12, 2002—STAY WITH RONNA & TED

Penny and I stayed with Ronna and Ted at their apartment on Camden. In the evening, we had dinner with Lynda and Herb Belinky and friends Brice and Lori Fuller, who were also living in Los Angeles at the time.

SUNDAY, JANUARY 13, 2004—SURPRISE BIRTHDAY PARTY

After breakfast, Ronna, Ted, Penny and I drove to Brea for an 11:45 a.m. surprise birthday celebration for Ted Jass. The event was held at the Mark and Jo Jass home in Yorba Linda. Mark Jass was seated on a chair looking out the window for Ted, Linda and Faith to arrive. He greeted Ted's daughter Faith first, then Ted walked through the door with a puzzled look on his face. Mark was on a chair laughing as Ted walked through the door.

There was a big crowd of Ted's friends and relatives at the party including his daughter Michele, Ted's mother, his brother, Harvey, nieces Rachel and Lisa Jass, Mark and Sharon Freilich and many others too numerous to mention.

SUNDAY, JANUARY 13, 2002—FLY BACK TO PHOENIX

Later in the day, Ted and Linda Jass drove Penny and me to Ontario Airport and we flew back to Phoenix on a Southwest Airlines flight.

MONDAY, JANUARY 14, 2002—FLIGHT BACK TO CHICAGO

Penny and I left the condo and dropped off our rental car at Phoenix Sky Harbor Airport and at 10:00 a.m. for our 12:35 p.m. a non-stop United Airlines flight to Chicago O'Hare. We arrived in Chicago at 4:51 p.m.

THURSDAY, FEBRUARY 21, 2002—FLIGHT TO LAS VEGAS

I was producing a client meeting at the Paris Hotel in Las Vegas so it was a perfect time for Penny to go with me. We departed Chicago to Las Vegas on a United Airlines flight at 10:35 a.m. and arrived in Las Vegas McCaren Airport at 12:28 p.m. IFMA's COEX '02 was held at the Paris Las Vegas. The meeting ended on Wednesday, February 22 and I rented a car so we could drive to Phoenix.

WEDNESDAY, FEBRUARY 27, 2002—PHOENIX MINI TRIP

Penny and I drove from Las Vegas to Scottsdale and stayed in our condo for the next few days.

SUNDAY, MARCH 3, 2002—DESERT BOTANICAL GARDEN

Kathy Morris, a Chicago friend, was staying in Scottsdale at the time and we met her at the Phoenix Desert Botanical Garden. We went to a butterfly exhibit and saw an afternoon concert with a female singer and a trio playing at the foot of a mountain

MONDAY, MARCH 4, 2002—FLIGHT BACK TO CHICAGO

Penny and I returned our rental car to Phoenix Sky Harbor Airport and departed Phoenix at 10:50 a.m. on a United Airlines flight to Chicago and arrived at 3:00 p.m. Executive Limousine picked us up at the airport and drove us home.

FRIDAY, MARCH 15, 2002—RONNA'S LOS ANGELES SHOWER

Penny and I flew to Los Angeles for Ronna's bridal shower. We departed for Los Angeles (LAX) on a United Airlines flight from Chicago O'Hare Airport at 11:55 a.m. and arrived in Los Angeles (LAX) at 2:17 p.m. Upon our arrival, we rented a car at the airport and drove to the Marina Beach Marriott in Marina del Rey.

SATURDAY, MARCH 16, 2002—SHOWER AND MY BIRTHDAY

Ronna's shower was held in Lynda and Herb Belinky's home. Ronna's close friends flew to LA to be at the shower.

MONDAY, MARCH 18, 2002—FLIGHT BACK TO CHICAGO

Penny and I dropped off our rental car at the Los Angeles International Airport and left southern California on a United Airlines flight at 1:50 p.m. and arrived at Chicago O'Hare at 7:37 p.m.

THURSDAY, APRIL 12, 2002—RONNA'S CHICAGO SHOWER

I picked up Penny's sister Lois on an American Airlines flight from Boston that arrived in Chicago at 1:48 p.m. and brought her back to our home.

FRIDAY, APRIL 13, 2002—RONNA'S SHOWER PICK UP

I picked up my sister Linda at 12:55 p.m. and Lynda Belinky at 4:29 p.m. and Ronna arrived at 1:25 p.m. from Los Angeles and Lynda Belinky at 4:29 p.m.

SATURDAY, APRIL 14, 2002—RONNA'S BRIDAL SHOWER

Ted flew into Chicago on an overnight flight from Los Angeles and I picked him up from Chicago's O'Hare Airport early in the morning. Around 11:00 a.m. Ronna's Bridal shower was held at a restaurant in Winnetka.

SATURDAY, MAY 25, 2002—RONNA & TED'S WEDDING

Penny and I decided to have a professional wedding planner, Reva Nathan, assist us with the planning of Ronna and Ted's wedding. After visiting Chicago's Knickerbocker Hotel, the Renaissance Hotel and the InterContinental Hotel, we decided on the InterContinental Hotel and the Memorial Day Weekend to have the wedding. We chose this hotel for the amazing beauty of the Grand Ballroom and the old world feel of the hotel. The InterContinental Hotel started out as a men's athletic club and was built in 1922. It had the largest indoor swimming pool on the twelfth floor where Johnny Weismuller, a Chicago native, trained for the 1932 summer Olympics. Penny and I had attended a wedding in February 2002 at the Fairmont Hotel and when we walked into the ballroom, the chuppah was in the round and it was a "Wow" factor. I suggested the idea to Ronna and she agreed her wedding would be in the round.

We chose Larry Eckerling's Orchestra, flowers from Keogh and Andre LeCour as our photographer. Andre was associated with Edward Fox, a 100-year-old photography studio in Chicago. We also hired videographer, Cory Torf, to capture the event. Reva also suggested not having table names put on small place cards but a scroll with everyone's name on it so there would be a record of the guests. A calligrapher made a beautiful keepsake of a scroll with everyone's table listed on it.

As Ronna was walking into the ballroom, she accidently got her dress caught on the door but it didn't rip. The wedding ceremony was beautiful and Rabbi Robert Schreibman was asked to perform it. At the reception, Ronna and I danced a jitterbug to the tune of Glenn Miller's *In the Mood*. We also decided to have a very small table for our family instead of a big head table. Reva added little "touches" to the process e.g., passing out flowers to the guests as they left the ceremony. The hotel did an outstanding job of pulling everything together.

FRIDAY, JUNE 14, 2002— THE RUBINS SOUTH HAVEN VISIT

Remey and Julie Rubin invited Penny and me to spend our 34th anniversary in South Haven, Michigan. The Rubins live at the corner of Webster and North Shore Drive. We left Northbrook after breakfast and arrived in time for lunch.

After lunch, we drove to Harbor Fest, an annual event. There were many vendors selling a variety of t-shirts, sweatshirts and other items. Julie and Penny walked around and looked at the different booths. There were also booths in one area that sold nothing but food. I took a photo of a woman holding two Pomeranians, one in each arm. We went home for dinner, then drove back carrying four folding chairs to the stage set up for the show that evening, featuring an Elvis impersonator with a band and female backup singers. We put down the chairs in a perfect spot and waited for the show to begin. The weather was cool, so Penny and Julie were wrapped in blankets. The show started at 7:30 p.m. and ended around 9:00 p.m.

SATURDAY, JUNE 15, 2002—DRAGON RACES & KAL-HAVEN PARK

After an early breakfast we drove to Harbor Fest and the Antique Market that was set up. The dragon boat races started around 8:00 a.m. and I took lots of photos of the races that took place in the South Haven harbor. About fifteen people were in each boat and each has an oar. There was a person at the front of the boat encouraging the rowers to go as fast as they can. Each participant wore life vests and each team had matching shirts. There was a person beating a large drum in the front of the boat to help with the race. Two boats, painted like dragons on the side competed at a time. We watched the races from the harbor wall and stayed until 11:00 a.m., then drove to the Rubins so Remey could show us his antique collections.

Remey has so many antique collections; he had two places to store them. One place is in the basement of the house and the other is a large room attached to their two-car garage. This place used to be a pool house before they filled in their pool. I took many photos of the downstairs and garage collections. Remey's vast collections represent museum quality exhibits because he's been collecting for many years. After lunch we drove to the Kal-Haven Trail State Park and walked to the Black River Covered Bridge. The bridge was rebuilt from an existing railroad trestle bridge into a 108-foot covered footbridge. We took photos in front of the covered bridge and walked through it. We also walked along a path back to the parking lot. After dinner we watch the sunset set over Lake Michigan starting at 8:17 p.m.

SUNDAY, JUNE 16, 2002—NEWCOME STREET LAKE BEACH

After breakfast, we walked to the beach across the street from the Rubin's home. Wooden stairs lead from the street to the beach and I took a photo of Remey, Julie and Penny at the top of the stairs. After our walk, we went to lunch at a harbor restaurant After lunch we went to the First Hebrew Congregation synagogue located at 249 Broadway Street in South Haven, then we drove home.

SUMMER VACATION JUNE 2002—LOS ANGELES
THURSDAY, JUNE 20, 2002—RONNA AND TED OPEN HOUSE

Herb and Lynda Belinky were having an open house in Los Angeles to honor Ted and Ronna's May marriage, so Penny and I decided to combine our trip to California for the open house with a vacation trip afterwards to northeastern Arizona. At 12:00 noon, we left Chicago's O'Hare Airport on United Airlines flight and arrived at LAX at 2:12 p.m. We picked up our rental car and drove to the Marina Beach Marriott Hotel and checked in around 4:00 p.m. We spent five days in Los Angeles with Ronna and Ted, saw Herb and Lynda Belinky, attended the open house and had a great time going to a variety of places and restaurants.

TUESDAY, JUNE 25, 2002—LOS ANGELES TO PHOENIX

At 1:00 p.m. Penny and I left LAX for Phoenix on United Airlines and arrived at Sky Harbor Airport at 2:19 p.m. We picked up our National Rental car and arrived at our condo around 3:30 p.m.

WEDNESDAY, JUNE 26—NORTHEASTERN ARIZONA TOUR

Penny and I spent two days in our condo buying supplies and a large ice cooler for keeping drinks and food fresh during our trip north. We were so looking forward to seeing new places in northeastern Arizona.

THURSDAY, JUNE 27—THE GRAND CANYON

After breakfast, Penny and I left for the Grand Canyon. We drove north on Interstate 17 to Flagstaff where we turned west Interstate 40 (the old route 66). We traveled on I-40 to Williams and drove north about 75 miles on route 64 to the south entrance of the Grand Canyon and the Grand Canyon Village.

We had made reservations to stay at the Yavapai Lodge. Yavapai Lodge is Grand Canyon National Park Lodges' largest facility and is surrounded by pine and juniper woodlands, about 1/2 mile from the south rim of the canyon. The rooms were modern with many services within a few steps and the location was convenient.

Yavapai East rooms had two-double beds with a private bath and fan. There was no air conditioning needed because it gets very cold at night. All rooms have television and telephone. The Lodge is located next to the Market Plaza that includes a general store, bank, and U.S. Post Office. The National Park Service

Visitor Center is within a short walk, approximately one-half mile. Yavapai Lodge features a cafeteria that is open for breakfast, lunch, and dinner. The curio shop has a wide range of gifts and a transportation/activities desk is located in the lobby. We checked in to our room at 4:00 p.m.

We ate an early dinner in the famous El Tovar Hotel that was fantastic. We tried making hotel reservations at El Tovar Hotel but we were too late because it gets booked well in advance. This premier lodging facility along the south rim of the Grand Canyon opened its doors in 1905 and was scheduled to go through a renovation in 2005. In the past, the hotel has hosted such luminaries as Theodore Roosevelt, Albert Einstein, Western author Zane Grey, and many other famous people. After dinner, we walked along a section of the south rim and I took lots of photos. After watching the sunset, we were exhausted, so we drove back to the Yavpai Motel and immediately fell asleep.

FRIDAY, JUNE 28—GRAND CANYON, PAGE, LAKE POWELL

After breakfast Penny and I took a scenic drive going east along the south rim before leaving for Page and Lake Powell. We drove east on route 64 to route 89, then drove north on 89 through Tuba City to Page. We arrived in Page in the late afternoon. Our three-night reservations were at the Courtyard by Marriott located close to the Glen Canyon Dam. There is a bridge that goes across the top of the dam and in order to get to the entrance of Lake Powell, you have to go over the bridge. It is very similar in structure to the Hoover Dam south of Las Vegas and Theodore Roosevelt Dam in Arizona. I believe they were models for the Glen Canyon Dam.

Lake Powell stretches from the Glen Canyon Dam in Arizona north along the Colorado River through Utah, past the San Juan confluence to Hite for a total of 186 miles. Including the numerous flooded canyons, Lake Powell has more than two thousand miles of shoreline, more than the entire west coast of the United States. The sheer size of this lake and the close proximity to many national parks draws visitors to its shores. I would imagine the rugged landscape and the surprising stillness of the area keeps visitors coming back for more. The fishing is supposed to be absolutely fantastic and is one of the best bass fishing lakes in the country. Lake Powell is abundant with largemouth, smallmouth and striped bass, walleye, channel catfish, bluegill and crappie. Over the years, I have seen many television fishing shows shot at Lake Powell and wanted to fish with a guide in Lake Powell.

Other than the National Park Service authorized concessionaire, you won't find the hotels, restaurants or other businesses hugging the shoreline and destroying the lake views. Except for Wahweap Lodge and Marina, hotels and shopping can only be found about fifteen minutes by car from the lodge in nearby Page, Arizona. When writing this book, more than eight thousand residents call Page, Arizona home. Many of the permanent residents are involved in tourism-related business activities or work for the nearby Salt River Project Navajo Generating Station.

SATURDAY, JUNE 29—BOAT TOUR TO RAINBOW BRIDGE

Penny and I had a terrific round-trip boat ride on Lake Powell to Rainbow Bridge. We arrived at the Wahweap Lodge and Marina around 7:30 a.m. and left about 8:00. The bridge is located in Navajo territory and is a sacred place. The boat ride was enjoyable with beautiful views of the mountains on each side of the boat. After we arrived at a dock, we had to walk quite a distance to view Rainbow Bridge. It was extremely hot but we didn't care. We arrived at the marina around 1:00 p.m.

LISA OWENS AND LAKE POWELL

After our tour to Rainbow Bridge, I had made arrangements to meet Lisa Owens, my teleprompter operator, whom I had been hiring for ten years and her husband Bob. It was a holiday weekend so Lisa and Bob were spending the weekend on the lake. They keep a houseboat and motorboat on Lake Powell so Penny and I met Lisa and Bob on their boat. We had a very nice visit and they took us for a short ride on Lake Powell in their motorboat.

SUNDAY, JUNE 30—LOOP AROUND SOUTHERN UTAH

Penny and I decided to do some exploring, so we took a two-hundred-mile drive in a loop on route 89 and 89A into southern Utah ending at Lees Ferry. Lee's Ferry is where they launch rafts that travel down the Colorado River in the Grand Canyon.

Lees Ferry has been the most important of the few canyon breaks along the Colorado River's stretch from southern Utah to western Arizona. Anyone with wagons or livestock that was planning to move between Utah and Arizona had to either make the river crossing at Lees Ferry or travel hundreds of miles out of their way. Today, Lees Ferry is the gateway to the Colorado River, the launching site for the tens of thousands of river runners who ride down the Grand Canyon every year. It is also a tourist destination and the location of one of the world's premier trout fisheries. Unfortunately, at the time, I was not into fly-fishing or I would have had my fishing equipment with me and done some fishing there.

MONDAY, JULY 1—CANYON DE CHELLY

After breakfast, Penny and I left Page and headed east on route 98, past Kaibito, then traveled north on route 160 to Kayenta on route 163 to Monument Valley, Utah. There is only one main road through Monument Valley, US route 163 that links Kayenta, Arizona with US 181 in Utah. The road approaching the Arizona/Utah border from the north gives the most famous image of the valley and possibly of the whole southwest. A long stretch of empty roads leads across a flat desert towards the one thousand foot high-unadulterated red cliffs on the horizon.

The highway cuts through the mesas at Monument Pass. Several dirt tracks leave both east and west and crisscross the red sandy landscape formations. These roads lead to Navajo residences so some discretion is necessary when visiting. This is also a good area for hiking, though there are no official trails. One possible route is around the group of formations on the southeast side of Monument Pass. This area is a cross-country trip of about four miles that involves traversing various small washes, cliffs and mesas. Monument Valley has the most amazing images of the American west. The isolated red mesas and buttes are surrounded by empty, sandy desert and have been filmed and photographed countless times over the years for movies, advertisements and holiday brochures.

The valley is not really a valley, but a wide flat, occasionally desolate landscape, the last remnants of the sandstone layers that once covered the entire area. This region is entirely within the Navajo Indian Reservation on the Utah-Arizona border. The Navajo Tribal Park continues to the San Juan branch of Lake Powell.

MONUMENT VALLEY NAVAJO TOUR GUIDE

Although you can appreciate the beauty from the main road, a lot more of the landscape is hidden from view behind long straight cliffs (the Mitchell and Wetherill Mesas), east of the road on the Arizona side. This is contained within the Monument Valley Navajo Tribal Park and reached along a short side road opposite the turn-off to Goulding. From the visitor center there are good views across three of the valley's most photographed peaks, East and West Mitten Buttes, and Merrick Butte.

For a self-guided tour of the valley, you can drive on the main road but once we got to the visitor center, Penny and I decided to take a Navajo guide for an off-road tour of Monument Valley. The three-hour road tour was in a canvas covered Jeep in blistering heat through the back roads that are off-limits to anyone not taking a Navajo tour. The view from the visitor center is spectacular enough, but most of the park can only be seen from the Valley Drive, a seventeen-mile dirt road that starts at the center and goes southeast among the towering cliffs and mesas, that include The Totem Pole, an often-photographed rock three-hundred feet high but only a few feet wide. Monument Valley is the place that famous movie director John Ford discovered when he made his Academy Award winning 1939 film, *Stagecoach*, with John Wayne. It is the place I always wanted to see from my early days of watching old cowboy movies. Ford went on to make many more films on-location in Monument Valley and our Navajo guide was able to point out various locations from these films. *The Searches*, released in 1956, also starring John Wayne, is supposed to be one of the best westerns ever made.

The road is very uneven and difficult for a non-4-wheel drive vehicle. It appears to be deliberately kept in such a condition to increase business for the many Navajo guides and four-wheel drive jeep rental cars that wait expectantly by the visitor center for tourists. I think we paid about thirty dollars per person for the tour and it was well worth the price. There were five of people in the Jeep; Penny and me, the guide and an older gay couple. Besides eroded rocks, this area also has many ancient cave and cliff dwellings, natural arches and petroglyphs.

Our guide grew up in the area, so he took us to places his family frequented when he was younger. He showed us places where he played as a youngster and where his family had picnics, where his cousin got married and where he used to go sled riding during the winter. The tour and our guide were very fascinating.

On the way back to the visitor's center, we stopped by a tent where Navajo women were selling their beads, stone necklaces and other hand-made jewelry. Our guide noticed one of his former teachers selling her wares but did not say anything to her. After our tour, we drove south on route 191 to Chinle and stayed in a Holiday Inn located on route 7 Chinle on the Navajo Indian Reservation.

TUESDAY, JULY 2—CANYON DE CHELLY TO WINSLOW

Most people we have spoken to have not heard about nor have they gone to Canyon de Chelly. This area is one of the longest continuously inhabited landscapes of North America. The cultural resources of Canyon de Chelly include distinctive architecture, artifacts and rock imagery. Canyon de Chelly sustains a living community of Navajo people who are connected to a landscape of great historical and spiritual significance. Canyon de Chelly is unique among National Park service units, as it is comprised entirely of Navajo Tribal Trust Land that remains home to the canyon community. NPS works in partnership with the Navajo Nation to manage park resources and sustain the living Navajo community. It was very interesting to listen to Navajo radio stations as we drove through the area. We couldn't understand a word but the speaking was fascinating nonetheless. After looking and walking by the canyon, we drove south on route 191 stopping at the Hubbell Trading National Historic Site. The Hubbell Trading Post is the oldest operating trading post on the Navajo Nation. The old wooden floors squeak as you enter the main door.

The trading post is like stepping back in time and experiencing this original 160-acre homestead, that includes the Trading Post, Hubbell home and Visitor Center with weavers. The Hubbell Trading Post offered a chance to become a part of this unique slice of history. We saw some very old Navajo baskets but they were too expensive to buy. After leaving the Hubbell Trading Post, we continued heading south on route 191 passing through Ganado in Apache County to Interstate 40.

WINSLOW, ARIZONA AND THE FAMOUS LA POSADA HOTEL

Our next stop for the night was Winslow, Arizona and a stay at the famous La Posada Hotel located at 303 E. Second Street. La Posada is the "last great railroad hotel," offering a unique cultural experience for southwest travelers. Built in 1929 for the Santa Fe Railway, La Posada is truly one of America's treasures and we were lucky to stay there overnight.

The La Posada story is quite captivating. It begins with Mary Colter, a famous architect and Fred Harvey, the restaurateur, who hired Colter to design the hotel. The hotel embodies her vision, from its architecture down to its finely crafted details. At one point, the Santa Fe Railroad turned this landmark hotel into corporate offices and sold all of its furnishings. Then in 1957, La Posada closed permanently and for the next forty years, its future remained uncertain.

In 1997 Allan Affeldt and his wife Tina Mion heard about the hotel and after much negotiation, purchased it, bringing with him a strong vision and commitment for returning La Posada to Colter's original concept. Restoration of the hotel started immediately and continues as I am writing this, thanks to Affeldt's efforts and the support of local preservationists, hotel guests, and a talented team of artisans and craftsmen. I believe as of our 2002 visit, some ten million dollars had been spent on the restoration. Each room is named for a famous movie star and

Penny and I stayed in the John Huston Room with a king-size bed. We explored downtown Winslow and there is a statue in the center of town that had one of *The Eagles* singing group with his guitar and the sign above it said *STANDIN ON THE CORNER*, with Winslow, Arizona painted on the building in the background. We had some tourist take our photo by the sign.

We had dinner in the hotel's famous Turquois Room and afterwards went to a fascinating lecture by a woman who was one of the original Harvey Girls. The Harvey Girls worked at the various hotels along the Santa Fe Railroad and were made famous by the 1948 movie musical starring Judy Garland called the *Harvey Girls*. The lecturer told the group that Harvey Girls were the women who brought respectability to the work of waitressing. They left the protection and poverty of home for the opportunity to travel and earn their own way in life while experiencing a bit of adventure. Fred Harvey also built hotels along the Santa Fe route and La Posada is the only one left from his vast empire.

WEDNESDAY, JULY 3—WINSLOW TO PINE, ARIZONA

After a restful sleep at La Posada and breakfast at a small coffee shop in Winslow, we took a tour of the old railroad station directly in back of La Posada. We also went to Kohlectiques; an antique shop in Winslow and Penny took a photo with the owner. I took a picture of Winslow's U.S. Post Office and the route 66 sign. We also stopped in Mother Road Antiques on one of the main streets where Penny bought a green 1940s designer beaded necklace.

We left Winslow and drove south on two-lane Arizona highway route 87, passing through the tiny town of Strawberry to see Allan and Julie LaMagna who had a log cabin house in Pine. Pine is a small town located about thirteen miles north of Payson. The weather is usually much cooler in this small community since it is about 5,400 feet above sea level. We arrived in Pine at lunchtime and a visit with Allan and Julie. After our visit, we drove back to our Scottsdale condo at 7:00 p.m. This trip had been a spectacular one covering 1,312.3 miles of northeastern Arizona.

THURSDAY, JULY 4, 2002—DIAMONDBACK BASEBALL

Steve Klein, who was working for the Tucson Chamber of Commerce, had free tickets to the Arizona Diamondbacks baseball game at Bank One Ballpark (The Bob for short) and we had a chance to see the San Francisco Giants play there at 3:00 p.m. The ballpark is now called Chase Field after Chase bought Bank One. Steve and Cindy stayed overnight with us at our condo and left the next day.

MONDAY, JULY 8, 2002—FLIGHT BACK TO CHICAGO

Around 9:30 a.m., we returned our rental car and left Phoenix Sky Harbor Airport on a non-stop United Airlines flight to Chicago at 12:45 p.m. and arriving at Chicago O'Hare at 6:15 p.m. This Arizona stay had been a great trip.

FRIDAY, JULY 26, 2002—FISHMAN WEDDING IN CLEVELAND

Penny and I flew to Cleveland for Doug Fishman and Biddy Hubman's wedding. Penny and I left Chicago O'Hare Airport on a non-stop United Airlines flight to Cleveland at 10:05 a.m. and arrived at Cleveland Hopkins Airport at 12:25 p.m. We rented a National car at the airport and drove to the Cleveland East

Beachwood Hilton at located at 3663 Park East Drive in Beachwood, Ohio.
SATURDAY, JULY 17, 2002—RONNA AND TED IN CLEVELAND
Ronna and Ted left LAX 11:50 p.m. and arrived in Cleveland at 6:50 a.m. The wedding was at a Cleveland Catholic Church and the reception and dinner was held at Cleveland's Thompson Auto Museum located.
SUNDAY, JULY 28, 2002—JOHN WAYNE AIRPORT FLIGHT
Penny and I got up early and left Cleveland on a United Airlines flight to Chicago. We left Cleveland at 6:50 a.m. and arrived in Chicago at 7:18 a.m. in time for a non-stop United Airlines flight that left Chicago at 8:05 a.m. to Orange County John Wayne Airport at 10:24 a.m. I rented a National car at the airport. My client did not want the crew to stay at the Ritz Carleton because it was too expensive so we stayed at the Doubletree Guest Suites in Dana Point. I was producing the Executive Conference for my client, *Chain Leader* magazine at the Ritz-Carlton Laguna Nigel Resort in Dana Point.
MONDAY, JULY 29, 2002—EXECUTIVE CONFERENCE
The conference was from 8:00 a.m. to 11:00 a.m. and the equipment was struck at 11:30 a.m. At 12:30 p.m., Penny and I drove Steve Dennison, my computer programmer/technician, to the John Wayne Airport for his flight back to Chicago and we were on our way to Phoenix the next day.
TUESDAY, JULY 30, 2002—FLY TO PHOENIX
Penny and I took a United Airlines Express operated by SkyWest flight that left LAX at 6:05 p.m. and arrived in Phoenix at 7:26 p.m. I picked up a car from National.
AUGUST 6, 2002—FLIGHT BACK TO CHICAGO
I dropped off our rental car at Phoenix Sky Harbor Airport and Penny and I left Phoenix on a United Airlines flight arriving in Chicago O'Hare at 6:15 p.m.
FRIDAY, AUGUST 30, 2002—LABOR DAY IN SOUTH HAVEN
Penny and I were invited to spend the Labor Day Weekend with Remey and Julie Rubin in South Haven, Michigan. We left Northbrook after breakfast and arrived in time for lunch.
SATURDAY, AUGUST 31, 2002—SOUTH HAVEN LIBRARY
After breakfast, we drove by the South Haven Public Library and I took a photo for Penny's library collection. In the afternoon, Remey had a friend who had a garage with some antique cars and memorabilia so we stopped by to check it out. There was a beautifully restored black 1929 Model A Ford pickup truck with a convertible top and a 1928 maroon painted four-door Studebaker sedan and lots of old car signs. The price tag on the window of the Studebaker was $25,000. In the evening, we watched the sunset over Lake Michigan.
SUNDAY, SEPTEMBER 1, 2002—THE HOUSE OF DAVID
After breakfast we drove to Benton Harbor, Michigan and went to a flea market. The flea market was right by Lake Michigan. There was an old military band organ parked on a trailer and the organ was playing music of a carousel. After we left the flea market, we drove by the Benton Harbor Public Library and I took a photo for Penny's library picture collection.

In the afternoon we drove to the House of David where a few people still lived. In March 1903, Benjamin and Mary Purnell co-founded a religious society called House of David in Benton Harbor, Michigan. This spiritual group also had a famous men's baseball team that played competitive exhibition games throughout the 1920s to the 1950s. All of the men had long beards.

In the 1920s, there was a sexual scandal against Benjamin Purnell and after Benjamin died in 1927, his wife Mary reorganized the group as the New Israelite House of David, better known as Mary's City of David. According to Wikipedia, as of 2010, the group had three surviving members.

So, in 2002 we went into a building with a printing press and a man with a long beard who was wearing a hat. This man was one of the last members of the House of David. He showed us what he was printing, *The New Shiloh Messenger* newspaper. There was also a woodshop there in a large building and the same man pointed to a brochure that showed a table saw. There was a building that had a sign on the side that read, Synagogue Gate of Prayer Congregation 1938. There was another sign that read Silver Queen 1883 of constantly running water coming from a spring.

MONDAY, SEPTEMBER 2, 2002—AUCTION

In the morning, we went to an auction and Penny and Julie Rubin were sitting on folding chairs looking bored. There was also an outdoor exhibit of old cars and trucks. Penny and I drove back to Northbrook but before we left, we stopped at Sherman's Dairy for delicious ice cream.

OCTOBER 2002—A FUNNY HAT STORY IN HIGHLAND PARK

Meredith Templeton, an aspiring actress and one of Bennett's friends from grade school, appeared in *Anna Christie* at the Apple Tree Theater in Highland Park, Illinois and Penny and I went to see her performance. I wore a coat and a brown fedora hat and before the play started, I hung up my coat and place my brown fedora hat on top of the coat rack. During the intermission, I noticed a man who was a member of Temple Jeremiah also attending the play. At the end of the play, I took my coat off of the rack and reached for my hat. I placed the hat on my head and noticed it seemed a little larger than my own hat but it still fit.

During that time, I took the Northwestern train from the Glencoe Station to my Chicago office. The day after the play, I was waiting for the train on the Glencoe platform and noticed the same man I had seen at the play the night before wearing my hat. I know it was my hat because it didn't fit him very well as it sat on top of his head in a funny way. Of course, he did not realize he had taken my hat by mistake. I'm not sure why, but I never told him we had switched hats. Every time I saw him waiting for the train, I got a chuckle seeing my smaller hat on top of his head. It was just one of those strange stories that I had to include in this book.

FRIDAY, OCTOBER 11, 2002—BOSTON TRIP AND CAPE COD

Penny and I were picked up at 7:45 a.m. by Executive Limousine and driven to Chicago O'Hare Airport for our trip to Boston. We flew on a non-stop United Airlines flight and left at 10:00 a.m. We arrived in Boston at 1:17 p.m. and Lois and Roy picked us up at Logan International Airport.

We went to a deli and bought some food to take to their house Falmouth,

Massachusetts on Cape Cod. Lois and Roy took us to the Coriander restaurant where we ate dinner.

SATURDAY, OCTOBER 12—FALMOUTH AND CAPE COD

After breakfast, we drove to their Falmouth house around 11:30 a.m. It was low tide when we got there. Their house is located on a marsh and has a great view of the entire area. The house had two levels with an upper and lower deck. The lower level had a couch, coffee table and two beach chairs. The upper deck had a better view of the marsh and also two bedrooms. I took many photos of the land in front of their house. The air was misty and the deck was still wet from having rained just before we arrived. Penny looked through binoculars at the beautiful landscape; afterwards, Lois took turns looking through the binoculars at the marsh. That evening, Lois and Penny had white wine and lobster for dinner while Roy and I had grilled cod with large potato wedges. After dinner we made s'mores.

SUNDAY, OCTOBER 13, 2002—CAPE COD ON A MARSH

We got up early, ate breakfast and afterwards, we looked out over the marsh and Roy pointed out different things to us. Around 10:30 a.m. we all took a walk on the beach near the house. Penny picked up some rocks and seashells to bring back to Chicago. We walked past a sign on a post that said, Closed Area, No Shell fishing per order of the Massachusetts Division of Marine Fisheries.

After our tour of the beach, we took a walk down Maker Lane, past an old grey shed and a house that had a place for the Cape Cod News and The Enterprise, two local newspapers. We took some photos of their house and of each of us. After lunch we walked on a wooden boardwalk along the marsh and by the Wing Fort house with a plaque in front of the house in memory of the owner, Frank Everett Wing.

SANDWICH, MASSACHUSETTS AND DRIVE TO NEEDHAM

Later, we drove by the Sandwich Public Library and I took a photo of Penny standing in front of it. We also went to Dexter's Grist Mill originally started on this site in 1637. The sign in front of the mill said the "mill we saw this day started operations in 1654." The mill and site were restored in 1961. There was a woman next to the mill filling large water bottles from the continuing running water coming from a well.

After the Dexter Grist Mill, we went to the Sandwich Glass Museum. There was a man inside giving a talk about various objects in the museum. After the museum we went into another old house but I can't remember anything about it and I didn't take any photos of the inside but I believe it was built in the 1600s.

We also took a tour of the 17th century Hoxie House built in 1675 in Sandwich. There was a working fireplace blazing and a docent explaining various objects in the house. The docent also told us how some of the common expressions we use today came about, e.g., a single woman who is old enough to be married but did not marry and who often spins yarn became a "spinster" and also "sleep tight" means to tighten the ropes on the bed before sleeping. Another phrase he mentioned was "don't let the bedbugs bite." A bedbug is a wrench so the expression means to don't pinch your fingers on the wrench. Around 2:30 p.m. we drove by the Mashpee Public Library and I took a photo of it as well as the Falmouth Public Library and then, the West Falmouth Library. After this, we drove back to Lois and Roy's house in Needham.

MONDAY, OCTOBER 14, 2002—FLIGHT BACK TO CHICAGO

Lois and Roy drove Penny and me to Logan International Airport and we flew back to Chicago on a United Airlines flight to Chicago. We left Boston at 3:15 p.m. and arrived in Chicago O'Hare Airport at 5:03 p.m. Executive Limousine picked us up at the airport and drove us to Northbrook.

FRIDAY NOVEMBER 1, 2002—FLY TO PHOENIX AND TUCSON

Penny and I flew to Phoenix on a United Airlines flight that left Chicago O'Hare Airport at 11:50 a.m. and arrived at Phoenix Sky Harbor Airport at 2:35 p.m. I rented a car for eleven days and we drove to Tucson for the set-up of the IFMA's 2002 Presidents Conference. The conference was held at the Loews Ventana Canyon Resort & Spa in Tucson, Arizona from Sunday, November 3 to Wednesday, November 6 with a final morning speaker. The conference was held at the Loews Ventana Canyon Resort & Spa in Tucson, Arizona. Paul Frank was my computer/audiovisual technician and Pati Hodges my teleprompter operator. For the Tuesday evening banquet, I hired Phoenix-based The Connection, a six-piece band with a female singer. After the event, the band drove back to Phoenix.

WEDNESDAY, NOVEMBER 6, 2002—VISITED THE KLEINS

After breakfast, Penny and I visited Steve, Cindy and Melissa Klein who lived down the street from the Loews Ventana Resort. After our visit, we drove to Scottsdale on another route through Florence and stayed overnight at our condo.

THURSDAY, NOVEMBER 7, 2002—PINE, ARIZONA VISIT

After breakfast, Penny and I went to Chompie's Deli and bought some bagels, potato salad and some other items and drove to Pine to visit with Allan and Julie LaMagna. Allan cooked salmon on the grill and we had a delicious lunch on their patio. Julie cared for a few horses in a nearby stable and I took photos of her with two of the horses. Penny and I also saw a farrier in action as she prepared to shoe a horse. It was the first time I saw how a farrier works with first cleaning a horse's hoof, trimming and balancing a horse's hooves, filing them, measuring the metal shoe and pounding the shoe to fit the horse and placing the shoes on the horse. It was an educational experience and I took many photos of the farrier in action. We drove back to Scottsdale in the early evening.

FRIDAY, NOVEMBER 8, 2002—RONNA IN PHOENIX

At 11:10 p.m., Penny and I picked up Ronna at Phoenix Sky Harbor Airport arriving from LAX on a United Airlines flight.

SATURDAY, NOVEMBER 9, 2002—RONNA IN SCOTTSDALE

After breakfast, Ronna, Faith Beall, Penny and me had lunch at Arcadia Farms. After lunch we drove to Fountain Hills, walked around the main street and saw the fountain in action.

SUNDAY, NOVEMBER 10, 2002—TEMPE AND RONNA TO L.A.

Kim Harrell, who worked with Ronna on *Union Square*, is a flight attendant and based in Tempe, Arizona. We got together with her for lunch a Z'Tejas restaurant off of Mill Avenue in Tempe. After lunch, Ronna, Penny and I went to the Phoenix Botanical Garden and walked around. I took a photo dancing with some children's statues after we entered the garden. At 7:00 p.m. Penny and I drove Ronna to Sky Harbor Airport and she left for Los Angeles on Southwest Airlines.

TUESDAY, NOVEMBER 12, 2002—FLIGHT TO CHICAGO

Our rental car was returned to the airport and we flew home on a United Airlines flight to Chicago at 12:40 p.m. and arrived at Chicago O'Hare Airport at 4:57 p.m. Executive Limousine picked us up at the airport and drove us back to Northbrook.

FRIDAY, AUGUST 8, 2003—WAUTERS & MELTZER WEDDING

Penny and I took a plane to Los Angeles to attend Nick Wauters and Aron Meltzer's wedding. When Ronna was in living in L.A, Nick and Ronna were writing partners for a short time. Nick was also a video editor for Pie Town Productions, a company that produced many of the Food Network shows. Several years later, Nick wrote and produced an NBC network television series that was broadcast for one season, called *The Event.*

We rented a car and stayed at the Courtyard Los Angeles on Maxella Avenue. Jan and Rich Aver happened to be in Los Angeles at the same time visiting their son Aaron, who had moved to Los Angeles. On the day they arrived, we went out to eat at a Brazilian Restaurant called the Bossa Nova. The restaurant was at the corner of Robertson and Santa Monica Blvd.

SATURDAY, AUGUST 9, 2003—NICK AND ARON'S WEDDING

At 11:30 a.m. before going to Nick and Aron's wedding, we met Ted and Linda Jass and the Avers for lunch in Pasadena at the Cheesecake Factory. That evening the poolside wedding took place at the Loews Santa Monica Beach Hotel on Ocean Avenue. It was a beautiful ceremony and we had a chance to meet Nick parents from Belgium and Aron's parents. The rest of the trip was filled with seeing friends

SUNDAY, AUGUST 10, 2003—BRUNCH AND COUSIN DINNER

Nick and Aaron's parents hosted a great brunch at Santa Monica's Il Fornaio on Ocean Avenue. We had a chance to get acquainted with both sets of parents. That evening, Penny and I had dinner with cousins Marilyn and Larry Levy, Samantha Deutsch and Lisa Levy Josefsberg at a Santa Monica Chinese Restaurant on Montana Street.

MONDAY, AUGUST 11—RANDI AND HOWARD RUBIN VISIT

Penny and I visited Randi and Howard Rubin who lived on Fuller Street in Los Angeles. Randi did the makeup for Ronna's wedding. Howard is a magician and heard I was from Youngstown. He freaked out because my home town reminded him of a Bruce Springsteen song, *Youngstown,* that he had on his computer so he burned me a copy. After our visit, we had lunch at King Pau Bistro near their house.

THURSDAY, AUGUST 14—*GOOD MORNING MIAMI* SHOW

At the time, Ronna was the Production Coordinator for *Good Morning Miami,* an NBC television sit-com. She got us tickets to see the filming of the show and

Jan and Rich Aver joined us. Before going to the show, we ate at Stanley's Restaurant on Ventura Blvd. in Studio City. We met Ronna in her office at 5:00 p.m. for the filming at 6:00 p.m. Penny and I had a chance to meet actors Mark Feuerstein and Suzanne Pleshette, the stars of the show. I was especially excited to meet Suzanne because of seeing her in movies and also on the Bob Newhart Show. She was bubbly and very friendly, as was Mark Feuerstein.

FRIDAY, AUGUST 15—DINNER WITH THE HARRELS

Penny and I checked out of the Marriott, had breakfast at Doughboys Bakery & Café, returned our rental car to LAX and took a taxi back to the hotel. Ronna picked us up and we ate dinner with the Harrells at Cameron's Restaurant near Pasadena.

SATURDAY, AUGUST 16—TED AND SANTA BARBARA TOUR

Ted, Ronna, Penny and I drove to Santa Barbara and Ted gave us a tour of the University of California at Santa Barbara campus. The campus is beautiful and we wondered how any student would be able to study in such an environment. We walked around Santa Barbara and took photos of several places.

SUNDAY, AUGUST 17—FLIGHT TO PHOENIX

Penny and I had brunch with Herb and Lynda Belinky and Ted and Ronna. After brunch, we flew to Phoenix to spend some time at our condo.

FRIDAY, AUGUST 22—CHICAGO CUBS BASEBALL

Allan LaMagna gave us tickets to a Chicago Cubs baseball game at Bank One Ballpark (now Chase Field). We saw the Cubs play the Arizona Diamondbacks with young twenty-two-year-old Carlos Zambrano pitching. There were more Cubs fans in the stadium than Diamondback fans. It was a hoot to hear the radio announcers after the game mentioning that fact on our way back to the condo.

SATURDAY, AUGUST 23, 2003—THE KLEINS

Steve and Cindy Klein drove to Scottsdale and we had lunch at the Coyote Grill in North Scottsdale. The Kleins left before dinner. After the Kleins drove back to Tucson, Penny and I ate dinner at the Paradise Bakery at Gainey Village.

MONDAY, AUGUST 25, 2003—FLIGHT BACK TO CHICAGO

Penny and I flew to Chicago arriving around 3:00 p.m. We had a great time seeing friends and spending time in our favorite place, Arizona.

FRIDAY, AUGUST 29, 2003—ALISON HAYES WEDDING

Penny and I drove to St. Louis, Missouri to attend the Alison Hayes and Jay Hoette wedding. We checked into The Ritz-Carlton located at 100 Carondelet Plaza St. Louis and I was able to upgrade to the concierge level.

SATURDAY, AUGUST 29, 2003—THE HAYES WEDDING

After breakfast at the hotel, we purposely left time to tour parts of St. Louis. Penny and I drove to the St. Louis Arch and went on a tour of the Lewis and Clark Expedition on the lower level of the famous arch. We saw two films about the Lewis and Clark Expedition that were quite interesting, but we chose not to take a tram ride to the top of the arch.

I also bought my Golden Passport card at the Arch gift shop. The $10.00 card is for people sixty-two years of age and older and it permits free admission for anyone in your party into any United States National Park for life. Such a deal!! After touring the arch, Penny and I walked along the St. Louis waterfront and stopped to take a picture in front of the sign that was under the Mississippi River Bridge. We toured the Cathedral Basilica of Saint Louis that housed the most mosaics in the world. We ate at the route 66 Brewery & Restaurant near St. Louis Union Station. Then we drove to the ice cream stand that Doc Molloy told Penny about, Ted Drewes Famous Frozen Custard where I had what they call a *Concrete*. It is a mixture of frozen custard and a candy, similar to a Dairy Queen *Blizzard* but much tastier. Since 1941, Ted Drewes Frozen Custard has been located along route 66 and has been a landmark in St. Louis since 1929.

In the evening, the wedding ceremony took place at the small chapel on the campus of Washington University in the city of Clayton, a suburb of St. Louis. The dinner reception was held in a multi-level art gallery near downtown.

SUNDAY, AUGUST 31, 2003—AFTER WEDDING BRUNCH

There was a wonderful brunch on Sunday morning. All of the Maxi-Pad girls were wedding attendants. Sarah and her husband Brent Rutter, Katie and Jeremy were there as well as Ronna and Ted. We sat with them at the brunch and were entertained by Brent. In the afternoon, we went to the Hoette's house and visited.

MONDAY, SEPTEMBER 1, 2003—DRIVE TO CHICAGO

Penny and I left St. Louis and drove back to Northbrook.

SATURDAY, OCTOBER 18, 2003—SAN ANTONIO

I had a client show (Flying J reception) in San Antonio so Penny and I flew on a non-stop United Airlines flight to San Antonio, Texas. Executive Limo picked us up at 7:30 a.m. We left Chicago's O' Hare Airport at 10:05 a.m. and arrived San Antonio Airport at 2:03 p.m. We took a taxi to the San Antonio Marriott Rivercenter located at 101 Bowie Street and was able to upgrade ro the concierge level.

Jan and Rich Aver drove south from Fort Worth and met us in San Antonio. We were able to take a walk on the Riverwalk that was right outside our hotel. We walked by the La Villita, Little Village of San Antonio and other places of interest along the way. We had frozen bananas and sat on some steps eating them.

SUNDAY, OCTOBER 19, 2003—SAN ANTONIO & AVERS

Penny and I had breakfast with Jan and Rich Aver and decided to take a Rio San Antonio River Cruise. The tour was fun and we got a chance to see many interesting sites along the way. We passed the back entrance to the La Villita. Many restaurants and cafes line the Riverwalk. After the river tour, we walked past the Bonham Exchange Dance Club and Bar and came to The Menger Hotel. This famous San Antonio hotel was built in 1859 and the home in 1907 where the section of the National Council of Jewish Women was organized with fifteen members. After passing The Menger Hotel, we walked in front of the International Accordion Festival with music and dancing on our way to see The Alamo. His historic building located on Alamo Plaza was the inspiration and a pivotal event for the establishment of the republic of Texas. Texas was under the control of Mexico and the people wanted to establish a republic. From February 23 to March 6, 1836, an attack took place at this mission by Mexican troops under General Santa Anna. The mission was finally overtaken and all of the Texans defending it inside were killed. Remember the Alamo was a battle cry that

MONDAY, OCTOBER 20, 2003—THE TEXAS HILL COUNTRY

I rented a midsize AVIS car and we drove to the Hill Country about ninety miles north of San Antonio. The area is characterized by tall, rugged hills of limestone and granite. This section of Texas was originally settled by Germans and Eastern Europeans and has a culture all its own. We stopped in the small town of Boerne, parked the car and walked into a few stores. We met a funny lady who was telling us about all the critters that are in the town. She went on and on and named a bunch of them.

We also went to Wimberley, Texas, a nearby town from Boerne and went to a glass factory there. Penny and I watched several men work on glass blowing projects. There was a retail store connected to the factory and we saw some beautiful examples of works created in this Wimberley factory.

TUESDAY, OCTOBER 21, 2003—SAN ANTONIO TO CHICAGO

Penny and I departed San Antonio for a non-stop United Airlines flight at 2:10 p.m. and arrived at Chicago O'Hare at 4:51 p.m. Executive Limo picked us up from the airport and drove us to Northbrook.

FRIDAY, DECEMBER 5, 2003—FLIGHT LOS ANGELES

Penny and I flew to Los Angeles on Friday, December 5 for Ted's MBA graduation that was held the next day.

SATURDAY, DECEMBER 6, 2003—TED GETS HIS MBA

At 10:30 a.m. Ted received a Master of Business Administration degree from The George L. Graziadio School of Business and Management at Pepperdine University. The ceremony was held on the Malibu campus. After the event a very nice luncheon was held for family and friends at Santa Monica's Il Forniao Ristorante on Ocean Drive, a wonderful Italian restaurant with delicious food.

SUNDAY, DECEMBER 28, 2003—PHOENIX TRIP

Penny and I flew to Phoenix a little late this year but I can't remember why. Our flight from Chicago left at 8:20 and we arrived at Phoenix Sky Harbor Airport a little after 11:00. We took a shuttle bus to pick up our car at National Car Rental off of 24th Street near the airport. We drove to our condo, dropped off our luggage and went back to the airport to pick up Jan and Rich Aver who arrived around 12:45 p.m.

TUESDAY, DECEMBER 30—DROVE TO PINE, ARIZONA

We all met Jeffrey, Susan and Jacqui at U.S. Egg in Tempe for their famous protein pancake (a great pancake with granola, nuts, cinnamon and currants). After breakfast, Jan and Rich met some friends and they went to a Robson community for a tour. Penny and I drove to Pine to see Allan and Julie LaMagna. We saw Allan's son Jimmy and his wife Marvy who were visiting.

WEDNESDAY, DECEMBER 31, 2003—NEW YEAR'S PARTY

The Spencers and Avers drove to Jacqui Schesnol's house in Phoenix for a New Year's Eve party.

THURSDAY, JANUARY 1, 2004—MYSTERY CASTLE TOUR

In the morning, we drove to the Scottsdale Marriott Suites in Old Scottsdale to eat breakfast and to tour the *Mystery Castle* with Jeffrey and Susan Schesnol and Jan and Rich Aver. Boyce Gulley built the castle in the 1930s for his daughter Mary Lou. It took Gulley from 1930 to 1945 to build this amazing but bizarre house. This castle has eighteen rooms and has three floors and is located at the foothills of South Mountain Park in Phoenix. At the time the castle was built, there was nothing around and it was completely isolated and in the middle no developments. Mary Lou had lived in the home since 1945 and actually gave us part of the tour. We were so happy to have met her when she was 81 years old and I was fortunate to have my photo taken with Mary Lou. She passed away at age 87 in November 2010. The house was placed on the Phoenix Historic Property Register. There is a great story behind the man and the building of his weird home and you can look it up on the Internet to find out all about it. After the Mystery House tour, we decided to drive to Dobbins Point at the top of South Mountain for a spectacular view overlooking the city of Phoenix. And an amazing view it was.

FRIDAY, JANUARY 2, 2004—DINNER WITH SCHESNOLS

Aaron Aver and a friend drove to Scottsdale from Los Angeles and arrived during the evening. We had dinner with Jeffrey and Susan at Pei Wei while Jan and Rich had dinner with friends. Aaron and his friend stayed at the Country Inn and Suites hotel around the corner from our condo.

SATURDAY, JANUARY 3—MESA FLEA MARKET

At 10:30 a.m. Penny and I drove to Mesa to our favorite flea market while Jan, Rich and the boys drove to Sedona. In the evening, Penny and I had dinner at the Village Tavern in the Gainey Village Shopping Center.

SUNDAY, JANUARY 4—PAPAGO PARK

In the afternoon, Penny and I went to Papago Park and explored it. We walked around and went to the Hole in the Rock for the first time. It was a fun day seeing the beautiful landscapes of the park.

MONDAY, JANUARY 5—AVERS FLY BACK TO FORT WORTH

Penny and I drove Jan and Rich to the Phoenix Airport and we ate an early pizza dinner at Patsy Grimaldi's Restaurant in Old Scottsdale. We finished packing our suitcases and got ready to leave Phoenix for Chicago.

TUESDAY, JANUARY 6, 2004—FLY BACK TO CHICAGO

Penny and I dropped off our rental car at Sky Harbor Airport and flew back to Chicago arriving around 8:00 p.m.

THURSDAY, APRIL 22, 2004—FLY TO PHOENIX

At 6:00 a.m. Penny and I were picked up by Executive Limousine and taken to the airport for our departure to Phoenix on a United Airlines flight. Our plane left Chicago O'Hare Airport at 8:10 a.m. and arrived in Phoenix Sky Harbor Airport at 10:01 a.m. After getting our luggage, we took a Super Shuttle to Glendale and picked up our car from National Car Rental for a five-day rental.

FRIDAY, APRIL 23,2004—PHOENIX BOTANICAL GARDEN

In the afternoon, Penny and I drove to the Phoenix Botanical Garden and walked around. There was a butterfly exhibit in a large tented area so we went inside and I photographed a number of beautiful butterflies. There seemed to be hundreds of these beautiful creatures either flying around or stationary sitting on leaves or other objects. The exhibit was not a permanent one.

SATURDAY, APRIL 24, 2004—HIKING IN THE DREAMY DRAW

In the afternoon, Penny and I decided to take a hike in an area just off the Arizona's 51 highway. It was a steep climb with a path leading to the top. As we climbed, we could see the parking lot below getting smaller and smaller. There were jagged rocks and boulders along the way with a definite path and small stones so we had to watch where we were walking for fear of tripping. The hike was picturesque and near the top, you could clearly see 51 highway in the distance.

SUNDAY, APRIL 25, 2004— FISHING ON SAGUARO LAKE

After breakfast, Penny and I drove to Saguaro Lake so I could fish. The parking lot overlooked the marina and a long fishing pier. From the parking lot you got a clear view of the store where you could rent a boat, buy gas, supplies and fishing tackle. There were many boats parked in the marina. We brought a folding chair for Penny and I fished on the pier. There were several people on watercrafts and speedboats going by as I fished. Beautiful mountains surrounded the lake. I didn't catch any fish but Penny and I enjoyed the afternoon.

TUESDAY, APRIL 27, 2004—FLY BACK TO CHICAGO

At 11:00 a.m. Penny and I returned our rental car to Phoenix Sky Harbor Airport. Our United Airlines flight departed Phoenix at 12:45 a.m. and arrived at Chicago O'Hare at 6:15 p.m.

FRIDAY, MAY 14, 2004—DRIVE TO CLEVELAND

Penny and drove to Cleveland and stayed with Linda for the Saturday wedding. The rehearsal dinner was held at a restaurant in Cleveland Heights.

SATURDAY, MAY 15, 2004—DEBORAH KOPPELMAN

The wedding was held at Landerhaven. The next day we drove home.

THURSDAY, JULY 8, 2004—FLIGHT TO LOS ANGELES

Today, Penny and I flew to Los Angeles on United Airlines leaving Chicago at 7:00 a.m. and arriving at LAX at 9:07 a.m. Ronna picked us up at the airport and we checked into the Marina del Rey Marina Beach Marriott. Our dinner plans consisted of celebrating Ronna's birthday at a favorite restaurant with Nick and Aaron, Heather, Liz Dickler and Ronna and Ted.

FRIDAY, JULY 9—RONNA'S 29th BIRTHDAY

In the morning, Ronna picked us up at the hotel and we went to breakfast at Doughboys in West Hollywood where I ordered a pancake similar to the protein pancake at Scottsdale's U.S. Egg. In the afternoon we drove to Brea and had dinner with the Jass family. At 8:00 p.m. a bachelorette party was held so Ronna stayed in Brea for the party.

SATURDAY, JULY 10—DRIVE TO BREA FOR WEDDING

Just before 12:00 noon, we departed the Marriott and drove to Brea to meet Ronna and Ted at the hotel for the rehearsal dinner. Penny and I arrived at the Embassy Suites Hotel Brea-North Orange County at 4:00 p.m. The rehearsal dinner started at 6:30 p.m. at Buca di Beppo in Brea.

SUNDAY, JULY 11—JASS AND HOUGHTON WEDDING

The guys went to lunch with Ted Jass at the Claim Jumpers restaurant in Brea. After lunch, we went back to the hotel to get dressed for the 6:30 p.m. Michele and Bruce's wedding and reception held at Summit House located at 2000 East Bastanchury Road in Fullerton, California.

MONDAY, JULY 12—DRIVE BACK TO LOS ANGELES

Penny and I checked out of the Embassy Suites Hotel and drove back to the Marina Beach Marriott 4100 Admiralty Way Marina del Rey.

TUESDAY, JULY 13—AUNT DOROTHY AND MARILYN LUNCH

We checked out of the Marina del Rey Marriott at 11:00 a.m. Ronna picked us up and drove us to have lunch with Marilyn and Aunt Dorothy at Arnold Schwarzenegger's Restaurant. Aunt Dorothy moved to Los Angeles to be closer to Marilyn after Uncle Morris passed away.

After lunch Ronna drove us to LAX for our trip back to Chicago. We left LAX at 4:00 p.m. and arrived Chicago O'Hare at 9:54 p.m.

THURSDAY, JULY 22, 2004—BOSTON TRIP

Penny and I took a trip to Boston to see Lois and Roy. We left Chicago O'Hare on a United Airlines flight at 11:00 a.m. and arrived in Boston at 2:19 p.m. Lois and Roy picked us up from Logan International Airport and we drove to their home at 1976 Central Avenue in Needham, Massachusetts.

SATURDAY, JULY 24, 2004—PEABODY ESSEX MUSEUM

After breakfast, we drove to Salem and went into the Peabody Essex Museum. They were having a special exhibit called American Fancy, Exuberance in the Arts 1790-1840. The exhibit was in the upper pavilion and Barton galleries. The museum had an amazing modern ceiling with wing and sail-like metal. Lois, Penny and Roy looked at some kaleidoscopes that were on display on the first floor. After viewing the exhibit, Roy took a photo of Penny and Lois outside on the brick walkway. After leaving the museum we passed by the Derby Waterfront District and the Derby House located at 168 Derby Street. The home is the oldest brick house still standing in Salem. Down the street from the Derby House is the House of the Seven Gables. This 1668 colonial mansion was made famous by American author Nathaniel Hawthorne's novel first published in 1851.

After leaving the Derby Waterfront District, we drove into Boston and drove by Boston's Custom House built in 1849. Then we went by Boston Harbor and Pier 1 West in the Charlestown Navy Yard. We walked next to the USS Constitution that is docked there. "Old Iron Sides" as it is called has been a United States icon for more than two hundred years. The ship was heavily involved in the War of 1812. This ship is the world's oldest commissioned naval vessel still afloat. The hull is made of wood and it has three masts. The amazing thing is the ship was originally launched in 1797. After leaving the Charlestown Navy Yard, we went by the Derby House, the oldest brick house still standing in Salem.

SUNDAY, JULY 25, 2004—DOVER, NATICK AND WELLESLEY

After breakfast, we drove to Dover Town and took a photo of its public library. Then we went to Natick, Massachusetts and saw the small dam and lake there. Then we drove to Wellesley and went to the Elm Bank Gardens, also known as the

 Massachusetts Horticultural Society. We walked around the various flower and vegetable gardens and took photos.

MONDAY, JULY 26, 2004—BLUE GINGER, THEN CHICAGO

Before Lois took us to Logan International Airport, we went to Wellesley's Blue Ginger restaurant for lunch. Chef Ming Tsai made this restaurant famous. When I was working at Williams/Gerard for my IFMA client, Ming Tsai won an award and I produced a video in his honor. Lois drove Penny and me to Boston's Logan Airport and we left at 5:15 p.m. on a United Airlines flight to Chicago O'Hare Airport, arriving at 7:00 p.m.

CHAPTER TWENTY-ONE
Bass Fishing And Other Adventures

NORMAN & ALAN—BASS FISHING ON THE POTOMAC RIVER

I can't remember the exact year, but it must have been in March or April when my cousin Norman hired a fishing guide and we went bass fishing on the Potomac River. It was so cold and we were freezing. I can't remember catching any bass. All I remember was we were not dressed properly and we froze speeding on the Potomac River in a bass boat with our hats turned backwards.

WEDNESDAY, AUGUST 27, 2004—BASS FISHING IN GALENA

Arnold Grauer, my internist doctor, has been an avid bass fisherman for a long time. For the past thirty-odd years, every time I went to his office for my annual physical exam, I would see fishing photos on his wall. I would always say that I liked to fish too. It wasn't until Penny went in for her physical exam in the summer of 2004 that Arnie said he would take me on a fishing trip to Galena, Illinois and teach me how to fish for bass.

DRIVE TO GALENA, ILLINOIS

This morning Arnie picked me up and we drove to Eagle Ridge, in "The Territory" as they call it. The area is a development about ten miles east of the historic town of Galena and we rented a three-bedroom house near Lake Galena. For nine years, Arnie and his family owned a house in "The Territory" plus a sixteen-foot Lowe aluminum fishing boat with a trolling motor and a nine-horse power Johnson outboard engine. He sold the house several years before 2004 when Laura, his oldest daughter, went to college. Arnie made a special deal with the new homeowner that as long as he paid for the winter storage and upkeep of the fishing boat, whenever a member of the new owner's family was not using the boat, then Arnie could fish in it. Lake Galena was a bass factory and Arnie knew exactly where the fish were in that lake. On a weekend, we would sometimes catch over one hundred largemouth bass. There are too many times Arnie and I went fishing in Lake Galena to mention between 2004 and 2009 but I'll list a few in the upcoming paragraphs. We'd usually take a photo of the catch, and then release the bass.

SATURDAY, APRIL 22, 2006—FISHING IN GALENA

Arnie caught the largest bass I had ever seen, a seven pounder. The bass had swallowed a hook and was bleeding, Arnie put the bass back in the water but he knew it would die so he took it home and had it mounted in May by local fisherman and taxidermy guy, Don Dubin who lived in Lincolnwood.

FRIDAY, AUGUST 18, 2006—FISHING IN GALENA

Arnie Grauer and his wife Sarah drove to Galena as did Penny and me and we rented a house in The Territory for the weekend. We used Arnie's Lowe aluminum boat and fished for three days and we caught so many bass.

SATURDAY, AUGUST 19, 2006—FISHING IN GALENA

We went fishing while Penny and Sarah went shopping in Galena. For dinner, we went to Cannova's Italian restaurant in Galena.

SUNDAY, AUGUST 20, 2006—FISHING IN GALENA

Arnie and I went fishing early in the morning and he caught a huge walleye. We drove home in the afternoon. We caught over one hundred bass over the weekend. It was so successful; we decided to rent a house and go back the next weekend for more fishing.

FRIDAY, JULY 20, 2008 TO SUNDAY, JULY 22—A HUGE WALLEYE

Arnie and I rented a house in The Territory and went fishing the entire weekend. On this particular day, we were fishing by a large chair on the land. It was a landmark where we caught many fish. At that spot I caught my largest walleye about eight pounds. It was an amazing catch and of course Arnie took a photo of the walleye and me.

MONDAY, SEPTEMBER 6, 2004—BELINKYS ARRIVE IN CHICAGO

On Friday, August 27, 2004, Ronna and Ted left California on a road trip to Chicago. Ronna's car was shipped to Chicago on a flatbed truck and they drove Ted's Ford Explorer packed to the ceiling. During the last part of their road trip, they attended a Maxi Pad reunion at Lake of the Ozarks. They arrived in the Chicago area on Monday, September 6, 2004 moving into a rental apartment in Amling Apartments at Chevy Chase in Wheeling. Penny and I were able to pick up the keys to their apartment ahead of time, so when Ronna and Ted arrived they had a surprise bag of goodies waiting for them. We had purchased toilet paper, paper towels and cleaning supplies for them.

SEPTEMBER 2004—BENNETT AND MARNI BUY A HOUSE

After living in the city for about five years, Bennett and Marni decided to move when Marni found out she was pregnant. Bennett's high school friend, Dan Kravitz, a real estate agent, found a great house in Deerfield and they bought it. Bennett and Marni moved to 235 St. Andrews Lane less than four miles from our house. Bennett has been a freelance video camera operator, audio engineer and lighting designer for film and video productions since graduation from Columbia College. He worked on projects that have appeared on CNN, PBS, HGTV, Oprah, Dr. Phil, Court TV and a variety of corporate and association video productions and some Chicago feature film work. Marni was a graduate of Cornell University and has been writing.

FRIDAY, NOVEMBER 19, 2004-GOMSHAY/PALEY WEDDING

Penny and I were off to another wedding and this time it was in New York City. Cousin Debra Gomshay, Arleen and Michael's daughter, would be getting married to Jonathan Paley at the Roosevelt Hotel. We departed Chicago O'Hare Airport at 9:00 a.m. on a non-stop United Airlines flight to New York City and arrived in LaGuardia Airport at 11:54 a.m. We took a taxi into Manhattan and stayed at the Roosevelt Hotel located at 45 East 45th Street at Madison Avenue. That evening at 7:00, there was a rehearsal dinner at Alfredo of Rome located at 4 West 49th Street.

SATURDAY, NOVEMBER 21, 2004—GOMSHAY WEDDING
The wedding took place at 7:00 p.m. with lots of dancing. Ronna and Ted joined us but Bennett and Marni had another wedding to attend in Philadelphia. It turned out her brother Mark and Pninah were to be married on the same day.

SUNDAY, NOVEMBER 21, 2004—GOMSHAY/PALEY BRUNCH
At 9:30 a.m., a brunch was held for all of the out-of-town guests in the hotel ballroom. Penny and I left LaGuardia Airport at 4:00 p.m. on United Airlines flight and arrived back at O'Hare Airport at 5:35 p.m.

WEDNESDAY, DECEMBER 29, 2004—FORT WORTH, TEXAS
Jan and Rich invited Penny and me to spend New Year's in Fort Worth. We departed Chicago O'Hare Airport on a non-stop United Airlines flight to Dallas/Fort Worth. Our plane left Chicago at 9:55 a.m. and arrived in Dallas/Fort Worth (DFW) Airport at 12:27 p.m. Jan and Rich picked us up from the airport and we drove back to their home.

SATURDAY, JANUARY 1, 2005—CENTRAL MARKET
Jan took Penny and me to the Central Market in Fort Worth. This grocery store is amazing and we walked out of the market with several items.

SUNDAY, JANUARY 2, 2005—BREAKFAST AND ART MUSEUM
Jan and Rich took Penny and me for breakfast at Lucile's, a famous Fort Worth restaurant. After breakfast, we went to the Modern Art Museum of Fort Worth. This museum is very modern in design with lots of glass and steel. We spent lots of time looking at the sculptures and art objects in their collection. There is pond outside of the museum. After the museum, we drove back to the Avers house and Jan showed us a quilt she made from old handkerchiefs.

MONDAY, JANUARY 3, 2005—FLY TO CHICAGO
Jan and Rich drove us to the Dallas Fort Worth Airport for our non-stop United Airlines flight to Chicago. Our flight left DWF at 9:43 a.m. and we arrived at Chicago O'Hare at 11:58 a.m.

SATURDAY, JANUARY 15, 2005—SHORT CLEVELAND VISIT
It was decided my mother could not live by herself anymore so we made arrangements to have her move to Beachwood's Stone Gardens. Before she moved, Penny and I drove to Beachwood for a visit and stayed at Linda's home.

SUNDAY, JANUARY 16, 2005—DRIVE TO NORTHBROOK
Before we drove back to Northbrook, Penny polished my mother's nails, and then we headed back to Chicago.

FRIDAY, FEBRUARY 11 TO SUNDAY, FEBRUARY 13, 2005
To celebrate my mother's 93rd birthday, Bennett, Marni and us drove in separately to Beachwood. During our stay we each stayed in the Beachwood Courtyard by Marriott

THURSDAY, MARCH 24, 2005—MOVE TO STONE GARDENS
My mother went to live at Stone Gardens, an assisted living facility located next to Menorah Park. Everything is provided including three meals in the dining room. Linda furnished her apartment beautifully. My sister and I hung pictures

everywhere on the wall of her new apartment. Penny and I drove into Beachwood to be with my mother when she moved.

SUNDAY, MARCH 26, 2005—DRIVE TO NORTHBROOK

After breakfast, Penny and I visited my mother before driving leaving Beachwood and drove back to Northbrook.

FEBRUARY 2005—RONNA AND TED BUY A HOUSE

On Saturday, April 2, 2005, after doing some painting and installing wood floors on the first floor, the Belinkys moved into their new home on Knolls Drive in Buffalo Grove, Illinois. It is a four-bedroom, three bath house. The fourth bedroom is used as Ted's office.

CHAPTER TWENTY-TWO
Grandchildren, Weddings & Birthdays

THURSDAY, JUNE 23, 2005—A CALL AROUND 10:15 P.M.

Penny and I got a call from Bennett saying Marni was in labor and they were driving to Chicago's Prentiss Women's Hospital on W. Superior Street. Ronna drove to our house and the three of us drove to Chicago. We arrived around 11:00 p.m. and decided to sit in the waiting room for the good news. Meanwhile, Marni's parents were notified and were planning on flying to Chicago the next morning.

FRIDAY, JUNE 24, 2005—DANIEL MILLER SPENCER IS BORN

Marni's parents, Alan and Jill Miller, arrived at the hospital around 10:30 a.m. just in time to see Bennett to tell us that Marni had given birth to our first grandchild, Daniel Miller Spencer around 8:30 a.m. The brit was planned for eight days later on Saturday, July 2 so the Millers had to fly back to Chicago. Marni's brother Mark, her sister Abby and her husband, Jason and their son Ben flew to Chicago for the event. My sister Linda also came into Chicago for the ceremony.

SATURDAY, JULY 16, 2005—MILWAUKEE ART MUSEUM

Penny and I along with Alan and Marilyn Appelbaum and Paul Mesnick drove to the Milwaukee Art Museum. Paul Mesnick who lives in Chicago drove to the Appelbaum house and parked his car. The Appelbaums along with Paul drove to my house and I drove to Milwaukee. We arrived at the museum around 11:00 a.m. and walked across a bridge over the expressway leading to the museum. The museum is a beautiful building with wings designed by renowned architect Santiago Calatrava. Large glass windows create a spectacular view of Lake Michigan from inside the building. There is a path in back of the museum with large rocks before the lake. A glass ceiling lets in natural light to the floor below.

A very large Dale Chilhuly glass sculpture is in the center of one of the galleries. In one part of the museum a row of chairs with a flower arrangement down an aisle were set up for a wedding to take place after hours. An event was happening along Lake Michigan and people were lined up and I don't remember why everyone was lined up.

We left the museum in the afternoon and drove to the Chicago Botanic Garden for the evening. We walked around the garden and I took a picture of Paul and Alan standing by the entrance holding on to a handrail. We saw the fountain go off and I also took a photo of Alan, Marilyn, Paul and Penny sitting on a brick wall and we watched the sunset over the water.

FRIDAY SEPTEMBER 23, 2005—HILTON HEAD WEDDING

Penny and I were invited to attend Jill Birnbaum and Michael Maremont Saturday, September 24, 2005 wedding in Hilton Head, South Carolina over a long weekend. Penny and I left Chicago O'Hare Airport at 9:25 a.m. for our flight to Savannah, Georgia on a non-stop United Airlines flight#5814 on a Canadair Jet arriving in Savannah Airport at 12:45 p.m. Upon our arrival in Savannah, I picked up a car rental around 2:00 p.m. for a three-day rental.

On the way to Hilton Head, we stopped in Beaufort, South Carolina and looked around. This is a very small town and we saw a store with the name Lipshitz written in the middle of the upper floor. There was also another store that had the same name. Beth Israel Congregation was a small temple on Beaufort's main street. The drive to Hilton Head from the Savannah Airport took about forty-five-minute drive. We stayed free for two nights at the Hilton Head Marriott Beach & Golf Resort in Hilton Head, South Carolina because of the hotel points I accumulated from Marriott Rewards and the American Express Rewards programs.

SATURDAY, SEPTEMBER 24—BIRNBAUM WEDDING

The Saturday wedding was an outdoor affair and was lovely. White wooden chairs were set up on two sides making for a wide aisle. Sam and his daughter, Jill, came out of a building and walked down steps to where the wedding was held. Our seats were right where they turned to walk down the aisle, so I was able to take several photos of Sam and Jill. White wooden chairs were set up on two sides making for a wide aisle.

Andrea Maremont, Michael's mother, was a familiar face to Penny and me because she was active in Lakeview politics in the early 1970s as we were. We hadn't seen Andrea in years and after the ceremony we were able to rekindle our old neighborhood memories. Her son Michael was surprised we knew his mother.

SUNDAY, SEPTEMBER 25, 2005—SAVANNAH TOUR

During the Sunday morning wedding brunch, I took a photo with Sam Roth and Sam Birnbaum, fraternity brothers from Ohio University and former Youngstown residents. Penny took a photo with Sam's sister, Charlene.

After brunch we drove to Savannah and checked into the Courtyard Savannah Historic District Hotel at 415 Liberty Street for a one-night stay. Around 1:00 a.m. we were awakened by a fire alarm and asked to evacuate the hotel. The Savannah Fire Department and Police arrived but it was a false alarm.

After we checked into the hotel, we took a trolley bus tour of the city and just happened to see two wedding guests, Sam's cousin Harris Roth and his girlfriend, Sarah who were on the same tour. Harris and his girlfriend live in Youngstown. I found out later they got married a year after the Birnbaum/Maremont wedding.

MONDAY, SEPTEMBER 26, 2005—LUNCH, FLY TO CHICAGO

At 11:12 a.m. Penny and I waited in line at The Lady & Son's restaurant located in an old building at 311 W. Congress Street and had a delicious lunch. This is a very famous low country plantation cuisine restaurant run by the now famous Paula Dean and her two sons. The food is real Southern cooking. After you are seated, they bring you hot hush puppies with honey and crispy and light buttermilk biscuits to fill you up before you order. Penny and I did not go to the buffet line but ordered from the menu. I think one of us ordered the mac n' cheese and for dessert, we split a key lime pie. Around 3:00 p.m. Penny and I returned our rental car with a grace period of one hour and departed Savannah, Georgia and flew back to Chicago on a United Airlines flight at 5:20 p.m. arriving at Chicago O'Hare Airport at 6:54 p.m.

SATURDAY, OCTOBER 15, 2005—BOSTON TRIP

I had a client project in Boston so Penny and I were able to fly there to see Lois and Roy and for me to produce a theme party for my client, Flying J. Penny and I stayed with Lois and Roy while I stayed at the Boston Marriott Copley Place for Sunday evening. We left Chicago for Boston on a non-stop United Airlines flight at 8:35 a.m. and arrived at Boston's Logan International Airport at 11:50 a.m. Lois and Roy picked us up at the airport.

SUNDAY, OCTOBER 16, 2005—FLYING J RECEPTION

After breakfast, Lois and Roy drove into Boston and dropped me off at the Boston Marriott Copley Place. At 1:00 p.m., the stage and room set up for the theme party took place in the Constitution Ballroom during the American Trucking Associations Convention. The theme for the evening was Streets of Boston-An Evening in Boston. I had two actors dressed up as Town Criers who stood outside the ballroom and invited guests inside. The entertainment was a string quartet playing light classical & Broadway show tunes. The event took place from 6:30 to 8:30 p.m. and was a huge success. After the event, I went back to my hotel room, watched some television and fell asleep.

MONDAY, OCTOBER 17, 2005—PICK ME UP AT HOTEL

After I ate a hotel breakfast, Lois, Roy and Penny picked me up at the Boston Marriott Copley Place and we drove back to their home and spent the day together.

TUESDAY, OCTOBER 18, 2005—FLY TO CHICAGO

Lois and Roy drove Penny and me to Boston's Logan International Airport for our flight to Chicago. We departed Boston on a United Airlines flight at 6:05 p.m. that arrived in Chicago O'Hare Airport at 7:53 p.m. Executive Limousine picked us up at the airport and drove us to our Northbrook home.

FRIDAY, NOVEMBER 11, 2005—PHOENIX AND PALM DESERT

I had a client show in Palm Desert, California so to spend more time in Arizona, Penny and I usually fly into Phoenix and drive to California. After the show, we drive back to Scottsdale and spend time in our condo. Executive Limousine picked us up from our home at 6:30 a.m. for our non-stop United Airlines flight to Phoenix that departed at 9:50 a.m. We arrived at Phoenix Sky Harbor Airport. After our arrival we picked up our luggage and boarded a Super Shuttle to pick up our rental car from National Car in Glendale for an eleven-day rental with unlimited miles.

SATURDAY, NOVEMBER 12, 2005—DRIVE TO PALM DESERT

Penny and I ate our breakfast in the car while we drove to Palm Desert, California on I-10. We arrived at the JW Marriott Desert Springs Resort located at 74-855 Country Club Drive in Palm Desert, California around 1:00 p.m. and checked into the hotel for IFMA's 2005 Presidents Conference. Meanwhile, Steve Dennison flew to Los Angeles and transferred to a small plane to Palm Springs and I picked him up at the Palm Springs Airport before our crew started our set-up our audiovisual equipment in the Springs Ballroom. The set-up was complete by 8:00 p.m. Meanwhile, Steve Dennison flew to Los Angeles and transferred to a small plane to Palm Springs and I picked up Steve at the Palm Springs Airport before our set-up started at 3:00 p.m.

SUNDAY, NOVEMBER 13 TO TUESDAY, NOVEMBER 15
SPEAKER REHEARSALS, GENERAL SESSIONS & BANQUET
WEDNESDAY, NOVEMBER 16, 2005—CLOSING SESSION

After breakfast Penny and I drove back to Scottsdale from Palm Desert and arrived at our condo around 1:00 p.m. At the time, our Florida friends, Yvette and Frank Zgonc, were staying at the Pointe Hilton Squaw Peak Resort in Phoenix. Penny and I picked them up at their hotel and we went to dinner at Kona Grill in Fashion Square and had such a great time with Yvette and Frank. After dinner, we drove them back to their hotel.

THURSDAY, NOVEMBER 17, 2005—DRIVE TO PINE

After breakfast, Penny and I drove to Pine to visit with Allan and Julie LaMagna. We arrived in time for lunch and drove back later in the afternoon.

TUESDAY, NOVEMBER 22, 2005—FLIGHT TO CHICAGO

At 9:00 a.m. I dropped off our rental car at the Phoenix Sky Harbor Airport for our United Airlines flight to Chicago at 12:10 p.m. and arrived in O'Hare at 4:36 p.m. Executive Limousine picked us up and we were driven home.

SATURDAY, DECEMBER 17, 2005—PHOENIX TRIP, TAKE ONE

Penny and I left in plenty of time to catch our flight to Phoenix but United Airlines had a shortage of people at the airport so many passengers missed their flight, including us. United apologized for their lack of staff and booked us on a next day flight to Phoenix.

SUNDAY, DECEMBER 18, 2005—FLIGHT TO PHOENIX

Executive Limousine picked up Penny and me at 6:00 a.m. for our non-stop United Airlines flight to Phoenix, Arizona. We left Chicago O'Hare Airport at 8:00 a.m. and arrived in Phoenix Sky Harbor Airport at 10:51 a.m. We took the Super Shuttle to pick up our rental car at National Car Rental in Glendale. It was a three weeks and one day rental. That evening we ate dinner at Pita Jungle.

FRIDAY, DECEMBER 22, 2005—MESA FLEA MARKET

After breakfast, Penny and I drove to the Mesa Flea Market at Signal Butte Road and spent several hours there. We always buy a few items every time we go. At 12:30 p.m. we drove to Gold Canyon and had lunch with Sylvia Waters and her husband Jim. Later in the evening, Jeffrey and Susan Schesnol arrived in Phoenix from Greensboro, South Carolina.

SATURDAY, DECEMBER 23—DESERT BOTANICAL GARDEN

Penny and I ate breakfast and didn't do much during the day. At 5:30 p.m. we met Jeffrey, Susan and Jackie Schesnol at the entrance to the Desert Botanical Gardens located at 1201 N. Galvin Parkway in Phoenix for the Las Noches de Las Luminarias. After the Luminaries at 7:45 p.m. we ate dinner with the Schesnols at the Paradise Café in Fashion Square.

SUNDAY, DECEMBER 24, 2005—STOMACH FLU

I was not feeling well and had the stomach flu all day, so I slept the entire day.

MONDAY, DECEMBER 25, 2005—PICKED UP AVERS

Penny and I picked up Jan and Rich Aver at Terminal 3 at Sky Harbor Airport at 9:25 a.m. on an American Airlines flight. They flew into Phoenix at 9:25 a.m. from Dallas/Fort Worth. At 12:30 p.m. the four of us went to lunch near our condo at Jade Palace on E. Shea Blvd. At 4:00 p.m. we met the Schesnols and saw the *Dreamgirls* movie and after the film ate dinner at Goldman's Deli.

TUESDAY, DECEMBER 26, 2005—PHOENIX ART MUSEUM

The Avers are staying with us so we hung out together. At 4:45 p.m. we drove to the Phoenix Art Museum at the corner of McDowell and Central and met the Schesnols there. We toured some of the exhibits and at 7:00 p.m. ate dinner with everyone at Fez Restaurant on Central Avenue.

THURSDAY, DECEMBER 28, 2005—WRIGLEY MANSION

At 9:30 a.m. Rich returned the rental car to Avis and I picked him up there. We had an 11:45 a.m. lunch reservation at Arcadia Farm with the Schesnols and Avers. After lunch, the Avers and Spencers took a Wrigley Mansion Tour.

SATURDAY, DECEMBER 30— FARMER'S MARKET

From 9:00 a.m. until 1:00 p.m. we were at the Farmer's Market for Breakfast at Vincent Market Bistro 3930 E. Camelback Road in Phoenix. The afternoon was open. In the evening, the Avers saw the Rosensweigs for dinner. Penny and I stayed at our condo and had dinner.

SUNDAY, DECEMBER 31, 2005—AARON AND A FRIEND ARRIVE

Jan and Rich picked up their son Aaron Aver and friend who arrived in Phoenix. In the evening, we drove to Jacqui Schesnol's house for New Year's Eve.

MONDAY, JANUARY 1, 2006—HIGH TEA

At 9:00 a.m. Jan and Rich Aver went to breakfast with Sherry & Sid Stern, meanwhile Harriet and Jay arrived from Tucson and are staying with Dan and Roseanne Murphy. At 2:30 p.m. the women met at the Phoenician Resort for High Tea. From 3:00 to 5:00 p.m. the guys were at Champs Restaurant to watch football games. At 5:30 p.m., the Murphys, Weintraubs, Avers and Spencers ate dinner at the Claim Jumper Restaurant.

TUESDAY, JANUARY 2, 2006—THE AVERS LEAVE PHOENIX

Before leaving for Sky Harbor Airport, Jan, Rich, Aaron and his friend ate at Chompie's. We left for the airport at 1:00 p.m. and the Aver's flight at 3:00 p.m. for Dallas/Fort Worth. At 5:30 p.m. we had dinner with Harriet and Jay Weintraub at Eden's Grill Inn in Phoenix.

THURSDAY, JANUARY 4—THE WEINTRAUBS LEAVE PHOENIX

In the morning, Harriet and Jay Weintraub left Phoenix for Chicago. In the afternoon Corky Weily arrived in Arizona from Denver. At 5:30 p.m. Penny and I had dinner with Faith, Matt & Maddy Beall at the El Zacolo in Chandler.

FRIDAY, JANUARY 5, 2006—MET CORKY WEILY FOR LUNCH

I had not seen my second cousin, Corky Weily in several years. At my Aunt Dorothy's funeral, I found out that Corky spent time in Arizona during the winter. I contacted Corky and he made arrangements for Penny and me to meet him at his Fountain Hills golf club for lunch. At 12:15 p.m. we met Corky for lunch at Fire Rock Country Clubhouse Grill. Penny and I had a great time with Corky and we took a photo at the end of lunch. We talked about getting together in the future. At

8:30 p.m. Penny and I drove into Phoenix to see the Phoenix Suns play the Miami Heat.

SATURDAY, JANUARY 6, 2006—LUNCH WITH THE PAZOLS

At 12:15 p.m. Penny and I met Bobby & Jim Pazol for lunch at Arcadia Farms at the Heard Museum North.

SUNDAY, JANUARY 7, 2007—GIMPLES & BEATLES CONCERT

At 10:00 a.m. Penny and I met Bonny and Ron Gimple for breakfast at Le Peep on N. Hayden. At 1:45 p.m. we met Jacqui Schesnol and Phil Voyce at Symphony Hall in Phoenix for a Beatles Concert. The afternoon concert featured the Phoenix Symphony Orchestra playing Beatles music.

TUESDAY, JANUARY 9, 2006—FLY BACK TO CHICAGO

At 9:00 a.m. Penny and I left for the Phoenix Sky Harbor Airport for our trip back to Chicago on a non-stop United Airlines flight. We departed Phoenix at 11:31 a.m. and arrived at Chicago O'Hare Airport at 3:53 p.m. Executive Limousine picked us up at the airport and drove us to Northbrook.

THURSDAY, FEBRUARY 23, 2006—PHOENIX FOR COEX'06

Any chance Penny and I have to get to Phoenix, we take. My client the International Foodservice Manufacturers Association (IFMA) was hosting COEX 06 (Chain Operators Exchange) in Phoenix so this was a perfect opportunity to go there and spend some time afterwards at our condo. Executive Limousine picked us up at 2:00 p.m. for our United Airlines flight. We left Chicago O'Hare Airport at 4:45 p.m. and arrived at Phoenix Sky Harbor Airport at 7:38 p.m. After our arrival, I rented a car at the airport for ten days.

SATURDAY, FEBRUARY 25, 2006—HOTEL EQUIPMENT SET-UP

At 7:30 a.m. the set-up of audiovisual equipment started at the JW Marriott Desert Ridge Resort & Spa in Phoenix. The set up was completed by 6:00 p.m. At 6:30 p.m. Ted and Linda Jass arrived in Phoenix from California.

SUNDAY, FEBRUARY 26 TO TUESDAY FEBRUARY 28, 2006 SPEAKER REHEARSALS AND GENERAL SESSIONS

WEDNESDAY, MARCH 1, 2006—DRIVE TO PINE, ARIZONA

After breakfast, Penny and drove to Pine to see Allan and Julie LaMagna. We drove back to Scottsdale in the late afternoon.

THURSDAY, MARCH 2, 2006—GIMPLES DINNER

In the early evening, I believe we went to dinner with Bonny and Ron Gimple but I don't remember where we went.

FRIDAY, MARCH 3, 2006—YVETTE AND FRANK IN PHOENIX

Yvette and Frank Zgonc arrived in Phoenix and were staying near the airport so Penny and I had dinner with them. They usually spend time in Sedona but were staying in Phoenix for a short time.

SATURDAY, MARCH 4, 2006—DRIVE TO TUCSON

In the morning, Penny and I drove to Tucson to visit with Steve, Cindy and Melissa Klein. We arrived in time for lunch. I don't remember where we ate.

SUNDAY, MARCH 5, 2006—FLY BACK TO CHICAGO

Penny and I left for Sky Harbor Airport at 12:30 p.m. We dropped off our luggage at the curb and I returned our rental car to the airport. Our non-stop United Airlines flight left Phoenix at 3:35 p.m. and arrived at Chicago O'Hare at 8:00 p.m. Executive Limousine picked us up at the airport and drove us to Northbrook.

TUESDAY, JUNE 13, 2006—CHARLEVOIX, MICHIGAN TRIP

Steve and Cindy Klein were in Southfield, Michigan visiting their families and they suggested driving to Charlevoix, Michigan and meeting there for three days. Penny and I decided to spend our wedding anniversary in Charlevoix and met up with the Kleins. We made three-day hotel reservations at the Weathervane Inn & Suites. We left Northbrook around 8:00 a.m., arrived in Charlevoix around 3:00 p.m. and checked into the hotel. Steve and Cindy Klein arrived a little after us.

THURSDAY, JUNE 15, 2006—CHARLEVOIX SUNSET

I don't remember what we did during the day but the sunset over Lake Michigan was beautiful.

FRIDAY, JUNE 16, 2006—DRIVE TO NORTHBROOK

Today is our 38th anniversary. After breakfast, Penny and I said goodbye to Steve and Cindy Klein and drove back to Northbrook arriving late in the day. The trip was lots of fun and spending time with the Kleins was a great idea.

TUESDAY, JUNE 27, 2006—GRAND RAPIDS, MICHIGAN TRIP

Penny and I were visiting Remey and Julie Rubin in South Haven, Michigan and we decided to go to Grand Rapids to see the Frederik Meijer Gardens and Sculpture Park. Remey drove and I took lots of photos and made a slide show.

FRIDAY, OCTOBER 27, 2006—FLY TO DALLAS, TEXAS

An Executive Limousine picked up Penny and me at 9:15 a.m. for a non-stop United Airlines flight to Dallas/Fort Worth, Texas. Our plane left Chicago O'Hare Airport at 11:55 a.m. and arrived in Dallas at 2:14 p.m. The client trip was for a Flying J theme party reception that was going to be held on Sunday, October 29 at the Gaylord Texan Resort and Convention Center during the American Trucking Associations Convention. Jan and Rich picked up Penny and me from the airport and we stayed in their Fort Worth home.

SATURDAY, OCTOBER 28, 2006—JAN AND RICH AVER

After breakfast, Rich and Jan drove Penny and me to Clark Gardens in Mineral Wells where we took a tour of the beautiful area.

SUNDAY, OCTOBER 29, 2006—FLYING J RECEPTION

Jan and Rich drove us to the Gaylord Texan Resort and Convention Center located at 1501 Gaylord Trail in Grapevine. The Flying J reception setup was at 12:00 noon and the reception was from 5:30 to 7:30 p.m. The theme was Jazz and Blues Nightclub and the entertainment was Benita Atterberry with her five-piece band.

MONDAY, OCTOBER 30, 2006—FLIGHT BACK TO CHICAGO

A limousine picked us up from the Gaylord Texan Resort for our non-stop United Airlines flight to Chicago. We departed Dallas/Fort Worth at 11:57 a.m. and arrived in Chicago at 2:14 p.m.

FRIDAY, NOVEMBER 10, 2006—FLY TO PHOENIX

My IFMA client was having their Presidents Conference in Tucson so whenever we have a chance, Penny and I fly to Phoenix and drive to Tucson for the show. Our non-stop United Airlines flight left Chicago's O'Hare Airport at 8:15 a.m. and we arrived in Phoenix at 11:07 a.m. When we landed, we took a Super Shuttle to National Car rental in Glendale and rented a midsize car and we stayed in our condo for one night.

SATURDAY, NOVEMBER 11, 2006—DRIVE TO TUCSON

After eating breakfast, Penny and I drove to Tucson and checked into Loews Ventana Canyon Resort located at 7000 North Resort Drive and IFMA's Presidents Conference. The equipment set-up was from 9:00 a.m. to 6:30 p.m. Penny and I had dinner with Steve and Cindy Klein.

SUNDAY, NOVEMBER 12 TO TUESDAY NOVEMBER 14
REHEARSALS, RECEPTION & GENERAL SESSIONS
WEDNESDAY, NOVEMBER 15-GS & STRIKE

The crew call was at 7:00 a.m. for the closing general session started at 8:00 that ended at 10:30 a.m. At the end of the closing general session, all of the audiovisual equipment was struck. Then we drove back to Scottsdale.

FRIDAY, NOVEMBER 17, 2006—DRIVE TO PINE, ARIZONA

After breakfast, Penny and I went to Chompie's and bought some bagels and cream cheese and drove to Pine, Arizona and paid Allan and Julie LaMagna a visit. We left after lunch and drove back to Scottsdale.

MONDAY, NOVEMBER 20, 2006—FLIGHT TO CHICAGO

I returned our rental car to the Phoenix Sky Harbor Airport and our non-stop United flight departed Phoenix at 3:27 p.m. and arrived in Chicago at 7:15 p.m.

NOVEMBER 25, 2006—MOM'S 95TH AND THANKSGIVING

Linda and I planned a celebration for my mother's 95th birthday to be held immediately after Thanksgiving on Saturday evening November 25, 2006. She didn't want the party to be called a birthday party because it was actually two months before her real birthday in January 2007 and since my mother is superstitious, this was her wish. This particular weekend was the only time every one of our Chicago family could drive into Cleveland. We choice the downstairs room of Charlie's Crab, a local restaurant on Richmond Road for the celebration. Ronna was eight months pregnant but she and Ted drove into Cleveland in our car. Bennett, Marni and Danny drove separately. Driving back from Cleveland on Sunday, November 26 was not fun. The Indiana Tollway coming into Chicago was totally backed up, so I decided to get off and drive through the back streets of Gary, Indiana that was not a good idea. The neighborhoods weren't the greatest but I managed to wind my way through Route 41 through Chicago and along the outer drive to Northbrook. After this trip, we decided never to drive to Cleveland during a Thanksgiving holiday.

TUESDAY, JANUARY 30, 2007—TALIA BELINKY BORN

Penny received a huge birthday present this year. On January 30, Ronna went into labor. It began around 6:00 in the morning with labor pains several minutes apart and lasting from thirty seconds to one minute. Ted stayed home from work and Ronna called her OBGYN doctor with the information. Her doctor told her to stop by the office around 5:00 p.m. to see if she should go to the hospital. During Ronna's visit to the doctor, she was dilated to four centimeters so it was recommended she go to the hospital. Ronna called Penny and me on the way to Evanston Hospital and we said we would be there in the atrium waiting room after dinner. Penny and I arrived at the hospital around 8:30 p.m. and Liz Gan joined us around 9:15 p.m.

Ted came out around 11:20 p.m. to tell us Talia Rose had been born at 11:07 p.m. Talia is named after Ted's grandfather, Thomas, and Rose, after Ronna's great-grandmother Rose. We found out that Talia Rose weighed 7 lbs. 7 oz. and was 19 inches long. Penny, Liz and I were able to go into the hospital delivery room around midnight to see Ronna and Talia. We took photos and left around 1:15 a.m. and got to sleep around 2:00. I did not go into the office on Wednesday, Thursday or Friday. Ted's parents, Herb and Lynda Belinky flew into Chicago on Thursday, February 1 and Penny and I picked them up at O'Hare Airport. The plane was delayed and we drove them to Ronna and Ted's home in Buffalo Grove where Marni had made food for us.

Ronna works for Hillel Foundation located on Evanston's Northwestern University's campus resigning a few weeks before her daughter, Talia, was born.

WEDNESDAY, MARCH 14, 2007—KEY WEST FISHING TRIP
In the morning, a taxi picked up Arnie Grauer and me and we left for Key West, Florida to do some ocean fishing. We departed Chicago O'Hare Airport on American Airlines flight non-stop to Miami, Florida at 10:35 a.m. and our flight arrived in Miami International Airport at 2:28 p.m. We had to transfer to a small plane for our flight into Key West. Our next flight was a small American Eagle plane that left Miami at 4:40 p.m. and arrived in Key West at 5:40 p.m. My cousin, Norman Lockshin, joined us there, flying in from Baltimore, Maryland. We stayed at the Paradise Inn, a quaint hotel one block off Duval Street where all of the restaurants and shops are located.

THURSDAY, MARCH 15 TO SATURDAY, MARCH 17, 2007
FISHING IN KEY WEST, FLORIDA
We fished for three days. Our guide on the first and second day was Mike Delph, Ralph Delph's oldest son. Ralph is supposed to be the top fishing guide in Key West and according to Mike, holds many fishing world records. Arnie had fished with Mike's younger brother Rob on some of his past Key West trips. On the first day of fishing, we took a taxi to Sunset Marina and met Mike around 7:30 a.m. A few days before, Mike bought a brand new 35-foot Sea Hunter boat with twin 275 Mercury Verado outboard engines. What a beautiful boat. The first morning on the Atlantic Ocean was a little rough and I felt nauseous. Both Arnie and Norman were also nauseous but not as bad as me. In the afternoon, Mike took us to calmer waters on the bay side and I was fine. We caught lots of fish, ten different species in all; mackerel, kingfish (King Mackerel), three different kinds of grouper, yellowtail snapper, black tip shark, barracuda and runners to use for bait.

CHINESE RESTAURANT FOR TWO NIGHT'S DINNERS
We took the yellowtail snapper and grouper to a Chinese Restaurant near the harbor and they prepared a fantastic dinner. Northbrook residents Larry Weinstock and his wife Karen joined us. The Weinstocks own a Key West condo and spend about five winter months there. The snapper was deep fried on the outside and smothered in garlic sauce. The grouper and yellowtail were prepared in a tomato sauce. Absolutely delicious!! In fact, the dinner was so delicious; we went back the next night with more freshly caught fish, this time without the Weinstocks.

SUNDAY, MARCH 18, 2007—FLIGHT FROM KEY WEST HOME
Arnie and I departed Key West for Miami on a small American Eagle flight that departed Key West at 4:30 p.m. and arrived in Miami at 5:25 p.m. Our next flight to Chicago was on an American Airlines flight that departed Miami at 7:10 p.m. and arrived at Chicago O'Hare at 9:25 p.m. This fishing trip was amazing.

FRIDAY, MAY 4, 2007—TRIP TO CLEVELAND WITH TALIA
Ronna, Talia, Penny and I drove to Cleveland to see my mother and sister, Linda. We picked up Ronna and Ted installed the car seat in our car. Ted couldn't join us because of work. Talia slept most of the way there and back. It was a wonderful weekend trip and my mother got a chance to see her great-granddaughter.

SATURDAY JULY 7, 2007—ANDREW'S GOING AWAY PARTY
Penny and I drove to Cleveland to celebrate nephew Andrew Waldman's move to Sydney, Australia. Andrew will spend two years there working for Deloitte. Linda had the party catered with some fabulous food. Andrew left for Australia on Saturday, August 11, 2007.

SUNDAY, JULY 8, 2007—YOUNGSTOWN TO SEE AUNT GERT
After the boys left, we drove to Youngstown to see my Aunt Gert and cousins Bruce and Suzyn Epstein. My Aunt Gert who can no longer take care of herself moved into Heritage Manor, a Youngstown Jewish nursing home for the aged. At age 91, she did not look good and her memory was fading.

SATURDAY, AUGUST 11, 2007—DISCOVERY WORLD
Paul Mesnick drove to the Appelbaums and parked his car. The Appelbaums and Paul drove to our home and I drove to Milwaukee's Discovery World Museum. We toured the many interesting exhibits and took photos of downtown Milwaukee and Lake Michigan. At 2:30 p.m. we left the museum for lunch at a downtown restaurant.

SUNDAY, AUGUST 26, 2007—TALIA ROSE'S BABY NAMING
Ronna and Ted had a baby naming ceremony for Talia Rose. Rabbi Josh from Hillel Foundation officiated at the event. Linda flew in from Cleveland, Lois and Roy came in from Boston, Sandy Belinky flew from Kodiak Island, Alaska and the Ted's parents arrived from Los Angeles. Ronna created the service and each of us had a part in a candle lighting ceremony. Bennett videotaped the event.

CHAPTER TWENTY-THREE
The Memory Jar

CHANUKAH PRESENT FOR PENNY

In the mid-1990s, I had Bennett and Ronna make a list of memories they experienced growing up in our family. I typed up the list on different colored sheets of paper, added my memories to it, organized the memories, cut them into small pieces of paper and put into two acrylic memory jars I bought at Crate and Barrel. I gave the jars with the cut-up memories inside to Penny as a Chanukah present. The idea was for Penny to take out one memory from a jar each day. We didn't make it to 365 memories but the following are the comments that went into the jar. Each statement had the following put in front of it: <u>Remember when</u> or <u>do you</u> <u>remember</u>.........

MEMORIES FROM ALAN

The first time I told you I loved you? And you told me that you loved me too. It was a great day in my life.

We got engaged? I didn't give you an engagement ring. My father took me to a local Youngstown jeweler the Saturday after Thanksgiving and I bought you a diamond necklace that I gave you in place of an engagement ring.

In December 1967, I gave you polka-dotted hosiery for a Chanukah present. Remember your orange dress? The one you had when we first started dating in Chicago. It came above your knees and you looked great in it.

We did not break the glass at our wedding and my cousin Shelly said that we weren't really married. The rabbi that married us didn't believe in breaking the glass so we listened to him.

Prince Arvind Singh who we met through Bonnie and Bernie Wilson? Arvind's father owned the Taj Lake Palace Hotel in Udaipur, India. Arvind was living in Chicago and studying the hotel industry so he could go back to India and help his father run the famous hotel. (Side Note: Arvind Singh Mewar is an Indian businessman and chairman of the HRH Group of hotels. After his father died, he took over the Palace Hotel in Udaipur, India and is now a maharajah. He also has a collection of antique cars).

We went pumpkin and apple picking at Sunny Acres on North Avenue with Bonnie and Bernie Wilson, Carter and Noreen Ross and Remey and Julie Rubin. It was October 1968.

We were first married and our parents came to our apartment at 441 W. Oakdale for Thanksgiving 1968? You dropped the turkey on the kitchen floor.

I was making the documentary film "The Wellington-Oakdale Old Glory Marching Society"? It was Memorial Day 1971 and we used your 1966 Chevy Impala Super Sport convertible for part of the filming.

Werner, who used to walk in our neighborhood, smoked a pipe and lived on the W. Briar Place

We sent my Grandmother Rose a winter picture of you wearing a big black hat in Lincoln Park? She thought your big hat looked like a new hairdo.

I squirted you on the face with toothpaste when you were in bed? You started laughing and I took a picture of you.

I came to your class at Schiller School and used my Super-8mm film camera during your kindergarten class in Chicago's Cabrini-Green housing project and one of your pupils danced like James Brown, the soul singer/dancer.

We toured Bellengrath Gardens in Georgia during our winter vacation Florida road trip in a 16-foot rented Winnebago motor home and the tour guide in Georgia talked about Meissen pieces of pottery with a southern accent.

We used to drive to Cleveland and Youngstown and Ronna and Bennett would fight in the back seat of the car? They drove us crazy.

You used to make cookies with Linda Jass. The kitchen table would be covered.

A Saturday morning ritual was my making pancakes for the children and Penny. I used to buy organic whole-wheat flour from the Bread Shop on Halsted Street in Chicago.

Bennett, Ronna, Mom and Dad used to go to Sally's Stage on Western Avenue in Chicago and Dewitt?

We took the children to the Museum of Natural History and the Museum of Science and Industry.

We put in a bid on our house in Tempe, Arizona in November 1991? You said you were going shopping with your aunt Helen and I said, "I'm going to buy a house."

Our trip to Spain you fell asleep on the park bench in Madrid after our plane ride from Chicago. You were probably still on a tranquilizer from the plane ride.

Guy Guilbert and I used to edit films and commercials in the back room off our kitchen on W. Briar Place? This took place from 1976 and ended when we moved to Northbrook.

Ray Pershing made your magnet boards for your tin collection? It was December 1995. You had seen the ones Ray made for Remey Rubin's typewriter ribbon tin collection.

Remember the James Taylor concert and how we had backstage passes? He signed your sweatshirt. Ronna made you cry when she told you what "Fire and Rain" was about.

A baby raccoon fell into our garbage can on the back patio and we had to call the Northbrook Animal Warden to come and get rid of it?

During our flight back to Chicago from visiting Ronna in Spain in April 1996 and we were watching the movie "Get Shorty." I was watching the film and laughing and you couldn't understand why I understood the film. We discovered you were listening to the film in Spanish. We had a good laugh.

We took a bus tour to Taliesin in Wisconsin and I thought the bus driver made a wrong turn. We were sitting in the front seat of the bus and you told me that I was not producing this show. It turned out the bus driver did make a wrong turn and we had to back track.

MEMORIES ABOUT BENNETT

Bennett ran into the dining room door that went into the bathroom and our bedroom and got a big bump on his head? We took him to Children's Memorial Hospital and the nurses gave him a Popsicle.

Bennett used to build cities out of blocks on our living room floor when we lived on W. Briar Place.

Bennett used to make matchbox cities? Ronna would almost always knock them down.

Bennett used to suck his thumb along with his blue blanket? The blanket shriveled into a small piece that we still have as a souvenir somewhere in the house.

You would buy Bennett sugar cereal when Dad was out of town.

You used to make Bennett wear a maroon sweater vest in his grade school class pictures.

Bennett collected cans and recycled them like a homeless person who had a home and lived with his parents.

Bennett loved cars and trucks? He had quite a collection of Matchbox cars and trucks and they are still in his old bedroom closet. I think we gave them to him to keep at his house.

You used to take Bennett to the YMCA on N. Marshfield in Chicago for swimming lessons.

We took both children to the Lincoln Park Zoo? Bennett used to call the farm, "The Sarm in the Zoo."
Bennett knocked the wind out of Amy Scott when he pushed her down the stairs in a sleeping bag.

We used to go to Bennett's karate classes to watch him practice.

Bennett shaved part of his finger in a 7th grade shop class.

We watched Bennett play baseball, soccer and gymnastics

Bennett used to go to "Black Bridge" in the woods underneath the railroad tracks and he floated in a homemade boat/raft.

Bennett camped out in the backyard with his friends.

Bennett was sledding with Mike Oya on Wood Oaks Hill and Bennett smashed into Mike's leg giving him a fat lip.

Bennett used to shoot off rockets in the field on Sunset Ridge. Several children in the neighborhood used to follow Bennett to the field to watch. He was like a Pied Piper.

Bennett learned how much money you spent on Ronna

MEMORIES ABOUT RONNA

Ronna was in a Brownie troop.

Ronna cried every day the first week at Camp Echo. She and Jana Schubert, Ronna's friend who lived a few houses from us on Dell Road, wrote letters to us and Nancy, Jana's mother, saying they wanted to come home. Then Ronna loved it and went back the next year.

Ronna and Faith Jass used to roller skate on George and Diane Hoffman's driveway.

Ronna went away to college. She didn't know how to do laundry or cook. So, she called you and asked you questions like "How do you get out chocolate stains?" And "How do I hard boil an egg?" And "How long should a bake potato bake?"

We were at a theater watching the play, *Peter Pan* and Ronna said "shit" out loud when Tinkerbell flew across the stage.

Ronna cried every day in nursery school and wouldn't let go of your leg. She never did graduate from nursery school.

Ronna scratched her cornea. Mike Kearns threw an ice ball at her eye and she had to wear a patch for a day.

You used to make Ronna French toast and toasted cheese sandwiches.

Ronna did not like to dial the telephone but would talk on it after it was dialed.

Ronna was in fourth grade in 1983 and we took a trip to Orlando and Disney World. Bennett twirled Ronna on a Dunkin Donuts stool and pulled her off it. We took Ronna to the hospital and she got a stitch in her head. We had a playhouse in the backyard when we moved into the house and before we built a garage in 1992.

Charlotte was a little girl who used to live on W. Briar Place and Bennett and Ronna used to play with her. She was at our house a lot.

We always were cheering Ronna on her gymnastics meets and soccer games. We were always there for her.

The day Ronna moved into the Chi Omega house in Madison? Emily had already moved her boxes in and her security box went off. We couldn't find it for a while and when we did, we didn't know how to turn it off. Everyone in the house came in to see what had happened.

Ronna directed Humorology at the University of Wisconsin and calling us all the time frustrated and crying. And then, their group placed in the running and none of the frustration mattered anymore.

Ronna called us in the middle of the night because she thought she was dying from inhaling Tile-X. We stayed on the phone with her until she was okay.

The telephone calls from Ronna after she moved to Los Angeles. Every other week she would be sad and crying to us, saying how much she did not like living there. Then things changed and she got a different job and started meeting people, then met Ted.

CHAPTER TWENTY-FOUR
Trips To Various Places

SATURDAY, OCTOBER 27, 2007—BOSTON TRIP
Penny and I flew to Boston to celebrate her sister Lois' sixtieth birthday. We had a limo pick us up at 6:00 a.m. for an 8:05 a.m. flight. We took off on time and arrived on time at 11:15 a.m. Lois and Roy met Penny and me at the Boston's Logan Airport and we drove to their house in Needham where we had a delicious lunch with items Lois bought. There was hummus, tuna salad, cucumbers and yogurt, seafood/crab salad, pita bread and many more delicious foods. We brought Lois and Roy a seedless rye bread from Leonard's Bakery in Northbrook.

WE TRIED SOME FISHING SPOTS
After lunch, about 3:00, Roy and I walked to the pond around the corner and behind their house. We fished a few places on the pond, and then went to the Charles River to try our luck. No luck either place. So, we went to a reservoir where Roy had taken his children many years ago. Still, we had no luck. We had to be back by 5:30 p.m. as we were going to Summerville to eat dinner and see a concert.

SUMMERVILLE CONCERT
We left for Summerville and ate dinner at Sagra, an Italian Restaurant. The weather was so warm, the floor length windows were totally open and we sat right by them. After dinner, we walked to the Summerville Theater. Lois and Roy bought tickets to a Greg Brown concert. We never heard of Greg Brown. The opening act was a huge surprise. Joe Price opened with an amazing guitar song and sang as he played. He was on the stage for about one hour. His wife joined him for a few songs. Both performers were from Iowa and were so impressed, we bought Joe's CD at the end of the show. After a twenty-minute intermission, we were less impressed with the headliner, Greg Brown.

SUNDAY, OCTOBER 28—FISHING AT SABRINA LAKE
After a hearty breakfast of an omelet and other goodies, Roy and I went fishing in several places and ended up at Sabrina Lake where we had gone fishing during our 2005 visit. It is a private lake next to a house Roy's client used to own. We had to go around the lake because the current owner did not want Roy to fish there. The fish in Sabina Lake were biting. I caught six largemouth bass and Roy caught three. I finally had a chance to take a photo of Roy with a bass. Two years before, I left my camera at their house so I wasn't able to take Roy's first bass catch. We used plastic wacky worms to catch the bass.

After fishing, Roy and I came back to their house where we ate an early dinner at Lee's Vietnamese Restaurant in a shopping mall in Chestnut Hill, Massachusetts. We drove back to Needham and stayed up to a little after midnight watching the Boston Red Sox win the World Series defeating the Colorado Rockies. The Red Sox swept the Rockies in four games.

MONDAY, OCTOBER 29—MANCHESTER, NEW HAMPSHIRE
After eating breakfast, we left for Manchester, New Hampshire at 10:35 a.m.

and arrived around 11:45 a.m. Penny read an article in the Chicago Tribune about Manchester's Currier Museum of Art being the only museum that owned a Frank Lloyd Wright Eusonian house. Eusonian was a term that Frank Lloyd Wright invented. It was supposed to mean a simple and an affordable house unlike some of the more expensive and elaborate houses he designed.

After arriving in Manchester, we parked the car in a public parking lot for $.50 per hour, and then walked one block to the Currier Museum of Art storefront located at 52 Hanover Street that housed the gift store and was the site of the tour. The actual museum, located in another part of Manchester, was closed for renovation and a new addition. The women at the Museum Store gave us a few restaurant recommendations and I picked Benvenuto's Lebanese/Italian restaurant about ½ block north of the museum.

TOUR OF THE ZIMMER HOUSE

After lunch we walked back to the museum store and waited until 2:00 p.m. when a docent approached us for a tour of the Zimmerman House. The house is the only residence in New England designed by the acclaimed American architect that is open to the public. Wright designed the Zimmerman house in 1950, planning its gardens, its built-in freestanding furniture, its textiles, and even the mailbox. The Zimmerman house offered a glimpse into the 1950s to 1960s and the private lives of Isadore and Lucille Zimmerman, who lived in the house for thirty-six years. When they died, the house was willed to the museum. An older woman from Florida and her younger daughter-in-law joined us on the tour. I found out later, she was born and raised in East Liverpool, Ohio, about thirty miles south of Boardman. We all got in a van and were driven to the house for a 1½-hour tour. Another docent met us at the house. The house and tour were quite fascinating.

After the tour, we drove back to Lois and Roy's house and had leftovers for dinner, then watched the Dancing With The Stars television program. Before we went to sleep, we said good-by to Roy who would be getting up early and going to work on Tuesday morning.

TUESDAY, OCTOBER 30, 2007—FLY TO CHICAGO

Roy went to work before we woke up. Lois, Penny and I had breakfast and finished packing for our trip back to Chicago. I loaded our suitcases into Roy's car and Lois drove us to a small antique store where we stopped to look around. This store had nothing but junk.

Lois and Penny stopped at a jewelry store to pick up an item Lois had left there while I fell asleep in the car. We then stopped at the Needham Free Library and I took a photo of the front of the library for Penny's library photo collection.

On our way to the Logan International Airport, Lois, Penny and I ate lunch at Farm Grille Rotissie, a Greek restaurant, in Newton. There was no traffic to Boston because thousands of people were at a rally and parade celebrating the Boston Red Sox after winning the 2007 World Series.

We arrived at the airport around 1:15 p.m. for our 3:35 p.m. flight. We arrived in Chicago about twenty minutes ahead of schedule and took a limousine home arriving around 5:45 p.m. We decided to have an omelet at George's, What's Cooking Restaurant in Deerfield. We were tired and went to bed early.

TUESDAY, DECEMBER 18, 2007—PHOENIX TRIP

Penny and I left for Phoenix on December 18 for three and one-half weeks away from Chicago. We were picked up by Executive Limousine at 6:00 a.m. and arrived at Chicago O'Hare Airport at approximately 6:30. The flight left from the B concourse so we didn't have to walk far to get to our gate. We bought our usual blueberry scone, blueberry muffin and coffee at Starbucks and waited for our flight to take off. Our United Airlines flight to Phoenix, Arizona was on time and we left at 8:20 a.m. arriving at Phoenix Sky Harbor Airport at 11:20 a.m. We were able to book free tickets using Frequent Flyer miles.

A skycap picked up our luggage and brought it to the curb to wait for a Super Shuttle so we could get our rental car at National Car in Glendale. The rental car facility is located at 5036 West Glendale Avenue at 51 Avenue, west from I-17 exit on Glendale Avenue. We go to Glendale to save over $250.00 by picking up the car away from the airport. Picking up a car at the airport is not economical because of the high taxes on top of the price of the car. After picking up our car, we decided to have lunch at the Paradise Café in the Gainey Village on N. Scottsdale Road. After lunch, the first task was to unload our suitcases and clean as much of our condo as possible. We ordered pizza at Oregano's To Go at Scottsdale & Shea and I picked it up around 7:00 p.m.

WEDNESDAY, DECEMBER 19, 2007—THE BEALL'S DINNER

In the afternoon, we drove to Terri's Consign & Design and immediately found a computer desk that will be delivered next Wednesday. Our garbage disposal was not working so I called our home warranty company who got me in contact with B & K Plumbing to have our disposal replaced. They are scheduled to come at 8:30 on Thursday. At 5:45 p.m., we met Faith, Matt, Maddy & Tyler Beall for dinner at Pita Jungle located at 1250 E. Apache Blvd. in Tempe.

FRIDAY, DECEMBER 21, 2007—STRICKERS IN SCOTTSDALE

In the morning we called my sister to wish her a happy birthday. At 11:30 a.m., Fran and Mike Stricker, good friends of Harriet and Jay Weintraub drove to Scottsdale from Tucson. Each December, they rent a condo in Oro Valley for a month and wanted to come to Scottsdale to see us and for a tour. We made lunch reservations at 12:30 our favorite restaurant, Arcadia Farms at 7014 E. 1st Avenue in Old Scottsdale. The lunch was delicious as always and after lunch we gave Fran and Mike a tour of the Phoenix and Scottsdale area. After the Strickers drove back to Tucson, Penny and I had dinner with Cindy Templer at Joyful Chinese Restaurant located at Mountain View and Hayden.

SATURDAY, DECEMBER 22—STU AND JACKIE TEMPLER

Penny and I made plans with Jac, 2007kie and Stu Templer to spend the day together. They drove to our condo and I met them in the parking lot and we ate lunch at Butterfield's on Shea. We drove all around Scottsdale, stopping at Cosanti and ended up going for pizza at 5:45 p.m. at Oregano's 3622 N. Scottsdale Road in Old Scottsdale. After dinner, the Templers drove back home to Sun City Grand.

SUNDAY, DECEMBER 23, 2007—TUCSON TRIP

At 9:45 a.m. Penny and I drove to Tucson to see my graduate school roommate Steve Klein and his wife Cindy. Melissa, their daughter had just had a nose job and was recuperating at home, so we got a chance to see her before we went to lunch at Bluefin Restaurant on Oracle Road. We went to a shopping mall and spent time eating at Blanco Tacos + Tequila for drinks and a late snack.

MONDAY, DECEMBER 24—NEW TOASTER AND ARIZONA ID

Penny and I drove to Radio Shack to buy a portable radio for her and a San Disk thumb drive for the digital photo album our children gave us for Chanukah. We then went to Linens & Things to buy a Cuisinart 4-slice toaster. I couldn't stand using our toaster oven because it took too long to make toast plus it kept on stopping and we would have to keep on running back and forth before the bagels actually got toasted. After breakfast, we drove to the Bass Pro Shops in Mesa to buy me a 2008 Urban Fishing license. A customer overheard me telling the clerk that I wish I could get a resident fishing license and avoid the out-of-state fee. The customer asked me if we owned any Arizona property. I said we owned a Scottsdale condo so he told me I could save money by going to the Department of Motor Vehicles and getting an Arizona State ID. If you own property you can get one. This ID would entitle me to get a resident fishing license. The Arizona State ID looks exactly like an Arizona driver's license except it has ID instead of driver's license on the card. Since I am over 65, the ID was free and it doesn't expire.

I didn't think of having Penny get one too, so a few days later we went back to the DMV and Penny now has her Arizona State ID. Around 2:30 p.m. we decided to have lunch at Islamorada Fish Company restaurant inside of the Bass Pro Shops. The meal was delicious and very reasonably priced. That evening we went to the Harkens 14 Theater on Shea and saw the movie Charlie Wilson's War. After the film, at 9:00 p.m., we stopped in Mimi's Café for dessert, just as they were closing. They were out of the dessert we wanted so we ended up ordering something else.

TUESDAY, DECEMBER 25, 2007—CHINESE FOOD

We had dinner back at the Joyful Chinese Restaurant.

WEDNESDAY, DECEMBER 26—ANNIE & DAN MURPHY

At 10:30 a.m. the deliveryman showed up with the computer desk we ordered from Terri's Consignment store the week before. At 4:30 p.m. Annie & Dan Murphy drove to our condo and we went to dinner at the Cafe Barrio on 16th Street, just south of Thomas in Phoenix. The meal was delicious as always.

THURSDAY, DECEMBER 27—PACKING FOR FORT WORTH.

We finished packing for our Fort Worth trip and ate dinner at a new restaurant recommended by the Gimples, called the Havana Café located on W. Bell Road in Phoenix. The food was terrific but the restaurant is now out of business.

FRIDAY, DECEMBER 28—FLY TO FORT WORTH, TEXAS

We left for Sky Harbor Airport around 2:00 p.m. and dropped off our National rental car at the airport. We took a non-stop American Airlines flight that left Phoenix at 6:00 p.m. for (DFW) and arrived at 9:15 p.m. Jan and Rich Aver met us at baggage claim. We stayed with them until we left on January 2, 2008.

Their home is at 7313 Lemonwood Lane Fort Worth, Texas.

SATURDAY, DECEMBER 29, 2007—DALLAS, TEXAS

While Penny and Jan went shopping, Rich and I watched sports on television. It was decided that on Sunday morning, we would drive to Dallas and see the Nasher Sculpture Center and indoor art museum. For dinner that evening we went to Lili's Bistro on Magnolia located at 1310 W. Magnolia Avenue in Fort Worth, about twenty-minutes from their home.

SUNDAY, DECEMBER 30, 2007—NASHER SCULPTURE CENTER

Around 11:30 a.m. we left for the Nasher Outdoor Sculpture Garden and Museum in Dallas. We spent about two hours there, and then decided to eat a late lunch at Olenjack's Grille in Arlington, a Dallas suburb.

MONDAY, DECEMBER 31, 2007—DINNER & WATCHED MOVIES

In the morning, we watched the first National Treasure movie that Jan had recorded. Since we were going to see the film's sequel in the evening, they thought it was a good idea to see the first film. It was a good idea as we decided to go to an early show at 3:40 p.m. to see National Treasure: Book of Secrets. After the film, we drove to Wasabi Sushi & Japanese Restaurant for an early dinner. We watched the film Waitress after we got home.

TUESDAY, JANUARY 1, 2008—COLLEGE FOOTBALL GAMES

Rich and I watched various college bowl games all day.

WEDNESDAY, JANUARY 2—FLY BACK TO PHOENIX

Rich drove Penny and me to the Dallas/Fort Worth Airport around 8:00 a.m. to get our flight back to Phoenix. We took an American Airlines flight that left at 11:20 a.m. arriving in Phoenix at 12:55 p.m. We took the Super Shuttle to pick up our rental car at National Car Rental for the next part of our trip. Upon arrival in Phoenix, we decided to eat a late lunch at Goldman's Deli.

THURSDAY, JANUARY 3—SAGUARO LAKE FISHING

I awakened early, went to Starbucks and bought two blueberry scones, a sandwich for lunch and a cup of coffee for the road. I drove to Saguaro Lake, about twenty-five miles from our condo, arriving around 8:15. I fished from the shore until the bait shop opened so I could rent a small fishing boat with a 9.9HP outboard motor. I met two guys at the bait shop. One of the guys was from Hubbard, Ohio, a suburb of Youngstown. It was an amazing coincidence.

I caught only one fish, my first yellow bass on a deep-diving green crank bait. The weather was brisk but sunny and it was a fun day. The scenery was spectacular and I took many photos of the rocky landscape. The Desert Belle paddleboat was also on the lake and I took a photo of it.

FRIDAY, JANUARY 4—LOST DOG TRAIL HIKING

Late in the afternoon, Penny and I went hiking at the Lost Dog Wash located at 124th Street and Via Linda in Scottsdale. We walked for about one hour and until it got close to dusk. The weather was warm so we were able to wear shorts. We got back to our condo around 5:30 p.m. with our four-door 2008 Chrysler Sebring rental car. We decided to have dinner at one of our favorite restaurants, the Eden's Grill Inn on Tatum just north of Thunderbird. We called and made sure they had catfish on the menu. The meal was delicious.

SATURDAY, JANUARY 5—PHOENIX FLEA MARKET

Around 10:00 a.m. we left for a new flea market in Phoenix. It was not a good choice as there was not much to buy and the people there were a little unsavory looking. We left the flea market around 12:15 and headed to Vincent's Marketplace for lunch. It is open from 9:00 a.m. to 1:00 p.m. every Saturday from October to April. We arrived around 12:50 p.m. The Marketplace is an outdoor event next to Vincent's Restaurant at 3930 East Camelback Road at 40th Street. There are a variety of local fresh produce vendors plus made-to-order stations set up where you can buy different kinds of food. I always get an egg white omelet and Penny orders a crepe. They also give you free tastes of dessert with the hope of you buying some.

After Vincent's we drove to the Scottsdale Center for the Performing Arts Museum Store at 7380 E. Second Street in Old Scottsdale to buy some sale items. Penny bought Mouse Paint, a big book that was in the ½ price section of the store. The book introduces colors to young children and Penny used it when she was teaching pre-school.

SUNDAY, JANUARY 6—SUNDAY A'FAIR

Almost every Sunday, at the Scottsdale Civic Center Mall, they hold a Sunday A'Fair starting at 12:00 noon. We went there but since the weather was a little chilly, not many people showed up and there really wasn't much to do. Penny looked at a jewelry booth but didn't buy anything,

TUESDAY, JANUARY 8—LOST DOG TRAILHEAD WASH HIKE

About 2:00 p.m., Penny and I took about a 1¾ hours hike in the desert at our favorite place located at the Lost Dog Wash located at 124th Street and Via Linda in Scottsdale. We took two trails we hadn't taken before and walked about three miles in total. We saw a beautiful sunset over the desert.

WEDNESDAY, JANUARY 9—CARPET CLEANING & PAZOLS

Doug from Ironwood Carpet Care arrived right on time at 8:30 a.m. to clean our condo's carpet. Penny and I went to the library and he called us around 10:30 to say he was done with his work. We called Bobbi and Jim Pazol to let them know we were on our way to have lunch with them at the Heard Museum North very close to Terra Vita where they have a home. We arrived around 11:30 and spent the entire day with them after lunch. Arcadia Farms caters the food at this museum.

SATURDAY, JANUARY 12, 2008—HIKE ON LOST DOG TRAIL

We called my mother on her 96th Birthday and took a long three-mile hike on a new trail at the Lost Dog Wash. Later in the afternoon, we drove to a different hiking trail off of Thompson Peak Parkway and McDowell Mountain Road and 104th Street. There is a 104th Street Access Area and Trailhead parking lot there. We had not been to this hiking location before. We walked for about 45 minutes until it got close to dusk. We also saw a beautiful rainbow in the sky.

SUNDAY, JANUARY 13, 2008—FLIGHT TO CHICAGO

We left for the airport at 9:15 a.m. and returned our rental car there. Fortunately, we were able to check our luggage with a skycap at the curb ahead of time rather than having to drag our four suitcases on the airport shuttle bus, then trying to maneuver to get them checked. Our non-stop United Airlines flight left Phoenix on time at 12:25 p.m. and arrived at Chicago O'Hare at 4:43 p.m. A limousine took us home to Northbrook.

SATURDAY, JANUARY 19, 2008--MOTHER'S 96TH BIRTHDAY

Since Penny and I were in Scottsdale on my mother's 96th birthday, I decided to fly to Cleveland by myself and be with her for the weekend. Penny took me to the airport and I caught a non-stop United Airlines flight on a smaller airplane at 9:00 a.m. to Cleveland. The plane was on time and landed at 11:13 a.m. Linda was having her hair done in the morning, so I took the Rapid Transit from the airport to downtown, then a transfer to the Van Aken line where Linda picked me up in front of Sand's Delicatessen. By the time I got to Sand's Deli, Linda was done with her haircut appointment and picked me up there. I stayed at Linda's home during my visit. For dinner that evening, we went to eat a Greek restaurant that was a complete disaster, because my mother didn't eat a thing.

SUNDAY, JANUARY 20, 2008—BEACHWOOD, OHIO

After breakfast, I visited my mother and spent the day with her at Stone Gardens. For Sunday dinner, we ate at Mitchell's Seafood Market and much better than the Saturday dinner at the Greek restaurant.

MONDAY, JANUARY 21, 2008—FLIGHT TO CHICAGO

Before eating breakfast, I drove to Bialy's to get bagels to take back to Chicago. For lunch, Linda, my mother and I went to Jack's Delicatessen on Cedar Road. Leaving Cleveland was another story. Linda drove me to the airport in plenty of time to catch my flight, but there were weather problems in Chicago, so my non-stop United Airlines flight got delayed. I was supposed to leave at 4:40 p.m. and ended leaving at 8:25 p.m. I kept on calling Penny with all of the flight delay news and updates. At one point during the delay, all the passengers who were on the plane were asked to deplane because the crew needed a break. They turned off the air conditioning so everyone got off the plane for a break.

ANNUAL PHYSICAL EXAM & PREVENTIVE MEDICAL TESTS

Annually around the beginning of February, I have a physical exam. I have been very fortunate as my health has been excellent. On Thursday, March 27, 2008, Dr. Grauer wanted me to have an exercise stress echocardiography test as a precaution. I passed the test with flying colors. It took place on a treadmill with wires hooked up to your body.

I have had at least four colonoscopy tests. The last time was on Monday, May 20, 2019 with Dr. David Shapiro at Lake Forest's Northwestern Hospital. It was an outpatient procedure. The tests showed no signs of polyps in my colon and all was clear. Every year I go to a urologist to check out my prostate. In 2008, I was diagnosed with BPH, an enlarged prostate, and a condition not uncommon for men over sixty. I have been going to a urologist since I was 58 years old. As a precaution, I have had three prostate biopsies. None of the procedures showed any signs of cancer. (There is more to read about my prostate later in this book).

WEDNESDAY, FEBRUARY 20, 2008—BROOKE SARA IS BORN

Marni's due date was February 17 and I was scheduled to leave Chicago on Thursday, February 21 to fly to Phoenix to produce an IFMA conference at the JW Marriott Desert Ridge Resort. Penny and I got a 4:10 a.m. call from Bennett on Wednesday, February 20 saying Penny should get dressed and go to their house to babysit Danny because they needed to go to the hospital. Penny immediately got dressed and drove to their house. As soon as Penny arrived, Bennett and Marni left for Prentice Women's Hospital in Chicago in less than 30 minutes. Brooke was born at 5:48 a.m., less than thirty-five minutes after their arrival. Brooke was 7lbs. 8 oz. and 20" long. In the meantime, I drove to my office and was there about 6:30 a.m. waiting for a call from Bennett because I wanted to see the baby before I left on my trip. I got a call from Bennett around 7:30 and took a taxi to the hospital arriving around 8:00 a.m. I held Brooke and Bennett took my picture with my camera so I could email photos to relatives before I left.

THURSDAY, FEBRUARY 21, 2008—PHOENIX TRIP

When I produce meetings in Phoenix Penny usually goes with me but not this time. She took me to Chicago's O'Hare Airport for my non-stop United Airlines Phoenix flight. The plane left on time at 8:00 a.m. and I arrived in Phoenix Sky Harbor Airport at 10:52 a.m. Upon arrival, I got my luggage at baggage claim and took a Super Shuttle to the National Car Rental in Glendale. I picked out a rental car for ten days with unlimited miles and then drove to our condo for a stay on Thursday, Friday and Saturday nights.

FRIDAY, FEBRUARY 22, 2008— EQUIPMENT SET UP

At 7:30 a.m. our crew was ready to begin the set-up of equipment at the JW Marriott Desert Ridge in Phoenix and we ended by 6:00 p.m. A security guard was hired to watch all of the equipment overnight. After the guard appeared, I drove back to our condo.

SATURDAY, FEBRUARY 23, 2008—TUESDAY, FEBRUARY 26
EQUIPMENT SET UP, REHEARSALS & GENERAL SESSIONS

I stayed at the JW Marriott Desert Ridge hotel during the show.

WEDNESDAY, FEBRUARY 27, 2008—FLIGHT TO CHICAGO

I got up early, covered all the furniture and drove to the Sky Harbor Airport, dropped off the rental car at the airport and boarded my non-stop United Airlines flight back to Chicago. The plane left Phoenix at 12:28 p.m. and arrived in Chicago at 4:50 p.m. Penny picked me up at the airport and we drove back to Northbrook.

WEDNESDAY, MARCH 19, 2008—FISHING IN LAKE AMISTAD

Arnie Grauer and I decided to try fishing in Lake Amistad, in Del Rio, Texas. Arnie drove his car to my house and I ordered a taxi to take us to Chicago's O'Hare Airport for our departure to Houston, for the first leg of our trip. Our non-stop Continental Airlines flight left Chicago at 9:48 a.m. and arrived in Houston Bush International Airport at 12:30 p.m. After our arrival in Houston, Arnie and I were hungry, so we ate lunch at Bubba's Bayou City Grill at the Houston Bush Airport before our second flight. We were on a very small non-jet Continental flight that left Houston Bush International at 2:30 p.m. and arrived in the Del Rio, Texas Airport at 4:15 p.m.

After landing in Del Rio, I rented an Enterprise Rent A Car at the airport for a midsize unlimited mileage four-day rental. Before we drove to the hotel, we stopped at a Fishing Headquarters to buy a Texas & Mexican Fishing Licenses located at 5245 W. Highway 90 in Del Rio. The cost was $15.00 per day times three days or $45.00 each. Our Mexican fishing license cost $34.00 for one week.

Our hotel was the Amistad Lake Resort located at 11207 Highway 90 West in Del Rio. We had separate rooms for the four nights. The cost of our Lake Amistad fishing guide, Jim Burkeen, was $525.00 each for the three days of fishing and at the end of the trip we tipped our guide $50.00 each. I had seen fishing shows on television that presented Lake Amistad as one of the best bass fishing lakes in North America, so that's how I decided to go here. The bass were supposed to be plentiful and a large size. Lake Amistad is part of Amistad National Recreation Area managed by the National Park Service. The dam and lake were formed in 1960 and were originally conceived a reservoir with a future toward recreational use. The first night we ate dinner at the hotel. After dinner we drove around the area and checked out where might be fishing the next day. The area was crowded with more pickup trucks and bass boats than we had ever seen.

THURSDAY, MARCH 20, 2008—FISHING LAKE AMISTAD

Arnie and I had an early breakfast and met our fishing-guide was Jim Burkeen at the dock where he launched his bass boat. Jim had been a guide on this lake for many years and was rated a top guide. The fishing on the first day was not good and our guide Jim was surprised at the lack of fish biting. We caught a few bass but nothing like we expected. So, after fishing, we treated our guide, Jim Burkeen, to dinner at The Herald restaurant located at 321 A South Main Street. We talked about the lousy fishing day, hoping for a better day tomorrow.

FRIDAY, MARCH 21, 2008—FISHING IN LAKE AMISTAD

The second day of fishing was no better and our guide was getting frustrated. We talked to some of the fisherman staying at the hotel and they said the fishing was slow. Arnie and I ate dinner at The Herald restaurant, one of the only good restaurants in Del Rio.

SATURDAY, MARCH 22, 2008—FISHING IN LAKE AMISTAD

On the third day of fishing, we ventured into Mexican waters because part of the lake stretched into Mexico. We did catch fish but it was very slow and Arnie and I were disappointed. Our fishing-guide, Jim, was so apologetic about the poor fishing; he told us he would give us a free fishing day if we returned. For the second night in a row, we ate dinner once again at The Herald restaurant in Del Rio. After dinner we went back to the hotel, relaxed and went to sleep early recounting the poor fishing experience before falling asleep.

SUNDAY, MARCH 23, 2008—FLIGHT BACK TO CHICAGO

Arnie and I got up early and drove to the Del Rio Airport and dropped off our rental car and the keys in the airport parking lot around 8:30 a.m. When we arrived, the airport was closed and we were in shock. We didn't realize the first flight out that morning was our non-Jet Continental flight departed from Del Rio, Texas to

Houston Bush International at 10:45 a.m. so the airport opened at 9:00 a.m. Our plane left Del Rio a little late and arrived in Houston at 12:34 p.m. Our non-stop Continental Airlines flight to Chicago left Houston Bush International Airport at 2:35 p.m. and we arrived at Chicago O'Hare Airport at 5:25 p.m. Overall it was a very disappointing fishing trip. The cost of the entire fishing trip including all expenses was about $1,506.00.

OUR 40TH WEDDING ANNIVERSARY TRIP TO ARIZONA
WEDNESDAY, JUNE 4, 2008—FLIGHT TO PHOENIX

Penny and I decided to spend a week in Arizona to celebrate our 40th wedding anniversary. We left on an early flight to Phoenix on Wednesday, June 4 and returned one week later on Wednesday, June 11. We arrived in Phoenix at 11:00 a.m. and took a shuttle to Glendale where we picked up our National rental car, then drove to Paradise Bakery for lunch and ate one of their great sandwiches. After lunch, we headed to our condo, unloaded our suitcases and started cleaning.

FRIDAY, JUNE 6—SHOW LOW AND PINETOP

At 8:00 a.m. Penny and I left for Show Low/Pinetop to explore the area before we checked into our bed and breakfast around 3:00 p.m. We checked into the Oakwood Inn Bed and Breakfast located at 6558 Wagon Wheel Pinetop-Lakeside, Arizona.

SATURDAY, JUNE 7—FISHING BUT NO LUCK CATCHING

In the morning, I was supposed to go fishing at Rainbow Lake but there were too many weeds in the lake and you couldn't rent a boat. I went fishing at Show Low Lake. I also fished at Fools Hollow Lake but had no luck at either place.

SUNDAY, JUNE 8—SCOTTSDALE THRU GLOBE

In the afternoon we drove back to Scottsdale from Pinetop-Lakeside via route 60, a very scenic road. The canyon views were spectacular and almost as scenic as driving to Payson. A little after 12:00 noon, we stopped in Globe and visited an old archeological site called Besh Ba Gowa and heard a lecture on Arizona birds by Jim Burns, a famous Arizona birder and author. The archeological site had been reconstructed as it was in 600 A.D. to 1400 AD. We left Globe intending to go the Boyce Thompson Arboretum State Park on route 60, three miles west of Superior, Arizona but the Arboretum closed at 4:00 p.m. so we just missed seeing it.

WEDNESDAY, JUNE 11, 2008—FLIGHT BACK TO CHICAGO

Penny and I left for the Sky Harbor Airport to return our National car rental at 12:00 noon. We departed from Phoenix Sky Harbor Airport to Chicago on our United Airlines TED flight that left Phoenix Sky Harbor Airport at 2:31 p.m. and arrived at Chicago O'Hare at 8:00 p.m.

THURSDAY, JUNE 19, 2008—FIRST BOUT WITH VERTIGO

My first episode of vertigo happened this morning. I woke up dizzy and could not go to work. I slept most of the day and had a mild headache.

FRIDAY, JUNE 27, 2008-O.K. BUT DIZZY ON SATURDAY

Today, Ronna and Ted dropped off Talia to stay at our house while they flew to California for Ted's cousin's wedding. I was O.K. until Saturday morning, June 28 when I had my second attack of dizziness. For the next two days I slept off while Penny was babysitting Talia. On Monday, June 30, I was O.K. again.

MONDAY, JUNE 30, 2008—DOCTOR'S APPOINTMENT

Today Penny drove me downtown to see Dr. Arnold Grauer, our internist, for an appointment to check out my dizziness. He examined me and determined I had Benign Positional Vertigo. He gave me several sheets that explained the condition, listed some exercises and said it might occur again. This condition is where tiny hairs in the middle ear break off and float down a tube causing dizziness. The hairs eventually disappear and the dizziness stops. Also, a quick jerk of the head can cause dizziness.

My third bout with dizziness came on Thursday afternoon, July 3. Penny and I attended a funeral for Sarah Grauer's mother and we went back to the Grauer house. That's when I started feeling dizzy again. We left and I went to sleep and woke up in the middle of the night and had trouble urinating because of my large prostate. In the morning I was still dizzy and had trouble urinating. I called the pager number of my urologist, Dr. William Lin who immediately called me back and told me to go the emergency room at Highland Park Hospital and have a catheter put in to relieve the pressure.

Penny drove me to the hospital around 10:15 a.m. I filled out paperwork while Penny parked the car and I was immediately admitted. A nurse came in and examined me and inserted the catheter. I was immediately relieved but still dizzy. Penny drove me home and for the next two days I was incapacitated. I was told to start taking a double dose of Flomax. On Monday, July 7, Penny drove me to the urologist's office where Dr. Lin removed the catheter.

My last episode with dizziness occurred on Monday, July 21. I was in my office when around 4:00 p.m. I started feeling dizzy again. I went home, ate a light dinner and went to sleep around 7:30. I woke up ten hours later completely O.K. with a mild headache. Since then, I have had no dizziness. On Monday, July 28, I had an appointment with Dr. Lin to see if everything was fine with my prostrate and everything was normal but large.

MONDAY, JULY 28, 2008—DR. ALAN SHEPARD EXAM

Just to make sure everything was O.K. with my dizziness, Dr. Grauer asked me to call for an appointment with Dr. Alan Shepard, a neurologist, for a more extensive examination. On Monday, July 28, I went to his office for an examination. I was thoroughly examined by Dr. Shepard's resident. He said I appeared to be normal but wanted me to make an appointment to have two other tests administered.

On Wednesday, August 6, I went to his office at 8:15 a.m. and had an ultrasound carotid artery and arm flow test. Both showed normal. So, the original diagnosis of Benign Positional Vertigo by Dr. Grauer was correct, an inner ear problem that hasn't come back. By the way to avoid any chance of dizziness, when getting out of bed each morning, I am careful without jerking my head.

MONDAY, DECEMBER 22, 2008—PHOENIX TRIP

Executive Limo picked us up at 6:30 a.m. and Penny and I departed from Chicago O'Hare Airport to Phoenix Sky Harbor Airport on a non-stop United

Airlines flight. The plane left Chicago at 8:47 a.m. and arrived in Phoenix at 12:00 noon. We picked up our luggage and took a Super Shuttle to get our rental car at Glendale's National car rental for thirty-seven days. We ate lunch at 2:00 p.m. at the Paradise Café in Scottsdale. We had pre-ordered Riviera pears from Harry & David Pears to arrive on Tuesday, December 23 but when we arrived at our condo the pears were sitting in front of our door.

THURSDAY, DECEMBER 25—THE AVERS PICK UP

Our breakfast consisted of take-out bagels at Chompie's. After breakfast, we drove to Sky Harbor Airport and picked up Jan & Rich Aver who flew into Phoenix on Southwest Airlines flight from Oklahoma City arriving at 11:55 a.m. We ate lunch at Goldman's Deli in Scottsdale and ate at dinner at Joyful Chinese Restaurant located on Hayden & Mountain View in Scottsdale.

FRIDAY, DECEMBER 26—NORDSTROM SHIRTS

At 11:00 a.m. we stopped at Border's before picking up Aaron Aver and bought the Beatles "Love" CD. At 11:45 a.m. we picked up Aaron Aver at Sky Harbor Airport. At 12:30 p.m. we all ate lunch at Maria Cantina in Tempe Marketplace. At 7:15 p.m. for dinner we went to the Village Tavern with the Avers and their son Aaron.

SATURDAY, DECEMBER 27, 2008—AVERS LOOK AT A CONDO

At 8:40 a.m. I drove to Chompie's for bagels to take-out and at 9:30 a.m. we went grocery shopping at Fry's on 90th Street. Jan and Rich went with Sylvia Waters to look for condos to buy as an investment. For dinner at 6:15 p.m., we went to dinner with Jan and Rich to La Fontanella Italian Restaurant in Phoenix.

MONDAY, DECEMBER 29—THE WEINTRAUB'S PICK UP

At 10:20 a.m. Penny and I picked up Harriet and Jay Weintraub at Sky Harbor Airport and drove them to Tucson to visit Fran & Mike Stricker. They flew into Phoenix on American Airlines that left Chicago at 7:25 a.m. The Weintraubs will stay with the Strickers for a few days, then rent a car and drive to Scottsdale. At 12:15 p.m. the Strickers, Weintraubs and the Spencers ate lunch at Tucson's Botanical Gardens, then Penny and I drove back to Scottsdale. From November 2008, my left foot had been numb since using the snow blower during a big snowstorm, so I decided to go to the Mayo Clinic Hospital Emergency Room at 5:00 p.m. after our return from Tucson. At 8:30 p.m. we finally left hospital and went to Walgreens for a prescription.

TUESDAY, DECEMBER 30— AARON AIRPORT DROP OFF

At 12:00 p.m. The Avers and Spencers ate lunch at Sushi Ko Restaurant next to Chompie's, and then at 1:30 p.m., we dropped off dropped Aaron at Sky Harbor Airport for his flight to Los Angeles. After taking Aaron to airport, we stopped at Trader Joe's for some groceries.

WEDNESDAY, DECEMBER 31—FOOD AND A MOVIE

The Avers and Spencers ate breakfast at our condo. At 12:00 p.m. we had lunch reservations at Arcadia Farms in Old Scottsdale. At 3:30 p.m. we decided to see the movie *Doubt* with Meryl Streep and Phillip Hoffman at the Harkins Camelback near Fashion Square. After the movie at 6:15 p.m. we ate dinner at

Patsy Grimaldi's Pizza in old Scottsdale.

THURSDAY, JANUARY 1, 2009—COLLEGE FOOTBALL

In the morning, Rich and I watched college football games while Penny & Jan watched Twilight Zone episodes. For dinner, we decided to go to the Jade Palace Chinese Restaurant for Take-Out.

FRIDAY, JANUARY 2, 2009—THE BELLA VISTA CONDO

For breakfast, we tried to go to Matt's Big Breakfast but it was too crowded, so we ended at U.S. Egg near Osborn and N. Scottsdale Road. At 4:00 p.m. we went to see the condo Jan and Rich bought at Bella Vista on 94th Street. Then at 5:30 p.m. we drove to meet the Murphys & Weintraubs at the Murphy's new house "Trilogy" in Peoria, Arizona. It was a real schlep from Scottsdale but the house was spectacular. The Murphy's had to sell the Peoria house before they could move-in because Dan's job transferred him to Charlotte, North Carolina.

At 6:00 p.m. the Murphys, Weintraubs, Avers and Spencers went to dinner at the Thee Pitt's Again in Glendale. This restaurant was featured on Diners, Drive-Ins & Dives, the Food Network's television show featuring host Guy Fieri.

SATURDAY, JANUARY—AVERS FLY TO OKLAHOMA CITY

For breakfast, I went to Chompie's for bagels to take-out. At 2:30 p.m. we had a late lunch at Chelsea's Kitchen in Phoenix, then at 6:30 p.m. we dropped off Jan and Rich at Sky Harbor Airport for an 8:20 p.m. flight to Oklahoma City on Southwest Airlines. They arrived in Oklahoma City at 11:25 p.m.

MONDAY, JANUARY 5—MRI AT THE MAYO CLINIC

My left foot was still numb so I wanted to get to the bottom of why it was feeling this way. At 8:30 a.m. I had an appointment for an MRI at the Mayo Clinic in Scottsdale campus. At 9:30 a.m., Penny and I left the Mayo Clinic. At 10:00 a.m. we ate breakfast at Scottsdale's Butterfield's on Shea Blvd. At 4:00 p.m. we shopped at Target for some Kleenex & bathroom tissue. At 5:10 p.m. Harriet and Jay Weintraub left for Chicago on American Airlines.

TUESDAY, JANUARY 6—AN INCIDENT AT WALMART

I didn't write anything in the morning. At 4:24 p.m. Penny and I were shopping at Walmart. While at Walmart, I was standing in the aisle minding my own business when a Walmart team member who was pushing a loaded product cart hit me in the back of my left leg. I let out a yell but did not fall. The manager was summoned and they got me a chair to sit on. I pulled down my white sock to reveal a scrape with some blood. The Salt River paramedics were called. They arrived within twenty minutes with a gurney and five firemen and paramedics. One of the paramedics took down information and my blood pressure that was higher than normal. After Walmart, we tried to go to the Spaghetti Factory on Central Avenue in Phoenix but there was a three-hour wait. For a limited time, the prices were rolled back to the 1950s and the place was jammed with people. So, at 6:00 p.m., we ended up at one of our favorite places, the Barrio Café on 16th Street just south of Thomas.

FRIDAY, JANUARY 9—MAYO CLINIC CONSULTATION

At 2:20 p.m. we drove to the Mayo Clinic where I had a consultation meeting with Dr. John Freeman who gave me the results of MRI, I had at the Mayo Clinic. The results showed I had some deterioration in my back that was causing the numbness. It was mainly due to aging. Dr. Freeman recommended physical therapy to possibly help the numbness. There was no pain in the left foot, just a little numbness. At 6:15 p.m. we ate dinner with Bonny and Ron Gimple at Flo's Chinese Restaurant, then went to Yogurtology, a new frozen yogurt place nearby.

SATURDAY, JANUARY 10—SUN CITY AND FISHING

At 10:00 a.m. I drove to Sun City to go fishing with Dick Krenzein. Dick was a patient of Arnie Grauer and a friend. He owns a Sun City house with a boat docked in back. We trolled the lake in his electric boat and caught nothing. At 2:30 p.m. Penny and I had a late lunch at Scottsdale's Wildflower, then at 3:50 p.m. we saw the movie *Slumdog Millionaire* at the Shea 14-Scottdale Road Harkins Theater. What an amazing movie and it won best picture at the 2008 Academy Awards.

SUNDAY, JANUARY 11—FLEA MARKET AND SYLVIA WATERS

From 10:30 a.m. to 12:30 p.m. Penny and I were at the Mesa Flea Market at Signal Butte Road. From 12:45 to 3:00 p.m. we were invited for lunch at Sylvia and Jim Water's home in Gold Canyon, Arizona, not far from the flea market.

At 5:30 p.m. on our way back to the condo, Penny and I ate dinner at the Islamorada Fish Company Restaurant inside the Bass Pro Shops. After dinner I bought some Panther Martin spinner baits while Penny bought a Skybar.

MONDAY, JANUARY 12—MOTHER AND PHYSICAL THERAPY

Penny and I called my mother to wish her a happy 97th birthday. From 8:00 a.m. to 9:00 a.m. I had my first physical therapy session with Christian Vanos at Scottsdale's Mayo Clinic. At 9:30, after my therapy session, Penny and I went to breakfast at Butterfield's in Scottsdale. Around 12:00 noon, we ate lunch at Paradise Café at Tatum and Shea Blvd. in Phoenix. At 5:30 p.m. we met Cindy Templer for dinner at the Joyful Chinese Restaurant.

TUESDAY, JANUARY 13—SAGUARO LAKE BOAT RENTAL

At 9:42 a.m. I went to Chompie's and bought two bagel sandwiches. Penny and I decided to try renting a boat on Saguaro Lake so I could do some fishing. So, we packed our cooler with the bagel sandwiches I bought at Chompie's and drinks. We arrived at the lake around 10:30 a.m. and rented a small boat with a 9.9 HP Mercury outboard engine. Penny was reluctant to go on the lake but and we were only on the boat for about twenty minutes when it was way too windy so we took the boat back and we got our money back for the short time on the lake.

WEDNESDAY, JANUARY 14—FAITH BEALL AND FAMILY

At 7:29 a.m. I took out Chompie's bagels for breakfast. At 11:30 a.m. Penny and I drove to the Chandler Mall and met Faith Beall, Maddy & Tyler for lunch. Then at 2:30 p.m. I had arranged a meeting at the Arizona Biltmore for a site survey to go over some perimeters for IFMA's Presidents Conference that would be held in November 2009.

THURSDAY, JANUARY 15—TEMPLERS AND SAKURA SUSHI

At 12:00 p.m. Penny and I drove to see Jackie & Stu Templer for lunch in Surprise, Arizona. At 4:30 p.m. Julie LaMagna who happened to be in Scottsdale, met us at our condo and we drove to Sakura Sushi Restaurant at Indian Bend and Hayden for Happy Hour sushi. It was really good and inexpensive.

SATURDAY, JANUARY 17—BARRETT JACKSON

From 11:15 a.m. to 4:15 p.m. Penny and I went to the Barrett Jackson Auto Auction. The weather was pleasant and I enjoyed the event much more than Penny but she was a good sport and humored me to go. At 4:00 p.m. we stopped at Costco and for dinner we ate leftovers from Eden's Grill.

SATURDAY, JANUARY 17—KLEINS STAY OVERNIGHT

At 11:15 p.m. Steve Klein flew into Phoenix from Detroit after spending his birthday there. His wife Cindy picked him up at Phoenix Sky Harbor Airport and at 12:15 a.m. Steve & Cindy arrived at our condo where they would stay with us overnight before driving back to Tucson.

SUNDAY, JANUARY 18—KLEINS SLEEPOVER & TEMPLERS

At 10:15 a.m. with our condo guests, Steve and Cindy Klein, we drove to Butterfield's Restaurant on Shea Blvd for breakfast. After breakfast, Steve and Cindy drove back to Tucson. At 1:00 p.m. At 4:15 p.m. Penny and I drove to Cheryl & Vince d'Aliessio house to meet with Stu & Jackie Templer. The d'Aliesio's home at Jomax and 41st street. At 6:00 p.m. the Templers, d'Aliessios and Spencers ate dinner at On the Border Restaurant located in the Desert Ridge.

MONDAY, JANUARY 19, 2009—THE APPELBAUMS ARRIVE

At 11:30 a.m. Penny and I drove to Sky Harbor Airport to pick up Alan and Marilyn Appelbaum who we invited to stay at our condo for a week. After meeting the Appelbaums, we decided to have lunch at the Paradise Café. Dinner was at the Pita Jungle at Shea and Scottsdale Road where we ate outside because of the beautiful weather. After dinner, we introduced the Appelbaums to Yogurtology located at Thompson Peak & Frank Lloyd Wright.

TUESDAY, JANUARY 20, 2009—BARACK OBAMA

From 8:00 to 9:00 a.m. I had a sales meeting phone call. At 10:00 a.m. Phoenix time, the Appelbaums and Spencers watched the inauguration of Barack Obama, the 44th president of the United States. Then had lunch at the Wildflower restaurant. I drove Alan and Marilyn to see Alan's Aunt Janice's house in Phoenix for a visit while we went to Post Office. I picked them up around 4:30 p.m. At 5:15 p.m. we drove to Alan's favorite restaurant, Scottsdale's Don & Charlie's to celebrate Alan's 68th birthday that was on this day. We met a man who told us about Riazzi's Restaurant in Tempe. It is one of his favorite places to eat Italian food. So, we decided to make reservations there for the next night before seeing *The Lion King* at the Gammage Theater on the campus of Arizona State University.

WEDNESDAY, JANUARY 21—GARDEN, DINNER & SHOW

From 7:00 a.m. to 8:00 a.m. I had another physical therapy session at the Mayo Clinic. When I was through, at 10:30 a.m., we decided to drive to the Phoenix Botanical Gardens to see the Dale Chilhuly blown glass sculptures scattered throughout the garden. At 1:00 p.m. we ate a light lunch at the Phoenix Botanical Garden Patio café. Around 4:45 p.m. we drove to Gammage Theater for an early dinner at 5:30 p.m. Riazzi's Italian Restaurant on South Mill Street in Tempe. *The*

Lion King started at 7:30 p.m. and we had four great seats in Row 9-Center on the aisle. The show was fantastic.

THURSDAY, JANUARY 22—LUNCH AND PHOENIX STADIUM

In the morning, we drove to Glendale and ate lunch at 12:00 p.m. at the Gordon Biersch Brewery near the Glendale stadium. We scheduled a 2:00 p.m. tour at the University of Phoenix Stadium, the home of the Arizona Cardinals football team. The Appelbaums and us took a most interesting tour of stadium. After the tour, we visited shops in Glendale, then ate dinner Goldman's in Scottsdale.

FRIDAY, JANUARY 23—FIRST METRO LIGHT RAIL RIDE

I had an 8:00 to 9:00 a.m. physical therapy session at the Mayo Clinic in Scottsdale. After my session, at 10:00 a.m., we all drove to the beginning of the Phoenix Valley Metro light rail line, got an all-day pass for $1.25. The first stop was the Central Library in Phoenix where we saw an exhibit of One-Hundred Years of Grand Canyon photos. After the library, we got back on the light rail and got off the train at Mill Street in Tempe and at 1:15 p.m. ate lunch at My Big Fat Greek restaurant, a close walk from the light rail station.

SATURDAY, JANUARY 24—TOUR AND TODD WALDMAN

In the morning, we decided to eat breakfast at U.S. Egg in Scottsdale. During the day, the Appelbaums and us spent time in Old Scottsdale taking a free trolley and walked around the area. Alan and I also went inside the Scottsdale Stadium, where the San Francisco Giants play Cactus League baseball games. At 5:00 p.m. our nephew Todd Waldman, who happened to be in Phoenix for a convention, visited our condo and followed us to the Z'Tejas restaurant in Tempe where we all ate dinner outside at 6:00 p.m.

SUNDAY, JANUARY 25—LOST DOG TRAILHEAD HIKE

For fifty minutes in the morning, Alan, Marilyn, Penny and I walked the Lost Dog Trailhead in Scottsdale. At 12:00 noon, we went to Yogurtology. Penny bought a birthday outfit at Accessories and More boutique located at 15029 N. Thompson Peak Parkway, next to Yogurtology. In the evening, for dinner Penny cooked seafood pasta from Trader Joe's at the condo.

MONDAY, JANUARY 26—LUNCH WITH THE APPELBAUMS

At 12:15 p.m. The Appelbaums and us ate lunch at Arcadia Farms. After lunch we drove Alan and Marilyn Appelbaum to Sky Harbor Airport. At 1:40 p.m. the Appelbaum left Phoenix on a United Airlines flight. Penny and I drove back to Borders in Tempe and bought children's books because the store was going out of business. We also went to Old Scottsdale and bought a cactus plant at Cactus Hut for our Northbrook next-door neighbors, the Diligs.

TUESDAY, JANUARY 27—CLEANED CONDO & PACKING

In the morning, our mission was to clean the condo and started packing for our trip back to Chicago. Earlier in the day, I went to the UPS Store to buy a box to send home clothes, shoes, books, etc. At 12:00 p.m. I went back to UPS Store to send the packed box to Northbrook.

WEDNESDAY, JANUARY 28, 2009—CHICAGO FLIGHT

We dropped off the rental car at the Transportation Center. Our departure from Phoenix Sky Harbor Airport to Chicago was on a non-stop United Airlines flight. We took off at 11:57 a.m. and arrived at Chicago O'Hare at 4:17 p.m. I had arranged for Executive Limo to pick us up and take us home to Northbrook.

FRIDAY, FEBRUARY 13, 2009—MOM'S 97th BIRTHDAY

I rented a minivan from Enterprise Rent-A-Car in Northbrook for a driving trip to Beachwood to celebrate my mother's 97th birthday. Since we were in Arizona during my mother's actual January 12th birthday, we decided to drive to Cleveland with Ronna, Ted and two-year old Talia. The Belinky's drove to our home and we left around 9:00 a.m. We arrived in Beachwood in the late afternoon and all of us stayed with Linda.

SATURDAY, FEBRUARY 14, 2009—MOM'S 97th BIRTHDAY

After breakfast, we all drove to Stone Gardens and visited with my mother. That evening for dinner we all celebrated my Mom's birthday at Bravo restaurant.

SUNDAY, FEBRUARY 15, 2009—DRIVE TO NORTHBROOK

After breakfast we left Beachwood and drove back to Northbrook. After arriving in Northbrook, the Belinky's drove back to their home in Buffalo Grove.

WEDNESDAY, APRIL 1, 2009—UNEXPECTED DENTIST VISIT

During dinner, I fractured a piece of my right second molar while eating a pomegranate seed. The tooth had a silver filling and it must have been weak and easily broke. The next day, I made an appointment to see my dentist, Dr. Arnold Gorchow to fix it. This is a significant event because what happened to me after having my tooth fixed was an unexpected experience I had to put into this book.

SATURDAY, APRIL 4, 2009—DENTIST TO FIX A TOOTH

I had an 11:00 a.m. appointment to see Dr. Gorchow. Since August 1966, Dr. Arnold Gorchow has been my dentist and I needed this broken filling fixed. During this visit, he informed me that I would need a crown because my tooth had been damaged beyond repair. A tissue reduction was required in order to restore the tooth with a crown. Instead of giving me a shot of nova Caine, Dr. Gorchow gave me a Robinul injection so I wouldn't feel the pain. In order to prepare my tooth for the crown, Dr. Gorchow used a laser to cut some gum tissue so the crown could fit properly and be made. The procedure took about one-hour for the gingivectomy to be done and stitches were put in my mouth to heal the tissue before a crown could be installed. A temporary filling was put to the tooth and an impression was made for my crown. I was to return the next week to see how my stitches were healing and it took a few weeks for the stitches to heal. My mouth creates a lot of saliva, so while I was in the chair, Dr. Gorchow decided to give me an injection in my left arm of the drug Robinul to reduce my saliva output.

Unbeknownst to me, the Robinul injection can produce certain side effects and adverse reactions including dry mouth, urinary hesitancy and retention and that is exactly what happened to me. I had an adverse reaction to this drug. With my large prostate, Robinul should never have been administered to me. I scheduled an appointment for Saturday, April 25 to have the crown installed.

SUNDAY, APRIL 5, 2009—HOSPITAL EMERGENCY ROOM

In the afternoon around 4:00 p.m., I had trouble urinating. I called our internist Dr. Grauer who told me to get in the bathtub with warm water and try to pee. That didn't work so I called him back and he told me to lie down in the bathtub with warm water and try to urinate. That didn't work either so by this time, around 9:00 p.m. I told Penny we had to go to the Emergency Room at Highland Park Hospital. Penny drove me there and upon entering the Emergency Room, a policeman who was standing at the door saw my distress and offered me a wheel chair. I immediately declined as I was in agony. I signed in and a nurse escorted me to a small room where she immediately inserted a catheter into my penis. I felt instant relief as the bag by the side of my leg filled up with urine. After the procedure, the nurse told me that when she saw the troubled look on my face and she knew we would immediately bond. Afterwards I was released with the catheter intact and Penny drove me home.

MONDAY, APRIL 6, 2009—DR. GORCHOW EXPLANATION

I called Dr. Gorchow's office to tell him what had happened to me over the weekend. He was so sorry I had to endure what took place. Each time I go to the dentist, they always ask what medications I am taking so a situation as described above will be avoided in the future. I also called my urologist to tell him what had transpired. He recommended I stop by the office on Tuesday morning, April 28 to have the catheter removed.

SUNDAY, APRIL 19, 2009—DICK REINAUER TRIBUTE

I had two connections with Richard "Dick" Reinauer. He was Dr. Arnold Grauer's patient and I met him briefly in the summer of 1970 at Zenith Cinema Service located on Chicago's W. Foster Avenue. I was completing the editing of music and mixing the soundtrack to my first 16mm film *Turn Off Pollution*. He had been Associate Producer of Mutual of Omaha's Wild Kingdom. The TV show produced their soundtracks at Zenith Cinema Services and his photo hung on the wall along with Don Meier, the Producer. Through the years, Penny and I had a chance to get to know Dick and his wife Kathryn. He was a master storyteller and a great friend. Dick passed away on December 6, 2008 at age 82. This afternoon, a gathering of his friends assembled at Chicago's Calo's Ristorante located on 5543 N. Clark Street. Arnie, his wife Sarah Grauer and their two daughters were also at the tribute this day.

SATURDAY, APRIL 25, 2009—DR. GORCHOW

I had a 9:00 a.m. appointment so Dr. Gorchow could check on the stitches he put in my mouth.

TUESDAY, APRIL 28, 2009—THE CATHETER WAS REMOVED

Penny drove me to my urologist's Chicago office and I was able to go into my office after the procedure, then Penny drove home. I took the train home at the end of the day and I don't want to have to go through that again.

SATURDAY, MAY 16, 2009—DR. GORCHOW

I had an 8:00 to 8:30 dentist appointment with Dr. Gorchow to have my new crown permanently put in place.

CHAPTER TWENTY-FIVE
Lake Carrol And Two Fishing Boats

FRIDAY, JULY 3, 2009—A TRIP TO LAKE CARROLL

One of Arnie Grauer's patients told him about fishing in Lake Carroll, a large lake about three-times the size of Lake Galena. Arnie asked me to look up the lake on the Internet to learn more about it. While on the website I found out Lake Carroll was a six hundred forty-acre lake. (Lake Galena is a two hundred twenty-acre lake) twenty-two miles of shoreline—deepest part of the lake is fifty feet. While looking at the website, I noticed an ad for pontoon boat rentals. The ad had a phone number so I called to find out about renting a pontoon boat on the lake. Duane Truckenmiller answered the phone and told me his son used to rent pontoon boats but they were all sold when his son went into the Army and there were no boats for rent at the time. Besides, he said, the lake is private and you can't fish in the lake unless you are a property owner. I asked him if he know of anyone selling an inexpensive lot and he said he was selling one of his undeveloped lots for $1,000.00. The lot was in Section 30-Lot# 33 and the property is about ¼ of an acre at the south end of the lake in a wooded area. I told him not to sell it before I talked to my fishing buddy, Arnie. I immediately called Arnie who said he'd consider buying the lot so we could fish the lake, although we did not own a boat.

DRIVE TO LAKE CARROLL

So, on Friday, July 3, 2009, Arnie and I drove to Lake Carroll to meet Duane Truckenmiller, check out the lot for sale and to see the lake. From the lake's office, I got the phone number of Lake Manager, Tom Wannick and told him we were thinking of buying some property so we could fish the lake and he offered to take Arnie and me on a tour of the lake in his boat. First, we met Duane at the lot on Brookside Drive and he drove us about 50 feet on a dirt road to the lot site. We got out of his Jeep and looked at the property. Arnie decided to buy it and shook Duane's hand to solidify the deal. I made arrangements with Denise from Assurance First Title & Escrow, a local Mt. Carroll title company, for the deal to go through and Arnie closed on the lot in one week. I also made a connection with Julie Bratner from The Lake Carroll Association and discussed the requirements associated with the lot purchase and the yearly membership fees.

In order to use a boat on the lake, there were certain requirements. Boat owners would need a certificate that showed you passed the Illinois Department of Natural Resources boating course. Also, a boat owner would need a certificate from the homeowners' association quiz and a required $500,000 in liability boat insurance. Although we did not own a boat at the time, in order to rent a boat slip at either marina, you had to register for a lottery that is held each March through the Lake Carroll Homeowners Association.

While waiting for Tom Wannick to take us on a boat tour of the lake, we saw a man fishing. I started talking to him and asked if he knew of anyone who was renting a marina boat slip. He said his brother had just sold his boat and was trying to sell his lot along with a deeded boat slip at the West Marina. The man gave me his brother's name, Mike Weber so I called Mike and left a message.

SATURDAY, JULY 11, 2009—ARNIE AND ALAN BUY A BASS BOAT

After our two-hour Lake Carroll tour, we stopped at Perdue Marine, a local marine dealer about four-miles from the lake to look around and ask additional questions about the lake. A sixteen-foot 1990 Smoker Craft Magnum fishing boat was for sale at the dealership. It was very clean and looked like it had been used infrequently. It came with a 90 HP 2-stroke Mercury engine, a trailer and two fish finders. The price was $4,500.00 plus state sales tax and titles to the boat and trailer.

Arnie and I talked about buying it and on Sunday, July 4, I called Hank Perdue, the owner of the dealership, to tell him we wanted to buy the boat. The next Saturday, on July 11, we drove to Lake Carroll and solidified the deal. By this time, the title for the lot had closed and Arnie now owned a small wooded and undeveloped lot near the lake. In the meantime, I called Mike Weber and made arrangements for us to rent his G-14 boat slip at the West Marina on a month-to-month basis for $75.00 per month, starting on July 15, 2009 until October 31 when all boats must be out of the marinas and off the lake.

THURSDAY, AUGUST 14, 2009—DRIVE TO CLEVELAND

Penny and I drove to Cleveland on Thursday, August 13 to be with my mother while Linda was involved with the wedding plans. We went to the Beachwood Courtyard By Marriott at 3695 Orange Place first, unloaded our suitcases, then we drove to Stone Gardens to pick up my mother.

Nephew Andrew was in Cleveland from Sydney, Australia so we got a chance to be with him. Rachel and Todd ate dinner with us that night at Linda's house. After dinner, we drove my mother back to Stone Gardens.

SATURDAY, AUGUST 15—TODD WALDMAN WEDDING

After having a continental breakfast at Starbucks on Chagrin Boulevard, we drove to Stone Gardens to see my mother. We drove to the Hyatt Regency Cleveland at the Arcade located in downtown Cleveland at 420 Superior Street and we checked into our room. Michael and Arleen Gomshay were in the lobby when we arrived and we also saw some other people who were attending the wedding. The Hyatt Regency Cleveland is inside one of the first indoor multi-floor shopping malls in the United States, built around 1892. In 2000, Hyatt Corporation renovated it and turned it into a hotel. Penny and I each took turns changing for the evening rehearsal and rehearsal dinner. The actual ceremony and rehearsal were held in the atrium lobby of the hotel.

Bennett, Marni, Danny and Brooke arrived in the afternoon and Ronna, Ted and Lynda Belinky also arrived about the same time. The casual dinner was held around the corner at a local restaurant. Although the restaurant was located a few short blocks away from the hotel, I drove my mother and Penny there and parked the car around the corner.

On Saturday, Shelly and Carol Pressler arrived and we were able to chat with them for a short time. It was a beautiful ceremony. A.J., Rachel's good friend from

Huntington Woods, husband, Rabbi Adam Cholom from Kol Hadash Humanistic Congregation in Lincolnshire, Illinois, performed the ceremony.

SUNDAY, AUGUST 16, 2009—DRIVE TO NORTHBROOK

There was a brunch in the morning and Penny and I drove back to Northbrook in the afternoon.

SUNDAY, SEPTEMBER 27, 2009—TRACKER BASS BOAT

Arnie and I were not happy with the sixteen-foot Smoker Craft Magnum fishing boat we purchased in July. It was difficult to fish and we kept on having problems with starting the 2-stroke Mercury outboard engine. Hank Perdue ended up replacing the fuel tank because parts of the original plastic tank would break off and clog the fuel line. We also had the front seat pedestal replaced with an adjustable one so Arnie could raise and lower the front seat. The tolling motor wasn't really powerful enough to move the boat and there were some other issues.

Arnie and I decided to drive to the Bass Pro Shops in Gurnee, Illinois and look at new boats. We met a salesman, Ted Koba, who worked in the new boats department. Ted told us he was interested in selling his 2003 Tracker Tournament V18 boat. He showed us a current version of the boat at the store and told him to drive the boat to the Bass Pro Shops so we could take a look at it. On Sunday, September 27, Arnie and I met Ted at the Bass Pro Shops and went to the parking lot to look over Ted's boat. We thought it was clean and well maintained and had some extras that Ted added to the boat; e.g., more powerful trolling motor, extra battery for the trolling motor, a GPS system, a more sophisticated Lowrance fish finder, an extra spare tire and wheel on trailer and other enhancements. He had purchased the boat used in 2007. Ted was asking $10,000 for the boat and Arnie offered to front the money. I asked Ted if he could deliver the boat to Lake Carroll and it was decided that Thursday, October 8 would be most convenient day for Ted since he had a day off work. Arnie offered to pay for his time and gasoline for the delivery.

THURSDAY, OCTOBER 8, 2009—DELIVERY OF TRACKER BOAT

Arnie and I drove to Lake Carroll where we met Ted at Perdue Marine around 9:00 a.m. Ted drove the boat to the lake where it was launched and put in the G-14 slip in the West Marina. Ted went over all of the accessories to make sure they worked, and then Arnie and I went fishing for a short time.

THURSDAY, APRIL 24, 2014—SELLING THE TRACKER BOAT

Arnie and I had fun with the boat but toward the fall of 2013, he lost interest in fishing and he also decided to sell his Jeep and bought a Mini Cooper so we had to sell the boat. The fishing in southern Wisconsin had not been good for the past two years and I think it beginning to be a hassle. I drove to Larsen Marine in Waukegan and removed all of our equipment from the boat. In October, I placed an ad in the *Boat Trader* and only had two inquiries. I would place another ad in the spring of 2014 to try and sell the Tracker.

In the middle of April 2014, I joined lake-link.com and placed an ad in the **lake-link.com**, hoping to sell the Tracker boat. I got a call on my cell phone from Jacob Nast from a western suburb of Milwaukee, Wisconsin. Jacob wanted to see the boat so we met at Larsen Marine in Waukegan. After looking over the boat, he made a firm offer. I called Arnie on the spot and he told me to sell the boat. Jacob gave me $60.00 cash up front. So, on Thursday, April 24, 2014, the deal was made for the Tracker for $7,500.00 to Jacob Nast. A few days later, Jacob came to Larsen Marine with his pickup truck and gave me a certified check for $7,440.00 made out to Arnold Grauer. I gave him all the boat title, the engine keys, the custom top we had made for Lake Carroll and a few other items I left in the boat.

FRIDAY, NOVEMBER 6, 2009—TO PHOENIX FOR IFMA

Penny and I departed Chicago's O'Hare Airport on a non-stop United Airlines flight at 9:23 a.m. and arrived at Phoenix Sky Harbor Airport at 12:15 p.m. In October, Jan and Rich Aver had permanently moved from Oklahoma City to Scottsdale, so they were able to pick up Penny and me from Sky Harbor Airport and drove us to the Scottsdale Avis Rent-A-Car store located at 7125 E. Shea Blvd. There were several people waiting for the owner to get back from another location. Rather than wait for the car, Rich decided to take Jan back to their condo and return to the store. Agency owner Scott Williamson returned and took care of us with a Pontiac Vibe for eighteen days.

SATURDAY, NOVEMBER 7, 2009—ARIZONA BILTMORE

IFMA knew we owned a Scottsdale condo, so in order to save money I had to stay at our condo and drive to the hotel each day. At 10:00 a.m., IFMA's 2009 Presidents Conference started the audiovisual equipment set-up in the Frank Lloyd Wright Ballroom. It was completed by 6:00 p.m. At 6:30 p.m. Jan and Rich picked up Penny and me and we ate dinner at Scottsdale's Pita Jungle at Shea Blvd.

SUNDAY, NOVEMBER 8—REHEARSALS AND RECEPTION

I left the condo around 7:00 a.m. to drive to the Arizona Biltmore. Pati Hodges, my teleprompter operator, arrived at 8:00 a.m. to set up her equipment. The crew call was for 9:00 a.m. and by 12:00 noon her equipment set-up was completed and she was working on some script changes. We had rehearsals and after the reception, I drove back to our condo.

MONDAY, NOV. 9 TO TUESDAY, NOV. 10, 2009
GENERAL SESSIONS AND CLOSING BANQUET
FRIDAY, NOVEMBER 13, 2009—A NEW TV STAND

After breakfast, Penny and I went looking for a TV stand at Costco off of Ray Road and to another Terri's. In the late afternoon, Jan and Rich took us to Greek Gyros on Northsight Blvd.

SATURDAY, NOVEMBER 14—FOUNTAIN HILLS FESTIVAL

In the morning we drove to Fountain Hills and went to the Fountain Hills Art Festival with Jan & Rich Aver. We love this art fair but we didn't buy anything.

SUNDAY, NOVEMBER 15—BEST BUY—NEW TELEVISION

At 9:30 a.m. we picked up Jan and Rich and had breakfast at The Breakfast Joynt on Northsight. After breakfast we went to Best Buy to purchase a Sony Bravia 46" TV set. I couldn't find a TV stand so we went to Ultimate Electronics & bought a TV stand that I had to put together. In the afternoon, we moved furniture around to get ready for the new television. I put together a new TV stand, which took about two hours.

MONDAY, NOVEMBER 16—TEMPLERS & SUN CITY GRAND
At 3:00 p.m. we drove to Surprise, Arizona to see Jackie and Stu Templer in Sun City Grand. Stu cooked chicken on the grill and salmon for me. We had a nice visit and got home around 9:30 p.m.

TUESDAY, NOVEMBER 17, 2009—NEW TV DELIVERED
At 8:30 a.m. the new television set was delivered and installed. Everything worked great. In the afternoon we went and looked for cushions for our cowboy bench and around 2:15 p.m. we found exactly what we wanted at Today's Patio located at 15500 N. Greenway-Hayden loop suite 102.

SATURDAY, NOVEMBER 21, 2009—DRIVE TO TUCSON
At 9:00 a.m. Penny and I drove to Tucson to visit with Steve and Cindy Klein. We ate lunch at The Westin LaPaloma Hotel, and then went to A.J.'s for dessert. We went back to Steve and Cindy's house and ate the dessert, then drove to Scottsdale arriving at 7:00 p.m.

SUNDAY, NOVEMBER 22—ARTS FESTIVAL AND NBA BASKETBALL
At 10:00 a.m. Jan and Rich Aver picked us up for the Scottsdale Arts Festival at the Scottsdale Civic Center. At 1:00 p.m. we decided to go to U.S. Egg for a late lunch with Jan and Rich where I ate a protein pancake. Around 6:00 p.m. Penny and I drove to Phoenix to see the Phoenix Suns vs. Detroit Pistons basketball game at the U.S. Airway Center. We had tickets through Central Michigan University. The seats were not very expensive or the greatest but we had a good time.

MONDAY, NOVEMBER 23, 2009—DESERT AND DINNER
Penny and I walked in the desert for about fifty minutes. After our walk we drove to Fountain Hills to buy Dr. Dennis Molloy his Christmas present at Chocofin Chocolatier and then headed back to the condo. I immediately took a nap in my brown leather recliner chair and wasn't feeling well when I woke up. We were scheduled to go to dinner with Jan and Rich at Un Bacio in Scottsdale. I told Penny I was "up" to going. We had a delightful meal with an interesting server who had her PhD in psychology with an emphasis on women's issues from a university in California. She couldn't get a job so she was waiting on tables. After dinner, we finished our final packing for our trip back to Chicago.

TUESDAY, NOVEMBER 24, 2009—FEELING SICK
We left for the airport at 4:30 a.m. for our 7:39 a.m. flight back to Chicago. By 6:00 a.m. we had returned our rental car to the Phoenix Airport's Transportation Center. We were on a United Airlines flight to Chicago that actually took off at 7:39 a.m. and arrived at Chicago O'Hare at 12:08 p.m. On the way back, I slept all the way to Chicago and was not feeling very well. I was weak and never sleep an entire flight. I knew something was wrong with me and Penny could tell I was sick and my body was achy after arriving home.

TUESDAY, NOVEMBER 24, 2009
LATER THAT THE DAY, A CALL TO MY DOCTOR

I was in bed for the rest of the day with no appetite. After work, Arnie came to our house to examine me. I had a fever, chills and breathing problems but upon examining me, Arnie did not believe I had the flu. Since he didn't have a stethoscope with him, he listened to my chest through a paper towel roll and said it sounded like I had pneumonia. He called in a prescription to Walgreens for 750 mg of Levaquin (an antibiotic) and said to come in to his office the next day so he could examine me more closely and to get a chest x-ray at the hospital. Penny picked up the prescription later that evening and I immediately started taking the Levaquin.

CHAPTER TWENTY-SIX
Valley Fever And Other Ailments

WEDNESDAY, NOVEMBER 25, 2009
DOCTOR'S OFFICE VISIT

I was very weak so Penny drove me to Chicago and dropped me off at Arnie's office. After examining me and listening to my chest, Arnie concluded I had a nasty case of pneumonia in my left lung and sent me to the fourth floor at Northwestern Memorial Hospital's Galter Pavilion for a chest x-ray. I didn't have to wait very long and the chest x-ray confirmed I had "according to Arnie" a nasty case of pneumonia in the lower lobe of my left lung. I was confined to the house until further notice. Arnie said this condition could take several weeks to clear up.

THURSDAY, NOVEMBER 26, 2009—THANKSGIVING

Bennett and Marni hosted Thanksgiving dinner but I was so sick I missed celebrating with my family From Wednesday, November 25 to Monday, November 30, I was on Levaquin but I wasn't getting any better. I could tell something serious was happening with me. I was also having trouble breathing.

TUESDAY, DECEMBER 1, 2009— HOSPITAL ADMITTANCE

The five days were up so Arnie called in a new prescription to Walgreen's in Northbrook and I started taking another dose of Levaquin at 10:30 in the morning. I was still having the chills, trouble sleeping, ran a fever and had shortness of breath. I felt terrible and was in pain. I went upstairs around 8:00 p.m. got into my pajamas and couldn't get comfortable. I called Arnie soon afterwards and said I had to go to the emergency room because I thought my condition was worse. Arnie agreed and said I should go to the hospital emergency room. He had arranged for a triage at Chicago's Northwestern Memorial Hospital and told me the hospital was expecting me there. I got dressed and Penny drove me to Chicago, arriving around 9:00 p.m. at Northwestern. Penny dropped me off at the emergency door entrance while she parked the car. Penny arrived soon afterwards and I was immediately taken into a small room. A triage nurse asked me many questions and a nurse took blood. They wheeled me into another room and I was given a chest x-ray. I was so weak and could not sit up so I laid flat on the gurney and the x-ray machine was brought up to my chest.

FINALLY GOT A HOSPITAL ROOM

Around 11:00 p.m., I still had not been assigned a hospital room so I encouraged Penny to leave and I would see her the next day. Penny left a little after 11:00 p.m. and was staying overnight at Renee and Sammy Sax's condo a few blocks away. Renee Sax is Arnie's sister. I got to room 1623 around 1:30 a.m. I did not sleep the entire night because I was very uncomfortable and restless. I don't remember being so sick in my entire life.

I was in the hospital from Tuesday, December 1 to Monday, December 7, 2009. During my stay I had a dose of antibiotics every morning. I had pain along my entire lower part of my back, had trouble moving my bowels and my prostate was giving me problems with pain when I urinated. Each morning at 3:00, I awakened and was given antibiotics intravenously. Sometimes I would be up when the nurse came in to administer the drug. It usually took about thirty minutes for the entire drug to complete. Two days before I left the hospital, a nurse inserted a pick point in my arm so Penny could administer more antibiotics at home. It was determined I had pneumonia in three of the four lobes of my lung or triple pneumonia. While in the hospital, I was visited by a service team of doctors from Arnie's practice led by Dr. David Kim along with Dr. Kuykendal, a resident and Dr. Benjamin Korman, an intern. After a few days, I was moved to the 18th floor to room 1829 because this floor was the floor where Arnie's hospital team was located. During my stay, I also got breathing treatments four times a day. Pulmonary consultation Dr. Ravi Kalhan and Dr. Michelle Prickett visited with me in the hospital. At this point, they just thought I had pneumonia and not valley fever.

MONDAY, DECEMBER 7, 2009—HOME FROM HOSPITAL

I was released from Northwestern Memorial Hospital around 3:30 p.m. That evening, Walgreens Home Care delivered a box of supplies and drugs to our home.

TUESDAY, DECEMBER 8—PENNY LEARNS A PROCEDURE

We received a call that Doug, a nurse from Health Resource Solutions, would be visiting to show Penny and me how to administer the antibiotic through the pick point in my arm. The schedule got messed up and a nurse, Lilyanna, called us around 5:15 p.m. saying she was in Aurora and would be at our house as soon as she could. She finally arrived at 6:15 p.m. Lilyanna took down information and showed us how to administer the drugs.

WEDNESDAY, DECEMBER 9—PENNY AND MY ANTIBIOTICS

For the next two days, Doug, another nurse came by the house and showed Penny and me how to administer the antibiotic. I had to take two different kinds of antibiotics for a total of eight days after my hospital release; azithromycin must be taken orally and ceftriaxone administered intravenously. I was also supplied with an inhaler that made me sick each time I tried to use it so I stopped after a few attempts. I was also prescribed norco for pain, tessalon perles for a cough and senokot for constipation. I knew I was too sick to produce an upcoming client holiday party so I called Williams/Gerard Executive Producer Don Duffy and asked him if he would produce my client's holiday party on Saturday, December 19th. Don agreed to take over for me producing the Cancer Treatment Centers of America 2009 holiday party at the Chicago Marriott Downtown.

WEDNESDAY, DECEMBER 9—RED MARKS & ANKLE BUMPS

When I got home and after my first shower, I noticed my right ankle was swollen and a red mark and bump appeared just above the ankle. I had no pain but the red mark and bump were tender. I told Arnie about this.

MONDAY, DECEMBER 14—NORTHWESTERN EXAM

Penny drove me to Northwestern Memorial Hospital's Galter Pavilion where I had a 4:00 p.m. appointment to see Dr. Ravi Kalhan and Dr. Michelle Prickett. Dr. Prickett examined me and removed my pick-point from my arm. A nurse assisted me as I walked around the office to make sure I was breathing properly and my oxygen level was good. She also gave me a lesson in properly breathing through my nose. Dr. Ravi Kalhan and Dr. Michelle Prickett, wanted me to have another CT-Scan in March.

WEDNESDAY, DECEMBER16—ADDITIONAL EXAMS

Arnie made an appointment for me to see Dr. Linda Mileti, a rheumatologist, in his office along with Dr. Toral Patel, a dermatologist both located on the twentieth floor of Arnie's office. Dr. Mileti had suggested some different blood tests so I first went to Arnie's office to have the blood drawn, and then went to the twentieth floor where both doctors examined me. Dr. Patel decided to do a biopsy on the red lesion on my leg so her assistant numbed the spot and Dr. Patel took two biopsies. I had four stitches where she made the incision and was told to come back in ten days to have the stitches removed.

TUESDAY, DECEMBER 29, 2009—DR. PATEL APPOINTMENT

I had an appointment with Dr. Patel to have the four stitches removed. I had another red bump near the other lesion, so Dr. Patel took a look at it. The Dermatology Report came back on Monday, December 28 and was non-specific; meaning, the biopsy did not reveal anything. The report said what I had was panniculitis that is an inflammation of the layer of subcutaneous fat underlying the epidermis of the skin.

MONDAY, JANUARY 4, 2010—SEEING ULOLOGIST, DR. LIN

Penny drove me to see my urologist, Dr. William Lin, who wanted to make sure I was not having difficulty urinating. He was going to scope my bladder but it was not necessary. They did an ultra sound on my bladder and he wanted to see me in one month.

THURSDAY, JANUARY 7—ANOTHER DOCTOR EXAM

Arnie called around 12:30 p.m. He spoke with Dr. Gary Noskin, an infectious disease doctor and Dr. Noskin wanted to see me. I called his office and the soonest he could see me was Wednesday, January 20. Arnie suggested I bring in the article to Dr. Noskin that Lois emailed to me.

WEDNESDAY, JANUARY 20—DR. NOSKIN & VALLEY FEVER

My appointment with Dr. Gary Noskin was at 1:00 p.m. A nurse drew blood and Dr. Noskin said he was going to send my blood to the Bakersfield, California laboratory to have my blood tested for coccidio mycosis that is another name for valley fever. After all that had happened to me, he had a suspicion I may have had the disease. The Bakersfield laboratory specializes in detecting coccidio mycosis. Several weeks went by and I received a call from Dr. Noskin's office saying I had been exposed to coccidio mycosis (valley fever) and this disease apparently caused my pneumonia. Valley fever also caused the red lesions and bumps on my leg and these are symptoms are part of the disease. After a while, the red lesions and bumps went away. I was told I have antibodies and am now immune to the disease so I don't have to worry about catching it again. It was a harrowing experience. I don't want to repeat.

SATURDAY, FEBRUARY 6, 2010—SELLING SMOKER BOAT

I spoke to Ron Belding from Kenosha, Wisconsin, a high school friend of Ted Koba, about buying our sixteen-foot Smoker Craft Magnum fishing boat. Ted who sold Arnie Grauer his 2003 Tracker V-18 Tournament boat, told his friend about our boat, so Ron was very interested in buying it. I drafted a letter of agreement and mailed it to Ron. He signed the letter February 20 and mailed two checks for $1,000.00 each made out to Arnie and me as a deposit on the boat. We later scheduled Ron's pickup of the boat at Perdue Marine for Saturday, April 24, 2010.

SATURDAY, FEBRUARY 20, 2010—BROOKE'S 2nd BIRTHDAY
PENNY FALLS DOWN FAMILY ROOM STEPS

Penny and I had a fun time at Brooke's second birthday party at Bennett and Marni's house. Marni's parents came in for the event. Talia, Ronna and Ted were there as well as a small group of Brooke's neighborhood friends.

Penny and I went home and were watching television in our downstairs family room when at 3:20 p.m. I heard a tremendous crash. Penny had tripped and fallen down the stairs of our family room. She was carrying a glass of tomato juice and the glass shattered leaving a large gash on her ring finger and tomato juice splattered on the wall and steps. Penny did not realize until sometime after the incident that her shoulder was bruised. She had also hit her head on the wall or floor, but it could have been a lot worse. I immediately rushed to Penny's aid as she was sitting upright in a daze on the basement floor. Blood was coming from a deep cut on her ring finger and I could see the deep gash would need stitches.

HIGHLAND PARK HOSPITAL EMERGENCY ROOM

I rapidly cleaned up the tomato juice on the wall and steps and drove Penny to the Emergency Room at Highland Park Hospital. At 3:50 p.m. we were at the hospital and they took Penny at 4:00 p.m. We were out of the hospital by 5:00 p.m. and I drove Penny home. In the corridor of the emergency room, a nurse practitioner gave Penny a few numbing shots and put six stitches in Penny's finger as I watched and took photos with my iPhone. Later Penny called Doctor Molloy and he insisted on having Penny come to his office to examine her. On March 6, when Arnie came to our house to go to the Bass Pro Shops, he said Penny could have broken her neck with the fall.

WEDNESDAY, MARCH 24, 2010—MRI APPOINTMENT

Penny had a 4:00 p.m. appointment to see Dr. Mark Bowen, an orthopedic surgeon at the Northwestern Orthopedic Institute office at 680 N. Lake Shore Drive. They x-rayed Penny's shoulder and after examining her, Dr. Bowen recommended getting an MRI. The office gave us a sheet with various MRI facilities listed but we wanted one closer to our home. After leaving the office, I found Upright MRI in Deerfield in the same complex as the Secretary of State's office on Lake Cook Road. Penny made an appointment for 5:00 p.m. on Thursday, March 25.

THURSDAY, MARCH 25, 2010—PRE-SCHOOL SEDER AND MRI

At 9:25 a.m., Penny and I drove to Talia's Passover sedar at her pre-school. We had a lovely time at the sedar. Ted had to go to work afterwards so Penny,

Ronna, Talia and I went to Butterfield's for lunch. After lunch we drove to Upright MRI office to look at the machine and to fill out paperwork for her 5:00 p.m. MRI.

SUNDAY, APRIL 4, 2010—DEPARTURE TO PHOENIX

After my bout with pneumonia and Valley Fever, Penny and I decided to fly to Phoenix for ten days of fun and to see friends, so we booked a flight on United Airlines. I called Uri at American Taxi to book a ride to O'Hare for a 7:00 a.m. pick up. We left Chicago at 9:35 a.m. and arrived in Phoenix at 11:25 a.m. We ate dinner at 5:45 p.m. at Pita Jungle with Jan and Rich Aver.

THURSDAY, APRIL 8—MORE URINARY PROBLEMS
BACK TO THE HOSPITAL EMERGENCY ROOM

In the morning the Avers and Schesnols left for a wedding in California. During the night I woke up to go the bathroom and was having difficulty urinating. After I awakened in the morning, I could not urinate and told Penny we should go to the Emergency Room at Scottsdale Healthcare. The hospital immediately took me into a room and Wayne, a male nurse, put in a catheter. Dr. David Gutman, the doctor on duty wanted me to leave it in but I insisted on having it removed after about one hour. They gave me water to drink but after about one hour, I still couldn't urinate so nurse Marla from Warren, Ohio consulted with Dr. Gutman and she put in a new catheter.

I was given the name of a urologist, Dr. Eric Kau and told to immediately make an appointment to see him on Monday morning to have the catheter removed. So, in the meantime, I am walking around with a catheter and bag inside my pants. I was so used to having one in place that it really didn't bother me. I had to walk a little slower and I was able to wear long shorts that covered the bulge in my pants. From 1:30 until 2:30 p.m. Penny and I went to the Phoenix Botanical Gardens to check out the new Wildflower Garden. We decided to order a pizza from Oregano's at Shea and Scottsdale Road and I picked it up around 6:50 p.m.

FRIDAY, APRIL 9— PHOENIX PUEBLO GRANDE MUSEUM

Penny and I ate breakfast and at 11:00 a.m. we decided to drive to the Pueblo Grande Museum and Archeological Park in Phoenix for a tour. At 6:30 p.m. we met Ron and Bonny Gimple and Bobby & Jim Pazol at the Pinnacle Peak Grille on Jomax Road for dinner. The Gimples told us to drive to their house and Ron would drive to the restaurant. So, Penny & I drove to the Gimples home, parked out car in their driveway and Ron drove us to the restaurant. After dinner we drove back to our condo and I was not feeling very well. I immediately went to sleep and woke up in the morning with diarrhea and a 100.5 fever.

SATURDAY, APRIL 10—NOT FEELING WELL

I was in bed all day with a slight fever and diarrhea. I felt really bad. We were supposed to drive to the Queen Creek Olive Factory & Restaurant to meet Ted and Linda Jass who happened to be visiting the Bealls. I was really feeling horrible, so Linda and Ted Jass & the entire family drove to see Penny at our condo. I think I had the stomach flu because in a day, my fever and upset stomach were gone.

SUNDAY, APRIL 11—FEELING BETTER

I woke up and immediately vomited and started feeling better. My temperature went down to 99.5.

MONDAY, APRIL 12—APPOINTMENT WITH DR. KAU

At 8:35 a.m. I had no temperature. I had an appointment with Dr. Kau who suggested I keep in the catheter until I returned home and have it removed by my urologist. Penny and I ate lunch at Wildflower and dinner was spaghetti by Penny.

TUESDAY, APRIL 13—WILDFLOWER

Later in the day we met the Avers at Wildflower for dinner. I started burning while urinating and decided to call Dr. Lin in Chicago to get a prescription for peridium. In the past, peridium eliminated the burning sensation.

WEDNESDAY, APRIL 14—THE SCHESNOLS NEW HOUSE

At 1:20 p.m. I picked up Rich Aver at his condo and we drove to see Jeffrey and Susan's new house off of Tatum not too far from the Musical Instrument Museum. After visiting the Schesnols, we picked up my prescription at Walgreens and drove back to our condo. For dinner, Penny & I ate leftover spaghetti.

FRIDAY, APRIL 16, 2010—PHOENIX ART MUSEUM

The Spencers, Avers and Schesnols went to the Phoenix Art Museum to see the Ansel Adams Photography exhibit, then decided to eat at Chelsea's Kitchen just north of Camelback Road on 40th Street.

SATURDAY, APRIL 17, 2010—CHICAGO REDEYE FLIGHT

Jan and Rich picked us up at 9:15 p.m. and drove us to Sky Harbor Airport. Our non-stop United Airlines flight departed for Chicago at 11:35 p.m. and arrived at Chicago O'Hare at 5:02 a.m. Meanwhile, I still am wearing a catheter. I slept for about two hours on the plane but Penny hardly slept. American Taxi driver Uri picked us up from the airport and drove us back to Northbrook and we got home around 5:40 and were in bed by 6:00 a.m.

That evening we saw *My Brother's Keeper*, the story of the Nicholas Brothers at the Black Ensemble Theater on 4520 N. Beacon Street in Chicago. Harriet and Jay Weintraub picked us up for a 5:30 p.m. with dinner reservations at L. Woods on N. Lincoln Avenue before the show.

MONDAY, APRIL 19, 2010—APPOINTMENT WITH DR. LIN

I had a 9:30 a.m. appointment with Dr. William Lin, my urologist. He took out my catheter and said he wanted to see me on Wednesday morning to evaluate my condition and told me to keep taking my antibiotic.

WEDNESDAY, APRIL 21—HIGHLAND PARK EMERGENCY

At 9:15 a.m. I met with Dr. Lin. I went back to my office and I was able to urinate for the rest of the day. Everything was working but in the middle of the night around 1:30 a.m. on Thursday, April 22 when I got up to go to the bathroom, I could not urinate. I tried but finally at 2:00 a.m. I told Penny I had to go to the Emergency Room at Highland Park Hospital. Nurse Lana immediately checked me in and put in another catheter. Here we go again. I must have been distracted because I realized I had forgotten to take my Flomax after lunch.

THURSDAY, APRIL 22—APPOINTMENT WITH DR. LINN

In the morning, I called Dr. Lin's office and left a message with the receptionist, and then I drove to the Bass Pro Shops to get the instruction manuals to the Tracker boat. After getting the owner's manuals from Ted Koba, I went to Lowe's to buy a gas can. Perdue Marine could only put in five gallons of gas into the Tracker. Dr. Lin called me back around 5:30 and told me to come in on Monday, April 26 because he wanted to size my prostate. He thought it would be a good idea to have surgery in the near future.

FRIDAY, APRIL 23, 2010—LAKE CARROLL & FISHING

Arnie and I drove to Lake Carroll around 9:30 a.m. We were going to check out the Tracker boat and complete the sale of the 16-foot Smoker Craft Magnum fishing boat we both owned on Saturday. Ronald Belding from Kenosha was the buyer and he was supposed to show up on Saturday with the rest of the money in cash with a truck to haul the boat back to Kenosha. It was extremely windy so we decided to not take the boat out on the lake. I fished off of the dock and caught three bass. Arnie tried and caught none.

Back in Freeport, we went to Menard's to buy a suction grip to try to attach to the boat to keep the cover down. The boat cover is really not made for a slip but for a trailer. I made reservations at the Country Inns and Suites in Freeport, Illinois, about twenty-two miles from Lake Carroll and checked into the hotel. We ate at Fieldstone Inn next to Cannova's Italian Kitchen, one of our favorite pizza restaurants. We both ordered walleye.

SATURDAY, APRIL 24, 2010—SMOKER BOAT NEW OWNER

Ron Belding, the potential owner of the Smoker boat, was supposed to meet Arnie and me at Perdue Marine around 9:30 a.m. Although I emailed Ron, very specific directions to Lake Carroll and Perdue Marine, his caravan of two cars got lost when they put directions into a GPS system. The cars went near Madison, Wisconsin, Dodgeville and Mineral Point, probably about 100 miles out of their way. A car with Ron and a friend and a truck with his son finally arrived at 11:15 a.m. After the transaction was complete, we drove back to the lake and I did a little fishing off the dock but had no luck. Arnie was tired and didn't fish. We tried to attach the suction grips to the boat, but they did not stick. The next day we returned the grips to Menard's. We got a rope and tied it around the bottom and top of the cover to prevent it from coming loose.

SUNDAY, APRIL 25, 2010—LAKE CARROLL HATCHERY

I got up early and went to breakfast without Arnie. He joined me a little later after I had eaten. We went to the boat for a short time. The weather was misty and cloudy. I fished from the dock and Arnie fell asleep. Lake Carroll's Hatchery had an open house that started at 10:00 a.m. so we decided to go around 10:30. We had a tour and saw how female walleye eggs are harvested along with male sperm. The millions of eggs are fertilized with a feather. The fry are put in the pond across from the hatchery, and then put into the lake every October. The tour and an accompanying video explaining the process were quite interesting. We left the lake around 11:15 and got a tour and price list at the Hickory Hideaway, a hotel with cabins located at 24366 Payne Road in Shannon, a small town near Lake Carroll. We drove back to Chicago on county roads suggested by the Hickory Hideaway's owner who said it would cut off 10 minutes of time from our trip. We would not travel on these roads again because if there was a car breakdown, you are in the middle of nowhere, then Arnie and I stopped for lunch at a Subway near Rockford.

MONDAY, APRIL 27, 2010—DR. LINN PROSTATE EXAM

I had an appointment with Dr. William Lin to have my prostate sized to see if I could have the TUNA or TURP surgical technique. After sizing my prostate two different times, Dr. Lin met with me in his office and told me the only way to fix my problem was to perform an open simple prostatectomy. My prostate size was between a Ping-Pong ball and a tennis ball, but closer to a tennis ball. A normal prostate is the size of a walnut. This surgery would require making an incision just below the belly button to just above the penis. The operation is like removing the core and meat of an apple and leaving the outside skin intact. I asked Dr. Lin if he does the laser method where you can go through the penis with a laser to accomplish the same thing. Dr. Lin said he does not do the laser procedure and gave me the name and phone number of Dr. Kevin McVary at Northwestern Medical Faculty Foundation because he works with lasers in these cases.

I immediately called Dr. McVary's office and was told the first time I could see him was the beginning of June. I mentioned that I had been wearing a catheter for the past two weeks and could not wait. The staff person who schedules his appointments said he could see me on Wednesday, May 20. I continued to press her to ask if he could see me sooner. Not knowing if I could see him sooner, I made an appointment for May 20. Meanwhile I had been speaking with my cousin Norman who had prostate cancer surgery six years before and he was surprised that the doctor could not squeeze me in at the last minute. I was hoping Dr. McVary might call me back sooner.

WEDNESDAY, APRIL 28—DR. McVARY WANTS TO SEE ME

Dr. Kevin McVary called my cell phone to let me know he could see me at 4:00 this afternoon. I had made a haircut appointment with Otto Bodner for 10:00 a.m. that morning. I arrived at Dr. McVary's office around 3:45 p.m. to fill out paperwork. I was very impressed with Dr. McVary and we talked about a few options before he examined me and sized my prostate. After my examination, he concluded my prostate was too large to do the laser technique and suggested the same procedure as Dr. Lin, an open simple prostatectomy. Dr. McVary told me he could cure my problem and I would be able to urinate with no problem ever again.

I asked Dr. McVary if he had any openings in his surgery schedule and he said next Tuesday, May 4 at 7:30 a.m. was open. I made an immediate decision and told him I would like him to perform the operation next Tuesday. I left the office a little after 5:00 p.m. but it was too late to get the information about a pre-op consultation so I decided to call Dr. McVary's office the next day. Dr. McVary said he would call Dr. Grauer to tell him of my decision and after I left, he did call.

FRIDAY, APRIL 30, 2010—PRE-OP SCHEDULE

In the morning, I called Dr. McVary's office to get the particulars and to schedule a pre-op for the following Monday. Dr. Grauer wanted to see me first thing on Monday morning and the scheduler at Galter Pavilion was able to give me an 11:00 a.m. appointment to get the paperwork for my operation.

MONDAY, MAY 3, 2010—PRE-OP APPOINTMENT

At 8:30 a.m. I had my first pre-op appointment with Dr. Grauer. He took my blood pressure, listened to my chest and said he would send a letter to the hospital clearing me. I went to my office to work on details for IFMA's Gold and Silver Plate Awards Celebration scheduled to take place at the Sheraton Chicago Hotel on Monday, May 24. Although they say my recovery will take six weeks, I am hoping to be able to complete the production and to attend this event.

I took a bus to Huron Street and arrived on the fifth floor of Galter Pavilion for my 11:00 a.m. appointment at 10:45 a.m. for the pre-op. Bridget, a nurses' aid, drew blood, took my blood pressure and finally got a urine sample by removing the connection to my catheter. Pat, a registered nurse, asked me a variety of family history and medical questions and entered the answers into a computer.

TUESDAY, MAY 4, 2010—DAY OF MY PROSTATE SURGERY

My surgery was scheduled for 7:30 a.m. and we were required to report to the fifth floor of Galter Pavilion at 6:00 a.m. Penny and I woke up at 4:45 a.m., got dressed and we drove to the hospital. Since it was so early, I got a great parking space on the second floor of the hospital, right by the Huron Street elevators and walkway to the Feinberg Pavilion. We had to walk to the Galter Pavilion and took the elevators to the fifth floor. I wanted Penny to have a short walk to the car after my surgery so this parking space was perfect.

I checked-in at the desk on the fifth floor of the Galter Pavilion a little before 6:00 a.m. and was assigned case 18. This number is important because there is a large screen in the hospital waiting room that displays each case number and what is happening with the patient, e.g., case 16 is in the operating room; case 18 is in recovery, etc. After checking in, I went to the public bathroom in the hall near the check-in desk and waited a very short time before I was called to go back to a preparation room in the Feinberg Pavilion. A worker took Penny and me to the room. The Feinberg Pavilion is the actual hospital and the Galter Pavilion houses doctor's medical offices. Once in the room, I removed my clothes and put on a backless hospital gown. After a brief time, two nurses, Colleen and Allan, arrived around 6:30 to ask me questions and to prepare me for the operation. They found out that this was my first surgery and they were excited to call me a surgical virgin.

Penny hung up my fishing pants, red short sleeve polo shirt and placed them into a black Northwestern Memorial Hospital garment bag along with my New Balance tennis shoes and socks that hung from a separate bag. The hospital had pre-printed labels with my name and an assistant stuck a few on the front of the garment bag. The labeled items would be delivered to my hospital room after the operation. At almost 7:30 a.m., the operating room nurse, Christine, and several resident doctors came into the room. Dr. Abbas Al-Qamari, the anesthesiologist, started the IV drip and I do not remember anything after that as I immediately fell asleep. I remember opening my eyes in the recovery room. I can't remember how long it took me to get back to my room but Penny was waiting for me there. During the operation, as a routine, a catheter was put in place. Around 6:30, Dr. McVary came into my hospital room, checked on me and discussed the operation.

WEDNESDAY, MAY 5—DR. KIM CHECKS UP ON ME

Dr. McVary was out of town for the next few days so his two residents paid me a visit around 7:30 in the morning. Dr. Dae Kim, along with another resident whose name I do not remember, came to my hospital room to look at me and to change the dressing on my incision. I was placed on a liquid diet, as my appetite was non-existent. Toward the dinner hour, I was starting to feel hungry, so I asked if I could go on solid foods. I was glad to have some solid sustenance. Janae was one of my night nurses and Art was my day nurse for several days.

After surgery, the anesthesia takes time to get out of your body and to "wake up." As a result, I was taking some different medications that included Norco for pain-every four to six hours. I was taking Dilaudid every two hours, another painkiller. I was getting bladder spasms that caused tremendous pain, so I was also taking Ditropan to relax my bladder. I also had pain when I urinated into the catheter. Surgery and the drugs can make you constipated, so I was also given Colace as a stool softener.

Dr. Abbas Al-Qamari, the anesthesiologist, came into my room and told me an interesting fact. He had difficulty putting a breathing tube down my throat before the operation, so they had to use a fiber optic tube. He mentioned that if I ever needed surgery again, I should tell them to use a fiber optic tube down my throat, instead of a regular tube.

THURSDAY, MAY 6—RELEASED TOMORROW

One of the resident doctors said it looks like I could go home today. I told him absolutely not. I was in no shape to go home. He told me it was time to remove the drain that was placed in the lower part of my abdomen, next to the incision. He said it would be a little pinch. Well, he almost had to scrape me off the ceiling as I let out a big yelp. The pain was intense but I survived. I told the resident that I thought tomorrow would be a better day for me to go home.

FRIDAY, MAY 7—HOME FROM THE HOSPITAL

Jackie, an older nurse replaced Art on the day shift and she started to prepare me to go home. Before I left the hospital, Terry Sweeney, the nurse practitioner, made an 8:15 a.m. Monday, May 10 appointment for me to see Dr. McVary's nurse to have my catheter removed and to check if my bladder was emptying.

MONDAY, MAY 10—FOLLOWUP WITH DR. McVARY

Penny and I arrived at 8:00 a.m. and Dr. McVary's physician's assistant, Valerie Gillis, greeting me at the door. Penny and I went into the examining room where Valerie talked to us. Then Penny left the room while Valerie removed my catheter. What a relief!! This operation would make it possible for me to never have to wear a catheter again.

Valerie wanted me to stay in the hospital area, drink lots of water, and then report back to her so she could observe if I could urinate. She would perform an ultra sound on my bladder to see that it was empty, and then I could go home. Valerie said it could take several hours for the water to reach my bladder. She told us to go to the hospital cafeteria, have some breakfast and drink lots of water. Penny and I walked to the cafeteria where I bought a croissant and Penny had a cranberry muffin. We both ordered coffee and I bought a quart of Ice Mountain bottled water. After breakfast, Penny and I went back to Dr. McVary's office where I continued to drink water. I finished the quart of Ice Mountain, and then Penny went to the drinking fountain and filled up about half of a plastic bottle with more water. Finally, around 10:45 a.m., I asked the receptionist at the check-in desk to page Valerie. In a few minutes, Valerie met me at the door and invited me to urinate in the toilet in the examining room. I had no problem urinating and she immediately did an ultra sound on my bladder. It showed I emptied my bladder and I was free to go home. I was wearing a man's *Depends* and a guard liner. I drank a quart and one-half of water that is the most I have every drunk in such a short period of time. On the way home in the car, I couldn't hold back and urinated into the *Depends* two different times. I made Penny laugh as I said, "here it comes" "yahoo!!" We arrived home around 11:45 a.m. Since being home, I have been very lucky as the last time I took pain medication was on Tuesday, May 11. My recovery has been without incident and complications.

TUESDAY, MAY 11, 2010—LAKE CARROLL EMERGENCY

Arnie received a call from Security Officer Luke on Lake Carroll Emergency that the back half of his 18-foot Tracker boat was underwater from a severe storm. Arnie called Hank Perdue and told him to tow the boat back to his shop, do an assessment of the damage and get back to him.

MONDAY, MAY 24, 2010—GOLD AND SILVER PLATE AWARDS

IFMA's Gold Silver Plate Awards Celebration I produce each year was held on this day. Penny suggested I rent a room at the Sheraton Chicago Hotel so I could rest during the day before rehearsals and spend the night there. She also insisted on driving me to the Sheraton Chicago for I had been working on this project before my operation and at home from the hospital. I arrived at the Sheraton Chicago around 6:50 a.m. and immediately checked into the hotel. My room was ready, unpacked my suitcase and rested until just before the 8:00 a.m. equipment setup in the Sheraton Ballroom.

The head table from the night before was set up so I had to have the hotel crew begin the process of removing the risers and re-setting our two-tiered head table. I was able to rest in my hotel room for about forty-five minutes before my client came to the ballroom to go over the music and the show flow. Robert Irvine, who had several shows on the Food Network, was the master of ceremonies for this event. He was a great guy and I had chance to have my photo taken with him. The event was a huge success and my client was very happy. I got to my room around 10:25 and was asleep by 11:00 p.m. The next morning, Penny picked me up at the hotel around 9:45 a.m. and I drove home.

THURSDAY, MAY 27, 2010—DR. McVARY APPOINTMENT

I took the Metra train to my 9:45 a.m. doctor's appointment with Dr. Kevin McVary at the Northwestern Medical Faculty Foundation. I arrived at his office on the 20th floor of Galter around 9:35 a.m. and was not taken into an examining room until 10:35 a.m. I gave a urine sample and they took a blood sample. The nurse also gave me an ultrasound to see if my bladder was empty, and it was. I asked Dr. McVary a few questions Penny had given me to ask him. He examined me. He said the pathology was normal on the tissue they took out from my prostate and I could travel anywhere. He said I was still healing and my urine flow should even get better than it has been. I felt great and thanked him.

SATURDAY JULY 10, 2010—THE LAKE CARROLL SAGA

Weather-wise, the summer of 2010 had been miserable because the temperatures had been in the 90s and it had rained just about every weekend. We have not had a chance to go fishing since last October when Arnie bought the Tracker boat. So, the saga continues with Arnie Grauer's Tracker Boat, Lake Carroll and the West Marina G-14 slip.

Arnie Grauer and I were excited to go fishing on Lake Carroll on Saturday, July 10 and Sunday, July 11. The Tracker boat had finally been repaired by Perdue Marine from the Tuesday, May 11, 2010 damage it sustained when the back half of the 18-foot Tracker boat was underwater. All repairs by Perdue Marine were now complete, a custom cover with snaps was made and we were finally going to be able to have Hank Perdue launch the boat in the West Marina's G-14 slip on Friday morning, July 9. The weather was going to cooperate with no rain and we were looking forward to our Saturday and Sunday of fishing. Hank launched Arnie's Tracker boat on Friday morning, July 9, 2010 and ran the boat around the lake to make sure the engine was working properly. Hank put about 5 gallons of gas in the tank back at his dealership to get us started for our arrival on Saturday morning, July 10.

Arnie and I got to the boat around 7:00 a.m. on Saturday, July 10. We removed the custom cover, loaded our fishing equipment onto the boat and the Mercury 4-Stroke engine started right up. At approximately 8:15 a.m., we drove the boat to the West Marina to fill up the tank with gasoline from the West Marina gas pumps. I spent $62.00 at the West Marina putting in a little over 15 gallons. We headed out into the lake and got about 150 yards from the West Marina when the engine suddenly died. We could not get the engine started.

We immediately called Perdue Marine and Hank arrived about fifteen minutes later with his tow/work boat. He tied his workboat alongside of the Tracker and tried unsuccessfully to get the engine started. Our fishing weekend was ruined.

Hank asked us if we had put any gas in the boat from the West Marina gas pumps and we said we had. He said there is a possibility of water getting into the gas from the West Marina tanks because other boats have had a similar problem. We were towed to his private house dock where we tied up the Tracker and Hank took us back in his boat to our car parked in the West Marina lot. We drove back to Hank's house to pick up our fishing equipment, then drove to Freeport, checked out of the hotel and drove back to Chicago.

The Tracker boat would be trailered to his dealership and tests would be conducted using fresh gasoline to determine if there was water in the tank from the West Marina gas, we pumped into the Tracker tank. Hank said he would let us know if that was the case and would communicate with the Association Office to let them know his findings.

If water from the West Marina gasoline tanks is the problem of why the engine would not start, I would like to get reimbursed for the $62.00 we spent on gasoline, plus the cost of towing the boat and repairing any damage caused by the tainted gasoline. The cost of our hotel room in Freeport was another expense not to mention the cost of driving to and from Lake Carroll for our busted weekend.

MONDAY, JULY 12 AT 4:35 P.M.—WATER IN THE GAS TANK

I just received a call from Hank Perdue. There was definitely water in the gas tank because they drained all of the gas from the Tracker gas tank and put it into a 55-gallon drum. Perdue Marine put in five gallons of new, clean gasoline into the Tracker boat. The engine immediately started at the dealership with the clean gas. They took the boat to the lake on Sunday morning and it ran it worked fine.

Apparently, a gasoline truck delivered gas to the West Marina's gas pumps early on Saturday morning before we filled up our tank with gasoline. Water is heavier than gas, so the water was on the top and had not settled to the bottom. We were probably the first boat to get gas on Saturday morning so apparently that is why we had a problem. Hank Perdue said this condition is a recurring problem and has happened before with the West Marina gas.

FRIDAY, JULY 23, 2010—LAKE CARROLL? NOT AGAIN!

Arnie and I were excited to finally be able to do some fishing on Saturday and Sunday. Hank Perdue was all set to launch the Tracker boat on Saturday morning at 8:00 when we were scheduled to meet him at the West Marina. The weather was supposed to be fine for Saturday and Sunday with only a 30% chance of rain on Saturday and a clear 0% chance of rain on Sunday.

Arnie picked me up at my house at 6:00 p.m. and we headed to Szechwan North at Pfingsten and Willow Road for some Chinese food before driving to Freeport and the Country Inns & Suites where I had booked a hotel room for two nights. It was drizzling and we were talking about our next two days of fishing. We checked into the hotel with our room on the first floor and I went to sleep after reading a few pages of Paul Schaffer's autobiography.

At 4:00 a.m., Arnie was wakened to thunder and lighting and a tremendous downpour with rain coming down in buckets. I slept through the entire ordeal. My alarm woke me up at 6:00 a.m. and the rain was steadily coming down. I woke up Arnie who had fallen back to sleep and he told me about what had happened a few hours earlier. He thought our day of fishing would be washed out.

We went to breakfast around 6:30 and were preparing to meet Hank Perdue at the lake at 8:00 a.m. At 7:10 a.m. I suggested calling Hank's house to find out if we could delay the launch and I left a message. Around 7:15 a.m. I called Perdue Marine and to my surprise, Ruth, Hank's wife answered the phone. Ruth had been at the dealership since 5:00 a.m. while Hank was at the West Marina surveying the damage to the docks. Apparently, the roads leading to the lake were flooded, some of the docks and slips had pull away or were on top of each other and boats were damaged. I spoke to Ruth on Monday, July 26 and she said they had twelve inches of rai\n and some lifts with boats pulled away from their moorings and some jet skis were still missing. The lake is closed and she doesn't know when it will reopen. Oh, well. It was another lost fishing weekend.

SUNDAY, JULY 25, 2010—MIDDLEFORK AND BILL KURTIS

After breakfast, Penny and I drove to Elawa Farm and parked the car around 11:00 a.m. We took a short walk in the Middlefork Savanna to the west of the farm. Around 1:30 p.m. we were at the 65-acre Bill Kurtis Estate in Mettawa, Illinois. There was an open house of the property in association with Garden Conservancy Open Days. Former Chicago CBS TV news anchor and investigative reporter, Bill Kurtis and Donna LaPietra, own the estate, known as Mettawa Manor. They have spent millions of dollars to reclaim prairie and ponds and adding new features and gardens to the property as well as enhancing what was already there. After parking in the lot, co-owner, Donna LaPietra, was near the entrance giving some comments to a group of people. Penny and I took a tour of the property, wondering through the various flowering gardens. I made a slide show to feature many of the areas we visited. The property consisted of a main mansion with surrounding structures. Toward the end of our tour, we saw Bill Kurtis The grounds are magnificent and the gardens beautifully landscaped. Today was a terrific way to spend a Sunday.

NOVEMBER, 2010—PHOENIX TRIP AND INDIAN WELLS

About three weeks before the event, I found out I would be producing IFMA's 2010 Presidents Conference at the Renaissance Esmeralda Resort in Indian Wells, California. As I have done in the past, I immediately made airline reservations to fly into Phoenix on Friday, November 5 and drive to Indian Wells on Saturday, November 6 for the equipment set up.

Unbeknownst to me, in order to save money, IFMA got a bid for equipment and labor from the hotel. Although the hotel did not have all the equipment or labor, they subcontracted Multi-Image Unlimited who provided the audio and video equipment plus the audio engineer, Albert Cox and the video projectionist, Scott Villani. T & S Hoist supplied the rigging and lighting and the hotel provided the rest of the gear and labor that consisted of the drapes, headsets, control drapes and miscellaneous equipment.

Los Angeles based, Robin Sloan, was hired by the hotel for teleprompter equipment and labor for the meeting. The audio engineer and the audio gear were good. The video projection equipment and Scott Villani were not up to William/Gerard's standards. My client did not know the video image could have been much better.

FRIDAY, NOVEMBER 5, 2010—FLY TO PHOENIX

Penny and I departed Chicago for Phoenix on our non-stop United Airlines flight. We left Chicago O'Hare Airport at 9:00 a.m. and arrived at Phoenix Sky Harbor Airport at 10:57 a.m. Rich and Jan Aver met us at the airport and drove us to pick up a rental car at Avis Car Rental (seventeen days) with a 2:00 p.m. located at 7125 E. Shea Blvd. For dinner that night, we ordered a Mediterranean platter at Pita Jungle and drove to pick it up.

SATURDAY, NOVEMBER 6—DRIVE TO INDIAN WELLS, CA

At 6:30 a.m. Penny and I drove to Indian Wells, California and stayed at the Renaissance Esmeralda Resort 44-400 Indian Wells Lane in Indian Wells, California for IFMA's 2010 Presidents Conference. We checked into the hotel at 10:45 a.m. and luckily our room was ready. From 12:00 p.m. to 6:15 p.m. I was involved with the audiovisual equipment set-up in the Emerald Ballroom.

SUNDAY, NOVEMBER 7—EQUIPMENT SET UP

At 8:00 a.m. Robin Sloan, the teleprompter operator, hired by the hotel, arrived to set-up her equipment. The rest of the crew arrived at 9:00 a.m. to complete the setup. At 12:00 p.m., the crew was released for lunch and back in the ballroom ready for a 1:00 p.m. speaker rehearsal that ended at 5:15 p.m. There was a reception from 7:00 to 9:00 p.m. in Emerald Ballroom.

MONDAY, NOVEMBER 8—GENERAL SESSION

The crew call was set at 7:00 a.m. in the Emerald Ballroom with the General Session beginning at 8:00 a.m. The General Session ended at 11:30 a.m. and the crew was turned excused. At 12:45 p.m. Penny and I ate lunch at the Daily Grill on El Paseo Drive in Palm Desert. I had to be back in the ballroom because at 6:45 p.m. there was a crew call for the 6:30 to 7:30 p.m. reception in ballroom Foyer.

TUESDAY, NOVEMBER 9—GENERAL SESSION

The crew call was set at 7:00 a.m. in the Emerald Ballroom with the General Session beginning at 8:00 a.m. At 11:30 a.m. the General Session ended. My crew removed the stage left podium for the evening's awards banquet and Robin Sloan took down her stage left teleprompter equipment to make room for the band that was setting up at 4:00 p.m.

At 12:30 p.m. Penny and I drove to Palm Desert and had a great lunch at Ristorante Mamma Gina's on El Paseo Drive. At 4:00 p.m. I went to the ballroom to meet Pat McCaffery, the leader of The Whiz Kids, the band that would be performing dinner and dance music that evening. At 6:30 to 7:35 p.m. there was a reception in the ballroom foyer and at 7:15 p.m. there was a speaker rehearsal for the evening's awards banquet. Dancing was scheduled from 9:15 to 11:00 p.m.

YOU WON'T BELIEVE WHAT HAPPENED
BEFORE THE SPEAKER REHEARSAL!

Right before our speaker rehearsal for the evening's awards banquet, my client talked to Robin Sloan, our teleprompter operator, to have her type into the prompter $1,800.00 for the amount of money the IFMA Educational Foundation made on the purchase of golf mulligans. My client smelled alcohol on her breath and Robin had a very difficult time typing in the amount of money into her computer.

My client came to me and said she thought Robin was drunk and would not be able to function during the speaker rehearsal. I talked to Robin and it appeared to me she was intoxicated. My client called hotel security and she admitted drinking a half bottle of Chardonnay before coming to the ballroom. Security arrived and removed her from the ballroom. Some of the on-site crew took down the remaining prompter gear and we went with a printed script for the awards banquet.

My client learned a big lesson that night. This incident was a "first" for my experience and the client never used labor or equipment supplied by a hotel for as long as I produced their events.

WEDNESDAY, NOVEMBER 10—DRIVE TO SCOTTSDALE

At 9:00 a.m. Penny and drove to Sherman's Deli & Bakery in Palm Desert and ate breakfast before driving back to Phoenix at 10:30 a.m. On our way back, about fifty-two miles from Palm Desert on I-10, there was an overturned truck in the median strip. It took us about one and one-half hours to get by the wreck. We finally arrived back in Scottsdale around 5:30 p.m. and stopped at Goldman's Deli to get sandwiches for dinner.

FRIDAY, NOVEMBER 12—COX COMMUNICATIONS STORE

In the morning, we went shopping at Walgreens and returned our DVR to Cox Communications on Williams Street. The woman at the Cox store said for $2.00 more a month, she convinced me to get a High-Definition DVR/Cable box instead of standard definition. At 1:30 p.m. we had a late lunch at our condo and I tried to hook up the new DVR box but were unsuccessful. A Cox Communications technician is scheduled for tomorrow afternoon between 3:00 and 6:15 p.m. We ate leftovers for dinner at our condo.

SATURDAY, NOVEMBER 13—COX TO THE RESCUE

At 2:45 p.m. Chris from Cox Communications called to say he was running early and wanted to know if he could come over and see how he can help with our new HD DVR. He arrived and found out it was a software problem. There is a new guide that went into effect about two weeks before and Cox has been having some problems with it. Chris went over how to record on the DVR and some of the new features. High Definition is amazing and the picture quality is outstanding. After Chris left, I programmed the recording of several television programs Penny and I wanted to see over the next few days.

At 6:40 p.m. we picked up Jan and Rich Aver and drove to the Schesnols for a poker party with some of their new Arizona friends. At 12:28 a.m. we got back to our condo, exhausted and immediately went to sleep.

SUNDAY, NOVEMBER 14—DESERT BOTANICAL GARDEN

At 8:15 a.m. Penny and I awakened and I walked to the front of the condo complex to get a Sunday newspaper from the newspaper machine. I made sunny side-up eggs and Penny & I had English muffins for breakfast. At 11:00 a.m. The Chicago Bears vs. the Minnesota Vikings played football on Fox channel 10. The Bears won 27 to 13. Their 2010 record so far is 6-3.

At 2:30 p.m. Jan and Rich Aver picked us up and we headed to the Desert Botanical Garden for Chiles and Chocolate. Penny found some cute chocolate bars for Doc as a Christmas gift. At 5:15 p.m. we drove to Flo's Chinese restaurant for everyday happy hour from 4:00 to 7:00 p.m. and ordered a variety of appetizers for our dinner. Afterwards, we walked a few doors to Yogurtology for dessert.

WEDNESDAY, NOVEMBER 17—CURRENT EVENTS

Penny and I ate breakfast at our condo and at 9:50 a.m. Rich Aver picked me up; then we drove to pick up Jeffrey Schesnol. Jeffrey had invited both Rich and me to attend a current events class he had been attending at Temple Chai located at 4645 E. Marilyn Road in Phoenix. The Mindful Center sponsors the class once a week for four to eight weeks. Afterwards, a group of the guys went to the Eden's Grill for lunch. At lunch I found out one of the guys, Larry Cohen, grew up in Youngstown and graduated from Rayen High School, class of 1960. I did not recognize him but after looking at his face during lunch, I began to see a resemblance of someone I had seen at Youngstown's Jewish Community Center. Larry is a Scottsdale resident.

FRIDAY, NOVEMBER 19—ART TOUR

In the morning, we drove to the Hidden In the Hills Art Studio tour in Cave Creek with Jeffrey Schesnol, Jan, Penny and me. A detailed studio map was provided because the studios were located in various locations and the only way to find them was with a map. The Sonoran Arts League of Cave Creek sponsored the event. We were able to go into artist's studios to watch them work and to ask each artist many questions. Their work was also for sale. The studios and houses were very interesting, some even remotely located. After dropping off Jeffrey and Jan, Penny and I had dinner back at the condo.

SATURDAY, NOVEMBER 20—DRIVE TO TUCSON

At 8:00 a.m. Penny and I drove to Tucson to visit Steve Klein and meet his girlfriend Hollie Pavloff and Steve's daughter, Melissa. At 11:45 a.m. Melissa met us for lunch at North restaurant in Tucson, a Fox restaurant. The restaurant is located in the La Encantata Shopping Center north on Campbell. There was a bicycle race on the very same weekend last year, so we had to make a few turns in order to get to Campbell going north. Hollie is a fantastic person and we had a wonderful lunch. After lunch we walked to A.J.s and picked up two chocolate desserts and drove back to Steve's apartment and ate the desserts.

SUNDAY, NOVEMBER 21—ART FESTIVAL AND THE TEMPLERS

At 12:00 noon Penny and I met Jan and Rich Aver at the Scottsdale Art Festival at the Scottsdale Civic Center. Penny bought two scarves, one for her sister Lois and a traveling scarf for herself. After the art festival, we drove to Le Grande Orange and ordered hot chocolate while the Avers and Schesnols ate a late lunch. At 4:00 p.m. Penny and I drove to Peoria's Arrowhead Shopping Center to meet Stu and Jackie Templer for dinner at The Elephant Bar. At 4:50 p.m. we saw Stu sitting by the front door. Jackie was in the bathroom and ran into Penny coming out. We had a very pleasant dinner with the Templers and will see them in January, when we return to Arizona.

MONDAY, NOVEMBER 22—OUR FLIGHT TO CHICAGO

In the morning we packed our suitcases, got ready to leave for Chicago and at 1:00 p.m. left for the airport and dropped off our luggage at the curb. At 1:30 p.m. I returned the Avis Rent-A-Car to the Phoenix Sky Harbor Airport Transportation Center. Our United Airlines non-stop flight departed Phoenix at 3:54 p.m. and we arrived at Chicago O'Hare at 8:22 p.m. We left Phoenix on time in spite of the inclement weather back in Chicago.

THURSDAY, NOVEMBER 25, 2010—THANKSGIVING

Penny got up early to sauté onions and mushrooms for her mother's delicious stuffing recipe that she will bring to Bennett and Marni's home for our family Thanksgiving dinner. I walked on the treadmill, helped Penny mix the stuffing concoction and ate a late breakfast. As always, we had a fun time with everyone and a wonderful family dinner at Bennett and Marni's home.

SATURDAY, DECEMBER 25, 2010—ARIZONA TRIP

Uri picked us up at 6:30 a.m. for our 9:45 a.m. flight from Chicago O'Hare Airport for Phoenix Sky Harbor Airport. We flew on a non-stop United Airlines flight and arrived in Phoenix at 12:43 p.m. The plane came in about thirty minutes ahead of schedule. As soon as we landed, I called Jan and Rich Aver who had just left their condo to pick us up. They were headed for the cell phone lot and I called them when we had our luggage. They met us at Door 7 at Terminal 2 (the original Sky Harbor Airport terminal).

We drove to Goldman's Deli at the corner of Hayden and Indian Bend for our traditional Phoenix arrival lunch and ordered sandwiches to bring back to our condo. It took Rich and I about forty-five minutes to get the order because the place was packed with people and the kitchen was overwhelmed. Bud Selig, the commissioner of baseball was at the restaurant. We finally got to our condo around 2:05 and ate lunch. We were supposed to see *The Kings Speech* film at 3:15 p.m. with the Schesnols, but the movie was sold-out, so we unpacked our suitcases and relaxed.

At 4:45 p.m. we drove to George & Son, an Asian restaurant for a 5:00 p.m. reservation. Michael Mehlman, a friend of the Schesnols, recommended this restaurant. The place was packed with people. The food was great but with had a limited menu. We would never go back to this restaurant on Christmas Eve because it was a madhouse. Harriet and Jay Weintraub joined us for dinner there.

SUNDAY, DECEMBER 26—PICK UP RENTAL CAR

Rich Aver drove me to pick up our rental car at Scottsdale's Avis Car Rental (thirty-two days) located at 7125 E. Shea Blvd. At 11:00 a.m. Rich Aver came to our condo to pick me up and we went to the Tavern Grill in Scottsdale to watch Chicago Bears vs. New York Jets at 8880 East Via Linda (90th St & Via Linda). Jeffrey Schesnol, David Bluhm and Lenny Flax joined us there. Meanwhile at 2:00 p.m. Jan Aver picked up Penny and joined the girls who were having "hIgh tea" at The Phoenician Resort in Phoenix.

TUESDAY, DECEMBER 28, 2010—LOIS & ROY TO PHOENIX

Lois and Roy left Boston and were on their way to visit us in Scottsdale. They first flew to Salt Lake City to visit Roy's brother Todd. They arrived in Phoenix at 3:13 p.m. and we picked them up at Sky Harbor Airport and drove to our condo.

WEDNESDAY, DECEMBER 29—PAYSON, THEN A PLAY

At 10:00 a.m. it was cold and rainy the entire day but we decided to drive to Payson, Arizona about ninety miles north of our condo. At 12:30 p.m. we ate lunch at the oldest family-owned restaurant in Payson, the Beeline Café located at 815 S. Beeline Highway. The restaurant started in 1962. We had homemade apple and banana cream pie for dessert. After lunch, there was a light snow and we drove back.

At 5:00 p.m. we met the Schesnols and Avers for dinner at Sam's Café in the Arizona Center before the show. At 7:00 p.m. we saw *Respect*, the musical play at the Herberger Theater Center located at 222 E. Monroe Street in Phoenix. All of us enjoyed the show, filled with great songs and four very talent female performers.

THURSDAY, DECEMBER 30—THE MIM

Lois, Roy, Penny and I ate breakfast at our condo, then at 10:25 a.m. we drove to the Phoenix Music Instrument Museum (MIM) at the 101 & Mayo Blvd. Lois and Roy really enjoyed the museum. After the museum, we drove to the Four Seasons at Troon to meet Murray and Karen Rosenbloom, friends of Roy. We had drinks and chatted, then drove back to the condo for dinner. I ordered two house salads from Oregano's on Shea and Roy went with me to pick it up.

FRIDAY, DECEMBER 31, 2010—NEW YEAR'S EVE DINNER

We arrived a little early for lunch at Arcadia Farms, so we went into two art galleries across the street from the restaurant. One of the galleries made custom jewelry and the other, right next door, was Jim Sudal, Ceramic Design where we got a huge surprise. The artist was working on a commissioned three hundred fifty-pound ceramic piece for Mohammed Ali's on January 17, 2011, his 69th birthday. Mohammed lives in a mansion in Paradise Valley.

At 1:00 p.m. we had made reservations for lunch at Scottsdale's Arcadia Farms located at 7014 E. 1st Avenue. After our delicious lunch we drove around Old Scottsdale and went into several art galleries. Roy spotted Hatuma African Gallery at 7033 E. Main Street and we stopped to browse. Roy bought two six-foot hand carved wooden Tanzanian figures for $700.00 including shipping. At 4:45 p.m. we went to Yogurtology for an appetizer before dinner. At 8:00 p.m. we drove to La Fontanella Ristorante for New Year's Dinner located at 4231 E. Indian School in Phoenix with the Spenschavers (Spencers, Schesnols and Avers) with Lois and Roy. Jacqui Schesnol and Phil Voyce also joined us.

SATURDAY, JANUARY 1, 2011—LOIS & ROY TO BOSTON

At 7:18 a.m. Penny and I left our condo to take Lois & Roy to Phoenix Sky Harbor International Airport for their flight to Boston. On the way back we stopped at U.S. Egg for breakfast and I ate my protein pancake. Their Boston plane departed at 9:55 am from Phoenix. The five hour and ten-minute flight arrived at Boston's Logan Airport at 5:05 p.m.

At 12:45 p.m. we picked up Jan and Rich Aver and went to Jeffrey & Susan Schesnol's home for a New Year's Day Open House at 4819 E. Villa Theresa Drive. We watched the Rose Bowl football game with Rich and some of the other open house guests. TCU beat Wisconsin 21 to 19.

TUESDAY, JANUARY 4—EATING AND MORE FOOTBALL

Today is Jan and & Rich's Anniversary. In the morning, Penny and I went grocery shopping at Fry's. We bought Jan and Rich a double chocolate chip cake to help them celebrate their wedding anniversary.

At 6:00 p.m. Penny and I picked up the Avers and we drove to Yume, a

Scottsdale sushi restaurant in the Promenade. The Avers had a $25.00 Internet coupon for $2.00. The restaurant was not as good as Hiro Sushi. We went back to the Avers condo where Rich and I watched the Sugar Bowl at the New Orleans Silver Dome. #6 Ohio State played #8 Arkansas in a tough football game Ohio State almost lost. The score was Ohio State 31—Arkansas 26. Meanwhile Penny & Jan watched a few episodes of the Twilight Zone. We ate the chocolate cake for dessert and left around 10:30 p.m. Jan gave me a heating pad for my stiff neck. I took some cough medicine with codeine before I went to sleep.

WEDNESDAY, JANUARY 5—LIBRARY AND EDEN'S GRILL

At 10:15 a.m. Penny and I drove to the Mustang Library to pick up a book Penny had ordered. At 11:30 a.m. I had lunch at the Eden's Grill with six of the fellas from the current events class.

THURSDAY, JANUARY 6—RONNA, A MOVIE AND DINNER

In the morning, Penny and I went shopping for yogurt and eggs so I could make pancakes for breakfast. At 2:00 p.m. we Skyped with Ronna and Talia and at 3:00 p.m. we met the Avers in the condo parking lot to go to the Camelview Theater to see *The King's Speech* movie. After the movie we had dinner afterwards.

FRIDAY, JANUARY 7—SHABBAT TEMPLE AND PIZZA

At 6:30 p.m. we went to an Or Adam temple service with the Avers and Schesnols, then after the service went to LGO for dinner and pizza.

SATURDAY, JANUARY 8—VINCENT MARKET BISTRO

From 9:00 a.m. until 1:00 p.m. we had breakfast in the Farmer's Market at Vincent Market Bistro located at 3930 E. Camelback Road in Phoenix. This farmer's market happens every Saturday morning during the winter season. It is a fun place to have breakfast and you can eat outside at tables under umbrellas.

SUNDAY, JANUARY 9—MESA FLEA MARKET

We picked up Jan and Rich Aver and drove to the Mesa Flea Market. We decided to eat a late lunch at Paradise Café in a shopping center around the corner from the flea market. It is always a fun place to shop.

MONDAY, JANUARY 10—TROUT-BUT NO PHOTO

From 2:00 to 3:00 p.m. I went fishing at the Evelyn Hallman Pond in Tempe and caught my first Rainbow trout on Roadrunner spinner bait. A man was standing next to me with his dog when I caught it, but the fish jumped off the hook and I couldn't get my picture with the fish. At 5:40 p.m. I picked up Rich and we drove to Jeffrey Schesnol's house to watch the BCS College Football Championship Auburn#1 vs. #2 Oregon at University of Phoenix Stadium in Glendale.

WEDNESDAY, JANUARY 12—MOM, CORKY AND NATALIE

I called my mother and wished her a happy 99th birthday. In the afternoon, Penny went with me while I fished at the Evelyn Hallman Pond. I caught another Rainbow trout but this time Penny was there to take a picture of me with the fish. After fishing, Penny and I went to AJs grocery store, bought dessert for tomorrow night and ordered cranberry raisin bread made by Simply Bread.

At 7:00 p.m. we had dinner plans with Corky Weily and his friend Natalie

Kane at the Eden's Grill located at the corner of Thunderbird and Tatum. All four of us ordered their famous catfish. After dinner Corky followed me back to our condo for dessert we bought at AJs the previous day.

THURSDAY, JANUARY 13—OATMEAL AND FISHING

Penny made oatmeal for breakfast. Yummy! At 9:25 a.m. we picked up the cranberry raisin bread from AJs. From 11:30 to 2:30 p.m. I went fishing again at the Evelyn Hallman Pond and caught another rainbow trout. I bought some stamps at Scottsdale's main post office on Scottsdale Road and got gasoline for the rental car at the Circle K near our condo. Dinner was with the Avers and Schesnols at Giuseppe's Italian Kitchen 2824 E Indian School Rd in Phoenix. The restaurant is located between N. 28th St and N 30th Street.

In the middle of dinner, I received an emergency call from my tenant, Ken Witham, that there was a water leak that went into the living room. He did not know where the leak was coming from so I told him to shut the water off and call the home warranty company to set up an appointment to diagnose the problem. Then we would call a restoration company to dry out the living room carpet. The next day I called Farmers Insurance Company to set up an appointment to access the damage.

FRIDAY, JANUARY 14—STEVE KLEIN AND HOLLIE ARRIVES

At 11:15 p.m. Steve Klein's friend, Hollie Pavloff flew into Phoenix from Atlanta. Steve Klein drove to Phoenix from Tucson and picked up Hollie at Sky Harbor Airport and drove her to our condo. At 12:00 midnight Steve and Hollie arrived and stayed overnight at our condo.

SATURDAY, JANUARY 15—STEVE AND HOLLIE BREAKFAST

Around 10:30 a.m. we ate breakfast with Steve Klein and Hollie Pavloff at Dragonfly restaurant located near AJ's Fine Foods on Via Linda near 96th Street. After breakfast, Steve and Hollie drove to Tucson. At 1:00 p.m. I picked up Jan and Rich and we went to Faith and Matt Beall's house to visit with Faith Beall, Maddy & Tyler. Ted and Linda Jass had driven to Chandler from Brea, California and we had a good lunch and a great visit. At 6:00 p.m. we had dinner reservations at My Big Fat Greek restaurant just north of Indian School in Old Scottsdale.

SUNDAY, JANUARY 16—FARMER'S MARKET

At 9:45 a.m. I took Penny to Jan Aver's condo and we drove to the Farmer's Market at City North near Desert Ridge to see Julie LaMagna and her partner Ray Stephens. Their new canning company is Urban Southwest. When I couldn't find Julie's booth, the head of the market told me they are usually set up by 6:00 a.m. I called Julie on her cell phone and left a message. Julie returned my call in the late afternoon saying they decided to go to another market in Peoria. Julie apologized for not telling me ahead of time that their plans had switched. They are planning on being at a farmer's market next Saturday at Warner and the 101.

I left Jan and Penny at the market and drove with Rich Aver to Morningside Office Bar and Grill at 116th Street just north of Shea arriving around 10:45 a.m. to watch the Chicago Bears play the Seattle Seahawks.

TUESDAY, JANUARY 18—BARRETT JACKSON AUCTION

At 9:30 a.m. I went to take photos at the Bluebell rental house where the water leak will be fixed. At 12:00 noon I met Jeffrey Schesnol at the Great Indoors at the Promenade and we drove to the Barrett-Jackson Auto Auction at West World. We spent almost four hours there and had a terrific time looking at the old cars for sale. After Barrett-Jackson, I drove Jeffrey to the Promenade to pick up his car.

THURSDAY, JANUARY 20—TALIESIN WEST AND CORKY

At 10:30 a.m. Jeffrey Schesnol picked up Penny and me and we drove to Taliesin West for a lecture. The granddaughter of Frank Lloyd Wright wrote a book about her father's love letters to her mother. Her father was Frank Lloyd Wright's son. Penny bought the book after the speech.

At 7:00 p.m. Penny and I joined Corky Weily, Natalie, Larry and Renee Yarov Cohen for dinner at the Village Tavern at Gainey Ranch in Scottsdale.

SATURDAY, JANUARY 22—GILBERT FARMER'S MARKET AND QUEEN CREEK OLIVE COMPANY

From 9:30 a.m. to 10:15 p.m. Penny and I picked up Jan and Rich Aver and drove to the 101 and Warner to meet Julie LaMagna and to see her new canning company, Urban Survival. We met her boyfriend, Ray Stephens and bought two of their canned products including Brussels sprouts and beets.

At 11:15 a.m. Penny and I met Jeffrey & Susan Schesnol at the Queen Creek Olive Company. They have a very nice café and we ate lunch outside. After lunch we took a 12:30 p.m. tour of the olive oil plant. At 3:30 p.m. we drove to the Pavilions Shopping Center where several thousand cars from the 1940s, 50s and 60s were on display in the parking lot. We stayed until 4:30 p.m.

TUESDAY, JANUARY 25—SYLVIA WATERS AND BRIAN GAN

At 11:30 a.m. we met Sylvia Waters for lunch at the Red Robin restaurant around the corner from our condo, then at 6:00 p.m. we drove south to meet Brian Gan in Tempe for dinner at Rustler's Roost at the Arizona Grand Resort. Brian is Brad Gan's brother and works in hospitality at the Arizona Grand Resort. Our dinner was comp'd at this restaurant that sits on top of a hill in back of the resort.

THURSDAY, JANUARY 27—FLY TO CHICAGO

In the morning Penny and I prepared our condo for the summer by putting sheets over the furniture, unplugging the lights, the washer and dryer and the electricity to the hot water heater. At 1:00 p.m. we left our Scottsdale condo and headed for Phoenix Sky Harbor Airport to return our rental car and fly back to Chicago on a non-stop United Airlines flight. We took off from Phoenix at 3:44 p.m. and landed at Chicago O'Hare at 8:03 p.m. Phil Lipchitz from American Taxi picked us up at the airport around 9:00 p.m. and drove us home.

SUNDAY, JANUARY 30, 2011—TALIA'S BIRTHDAY PARTY

Penny and I celebrated Talia 4th birthday at a party place for children in Deerfield.

SATURDAY, MARCH 5, 2011—SPENCER BELINKY IS BORN

About 2:00 a.m. Penny and I received a phone call from the Belinky home so we quickly got dressed and drove to Ted and Ronna's house where Talia was asleep. Just before 3:00 a.m. Ted and Ronna left for Evanston Hospital and Spencer was born at 9:18 a.m. He weighted 6 lbs. 1 oz. and was 20 inches long. In the afternoon, Penny, Talia and I drove to Evanston Hospital to see Talia's baby brother. Bennett came to the hospital a little while after us. We took photos and held the little guy.

SUNDAY, MARCH 13, 2011—SPENCER'S BRIS

We arrived at Ronna and Ted's home around 9:30 and the rest of the family and friends gathered around 10:30 a.m. for Spencer's bris. Lynda Belinky had flown into Chicago on Tuesday, March 8 and Herb flew here on Friday. March 11.

MONDAY, JULY 18, 2011—DRIVE TO CLEVELAND

Penny and I drove to Cleveland in our 2005 black Toyota Camry and spent the night at my sister Linda's home. The next day we would drive to Geneva-on-the-Lake for the seventieth birthday party and 1959 class reunion of Boardman High

TUESDAY, JULY 19, 2011—HIGH SCHOOL REUNION

After breakfast, Penny and I left Linda's home and drove to Geneva-on-the-Lake, Ohio and arrived in town around noon. Before checking into the hotel, we went to Madsen's Donut shop and got two coffees and donuts to go. We drove to a park and sat at a picnic bench and ate the donuts and drank coffee. We wanted to see the many covered bridges in Ashtabula County, so we drove around the area. We first stopped at the Harpersfield covered bridge and stopped to take some photos. We saw the Smollen Gulf covered bridge on highway 25 and several other bridges in Ashtabula County. We also drove by the Grand River Manor founded in 1847 in Geneva, Ohio.

Later in the day, we checked into the The Lodge At Geneva-on-the-Lake, Ohio. There was a get together with my high school classmates in the evening. Bill DeCicco and I took a photo with our senior prom dates, me with Ann Brandmiller and Bill with Eva Massaro. Penny and I had a great time at this event and it was fun reminiscing with everyone. Our high school classmates are closer now than when we were in high school, thanks to a Google Group that classmate David Beede created a year before our 50th high school reunion.

WEDNESDAY, JULY 20, 2011—ASHTABULA & CONNEAUT

Penny and I drove to Ashtabula to see the river and waterfront. We stopped at the Hubbard House. This house was an important terminus for the Underground Railroad in the years before the Civil War. We took a tour inside the building. We also stopped to take a photo of the Harbor Topky Memorial Public Library and the Carnegie Library. Our next stop was Conneaut, Ohio and the Conneaut Historical Railroad Museum. This building was the old Conneaut Railroad Station and they turned it into a museum. The old New York Central Railroad used to pass through this small town on the way from New York City to Albany, Buffalo, Cleveland, Cincinnati, Detroit and Chicago. A steam engine with one freight car and a caboose were on display next to the station. We drove back to Cleveland arriving in time for dinner and staying overnight at Linda's home.

THURSDAY, JULY 21, 2001—DRIVE TO CHICAGO

After breakfast, Penny and I drove to Northbrook arriving around 3:00 p.m.

CHAPTER TWENTY-SEVEN
Door County, Wisconsin And Other Trips

FRIDAY, JULY 22, 2011—ARNIE & I FISH IN DOOR COUNTY
Arnie picked me up in his Jeep Commander and we left around 3:30 p.m. to hitch the Tracker bass boat at Larson's Marine in Waukegan. By the time we left Waukegan it was around 4:30 p.m. We ran into traffic in Milwaukee and arrived at the Open-Hearth Lodge in Sister Bay around 10:45 p.m., unhitched the boat trailer near an electrical outlet in the parking lot and charged the two marine batteries.

SATURDAY, JULY 23, 2011—BREAKFAST AT AL JOHNSON'S
Arnie and I ate breakfast at Al Johnson's Restaurant, the home of the goats on the roof. We both had Swedish pancakes with their famous lingonberry sauce. After breakfast we drove to Fish Creek and stopped in at a bait shop, bought a detailed fishing map of the region, some leeches and worms. We launched the boat in Fish Creek Marina and were out in the choppy waters for about fifteen minutes and decided it was too windy and rough, so we decided to come back without throwing out a line.

SUNDAY, JULY 24, 2011—BAILEY'S HARBOR
In the morning we drove to Bailey's Harbor to launch the boat but we didn't have a chance to do much fishing. Later in the afternoon we took a ride to Peninsula State Park to check out the launch area to see where we might launch the boat the next day.

MONDAY, JULY 25, 2011—SISTER BAY & PENINSULA PARK
We launched the boat at Sister Bay's Marina, then motored to Peninsula State Park and launched the boat. We went to Horseshoe Island and caught a few perch but no bass.

TUESDAY, JULY 26—LITTLE STURGEON BAY & HOME
Since we hadn't had much luck with fishing, we decided to leave a day early so we drove to Sturgeon Bay arriving around 10:30 a.m. to get three new tires for the boat trailer at LeFevre Tire. The owner's son installed two new marine batteries and three new tires, then told us of a place to fish in Little Sturgeon Bay. He gave us directions and off we went. Before we launched the boat, we ate lunch at the Gizmo restaurant part of a large hotel right by the launch area. We launched to boat and I caught the largest smallmouth bass but Arnie was skunked. We also used Lindy rigs and drop shots but had no luck. We headed back to Larsen Marine and after dropping off the Tracker boat trailer; we arrived home around 12:45 a.m.

FRIDAY, AUGUST 19, 2011— DOOR COUNTY GAN WEDDING
Penny and I drove to Sister Bay and arrived in the afternoon. We stayed at the Open-Hearth Lodge and Ronna and Ted were already there. We were in the only suite in the hotel. Brad and Brian Gan's sister was getting married. That night we were invited to join the bride to be and her fiancé for a whitefish boil at the Gan's family home located about four miles from our hotel.

SATURDAY, AUGUST 20—AL JOHNSON'S RESTAURANT

The Belinkys and Spencers went to breakfast at Al Johnson's Restaurant, the home of the goats on the roof. We all sat at a corner table and had Swedish pancakes with their famous lingonberry sauce. Talia went to the beach in Sister Bay and Penny and I hung out with Ronna and Talia. I brought my fishing equipment and fished in the harbor for about thirty minutes actually off limits to fishing and caught nothing. We babysat for Talia and Spencer while Ted and Ronna went to the wedding in the evening.

SUNDAY, AUGUST 21—SHOPPING IN FISH CREEK

Ronna, Ted and the children left for home while Penny and I drove to different places. We went shopping in Fish Creek and I bought a pair of Merrell shoes on sale and a felt hat for the winter also on sale. After shopping we drove back to the hotel.

MONDAY, AUGUST 22—OLIVE LOAF BREAD AND HOME

After breakfast, Penny and I went to Door County Bakery, a famous local bakery and bought a large chunk of their delicious olive loaf bread. We also saw WGN radio's Spike O'Dell's cup museum in a small building behind the bakery. We left for Northbrook by the way of Little Sturgeon Bay and ate lunch at the Gizmo restaurant that is part of a large hotel right by the boat launch area, then left for home arriving in the evening.

MONDAY, OCTOBER 10, 2011—TRIP TO CLEVELAND

Penny and I drove to Cleveland to see my mother. We left Northbrook at 5:30 a.m. Chicago time and got to Stone Gardens in Beachwood, Ohio at 12:45 p.m. in time to see my mother who had returned from lunch.

THURSDAY, OCTOBER 13, 2011—DRIVE TO CHICAGO

We drove to Stone Gardens to see my mother, then left around 8:30 a.m. Cleveland time to drive back to Northbrook.

FRIDAY, OCTOBER 15, 2011—MOM IN THE HOSPITAL

My mother's blood pressure was very high and she was having trouble breathing, so the Stone Gardens nurse called an ambulance and had her taken to Ahuja Medical Center in Cleveland.

TUESDAY, OCTOBER 18, 2011—NORTH SHORE CENTER

I went to the North Shore Senior Center in Northfield, Illinois to hear Clark Weber, a disc jockey on WLS radio in the 1960s to the 1980s. He had written a book and shared some of the interesting stories from his career. Although the retired 82-year-old is not regularly on the air, his voice is periodically heard on radio commercials.

TUESDAY, OCTOBER 25, 2011—DENNIS SHERE TALK

I went to the North Shore Senior Center to hear a fellow Ohio University graduate, Dennis Shere, give a speech on being a defense attorney on a famous Chicago murder trial. Dennis graduated with me and was an editor on the *Ohio University Post* newspaper while in college. Dennis, wrote *The Last Meal, Defending an Accused Mass Murderer*, about the Brown's Chicken & Pasta Restaurant murder that took place on January 8, 1993 in Palatine, Illinois. He spoke for about fifty minutes giving case studies and talking about defending Juan Luna, who was convicted of the mass murder, then answered questions from the audience. After Dennis' speech, Alan Appelbaum, his wife Marilyn, Dennis and I went to lunch at Baker's Squarer restaurant in Wilmette.

TUESDAY, NOVEMBER 1, 2011—TOM RICKETTS TALK

Alan Appelbaum and I went to the North Shore Senior Center to hear Tom Ricketts, President of the Chicago Cubs, give a thirty-minute presentation on the direction the Cubs will be going in the future with the hiring of Theo Epstein and others. The presentation contained a video put together for this occasion and Tom's insight into the Cub's future.

CHARLOTTE, NORTH CAROLINA TRIP
NOVEMBER, 2011—DAVID ABRAMOVITZ WEDDING

David Abramovitz, son of Les and Ronni Abramovitz, lives in Charlotte, North Carolina and is a graphic artist. His father, Les and I sold shoes together at Youngstown, Ohio's Baker's Shoes Store during our junior and senior year of high school. Les lived on the north side of Youngstown and attended Rayen High School with my cousin Norman Lockshin. I knew Les through Norman and the shoe store. Over the years, we kept in touch with Les and family and were very friendly with them in the 1980s when they lived in Arlington Hts., Illinois. David, now known as Dave, is their youngest child. Their daughter Pam is the oldest and Amy the middle child. Pam is married to Bill and lives in Syracuse, New York with her two children, Natalie, age 16 and her son about 11 years old. Amy lives in St. Charles, Illinois with her husband Mike Brasley and their two children, Ryan age 14 and Sarah age 10.

Les and Ronni moved to Baltimore, Maryland, then Rochester, New York. Over the years, Penny has been in contact with Ronni and we found out about one-year ago that Ronni has ALS, Lou Gehrig's disease, and is confined to a wheel chair and has constant care. She could not travel to North Carolina and attend the wedding so the ceremony was sent via Skype to her iPad. Penny and I decided to go the wedding since we are Dave's Godparents.

THURSDAY, NOVEMBER 3, 2011—CHARLOTTE DRIVE

At 7:20 a.m. Penny and I picked up a rental car from Enterprise Rent A Car. It was a 2012 Nissan Altima, drove the car to our house, loaded the trunk with two small suitcases and a small shoe suitcase along with hanging clothes for the upcoming wedding. We left Northbrook at 8:15 a.m. and it took us about one-hour thirty minutes to drive through Chicago. On the Indiana Toll Road, we exited at Interstate 65 South and followed the highway to Indianapolis, Indiana. At 1:30 p.m. we arrived in Indianapolis and continued on I-65 to Louisville, Kentucky having arrived there at 3:15 p.m. At that point we had driven 310 miles from our Northbrook home. From Louisville, we picked up I-64 headed toward Lexington, Kentucky.

At 4:50 p.m. we were 390 miles from Northbrook, approaching Lexington, Kentucky. At Lexington, we followed Interstate 75 south toward Knoxville, Tennessee. At 8:10 p.m. after driving ten hours and three minutes and 547.5 miles, we arrived at Country Inns & Suites in Knoxville, Tennessee for the night.

FRIDAY, NOVEMBER 4—CHARLOTTE, NC

Penny and I ate breakfast at the hotel and left Knoxville at 7:51 a.m. headed east on I-40 toward Charlotte. After leaving the hotel, we realized we left our coffee carafe in the hotel room so I decided to call the hotel when we returned to Chicago to see if they had found it in our room. (Side note: On Tuesday, November 8, after returning to Northbrook, I called the hotel and the hotel manager found the carafe. He took my credit card, boxed the coffee carafe and sent to us via FedEx and we received it on Thursday, November 10, 2011).

SMOKY MOUNTAINS, PIGEON FORGE AND CHARLOTTE

We wanted to drive through the Smoky Mountain National Park so we picked up route 441 south and drove through Sevierville and Pigeon Forge, Tennessee, home of Dolly Parton and Dollywood, and stopped at an information center in Gatlinburg, Tennessee, at the entrance to the Smoky Mountains National Park. Out of the parking lot, we traveled on the Newfound Gap Road that stretched between Gatlinburg and Cherokee, the only paved road through the park. The road climbs from 1,300 feet above sea level to an elevation 5,046 feet.

It took us about forty-five minutes to drive the thirty-one miles through the park. The fall colors were spectacular and we even ran into some snow at the upper elevations. After arriving in Cherokee, North Carolina, we headed east on North Carolina route 19 to I-40 toward Ashville. We were going to stop for lunch in Asheville, about 700 miles from Northbrook, and even pulled into a parking lot, but I was hesitant about leaving the car with our belongings exposed in the back seat, so at 1:00 p.m. we headed south on route 74 and I-26 toward Charlotte. We stopped for lunch at a Waffle House restaurant in honor of Larry Fishman who always liked to eat at one when he was traveling from Florida to Cleveland.

About 3:30 p.m., we arrived at the Marriott City Center Hotel in Charlotte, North Carolina. It was about 800 miles from our Northbrook home. We checked into the hotel and relaxed before we got dressed for the evening with Steven and Karen Kropp, the home of the bride's parents. We met Amy Brasley, her husband Mike and their children in the hotel's parking lot and we followed them to the Kropp's house. Les Abramovitz went with us in our car.

SATURDAY, NOVEMBER 5—THE MURPHYS AND THE WEDDING

Dan and Annie Murphy, who lived in Charlotte at the time, picked us up at our hotel around 9:35 a.m. and we drove to the Pewter Rose Bistro for brunch. Although the restaurant did not open until 10:00 a.m. we were seated outside ahead of time. Susan Schesnol, who used to live in Greensboro, North Carolina and occasionally worked in Charlotte, recommended this restaurant and it was a good choice. We had a wonderful brunch. After brunch, Dan drove us to various Charlotte neighborhoods and gave us a tour of the city. They dropped us off around 1:30 p.m. and I watched various football games until it was time to get ready for the wedding located right across the street at the Charlotte City Center Club. The wedding was very nice and Ronni Abramovitz was able to watch it on her iPad from Rochester, New York.

SUNDAY, NOVEMBER 6, 2011—DRIVE TO CLEVELAND

Penny and I were supposed to go to a 9:30 a.m. brunch at the Kropp house but she was feeling very sick, so we decided to pack the car and leave for Cleveland. I made several trips to the car and we left the hotel around 9:15 a.m. We followed Interstate 77 goes north and it ends in Cleveland, our final destination before heading back to Northbrook. I wanted to see my mother who had just returned from rehab at Menorah Park. We stopped at Exit 16 and went to Panera Bread for coffee, a muffin and scones for breakfast and immediately left to eat in the car. At 2:05 p.m. we stopped at a Pizza Hut for lunch about forty miles south of Parkersburg, West Virginia. As we approached Cleveland, we stopped for gasoline off of I-271 just outside of Cleveland in Northfield Road, Ohio and Route 8. I paid $3.16.9 for a gallon of gasoline, a bargain at the time compared to Chicago gasoline prices. We arrived in Cleveland around 6:30 p.m., unloaded two small suitcases and some of our clothes at Linda's home. The distance from Charlotte, North Carolina to my sister's house was 515.3 miles. At 6:50 p.m. I left to see my mother at Stone Gardens. Penny was feeling lousy and did not go to Stone Gardens with me.

MONDAY, NOVEMBER 7, 2011—PENNY NOT FEELING WELL

I went to Bruegger's Bagels to get coffee and took my mother to Pearl Vision to have her glasses adjusted. I picked up Penny at Linda's house and took my mother back to Stone Gardens. After dropping off my mother, we left Beachwood at 10:34 a.m. I drove the entire way because Penny was not feeling very well. She had a nasty cough and a temperature of 101. Toward the end of the trip, Penny called Dr. Grauer's office to make an appointment for the next day, Tuesday at 9:45. We arrived home at 3:43 p.m. having driven a total of 1,736.6 miles since we left last Thursday and spent a total of 32.17 hours in the car.

TUESDAY, NOVEMBER 8, 2011—PENNY'S PNEUMONIA

We left for Arnie's office at 8:00 a.m. and arrived in plenty of time for her 9:45 a.m. appointment. Arnie determined Penny had bronchitis but did not recommend an antibiotic since Penny had a bad reaction to it the last time. We got home around 11:15 and Penny went right to bed and stayed there for the next two days with her temperature going up and down after taking Tylenol. Actually, Penny had pneumonia and it took many weeks before she felt better.

MONDAY, DECEMBER 19, 2011—ARIZONA ROAD TRIP

Our friends drive to Arizona, so we decided to give it a try this time. I packed the trunk of our 2005 black four-door Toyota Camry with two large suitcases and a very large duffle bag with wheels and got to bed early.

TUESDAY, DECEMBER 20, 2011—TULSA, OKLAHOMA

Penny and I woke up at 12:00 midnight with a sweat and I started coughing and could not go back to sleep. I took some cough medicine and went downstairs in the family room around 12:30 or 12:45 a.m. and fell back to sleep around 2:00 a.m. I set the alarm for 3:15 and woke up at 3:15. Penny was up, so we started to get ready to leave for Scottsdale.

It was 4:13 a.m. and 40 degrees in Northbrook as Penny and I pulled out of our driveway headed for Phoenix, Arizona. We took the Edens Expressway downtown to I-94 and got on the Stevenson Expressway, I-55 going south. The speed limit was 65 on I-55. At 7:25 a.m. we had gone 203.1 miles and stopped at a Love's gas station. At 9:15 a.m. right before you get to St. Louis, I-55 merges with I-70. At 308 miles, we arrived in St. Louis and followed 55/70 until I-44 toward Springfield, Missouri. Sometimes the speed limit goes down to 60 miles per hour.

Penny took over driving at mile 308.

10:08 a.m. 391.8 got off I-44 at Cuba, Missouri to get gasoline.

12:29 p.m. 509.5 miles stopping by Stafford, Missouri outside of Springfield, Missouri.

12:53 p.m. We went to the bathroom, ate some leftover salads for lunch in our car and left the gas station.

1:59 p.m. we've driven 584.1 miles and arrived in Joplin, Missouri

2:10 p.m. the mileage was 597.1 miles and we were about to enter the Will Rogers Turnpike in Oklahoma. The road went down to one lane in each direction because they were repairing the road right before you enter the Turnpike. The turnpike charges $4.00 for the first segment that is about 47 miles after you enter the Turnpike from the Missouri border to Tulsa. The speed limit is 75 miles per hour. The second segment is from Tulsa to Oklahoma City. The turnpike does not accept Illinois' IPass.

3:16 p.m. we stopped at a free rest room at a McDonald's went to the bathroom and bought Blue Bonnet Ice Cream. Leaving for Tulsa

4:02 p.m. at 689.4 miles we arrived at the Country Inns & Suites in Tulsa. Penny and I are not hungry and ate some leftovers and went to sleep early.

WEDNESDAY, DECEMBER 21—ALBUQUERQUE

At 6:36 a.m. we drove to Walgreens to get me cough medicine and after Walgreens we filled up with gasoline. At 6:59 a.m. we're headed to Oklahoma City arriving around 8:30 a.m. and the mileage is 109.00 from Tulsa. I-44 and I-40 merge through Oklahoma City and we're headed west on I-40 to Albuquerque.

We stopped at 10:30 a.m. at a TA Travel and the mileage is now 235 miles from Tulsa. We are almost in Texas in about 10 miles. We were about 35 miles from Amarillo, Texas with minor traces of snow.

At 12:20 p.m. Penny and I arrive in Amarillo, Texas. The mileage is 359 miles from Tulsa, Oklahoma.

1:05 p.m. we stopped for a Subway sandwich and the mileage is 369 miles.

2:10 p.m. we stopped at the information area in New Mexico, got a map and some brochures.

5:03 p.m. we arrived at 636.5 miles and entered the city limits of Albuquerque. The time changes to Mountain time so we gained one hour.

4:40 p.m. we took I-25 south and got off at exit 222 and arrived at Country Inns & Suites in Albuquerque and the mileage was 653.1. It took us a little extra time to find the hotel because the directions were not very specific.

We checked into the hotel and decided to go to dinner at the Standard Diner at 5:20 p.m. for dinner and got great directions from the host of the restaurant. The location is 320 Central Avenue SE. off of I-25 and exit 224.

THURSDAY, DECEMBER 22—ARRIVAL IN SCOTTSDALE

5:11 a.m. The odometer reads 1,351.8 miles. I found a Starbucks.

5:41 a.m. we got coffee and scones at Starbucks and we're headed to Phoenix.

6:50 a.m. We stopped at 75 miles to go the bathroom because of all the coffee we drank. Penny switched driving and it started to snow a little so I decided to switch back and I drove.

8:30 a.m. we stopped at a Rest Area just inside the border of Arizona. The odometer reads 163.8 miles since leaving Albuquerque.

10:05 a.m. we arrived in Winslow, Arizona and entered the La Posada Hotel for a late breakfast/brunch in the Turquoise Room and the mileage is 266.5 from Albuquerque.

11:16 a.m. we left La Posada after taking a short tour on our own of the hotel that has had extensive renovation since our last visit in 2002. Penny is driving and we drove down the main street in Winslow.

At 12:45 p.m. we stopped at a rest stop. At 2:07 p.m. we were inside the city limits of Phoenix and 435.00 miles from Albuquerque.

2:37 p.m. the mileage is 463.4 miles from Albuquerque and Penny and I arrived at our Scottsdale condo for a grand total of 1,815.2 miles from Northbrook, Illinois. We unpacked the car, uncovered the sheets from the furniture and started cleaning.

SATURDAY, DECEMBER 24—FLO'S RESTAURANT

At 6:00 p.m. Penny and I picked up Jan and Rich drove to Flo's Chinese Restaurant for dinner where we met the Schesnols.

SUNDAY, DECEMBER 25—MOVIE & BULLS BASKETBALL

At 1:15 p.m. Jan & Rich picked us up for *The Artist* playing at the Camelview movie theater. From 4:00 to 10:00 p.m. we watched the Chicago Bulls vs. Los Angeles Lakers and the Chicago Bears play the Green Bay Packers on NBC's Sunday Night Football at Jeffrey and Susan Schesnol's house.

MONDAY, DECEMBER 26—HIGH TEA—BELINKYS ARRIVE

At 2:00 p.m. Penny picked up Jan Aver for High Tea with the "girls" at The Phoenician Resort in Phoenix. Ronna and family arrive in Arizona.

THURSDAY, DECEMBER 29—ARCADIA FARMS LUNCH

From 10:15 to 10:45 p.m. Penny and I took a walk in the neighborhood, then, afterwards went to Walgreens to buy Kleenex on sale. We were introduced to Charlene our upstairs neighbor in unit number 2030. Charlene lives in Sun Valley, Idaho for six months of the year. At 11:45 a.m. I called Bobby Pazol and made a date with the Gimples for Monday, January 9 to go to dinner at Saigon Night 12:30 p.m. Jan to picked up Penny for lunch at Arcadia Farms located at 7014 E. 1st Street in Scottsdale. From 1:00 to 1:45 p.m. Darren Hamilton from Denali Services came to service our microwave oven that had a bad fuse. He replaced the fuse and it works great. The dishwasher was not working so he showed me how to start it. I ran it twice with Dishwasher Magic, and then Penny noticed it was leaking water, so I will call Denali back in the morning.

FRIDAY, DECEMBER 30— EFFICIENCY MECHANICAL
At 9:30 a.m. Jeremy from Efficiency Mechanical came to show us where the filter was and to give us a lesson on the thermostat. At 11:15 a.m. we drove to Bashas on Bell Road for groceries. At 1:15 p.m., we picked up Jan Aver and went to Al's Chicago Beef for lunch. Rich Aver started working there in the early part of December. After lunch, Penny dropped me off and she & Jan went to Sunflower Market for shopping. From 4:00 to 6:00 p.m. I called Darren Hamilton at Denali Services and the home warranty company and got a new work order # for Darren's return visit to check out the leak.

SATURDAY, DECEMBER 31, 2011—FISHING AND NEW YEARS
From 12:45 p.m. to 2:30 p.m. I went fishing at Evelyn Hallman Pond near McKellips and College Avenue and caught nothing. I stopped at Starbucks after fishing. Later in the day, Penny and I watched one Twilight Zone episode and part of the Jerry Lewis documentary that I had recorded on our DVR.

At 8:00 p.m. we picked up Jan and Rich and drove to La Fontanella Ristorante for New Year's Dinner with the Spenschavers. One of our favorite Italian restaurants is located at 4231 E. Indian School in Phoenix. For the past several years, our group has celebrated New Years at this restaurant.

SUNDAY, JANUARY 1, 2012—SCHESNOL'S OPEN HOUSE
From 12:45 p.m. to 5:00 p.m. Penny and I picked up Jan and Rich and we drove to the Open House at the Schesnol's home at 4819 E. Villa Theresa Drive in Scottsdale. Later in the day, we watched some football games, while Penny and Jan watched a few Twilight Zone episodes. We also watched bowl games and the Rose Bowl. Ronna, Ted and family rented a car and drove from Los Angles to Chandler, Arizona to stay with Faith and her family.

MONDAY, JANUARY 2—RONNA AND FAMILY IN ARIZONA
At 11:30 a.m. we met Ronna, Faith and families at the Wildflower Bread Company in the Scottsdale Seville on the northeast Corner of Scottsdale Road & Indian Bend for lunch. After lunch we drove across the street to the McCormick-Stillman Railroad Park [carousel & train] at 7301 East Indian Bend Road in Scottsdale for $2.00 per person, children under 3 free. We stayed there from 12:00 p.m. to about 1:30 p.m. Then Stu and Jackie Templer met us at this park along with their daughter Cheryl and her three children, Noah, Mathew and Sophie.

TUESDAY, JANUARY 3—CHANDLER AND LINDA IN PHOENIX
At 2:15 p.m. I got gas for the rental car, then at 2:45 p.m. we met Ronna & Talia & Faith at a park in Chandler. At 4:00 p.m. we drove to Faith Beall's home where we ate dinner with Faith and her family at 7:20 p.m. my sister Linda flew into Phoenix Sky Harbor Airport from Cleveland on Continental Airlines and we picked her up from the airport.

WEDNESDAY, JANUARY 4—RONNA BACK TO CHICAGO
Today is Jan and & Rich's wedding anniversary. In the morning, Harriet and Jay Weintraub arrived in Scottsdale. At 12:00 p.m. we went with Linda to the Old School House by the Scottsdale Mall. At 1:00 p.m. we ate lunch with Linda at Arcadia Farms in Scottsdale.

After lunch, we went to Old Scottsdale and the Cactus Hut where Linda bought a pottery pot. At 2:10 p.m., Ronna, Ted and family flew back to Chicago from Phoenix Sky Harbor Airport on American Airlines flight #510 and arrived in Chicago at 6:45 pm. At 5:00 p.m. I went to the Bluebell rental house for the repairman for the dishwasher. The door to the dishwasher had come off its hinges.

THURSDAY, JANUARY 5—PANCAKES, MIM AND CHINESE

In the morning before breakfast, Linda and Penny went walking in the neighborhood while I prepped pancakes. When they returned from their walk, I made blueberry pancakes for breakfast. At 10:30 a.m. we drove to the Musical Instrument Museum on North Tatum in Phoenix. At 1:00 p.m. we ate lunch at the Musical Instrument Museum café. At 6:30 p.m. we decided to have dinner at George & Son Asian Restaurant. We ordered the spinach fried rice among other items and after dinner at 7:45 p.m. we went for frozen yogurt at Yogurtology

FRIDAY, JANUARY 6—DINNER WITH CORKY AND NATALIE

At 7:15 p.m. Penny, Linda and I ate dinner with Corky Weily and Natalie Kane at Scottsdale's Village Tavern. It's always a fun time with Corky and Natalie and they enjoyed talking to Linda.

SATURDAY, JANUARY 7—VISIT COUSIN GERT

From 10:00 am until 1:00 p.m. Penny and Jan Aver went to the Farmer's Market at Central and Northern. Afterwards Penny, Linda and I drove to visit cousin Gert Phillips at the Heritage Palmeras Senior Living facility in Sun City, Arizona and had a great visit.

SUNDAY, JANUARY 8—LINDA GOES BACK AND WEINTRAUBS

At 6:30 a.m. Penny and I drove Linda to the Phoenix Sky Harbor Airport where her non-stop Continental Airlines flight took off at 8:05 a.m. and arrived in Cleveland at 1:52 p.m. At 6:30 p.m. we ate dinner with Harriet and Jay Weintraub at the New York's Best Italian Bistro.

MONDAY, JANUARY 9—PAZOLS AND GIMPLES DINNER

At 6:30 p.m. Penny and I met Jim and Bobby Pazol and Ron and Bonny Gimple at Scottsdale's Vietnamese restaurant; Saigon Nites located at 15111 N. Hayden Road in Suite 110. The food was excellent and we will no doubt go back the next time we are in Scottsdale but we never did go back.

TUESDAY, JANUARY 10—MANI-PEDI AND LUNCH

At 10:00 a.m. Penny picked up Harriet Weintraub and they went for a pedicure & manicure, then to lunch at Vermont Sandwiches. At 1:05 p.m. Rich Aver and Jay Weintraub picked me up and we went to the Vermont Sandwiches where we saw the girls. I had already eaten my leftovers from Saigon Nites, so I only had a cookie. At 6:15 p.m., we picked up Jan and Rich and went to Harriet & Jay's rental townhouse for dinner that Jay made on the grill.

WEDNESDAY, JANUARY 11, 2012—STONE GARDENS CALL

At 8:00 a.m. I had a conference call with Linda Holpuch from Stone Gardens (10:00 a.m. Cleveland time). All morning I sent emails and did W/G business.

THURSDAY, JANUARY 12, 2012—MOTHER IS 100 YEARS OLD

Today is my Mother's 100th Birthday and Penny and I called to wish her a

Happy Birthday. After our birthday phone call, I decided to go fishing in Dobson Ranch Lakes and caught two largemouth bass. I almost got caught by the local men working on putting gravel alongside the lake wall because I found out you must be a resident of Dobson Ranch in order to fish there. Little did I know but it didn't stop me from fishing.

FRIDAY, JANUARY 13—APACHE JUNCTION & MINING CAMP

At 10:00 a.m. Harriet and Jay Weintraub picked up Penny and me and drove to the Historic Mining Camp Restaurant for lunch and a show. The restaurant is located at 6100 E. Mining Camp Street in Apache Junction. The "live" show featured the McNasty Brothers. These crazy "brothers" were entertaining, terrific musicians and very funny. After lunch, Jay drove us to Tortilla Flat where we saw Canyon Lake and the beautiful scenery along the way. At 6:15 p.m. Harriet and Jay came to our condo for dinner. At 8:30 p.m. Jan and Rich Aver came to our condo for dessert.

SATURDAY, JANUARY 14—VINCENT MARKET BISTRO

From 11:00 a.m. until 1:00 p.m. Penny and I drove to the Farmer's Market at Vincent Market Bistro for brunch. The restaurant is located at 3930 E. Camelback Road in Phoenix. It is a fun place to go and we always try to eat brunch at this place once during our Scottsdale stay. In the afternoon, Penny, Jay, Harriet and Jan went to the Art Show in the tents on the 101 and I stayed at the condo.

SUNDAY, JANUARY 15—BRUNCH AND THE GOLDEN GLOBES

At 11:00 a.m. Penny and I picked up Jay and Harriet Weintraub at their rental townhouse and ate brunch at the Dragon Fly restaurant. In the afternoon, we drove to the Carefree Art and Wine Show. For dinner we decided to pick up a pizza and apple pie at Costco. Then at 5:45 p.m. we drove to Jan & Rich Aver's condo to eat dinner and watch the Golden Globe Awards. In the evening, Betty Koppelman arrived from Cleveland and was picked up at Sky Harbor Airport by her Cleveland friend Beverly, who owns a house in Scottsdale.

MONDAY, JANUARY 16—RENTAL HOUSE, CHINESE FOOD

Today is Steve Klein's Birthday. At 9:00 a.m. I met Bob Lafferty at the Bluebell house. Bob was a former tenant and is currently a real estate broker who will be leasing the Tempe house on my behalf. Al Mollsen, the handyman, met us at the house and along with Bob did a walk-through and went over items that needed to be repaired before the house could go on the market for leasing. After leaving the house, at 11:15 a.m. I went to Home Depot and bought a GE refrigerator for the Bluebell rental house. At 5:30 p.m. Penny and I met Cindy Templer and Brian Gan for dinner at Scottsdale's Joyful Chinese Cuisine.

TUESDAY, JANUARY 17—COUSIN GERT AND SPRITZERS

Our Federal income tax estimate is due today, so I mailed it from the Scottsdale branch Post Office. At 5:00 p.m. Penny and I drove to Sun City and met Gert Phillips at The Heritage Palmeras. Cousins Hal and Joyce Spritzer were flying into Phoenix from Denver but their plane was late so they didn't get to see Gert until 6:00 p.m., then Hal drove us to Line Thai restaurant in Sun City for dinner.

WEDNESDAY, JANUARY 18—PENNY'S FRIEND'S LUNCH

In the morning, Harriet and Jay started their drive from Scottsdale for Northbrook. I drove Penny to Vincent's Market Bistro for lunch where she was joined by Betty Koppelman, Betty's friend Beverly and Bonny Gimple. At 3:00 p.m. we met the Templers for dinner at the Pacific Rim restaurant in Glendale.

THURSDAY, JANUARY 19—NATIVE TRAILS AND DINNER

Steve Klein was supposed to drive to Scottsdale to have lunch with us but was too sick to come, so instead, Penny and I went to the Native Trails show at the Scottsdale Civic Center. The performance was fantastic. Several times a month, Native Americans put on an entertainment show that highlights their life. There is singing, lots of music, dancing and hoop dancing. The city of Scottsdale sponsors these free concerts. At 6:00 p.m. Penny and I met Bonny and Ron Gimple, Betty Koppelman and their friend Beverly at the Havana Café in Scottsdale for dinner.

SATURDAY, JANUARY 21—BARRETT-JACKSON & DINNER

From 11:00 a.m. to 3:15 p.m. I went by myself to the Barrett-Jackson auto auction at Scottsdale's Westworld. I ran into Jan and Rich Aver and their friends Jerry and Eileen. Jerry and I walked around for a short time, and then I drove home around 4:00 p.m. At 6:00 p.m. Penny and I met Jeffrey and Susan Schesnol at the Elephant Bar in North Scottsdale for dinner.

MONDAY, JANUARY 23, 2012—NORTHBROOK PACKING

Penny and I finished packing for the drive back to Northbrook. I loaded the car in the evening so I didn't have to bring a lot of items to the car in the dark for the next morning because we were planning on leaving very early.

2012 ROAD TRIP BACK TO NORTHBROOK
TUESDAY, JANUARY 24 TO THURSDAY, JANUARY 26, 2012

4:19 a.m. We left our Scottsdale condo headed for Chicago.

5:51 a.m. Driven 101 miles so far and we just passed Sedona.

6:27 a.m. We've driven 139.6 miles and we are now on I-40 headed east toward Albuquerque.

6:59 a.m. We have driven 178 miles we made our first stop in a rest area.

8:53 a.m. We're driven 300.5 miles from Scottsdale and we are now in New Mexico.

9:25 a.m. We've driven 339 miles making our second stop for the day at a Pilot gas station where the gas is $2.99.9 per gallon

11:17 a.m. We were approaching the outskirts of Albuquerque and the mileage is 453 miles. Our odometer reads 453 miles from our condo to Albuquerque and making our third stop.

12:54 p.m. made a stop to eat lunch in Santa Rosa, New Mexico. We have driven 570 miles from our Scottsdale condo.

1:45 p.m. After eating lunch in Santa Rosa, we're off to Amarillo, Texas. Penny is driving and the mileage is 578 miles.

4:04 p.m. (Central Standard Time) we just entered Texas and the mileage is 667.4 miles and Penny is still driving.

Amarillo is about 72 miles after we crossed the Texas border.

5:00 p.m. We've driven 731.4 miles from our Scottsdale condo arriving at the Courtyard by Marriott. We ate dinner at Carrino's Italian Restaurant nearby.

WEDNESDAY, JANUARY 25, 2012—AMARILLO, TEXAS

We got up at 5:17 a.m. and drove to a nearby Starbucks to buy coffee and scones. Filled up the tank with gasoline and are left Amarillo, Texas around 5:45 a.m.

At 6:34 a.m. the total mileage is 736.3 miles from Scottsdale and it is 359 miles from Amarillo, Texas to Tulsa, Oklahoma.

8:22 a.m. Arrived in Oklahoma the total mileage is 846.00 miles from Scottsdale.

10:05 a.m. 966.4 miles second stop. El Reno, Oklahoma.

10:28 a.m. 975 miles we reached the city limits of Oklahoma City.

12:25 p.m. We're in Tulsa, Oklahoma and the mileage is 1,101.3 miles

1:34 p.m. Leaving Tulsa, Oklahoma after eating lunch at a Cracker Barrel Restaurant.

2:55 p.m. We're about 10 miles from Joplin, Missouri and the total mileage is 1,197.3 miles. We stopped at a Visitor's Center to get some information about Missouri.

4:09 p.m. The mileage is 1, 270.5 miles to the city limits of Springfield. Missouri.

4:11 p.m. The mileage is 1, 271.7 miles and we arrived at the Courtyard by Marriott in Springfield, Missouri.

6:00 p.m. We ate dinner inside the Bass Pro Shops in the Hemingway restaurant.

THURSDAY, JANUARY 26, 2012—SPRINGFIELD, MISSOURI

6:52 a.m. It's 37 degrees in Springfield and 1,296.3 miles so far. We got started a little late today.

9:07 a.m. 1,453 miles, we stopped to go to the bathroom at a rest stop where we are very close to St. Louis.

9:51 a.m. The mileage is now 1,493.5 miles and we tried getting onto I-270 around St. Louis that goes into I-55 in Illinois

10:19 a.m. We are crossing the Mississippi River and the mileage is 1,522.1 miles from our Scottsdale condo.

10:20 a.m. We're in Illinois and the mileage is 1,523.5 miles

10:38 a.m. 1,540 miles we stopped for gasoline.

11:55 a.m. Stopped at a rest stop in Illinois. 1,618.4 miles

11:40 a.m. Stopped in Williamsville, Illinois and ate lunch at a Subway 1,625.7 miles from our Scottsdale condo.

2:40 p.m. Stopped in Coal City to get gasoline. The mileage is 1,750.4 miles. Coal City is about 70 miles from Chicago.

4:02 p.m. Penny and I arrive in Northbrook having driven 1,823.3 miles from our Scottsdale condo. Since we left our Northbrook home on December 22, the total miles we've driven was 4,879.9 miles.

SATURDAY, JANUARY 28, 2012— ALAN & PENNY HAIRCUTS
Penny and I drove into Chicago for our haircuts. I had a 10:30 a.m. haircut appointment with Otto Bodner in the Hyatt Regency Chicago hotel and Penny's hair appointment with Cheryl was scheduled at 11:00 a.m. at J Gordon Designs located at 2322 N. Clark Street. At 12:15 p.m. I took a city bus and met Penny at J Gordon Designs. We drove back to Northbrook after Penny's haircut.

THURSDAY, FEBRUARY 2, 2012—CLEVELAND & BIRTHDAY
My sister and I decided to have a luncheon for my mother's 100th birthday. We planned the luncheon while Linda was in Scottsdale visiting Penny and me during her winter break from school. After looking at several restaurants and luncheon menus, we decided on Mitchell's Fish Market located at 28601 Chagrin Boulevard in Woodmere, Ohio, a Cleveland suburb next to Beachwood. Penny and I drove into Cleveland on Thursday, February 2 and I made a hotel reservation at the Beachwood Courtyard by Marriott.

FRIDAY, FEBRUARY 3, 2012—FRIDAY NIGHT DINNER
Our first cousin Arleen Gomshay flew into Cleveland from New York and Linda picked her up from the airport. My first cousin Shelly Pressler made arrangements to fly into Cleveland on Friday so he could have dinner with us at Linda's but had to fly back to Palm Beach on Saturday morning for a previous dinner engagement on Saturday evening.

For Friday night dinner, Bennett, Marni, Danny and Brooke drove into Cleveland, as did Ronna, Ted, Talia and Spencer in separate cars. We ordered food from Maggiano's Little Italy and picked up pizza for Talia and the children at California Pizza Kitchen located in Legacy Village. Maggiano's sent a person to deliver and set up the food. We ordered lasagna and eggplant Parmesan plus a pasta dish. It was a great evening of laughter and reminiscing. After dinner, Penny and I went back to the Beachwood Courtyard by Marriott and went to sleep.

SATURDAY, FEBRUARY 4, 2012—MOM AT HOSPITAL
The telephone rang at 4:30 a.m. from Linda who said my mother had been taken to Ahuja Medical Center Hospital during the night due to trouble breathing. My mother had pressed the call button in her apartment and a Stone Gardens nurse went to examine her. The nurse took her blood pressure that was very high. The nurse called for an ambulance and my mother was whisked off to the hospital. Stone Gardens called my sister and Linda called us. Penny and I got dressed and met Linda and Arleen at the hospital. We were worried about my mother and if we might have to call off the luncheon celebration. After a few hours, my mother's condition had improved, so she was released and taken back to Stone Gardens in an amulet. During the luncheon, my mother had to wear oxygen just in case.

MOM'S 100th BIRTHDAY LUNCHEON
We arrived at Mitchell's Fish Market restaurant around 11:45 a.m. and saw Norman and Sheila getting out of their car in the parking lot. The restaurant printed a special menu that said Happy 100th Birthday Esther!! On the menu, our guests had a choice of soup or salad: Little Neck Clam Chowder, Seafood Gumbo, Maine Lobster Bisque or The Market's Famous House Salad or the Classic Caesar

Salad. Entrée selections were Blackened or Grilled Salmon Salad, Fresh Grilled Seasonal Fish, Garlic Shrimp Scampi or Parmesan Crusted Chicken. Linda bought a birthday cake and the restaurant cut it into slices for our guests.

The following people were at the celebration; my mother, Penny, me, Linda, Todd Waldman, Rachel Jacobs, Bennett, Marni, Danny and Brooke Spencer, Ronna, Ted, Talia and Spencer Belinky, Arleen Gomshay, Norman and Sheila Lockshin, Bruce and Suzyn Epstein, Bob Weily for a total of 24 people. It was a great day in spite of my mother having to go to the hospital in the middle of the night.

SUNDAY, FEBRUARY 5, 2012—DRIVE TO NORTHBROOK
Penny and I saw my mother in the morning before we left to drive back to Northbrook just in time to watch the Super Bowl.

FRIDAY, MARCH 16, 2012—PENNY HAS A SINUS INFECTION
We couldn't get together with the entire family to celebrate my birthday because Penny was sick with a sinus infection. We brought a mint chocolate chip ice cream pie from Baskin Robbins and put it the freezer for a later celebration.

SUNDAY, OCTOBER 21, 2012—MOM'S HEALTH DECLINING
My mother was in the hospital and Penny and I drove into Cleveland to see her. Her health was failing and Dr. Narcia, the doctor on duty, came into her room to discuss my mother's condition. He said she is not going to get better and told me to discuss her condition with Dr. Steiner about putting my mother in hospice, or either at home in Stone Gardens. Maryellen Lash, the Stone Gardens social worker on duty left for the day so I couldn't talk to her. At 4:15 p.m. Dr. Steiner who had been out of town came by the hospital and examined my mother. I spoke to him about my mother's condition. He said my mother was shutting down and he mentioned hospice. He will be back at 7:30 tomorrow morning to further examine my mother and I will meet him at the hospital. My mother was not eating.

MONDAY, OCTOBER 22, 2012— MOM'S HOSPICE CARE
I got to the hospital at 7:00 a.m. and Dr. Steiner examined my mother at 7:30 a.m. He mentioned hospice again. He will be back at 7:30 a.m. on Tuesday and I'll be there again to meet him. I called Stone Gardens and explained the situation to them. I also called Aetna to see if hospice was covered on my mother's insurance policy. I also call Shriver Alyson Funeral Home in Youngstown and spoke with David.

I spoke to Colleen Abate the hotel social worker before lunch. Linda Holpuch from Stone Gardens called and Tina G. from Menorah Park called at 3:30 p.m. Medicare pays for the Menorah Park hospice care team but not for a 24-hour private caregiver. If a hospital bed is available, then Menorah Park Hospice & Home Health pays for it. My mother is only drinking GFS Nectar, a thickened apple juice or orange juice and not much else. Hormel makes a thick and Easy Hydrolyte Nectar consistency that my mother will drink. I could see she was failing.

TUESDAY, OCTOBER 23, 2012— MENORAH PARK HOSPICE
Dr. Steiner came to the hospital at 7:15 a.m. on the first floor and we rode the elevator to my mother's floor together. I spoke to Colleen Abate, the hospital social

worker again, and it was decided that my mom should be taken to Menorah Park and put under hospice care. I also called Linda Holpuch at Stone Gardens and explained the situation.

WEDNESDAY, OCTOBER 24, 2012—HOSPICE CARE

My mother was released from the hospital and went to Menorah Park Hospice care. Her condition was deteriorating but we drove back to Northbrook and waited to hear about my mother's condition. Linda kept us up-to-date.

TUESDAY, OCTOBER 30, 2012—DRIVE TO CLEVELAND

Penny and I drove to Cleveland and helped Linda start to dismantle my mother's apartment and we visited my mother in Menorah Park.

WEDNESDAY, OCTOBER 31, 2012—DISMANTLING APT.

Penny, Linda and I completed the dismantling of her apartment and we again visited my mother in Menorah Park.

THURSDAY, NOVEMBER 1, 2012—FURITURE PICK UP

Linda arranged for Shawn to pick up the apartment furniture that was being donated. Penny and I visited my mother in Menorah Park and I could tell she was dying because she refused to eat.

FRIDAY, NOVEMBER 2, 2012—DRIVE TO NORTHBROOK

Penny and I drove to Northbrook after seeing my mother in Menorah Park.

THURDAY, NOVEMBER 8, 2012—MOTHER PASSES AWAY

Linda called us at 5:00 a.m. Chicago time to tell us that our mother had passed away at 5:45 a.m. I immediately called Shiver Alyson Funeral home and arranged everything. We decided to have the funeral the next day in Youngstown. Ronna and Bennett drove into Cleveland together around 1:00 p.m.

FRIDAY, NOVEMBER 9, 2012—MOTHER'S FUNERAL

At 11:00 a.m. Penny, Linda and I drove into Youngstown for my mother's funeral. Bennett and Ronna drove separately and left for Chicago from Rodef Sholom Temple following the luncheon after the funeral. Norman and Sheila Lockshin drove into Youngstown from Maryland. Bob Weily and my high school friend Bill DeCicco also came to the funeral along with cousins Bruce and Suzyn Epstein. Charles McCabe, a teacher who also taught with my father at Woodrow Wilson High School was also at the funeral.

It's a small world. Just before leaving the temple, we thanked the kitchen staff and found out Lisa Lowendorf Levy was Maxine Lowendorf's sister. Lisa is married to Blondie Levy. They have a condo in Boca Raton, Florida and one of the women who attend Joyce Schrager's current events lectures also has a condo in the same complex as Lisa and her husband and they became friends. Meanwhile, I gave Lisa my email address and Maxine emailed me. I became friends with Maxine at Ohio University but I had lost contact with her. She was one year older than me and lives in Israel with her family.

MONDAY, DECEMBER 17, 2012—TRIP TO SCOTTSDALE

Uri picked us up at 2:30 p.m. and we arrived at Chicago O'Hare Airport a little after 3:00 p.m. Our departure to Phoenix Sky Harbor Airport was on a non-stop United Airlines flight. Penny and I left Chicago O'Hare Airport at 5:43 p.m. and arrived around 8:35 p.m. Phoenix time. We had free awards tickets for both of us. Rich Aver picked us up at the Sky Harbor Airport and drove us to our condo.

TUESDAY, DECEMBER 18, 2012—RICH AVER TO AVIS

At 12:45 p.m., Rich Aver picked me up to go to the Avis for a thirty-seven-day rental located at 7125 E. Shea Blvd. in Scottsdale. We rented a 2012 Kia Optima that was a great car. First, we drove to Rich's storage locker to pick up a dolly so I could drive directly to his condo to pick up the two boxes we had shipped from Northbrook. At 5:45 p.m. we picked up Jan, Harriet and Jay Weintraub and drove to Via Linda and Frank Lloyd Wright and ate pizza at Spinato's Pizza.

THURSDAY, DECEMBER 2012—FISHING IN ROOSEVELT LAKE

Roosevelt Lake is eighty miles from our condo and Jay Weintraub agreed to go fishing with me. Jay drove to our condo, parked his car and I drove to the lake at 7:00 a.m. I had pre-arranged to meet our guide, professional bass fisherman Clifford Pirch, at 9:00 a.m. at the lake marina. Unfortunately, there was a cold front overnight and it was not a good idea to go fishing because fish do not bite in this type of weather condition. Jay and I watched Clifford launch his bass boat and we fished until 4:00 p.m. but didn't catch a bass. Clifford caught one 3 lb. bass and he gave the rod to Jay to bring the fish to the boat and I took a photo of Jay holding the fish. In spite of getting skunked, Jay and I had a good time. The next time I go fishing with a guide, it will be in warmer weather and not a cold front.

FRIDAY, DECEMBER 21, 2012—LUNCH AT EDEN'S GRILL

I dropped off Penny at Jan's condo at 11:15 and picked up Rich. We drove to the Eden's Grill and met Jeffrey Schesnol there for lunch. After lunch Jeffrey showed us his new Mini Cooper he had just leased.

SATURDAY, DECEMBER 22, 2012—TEMPE HOUSE & ABE'S DELI

I left at 7:50 a.m. and drove to meet at 8:15 a.m. my new Bluebell rental house tenant Attorney Rob Webb. Rob had recently lost his house because of the 2008 financial crisis and the bank would not refinance his house. He decided to rent and realtor Bob Lafferty was able to rent Rob the Bluebell house. Rob turned out to be a great tenant and three years later bought the house from me.

At 10:30 a.m. Penny and I met the Avers and Schesnols at Abe's Deli for breakfast at the corner of Gold Dust and Scottsdale Road. The restaurant wasn't that good and I found out later that it was no longer in business. After breakfast, Penny and I drove to The Promenade, went into Lowes and bought a Samsung above the range microwave oven. It will be delivered and installed in our condo sometime during next week. I picked up Harriet and Jay Weintraub at 4:00 p.m. and we drove to a 4:30 p.m. holiday party at Dan and Annie Murphy's house in Winfield at 7348 E. Crimson Sky Trail in North Scottsdale.

MONDAY, DECEMBER 24, 2012—A MOVIE AND DINNER

With Jan and Rich Aver at 1:00 p.m. we saw *Hyde Park On the Hudson* with Bill Murray and Laura Linney. We couldn't wait until our 5:00 p.m. dinner reservations, so we went to the Seasons 52 restaurant around 4:15 p.m. and they seated us along with Jeffrey and Susan Schesnol.

TUESDAY, DECEMBER 25, 2012—MOVIE AND CHINESE FOOD

At 1:00 p.m. Penny and I left to see the film *Les Miserable*. We picked up Jay and Harriet Weintraub around 1:15 p.m. and met Jan and Rich Aver, Jeffrey, Susan and Jacqui Schesnol at the Desert Ridge AMC Theater at 2:40 p.m.

At 6:30 p.m. nine of us went to dinner at Scottsdale's George & Son Asian Cuisine at 11291 E. Via Linda where we had reservations made by the Mehlmans, friends of the Schesnols. The restaurant was a mad house and I got wine spilled on my shirt and pants by Susan. We left around 8:40 p.m. It was not a good idea to go to this restaurant on Christmas Eve because the restaurant had a limited menu and was chaotic. This will be the last time we go to George & Sons on Christmas Eve. From now on it is a good idea to not go to a restaurant but order Chinese food and bring it into a friend's house.

WEDNESDAY, DECEMBER 26, 2012—FIREWOOD AND HIGH TEA

Penny and I had breakfast and left the condo around 8:15, heading to Berry Brothers to buy firewood. Around 11:15 I brought in the firewood from the car and put it in our patio storage locker. At 2:30 p.m. Penny picked up Harriet and Jan and drove to the Phoenician Resort for High Tea with Susan and Jacqui Schesnol and two other women I did not know.

SATURDAY, DECEMBER 29, 2012--STEVE KLEIN AND GIRLFRIEND

Around 11:15 a.m. Steve Klein and his new girlfriend Lisa Ash drove to Scottsdale and we ate at one of our favorite Phoenix restaurants, Chelsea's Kitchen, where we both had a kale salad that was delicious. After lunch, Steve and Lisa drove back to Tucson.

MONDAY, DECEMBER 31, 2012—NEW YEAR'S EVE

Around 7:30 p.m. we picked up the Avers and drove to La Fontanella Ristorante where we had an 8:00 p.m. reservation for the Spenschavers at our favorite Phoenix Italian restaurant located at 4231 E. Indian School. Jacqui Schesnol and her friend Phil Voyce also joined our dinner party.

TUESDAY, JANUARY 1, 2013—ARCADIA FARMS

At 12:00 p.m. Jeffrey, Susan and Jacqui Schesnol, Jan Aver and us had lunch at Scottsdale's Arcadia Farms.

WEDNESDAY, JANUARY 2, 2013—WALK & SIMON'S LUNCH

In the morning Penny and I went walking in the neighborhood. At 4:00 p.m. we were invited for dinner at Harriet and Jay Weintraub's rental condo with their guests Carol and John Simon, Annie and Dan Murphy and the Avers. Carol and John were in Scottsdale for a few days visiting Jay and Harriet.

THURSDAY, JANUARY 3—TUCSON TRIP

At 9:00 a.m. Penny and I drove to Tucson to visit Lisa Ash and Steve Klein and ate lunch at Ghini's French Market Caffe. We also bought a loaf of bread to take back to Scottsdale. We left in the early evening. On the way back to Scottsdale, I was very hungry so I stopped at a Tucson Subway but Penny did not eat anything.

SATURDAY, JANUARY 5, 2013—SPENCER FILM FESTIVAL

In the morning, I bought Einstein's Bagels and then went to Sprouts for groceries. We ate lunch at Wildflower and did some last-minute shopping to get ready for the film festival that night.

At 7:00 p.m. I invited our friends to show some of my films at The Alan Spencer Film Festival in our condo. The Weintraubs, Murphys, Avers and Schesnols were at our little get together. Penny served popcorn and dessert.

SUNDAY, JANUARY 6, 2013—*DOWNTON ABBEY*

Penny and I are huge *Downton Abbey* fans so at 5:00 p.m. *Downton Abbey* started season 3 and the Avers invited the Murphys and us to a *Downton Abbey* party at their condo. Jan made English food. Rich ate the food but did not watch the show.

TUESDAY, JANUARY 8, 2013—DINNER AT PASTA BRIONI

Penny and I had dinner with the Weintraubs at Scottsdale's Pasta Brioni restaurant. Penny was disappointed because they didn't have the exact chicken dish they usually had. We later discovered it was Chicken masala that used to be on the menu so you have to request it. We went to Yogurtology after dinner.

THURSDAY, JANUARY 10, 2013—GERT AND JEWISH FILMS

At 11:00 a.m. Penny and I drove to Sun City to visit with cousin Gert Phillips. She treated us to lunch at nearby Line Thai restaurant located at 9803 W. Bell Road in Sun City. After Sun City, Penny and I went to AZ Yo Co for a snack.

At 6:30 p.m. we went to the Scottsdale Jewish Center and the Jewish Film Festival-*Three Generations of Funny Jewish Women*. The tickets cost $10.00 each, pre-paid to Susan Schesnol. After the film festival, we went to Sauce for dinner with the Spenschavers.

FRIDAY, JANUARY 11, 2013—MARTIN MUSEUM AND LUNCH

At 10:00 a.m. Jeffrey Schesnol and I drove to the Martin Auto Museum in North Phoenix. I also drove Jeffrey in north Scottsdale to see Desert Auto Wreckers, a reality television show that was featured on the Speed channel. At 12:30 p.m. Jeffrey and I had lunch at Pappadeaux's restaurant near the auto museum. In the early evening we all went to Uncorked for dinner in Scottsdale.

SATURDAY, JANUARY 12, 2013—FARMER'S MARKET & DINNER

Today would have been my mother's 101st birthday. In the morning, Jan, Rich, Penny and I drove to Gilbert to the Farmer's Market. We saw Julie LaMagna and Ray Stephens at their booth and ate some vegan burgers at the Uprooted Kitchen food truck owned by friends of the Weintraubs. In the evening, we met the Schesnols and Avers at the Blue Wasabi restaurant near Hilton Village for sushi. We went to AZ Yo Co for a snack after sushi.

MONDAY, JANUARY 14—BARRETT JACKSON & DINNER WITH THE PAZOLS AND GIMPLES

At 8:00 a.m. I drove to the Barrett Jackson auto auction and had a great time by myself. At 6:00 p.m. we met Bobby and Jim Pazol and Bonny and Ron Gimple for dinner at the Pita Jungle by Desert Ridge Shopping Center. We try to see these two couples at least twice during our Scottsdale trips.

TUESDAY, JANUARY 15, 2013—BARRIO QUEEN TACOS

In the morning, I went to Einstein Bagels for breakfast goodies. For lunch, Penny and I went to the Barrio Queen in Old Scottsdale for taco Tuesday and it was delicious. We had a great server who made the meal very enjoyable.

At 6:00 p.m. we picked up Jan and went to Al's Italian Beef for dinner where Rich Aver worked.

WEDNESDAY, JANUARY 16, 2013—RUSSO STEELE AUCTION THEN CORKY AND NATALIE FOR DINNER

Today is Steve Klein's birthday. After breakfast I went to the Russo Steele Auto Auction on Scottsdale Road and was there the entire day. I met Eddie Matney there at his food stand and said hello. I reminded him we gave him the Bulls poster many years ago. He gave me his ex-partner Larry Cohen's mobile number. I taught Larry in fourth grade at Winnetka's Crow Island School. I had great fun at this event. At 7:00 p.m. Penny and I met Corky Weily and Natalie Kane for dinner at the Elephant Bar Grill.

THURSDAY, JANUARY 17, 2013—NATIVE TRAILS SHOW

At 12:00 noon Penny and I drove to Old Town Scottsdale to see the Native Trails show at the Scottsdale Civic Center. At 6:00 p.m. We went to dinner with our upstairs neighbors Dave and Sylvia Tucker at the Elephant Bar.

SATURDAY, JANUARY 19, 2013—THE SPENSCHAVER'S DINNER

Penny and I drove to Carefree in the afternoon and ate dinner at Nick's Italian Restaurant in the evening with the Avers and Schesnols.

SUNDAY, JANUARY 20, 2013—THE BEALLS AND MEXICAN FOOD

At 11:15 a.m. we met the Bealls at Chompie's in Tempe but the wait was too long so we went to a quick serve Panchero's Mexican restaurant located at 2051 W. Chandler Blvd. in Chandler instead.

WEDNESDAY, JANUARY 23, 2013—BOXES AND DINNER

In the morning, I took two large boxes of clothes and "stuff" to the UPS store on Shea Blvd and sent them to Northbrook. I also went to the Scottsdale Post Office and mailed Andrew Waldman's birthday card and gift and we finished packing for our trip to Chicago. This evening Penny and I ate dinner with the Avers and Schesnols at La Grande Orange in Phoenix. After dinner, we to the Aver's condo where Penny opened her birthday presents from Jan.

THURSDAY, JANUARY 24, 2013—FLIGHT TO CHICAGO

Penny and I are left our condo at 11:30 a.m. on a non-stop United Airlines, flight to Chicago. We departed from Phoenix Sky Harbor Airport at 3:39 p.m. and arrived at Chicago O'Hare at 8:00 p.m. Uri picked us up and drove us home.

JULY 25 TO JULY 28, 2013— BOSTON FAMILY REUNION THURSDAY, JULY 25, 2013—FLIGHT TO BOSTON

Penny and I departed from Chicago O'Hare Airport to Boston on a non-stop United Airlines flight at 6:00 a.m. and arrived at Boston Logan Airport at 9:16 a.m. Lois and Roy picked us up from Logan Airport and drove us to their home.

This trip was a family reunion with Lois Camberg, Roy Cramer, Leah and Aaron Cramer, Mara, Christian and Samantha Centanni, Sandy Fishman, Bennett and his family, Ronna and her family and Penny and me. All of the out-of-towners stayed at the Sheraton Needham Hotel located at 100 Cabot Street in Needham, Massachusetts. This trip was the first time we had a chance to meet Leah's boyfriend, Josh Eaker.

FRIDAY, JULY 26, 2013—RAIN AND DOUG'S DINNER

It rained all day so we stayed in the hotel and the children and some adults swam in the indoor pool. After swimming, everyone went back to Lois and Roy's house and Doug Fishman made a delicious pasta dinner.

SATURDAY, JULY 27, 2013— LOIS & ROY'S POOL PARTY

The weather was warm today so everyone gathered at Lois and Roy's house for lunch and a pool party. It was a fun day.

SUNDAY, JULY 28, 2013—FLY BACK TO CHICAGO

Penny and I departed from Boston to Chicago on a non-stop United Airlines flight. We left Boston at 5:25 p.m. and arrived in Chicago at 7:08 p.m. Uri picked us up from O'Hare Airport and drove us to Northbrook.

THURSDAY, SEPTEMBER 19, 2013—COLORADO WEDDING

Penny and I were invited to Laura Grauer's wedding to Brian Burnham in Beaver Creek, Colorado and we decided to go. Our non-stop United Airlines flight#1429 departed Chicago O'Hare Airport at 8:47 a.m. to Denver. We left on time and arrived in Denver International Airport at 10:22 a.m. Upon our arrival in Denver, we rented an Avis car with unlimited miles for $226.36. We drove to the Beaver Creek and checked into the The Osprey at Beaver Creek located at 10 Elk Track Lane in Beaver Creek. The cost for three nights stay was $554.97. The hotel, located on a mountain, was beautifully furnished and very accommodating.

Penny and I were excited because our plan after the wedding was to drive through Rocky Mountain Nation Park and spend Saturday night at Murphy's River Lodge located at 481 W. Elkhorn Avenue in Estes Park, Colorado. Unfortunately, there were torrential rains that washed out roads through the park including the overflow of the Thompson River that runs through Estes Park. All of the roads were washed out and closed so I had to cancel our hotel reservations.

FRIDAY, SEPTEMBER 20, 2013—GRAUER WEDDING

In the morning, Penny and I walked across the street and went into the town of Beaver Creek. Penny noticed the thin air and had a little trouble breathing but the air didn't affect me. We ate lunch in a small restaurant in the town. Later in the day, we got dressed for the wedding. A ride was provided for the guests to go up the mountain outside of the hotel to the wedding site. The wedding site overlooked the entire valley and the view was spectacular. A lodge was at the top of the mountain. After the wedding, a delicious dinner was served inside the lodge. A ride was supplied to drive down the mountain to our hotel.

SATURDAY, SEPTEMBER 21, 2013—FLY FISHING IN AVON

After breakfast, Penny and I drove down the mountain to the town of Avon and I went into Fly Fishing Outfitters a store that sold fly fishing equipment and clothing. The Avon store was located at 1060 W. Beaver Creek Blvd. On this trip I brought my travel fly rod with me just in case I could go fishing. The store had some fly-fishing shirts on sale, so Penny bought one and I purchased two long-sleeve shirts with insect repellent built into the fabric. I also bought a one-day fishing license and the knowledgeable friendly and experienced staff told me the exact spot to fish, by a big rock underneath the bridge on the Eagle River, a tributary of the Colorado River. I was at this fishing spot for about one-hour and caught my first brown trout on a wooly bugger.

SUNDAY, SEPTEMBER 22, 2013—JERRY ARONSON

Since we could not go to Estes Park because the flooding, we texted Jerry Aronson and made arrangements to drive to Boulder to visit with him. So, after breakfast at the hotel, we drove to Boulder and met Jerry at his rental house. We spent some time with him, and then went to lunch at his favorite nearby restaurant. After lunch we had time to drive to the Denver Airport for our evening flight back to Chicago. We arrived at the airport around 5:00 p.m. and returned our rental car. Our non-stop United Airlines flight#1403 was on time and left Denver International Airport at 7:37 p.m. and arrived at Chicago O'Hare Airport at 10:58 p.m. Uri picked us up at the airport and drove us to our home in Northbrook.

TUESDAY, DECEMBER 24, 2013—SCOTTSDALE TRIP

Uri picked up at 6:15 a.m. and we arrived at the airport a little after 6:45 a.m. for our departure from Chicago O'Hare Airport to Phoenix Sky Harbor Airport. We were on our non-stop United Airlines flight. We left Chicago O'Hare at 8:11 a.m. and arrived in Phoenix at 11:10 a.m.

Jan and Rich picked us up at the airport and we drove to Goldman's Deli for lunch. After lunch we drove to Einstein Bagels to buy breakfast for the next day, then before going to the condo, we went to Basil and Garlic, a pizza restaurant and picked up two small loaves of bread to go with the soup Jan made for dinner.

WEDNESDAY, DECEMBER 25, 2013—A MOVIE, THEN FLO'S

Penny and I ate breakfast at the condo with coffee Ronna brought back from the Caribbean. At 2:45 p.m. Jan and Rich picked us up and we went to the Harkins Theater at the 101 and Scottsdale Road to see *American Hustle*. The place was packed and we could only find four seats in the last row. I saved two seats up front for Jeffrey and Susan. After the movie, the girls went with Jan to their condo and Jeffrey drove to his house to pick up his pills, then we went to Flo's Chinese restaurant to pick up food Rich had ordered ahead of time. The place was a zoo when we arrived. After dinner, we got back to our condo around 9:45 p.m.

THURSDAY, DECEMBER 26, 2013—PICK UP RENTAL CAR

I got up around 7:30 and Penny slept until about 8:15 a.m. We ate breakfast and at 10:10 a.m. Penny and I took a thirty-minute walk around the neighborhood. At 1:10 p.m. Rich Aver picked me up and we drove to get our rental car with unlimited miles at Avis rental car for thirty-seven days. Chris Freh, owner of the Avia franchise set me up with a 2014 Kia Optima.

SATURDAY, DECEMBER 28, 2013—FARMER'S MARKET

Penny and I had breakfast at the condo, and then picked up Jan and Rich at 9:30 for a trip to the Gilbert, Arizona Farmer's Market to see Julie LaMagna and Ray Stephens who exhibit their pickled food products there. We bought Julie's pickled beets and onions, pickled Brussels sprouts and big dill pickles. We also purchased raisin bread and Italian cookies from other vendors. Penny bought five greeting cards from a woman whose autistic son Sam is an artist.

After leaving the farmer's market we drove to Paradise Café in Mesa and ate lunch. After lunch we drove around the corner to the Mesa Flea Market and bought a variety of items for the condo and Northbrook home. Afterwards we dropped off Jan and Rich at their condo At 6:45 p.m. we picked up Jan and Rich and met Jeffrey and Susan Schesnol for dinner at Coconuts Fish Café at 16640 N. Scottsdale Road. Penny and I ordered calamari and a taco mountain and shared each. We met the owner, Kim Kuhljuergen, who bought the Arizona franchise. The original café is located in Kihei, Hawaii.

SUNDAY, DECEMBER 29, 2013—CHICAGO BEARS

Rich Aver picked me up at 12:10 p.m. to watch the Chicago Bears play the Green Bay Packers at the Tavern Grille Sports Bar at 8880 E. Via Linda.

At 12:15 p.m. Penny picked up Jan and drove to Susan Schesnol's home, and then they all went to the Phoenix Art Museum. At 2:25 p.m. Chicago Bears played the Green Bay Packers and at 8:00 p.m. we watched Kennedy Center Honors.

MONDAY, DECEMBER 30, 2013—DISHWASHER AND FIREPLACE

Penny and I ate breakfast and took a thirty-minute walk on the new bike and walking path just east of our condo. After breakfast, we drove to Lowes looking for a new dishwasher. Our old dishwasher still worked but not well. It is an original dishwasher from 1984 and not very energy efficient. After talking to a Lowes sales person, we decided to go to Spencers Appliances at Acoma and Scottsdale Road. Matt Osborne, a very nice salesman, talked to us about various dishwashers. We settled on a quiet GE dishwasher that was on sales for $399.00. The total cost was $535.00 including a $100.00 delivery and an installation charge. The delivery and installation were scheduled on Tuesday morning December 31, 2013.

At 2:30 p.m. Arizona Chimney Sweep inspected and cleaned our condo's chimney. The chimney was dirty. On a scale of 10, the chimney was a 6, not overly dirty but warranted a cleaning. After the chimney cleaning, we went to Sprouts Market for additional grocery shopping of salad, eggs, broccoli, and Bob's Gluten Free Pancake mix, trail mix, popcorn and some other items.

TUESDAY, DECEMBER 31, 2013—NEW YEAR'S DINNER

I woke up at 5:25, shaved and got dressed. Penny was still sleeping and I made pancakes for breakfast. Our new GE Dishwasher was delivered and installed in the morning. After the installation, I went shopping at Fry's for some groceries.

At 7:30 p.m. Jan and Rich Aver picked Penny and me up for an 8:00 p.m. for New Year's dinner reservations at our favorite Phoenix Italian restaurant at La Fontanella Ristorante. The reservation was for Jan and Rich Aver, Jeffrey and Susan Schesnol, and Jacqui Schesnol's friend, Phil Voyce. After dinner we drove to the Schesnols where we celebrated New Year and got home at 1:35 a.m.

WEDNESDAY, JANUARY 1, 2014—COLLEGE FOOTBALL

At 9:39 a.m. Penny and I woke up after getting home late the night before. I had leftover pancakes for breakfast from the previous day. I watched Wisconsin lose to South Carolina in the Capital One Bowl in Orlando, Michigan State 24 defeated Stanford 20 in the Rose Bowl in Pasadena and University of Central Florida 52 beat Baylor 42 in the Fiesta Bowl held in Glendale, Arizona. I also watched some of the recorded *Twilight Zone* episodes in between. In the afternoon,

Penny drove to Jan's to watch recorded figure skating.

FRIDAY, JANUARY 3, 2014—RAINBOW TROUT AND HIGH TEA

Today is Jan and & Rich Aver's Anniversary. Around 8:45 a.m. after eating breakfast, I drove to my favorite Tempe fishing place, the Evelyn Hallman Pond off of College Avenue and McKellips. On the first cast with my fly rod, I caught a 13" rainbow trout on a woolly bugger fly. I brought a thermal ice container with me because Jan Aver said if I caught a fish, she would clean it. Around 10:30 a.m. I left the pond and drove back to the apartment with the fish and my rods and reel. At 2:15 p.m. Penny picked up Jan to have High Tea at the Phoenician Resort with the girls. Susan Schesnol was at The Promenade and Susie Flax joined the group for their annual high tea adventure.

SUNDAY, JANUARY 5, 2014—TROUT AND *DOWNTON ABBEY*

For breakfast I cooked the trout I caught and made sunny side up eggs. At 11:30 a.m. we went to Fry's to pick up ingredients for the *Downton Abbey* party and other grocery items. I watched the Cincinnati vs. San Diego football game and the Green Bay and San Francisco game before picking up Jan and Rich at 6:45 p.m. to go to the Schesnols home for a *Downton Abbey* party. We got back to our condo at 11:35 p.m.

MONDAY, JANUARY 6, 2014—WALK AND COUSIN GERT VISIT

I made French toast on our new large electric skillet. After breakfast, we went for a one-hour walk in our neighborhood. I called cousin Gert Phillips who hadn't been feeling well. She said she hoped we could see her before we left. We went to the Scottsdale Library at 2:00 p.m.

TUESDAY, JANUARY 7—LUNCH AND SUNNYSLOPE

. We decided to have a late lunch at Barrio Queen at 7100 E. Stetson in Old Scottsdale. The restaurant has $3.00 Margarita's on Taco Tuesdays and small bite-size tacos for $2.50 each. During lunch Penny mentioned driving to Sunnyslope, an old section of Phoenix she read about several years ago in the *Arizona Republic*. Before our lunch was serviced, I looked up Sunnyslope on Google and found the Sunnyslope Historical Society Museum. They were closed but a woman named Juanita answered the phone, gave me her cell phone number and said she would give us a private tour of the museum. I told her we were eating lunch but would drive to Sunnyslope in one hour.

So, after lunch, Penny and I drove to the Sunnyslope Museum and met Juanita and Connie there. We got a private tour of the museum and the house next to the museum. I bought a pamphlet about the 1954 creation of the S painted on the wide of a mountain by the students at Sunnyslope High School. The museum was originally a drug store and was moved to its current location in 1999 along with the small house next to it. After our tour, we drove around the neighborhood, took photos and looked at the different houses on the side of the mountain.

WEDNESDAY, JANUARY 8—TEMPLER VISIT

At 2:30 p.m. Penny and I left for Jackie and Stu Templer's home in Sun City Grand located in Surprise, Arizona about thirty-eight miles from our condo. Jackie made dinner and Penny brought brownies for dessert.

THURSDAY, JANUARY 9—BREAKFAST FOR FRIENDS

At 9:15 a.m. Penny went to Sprouts to buy turkey sausage, hash brown potatoes and an extra orange juice for the breakfast I planned for our friends. At 10:00 a.m. the Schesnols´ and Avers came to our condo and I made protein pancakes for them for breakfast. We talked until 1:35 p.m. After eating a late lunch, Penny and I went for a twenty-minute walk around the condo complex. I called Steve Klein who had knee surgery in the morning. We Skyped with Ronna, Spencer and Talia, and then with Bennett, Marni, Danny and Brooke.

FRIDAY, JANUARY 10—IRON STAND AND SHABBAT

Penny and I woke up late and didn't get out of our home until 1:30 p.m. We drove to several consignment stores and bought a blue patina pedestal iron plant stand at Consign2Design located at 7342 E. Shea Blvd. We stopped by Jan and Rich's condo and were there for a few minutes when Jay and Harriet arrived in Scottsdale from Tucson. We stayed until 4:30, and then came back to our condo. Penny put on a frozen pizza and we ate dinner around 5:15 p.m.

Penny and I left our home at 6:10 p.m. for our drive to the Arizona Jewish Historical Society located on Culver Street in Phoenix, where the Or Adam Friday night service was held. We took Shea Blvd. west to the 51 south and got off at McDowell going west to 2nd Street. We turned left on 2nd Street to the bungalow currently used for the service. The historical society is 18.6 miles from our condo and it took about forty-five minutes to get there. There was an accident at McDowell so the traffic was slow moving until we got off the 51. Penny and I met Susie Ernst and her husband Tim, both graduates from Cleveland Height High School ten years after Penny. What a small Jewish world.

The service started about 7:10 p.m. and lasted one hour. Penny and I were asked to take part in the service. I read a passage from the printed service and Penny read a short poem. An Oneg Shabbat immediately followed the service and a discussion of Jewish values. We got back to our condo around 10:30 p.m.

SUNDAY, JANUARY 12—*DOWNTON ABBEY AND THE* GLOBES

From 7:00 to 10:00 p.m. Jan and Rich Aver invited Dan and Annie Murphy along with Jay and Harriet Weintraub for dinner. She served Shepard's pie and we watched the Golden Globe Awards, then the Murphy's left before we watched *Downton Abbey.* Rich wasn't interested so it was Jan, Penny and me watching one of our favorite PBS television series.

MONDAY, JANUARY 13—BARRETT JACKSON AUCTION

I woke up early, ate a small breakfast, drove to the Barrett Jackson Auction and spent the entire day there arriving around 8:30 a.m. and leaving around 3:15 p.m. There were 1,400 cars on display and I had a great time taking photos of several of my favorite cars. On the way home I stopped at the Chase bank to get some cash and at Safeway to buy bottled water since the water was turned off at the condo for some repairs. When I got home the water had been turned back on.

We picked up Jan and Rich Aver at 5:30 p.m. and met Jeffrey and Susan Schesnol for dinner at the Eden's Grill. I ordered catfish for the four of us and made sure they had it for our upcoming Thursday evening dinner reservations with

Corky Weily and Natalie Kane. After dinner, we drove to Rita's Frozen Custard on north Tatum to get their frozen custard and Italian ices concoction for dessert.

TUESDAY, JANUARY 14—BREAKFAST AND PAZOLS-GIMPLES

We met Jay and Harriet Weintraub at Butters Café, a breakfast restaurant located at Hayden and Via Ventura. I wasn't very impressed with the breakfast and we probably won't go back here in the future. At 6:00 p.m. we had a get together with Jim and Bobby Pazol and Bonny and Ron Gimple at the Pita Jungle just north of the 101 on Tatum. It is always fun to get together with our Youngstown friends.

WEDNESDAY, JANUARY 15—LUNCH AND DESERT GARDEN

Harriet and Jay picked us up at 11:30 a.m. and we went to Chelsea's Kitchen for lunch. After lunch we went to the Desert Botanical Garden to see the Chilhuly exhibit. For dinner, I ate leftovers from Monday evening and Penny had popcorn.

THURSDAY, JANUARY 16— WEINTRAUBS BRUNCH, A MOVIE, AND CORKY WEILY DINNER

At 11:15 a.m. Jay and Harriet picked us up and we ate brunch at Le Petite France in the Seville Shopping Center at the corner of Scottsdale Road and Indian Bend. After lunch we drove to the Camelview Theater and watched the movie *Nebraska*, starring Bruce Dern. The movie was fabulous and was nominated for an Academy Award along with June Squibb for best supporting actress. She played Bruce Dern's wife in the film. After the film, Penny and I called Steve Klein and wished him a happy 70th birthday.

At 7:00 p.m. Penny and I met cousin Corky Weily and Natalie Kane for dinner at the Eden's Grill. I called on Monday to make sure the restaurant had four catfish dinners. One time, the restaurant was out of catfish and they told us to call ahead of time to make sure they had it. Nahreen took a photo of us at the end of the dinner.

FRIDAY, JANUARY 17—PENNY AT JAN'S CONDO AND FISHING

I drove Penny to the Aver's condo around 9:50 a.m. and then Jan, Harriet and Penny drove to Cave Creek & Carefree to shop while I went fishing at Papago Park in several ponds until 2:00 p.m. I had one hard hit on my fly rod, but did not catch a fish. I returned to the condo around 2:20 p.m., ate lunch and was on the computer to pay some bills. Penny got home around 4:45 p.m. and showed me some of the items she purchased.

SATURDAY, JANUARY 18—TED JASS 65TH BIRTHDAY

This morning, Penny and I ate breakfast around 9:00. Linda and Ted Jass were visiting Arizona to celebrate Ted's 65th birthday so the plan was to meet at Chompie's Deli in Chandler at 11:45 a.m. for a birthday brunch. Penny and I picked up the Avers and we met Faith, Matt, Maddy and Tyler Beall and the Jass family at the restaurant to help celebrate Ted's birthday.

SUNDAY, JANUARY 19, 2014—VISTAL GOLF CLUB

Rich Aver and Jay Weintraub wanted me to play golf with them but I hadn't played in over twenty years. I decided why not, so at 9:00 a.m. Jay, Rich, our friend Dan Murphy and I drove to Vistal Golf Club at the base of South Mountain and played 18 holes. Since I did not own golf clubs, I had to rent a set along with six golf balls at the golf course. Golf club drivers and fairway woods had become larger since I last played so with the new type of larger golf clubs, I was able to hit the ball and decided that perhaps on our next Arizona visit, I would buy a set of golf clubs.

Originally, I started playing golf as a teenager in Boardman, Ohio with my friend Bill DeCicco. We would play nine holes at Mill Creek Golf Course not too far from my home. Bill and I tried out for the Boardman High School Golf Team, but we weren't that good and neither of us made the golf team. I introduced golf to Bennett when he was ten years old and we used to play at Northbrook's Sportsman Golf Club. Rich Aver and I would also play before he moved to Fort Worth, Texas. I gave up playing many years ago because I became interested in bass fishing with Arnie Grauer. From 10:00 a.m. to 12:00 noon, Penny, Jan and Harriet went to a glass fusion plate making class located at 1202 N. 3rd Street in Phoenix. They created some beautiful looking glass plates and the one Penny made sits on a shelf in our condo.

MONDAY, JANUARY 20—SUNNYSLOPE AND MacALPINE'S

Today is Martin Luther King's birthday, a national holiday as well as Alan Appelbaum, Remey Rubin and Ted Jass birthday. Harriet and Jay Weintraub had not been to Sunnyslope so I drove the Weintraubs around the Sunnyslope area in Phoenix and parts of Tempe new to them. We had lunch at a new restaurant on Central Avenue, Pane Bianco. It was delicious. Then we drove around some Phoenix historic neighborhoods and ended at Phoenix's MacAlpines Diner and Soda Fountain and antique store located at 2303 N. 7th Street. Penny and I had been to MacAlpines last year. MacAlpines Diner and Soda Fountain was originally a Rexall drug store. This famous Phoenix landmark has been around since 1928. It has vintage décor and serves retro food, drinks and ice cream concoctions. Devon was our server and one of her co-workers took a photo of the Weintraubs and us at a booth. Jay ordered a chocolate soda and Harriet and Penny ordered a chocolate sundae. I ordered a chocolate sundae with pecans. We bought a teapot to add to our condo collection that sits on the top of our kitchen cabinets. Unbeknownst to us, Harriet and Jay bought the other teapot that Penny admired and gave it for her birthday.

We met a retired Chicago homicide detective and his wife who were eating ice cream at a table near the back of the store. They bought a place in Scottsdale and were enjoying the great weather. We chatted with them for quite a while and one of the photos I took inside the store had the Chicago couple seated at a table.

TUESDAY, JANUARY 21—GILBERT, LUNCH AND DINNER

Jay and Harriet Weintraub drove Penny and me to Gilbert and Chandler to go antiquing. We first stopped at Antiques in the Garden and ate lunch at Gilbert's Farmhouse Restaurant. After Gilbert we drove to Chandler and went antiquing at Merchant Square. After buying a variety of items, we drove to a gigantic furniture store that had just opened to look at a turquoise dining room cabinet Penny had seen in a newspaper ad. The cabinet was not turquoise and the front was too yellow, so we didn't buy it. At 6:30 p.m. the Avers met Jay, Harriet and us for dinner at the Elephant Bar Restaurant. After dinner we went to Yogurtology for dessert.

THURSDAY, JANUARY 23—BREAKFAST AND THE SPRITZERS

At 9:45 a.m. Penny and I picked up Jan and Rich Aver and we met the Weintraubs at Tom Thumb's Fresh Market for breakfast. After dropping off Jan and Rich, we went to Savers and found some plates that sort of matched our dishes and bought them. At 3:45 p.m. Penny and I met 2nd cousin Ron Spritzer, his wife Carol and Ron's mother, cousin Gert Phillips for dinner at Pasta Brioni. Ron and Carol were staying at the Scottsdale Cottonwood Resort located at 6160 N. Scottsdale Road. They flew into Phoenix to see Ron's mother, Gert, who lives in Sun City. We had a terrific meal and told family stories and caught up of life.

SATURDAY, JANUARY 25—FISHING AND DON & CHARLIE'S

I went fishing at Evelyn Hallman Park in Tempe. Penny joined me, sitting and reading a book while I fished. After fishing I bought gasoline for the rental car. We got back to the condo around 1:00 p.m., ate lunch and relaxed before our dinner with Jay and Harriet Weintraub. At 6:10 p.m. Jay and Harriet Weintraub picked up Penny and me for our 6:30 dinner reservation at Scottsdale's Don & Charlie's restaurant on Camelback Road.

SUNDAY, JANUARY 26, 2014—WEINTRAUB CONDO, BREAKFAST AND DINNER AT JALAPENO INFERNO

I invited Jay and Harriet for breakfast for 9:30 a.m. and I made my version of protein pancakes. After breakfast, I drove to Jan and Rich's condo and Susan and Jeffrey Schesnol met us there. Jeffrey, Rich and I picked up Jay and we met Dan Murphy at Jalapeno Inferno on Scottsdale Road for a 2:30 p.m. lunch. After lunch we went to the Murphy's to celebrate Penny's birthday. In the meantime, Penny, Jan and Susan picked up Harriet and they went to high tea in at the English Rose Tea Room in Carefree.

MONDAY, JANUARY 27—OLD SCOTTSDALE AND A WALK

Penny and I ate breakfast around 9:00 a.m. and drove to Old Scottsdale to buy post cards and gifts for Talia and my sister Linda. We came back to the condo, ate lunch at 1:15 p.m. and relaxed for the rest of the day until we went for a walk in back of our condo. We met Vic Lewis by the Paradise Gardens cemetery who mistook us for a short Italian couple he met in our condo complex. Vic moved here from Minnesota and spends approximately six months in Scottsdale. He lives in the La Contessa condo units immediately to the south of Mission de los Arroyos.

THURSDAY, JANUARY 30, 2014—FLIGHT TO CHICAGO

Happy Birthday Penny!! At 9:30 a.m. Jan Aver came to our condo to watch figure skating with Kurt Browning and to get some of our leftover food items before our trip back to Chicago. Penny and I were going to be back in Scottsdale in March for Melissa Klein's Tucson wedding, so we did not unplug our refrigerator because we had items in the freezer for our return.

Penny and I left for the airport at 11:45 a.m. We dropped off our rental car at Avis, told the representative the overhead light did not work and the windshield could not be cleaned. The plane was thirty minutes late arriving from Chicago, so we left Phoenix at 5:45 p.m. Chicago time on a non-stop United Airlines flight and arrived in Chicago at 8:02 p.m. Uri picked us up and drove us home.

ONE CRAZY WEEKEND—TWO WEDDINGS IN TWO DAYS IN TWO DIFFERENT PARTS OF THE UNITED STATES
FRIDAY, MARCH 21, 2014—TRIP TO WASHINGTON, DC

Uri picked Penny and me up at 6:30 a.m. and we arrived at the airport a little after 7:00 a.m. We took a non-stop United Airlines flight to Washington, D.C. (National-Reagan). The plane left Chicago O'Hare at 9:00 a.m. and we arrived in Washington around 11:50 a.m. The cost was $37.00 total plus 20,000 Award Miles. Penny and I took a taxi to the Fairfax at Embassy Row located at 2100 Massachusetts Avenue NW and arrived around 12:00 p.m. The Starwood hotel room cost $159.00 per night.

We met my sister Linda in the lobby and had lunch at Le Pain Quotidian around the corner from the hotel. Then we took the Metro to the National Museum of Art where we saw the only Leonardo DaVinci painting in America. The young Florentine lady is the portrait of Ginevra de' Benci who was much admired by contemporaries for her culture, beauty and character and appears on a double-sided wooden panel. This panel was painted before the Mona Lisa. We ate lunch in the Cascade Cafe downstairs in the National Gallery of Art museum.

Bruce and Suzyn Epstein and Marilyn and Larry Levy were also staying at the same hotel and we had dinner with them at Grillfish within walking distance of the hotel along with Jacqui Schesnol who was living in Washington, D.C. at the time.

SATURDAY, MARCH 22, 2014—TROLLEY TOUR AND WEDDING

We got us early and had a quick breakfast at a Starbucks across the street from the pickup of the Trolley Tour bus. The trolley was supposed to arrive at 9:30 a.m. but just as we were crossing the street, we noticed it pulling up to the photo shop stop. Linda ran and stopped the trolley just in time and we boarded it. We also went to Air and Space Museum.

We got back to hotel around 4:00 p.m. and got dressed for the wedding. The Alexis Lockshin and Harrison Gyurko reception and wedding were at The Cosmos Club located at 2121 Massachusetts Avenue NW in Washington, D.C. At 5:00 p.m. we walked a short distance to the Cosmos Club where Norman and Sheila and Sheila's mother, Ethel, were in a small room near the ballroom. We visited with them and saw Ben, Diana and Steven and his wife Allison and spoke with them.

SUNDAY, MARCH 23, 2014—PHOENIX AND TUCSON WEDDING

Penny and I got up at 3:45 a.m. and were picked up at 4:50 a.m. by Angie Scott, owner of Scott Enterprises and driven to Baltimore/Washington Airport for 75.00 in a Jeep Liberty. I found Scott Enterprises on the Internet and everything worked out great. We were flying from Baltimore/Washington Airport to Phoenix Sky Harbor Airport. We left Baltimore on time at 7:35 a.m. and arrived in Phoenix at 9:50 a.m. on a non-stop Southwest Airlines flight.

At 10:25 a.m. Jan Aver met us at the Southwest terminal and she drove us to pick up a rental car at Avis car rental at 7125 E. Shea Blvd. Scottsdale (20 days rental) through Costco Travel & AARP for a total cost of $728.21. Since we were already in Tucson for Melissa and Matt Landau's wedding, we would drive back to Scottsdale to stay for twenty days at our condo. We left Avis at 11:45 a.m. went to Starbucks across the street on Shea Blvd. and each of us bought an ice tea to take on the road. At 2:00 p.m. we arrived at the Fairfield Inn and Suites by Marriott Tucson North. The hotel is located at 10150 N Oracle Road at Oro Valley.

The beautiful outdoor reception and wedding of Matthew Landau and Melissa Klein was held at 5:30 p.m. at Reflections at the Buttes at 9800 N Oracle in Oro Valley, Arizona down the street from our hotel. The weather was perfect and the Melissa and Matt made a terrific couple. We met many relatives and friends of Steve Klein and had a great time at the reception and wedding.

MONDAY, MARCH 24, 2014—DRIVE TO SCOTTSDALE

At 9:00 a.m. Steve Klein met Penny and me and his friend Jan in the hotel lobby. I drove all of us to Beyond Bread for breakfast that was at the corner of Ina and Oracle Road. After breakfast, we drove back to hotel and checked out around 11:15 a.m. We drove to Scottsdale and stopped at the Picacho Peak State Park on I-10. We toured the park and bought some coloring books for the grandchildren.

After returning to Scottsdale, Penny and I went shopping for food at Fry's. We ate dinner around 5:30 from leftover eggplant Parmesan and spaghetti that was in the freezer from our January trip. We left for the Mustang Library around 6:30 p.m. for a 7:00 p.m. for the Mission de los Arroyos Annual Meeting held in the auditorium of the Scottsdale's Mustang Library on 90th Street.

WEDNESDAY, MARCH 26, 2014—PANEL DISCUSSION

At 6:40, Penny and I picked up Jan Aver at her condo and we drove to the Valley Beit Midrash where our friend, Jeffrey Schesnol, was invited to participate in a panel discussion from 7:00 to 8:00 p.m. The facility is just north of Shea Blvd. and just west of Scottsdale Road. The panel consisted of an Orthodox and Reform Rabbi and was moderated by an Arizona State University professor. The evening was very educational and Jeffrey did a great job of expressing his views.

THURSDAY, MARCH 27, 2014—SPRING TRAINING

I picked up Rich Aver at 10:00 a.m. and we drove to the Arizona Jewish Historical Society to pick up Susan and Jeffrey at 10:30 a.m. We arrived at Cubs Park in Mesa around 11:15 and got a close parking spot. Our seats were three rows from the field on the first base side. The game started at 2:05 p.m. and I had a veggie sandwich for lunch. The Chicago Cubs were playing the Chicago White Sox and the Cubs won 4 to 3. I called Chicago radio personality, Bruce Levine and left a message on his cell phone but he did not return my call. I met Bruce after his speech at Max and Benny's in February and told him I'd be at the game. He gave me his cell phone number and so I decided to call him at the game. While we were at the game, Jan and Penny went shopping at Kohl's and other stores. Later that day we ate dinner at Spinato's with the Spenschavers.

FRIDAY, MARCH 28—ART FAIR AND SCHESNOL DINNER

Penny and I picked up Jan and Rich Aver and drove to a Park and Ride parking lot at 38th Street and Washington Streets to catch the Phoenix Valley Metro light rail to Tempe. We paid $2.00 each and took the light rail to Mill Avenue in

Tempe for the Tempe Art Fair. We spent five hours there and took the light rail back to the parking lot. At 7:00 p.m. we met Susan and Jeffrey at George and Son for dinner.

SATURDAY, MARCH 29—FISHING, A MOVIE AND DINNER

I got up at 5:45 a.m. ate breakfast and went fishing until 1:15 p.m. at the McCormick Ranch lake. We went to see *The Grand Budapest Hotel* film at the Harkin's Camelview Theater and ate dinner at The Twisted Sister that was empty and not a good meal for the price.

SUNDAY, MARCH 30, 2014—JEROME AND MURPHY DINNER

At 9:15 a.m. Penny and I picked up Jan and Susan and Jeffrey and drove to Jerome, Arizona for the day and ate lunch at the Haunted Hamburger. We visited Nellie Bly and looked at all of the kaleidoscopes. On the way home we got off I-17 at exit 242 and stopped at the Rock Springs Pie Café to buy a slice of cherry peach pie. Later we met Dan and Annie Murphy at the Elephant Bar for dinner.

MONDAY, MARCH 31, 2014—DESERT GARDEN AND CHILHULY

After breakfast, I picked up bananas, blueberries and hummus at Sprouts. Didn't do much during the day. We had an 8:00 p.m. reservation to see the Chilhuly exhibit at night at the Phoenix Botanical Garden. Penny and I picked up Jan and met Jeffrey, Susan and Jacqui Schesnol there. Rich was not interested so he did not join us.

TUESDAY, APRIL 1, 2014—BARTLETT LAKE AND PICNIC

Penny and I drove to Bartlett Lake about thirty-five miles north and east from our condo. We took Pima Road north to Cave Creek Road and turned right. There was a Ranger station before the entrance to Tonto National Forest and the fee was $6.00 per car. Since I had a United States National Parks Golden Passport, our fee for the day was reduced to $3.00. I went fishing, caught nothing and had a picnic lunch on a park table and bench, and then drove back to our condo. The scenery was spectacular and the day was fun even though I didn't have a bite. We are hoping to drive back to Bartlett Lake on a future visit to Scottsdale.

WEDNESDAY, APRIL 2—CONCERT, CORKY AND NATALIE

During the day, Penny watched figure skating at Jan and Rich Aver's condo. At 6:15 p.m. Penny and I met Corky Weily and Natalie Kane at the Wildflower restaurant located at the Seville shopping center on Scottsdale Road and Indian Bend before a jazz concert. We left Wildflower at 7:00 to pick up our tickets.

By 7:30 p.m. we were at Scottsdale's Kerr Institute located at 6110 N. Scottsdale Road [Section B, Row 2, Seats 1 & 2] to see the Amazing Piano Players. Corky and Natalie joined us there. We heard three amazing pianists, each with their own style. Nicole Pesce was one of the pianists and a favorite of ours. Since this performance, we've seen Nicole Pesce on many occasions in a variety of Scottsdale venues. Nicole is so talented and can play anything on the piano.

FRIDAY, APRIL 4, 2014—ART MUSEUM AND DINNER

At 1:00 p.m. we picked up Jan Aver and drove to the Phoenix Art Museum for the Hollywood Costumes Exhibit and met Jeffrey and Susan Schesnol there. Rich did not want to go. The exhibit was quite interesting because it contained a wide variety of elaborate costumes worn in famous movies. We wandered through the exhibit, walked around the museum for several hours and left around 3:30 p.m. At 7:30 p.m. we picked up Jan and Rich Aver met for dinner at The Habit Burger Grill with the Spenschavers. A young couple had a bull dog named Stella who was very friendly and so we took a photo with Stella and the Spenschavers.

SATURDAY, APRIL 5—FARMER'S MARKET AND FISHING

Jan Aver and Penny went to the Farmer's Market and the Modern Phoenix Marketplace at the Center for the Performing Arts and a free entrance fee to the Scottsdale Museum of Contemporary Art. They ate lunch at Farmer's on the Edge on the Scottsdale Mall. In the meantime, I went fishing at the McCormick Ranch Lake and caught nothing. For dinner, Jan and Rich Aver picked us up and we went to Joyful Chinese Cuisine . After dinner we went for frozen yogurt at Yogurtology.

SUNDAY, APRIL 6, 2014—PHOENIX AND SUNDAY A'FAIR

After breakfast, Penny and I were up for an adventure, so we took a drive to see the old DeSoto Building near 7th Street and Central Avenue in Phoenix. Around 11:00 a.m. we drove to the Scottsdale Civic Center Mall where we saw some amazing acts. The program was called OrigiNation, a festival of native cultures. The program started at 12 noon and lasted until 4:00 p.m.

The program was presented as part of the Discovery Series and Sunday A'Fair. The entertainment event offered the opportunity to learn about native cultures in Arizona and Brazil through music, song, dance and storytelling. We saw and heard Sambatuque, Native American championship artists through dancing and music. Capoeira Brazil Arizona performed as well as samba dancers. The show was terrific and I took videos of a few acts and edited them into my "shows." Around 12:15 p.m. I was hungry so I had a veggie burger at The Blue Moose Restaurant next to the Scottsdale Center for the Performing Arts. Penny wasn't hungry and had an Arnold Palmer and some of my sweet potato fries.

MONDAY, APRIL 7—DINNER AT LOS SOMBREROS

In the afternoon our comforter was ready at Continental Dry Cleaners so I stopped by to get it. In the early evening, I picked up Jan and Rich Aver where we met Jeffrey Schesnol for dinner at Scottsdale's Los Sombreros Mexican Restaurant. Jeffrey's wife Susan was out of town.

TUESDAY, APRIL 8, 2014—DINNER WITH THE PAZOLS

At 6:00 p.m. Penny and I drove to Cave Creek where we met Bobby and Jim Pazol for dinner at the Tonto Bar and Grill overlooking the golf course. The restaurant has a great view of the golf course and the food is delicious. We had a terrific dinner and good conversation. The Pazols usually go back to Youngstown at the end of April.

WEDNESDAY, APRIL 9, 2014—ANTIQUES, BASIL AND GARLIC

In the afternoon, Penny and I went to the Antique Trove on Scottsdale Road and found some teapots to put on top of our kitchen cabinets. At 6:30 p.m. Penny and met Jan and Rich Aver and Jeffrey Schesnol for dinner at Basil and Garlic. We sat on the outdoor patio and I brought a bottle of Merlot.

THURSDAY, APRIL 10, 2014—SNOOZE AND MARGIE HAYES

At 9:40 a.m. Rich and Jan Aver picked up Penny and me and we drove to Snooze, an AM Eatery located at 2045 E. Camelback Road in Phoenix. The restaurant opened in Phoenix on November 25, 2013 and the breakfast was amazing. Each of us had pancakes that came in two six-inch pancakes to an order. Rich ordered his own a banana-nutella pancake and Penny, Jan and I split a pineapple-upside down pancake, a sweet potato pancake and a blueberry pancake. Our server brought three plates and we put all of the pancakes in the middle and helped ourselves. This place was amazing. We had leftovers for tomorrow morning's breakfast. We left Snooze at 12:15 p.m. and drove to 441 E. Bluebell Lane where I placed a $65.00 check under the backdoor floor mat for a service call on the garage door. The Tempe rental house garage door was having difficulty raising and lowering and it turns out the springs were shot and needed replacement so the home warranty company replaced the garage door springs.

Penny and I went to Sprouts to buy Harriet and Jay some dark chocolate almonds, cashews and cocoa covered almonds. And then we went to AJs to buy some chocolate for our Northbrook next-door neighbors, the Diligs. We drove to Two Plates Full and Penny bought a few greeting cards. We left the condo at 5:30 p.m. to meet Margie Hayes at Pasta Brioni. We had a delicious dinner and a wonderful get together with Margie. We took a selfie and emailed it to Margie, her daughter, Alison, Penny and Ronna.

FRIDAY, APRIL 11, 2014—UPS STORE

We woke up at 6:55 a.m. and ate leftovers from yesterday's breakfast. I took two boxes to the UPS Store on Shea Blvd. to ship back to Northbrook. The two boxes were delivered to Northbrook the next Thursday afternoon.

SATURDAY, APRIL 12, 2014—FLIGHT TO CHICAGO

Penny and I left for the Phoenix Sky Harbor Airport a little earlier than usual because the bus drivers from the car rental terminal were on strike and we heard there was a ten-to-fifteen-minute delay in getting back to the terminal. Since I had two free passes to the United Airlines Red Carpet Club, we spent several hours in the lounge before boarding our flight. We departed a little late from Phoenix Sky Harbor Airport to Chicago because the plane arriving from Chicago was delayed. We were on a non-stop United Airlines flight that left Phoenix at 3:50 p.m. and arrived in Chicago O'Hare a little after 7:00 p.m.

MONDAY, APRIL 14, 2014—PASSOVER DINNER

In the morning I dropped off our signed 2013 income tax forms to David Friedman's office on Skokie Blvd. Penny and I prepared for our family sedar that evening and our family of ten celebrated Passover at our home and grandson Danny read the Four Questions. After dinner, Penny and I decided that we would not host a Passover dinner after returning from Phoenix a few days earlier. It was a little much for us and I guess our age had something to do with our decision.

THURSDAY, JUNE 27, 2014—TEN CHIMNEYS, WISCONSIN TRIP

Penny and I decided to drive to Genesee Depot, Wisconsin for a tour of Ten Chimneys. This historic site was the summer home of Alfred Lunt and Lynn

Fontanne, two of Broadway's most famous actors during the 1920s, 30s, 40s and 50s. On Monday, June 23, I called and arranged for a Thursday, June 27 11:00 a.m. tour of the house and property. We arrived at the visitor's center around 9:45 and decided to drive around for a short time before parking in the visitor's lot. The trip was exactly ninety-five miles from our Northbrook home. A man at the reception desk greeted us and mentioned the only film the Lunts made was in 1932 and was called *The Guardsman.* The film was playing in the next room so we decided to watch as much of the film waiting before our tour was to begin.

Much to our surprise, we were the only ones on the tour. The couple that was supposed to join us on our tour arrived early and went on the 9:00 a.m. tour. Beth, our docent and Bonnie who was a volunteer at the Foundation, took Penny and me on a great tour that lasted a little over 2 hours. The tour consisted of the Lunt's house, some of the grounds and the Swiss cottage where the famous couple first occupied after their marriage. The house was fascinating. Many famous actor guests spent summers with the Lunts. Helen Hayes, Noel Coward, Katherine Hepburn and Sir Lawrence Olivier and many other friends were guests of the Lunts. After the Lunts passed away, the Ten Chimneys Foundation, a non-profit organization, took over the sixty-acre property and restored the houses and grounds. Tours started in 2009.

THE TOWN OF GENESEE DEPOT

After our private Ten Chimneys tour, we were hungry, so we decided to drive into the small town of Genesee Depot for lunch. Before we left, we asked where we could eat and our tour guide Beth suggested the Cornerstone restaurant and not to forget to stop at Sally's Sweet Shoppe, a bakery right across the street from the restaurant that closes at 2:00 p.m. We took Beth's advice and stopped at the bakery before lunch. We bought bread and a canola cupcake. Luckily, we brought our Igloo cooler to keep our new purchased goodies fresh. At the Cornerstone restaurant, Penny and I ate different salads for lunch. I had a granny apple, walnut and cranberry salad and Penny had a chopped salad. Both were good especially eating the bread we had just purchased at the bakery across the street.

After lunch, we wondered across the street and went inside to Bonjour Again, an upscale resale shop where Penny bought a pair of socks. We headed to Delafield, Wisconsin to check into the LaQuinta Inn and Suites. Delafield is about thirty-five miles west of Milwaukee and the home of St. John's Military Academy.

Upon arriving, we checked into our hotel, changed clothes and went out exploring for an evening "on the town." We stopped at Angel's Place, a store that gave back to cancer survivors. We bought a gift for Harriet Weintraub's next birthday and a plate rack for us. The owner told us the Mazatlan, a Mexican restaurant, was four stores down the street. We took the owner's advice and we went to the Mazatlan. We ordered two margaritas and shared a red snapper flaming fajita and plenty to eat, then drove to the hotel for the evening.

FRIDAY, JUNE 28, 2014—DRIVE BACK TO NORTHBROOK

The next morning, the breakfast at the hotel was not very good, so we headed to Starbucks on route 83 north before I went fishing at Nagawicka Lake. I caught perch by St. John's Bay and headed north to Lake Okauchee, Wisconsin where I had fished with Arnie for the past two summers. I caught a rock bass off the loading dock and then we headed east on route 16 to Pewaukee about ten miles away from Okauchee. In Pewaukee, Penny and I went into a consignment store called DesignXchange and bought a plate for our Scottsdale condo. I took a photo of the Pewaukee Library and tried fishing in Pewaukee Lake but had no luck. Before leaving Pewaukee, I stopped for gasoline at a BP station.

After Pewaukee, we drove south to Waukesha and ate lunch at the Rochester Deli. Then we ate a gelato at the Divino Gelato Café on West Main Street. The Waukesha County Historical Society and Museum and former Court House was our next stop, so we could see the Les Paul exhibit. Les Paul was born in Waukesha, Wisconsin and he and Mary Ford made some amazing recordings in the 1950s and early 60s. Les invented multi-track recording with a crude Ampex tape recorder and made the electric guitar famous. He is known as the Wizard of Waukesha. The Les Paul exhibit was quite interesting and we enjoyed seeing the various historic items on display.

After the museum, I went fishing on a river in Waukesha. We decided to head home by local routes instead of traveling on the interstate. We went through Burlington and I took a photo of the Burlington Public Library for Penny, then we drove south on route 36 ended our day just before dinner in Lake Geneva. After taking a photo of the Lake Geneva Public Library, we found a parking space on the main street and walked around before ending up at the Scuttlebutt's Restaurant After dinner we went to Kilwins chocolate store and bought our neighbor's, the Diligs, some chocolate covered pretzels as a thank you for putting out our garbage and taking in our newspaper while we were gone. What a great trip. We had talked about going to Ten Chimneys and thoroughly enjoyed our Wisconsin adventure.

CHAPTER TWENTY-EIGHT
Fishing Trips To Maryland

FRIDAY, JULY 1, 1988—FISHING ON THE POTOMAC RIVER

Cousin Norman chartered a boat to go fishing at the mouth of the Potomac River and Chesapeake Bay. The charter was out of Stevensville, Maryland. Norman, Arlyn, Ben, a friend of Arlyn's and me were fishing on the boat. A husband and wife were the captain and first mate. On the way back to the dock, Norman and I feel asleep sitting up in a chair. We caught several Bluefish on this trip. After our trip and back at the dock, the first mate filleted some of the fish we caught and we brought them back to Norman's home. We made an attempt to cook the Bluefish for dinner but we didn't know how to cook them, so they weren't very tasty.

THURSDAY, JULY 31, 2014—FIRST CHESAPEAKE BAY TRIP

My first cousin Norman Lockshin invited me to go fishing on a charter boat in Chesapeake Bay and to stay at his condo in Annapolis, Maryland. Chesapeake Bay was famous for large striped bass, called rockfish in Maryland. Norman had fished with Arnie Grauer during our Key West trip in 2007, so he invited Arnie to join me for the fishing trip. I was able to buy two tickets on a non-stop Southwest Airlines flight to Baltimore International Airport (BWI).

Driving our 2005 Toyota Camry, I picked up Arnie at his Wilmette condo at 10:30 a.m. and I drove to Midway Airport. I found an inexpensive parking lot online, Airways Parking, about 2 blocks away from Midway Airport. We unloaded our luggage for the van to take us to Midway and I parked the car with the assistance of the parking attendant and the parking lot's shuttle took us to Midway. There is a large food court inside of Midway Airport and for lunch before our Baltimore flight, I had some hummus and pita bread at Pegasus. Southwest Airlines flight left Chicago at 1:30 p.m. and we arrived at the Baltimore International Airport (BWI) on time and Norman picked up Arnie and me at 4:33 p.m.

We drove to Norman's three-bedroom condo in Annapolis, Maryland where his wife Sheila was waiting for us. We arrived at the condo around 6:00 p.m. Diana, Ben Lockshin's wife, made a 7:30 p.m. dinner reservation at a Spanish restaurant. After dinner we drove to Norman and Sheila's condo and went to bed because we were going to get up early for our next day's fishing trip.

FRIDAY, AUGUST 1, 2014— CAPTAIN RANDY DEAN

I got up at 4:15 a.m. and Ben Lockshin met us at Norman's condo. At 5:10 a.m. Norman drove for the one-hour trip to Chesapeake Beach, Maryland, where the Bay Hunter, a forty-two-foot charter boat, captained by Randy Dean, was docked. Once underway, it took us awhile to get to a fishing area where we started catching baitfish called Spot. Spot is the "live" bait used to "live-line" for rockfish. The charter captain provided the fishing equipment. The first mate cut up bloodworms that were put on two hooks to catch the Spot. We weren't that successful catching Spot but caught enough to move to another location to catch the rockfish. The four of us, Arnie, Ben, Norman and me were fishing on this trip.

We caught our limited of stripers and ended the trip around 12:15 p.m. Norman paid to have the seven rockfish filleted at the dock. The cost of the half-day charter was $650.00 plus $100 for the first mate. I gave the captain $200 in cash for my part and Arnie also gave the same. We drove back to Annapolis and had a late lunch at Rocco's Pizzeria where Sheila joined us. Sheila left Annapolis after lunch and drove back to Rockville.

Jack's Fortune Chinese Restaurant is next-door Rocco's Pizzeria, so Norman and I walked to the restaurant to find out if they would prepare the fillets for dinner. We met May, the restaurant owner's wife who said her husband, chef Jack, would cook the fish. That evening Norman, Arnie and I took the 3 rockfish fillets to Jack's Fortune Chinese restaurant where Jack prepared the fillets, three different ways; steamed, black bean garlic sauce with peas and sweet and sour style. The meal was absolutely delicious, reminiscent of our Key West trip when we took grouper and yellow tail snapper to a Chinese restaurant and the chef prepared them for us.

SATURDAY, AUGUST 2—NORMAN'S BOAT AND DINNER

Norman has an Edgewater twenty-two-foot fishing boat docked by the condo on Spa Creek. We fished on Norman's boat for several hours near the Chesapeake Bay Bridge but had no luck catching stripers but we did catch some Spot and several croaker fish. Croakers actually make a croaking sound. We saw the United States Navy doing maneuvers on Chesapeake Bay in a large boat. We also saw film director Barry Levinson's house and boat on Spa Creek, not far from Norman's condo.

Norman drove us to have dinner at the Edgewater Restaurant in Edgewater, Maryland. This restaurant served the best crab cakes I've ever eaten. The crab cakes were so large you could only eat one. After dinner we drove back to Annapolis, parked the car in a free lot off of Main Street and walked around the downtown area, stopping for ice cream at Kilwins Ice Cream shop. Kilwins has other locations around the country; one in particular is in Lake Geneva, Wisconsin. Right near Main Street is the Kunta Kinte-Alex Haley Memorial. Alex Haley, the author of the popular book, *Roots*, and the television series, is seated reading to three children. Norman took a photo of Arnie and me seated next to Alex Haley.

SUNDAY, AUGUST 3, 2014—NORMAN'S BOAT AND LUNCH

Fishing again on Norman's boat. Arnie, Norman and I had luck catching small Spot, one after another. Norman drove us to Mike's Restaurant in Riva, Maryland for a late lunch. Each of us ordered a soft-shell crab sandwich that was fresh and absolutely delicious.

MONDAY, AUGUST 4, 2014—NAVAL ACADEMY TOUR

Before Norman drove back to his home in Rockville, he drove Arnie and me to downtown Annapolis. Arnie and I ate breakfast at Chick & Ruth's Deli, a mom-and-pop restaurant on Main Street. After breakfast, we walked to the United States Naval Academy founded in 1845. Once inside the visitor's center, we walked around on the first floor, and then paid $9.00 for a guided tour of the campus. Our tour guide was a retired Navy doctor and the tour lasted for one hour forty-five minutes. We saw first year plebs marching to a very large aquatic center for training. A display of footballs from the Army/Navy football games plus a glass case with the two Navy Heisman Memorial Trophy winners were inside the aquatic center. Joseph Bellino from 1960 and Roger Staubach in 1963 were two Navy men who won the Heisman. The Heisman trophy is awarded to the outstanding college football player and is presented at the downtown Athletic Club of New York City at the end of the college football season. We also saw a large amphitheater used for special events and an early 1905 biplane hanging from the ceiling at one end of the building. While walking, we saw a captured World War II Japanese aerial type 91 torpedo from Okinawa. There was a statue marking the centennial of the United States Navy submarine force dedicated to those who serve beneath the seas, families and support personnel.

Our tour took us by the world's largest dormitory that houses some four thousand Naval cadets and went inside Bancroft Hall that feeds them. The hall was named after George Bancroft, Secretary of the Navy from 1845 to 1846, who established the United States Naval Academy on October 10, 1845. In front of Bancroft Hall were two large bells. The ship's bell was from the World War II USS Enterprise battleship and was presented to the Academy by the class of 1921. The other bell came from a World War II Japanese ship. We toured the campus main chapel and saw a statue of the Navy's mascot, a goat. Arnie took a picture of me in front of the goat statue.

After we left the tour guide at the visitor's center, Arnie and I walked to the Commodore Uriah P. Levy Center. Inside was the Jewish chapel and many interesting exhibits all related to Jews in the U.S. Navy. Uriah Phillip Levy was well known for his efforts to end flogging in the Navy and was also a champion for education and professional development with the enlisted ranks and officer corp. Levy also wrote the Manual of Rules for Men of War and his work is considered a "contemporary classic for its description of regulations in a modern navy." The Jewish chapel has Aramaic letters instead of Hebrew letters on each side of the arch. There was also an exhibit and tribute to Jewish women in the Navy. Finally, we saw the crypt of Naval hero John Paul Jones who is buried at the academy.

After the Naval Academy, we went to the State capital building for a quick look. Then we walked to Buddy's restaurant. Buddy's was an upstairs restaurant on Main Street and we ate lunch at the buffet. Arnie and I waited for the water taxi to take us back to condo to get our luggage. There was a lock box on the condo, so we were able to get into it. After doing our final packing I called a taxi for a 3:00 p.m. pick up to take us to Baltimore International Airport for our trip back to Chicago. We were flying on a non-stop Southwest Airlines flight scheduled to leave Baltimore at 5:55 p.m. and arrive at Midway Airport at 7:04 p.m. At the airport, there was a little fiasco. Arnie took a seat by our gate facing the runway. Our plane was scheduled to leave at 5:55 p.m. but there was an announcement that it would be delayed and would not leave until 6:10 p.m.

Around 6:15 p.m. I went back to the gate counter to check again when our plane would be leaving and the gate attendant said the plane had already departed. I did not notice that our gate had been switched to a gate near our gate nor did I hear any announcement about the switch or our flight number. I was quite upset and shocked to find our flight had departed without us. The gate attendant got us on a one-stop flight to Chicago stopping in Columbus, Ohio and arriving at Midway around 10:00 p.m. It was pouring rain so I called Midway Parking and a van came to get us in approximately 20 minutes. Arnie stayed underneath the office overhang while I was driven to my car where I put the luggage in the trunk. I was fairly soaked by this time. I went inside and paid the $68.00 for the parking. We headed back to Wilmette to drop off Arnie at his condo and I finally arrived home around 11:30 p.m. I couldn't believe how we could miss our flight in Baltimore.

THURSDAY, JULY 30, 2015—<u>SECOND</u> CHESAPEAKE BAY TRIP

Arnie Grauer, Penny and I flew to Annapolis, Maryland so Arnie and I could go fishing with my cousin Norman Lockshin. Arne drove to our house at 10:45 a.m. and Uri, our taxi driver, picked us up at 11:00 a.m. We were taking a round trip non-stop United Airlines flight to Baltimore International Airport. We arrived at O'Hare Airport around 11:35, dropped off our luggage outside with a skycap and continued to whiz through security as we each had TSA clearance with only a few people were ahead of us in the security line.

We had plenty of time before our plane took off from Terminal C, so we ate lunch at the food court. I had some hummus and pita bread at Pegasus. We left Chicago at 2:10 p.m. and arrived at the Baltimore International Airport (BWI) on time at 5:10 p.m. Norman us picked up around 5:30 p.m. and we drove to his three-bedroom condo in Annapolis, Maryland around 6:00 p.m. where his wife Sheila was waiting for us. We unloaded our suitcases and drove to Cantler's for steamer clams and hard-shell crabs. Penny and I had never eaten steamers. They had little tails that we pulled so they could be removed them from their shell. We dipped the clams in water to remove any sand, and then dipped them in butter or Old Bay, a spice made for crabs and steamers. After eating, Penny, Norman and I walked down steps to where the crabs and steamers were kept in huge water-filled bins. The lower level of the restaurant is right by the water. After dinner we drove back to Norman and Sheila's condo. We talked until 10:30 p.m. and we all went to sleep because we were going to get up early for our next day fishing trip.

FRIDAY, JULY 31, 2015—CHARTER CAPTAIN JOHNSON

I got up at 4:20 a.m., got dressed and brushed my teeth. By that time, Norman and Arnie were up and ready to go. We left the condo at 5:10 a.m. for the one-hour drive to Chesapeake Beach, Maryland, where the Semper Fidelis boat was waiting for us. Steve Exelbert, a friend of Norman, met us at the boat dock. Captain Don Johnson and his wife, Maydie who was his first mate, met us on their 46-foot charter boat. Don is Randy Dean's business partner. Randy will be our captain on day two of our fishing trip.

It took us awhile to find a location where we started catching baitfish called Spot. Spot is the "live" bait used to "live-line" for rockfish. The charter boat supplied all the equipment. Our first mate, Maydie cut up bloodworms that were put on two hooks to catch the Spot. I caught the most Spot, around thirty-five or so. After catching Spot, we moved to another location to catch the rockfish.

Unfortunately, we had to travel ten miles north of the Chesapeake Bay Bridge that cost another $120.00 in fuel charges. The fish we caught were larger than the ones we caught on last year's trip. Our limited of stripers [rockfish] was caught and our trip ended around 2:30 p.m. Arnie caught the largest fish, about a fifteen pounder. The cost of the day was $600.00 plus $150.00 for the first mate who worked her tail off for us. Norman and I paid for the rockfish filleted at the dock.

We drove back to Annapolis and dropped off the fish at Jack's Fortune Chinese Restaurant. May, the owner/chef's wife, remembered us from last year. She was happy to take the fish and Chef Jack would prepare the fillets four different ways; steamed, black bean garlic sauce with peas, sweet and sour and Szechwan-style with vegetables. We went back to the restaurant at 6:30 p.m. for dinner and like last year, the meal was absolutely delicious, reminiscent of our Key West trip when we brought grouper and yellow tail snapper to a Chinese restaurant and they prepared them for us. Steve Exelbert's wife, Ellen, drove to Annapolis from Rockville and joined us for dinner. After dinner we had ice cream at Main Street's Annapolis Ice Cream Shop.

While we were fishing, Sheila and Penny had a great day of Annapolis site seeing with a tour of the Maryland state capital and the house of one of the signers of the Declaration of Independence.

SATURDAY, AUGUST 1, 2015—CAPTAIN RANDY DEAN

Once again, I got up at 4:20 a.m. I got dressed and brushed my teeth. Norman was up but Arnie did not feel well, so he decided to stay back at the condo instead of fishing. Larry Nordhauser, Norman's next-door neighbor met us at the condo and joined us for a day of fishing. We left the condo about 5:05 a.m. for the one-hour drive to Chesapeake Beach, Maryland, where met Captain Randy Dean was waiting for us at the dock with his 42-foot charter boat, Bay Hunter. Norman's son-in-law, Maurice Amsellem and his fourteen-year-old son Mikey were waiting for us at the dock.

We left the dock around 6:30 a.m. and sun was just appearing over the horizon so I took a photo to include in my slide show. It took a while to find the best location to catch the baitfish, Spot. Once we had about eighty or so of Spot, it took about one and one-half hours to get to a location where the rockfish were biting. Maurice had been out late the night before, so he slept most of the way to our fishing location. Our fishing location was about ten miles north of the Chesapeake Bay Bridge, almost in the same location as yesterday's fishing. In a matter of forty-five minutes, we had caught our limit of two fish per person. To be a keeper, each fish must be at least twenty inches in length. The fish were much larger than the ones we caught the day before. Randy is a fantastic captain and knows how to find the fish. The cost of the charter was $650.00 plus $100 for the first mate.

Randy had been in constant contact with Don Johnson who also had a full boat of fishermen. As soon as we caught our limit, Don's boat moved into our spot and starting catching rockfish. We headed back to Chesapeake Beach arriving at the dock around 2:30 p.m.

Instead of having fillets made of all of the fish, we left three fish whole without even gutting them so the owner/chef at Jack's Fortune Restaurant could prepare them his way. After the fish were filleted, we drove back to Annapolis where we immediately went to Jack's Fortune Restaurant, gave the fish to chef Jack's wife, May. Norman's daughter Alexis and son-in-law Harrison Gyurko drove to the condo to join us for dinner. Norman's oldest daughter, Arlyn Amsellem, her daughter Rachel and a friend, also joined us for dinner at Jack's. We had fourteen people all together for a fantastic fresh rockfish dinner. The chef outdid himself by making the rockfish five ways. Everyone agreed, the Szechwan-style dish was the tastiest one. After dinner we drove to Kilwins on Main Street and ate ice cream.

SUNDAY, AUGUST 2, 2015—GRUMP'S CAFÉ AND CHICAGO

Arnie, Penny, Sheila, Norman and I went for breakfast at Grump's Café in Annapolis located very close to their condo. The servers were all wearing pajamas. The restaurant was unusually decorated with splattered paint on the floor, posters on the wall, water skis, a surfboard and a mini bar area with bar stools. You ordered the food from a guy at a cash register and the food was brought to your table. The "locals' go to this restaurant and the food was delicious.

After breakfast, we went for a one-hour ride in Norman's twenty-two-foot Edgewater fishing boat on Spa Creek looking toward Chesapeake Bay. Along the way, we saw two people paddle boarding and passed several large yachts docked along Spa Creek. One yacht in particular, "Winning Drive" is owned by Steve Biscotti, the owner of the Baltimore Raven's National Football League football team. We took a short ride on the Severn River to just above the Chesapeake Bay Bridge where I caught croaker fish the year before. Penny enjoyed the ride that was calm for the most part. Arnie decided to stay at the condo instead of going with us.

FLIGHT BACK TO CHICAGO

Around 2:30 p.m. Norman drove us to the Baltimore International Airport for our 5:02 p.m. flight to Chicago. With very little Sunday traffic, we arrived at the airport around 3:15. We had time at the airport so we were able to have an early dinner at The Green Turtle inside the airport. Our non-stop United Airlines flight left Baltimore on time at 5:25 p.m. and we arrived in Chicago at 6:30 p.m. When we arrived in Chicago, we had to wait about thirty-minutes for a gate. Once we pulled into the gate, we had to wait another fifteen minutes because sixty pieces of luggage had to be unloaded first for fear of the plane tipping back. It was the first time anyone on the plane had ever heard of this bizarre circumstance. No one on the plane could believe what was happened.

THURSDAY, JULY 28, 2016—THIRD CHESAPEAKE BAY TRIP

Uri picked up Penny and me around 10:30 a.m. for our United Airlines flight to Baltimore. For lunch, I bought a croissant and Arctic water at Brioche Doree and Penny ate a yogurt parfait from Fresh Market. Penny also bought popcorn at Nuts on Clark. Our plane left Chicago's O'Hare Airport at 1:45 p.m. and arrived in Baltimore at 4:48 p.m. Cousin Norman picked us up at the Baltimore International Airport and we drove to his condo in Annapolis where his wife Sheila was waiting for us. For dinner, we went to Reggio's C-22. After dinner we went to the condo, talked awhile, then went to sleep because we had to get up early the next day.

FRIDAY, JULY 29, 2016—WITH CAPTAIN RANDY DEAN

Norman and I got up early, had a light breakfast and we drove to meet Ben Lockshin and friend Steve Exelbert at the dock for our one-half day of fishing with Captain Randy Dean and his Bay Hunter charter. In order to find the fish, we had to travel about two miles north of the Chesapeake Bay Bridge. We passed Thomas Point Lighthouse on our way to our fishing spot. We caught our limit of rockfish and headed back to the dock. At the dock, we had the fish cleaned and some made into fillets. Other rockfish were cleaned only. We took four whole rockfish to Jack's Fortune Restaurant and gave May, the owner's wife, the rockfish so they could be cooked by Jack for our dinner later in the day. After dropping off the rockfish at Jack's Fortune, Sheila, Norman, Penny and I had a late lunch at Wild Country Seafood where we sat outside on a picnic table.

At 7:00 p.m. we drove to Jack's Fortune Chinese restaurant where we met Ben Lockshin, his girlfriend Courtney, Steve and Ellen Exelbert and neighbor Mary Nordhauser for dinner. Jack prepared the rockfish six different ways: rockfish steamed with ginger and scallions, whole rockfish fried with broccoli, Szechwan-style, sautéed with vegetables, Hunan-style and I can't remember the sixth way. A photo was taken of our dinner group. Jack only charged $54.00 for the ten people.

SATURDAY, JULY 30, 2016—NORMAN'S BOAT

Norman and I went fishing in Chesapeake Bay on his twenty-two-foot Edgewater fishing boat. Norman's boat was docked by his condo on Spa Creek. As we left his dock, we saw paddle boarders and large yachts. We also passed film director's Barry Levinson's house and the U.S. Naval Academy in the distance. Osprey nests on poles dot the bay. Norman followed the birds and I had a lot of luck catching about fifty small rockfish in total. I brought my GoPro and had it mounted on my head. After fishing, Penny, Sheila, Norman and I went to Eastport Kitchen for lunch and I treated Sheila and Norman for breakfast instead of lunch. Later in the day, we drove to Mike's where we met Ben Lockshin and his girlfriend Courtney. We ordered jumbo crabs, steamer clams and steamed shrimp for dinner. After dinner we had ice cream at Annapolis Ice Cream. Ben showed us his condo several units from Norman and Sheila's condo. I took several inside photos and also looking out the window on Spa Creek.

SUNDAY, JULY 31, 2016—FLIGHT TO CHICAGO

Norman drove Penny and me to Baltimore International Airport for our non-stop United Airlines flight back to Chicago. Our flight departed Baltimore on time at 5:48 p.m. and we arrived at Chicago O'Hare Airport at 7:02 p.m. Uri picked us up at the airport and drove us to Northbrook.

THURSDAY, JULY 27, 2017—FOURTH TRIP WITH BENNETT

Bennett decided to join Penny and me on our trip to Maryland. He seemed to be excited about seeing his cousins and to catch some big fish, especially after hearing my stories and seeing photos from past years. Around 8:00 a.m. Bennett picked up Penny and me, drove to Midway Airport and parked the car in the airport garage. Our non-stop Southwest Airlines flight to Baltimore International

Airport was $400.00 cheaper than United Airlines, so we decided to fly out of Midway instead of O'Hare Airport. Before our flight, we had lunch at Pegasis, a Greek restaurant inside the airport.

Our flight left Chicago's Midway at 11:45 p.m. and arrived in Baltimore at 2:30 p.m. Cousin Norman picked us up at the airport and we drove to his condo in Annapolis. Penny would not be fishing but would spend the days with Norman's wife, Sheila.

FRIDAY, JULY 28, 2017—FISHING ON CHESAPEAKE BAY

Bennett, Norman and I got up at 4:45 a.m. and left the house at 5:15 to meet our charter captain Randy Dean at his boat Bay Hunter at 6:00 a.m. Steve Exelbert and Ben Lockshin met us at the boat so there were five of us on this trip. Bennett caught some nice rockfish [striped bass] near Thomas Point Lighthouse. The fishing was so good we caught out limit by 8:30 a.m. You are allowed two fish at least 20 inches in length per person. Anything smaller gets released. Since we got done early, the first mate cut up bloodworms so we could catch "Spot" baitfish used for Randy Dean's afternoon charter group of fisherman. My portion of the trip was $200 and I put the charge on a credit card. I gave Bobby our first mate, a $100 tip in cash.

When we docked, our first mate, Bobby, cleaned the rockfish and made fillets for our dinner later in that evening. We left the dock and drove to Jack's Fortune Restaurant, left the fish with chef/owner Jack's wife, May, so Jack could cook the fish for our 7:00 p.m. dinner. That evening we had rockfish steamed with scallions and ginger, rockfish salt & pepper-style, rockfish Human-style and my favorite, rockfish Szechwan-style. Jack also made rice to go along with the rockfish and the meal was delicious.

SATURDAY JULY 29, 2017—NAVAL ACADEMY TOUR

After breakfast, Bennett, Norman, Penny and I took a mini walking tour of the U.S. Naval Academy. We went through an entrance and showed our IDs to the military policeman standing by a guardhouse. We saw the Chapel Dome, the burial crypt of Naval Hero John Paul Jones, went inside Bancroft Hall, went by the site of the old Fort Severn erected in 1808 and watched plebes dressed in whites [first year cadets] march through drills. Another group of plebes dressed in blue had rifles and were marching. I don't remember where we ate dinner. Later in the day, there was a beautiful sunset taken from Norman's condo.

SUNDAY, JULY 30, 2017—NORMAN'S BOAT AND HOME

After breakfast, Bennett, went on Norman's twenty-two-foot Edgewater fishing boat. First, we motored down Spa Creek where the boat was docked passed the U.S. Naval Academy looking for some fishing spots. We followed the birds and were lucky to catch many decent size rockfish. Jan Scruggs, Norman's neighbor, joined us on the boat. Jan organized and helped to raise money for the design and construction of Washington's Vietnam War Memorial.

After fishing, we ate avocado toast for lunch at Eastport Kitchen before heading to the Baltimore Airport. Our Southwest Airlines non-stop flight #5194 left Baltimore International Airport at 3:25 p.m. and we arrived back at Chicago

Midway Airport at 4:25 p.m. We got our luggage in baggage claim and walked to the parking garage. Bennett drove Penny and me to Northbrook. It was a great weekend of fishing in Chesapeake Bay.

THURSDAY, JULY 26, 2018—FIFTH CHESAPEAKE BAY TRIP

I went on my fifth fishing trip to Maryland by myself. Penny drove me to the airport and I took a non-stop United Airlines flight to Baltimore International Airport. My plane left Chicago at 2:20 p.m. and arrived in Baltimore International Airport at 5:15 p.m. Norman picked me up from the airport and we drove to his Annapolis condo. We went to a crab cake dinner at the Edgewater Restaurant located at 148 Mayo Road in Edgewater, Maryland. The crab cakes are so large you can only eat one and they are the best I have ever eaten.

FRIDAY, JULY 27, 2018—FISHING ON CHESAPEAKE BAY

Norman and I got up at 4:45 a.m. and left the house at 5:15 to meet our charter captain, Randy Dean, at 6:00 a.m. his boat the Bay Hunter for one-half day of fishing. Norman, his son, Ben, Larry Nordhauser, Jay Bernstein and I were on the boat so there were five of us on this trip. The first thing we did was fished for Spot. First mate, Bobby, cut up bloodworms so we could catch "Spot" used as baitfish. We started fishing by Thomas Point Lighthouse but had no luck with any keepers, just some small ones that we threw back. Next, we travelled north of the Chesapeake Bay Bridge. We had a touch morning of fishing and we started catching rockfish around 9:35 a.m. and only caught two keepers. This is the first time since I started fishing in the Chesapeake in 2014 that we had a challenge catching keepers. You are allowed two fish at least twenty inches in length per person. Anything smaller gets released.

We got back to the dock around 12:30 p.m. Ben went to his condo and cleaned the two-keeper rockfish. Norman and I went to lunch at East Point Kitchen where we ate delicious avocado toast. After lunch we went back to Norman's condo, we saw Rachel Amsellem and Grant Gyurko. A photo was taken of Grant, Rachel and me sitting on the condo's sofa.

For dinner, we went to Sammy's Italian Pizza Kitchen. I took a photo of Ben and his daughter Noa. Grant, Noa, Ben and me were at the restaurant. After dinner, Norman and I went walking into downtown Annapolis passing the entrance to the U.S. Naval Academy, the Water Witch Fire Station, the James Brice House Restoration Project, the William Paca House & Garden and 41 Cornhill Street, a famous house opened as the King's Arms Tavern in 1773.

SATURDAY, JULY 28, 2018—NORMAN'S BOAT

After breakfast, we took out Norman's twenty-two-foot Edgewater fishing boat into Chesapeake Bay. Larry Nordhauser and Jay Bernstein joined us. On Spa Creek, we saw a jet ski equipped with a cooler on the back and totally rigged for fishing, a first for us. We fished under the Chesapeake Bay Bridge and saw two men fishing in Hobie kayaks under the bridge. We were looking for birds and didn't have much luck catching any fish but it was fun. After fishing, Norman, Jay, Larry and me went to Wild Country Seafood for a softshell crab sandwich.

For dinner, Courtenay and Ben, prepared the rockfish in their condo, we had caught the day before plus shrimp tacos and guacamole and chips. One year old Noa was in her highchair eating dinner with us. Ben gave me a demonstration of his drone but there was interference and the drone got lost over Spa Creek. After dinner Ben, Courtenay, Noa, Norman and I went to Annapolis Ice Cream Company for dessert.

SUNDAY, JULY 29, 2018—NORMAN'S BOAT & CHICAGO

Norman and I took out his fishing boat into Chesapeake Bay looking for birds but had no luck. On the way back to Norman's dock we saw a huge yacht named the Minderdella with a helicopter perched on top. We also saw two paddle boarders with one of them and her dog on the board. A kayak tour of seven kayaks was also on Spa Creek.

Before Norman took me to the airport, we stopped for lunch at East Port Kitchen and another delicious avocado toast. We left for Baltimore International Airport at 2:30 p.m. for my 5:15 p.m. non-stop United Airlines flight to Chicago. My plane arrived at 6:22 p.m. at Chicago's O'Hare Airport. Penny picked up and we drove back to Northbrook.

CHAPTER TWENTY-NINE
Life Goes On

THURSDAY, AUGUST 28, 2014—55TH YEAR CLASS REUNION

Penny and I left Northbrook around 9:00 a.m. stopping at Starbucks on Skokie Boulevard around the corner from our home for some scones as well as two tuna sandwiches for our lunch. We drove leisurely to Huron, Ohio for our *Stayin Alive at 55*-class reunion. Before checking into the Sawmill Resort, I stopped by a yacht club and bought a three-day Ohio fishing license, then checked into the Sawmill Resort around 4:30 p.m. We then headed to Sandusky to meet the Boardman reunion group at 7:15 p.m. at the Zinc Brasserie on Water Street. About twenty of my high school classmates had been on a tour of Put-In-Bay and Kelley's Island the entire day.

Jim Jones and his wife Madonna were the first to arrive and we talked until the rest of the group came. Jim graduated from Boardman High School in 1958, a year ahead of our class, has attended several other reunions and remains in contact with our class. Around 7:20 p.m., the rest of our group arrived at the restaurant. It was fun to see everyone and we talked about the next few days of activities.

FRIDAY, AUGUST 29—THREE DIFFERENT CITIES

We checked out of the Sawmill Resort and drove into Sandusky and found a Cracker Barrel for breakfast before heading to the tourist center right next door to the restaurant. Penny found a brochure showing houses associated with the Underground Railroad. We drove around and saw several houses and then headed to the peninsula north of Sandusky.

After driving around Sandusky looking at the various Underground Railroad houses, we drove to the Marblehead peninsula on route 2, then Ohio route 163 to get to Lakeside Chautauqua. The Methodists originally established this historic community about one hundred forty years ago on the shores of Lake Erie. The community offers an abundance of spiritual opportunities, educational lectures, cultural arts performances and recreational activities during its ten-week summer programming season. There was an entrance gate before you go into the grounds and we got a free three-hour visitor's pass. We had to buy something at a store and have our receipt stamped in order to get the free pass. We stopped at Oh La Gelato and had our receipt stamped.

After Chautauqua, we drove to Boardman and checked into the Holiday Inn on South Avenue. Bill DeCicco and Carol Bender Gordon were in the lobby when we checked in. An attendant helped us with our luggage from the car to our room. After checking into our room, we headed to the Magic Tree bar at 5:00 p.m. to have some food and drink before the Boardman High School football game between Boardman and Mentor, Ohio.

SATURDAY, AUGUST 30, 2014—BOARDMAN, OHIO TOUR

Penny and I had breakfast at the Boardman Holiday Inn and we went to the Canfield Fair for about one and one-half hours. Our high school marching band would always play over the Labor Day weekend and I hadn't been to this fair in over fifty years. After the fair we drove to Mill Creek Park, went by the golf course and stopped by Lake Newport where I attempted to fish from by the dam. First, I walked down the steep steps below the dam but it was too shallow so I walked up the stairs to the dam and casted. Two teenage girls were hanging out on top of the dam but the fishing was not good so I went back to car where Penny was reading.

We then drove to the uptown area and Indianola Blvd. where I took a photo of where my father's store was located at 2633 Market Street. The building now houses a tax office and looks nothing like it did when my father owned Jack & Jill Kiddie Stores. It was very depressing to see those stores.

We drove back to hotel to get ready for the evening's dinner and festivities. Penny and I arrived at the Tippecanoe Country Club around 6:15 p.m., the site of past Boardman reunions. The last reunion was held at this club in 45th in 2004 our 45th reunion. It was a fun evening seeing my Boardman classmates with a special program hosted by our class president, Don Samuels and others who were on the planning committee.

SUNDAY, AUGUST 31, 2014—TRIP TO CLEVELAND

Penny and I packed our suitcases and I decided to load the car before going to breakfast downstairs in the hotel's restaurant. Everyone was supposed to meet there for breakfast at 9:00 a.m. When we arrived, there was a table already full of classmates so we sat with Dave Phillips and Norman Chevany who joined us. After breakfast we joined the other table and eventually broke up around 10:15 a.m.

KNOX STREET JEWISH CEMETERY IN YOUNGSTOWN

We went back to our room for a few items and headed to the Knox Street Jewish Cemetery where my great-grandmother and great-grandfather are buried along with other relatives. I was very disappointed to see the cemetery was totally overrun with weeds and bushes and was fenced in with a lock so I could not go inside or even get near the cemetery. In fact, if you did not know there was a cemetery at that location the area looked like a woods. Knox Street is near downtown Youngstown off of South Avenue. Radio station WBBW's tower and the building housing its transmitter are located right near the cemetery. A lonely wooden house is across the street from the radio station building. I took photos of the cemetery and emailed them to my first cousin Bruce Epstein. In 1897, the Youngstown Benevolent Association Cemetery of the Order of Benjamin David Lodge 58, established the cemetery. After Bruce received my photos, he told some Youngstown people about the condition of the cemetery and volunteers cleaned it up. Several months later, Bruce sent me a newspaper article about the volunteer cemetery cleanup project. I was very proud I was able to have something to do with this meaningful cemetery.

TODD CEMETERY, THEN MET BRUCE AND SUZYN EPSTEIN

Penny and I then drove to Tod Cemetery where we went to pay respects to my father David, mother Esther and grandparents, Ben and Rose Shwartz who are buried in the Rodef Sholom Temple portion of the cemetery. At 12:45 p.m., we met Bruce and Suzyn Epstein at the Squaw Creek Country Club for lunch. After lunch we drove to Cleveland to stay with my sister for a few days before heading back to Northbrook.

MONDAY, SEPTEMBER 1, 2014—LABOR DAY AND BASEBALL

Around 12:15 p.m. Betty Koppelman picked up Penny, ate lunch at California Pizza Kitchen in Legacy Village and spent the two spent the afternoon together. Meanwhile, around 2:15 p.m. Linda and I drove to the Rapid Transit station at Shaker Blvd where we met her friend Rory Sanders. We waited a short time for the Rapid that left us off underneath in the old Terminal Tower building. We walked about fifteen minutes to Progressive Ballpark to watch the Cleveland Indians play the Detroit Tigers. We left the ballpark in the eighth inning.

TUESDAY, SEPTEMBER 2, 2014—DeCICCO'S AND NORTHBROOK

At 9:10 a.m. Penny and I left Linda's home on our way to Northbrook by the way of stopping to see my high school friend, Bill DeCicco and his wife Carole. Bill gave us directions and we arrived at the parking lot by their apartment around 10:00 a.m. where Bill met us and we took the elevator to Bill's apartment. Bill and Carole live in Westlake, Ohio in the Crocker Park Shopping complex about forty-five minutes from Beachwood and a little out of our way to the Ohio Turnpike. About three years ago, Bill and Carole sold their house in Boardman and decided to move to Westlake. They rent an apartment to be close to their son and his family.

MONDAY, DECEMBER 22, 2014—SCOTTSDALE TRIP

For this trip, Penny and I took a later flight to Phoenix. We were picked up at 4:20 p.m. and arrived at the Chicago O'Hare Airport a little after 5:00 p.m. We breezed through security because of our TSA clearance and decided to eat dinner at Wolfgang Pucks. I had a margarita pizza and Penny had a salad. After dinner we went to the United Airlines Red Carpet Club to wait until our Phoenix flight.

About 7:45 p.m. we walked to gate B-10 and it was about a thirty-minute wait until we started to board our plane. Our departure to Phoenix was around 9:00 p.m. on our non-stop United Airlines flight and we touched down at Phoenix Sky Harbor Airport at 11:08 p.m. Phoenix time. After picking up our luggage from baggage claim, Jan and Rich drove to terminal two and they drove us to our condo, arriving around 12:00 midnight. After making our bed, we went to sleep exhausted.

TUESDAY, DECEMBER 23, 2014—RENTAL CAR

. At 12:50 p.m. Jan took us to pick up our rental car at Avis located at 7125 E. Shea Blvd. Suite 101. Unfortunately, our rental car, a 2015 Nissan Altima, had been sitting in their parking lot since Saturday, waiting for an oil change from one of the airport service guys. They gave me Hyundai Elantra loaner until the oil change was made. Our Avis Car rental was for 99 days rental. Chris Freh, owner of the Avis franchise, apologized for not having the car ready for me. After picking up the loaner, for dinner, I made pan-seared salmon, sweet potatoes and steamed broccoli.

WEDNESDAY, DECEMBER 24, 2014—OIL CHANGE

After breakfast, Penny and I drove to the Scottsdale Post Office where I found out I did not have to fill out anything in order to receive mail at our condo. There is a green card in our mailbox and all you have to do is fill it out and mail can be delivered to the mailbox. After the post office we drove to Kohl's where I bought six pairs of black, argyle and beige/brown socks that I had inadvertently left in Northbrook. I decided to call Avis and asked them if the oil had been changed in the rental car. Since nothing had been done, I decided to ask them if it would be OK for me to have the oil changed on the Nissan Altima at a Jiffy Lube. They had no problem with that idea and would reduce the rental of the car, so I returned the Hyundai Elantra loaner and went to Jiffy Lube around the corner for an oil change on the 2015 Nissan Altima.

After the oil change, I arrived at the condo around 12:45 p.m. and we had lunch. I called Cox again and they scheduled a repairman to come to our condo on Friday morning, December 26 between 10:00 and 12:00 p.m. Penny got a horrible text from Lois about Ronna's friend, Heather, dying suddenly in New York. Penny spoke to Ronna after she got home from work and she was devastated with the sad news.   Ronna and Ted were supposed to get together with Heather and her husband in Los Angeles this coming weekend.

For dinner, we went to Jan and Rich's condo and ordered pizza from Spinato's and Jeffrey and Susan Schesnol joined us.

THURSDAY, DECEMBER 25, 2014—CHINESE FOOD

After breakfast, Penny and I walked in the neighborhood for one-hour down Cholla. We came back tired and ate lunch. After lunch I fell asleep in my brown leather chair watching Chasing Classic Cars on the Velocity channel.

Jan was dog sitting at David and Becky Bluhm's house at 9745 Desert Cove almost around the corner from our condo. She invited the Jeffrey, Susan and Jacqui Schesnol plus Suzy Flax to the house to order Chinese food. We were talking too much and failed to place a take-out order at Flo's. So, someone suggested Chompie's but there was a two-hour wait, so that wouldn't work. I suggested calling Joyful Chinese Dining and took our order. Susan wasn't feeling very well so Jeffrey drove her home and returned just in time to join Rich and me to pick up the Chinese food at 8:15 p.m. We left the Bluhm house around 11:30 p.m.

TUESDAY, DECEMBER 30, 2014—BELINKYS ARRIVE

After breakfast I drove to Costco to buy a paper shredder but saw an Oster blender and a Brother's labeler I had to buy. Around 4:30 p.m. Ronna, Ted, Talia and Spencer arrived in Phoenix from Los Angeles in a rental car. Ted showed me how to blow up two Aerobeds and we moved furniture in the guest bedroom so Spencer could sleep. Ronna and Ted had 7:15 p.m. dinner reservations with Faith and Matt Beall at Malee's Thai restaurant in Old Town Scottsdale. The Belinky's stayed overnight at a Hampton Inn in North Scottsdale while our grandchildren stayed at our condo. Talia read until around 8:45 and Penny read stories to Spencer who went to sleep as soon as his head hit the pillow. It was the first time he used a pillow and a blanket because he has been sleeping in a crib.

WEDNESDAY, DECEMBER 31, 2014—NEW YEAR'S DINNER

The kids slept until 7:20 this morning. I took a shower and started to prepare a pancake breakfast because Talia said she was hungry. Ronna and Ted arrived at 9:00 a.m. for my pancake breakfast I prepared and Jan Aver came over around 9:30 p.m. I had to go into our bedroom to finalize and sign the paperwork for the apartment building sale. At 6:20 p.m. Jan and Rich picked up Penny and me and we drove to Jeffrey and Susan Schesnol's home for our New Year's Eve dinner and get together. Each of us brought a dish to the party. Jeffrey made lamb chops and salmon. Penny made a salad and Jan brought her famous chocolate dessert. We played Heads Up game and the dictionary game, a lot of fun. We went to sleep around 2:00 a.m.

THURSDAY, JANUARY 1, 2015—NEW YEAR'S DAY

Penny and I slept to 8:30 a.m. and didn't have breakfast until close to 10:30 a.m. After breakfast, Penny picked up Jan Aver around 12:30 p.m. to go shopping at Kohl's and I watched the Outback Bowl with Wisconsin vs. Auburn football game. I relaxed the entire day watching the Rose Bowl Parade and various football games. We left at 5:00 p.m. to have dinner at Faith and Matt Beall's home in Chandler with Ronna, Ted, Talia and Spencer. Before going to the Bealls, we made a stop at Walgreens to buy miscellaneous household goods and cough medicine for Penny. We watched the Sugar Bowl with Ohio State vs. Alabama. Ohio State won 42 to 35. We got home around 11:00 and were in bed by 11:30 very tired.

FRIDAY, JANUARY 2, 2015—DAVE FRIEDMAN AND HIGH TEA

Penny and I got up around 8:15 a.m. and had breakfast. Penny's throat was scratchy so she had some scrambled eggs and lox for breakfast. Dave Friedman called me at 10:30 a.m. regarding my Federal income tax liability. Ronna, Ted, Talia and Spencer flew back to Chicago from Phoenix.

Rich Aver picked me up at 12:45 p.m. and we met Jeffrey Schesnol at The Habit Burger Grill for lunch. Jeffrey was already at the restaurant because of our traffic delay. After lunch Rich drove me to Cracker Jax, a driving range on North Scottsdale Road by Paradise. Rich had an extra pair of golf shoes that he gave to me. Luckily, we take the same size shoe. After the driving range, Rich dropped me off and I cleaned the golf shoes he gave me. Meanwhile, Penny picked up Jan Aver at 1:45 p.m. for their 2:30 p.m. High Tea with the girls at The Phoenician Hotel. During High Tea, Susan Schesnol started having chest pains and an ambulance was called and Susan was taken to Scottsdale Healthcare for tests and observation. I had a light dinner and Penny wasn't hungry from the High Tea.

SUNDAY, JANUARY 4, 2015—*DOWNTON ABBEY* PARTY

Today is Jan and & Rich's Anniversary. I watched some of the NFL playoff games during the day. Jan Aver drove to our condo around 5:00 p.m. to help Penny and me get ready of our *Downton Abbey* dinner and the premiere of the fifth and final season of the PBS television program.

At 6:30 p.m. Rich Aver placed an order at the Skeptical Chymist for fish and chips. Penny and I hosted the *Downton Abbey* party. At 7:00 p.m. Rich, Jay Weintraub and I drove to the Skeptical Chymist to pick up our order of fish and chips and came back to our place to eat dinner and watch *Downton Abbey.*

WEDNESDAY, JANUARY 7, 2015—THE SALMONS

After breakfast, at 10:20, Penny and I met Jeff and Michelle Salmon in the parking lot before taking a thirty-minute walk. After lunch I went to Anna's Linens to buy the last eighty-four-inch room blackout curtains for the guest bedroom. And then I drove to the Apple store to ask about iPhone transfers and saw NASCAR and INDY race driver Tony Stewart talking to a sales person but I did not approach him. After the Apple store I went to Cracker Jax driving range to hit some golf balls. After the driving range, I drove to the Trader Joe's to buy some food for the Golden Globe party on Sunday. We ate leftovers at home for dinner.

THURSDAY, JANUARY 8, 2015—ORANGE TREE GOLF

I woke up at 6:00 a.m. took a quick shower, ate an English muffin and Jay Weintraub picked me up at 7:10 a.m. to go to the Orange Tree Golf Club to play golf with Dan Murphy. Dan had arranged for an 8:08 a.m. tee time. The cost was $56.32 including tax. We had a great time. Penny and Harriet Weintraub went for an $11.00 manicure at a new place near Fry's. After the manicure, they went for a delicious lunch at Andreoli's and went to the Dollar Store and Steinmart. After golf at 1215 p.m. Jay, Dan and I decided to go to Arizona Bread Company for lunch.

FRIDAY, JANUARY 9, 2015—VERIZON AND NEW IPHONES

I went to the Verizon store in The Promenade to buy two new iPhone 6s for Penny and me. I also purchased a case for my new iPhone 6. After the Verizon store, we drove to the Apple Store to buy Apple Care for the two new iPhone 6s.

Later in the day, we picked up the Avers and Susan Schesnol and drove to the Or Adam's service for "Jewish Music of Europe." The curator of the service was presented at an exhibit at the Musical Instrument Museum. We met Susie Dorfman Ernst and her husband, Tim, both from Cleveland Heights, Ohio.

SATURDAY, JANUARY 10, 2015—BOUGHT MACBOOK AIR

After breakfast, I went to the Apple Store at the Scottsdale Quarter to buy a new MacBook Air computer. My old black MacBook was outdated and I decided to buy a new computer for updated technology.

MONDAY, JANUARY 12, 2015—TAMPA TRIP PLANNING

Penny got a pedicure at She's Nails in Scottsdale. After a call to Granite Reef Senior Center, Penny found out all of the yoga classes were filled. She looked up studios and found a lot of Kripalu yoga centers that were probably expensive but could follow videos. Lois and Roy will go to Florida for Mara's wedding reception. I looked up flights to Tampa.

TUESDAY, JANUARY 13, 2015—BARRETT JACKSON

I left around 8:15 a.m. for the Barrett Jackson Auto Auction by myself and spent $80.00 on six model 1930 Ford cars; 1930, 1931, 1932, 1934, 1939 and 1940 model Ford cars for my collection that I put on the top shelf of the bookcase in the guest bedroom. I parked next to where the shuttle busses park in a spot off of Bell Road by Hayden. The water was turned off in the condo while I was at Barrett Jackson but when I got home the water had been turned back on.

WEDNESDAY, JANUARY 14, 2015—OLIVE MILL

Jay and Harriet Weintraub picked up Penny and me up and we drove to the Olive Mill in Queen Creek, Arizona, took a $10.00 tour and had lunch there. It was the second time we had been there. We bought some lemon olive oil, then stopped in downtown Chandler and went to the Antique Market Square but bought nothing. We went into a few shops and bought some post cards. That night I picked up dinner at the Pita Jungle by Scottsdale Road and brought it back to our condo.

THURSDAY, JANUARY 15, 2015—ORANGE TREE GOLF

Jay Weintraub picked me up and we met Dan Murphy at Orange Tree Golf Club. Penny, Jan Aver and Harriet Weintraub tried to go to Simple Farm but it was not open. On the way to Jewel's Gluten-Free Bakery they saw a $10.88 shoe store. Jan bought suede butterfly sandals and pedi sandals and a beige slip, and then they went to LGO for lunch.

FRIDAY, JANUARY 16, 2015—VERTIGO

I woke up dizzy. My dizziness feels like Benign Paroxysmal Positional Vertigo, a condition I had about ten years ago. I slept most of the day with very little hunger. If I sleep the entire day, it usually goes away the next day or soon after.

SATURDAY, JANUARY 17, 2015—STILL DIZZY

Penny ran errands while I was still dizzy. Penny and I were supposed to go out with the Jackie and Stew Templer but we had to cancel reservations. Gene Purkhiser, our condo board president, came by our condo and fixed Penny's toilet that kept on running. Gene replaced the inside workings of the toilet. Later in the day, I was feeling much better, so we went to The Habit Burger Grill for dinner, not one of Penny's favorite restaurants.

SUNDAY, JANUARY 18—NO DIZZINESS AND PANCAKES

I was fine today so I decided to make blueberry pancakes. After breakfast we went on a forty-minute hike at Lost Dog Preserve off of 124th Street.

TUESDAY, JANUARY 20, 2015—FISHING AND DINNER

We decided to drive to Riverview Park and I went fishing in the lake. I took my fishing equipment but had no luck catching anything, not even a bite. We explored a great playground in the park for a possible destination for Danny and Brooke when they come to visit in February.

At 7:00 p.m. Penny and I met Natalie Kane and Corky Weily for dinner at the Village Tavern.

THURSDAY, JANUARY 22, 2015—PHOENIX THEATER

In the evening, Harriet, Jay, Rich, Jan and Penny and me saw *Four Hands Two Pianos* at the Phoenix Theater next to the Phoenix Art Museum. We had great seats. The performance was terrific and very entertaining. Two guys talked about piano lessons and kids and played some amazing piano.

After the show we drove to Switch, a gay restaurant, for dessert. Jay and I shared a fantastic bread pudding while Jan, Harriet and Penny shared a different dessert.

FRIDAY, JANUARY 23, 2015—GOLF AND HANDLEBAR J

I got up early because at 7:15 a.m. Jay Weintraub picked me up and we met Dan Murphy at the 101 and Mayo to play golf at Coyote Lakes Golf Club in Surprise, Arizona. It took about forty minutes to drive to the course and the green fees with a cart were $49.91 for 18 holes. We saw two coyotes on the golf course. Coyote Lakes is very close to Sun City, so after golf we went to Line Thai in Sun City for lunch. The restaurant has a luncheon special for $9.95 that includes soup, egg roll, a main course with rice and it was good. This restaurant is where we usually go with my cousin Gert Phillips because it is right around the corner from her residence.

That evening the Avers picked up Penny and me and we met the Murphys and Weintraubs at the Handlebar J Restaurant in Scottsdale at 71st and Shea Blvd for fish and chips. Each Wednesday and Friday nights, they have a special fish n chips for $9.95. Penny and I tried a delicious beer. The food was really good and a "live" band started to play, as we were leaving. Afterwards, we all stopped at Yogurtology.

SATURDAY, JANUARY 24, 2015—COUSIN GERT VISIT

Penny and I drove to Sun City to visit my cousin Gert Phillips and her son Hal Spritzer and his wife Joyce arrived from Denver at 11:30 a.m. We talked in the lobby for one hour, and then went to Line Thai for lunch. Joyce suggested several books to read, including *Once We Were Brothers* written by Chicago attorney, Ronald Balson and *Sutton*, about the bank robber Willie Sutton.

After lunch Penny and I stopped at a consignment store down the street from where Gert lives and saw a cute mission side table but no price. We put our name on a list for the table but we never received a call to buy it. On the way back to our condo, we stopped at Half Price books and I bought *Sutton* and ordered *Once We Were Brothers* at another Half Price Books store. Penny had no luck finding a book.

MONDAY, JANUARY 26, 2015—GLOBE, AZ AND THE WEINTRAUBS

The Weintraubs picked us up at 10:30 a.m., drove eat on route 60 to Globe, Arizona and stopped at the Pickle Barrel Trading Post there. Jay's cousins Barry and Nancy Slavin had mentioned this place where they bought a copper bowl that the Weintraubs admired in their living room. The Pickle Barrel Trading Post was a little more formal than The Town Dump. The price and choice of copper bowls was not exactly like Jay's cousins had described but the Weintraubs bought one anyway. Penny and I found a copper piece that looked like a fish, so we bought it for $45.61 and put it on a shelf in our condo's living room. Afterwards, we stopped for lunch at DeMarco's Italian Restaurant on the main road in Globe and our server took our photo of us after lunch. The meal was very good.

After lunch and on the way back to Phoenix, we drove to Miami, Arizona, a small town just west of Globe. We went into several stores and walked around the town then drove back to Scottsdale.

TUESDAY, JANUARY 27, 2015—VERTIGO AGAIN

I woke up dizzy, stayed in bed and slept for most of the day. We were supposed to go out with the Templers but I had to cancel. My sister Linda called to tell us Todd Kay, the husband of Jennie Waldman unexpectedly died in his sleep. He was the executive director of Cleveland's BBYO and was thirty-eight years old.

WEDNESDAY, JANUARY 28, 2015—DIZZINESS IS GONE

I felt much better today because my dizziness went away. Penny and I went to US Egg for breakfast and did some grocery shopping at Fry's. In the afternoon, we went to see *Mortdecai* with Johnny Depp at the Harkins 14 Theater on Shea Blvd. The movie wasn't that good but it's always fun to get out and see films. For dinner, Penny made salmon patties.

THURSDAY, JANUARY 29, 2015—BELLAIR CLUB GOLF

Jay Weintraub and I met Dan Murphy in the parking lot at the 101 and Mayo and we drove in Dan's car to the Bellair Golf Club in Glendale, Arizona, an executive course, meaning a par three course. Dan's buddies usually go to this place. The green fee was $30.00, a very reasonable charge that included a golf cart. Rich did not join us. After golf we had lunch at MiComida, an Ecuador restaurant, not far from the golf course at 4221 W Bell Road in Phoenix. The lunch was delicious and I asked the owner if he would take a photo of us. During golf, Penny picked up Jan and Harriet and drove to Fountain Hills where there were more artists. Penny bought a lazy Susan granite cheese duo for the condo. Good artists there. Penny controlled herself but overate a burger for lunch. We met the Schesnols and Avers at Flo's Restaurant for Happy Hour and the Murphys joined us there. Afterwards we walked to Yogurtology for dessert.

SATURDAY, JANUARY 31, 2015—MESA FLEA MARKET

I picked up Jan and Rich Aver and I drove to the Gilbert Farmers Market where we saw Julie LaMagna and Ray Stephens selling their food in mason jars. We bought sauerkraut, beets and a bottle of wine from their booth. Ray had started making wine. After the farmer's market, I drove to Paradise Bakery where we ate lunch.

After lunch I drove around the corner to the Mesa Flea Market where Rich and I split up from Penny and Jan. We decided to meet at 2:00 p.m. at the same entrance where we walked into the Flea Market. Penny and Jan got mixed up and were waiting at the wrong end of the market so we called them to find out where they were. They walked to our entrance and we left around 2:30 p.m. I don't remember buying anything significant except for a few kitchen utensils. We drove back to the Avers where we ate appetizers and dessert. Jan had recorded a PBS Special, *A Tribute to Mel Brooks,* so we watched it.

TUESDAY, FEBRUARY 3, 2015—HISTORIC PHOENIX

In the morning I went to Einstein Bros for bagels. Harriet and Jay Weintraub spent the day with us. I drove to two different historic Phoenix neighborhoods including Encanto-Palmcroft Historic District and well as Willo Historic District at North 5th and West Palm Lane. The houses in these two neighborhoods are very different. We have done on a self-guided tour of the Willo neighborhood. For dinner, we went to Joyful Chinese with the Avers and Weintraubs.

WEDNESDAY, FEBRUARY 4, 2015—HAIRCUT AND CONCERT

I drove Penny to Mane Attraction Salon in Phoenix for her haircut appointment with Chris Knudsen and she was introduced to the owner. While Penny was getting her haircut and colored, I went to the Biltmore Mall and went to Starbucks inside of Macy's for some coffee and sat reading a book. After her appointment, Penny looked great and I had a chance to meet Chris for the first time.

At 6:00 p.m. we met cousin Corky Weily at Wildflower at Scottsdale Road and Indian Bend. Natalie Kane did not join us for dinner but met us for the concert. After dinner Corky followed us to the ASU Kerr Institute Cultural Center located at 6110 N. Scottsdale Road. The show featured brilliant saxophonist and leading authority on Stan Getz, Greg Fishman, along with his wife Judy Roberts (piano/vocals), Scott Black (bass) and Pete Swan (drums). This show was an ASU Kerr favorite, with remarkable music and endless insights into Stan Getz's genius. We paid $34.50 per ticket that included a $1.50 per ticket charge for a phone order. Our seats were 5 & 6 in Row 2, the premium section. I had previously ordered the tickets in October.

THURSDAY, FEBRUARY 5, 2015—THE APPELBAUMS ARRIVE

Penny and I left to pick up Alan and Marilyn Appelbaum for their arrival at 7:55 a.m. in Phoenix. They flew on a non-stop US Airways flight #602. We sat in the cell lot on the west side of the airport and made an easy pick up. On the way back to our condo, we stopped for breakfast at US Egg on Scottsdale Road and Osborn. After breakfast we drove to the condo. Alan and Marilyn changed clothes and we went to Pinnacle Peak where we hiked to the top. After our hike, we had lunch back at our condo. After lunch we drove to Papago Park, the location of the Hole-In-The-Rock near the Phoenix Zoo and hiked to the top. I think the Appelbaums really enjoyed our full day of activities.

FRIDAY, FEBRUARY 6, 2015—MESA'S SLOAN PARK TOUR

After breakfast at our condo, I drove Alan and Marilyn Appelbaum to Mesa's Sloan Park, the spring training baseball stadium of the Chicago Cubs for a $5.00 and two-hour tour. Our tour guide was Clyde Allen who recently bought a condo in Arizona to work for the Cubs throughout Spring Training. During the baseball season he lives in Pleasant Prairie, Wisconsin and commutes to Wrigley Field during game days. After the Sloan Park tour, we ate lunch at our condo and at 3:30 p.m. I drove Alan and Marilyn to pick up their Budget Rent-A-Car at the Doubletree Paradise Valley Resort located at 5401 N. Scottsdale Road. The Appelbaums went out to dinner by themselves at Don & Charlie's on E. Camelback Road.

Meanwhile, I picked up Jan and Rich Aver and we drove to Dan and Annie Murphys for a Jewish Party. At 6:00 p.m. The Murphys had invited all of their Jewish friends to a party that we called "The Jewish Party." A couple, Alan and Linda Rossell, had to leave a little early because they had concert tickets. The catered food was from Chompie's and was delicious with no leftovers.

SUNDAY, FEBRUARY 8, 2015—FOUNTAIN HILLS

After breakfast I drove Alan and Marilyn Appelbaum to Fountain Hills to see the fountain and to walk around the area and saw the Civic Center Trail map by a playground. After Fountain Hills, I drove to the small golf community of Rio Verde, Arizona where we went inside the Rio Verde Community & Welcome Center and saw a small library. I took some photos that I put into my slide show.

MONDAY, FEBRUARY 9, 2015—APPELBAUM'S HOTEL

In the afternoon, Alan and Marilyn Appelbaum checked into the Hampton Inn Phoenix/Scottsdale located at 10101 N. Scottsdale Road at Shea Blvd. We picked up the Appelbaums and drove to the Arizona Jewish Historical Society located at 2nd Street by McDowell in Phoenix for a 7:00 p.m. Czech Torah

Dedication. We saw Patti and Bob Schriebman there. There was a huge crowd of religious holocaust survivors and Jeffrey Schesnol was recognized for putting together the dedication.

TUESDAY, FEBRUARY 10, 2015—CALL AND TEMPLERS

At 9:00 a.m. I had a conference call for the recording of the voice-over narration for the 2015 *gia* Awards that will take place in Chicago in March. She also went to the pool but it was too hot. At 4:00 p.m. Stu and Jackie Templer came to our condo and we ate dinner at The Village Tavern.

THURSDAY, FEBRUARY 12, 2015—MESA WITH FRIENDS

At 10:00 a.m. Penny and I drove to Mesa to meet Mike and Fran Stricker, Carol and John Simon, Jay and Harriet Weintraub and Rich and Jan Aver at Crackers Restaurant for breakfast. After breakfast, they all went on a paddleboat ride on Saguaro Lake. After the boat ride, the Tucson people drove to Globe to the Pickle Barrel Trading Post, and then drove back to their home.

After breakfast at Crackers, Penny and I went shopping at Trader Joes, the Vitamin Shoppe and Fry's. In the afternoon, Alan and Marilyn Appelbaum flew back to Chicago at 7:40 pm

FRIDAY, FEBRUARY 13, 2015—THE SPENCERS ARRIVES

It's the start of President's Day Weekend and Bennett, Marni, Danny and Brooke arrived in Phoenix and rented a car at the airport. In the meantime, Penny and I went to Whole Foods to stock up on some food items for the grandchildren and afterwards then drove to the Fire Sky Hotel at the corner of North Scottsdale Road at Chaparral and waited for their arrival. There were soft seats in front of the hotel so Penny and I waited for them. They arrived around 4:00 p.m. and we met them outside the lobby. They unpacked and went in the hotel's pool. I made dinner reservations at Z'Tejas in Tempe. At 5:45 p.m. we drove to dinner with Bennett following us. After dinner, Danny and Brooke had a sleepover at our condo.

SATURDAY, FEBRUARY 14—WAFFLES AND PINNACLE PEAK

I made waffles for the grandchildren and Bennett and Marni came for bagels. The Spencers sent us chocolate covered strawberries that arrived on Friday, so we ate them for breakfast too. At 10:30 a.m. Penny and I and Bennett and family drove to hike at Pinnacle Peak in North Scottsdale. The place was very crowded but we all hiked to the top with Penny going most of the way.

We all ate dinner at Goldman's Deli in Scottsdale. After dinner Bennett, Danny and I went to a car show at the McDonald's at Pavilion's Shopping Center while Marni drove Penny and Brooke back to our condo. After the car show we all met back at the condo. It was a very fun day.

SUNDAY, FEBRUARY 15—DESERT BOTANICAL GARDEN, HOLE IN THE ROCK AND RIVERVIEW PARK

The family went to the Phoenix Botanical Gardens for a walk. After the Garden, we drove to the Hole-In-The-Rock Archaeological Site where Bennett, Marni, Danny, Brooke and I climbed to the top and took photos through the hole. And then, we drove to Riverview Park where Brooke climbed on a few devices and had a blast. After the park we all drove back to the hotel where Bennett and family went swimming in the pool. Bennett and Marni had dinner at Tommy V's while Danny and Brooke ate dinner with us at our condo and had a sleepover where we celebrated Brooke's 7th birthday with a cake from Fry's Grocery.

MONDAY, FEBRUARY 16, 2015—THE SPENCERS LEAVE ARIZONA

Around 10:30 a.m. Bennett and Marni came by our condo and picked up Danny and Brooke to fly back to Chicago. In the evening we met The Spenschavers and Jacqui Schesnol at Rusconi's Kitchen for dinner. The service was not good and the food was just OK. Susan was not very happy with our server and mentioned it to the owner. The Schesnols like this restaurant but we won't go back.

THURSDAY, FEBRUARY 19, 2015—AZ GRAND GOLF

Dan Murphy, Jay Weintraub, Rich Aver and I went to play golf at the Arizona Grand Hotel. Dan drove to Rich's house, then Jay picked up Dan and Rich and then me. I called Brian Gan to let him know we were going to be at the hotel. As we were walking in the door, I spotted Brian and we exchanged greetings and I introduced everyone to him. Meanwhile, Penny walked down Desert Cove 3,265 steps and 1.2 miles burned 185 calories in twenty-five minutes.

TAMPA—CENTANNI-KNAPP WEDDING AND RECEPTION
FRIDAY, FEBRUARY 20, 2015—FLY TO TAMPA

At 7:45 a.m. Jan Aver picked up Penny and me and drove us to Phoenix Sky Harbor Airport for a 9:55 a.m. flight to Tampa, Florida on a non-stop US Airways flight for Mara Centanni and Mike Knapp's wedding reception. We ate breakfast at Peet's Coffee & Tea at the airport and arrived in Tampa close to 5:00 p.m. Doug and Sandi Fishman picked us up at Tampa International Airport and we were driven to the Circles Bistro for dinner with Mara, Mike, Christian, Samantha and Mike. This get together was a nice opportunity to meet several of Mike's family.

After dinner, we drove back to the Tampa International Airport where we picked up Lois and Roy who arrived around 8:00 p.m. Then we all drove to the Hilton at Carillon Park in St. Petersburg, Florida to drop off our luggage and check into the hotel. Doug left Sandi's car with us at the hotel so we would have transportation during our visit.

SATURDAY, FEBRUARY 21, 2015—BREAKFAST AND DINNER

We met Lois, Roy and Sandi for breakfast at the hotel and Samantha joined us. The hotel was built on beautiful marshlands and after breakfast, Roy and I walked on a boardwalk behind the hotel that is part of a nature preserve and I took some photos of wildlife. We saw some alligators, turtles and beautiful birds sunning themselves. After our walk, Lois, Penny, Roy and I had lunch at Panera Bread almost across the street from the hotel. After lunch, we took Sandi's car and drove to St. Petersburg and looked around the city and that was fun.

Later in the afternoon many of the invited guest and family gathered outside in back of the hotel to take photos with the nature preserve in the background. After photos, we took the hotel shuttle to dinner and the wedding ceremony at Bascom's Chop House (Steaks & Fresh Seafood) in St. Petersburg. Doug Fishman conducted the wedding ceremony as a minister and he did a great job.

SUNDAY, FEBRUARY 22, 2015—BREAKFAST AND BRUNCH

Around 8:00 a.m. Penny and I drove to Panera Bread for a quick breakfast. At 11:00 a.m. we met for brunch at the Clearwater Yacht Club. We had a table with a water view and yachts in the harbor with Sandi, Mike, Mara and family. The brunch was delicious and after brunch we went to Sandi Fishman's condo and walked on the beach. Samantha put on a mermaid outfit and swam in the pool. Doug and Biddy invited us to their home for a delicious dinner of brisket, mac n cheese and grouper that Doug cooked especially for me.

MONDAY, FEBRUARY 23, 2015—BREAKFAST AND PHOENIX

Today is my cousin Norman's 74th birthday. I drove Roy to Panera Bread where we ordered breakfast and left for the airport around 2:00 p.m. for a 5:20 p.m. non-stop US Airways flight back to Phoenix. I made arrangements to be taken back to our condo from a Super Shuttle.

TUESDAY, FEBRUARY 24, 2015—EYE DOCTOR APPT.

At 9:00 a.m. I had an eye doctor appointment with Dr. Dennis Cooper, an ophthalmologist who looked at my chalazion [an inflamed swelling of a sebaceous gland of the eyelid. He said it wasn't ready to be drained. I had a 2:00 p.m. appointment at the Apple Store for new features on my MacBook Air computer.

WEDNESDAY, FEBRUARY 25, 2015—SENIOR EXPO

At 9:00 a.m. I went for my first pedicure at Pauline's Nails. After my pedicure, Penny and I went for a twenty-five-minute walk in the neighborhood. In afternoon, Penny and I went to a senior expo held at the Scottsdale Center for the Performing Arts building. Vendors from all over the Phoenix area were there. We got cloth bags of lots of goodies inside. After the expo, Penny bought some items at the Museum Store. In the evening, we were invited along with the Murphys and Avers to a going away party at Jay and Harriet's condo. Jay's cousin Barry and Nancy Slavin were also there.

THURSDAY, FEBRUARY 26, 2015—ORANGE TREE GOLF

At 7:15 a.m. I picked up Jay and we went to the Orange Tree Golf Club where we met Dan Murphy. Harriet picked up Penny and went to various places. After golf we met Penny and Harriet for lunch at Perk Eatery in Scottsdale. After lunch, Penny went for a walk and I rested from golf.

FRIDAY, FEBRUARY 27, 2015—WEINTRAUB BREAKFAST

We had a goodbye breakfast for Jay and Harriet Weintraub at the Soul Café along with the Murphys and Avers. After breakfast I bought a 1930 Ford model at the Antique Emporium plus three green iron stands. I filled the car with gasoline so Penny would have a full tank while I was back to Chicago to produce the International Housewares Association's *gia* Awards.

SATURDAY, FEBRUARY 28, 2015—FLY TO CHICAGO

We got up early because Penny drove me to the Phoenix Sky Harbor Airport at 5:15 a.m. for a 7:35 a.m. non-stop United Airlines on flight to Chicago O'Hare Airport. The plane left on time and I arrived in Chicago at 11:57 a.m. The flight was a little early but Alan Appelbaum insisted on picking me up at the airport and drove me to Northbrook. I phoned Penny to let her know I arrived safely. At 5:30

p.m. I had dinner at Bennett and Marni's home with Danny and Brooke.

SUNDAY, MARCH 1, 2015—BRUNCH AND RONNA DINNER

At 10:00 a.m. Bennett and Marni invited me for brunch at their home and later in the day I had dinner at Ronna and Ted's home.

TUESDAY, MARCH 3, 2015—EYE DOCTOR APPOINTMENT

At 1:45 p.m. I had an eye doctor appointment with Dr. Mark Buranosky. I developed a chalazion while in Scottsdale and went to see Dr. Dennis Cooper for treatment. The redness was very apparent so Dr. Buranosky gave me a numbing shot and drained it. At 6:15 p.m. I met Arnie Grauer for dinner at Northfield's Happ Inn.

WEDNESDAY, MARCH 4, 2015—PROGRAM REVIEW AT W/G

I took the Metra into Chicago for the program review for the IHA. At 10:00 a.m. all of my clients arrived for a program review of the International Housewares Association's Exhibitor Innovation Awards Slides at William/Gerard's office. My clients were Perry Reynolds, Connie Chantos, Derek Miller, Master of Ceremonies, Dan Gately, Art Director, Tony Sanchez & me.

At 10:30 a.m. we had a program review of the modules for the *gia* graphics and Discover Design. The review was successful. At 3:00 p.m. I had my haircut with Otto Bodner on the lower level of the Hyatt Regency Chicago.

THURSDAY, MARCH 5, 2015—SPENCER'S 4th BIRTHDAY

Today is Spencer's 4th birthday and I went to Ronna and Ted's home to celebrate and had dinner there. Ronna bought an ice cream cake for Spencer's birthday.

FRIDAY, MARCH 6, 2015—BENNETT AND MARNI'S DINNER

In the late afternoon I was invited to Bennett and Marni's home to have dinner.

SATURDAY, MARCH 7, 2015—McCORMICK PLACE

4:30 p.m. IHA Exhibitor Innovation Awards in the E-350 Innovation Display Auditorium.

SUNDAY, MARCH 8, 2015—LOAD-IN, EQUIPMENT SETUP, SPEAKER REHEARSAL & *gia* AWARDS CELEBRATION
MONDAY, MARCH 9, 2015—FLY BACK TO PHOENIX

Uri picked me up at 9:15 a.m. and we arrived at Chicago O'Hare Airport a little after 9:45 a.m. My United Airlines flight departed Chicago at 12;00 p.m. and arrived in Phoenix at 1:59 p.m. The plane was on time and Penny picked me up. At 6:00 p.m. Penny and I met Susan and Jeffrey Schesnol for dinner at Zappa's in the Desert Ridge Shopping Center.

THURSDAY, MARCH 12, 2015—WALK AND PENNY HAIRCUT

In the morning, Penny and I walked for thirty-minutes around the bike path 1.4 miles and we saw our upstairs neighbor, Sylvia Tucker walking on our way back. After our walk, we ate a light breakfast.

At 2:00 p.m. Penny had a haircut appointment with Chris at Mane Attractions and I drove her there. During Penny's appointment I drove to Starbuck's inside Macy's and drank a cup of coffee and read on my iPad.

FRIDAY, MARCH 13, 2015—PIZZA AT THE PARLOR
Jan, Rich and us ate pizza at The Parlor. We love this Phoenix restaurant. Then I drove to the Phoenix Art Center on Central Street to see *Radio Waves*, a musical. We didn't realize it was a LGBTQ chorus singing old songs from the radio. We enjoyed the evening of songs.

SATURDAY, MARCH 14, 2015—FOUNTAIN HILLS FAIR
The Avers and Spencers went to the Fountain Hills Art Fair. We bought a desert landscape made out of rocks from Jerry Locke for $151.37 and decided to have it shipped to our Northbrook home through the UPS Store instead of having Jerry Locke send it. We ate lunch at Sofritas, a colorful, folk-art Latin American restaurant with tapas, bruschetta, sangria and outdoor seating. We originally saw this restaurant on Check Please Arizona. We enjoyed the rest of the day.

SUNDAY, MARCH 15, 2015—MY 74th BIRTHDAY
We celebrated my 74th birthday at our condo with the Avers, Murphys and Susan Schesnol. Jeffrey was in Chicago attending a seminar for his Jewish studies. I ordered Nello's Pizza and Rich went with me to pick it up.

MONDAY, MARCH 16, 2015—MY HAPPY 74th BIRTHDAY
To celebrate my birthday, Penny and I went to breakfast at U.S. Egg on Scottsdale Road and Shea Blvd. And then, we went to Ginny's Laundromat to wash some rugs and also did some shopping at New York Bagel and Bialys, Sprouts & Fry's plus filled up the rental car with gas at Circle K. What an exciting day to celebrate my birthday.

TUESDAY, MARCH 17, 2015—SISTER LINDA FLIES TO PHOENIX
From 7:40 a.m. to 9:04 a.m. Penny and I picked up my sister Linda on a non-stop US Airways flight from Cleveland. We drove back to our condo and ate breakfast. We ate breakfast and afterwards, Linda and I drove to Goodyear Park located at 933 S. Ballpark Way in Goodyear for a 1:05 p.m. spring training game between the Cincinnati Reds and Cleveland Indians. The ballpark is located at the southwest corner of the greater Phoenix area. From I-10, take Estrella Parkway South and continue on Estrella Parkway; you'll see the ballpark on your left after you pass Van Buren. While Linda and I were at the game, Penny and Jan Aver had lunch at Portillos, went to Two Plates Full and to the Tina's Treasures on Shea.

WEDNESDAY, MARCH 18— PUEBLO GRANDE MUSEUM
Linda, Penny and I drove to the Phoenix Pueblo Grande Museum for a film and tour of the property. I also picked up some firewood for next winter at Berry Brothers on Washington Street. Afterwards, we had lunch at Phoenix's Chelsea's Kitchen at 40th and Camelback Road. For dinner, Penny made turkey meatballs and spaghetti.

THURSDAY, MARCH 19—MYSTERY CASTLE AND DINNER
Linda, Penny and I drove to the Mystery Castle for a tour. The eighteen-room house is built on a forty-acre plot of land, located at the foothills of South Mountain Park in Phoenix. This house tour was better than the first time we visited the place on January 1, 2004. On our first tour, we had a chance to meet Mary Lou Gulley, the daughter of Boyce Luther Gulley, who built the house in the 1930s.

Mary Lou gave us a personal tour in 2004. She died on November 3, 2010 at age 87. At 7:00 p.m. Linda, Corky Weily, his friend Natalie Kane, Penny and I sat on the Pasta Brioni's outdoor patio and ate dinner.

FRIDAY, MARCH 20, 2015—A DAY IN CAREFREE

After breakfast, Linda, Penny and I drove to Carefree and ate lunch outside at The Grotto. We sat under a tree and had a delicious lunch. After lunch, we stopped at The Dump, and then went to The Rare Earth Gallery. This place has a collection of unbelievable items including unique stone pieces, rare gems, jewelry, crystals, geodes, minerals and fossils from all over the world and they are all for sale. This store is a museum with quality merchandise made by nature. The sales people are very knowledgeable and helpful. We bought a small two-piece geode that we display on a shelf in our condo. The prices for the larger pieces are outrageously expensive but it's a fascinating destination and worthy trip. For dinner, we ate leftovers and met the Avers at Yogurtology.

SATURDAY, MARCH 21, 2015—GOODYEAR AND INDIANS

After breakfast, Linda and I drove back to Goodyear to see the Colorado Rockies play the Cleveland Indians in spring training that started at 1:05 p.m.

SUNDAY, MARCH 22, 2015—CUBS SPRING TRAINING

At 11:15 a.m. Penny, Linda and I left to see the San Diego Padres play the Chicago Cubs at Mesa's Sloan Park. The Cubs lost the game. Penny was not thrilled with the game and was actually bored. While leaving the ballpark I drove over a curb and the car bumped. Penny's neck started aching after my little encounter with the curb. We picked up Chinese food for dinner from the Jade Palace.

MONDAY, MARCH 23, 2015—LINDA FLIES HOME

At 11:30 we drove Linda to the Phoenix Sky Harbor Airport for her non-stop US Airways flight to Cleveland. The flight left at 3:00 p.m. and she arrived in Cleveland at 9:55 p.m. In the afternoon, Penny sat outside and read. She talked to Chris and Dave Tucker. It was 88 degrees this day. She made chili for dinner.

WEDNESDAY, MARCH 25, 2015—GATEWAY WALK

We were supposed to drive to Tucson to see Steve Klein but I got a chalazion in the other eye so I cancelled our trip there. Instead, we walked in the Nature Trail at Gatehead at the Sonoran Preserve. The walk and scenery were spectacular. Penny's neck was still aching from the Sunday curb incident. For dinner, Penny and I went to Z'Tejas with the $35.00 gift certificate the Appelbaums had given us.

THURSDAY, MARCH 26, 2015—NATIVE TRAILS

After breakfast, Penny and I decided to go to the Native Trails show at the Scottsdale Civic Mall. During the winter, various Native American tribes put on a show of music and dancing and talk about native customs. The crowd was small but the show was great. We have gone to several of these shows over the years. Derek is still doing his hoop dances and I shot video of him in action and included him in my "show." Derek is ranked as one of the best Native American hoop dancers in the world. For dinner, we were invited to Jan and Rich Aver's for paella and to watch a three-hour salute to Saturday Night Live the Avers had recorded.

FRIDAY, MARCH 27, 2015—GOLF AT VISTAL GOLF CLUB

At 7:00 a.m. Dan Murphy picked up Rich, Jay and me to play golf at Vistal Golf Club in south Phoenix. After golf we ate at Goldman's Deli and I had a white fish sandwich on challah with lettuce, tomato and onion. Meanwhile, Penny did some yoga exercises, went to Scottsdale's Mustang Library to drop off a library donation book, and then went to Sprouts to buy nuts.

SATURDAY, MARCH 28, 2015—EISENDRATH HOUSE

Penny and I celebrated Rich Aver's 69th birthday at the Soul Café in north Scottsdale where we ate delicious banana pancakes for breakfast. After breakfast, we dropped off the Avers. Penny and I drove to Tempe's Eisendrath house for an outside look as it is being rehabbed and under construction by the Rio Salado Foundation and the city of Tempe. The historic Tempe house is located at 1400 N. College Street. When the renovation is finished, it will be turned into city offices. This coming December, when Penny and I return to Scottsdale, we'll be sure to get a personal tour of the property.

The history of this notable adobe house is fascinating. Early in 1930, a Jewish woman from Chicago, Ruth Eisendrath, whose late husband was in the glove business, had spent winters in Arizona. On April 23, 1930 she acquired a forty-four-acre parcel in the hills above the Salt River in North Tempe. Mrs. Eisendrath had been refused accommodations at a valley resort because of her religion. So, she decided to build a house on nine-acres of pristine Sonoran Desert that sits on top of a hill. She commissioned famed Arizona architect, Robert Thomas Evans to design this adobe revival house. We also drove to the Steve Sussex house that is a mess near downtown Tempe. The city has been trying to condemn the property because it is an eye sore on the community. Junk is strewn all over the property and is visible from the street. Afterwards, we went to Cool Gelato for a snack.

SUNDAY, MARCH 29, 2015—TEMPE ART FAIR

At 9:00 a.m. we picked up Jan Aver and I drove to the 32nd Street parking lot in Phoenix and we took the light rail to the Tempe Art Fair. We wondered in the direction of Robert Shield's booth. He is Shields of Shields and Yarnell television and stage fame from the 1970s. We bought a piece of his artwork for our condo's kitchen. The artwork was a long horizontal piece with teacups. He is such a character and he told us Jewish jokes. After returning from the Tempe Art Fair, we picked up the Avers and had farewell a dinner with the Murphys and Avers at the Jalapeno Inferno restaurant in north Scottsdale.

MONDAY, MARCH 30, 2015—UPS STORE AND TEMPLERS

I took four boxes to the UPS store in Scottsdale to be shipped back to Northbrook. The Templers came to our condo at 3:30 p.m. and I drove them to Cosanti where they bought a bell for each of their daughters since Cindy and Brian bought a house. Cosanti closed at 5:00 p.m. so we had to leave.

We went on a little drive up the mountain by the JW Marriott Camelback Inn and a drive along Lincoln Avenue. We stopped at My Sister's Attic by the Borgota, and then had dinner at the Village Tavern, Stu Templer's favorite restaurant.

TUESDAY, MARCH 31, 2015—LOST DOG TRAILHEAD
Penny and I went walking in the desert at Lost Dog Trailhead and the Kovach Family Nature Trail that is named after a family who donated $60,000 for its creation. The trail wasn't that great. Interpretive trails are generally short to moderate in length and provide an opportunity for walkers to study interesting features and plants along the trail. This particular path is divided into two loops, each roughly a quarter-mile long.

The next time we'll try the one-half mile Jane Rau Interpretive Trail at Brown's Ranch in the McDowell Sonoran Preserve. We drove down Cactus looking at various houses on side streets and caught up on some recorded television shows. We finished packing to get ready to leave Scottsdale the next day for Chicago.

WEDNESDAY, APRIL 1, 2015—FLIGHT TO CHICAGO
At 11:30 a.m. Penny and I left our condo for Phoenix Sky Harbor Airport and I returned the car to the transportation center. Our non-stop United Airlines flight departed Phoenix at 2:15 p.m. and we arrived at Chicago O'Hare Airport at 7:37 p.m. Uri picked us up at the airport and drove us to Northbrook.

FRIDAY, APRIL 3, 2015—PASSOVER DINNER
We had the family over for Passover dinner. Everyone came to our house around 4:00 p.m. Since three of the children can read, they participated in the reading of the Haggadah that we created over the years. It is always exhausting to have a Passover dinner a few days after returning from Phoenix.

TUESDAY MAY 12, 2015—A FAMILY TRAGEDY
Rachel Jacobs, our nephew Todd Waldman's wife, was killed in the Philadelphia Amtrak train crash on Tuesday evening, May 12, 2015. Todd is my sister Linda Waldman's son. As CEO of ApprenNet.com, Rachel had been in Philadelphia attending a meeting and was on her way back to New York when a horrible train accident occurred. Initially after the crash, Rachel was unaccounted for and trying to find what happened to her made national news. It was a horrific day and our family was devastated by the news. We could not believe this misfortune. A funeral was set for Sunday in Detroit.

SUNDAY, MAY 17, 2015—DRIVE TO DETROIT
Bennett and Marni, Ted and Ronna and Penny and I drove separately to Rachel's hometown Detroit for the funeral. Penny and I arrived at 6:15 p.m. at John and Gilda Jacobs' home, Rachel's parents, located at 8353 Hendrie Blvd. in Huntington Woods, a suburb of Detroit. We stayed until 9:00 or so. Arleen and Michael Gomshay came in from New York. Bennett and Marni arrived a little later and stayed later. We all stayed at the Embassy Suites located at 28100 Franklin Road in Southfield.

MONDAY, MAY 18, 2015—RACHEL JACOBS FUNERAL
The 10:00 a.m. funeral service was held at the Ira Kaufman Chapel in Southfield, Michigan and the funeral procession to the cemetery was about sixty-five cars in length. After the funeral, we went to John and Gilda's home. The entire weekend was disbelief, a blur, sad and shocking. It will take Todd a long time to heal.

TUESDAY, MAY 19, 2015—TODD, ANDREW AND JACOB

Before we drove back to Northbrook, Penny and I met Todd, Andrew, Jacob and Linda for breakfast at the Original Pancake House near the hotel. We contributed to two projects made in memory of Rachel. One of the projects was a scholarship created by New York's Columbia University Business School established in Rachel's name, as well as a bench dedicated in New York's Central Park in Rachel's memory.

SATURDAY, JUNE 13, 2015—SUE'S ST. LOUIS ORDINATION

David and Marcy Levinson picked up Penny and me at 5:10 a.m. for our trip to St. Louis, Missouri for Sue Vaickowski's Ordination as a Deacon in the Roman Catholic Church. At approximately 7:00 a.m., we stopped at a Cracker Barrel in Bloomington, Illinois for breakfast. I had called the St. Louis Hampton Inn & Suites several days ahead of time to see if we could have an early check-in so we could change before for the 2:00 p.m. ordination. At 11:30 a.m. we arrived at the six-year-old Hampton Inn and Suites of Forest Park and our rooms were ready. The hotel was located at 5650 Oakland Ave in St. Louis. Elsie McGrath, an ordained priest, arranged for a special rate of $149.00 plus tax for a $174.22 total cost. Elsie also took a major part in the ceremony. Most of the people involved in the ordination stayed at this hotel. The site of the hotel was originally the Forest Park Amusement Park, now, luxury apartments and some restaurants dot the entire area.

At 1:40 p.m. we arrived at the ceremony's site at the First Unitarian Church located at 5007 Waterman Blvd. at Kings Highway. The Hope Chapel was at the rear alley of the church where the ordination was held. We were greeted at the main door and showed where to go for the ceremony. At slightly after 2:00 p.m. the sign of the cross and greeting started the liturgy of the word and ordination. Three women were ordained. The organization was Roman Catholic Women priests— USA, Great Waters Region. The actual program was a celebration of Ordination to the Roman Catholic Diaconate. I didn't know what the word meant, so I looked it up in the Merriam-Webster dictionary. "A diaconate is the office or period of office of a deacon or deaconess or an official body of deacons." Then I looked up the word deacon that is defined as "an official in some Christian churches whose rank is just below a priest and in this particular case a Roman Catholic cleric ranking next below a priest."

The three women who were ordained were Mary Michele Regina Foley, Susan Mary Mielke and Susan K. Vaickowski who went under the assumed name of Susan Martin for fear of discovery and being excommunicated from the Church. Women are not permitted to become deacons or priests in the Catholic Church so Sue took her vows under an assumed name.

THE ORDINATION CEREMONY

A woman bishop started the ceremony that was quite elaborate. There was a great amount of singing, responsive reading and a reference to Jesus, the Christ throughout the ceremony. Two guitars, a flutist, a pianist and several singers led the singing. For each ordained woman, someone spoke and gave a testimony on why they should become a deacon. The investiture of the deacon stoles was interesting as a handmade stole was placed over the shoulders and in front of each person to go over their white robes. The entire ceremony took about one hour thirty minutes and was dismissed. At approximately 3:30 p.m. after congratulations, we went into a room in the basement of the church for cheese, crackers, cookies and soft drinks until approximately 4:45 when we went back to the same room for the 5:00 p.m. mass that lasted about one hour. All four of us agreed that sitting through the ceremony and mass were a little painful and boring. The Jesus references and content were totally against anything we could relate to but the experience was worthwhile, once. We did it for Sue.

BUFFET DINNER AFTER THE CEREMONY

Following the mass, we headed toward Chris Pancake House for a 7:00 p.m. buffet dinner. The buffet consisted of a Caesar salad with two types of pasta, cooked peas and carrots and fried chicken that I didn't eat. At approximately 8:30 p.m. we drove back to the Hampton Inn to watch the conclusion of the Blackhawks versus the Tampa Bay Lighting playoff hockey game that the Blackhawks won 2 to 1.

SUNDAY, JUNE 14, 2015—DRIVE TO NORTHBROOK

Penny and I got up around 7:00 a.m., showered and about to take a walk when Marcy Levinson knocked on our door. We went for a twenty-minute walk while David got up. We ate breakfast on the first floor of the hotel and left for our drive to Chicago around 10:00 a.m. Around 11:40 a.m. we stopped in Springfield, Illinois for gasoline and lunch at Panera Bread and arrived in Northbrook at 4:16 p.m. Overall it was an interesting, educational and a quick trip.

SATURDAY, JUNE 27, 2015—DICK ORKIN INTERVIEW

Penny and I drove to Chicago and the Museum of Broadcast Communications to hear Dick Orkin being interviewed by local WGN radio talk show celebrity Bob Sirott. I went online and ordered Park Whiz, a discount parking app and got a $14.00 price to park at 20 W. Kinzie in front of the Kinzie Hotel. It made sense to join the museum as family members for $60.00 since the individual tickets to the interview were $12.00 each.

We arrived about one and a half hours early and I saw Bruce Dumont, president of the museum, who happened to be standing near the audio console as we exited the elevator. I introduced myself and I told him I used to listen to him on Evanston's WCGO radio, 1590 on the dial, in the mid 1970s. I introduced him to Penny and when he asked what I did for a living, he took us to the fourth floor where the museum is trying to sell the space for special events. Blue Plate Catering and Frost are the contractors for the room.

I worked with Dick Orkin in 1975 on the *Multiplication* film when employed by Larry Levy. We wrote the script and Dick and his team added the humor and the audio production. The film's soundtrack was recorded at Dick Orkin Creative Services studio. In a previous section of this book, I wrote about meeting Dick when he spoke at IFMA's COEX 83, a meeting I produced in February 1983 at the Fontainebleau Hotel in Miami Beach. Since Dick was into Jewish genealogy and he knew about *Search* and my name, I contacted him ahead of time and we had dinner together the night before his Miami Beach speech.

The last time I spoke to Dick was at the 1990 Jewish Genealogical Seminar in Los Angeles, California. Dick gave the opening night address along with comedian Shelly Berman and I met his wife Bunny. During the interview, Dick brought some video and radio clips from his Chickenman radio serial and a humorous radio commercial. After the interview, it was a mini-reunion with some of Dick's Chicago friends and colleagues with whom I had worked in the past. Penny Lane and Joel Cory were among the crowd and I had a chance to reminisce. Penny Lane was married to Wayne Juhlin who died suddenly of a heart attack at age 77 on April 17, 2014. Wayne was Penny's husband and partner in life, love and laughter of Sandi (nee Marcus) professionally known as Penny Lane. I knew Wayne and Penny from the commercial industry in the mid 1970s. Penny was originally part of the all-female WSDM-Chicago [97.9 FM] line-up in the 1970s, but has been in the advertising/voice-over world for many years.

(As a side note, Penny met Wayne while he was writing a comedy album on the late Mayor Richard J. Daley. He needed a female on the *"CHICAGA"* album and since he was also a record promotion man and knew [WSDM] Penny's boss, Burt, he asked Wayne for a suggestion. Because of Penny's theater background, Burt suggested Penny and it also led to Penny leaving WSDM and going on the air to WFYR with Wayne as the morning duo. They also did many commercials and syndicated radio shows first for Dick Orkin (*Chicken Man* and the *Tooth Fairy*) and then we went out on our own with Penway Productions).

Joel Cory (original name Cohen) was a singer and originally in the New Wine Singers, a folk group based out of Chicago. Guy Guilbert, my ex-partner in The Spot Shop, knew Joel from Chicago's folk scene days. I used Joel as a narrator in a Rand McNally filmstrip when Guy and I were partners. Joel made lots of money as a voice-over talent and at one-time lived with Robyn Douglass, the movie actress who was in the film *Breaking Away*. It was great seeing both of them after the Orkin interview.

I also had a chance to speak briefly to Dick Orkin and Bob Sirott. I told Bob I met him in 1971 when he was a disc jockey on WBBM-FM. Bernie Wilson, my friend and upstairs neighbor on W. Oakdale who sold advertising time on WBBM AM, introduced me to Bob in between records while he was on the air. I also introduced myself to Dick's second wife, Deedee. Dick's first wife, Bunny had passed away in 2007 after a long illness. Dick passed away on December 24, 2017 at age 84.

At 5:00 p.m. Jay and Harriet Weintraub picked up Penny and me and drove us to Des Plaines and the Boston Fish Market, a restaurant with the freshest fish. The portions were huge. We ordered a small Greek salad one pound of Red Snapper that was grilled and a Blue Moon beer to share. The meal was absolutely delicious. We took home half of the fish and had it for dinner on Sunday evening.

FRIDAY, JULY 2, 2015—CHICAGO ART MUSEUM

Penny and I had a terrific day today. At 10:45 a.m. we drove downtown

Chicago and valet parked the car at the Art Institute. After going through a few of the museum exhibits, we walked across the street and down one block to the new Maggie Daley Park. We walked through the park a short way and heard some music coming from the Pritzker Pavilion. So, we walked across the bridge and sat until 1:00 p.m. listening to the Grant Park Orchestra rehearsing for an evening concert. After the rehearsal we walked back to the Art Institute to view the Charles Ray sculpture exhibit on the second floor. Then we bought some lunch at the Museum Café on the lower level and ate outside by the water fountain.

After lunch we walked to the Michigan Avenue side of the museum to view the Degas exhibit that was very impressive. The museum store was right by the entrance so we spent a few minutes wondering the store before walking to the Chicago Cultural Center located by Washington Street.

The Chicago Cultural Center had two exhibits of interest both involving African-American artists; the graphic art of Valmor Products, a Chicago company and the paintings of Archibald Motely, a Chicago artist in the 1920, 30s and 40s. Of particular interest was the African American artist, Charles Dawson who designed the artwork for the Valmor Products Company. Many of his works were on display. While walking to go to the bathroom on the first floor, Penny and I ran into Marilyn Appelbaum in the corridor. She was looking at photographs while Alan was resting in the lobby. They were downtown to celebrate their wedding anniversary, having dinner at Catch 35 and to see the musical *On Your Feet* at the Oriental Theater.

SPRINGFIELD, ILLINOIS ROAD TRIP
THURSDAY, OCTOBER 22, 2015—DRIVE TO SPRINGFIELD

For many years, Penny and I had been talking about going to the Illinois state capital and we finally decided to go there in the fall of 2015. We left early in the morning for a full day of travel and touring. Our first stop was the Springfield Convention & Visitors Bureau located at 109 N. Seventh Street. The Visitors Bureau gave away Free Guest Parking Passes for parking meters as well as a $5.00 off coupon per adult for the Abraham Lincoln Presidential Library.

After leaving the Visitors Bureau we drove to the Old State Capitol located at #1 Old State Capitol Plaza for a 1:00 to 1:35 p.m. tour and our tour guide Stephanie Thomas. Close to the Old State Capital was the Chase Bank formerly the Springfield Marine Bank to see a plaque that read Abraham Lincoln's ledger showing his account at the bank.

We walked one block from the Old State Capital and bank to the Lincoln-Herndon Law Office located at 1 South Old State Capitol Plaza. Unfortunately, we couldn't go inside because the building was under renovation. We drove by the Springfield train station, parked the car and had a picnic lunch with food near the station with food we had brought with us.

After lunch our next stop was a drive to the Oak Ridge Cemetery and Lincoln's Tomb located at 1500 Monument Avenue in Springfield. We were able to go on a self-guided tour from 2:30 to 3:05 p.m. The grave is the final resting place of Abraham Lincoln and his wife Mary and three of their four children. Members of the Lincoln family chose the site in May 1865.

The day's final stop was the Dana-Thomas House located at 301 E. Lawrence Avenue. The sign in front of the house said it is a state historic site. In 1902, famous architect Frank Lloyd Wright designed the house for Susan Lawrence Dana, a forward-thinking socialite living in Springfield. The home, the seventy-second building designed by Wright, contains the largest collection of site-specific, original Wright art glass and furniture. Wright's first "blank check" commission, the home has thirty-five rooms in the 12,000 square feet of living space that includes three main levels and sixteen varying levels in all.

This magnificent home is regarded as a Springfield treasure and is a gorgeous house museum. The Illinois State Historic Preservation Agency bought the home and undertook a major restoration project. The results yielded a beautifully preserved example of Wright's genius. The home is a brilliant showcase of craftsmanship in glass doors, windows and light fixtures, terra cotta sculpture and an exquisite mural. The house is beyond an architectural masterpiece and has international significance. This home is the best preserved and most complete of Frank Lloyd Wright's early "Prairie" style houses. The house is open 9 a.m. until 5 p.m. Wednesday through Sunday each week. At approximately 3:45 p.m., we were able to get in the last tour that started with a video introduction.

Before checking into our hotel, we drove by the Lincoln Depot Train station located at 930 E. Monroe Street. The Lincoln Depot that is now a law office. This is the building where Abraham Lincoln departed on February 11, 1861 to assume the Presidency of the United States. The sign in front says Great Western Railroad Depot [Lincoln Depot] and is on the National Register of Historic Places by the Department of the Interior. At 5:15 p.m. we checked into Hilton Garden Inn Springfield located 3100 S. Dirksen Parkway.

FRIDAY, OCTOBER 23, 2015—LINCOLN'S HOME

After breakfast at the hotel, we drove to the Abraham Lincoln Home, a National Historic Site and the visitor's center in front of home. The Lincoln home is located at 426 S. 7th Street in Springfield. The tour of the house was free conducted by a National Park Service employee. The tours are from 9:30 a.m. to 11:00 a.m. It was hard to believe they did not have indoor plumbing in the house.

Directly across the street from the Lincoln home was the Harriet Dean House. We went inside of the house for a short tour. After the Harriet Dean house, we drove to Springfield's Abraham Lincoln Presidential Museum located at 212 N. 6th Street. The admission fee was $12.00 for adults with seniors less with the $5.00 off coupons for the Abraham Lincoln Presidential Library per adult. Our senior admission price was $9.00 each. Inside the museum I asked a person to take a photo of Penny and me standing in front of life size figures of Abraham Lincoln and his three children. We also saw the Abraham Lincoln & The Jews Exhibit that was from August 3 to November 15, 2015. The tour was from 11:15 to 12:35 p.m.

After touring the Presidential Museum, we headed to Maldaner's for lunch located at 222 S. 6TH Street from 12:45 to 1:35 p.m. This restaurant is expensive and recommended by Alan Appelbaum where our state's politicians go. We had to make a reservation from 12:45 to 1:35 p.m. After lunch we went back to the museum to complete our tour from 1:45 to 2:55 p.m.

Our next stop was the Abraham Lincoln Presidential Library located at 212 N. 6th Street. The library was free and mainly used as a research library for Lincoln scholars. You couldn't go into the book stacks unless you were doing Lincoln research so we were only in the main part of the library. From 3:20 to 4:00 p.m. the current Illinois State Capitol building located at 301 S. 2nd Street was our next tour. After going to the state capital, we took a drive to Lake Springfield Marina located at 17 Waters Edge Blvd at Interstate 55 at Exit 88. I visited the marina from 4:50 to 5:35 p.m. and got map of lake at marina and they showed me where to fish.

We also drove north part of Springfield Lake to Bridgeview Park, where I was told you could catch crappie and largemouth bass. The park is 19.78 acres and is located at 149 N. Lakewood Drive, in Chatham, IL. The park has playground equipment, one pavilion that accommodates seventy-five people, and a small boat dock for easy access from the lake. This park is the site of the Bridgeview Building that is available to rent by the public. I tried to fish but had no luck.

Harriet Weintraub recommended having dinner was at the Chesapeake Seafood House, located at 3045 E. Clear Lake Avenue. Penny and I arrived at 5:35 and had to wait for thirty minutes because we did not have a reservation. We had a delicious dinner and left at 7:35 p.m. for the ride back to our hotel.

SATURDAY, OCTOBER 24—EXECUTIVE MANSION

At 9:25 a.m. Penny and I arrived at the Executive Mansion Governor's Mansion for a free 9:30 tour given by the Governor's butler because the regular tour guide did not show up. The Executive Mansion is located at 410 E. Jackson Street and the tour was from 9:30 a.m. to 10:30 a.m.

After the Executive Mansion tour, we drove to the nearby Vachel Lindsay House located at 603 S. Fifth Street In Springfield and called (217) 524-0901 to set up a private tour of the house. We waited for about twenty-five minutes before our tour guide, Troy Gilmore, arrived. The house was restored by the Illinois Historic Preservation Agency and reopened to the public in October 8, 20014. We were the only two people on the tour. Vachel Lindsay was an American poet who was known as the founder of modern singing poetry with verses meant to be sung or chanted. The house was the site of his birth and death.

After our tour of the Vachel Lindsay house, we saw the outside of the Elijah Iles House, Springfield's oldest house and a museum of Springfield's history. It was not open for a tour so we only saw the outside of the house. We had lunch at the Obed & Isasc's Microbrewery & Eatery in an old Springfield mansion.

After lunch, we drove to Lincoln's New Salem Historic Site located at 15588 History Lane route 97 and did a walking self-guided tour from 12:45 to 3:15 p.m. There was a visitor's center and statues of Lincoln as a young man. In the village, volunteers, dressed in period clothing and worked outside and inside some of the houses and shops. A woman was making a candle and a man was cooking something on an outdoor fire. A woman was spinning cotton inside one of the houses and another was making soap. A blacksmith's shop with a man pounding on an anvil was also in the village as well as the New Salem Museum Store. It was a very interesting place and gave you a sense of what it was like living in such a place when Lincoln was a young man.

SUNDAY, OCTOBER 25, 2015—DRIVE TO NORTHBROOK

Penny and I drove to Springfield's Charlie Parker's Diner for breakfast located at 700 North Street. The restaurant was featured on the Food Network's *Diners, Drive-ins and Dives*. After breakfast, we left Springfield and drove to Peoria. We arrived at 11:15 a.m. in time to buy six loaves of Avanti's bread for Harriet Weintraub, one loaf for the Murphys and one loaf for us. The restaurant is located at the corner of Main and University at 1301 W. Main Street in Peoria. This Italian restaurant was a frequent hangout for Harriet and the Murphys while they went to college at Bradley University. After locating Avanti's, we did a short driving tour of Bradley University at 1501 W Bradley Avenue.

Before lunch at Avanti's we stopped at Luthy Botanical Garden located at 2520 N. Prospect, turn at the corner of Prospect & Gift), in Peoria and drove around the riverfront. At 12:30 p.m. we arrived back at the Avanti for lunch. After lunch we drove to Glen Oak Lagoon located on the east central side of Peoria in Glen Oak Park at Prospect and McClure where I went fishing for about forty-five minutes. This three-acre pond fed by runoff water has the entire shoreline accessible to anglers with a paved surface. This pond is also an urban fishing clinic site for children each summer. The park is also home to the Peoria Zoo. I caught nothing at this pond, not even a nibble.

TUESDAY, DECEMBER 25, 2015—PHOENIX TRIP

Uri pick us up with at 6:30 a.m. and we arrived at Chicago O'Hare Airport a little after 7:00 a.m. for our non-stop United Airlines flight to Phoenix Sky Harbor Airport. We departed on time at 9:05 a.m. and arrived in Phoenix at 12:04 p.m. Phoenix time. Jan and Rich picked up Penny and me from the Sky Harbor Airport and we ate lunch at Goldman's Deli. After lunch the Avers dropped us at our condo and brought in our three suitcases and carry-ons. Around 3:30 p.m. Jan drove us to Spencer's Appliances and we bought an Amana refrigerator because the one at our condo was not working when Jan tried to plug it in. At 4:30 p.m. the two boxes of pears I ordered from Harry and David arrived.

WEDNESDAY, DECEMBER 16, 2015—NEW REFRIGERATOR

Our *Arizona Republic* started delivery and at 9:30 a.m. our new Amana refrigerator was delivered and the old one taken away. At 11:40 a.m. Jan picked both of us up and drove us to pick up the Avis Car Rental for a one-hundred twenty-four day mini-lease rental with unlimited miles through Costco. Chris Frieh, owner of the Avis franchise signed us in and we rented a 2016 Toyota Camry. Around 12:10 Penny and I went to New York Bagels and Bialys and bought one-day old bagel sticks and bialys. Then we drove to Fry's to do grocery shopping, got back to the condo around 1:30 p.m. and ate lunch. At 3:45 p.m. I drove to Jan and Rich Aver's condo to pick up the four boxes we sent from Northbrook. I made a fire and we were both not hungry from a late lunch, so for dinner we had salad and a sliced pear and cheese.

SUNDAY, DECEMBER 20, 2015—NEW STOVE AND OVEN

At 11:00 a.m. Penny and I drove to Spencer's TV and Appliances and bought a GE stove and oven to replace our original one. At 1:30 p.m. I made guacamole and we relaxed in the evening.

TUESDAY, DECEMBER 22, 2015—STOVE AND OVEN ARRIVE

At 9:05 a.m. our new GE stove and oven were delivered. At 10:20 a.m. Penny was picked up by Jan and I went shopping at Trader Joe's and Whole Foods.

FRIDAY, DECEMBER 25, 2015—CHINESE FOOD

At 11:00 a.m. Penny watched the Chicago Bulls play the Oklahoma Thunder. The Bulls won, then at 2:00 p.m. she watched the Cleveland Cavaliers play the Golden State Warriors. At 6:30 p.m. Penny and I went to Jan and Rich Aver's condo. Jan ordered food from Flo's and Rich and I went to pick it up at 7:00 p.m. Although I placed food order in the afternoon for a 7:00 p.m. pick up, there was a huge mix-up. Finally, at 8:05 p.m. we received our order. Because of the huge delay and oversight, we were given a $40.00 future meal voucher for our messed-up order. We will never order Chinese food from Flo's on Christmas Eve.

TUESDAY, DECEMBER 29, 2015—TERRI'S STORE

At 1:30 p.m. Penny and I went to Terri's Consignment store to look for a chair for our guest bedroom, so Penny would be able to read while I was watching football games. We found a small black leather chair for under $200.00 so we bought it. At 2:45 p.m. we drove to Bashas to grocery shop and in the evening, I made a fire in our fireplace, then Penny and I watched Kennedy Center Honors.

THURSDAY, DECEMBER 31, 2015—NEW YEAR'S EVE

During the day, I watched various college football games. At 7:00 p.m. Rich and Jan Aver picked up Penny and me and we drove to the Schesnols for our annual New Year's Eve party with Jacqui and Phil Voyce. Aaron Aver and his fiancé Stacy Gorman came to Scottsdale from Los Angeles and joined the Avers and us. It was a fun evening with lots of laughing and celebrating the arrival of 2016. I kept on making Stacy laugh for no apparent reason. We were exhausted so we left the party and got home at 2:30 a.m. We got to sleep it was after 3:00 a.m.

FRIDAY, JANUARY 1, 2016—WALK AND A MOVIE

At 9:30 a.m. My sister, Linda, woke us up with a Happy New Year's call. After breakfast, we walked for thirty-five minutes and watched the *Theory of Everything* that I had previously recorded.

SATURDAY, JANUARY 2, 2016— CAREFREE HIGH TEA

We woke up at 7:25 a.m. and Penny fell back to sleep until 8:30 a.m. Penny picked up Jan Aver for her 2:30 p.m. High Tea with the girls at the Rose Tea Room in Carefree. I stayed home.

SUNDAY, JANUARY 3, 2016—*DOWNTOWN ABBEY* PARTY

At 6:00 p.m. Jay and Harriet Weintraub picked up Penny and me and we drove to Jan and Rich's condo for our *Downton Abbey* party. For dinner, Jay and I drove to the Handlebar J restaurant to pick up fish n chips at $20.00 per person.

MONDAY, JANUARY 4, 2016—EFFICIENCY MECHANICAL

Today is Jan and & Rich's forty-sixth Anniversary. At 1:00 p.m. Jason

Harrington from Efficiency Mechanical came to our condo to inspect and service our heat pump and air conditioner. It was raining, so he had to reschedule an inspection for Thursday, January 14th to go on the roof to complete the job.

WEDNESDAY, JANUARY 6, 2016—CORKY AND CONCERT

At 6:00 p.m. we met Corky Weily for dinner at Wildflower in the Seville Shopping Center before the concert at the Scottsdale ASU Kerr Cultural Center located at 6110 N. Scottsdale Road. Natalie Kane was supposed to join Corky but she was sick with a bad cold and was not able to be at dinner or the concert. After dinner, Corky followed us to the Kerr Cultural Center and the concert began at 7:30 p.m. We had premium seats in section B, row 2, seats 1 & 2. Nicole was joined on stage by saxophonist, Jerry Donato, Bob Lashier on bass and Dan Tomlinson on drums and performed an unbelievable concert. Nicole Pesce is an absolutely amazing pianist and she presented a program of jazz, blues and swing with selections from the Great American Songbook. There was also a section of the concert dedicated to audience requests and a feature performance by each band member. Nicole asked the audience for their favorite songs and asked that they yell them out from the audience. She picked ten songs and created a medley where one song blended into the next song.

FRIDAY, JANUARY 8, 2016—CUBS SPRING TRAINING

A few minutes before 10:00 a.m., I called Alan Appelbaum so he could advise me about buying Chicago Cubs spring training tickets. While I was on the phone with Alan, Rich and Jan Aver came to our condo. Rich thought he might want to go to a Cubs pre-season game and wanted to know the ticket price. At 10:00 I got online and ordered Chicago Cubs Spring Training tickets for Alan Appelbaum and me for Tuesday, March 4 and for Tuesday, March 8 at Sloan Park.

SATURDAY, JANUARY 9, 2016—HERB AND LYNDA ARRIVE

Herb and Lynda Belinky were driving to Scottsdale from Los Angeles to spend some time with Penny and me in our condo. They finally arrived around 7:30 p.m.

SUNDAY, JANUARY 10, 2016—PHOENIX HOME TOUR

All of us ate breakfast at our condo and around 11:30 a.m. we drove for a "Modern Phoenix" home tour with the Belinkys. The southern Scottsdale Innovations Mod home tour benefitted the Coronado High School. The houses we toured were amazing from the inside but looking at the outside you would not know that these houses had been remodeled. The modernization and furnishings were terrific. We toured ten homes. We drove from one home to another, parked the car while some were within walking distance of each other.

MONDAY, JANUARY 11—CAVE CREEK, LUNCH, DINNER

The Belinkys and Spencers drove to Cave Creek and ate lunch at the Grotto. After lunch, we took the Belinkys to Rare Earth Galleries where Betsy gave us a tour. We drove to Little Thaiger for a Thai dinner and we met the owner.

TUESDAY, JANUARY 12, 2016—LUNCH AND DINNER

We all drove Herb and Lynda to the Scottsdale Civic Center Mall but the Schoolhouse Museum was closed. We walked around the Civic Center mall but Lynda Belinky had difficulty so we didn't do too much. We had a terrific lunch at

Arcadia Farms and a fabulous dinner at the Eden Grill with three of us ordering their delicious catfish entre.

WEDNESDAY, JANUARY 13, 2016—BELINKYS LEAVE

The Belinkys left around noon to stay with their Phoenix friends for a few days. They talked about coming next year for a stay. Penny and I cleaned the condo and she did many loads of wash.

THURSDAY, JANUARY 14, 2016—FOUNTAIN HILLS FAIR

The Weintraubs picked us up and we drove to the Fountain Hills art fair. We saw the granite lady selling slabs for $50.00 each. We called the Belinkys and told Lynda about the granite lady, but she didn't want to go to the art fair. Lynda had expressed interest in the granite turntable Penny purchased from the granite lady. We bought a wooden turning trivet and ate lunch at DJ's Bagel Café.

FRIDAY, JANUARY 15, 2016—CAREFREE AND GOLF

Penny picked up Harriet Weintraub and Jan Aver and drove to Carefree for the day. Jay Weintraub picked me up and we drove to Starfire Golf Course where we met Dan Murphy and played eighteen holes.

SATURDAY, JANUARY 16, 2016—TUCSON AND LUNCH

Penny and I left at 9:00 a.m. and drove to Tucson to celebrate Steve Klein's 72nd birthday with Steve's daughter Melissa and her husband, Matt Landau. We parked our car at Steve's apartment and we drove to Trail Dust Town located at 6541 E. Tanque Verde Road. The shopping mall was built for the abandoned set of an unfinished Glen Ford western movie that was left outside of the populated area of Tucson in the 1950s. This area is a historic outdoor shopping center and it houses some historic artifacts including a Museum of the Horse Soldier that chronicles the history of the U.S. mounted military service. We had not been to this part of Tucson. We ate lunch at the Dakota restaurant in the shopping center.

THURSDAY, JANUARY 21, 2016—GOLF AT SILVERADO

At 10:45 a.m. I went golfing at Silverado Golf Course with Jay Weintraub and Dan Murphy. Dan picked up Jay and then me and we drove to Silverado.

SATURDAY, JANUARY 23, 2016—COUSIN GERT VISIT

Around lunchtime, Penny and I visited my cousin Gert Phillips in Sun City. Gert insisted on treating us to lunch at Line Thai restaurant, one of her favorite restaurants. Gert is 101 years old and doing well except for her hearing.

SUNDAY, JANUARY 24, 2016—CAREFREE

At 12:15 p.m. I drove Harriet and Jay Weintraub to the Indian Art Fair in Carefree. Later in the day at 5:00 p.m. we met Jan and Rich Aver for dinner at Lo Lo's Chicken and Waffles in Scottsdale. I ate waffles and they all had the fried chicken and waffles.

MONDAY, JANUARY 25, 2016—BARRETT JACKSON

At 8:00 a.m. I left for the Barrett Jackson Auto Auction until 2:15 p.m. At 3:30 p.m. Penny and I made a trip to Costco to get her glasses fixed after I accidently stepped on them in the morning. At 4:30 p.m. we went to the Flower Child restaurant for dinner. I thought the food was delicious food but Penny didn't care for it.

TUESDAY, JANUARY 26, 2016—CASA GRANDE GOLF

In the morning, Jay Weintraub picked up Dan Murphy and me and we drove to Casa Grande to meet Mike Stricker to play golf at the Francisco Grande Golf Resort. Mike arranged for the tee time. It was a fun day. After golf we drove back to Scottsdale. In the evening we ate dinner at the condo.

WEDNESDAY, JANUARY 27, 2016—YOUNGSTOWN REUNION

From 4:30 to 6:30 p.m. Penny and I went to a "Hometown Reunion" of Youngstown people at the home of Marsha Burdman who lives at 4436 E. Camelback Road #37 in Phoenix. The Youngstown Jewish Federation sponsored the event. The Pazols gave our name to the Federation and we were put on the invitation list. Penny and I met interesting Youngstown people who I didn't know.

THURSDAY, JANUARY 28, 2016—BREA, CALIFORNIA TRIP

My cousin Norman and his wife Sheila were going to be in Los Angeles for a few days before traveling on a vacation to Hawaii so Penny and I decided this would be a good weekend to drive to Brea, California to see the Linda and Ted Jass. We would be able to stay with Ted and Linda Jass and see Norman and Sheila too. We left Scottsdale early in the morning and arrived in Brea by the afternoon.

FRIDAY, JANUARY 29, 2016—SHOPPING IN BREA

Ted and I spent time sitting on a bench on Birch Street in downtown Brea while Linda and Penny went shopping at Chico's and ate dinner at a nearby restaurant.

SATURDAY, JANUARY 30, 2016—DRIVE TO LOS ANGELES

After breakfast, Penny and I drove to Los Angeles and met cousin Norman and his wife Sheila for lunch at the Bergamot Café in Bergamot Station. Inside the café, you ordered from a menu board. They offered cold and warm sandwiches, salads and a variety of beverages. After lunch we went back to Steven Lockshin's apartment and unloaded our luggage. Norman, Sheila, Penny and I were staying in Steven and Allison's condo in Century City because they were away.

In the evening we drove to Soritas restaurant where we met Marilyn and Larry Levy, Ken, Lisa and Stella Josefsberg and Samantha, Jason and Sofia Deutsch. We were also celebrating Penny's Birthday at the restaurant and they had a special dessert for her after the meal.

Penny had a urinary tract infection and she had to get up during the night. One of those bathroom times during the night, Penny dropped a book on the top of her foot and it really hurt.

SUNDAY, JANUARY 31, 2016—NORMAN'S BIRTHDAY

In the morning, we went to Cedars-Sinai Urgent Care so Penny could be treated for her urinary infection. In the meantime, the top of her foot was really hurting. We celebrated Norman's upcoming birthday but I don't remember any other details. We were invited to stay overnight with Marilyn and Larry Levy.

MONDAY, FEBRUARY 1, 2016—DRIVE TO SCOTTSDALE

We got up and the Levy's made a terrific breakfast. We had a wonderful visit and Larry also showed us some of the wooden furniture he made. Penny and I drove back to Scottsdale from Los Angeles.

WEDNESDAY, FEBRUARY 3, 2016—LUNCH AND CONCERT

Jan and Rich joined us for lunch at the Angry Crab. For the cost of the lunch, we thought it wasn't worth it. Later in the day, I ordered a clock radio, Steven Lockshin's book *Get Wise To Your Advisor* and house slippers on Amazon.

We had an early dinner at the Village Tavern before our concert. At 7:30 p.m. Penny and I attended Scottsdale's ASU Kerr Institute Cultural Center located at 6110 N. Scottsdale Road for a concert featuring brilliant saxophonist and leading authority on Stan Getz, Greg Fishman along with his wife Judy Roberts on piano and vocals. Scott Black on bass and Pete Swan on drums joined Roberts and Fishman for the concert. Greg Fishman gave his endless insights into Getz's genius. Greg Fishman explored some of the great Kenny Barron-Stan Getz piano-sax duo material that Getz recorded on his final album, "People Time."

SATURDAY, FEBRUARY 6, 2016—*STAR WARS* MOVIE

Penny and I met Jeffrey Schesnol and the Avers at the AMC Theater in Desert Ridge and saw the latest *Star Wars* movie. Penny and I decided to try eating dinner at Red House Chinese restaurant on 90th Street. We thought it wasn't very good so we're not going back.

SUNDAY, FEBRUARY 7, 2016—TRAIL AND TILE SHOP

The weather was beautiful so Penny and I went for a walk at The Gateway Trailhead. We also went to The Tile Shop to look for tiles for our condo floor, took some samples and bought groceries at Sprouts.

TUESDAY, FEBRUARY 9, 2016—BELINKYS VISIT AZ

Ronna and her family flew to Phoenix on a non-stop United Airlines flight. Ronna and family left Chicago O'Hare at 4:08 p.m. and arrived in Phoenix Sky Harbor Airport at 7:10 p.m. After we picked them up at the airport, we drove back to our condo for dinner. That evening we celebrated Talia, Penny, Spencer and my birthday. Spencer and Talia slept overnight in our condo.

WEDNESDAY, FEBRUARY 10, 2016—RAILROAD PARK

After breakfast we hung around the condo. Around 12:00 noon we met Faith with Maddy and Tyler for lunch at Sweet Tomatoes. After lunch we drove to the McCormick Stillman Railroad Park where we took a train ride around the park and the children played. After the train park we went back to our condo and went in our pool with the Beall and Belinky children for a good time.

THURSDAY, FEBRUARY 11, 2016—NATIVE TRAILS

At 10:00 a.m. Chicago Time, I had a phone call for the recording of the IHA *gia* Awards voice-over narration at the WG audio studio. The recording lasted about one-hour. At noon we drove to the Scottsdale Civic Center Mall to see the Native Trails show. We took a selfie while watching the performance. After the show, we headed back to our condo for more pool time with grandpa. Meanwhile, Ronna and Ted went to see Cindy Gan and had dinner with Faith and Matt Beall at the Barrio Queen in Gilbert.

FRIDAY, FEBRUARY 12, 2016—PINNACLE PEAK AND HOLE

It's President's Weekend and Ronna and family drove to Pinnacle Peak to hike to the top and I hiked with them. After the hike we ate lunch at Chelsea's Kitchen in Phoenix. After lunch we hiked to the top of Hole in the Rock and took lots of photos at the top.

SATURDAY, FEBRUARY 13, 2016—FAREWELL BREAKFAST

We met Faith, and Maddy at New York Bagel N Bialy for breakfast before Ronna and her family flew back to Chicago from Phoenix. We got together with Dan and Annie Murphy, Jay and Harriet Weintraub and us for dinner.

SUNDAY, FEBRUARY 14, 2016—COUSINS AND DINNER

Penny and I drove to Sun City to see cousin Gert Phillips. Cousins Hal and Joyce Spritzer were visiting Hal's mother so we had a very nice mini-reunion. We had lunch at JB's restaurant and took a selfie photo.

In the evening, we ate dinner at Basil and Garlic with Chicago friends Linda and Jerry Bernstein, Alan and Ellen Magit, Jay and Harriet Weintraub, Jan and Rich Aver and Penny and me. After dinner we went to Deedee and Dan Flores home where the girls looked at Deedee's jewelry and the men talked.

TUESDAY, FEBRUARY 16, 2016—TSA CLEARANCE

Penny and I schlepped to Tempe and enrolled in TSA security. Penny had some difficulty with her fingerprints so it took a few months for her application to get approved. For dinner, we went to Humble Pie on Scottsdale Road.

THURSDAY, FEBRUARY 18, 2016—GOLF AT SILVERADO

Jay Weintraub, Dan Murphy, Larry Hughes and me played golf at Silverado Golf Club and we took a group photo after our game. Jay and I were wearing the western hats we bought in Carefree. In the meantime, Penny, Jan Aver and Harriet Weintraub went to lunch at the VU Bistro that overlooked Fountain Hills.

In the evening, we had dinner at The Thumb restaurant with Rich and Jan Aver, Susan, Jeffrey and Jacqui Schesnol and Penny and me.

FRIDAY, FEBRUARY 19, 2016—MUSEUM OF THE WEST

Penny and I went to Scottsdale's Museum of the West to see the Lewis and Clark Expedition. We had lunch at Cowboy Ciao and ordered their famous salad.

SATURDAY, FEBRUARY 20, 2016—THE BARLEENS

Cousin Corky Weily and Natalie Kane invited Penny and me to join them at the Arizona Opry to see the Barleen's rock n roll show in Apache Junction. Their friends were supposed to go but had to cancel at the last minutes so they asked us to go with their friend's tickets. In all the years Penny and I have been visiting Arizona, we had never heard of the Barleens or their show. Corky picked us up in the late afternoon and drove us to Apache Junction located in the middle of nowhere. The doors opened at 5:00 p.m. for the 7:30 p.m. show. The theater building seats at least seven hundred people including the dinner and a show. Dessert was on the table before the meal was served. The rock n roll show was very entertaining and it will be a place to bring our friends in the future. The Barleens family built a theater building, own, star-in and run the entire event.

SUNDAY, FEBRUARY 21, 2016—TEMPLERS AND CAREFREE

In the afternoon, Penny and I met Jackie and Stu Templer in Carefree at a free big band concert at the Sanderson Lincoln Pavilion. After the concert we had dinner at the Pita Jungle at North Tatum Road in Desert Ridge.

MONDAY, FEBRUARY 22, 2016—NEW CONDO TILE FLOOR

Alan and Marilyn Appelbaum arrived in Phoenix on a non-stop American Airlines flight. They left Chicago O'Hare at 9:35 a.m. and arrived at 12:30 p.m. in Terminal 4 at Sky Harbor Airport. Penny and I picked them up and we ate lunch at Goldman's Deli. After lunch, we drove the Appelbaums to pick up their rental car at the Scottsdale Doubletree Resort on Scottsdale Road. In the meantime, Impressions of Arizona started to remove carpet in our dining area and began installing our new tile flooring.

In the evening we took the Appelbaums to Joyful Chinese Cuisine to have dinner. After dinner we drove to Yogurtology for frozen yogurt.

WEDNESDAY, FEBRUARY 24, 2016—TILE AND CONCERT

Penny and I had dinner at Paradise Café in Desert Ridge. At 7:00 p.m. we went to the Musical Instrument Museum located at 4725 E. Mayo Boulevard to see Kurt Elling's Passion World Concert. We sat in the 4th row center. The concert was very entertaining. Our new title floor was completed by Impressions of Arizona and Gary Hyndowitz, owner.

THURSDAY, FEBRUARY 25, 2016—DAVID WRIGHT HOUSE

We had a very interesting day with Alan and Marilyn Appelbaum as we took a tour of the David and Gladys Wright house in a street off of Camelback Road in Phoenix. We entered the 6.1-acre property through a fence in the church parking lot next door. In the evening, we had a going-away party at our condo for Jay and Harriet Weintraub who were about to drive back to Northbrook.

SATURDAY, FEBRUARY 27, 2016—FLY TO CHICAGO

Penny drove me to the Phoenix Sky Harbor Airport for my departure to Chicago O'Hare on a non-stop United Airlines flight. I left Phoenix at 12:04 p.m. and arrived in Chicago at 4:26 p.m. Uri picked me up from the airport and drove me to Northbrook. No dinner plans this evening.

SUNDAY, FEBRUARY 28, 2016—RONNA AND FAMILY DINNER

In the afternoon and evening, I went to Ronna and Ted's for dinner and we watched the Academy Awards.

MONDAY, FEBRUARY 29, 2016—VOTED & ARNIE

At 9:00 a.m. I went for early voting in the primary at Northbrook Village Hall. At 10:30 a.m. I had an appointment with accountant David Friedman in Palatine to hand over 2015 income tax documents. At 12:15 p.m. I had lunch with Arnie Grauer at Panera Bread and the evening was open.

TUESDAY, MARCH 1, 2016—TEST DROVE TWO CARS

I went looking for cars all day. I test drove a 2016 Kia Optima, a 2016 Toyota Camry both at Grossingers in Skokie and a 2016 Chevrolet at Jennings Chevrolet. The Malibu was superior to the other two cars I had driven.

I was invited for dinner with Bennett, Marni, Danny and Brooke.

WEDNESDAY, MARCH 2, 2016—PROGRAM REVIEW

After breakfast, I took a Metra train into Chicago and a bus to my office. At 10:00 a.m. a successful program review of modules and slides was held at the Williams/Gerard office. At 3:00 p.m. I got a haircut with Otto Bodner at the Hyatt

Regency Chicago. While I was in Chicago at my program review, Penny ate breakfast in Old Scottsdale with Alan and Marilyn Appelbaum at the Breakfast Club on Scottsdale Road.

THURSDAY, MARCH 3—BENNETT AND I DROVE A CAR

Nothing was happening during the day so I asked Bennett to test drive a 2016 Chevrolet Malibu at Bill Stacek Chevrolet in Wheeling. Bennett agreed that the Malibu was a great car. After school and in the evening, I was invited for dinner with Bennett, Marni, Danny and Brooke.

FRIDAY, MARCH 4, 2016—BREAKFAST WITH RONNA
SATURDAY, MARCH 5, 2016—IHA *GIA* AWARDS
SUNDAY, MARCH 6, 2016—SPENCER'S BIRTHDAY PARTY

In the afternoon and evening, I spent Spencer's 5th birthday party at Buffalo Grove Gymnastics.

MONDAY, MARCH 7, 2016—TRIP TO PHOENIX

Uri picked me up at 9:15 a.m. and we arrived at the O'Hare Airport a little after 9:45 a.m. for my non-stop United Airlines flight to Phoenix Sky Harbor Airport. The plane departed Chicago O'Hare Airport at 12:29 p.m. and arrived in Phoenix at 3:24 p.m. Penny picked me up at the airport.

TUESDAY, MARCH 8, 2016—LINDA FLIES TO PHOENIX

In the morning, Linda flew to Phoenix and we picked her up at Sky Harbor Airport. At 1:05 pm. I picked up Alan Appelbaum and drove to Sloan Park for a spring training game between the Chicago Cubs and the Los Angeles Dodgers. We sat in section 109, row 19, seats 12 & 13.

WEDNESDAY, MARCH 9, 2016—SPRING TRAINING CLEVELAND INDIANS VS. CHICAGO CUBS

At 1:05 p.m. Linda and I drove to Sloan Park to see the Cleveland Indians play the Chicago Cubs in a spring training game. While seated I said to Linda, "wouldn't it be something if the Cubs played the Indians in the World Series?" We both said no, it won't happened. The Cubs lost the spring training game and the score was the Indians 5 and the Cubs 3. It is hard to believe but the Cubs did play the Indians in the World Series and the Cubs won the World Series in seven games.

THURSDAY, MARCH 10, 2016—APPELBAUMS LEAVE

Alan & Marilyn left Phoenix for Chicago. Penny, Linda and I went to the Scottsdale Museum of the West to see a lecture by Dolan Ellis the official Arizona State Balladeer. In the evening, we went to the Desert Botanical Garden to see the Sonoran Lights display.

FRIDAY, MARCH 11—INDIANS VS. ROCKIES

After breakfast, Linda and I had a spring training game at Salt River Field at Talking Stick where we saw the Cleveland Indians play the Colorado Rockies. For dinner, we met cousin Corky Weily and Natalie Kane at Wally's American Pub'n Grille in Scottsdale.

SATURDAY, MARCH 12, 2016—CUBS VS. WHITE SOX

At 1:05 pm. Rich Aver, Jeffrey Schesnol, Linda and I saw the Cubs play the White Sox at Sloan Park. Meanwhile, Jan picked up Penny and Ann Dyer and went to resale shops.

SUNDAY, MARCH 13—EGGSTACY AND FOUNTAIN HILLS

We went to Eggstacy for breakfast and I wasn't too happy about waiting ten to fifteen minutes for a table. After breakfast, Linda, Penny and I drove to Fountain Hills for the Thunderbird Artists Fine Art & Wine Affair. We bought a Chip N Dip handmade ceramic bowl for salsa and guacamole. For dinner we went to Z'Tejas.

MONDAY, MARCH 14, 2016—LINDA FLIES TO CLEVELAND

I took Linda to Sky Harbor Airport for her flight to Cleveland. There was a breach of security at the airport and lots of traffic.

WEDNESDAY, MARCH 16, 2016—BIRTHDAY DINNER

I worked all morning on my computer catching up on bills. We went to Costco and bought a new Shark steamer. We also went looking for shoelaces at two shoe repair shops. We both took a short nap and at 5:00 p.m. went to dinner at Scottsdale's Culinary Dropout located on Camelback Road and had one of the best rainbow trout dinners I have ever eaten.

FRIDAY, MARCH 18, 2016—HIGH TEA AND BASKIN ROBBINS

Penny went to High Tea at the English Rose Tea Room in Carefree. After high tea, we also went to Baskin Robbins to get some ice cream for two pies Penny made for my birthday celebration the next day. In the evening, we went to the Arizona Jewish Historical Society building to hear Larry Bell, the director speak. His talk was part of the Or Adam Friday evening service.

SATURDAY, MARCH 19, 2016—75TH BIRTHDAY

We cleaned the condo for my birthday celebration. The Avers, Schesnols and Spencers went to Flo's Chinese restaurant for Happy Hour. After Flo's we all came back to our condo for ice cream pie.

SUNDAY, MARCH 20—SUNDAY A'FAIR AND BETYS SAAR

Penny and I spent a full day by first having breakfast at U.S. Egg in Scottsdale. Our server was from New Lennox, Illinois and I took a photo of her. After breakfast we drove to the Scottsdale Civic Mall to see the entertainment at Sunday A'Fair. Since we were close to the Scottsdale Museum of Contemporary Art, we decided to see the Betys Saar "Bridge of Memory" Exhibit. This exhibit was amazing and we were so happy to have seen it. As part of the display, there was a film interviewing Betys created art from found objects and her collection was outstanding. Her art was very interesting and quite extensive.

MONDAY, MARCH 21, 2016—CHOLLA WALK AND MOVIE

In the morning, Penny and I walked down Cholla for thirty minutes but at 9:30, it was too hot. For lunch we met Jeff and Michaele Salmon for lunch at Noci restaurant, one of their favorite lunch places. After lunch we went to the Harkins and saw the movie, *My Name Is Doris*, featuring Sally Field.

TUESDAY, MARCH 22, 2016—MOVIE CLASS AND POOL

Penny and I went to the last movie group discussion was about the film *My Name is Doris* at the Mustang Library, then after lunch, we went to condo pool for one and one-half hours. Penny made cauliflower pizza for dinner. At 6:45 p.m. we walked to Cholla to see the sunset.

WEDNESDAY, MARCH 23, 2016—ANASAZI STONE COMPANY

I overdid it by going to Anasazi Stone Company located at 7486 E. Adobe Drive in Scottsdale and buying two fifty lb. bags of river rocks. A man loaded the bags of stones to the car trunk and we drove back to the condo. I schlepped the heavy stones from the car and put them in the rock garden in front of our condo. I was so tired I took a nap and afterwards we met the Gimples for dinner at Jalapeno restaurant on North Scottsdale Road.

FRIDAY, MARCH 25, 2016—FLEA MARKET AND BELTS

I drove the Avers and us to the Mesa Flea Market where Rich and I bought Perfect belts from Grizelda Celaya and we took a photo with her. In the evening, the four of us ate a Chinese dinner at Nee House restaurant located a few doors down from Eden's Grill in Phoenix. After Chinese food we went to Yogurtology.

SATURDAY, MARCH 26, 2016—DRIVE TO PINE, AZ

I picked up Jan and Rich and we drove to Pine to see Julie LaMagna and Ray Stephens, who moved there. We had lunch at the Pine Deli, and then we visited with Julie and Ray. Penny got a disturbing email from Jill Cole saying her husband Jeffrey had a brain bleed and was recovering. We drove back to Scottsdale later in the day.

SUNDAY, MARCH 27, 2016—INGO'S AND HUNT'S TOMB

I made eggs and sausage for breakfast and decided to go to Encanto Park but it was too crowded. Penny and I had lunch at Ingo's (the round restaurant) on 40th Street and Campbell. After lunch we went for a short hike up some stone steps to Hunt's Tomb that sits on top of a hill and is shaped in a triangle with a metal fence around it. In 1912, George Hunt was the first governor of Arizona when it officially became the 48th state. From the tomb's site, you could look down on several of the Papago Park ponds the sandstone rock formations near the Phoenix Zoo and parking lots. In 2004, the marker was relocated at this location.

TUESDAY, MARCH 29, 2016—BASIL AND GARLIC

Penny and I drove to Michaels for a picture frame. For dinner, we celebrated Rich Aver's birthday at Basil and Garlic with Dan and Annie Murphy. The Rags Allen Trio performed on the patio that evening.

WEDNESDAY, MARCH 30, 2016—TOM THUMB HIKE

Penny and I decided to try a hike at Tom Thumb Trailhead in North Scottsdale. It took us awhile to drive there because it is located at the northern boundary of Scottsdale. I put on my GoPro to record part of our hike. We started out walking on the rough Tom's Thumb Trail with lots of rocks in the path and we turned back after ten minutes. The smoother trail was the Marcus Landslide Interpretive Trail that was much easier to walk. Afterwards, I had an appointment at the Apple Store and Penny bought white jeans at the Gap.

THURSDAY, MARCH 31, 2016—SALUT KITCHEN BAR

Penny and I ate a late lunch at Tempe's Salut Kitchen Bar where we ate our usual sampler plate of a capese salad, hummus nachos, quinoa fritters, mac and cheese and the salut fries. We seem to order the same food every time we go to this restaurant. Yummy! Jeff and Michaele Salmon came to see our condo and gave us a western metal candleholder.

SATURDAY, APRIL 2, 2016—PRESCOTT TRIP WITH THE AVERS

After breakfast I picked up Jan and Rich and we drove to Prescott, Arizona. We arrived around 11:30 a.m., parked the car and stopped at the Old Firehouse Plaza to look around. The plaza sign in front said "Prescott's Hot Spot for shopping and dining with a bakery, boutiques, shops, salons and restaurants."

LUNCH AT EL GATO AZUL RESTAURANT

Jan had made a 12:15 p.m. lunch reservation at the El Gato Azul restaurant. Outside of the restaurant, we saw El Gato Azul's Little Free Library box. As we were walking into the restaurant, a server watering plants by the entrance. The weather was a little cooler so we were each wore a light jacket except Rich who was wearing a long-sleeve shirt and I wore my western hat. The food was delicious and our server took several photos of our table. After lunch we walked by a small creek next to the restaurant and then drove to Van Gogh's Ear and Art Gallery. This eclectic store was amazing because it had all kinds of hand-made pottery, glass works, Cosanti bells, homemade colorful shoes and artistic lamps. While the girls were shopping and going through the store, Rich and I wondered across the street to in front of the Prescott Courthouse Square to attend a Hero's Honor Rally that supported U.S. Military Service Organizations and a fund-raising goal of $5,000. We sat on a bench listening to a band play. The keyboard player was wearing a t-shirt that said on the back "Home of the Free Because of the Brave." After listening to the band for a while, Rich and I walked back to Van Gogh's Ear and met the girls.

Afterwards we all walked up and down Montezuma Street and saw many bikers at the corner of Montezuma Street and W. Gurley Street. On the way home from Prescott, we stopped at the Rock Springs Pie Company to buy pie for dessert.

SUNDAY, APRIL 3, 2016—WINDSOR SQUARE TOUR

Penny and I had a great day today because we went on the historic Windsor Square Home and Garden Tour. Windsor Square is located off of Central and Camelback Road in Phoenix. We saw ten home and gardens. After the tour, we had dinner at The Parlor restaurant located at 1916 E. Camelback Road, close to the Windsor Square neighborhood. After we got back from dinner, I started to create a slide show of the day.

THURSDAY, APRIL 7, 2016—BARTLETT LAKE

I hired a fishing guide, Derrick Franks, to go fishing on Bartlett Lake. We met Derreck at the gas station at the corner of Darlington and Cave Creek highway in Carefree where we purchased a daily pass to get past the ranger station at the entrance to the lake. Dan Murphy joined me and he asked his former neighbor in Winfield, Alan Rossell, to also join the group. Our guide supplied us with all of the gear. We were all using the same light blue shallow running crank bait lure. I caught the most bass, a total of six, losing the first bass that jumped off the lure. Dan and Alan also caught about four bass each. Dan caught the largest bass of the day. I brought my GoPro with me on the boat and took some video. We saw a bald eagle on top of a hill. After fishing we ate dinner at Coconuts Fish Café.

FRIDAY, APRIL 8, 2016—ANDREOLI'S AND THE PARLOR

Penny bought some clothes at Fountain Fashions. Rich and I had lunch at Andreoli's and I had an eggplant Parmesan sandwich. Jan, Rich and the Spencers had dinner at The Parlor on E. Camelback Road in Phoenix. After dinner we drove to the Phoenix Theater to see the play, *All Night Strut!*

SATURDAY, APRIL 9, 2016—CUBS VS. DIAMONDBACKS

Dan Murphy drove to our condo and I picked up Jeffrey and Susan Schesnol at the Arizona Jewish Historical Society parking lot. We drove to Chase Field for the 5:10 p.m. start of the regular baseball season with the Arizona Diamondbacks playing the Chicago Cubs. I used Park Whiz and paid $12.00 for parking directly across from the ballpark. Outside the ballpark and before the game, there was a salsa band playing and dancers in native Mexican costumers were performing to the music. A D-Backs cereal bowl was given away when you entered the Chase Field.

We sat in section 130, row 30 and seats 9, 10, 11 & 12. A local high school band played the national anthem. Who would have predicted us watching the season beginning with the Chicago Cubs ending up winning the October 2016 World Series against the Cleveland Indians in game seven?

In the meantime, Jan Aver picked up Penny at noon and drove to the Front Porch Pickens at Glendale's University of Phoenix Stadium, home of the Arizona Cardinals football team. Penny bought a heart for Harriet and a large yard art piece of a large sunflower on a stand for $50.00. The Strickers brought back the sunflower part and several days later, I sent the tall metal piece of the yard art packed by the UPS store back to Northbrook.

MONDAY, APRIL 11, 2016—PAZOL AND GIMPLE DINNER

After breakfast, Penny and I went to Ginny's Laundromat to wash rugs and we sat outside while the rugs were being washed. At 5:30 p.m. Penny and I met Jim and Bobby Pazol and Bonny and Ron Gimple at Nee House several stores down from Eden's Grill on Tatum and Thunderbird for a terrific Chinese dinner. It's always fun to go out with the Youngstown couples.

WEDNESDAY, APRIL 13, 2016—TRIP TO TUCSON

After breakfast, Penny and I drove to Tucson to see Steve Klein. We arrived at his apartment around 11:30 a.m. and parked our car. For lunch, Steve drove us to Relish Kitchen & Wine Bar located at 4660 E. Camp Lowell Drive. After lunch we drove Steve back to his apartment and visited for a while. And then, we went to visit Mike and Fran Stricker at 1540 E. Ram Canyon Drive in Oro Valley. We had a very nice visit with the Strickers. Before leaving Tucson, we stopped to fill up our rental car with gas at Circle K because gas is always less expensive in Tucson. When we returned from Tucson, we met Jeffrey and Susan for dinner at the Habit Burger Grill located at 16495 N. Scottsdale Road at The Promenade.

THURSDAY, APRIL 14, 2016—ORANGE TREE GOLF

Dan Murphy, Glen Kanenwisher, Alan Rosell and me went golfing at Orange Tree Golf Club. After golf we packed for our trip back to Northbrook.

FRIDAY, APRIL 15, 2016—PENNY'S HAIRCUT AND CHINESE

I went to the UPS Store and sent back four boxes to Northbrook. Penny and

Alan, along with Dan and Annie Murphy, Rich and Jan Aver had a goodbye dinner for us at George & Sons Asian Cuisine before our flight back to Chicago.

SATURDAY, APRIL 16, 2016—BROWN'S RANCH WALK

Before heading back to Northbrook in a few days, Penny and I decided to have breakfast at Soul Café and went on a short eighteen-minute walk at The Gateway Trailhead off of Bell Road to get our fill of the blooming desert. After The Gateway Trailhead walk, we drove to Brown's Ranch Trailhead for another eighteen-minute walk. Brown's Ranch Trailhead was flat and an easy walk.

SUNDAY, APRIL 17, 2016—HISTORIC TEMPE

After breakfast, at US Egg, we saw our favorite US Egg sign guy flipping his US Egg sign on Shea Blvd. and I had to stop and take photos and a video of him. We also took a drive to the Borden Homes Historic District in Tempe to look around. Bright and beautifully colored mosaics dot the entire neighborhood and of course I took pictures of them for my "show." We also drove by the old Borden Factory in historic Creamery Village. The building was being rehabbed.

We went to another historic neighborhood nearby Borden Homes; Tomlinson Estates Historic District. Later in the day, we stopped by Carl Hayden's home that is now a defunct Monti's restaurant. Across the street from the Hayden home is the old Tempe grainery scheduled to be torn down in the future for the building of a high rise. Penny and I decided to check out the Xeriscape Garden. The ecological park is located at 8111 E. McDonald Drive in Scottsdale. We walked around this beautiful park and was had no idea it was here. It had lots of desert foliage, succulents and a good example of limited water usage for lush landscaping. And it was a nice place to take a walk. It is next to the Chaparral Dog Park.

MONDAY, APRIL 18, 2016—MIM FOR VIOLINS

Penny and I decided to go to the Musical Instrument Museum to see the *Stradivarius Exhibit, Origins and Legacy of the Greatest Violin Maker*. We had lunch at Café Allegro inside the museum and a farewell dinner at the Pita Jungle on Shea.

TUESDAY, APRIL 19, 2016—FLIGHT TO CHICAGO

Penny and I drove to Phoenix Sky Harbor Airport around 11:30 a.m. for our departure to Chicago O'Hare Airport. We dropped off our luggage at curb side at Terminal 2 and I took our rental car to the Transportation Center and returned to the terminal in the bus. Before our flight, we ate lunch at Paradise Cafe inside the airport. Our non-stop United Airlines flight left Phoenix at 2:15 p.m. and we arrived at Chicago O'Hare at 7:37 p.m. Uri picked us up at the airport.

THURSDAY, APRIL 21, 2016—PASSOVER DINNER

I went to Binny's to buy Passover wine and also bought gefilte fish at Max's Deli for our Passover dinner at our home. The entire family was at our seder.

FRIDAY AUGUST 12, 2016—KANKAKEE TRIP AND WRIGHT

After breakfast, Penny and I left Northbrook headed to Kankakee for the 1:00 p.m. tour the B. Harley Bradley House, a home designed by Frank Lloyd Wright. This home was the first prairie-style house in Kankakee, Illinois. Outside of the tour entrance were two wooden benches with two different prairie designs. There was a large porte-cochere on the west side of the house leading to a carriage house in back. There was a plaque outside that read in part, "Residence for B. Harley Bradley, Frank Lloyd Wright, Architect, circa 1900." According to the sign, the house was restored in 1990. The cost of our tour was $30.00. Once inside the entrance we saw a poster of historical places in Kankakee County. We were not allowed to take photos of inside the house.

Next to the Bradley House was another Frank Lloyd Wright designed home. I took a photo of the side of that house. After the tour we checked into Riverview Bed & Breakfast located at 641 S. Chicago Avenue and was greeted by the owner and innkeeper, Nita Kloska. We stayed in The Library Room and the total cost was $139.85 for one night. The bedroom was spacious with a queen-size bed and a red circular sofa. Two wicker chairs were placed on an angle in front of a stain-glass picture window. A small dresser with a lamp and plant was placed between the two chairs. The small bathroom was adequate. Outside of our bathroom was a breakfront that stored towels and washcloths.

Nita told us to eat dinner at Rigos Place restaurant at 164 N. Schuyler Avenue in Kankakee. I immediately called for a 6:00 p.m. dinner reservation and was lucky a table was open at the last minute. The restaurant is known for its culinary excellence and internationally inspired dishes. The restaurant dining area was huge with a wonderful atmosphere, a fabulous staff and incredible food, a real surprise to find in Kankakee. I can't remember what we ordered but the food was delicious and we were happy Nita recommended it.

SATURDAY AUGUST 13—FARNSWORTH HOUSE

Penny and I got us early and came downstairs to find Nita cooking our breakfast and Penny started talking to her. The kitchen was large and well organized. A small round table with four chairs was in one corner and an island with a sink and counter was in the middle of the kitchen with two stools underneath. There was a backyard view from the kitchen with an iron table and chairs on a deck. Our breakfast was set up in the dining room. Sunflowers in a vase sat on top of a wooden cabinet in front of a window. The walls were painted red and a large poster of Maurice Chevalier was on one wall. Festive place mats with cloth napkins inside a ring were placed on the table. A croissant sandwich with roasted potatoes was served along with coffee. Nita was a perfect innkeeper and hostess. The living room had a sofa and two chairs and a breakfront and Tiffany lamp on an end table next to the two chairs and sofa. A grand piano was by a large picture window. There was also a large staircase leading upstairs.

After breakfast we loaded our car and drove to Plano, Illinois for a 12:00 p.m. tour of the famous Farnsworth House, a Ludwig Mies Van der Rohe designed and constructed home. The house was constructed between 1945 and 1951 and built in a rural setting fifty-five miles from downtown Chicago on a sixty-acre estate site next to the Fox River and south of Plano. The house is made of steel and glass and was commissioned by Dr. Edith Farnsworth, a prominent Chicago nephrologist, as a place to enjoy her hobbies, nature and a location to get away on weekends. A plaque in front of the house read "Historic Site of the National Trust for Historic Preservation." The house was designated a National Historic Landmark in 2006 after being listed in the National Register of Historic Places in 2004. The house is built on stilts and over the years has had water damage from the flooding of the Fox River.

We parked our car and signed-in for our tour in a small building next to the parking lot. After paying $50.00 for the tour, we walked one-half mile to the house on a clear and well-marked path. Along the way, there was a creek leading to the house and about eight visitors walking in front of us. Once we got there, Pam Williams, a docent, greeted us in a clearing in front of the house. She also spoke to us from the top of the steps leading into the house and gave an introduction of what we were about to see. The steps leading to the home are made of travertine both inside and outside of the house. I took many photos and put together a slide show of the house. After our tour, we drove back to Northbrook. This mini-trip was a terrific one.

TUESDAY, DECEMBER 13, 2016—SCOTTSDALE TRIP

Uri picked up Penny and me at 6:30 a.m. and we arrived at Chicago O'Hare Airport a little after 7:00. Our non-stop United Airlines non-stop flight to Phoenix Sky Harbor Airport departed on time at 12:40 p.m. and we arrived in Phoenix at 3:39 p.m. Rich and Jan Aver picked up Penny and me from the Sky Harbor Airport and dropped us at our apartment where we brought in our three suitcases and carry-ons. Around 3:30 p.m. Jan drove us to Spencer's Appliances and we bought an Amana refrigerator. At 4:30 p.m. the two boxes of pears I ordered from Harry and David arrived at our door. At 6:00 p.m. Rich picked up Penny and me and we drove to Goldman's Deli for dinner.

WEDNESDAY, DECEMBER 14, 2016—RENTAL CAR

Today the *Arizona Republic* started delivery. At 10:15 a.m. Jan picked us up and drove us to pick up our unlimited miles Avis car rental [one-hundred thirteen-day rental] located at 7125 E. Shea Blvd. Suite 101 in Scottsdale. Chris Frieh, the owner of the Avis franchise rented us a 2017 Toyota Camry LE. After picking up the rental car, we went to Fry's to buy basic groceries. After Fry's I drove to Discount Tires to get the tires pumped up on our dolly. We started cleaning the condo, and after a while I picked up six cardboard boxes at the Aver, we shipped from Northbrook.

THURSDAY, DECEMBER 15, 2016—MURPHY DINNER

After breakfast, we continued cleaning the condo. In the afternoon, Penny and I went to Sprouts grocery shopping. At 6:00 p.m. we picked up Rich and Jan and ate dinner at Hot Ramen and Cold Saki off of Raintree where we met Dan and Annie Murphy. This restaurant was not good.

FRIDAY, DECEMBER 16, 2016—EFFICIENCY MECHANICAL

From 8:00 to 10:00 a.m. Efficiency Mechanical was at the condo to inspect our heat pump and air conditioning unit.

SATURDAY, DECEMBER 17, 2016—DINNER AND THEATER

During the day, Penny and I continued to clean the condo. At 5:00 p.m. we I picked up Jan and Rich Aver and drove to Fez restaurant for a 5:30 p.m. dinner reservation. At 7:30 p.m. we saw *Billy Elliott*, the musical at the Phoenix Theater. It was great show and extremely entertaining. The Avers knew the parents of one of the boy cast members.

SUNDAY, DECEMBER 18, 2016—CHIMNEY CLEANING

After breakfast and at 10:15 a.m., Justin from Arizona Chimney & Duct Cleaning came to our condo and cleaned our fireplace and chimney for $125.00.

MONDAY, DECEMBER 19, 2016—WEINTRAUBS ARRIVE

Harriet and Jay Weintraub arrived in Scottsdale and stayed with Jay's cousins, Barry & Nancy Slavin. At 10:00 a.m. one box of pears from Harry and David arrived at our condo. Around noon, I met some Phoenix area Central Michigan University alums at the Blue 32 Sports Grill located at 7000 E Mayo Blvd in Phoenix. The football game was CMU vs. Tulsa in the Miami Beach Bowl and started at 12:30 p.m. on ESPN. At 3:30 p.m. I picked up Rich Aver from Walgreens and drove him to his car at Rayco.

WEDNESDAY, DECEMBER 21, 2016—THE MURPHYS

At 9:30 a.m. I got gasoline for the rental car and at 11:40 a.m. we met Dan and Annie Murphy at their new house [Trilogy at Vistancia] in Peoria and had a quick tour. They live about thirty-five miles from Scottsdale in a brand-new development. Then we went to lunch at V's Taproom on the Trilogy golf course. At 6:40 pm we went to the Hallmark store on Via Linda to buy greeting cards.

THURSDAY, DECEMBER 22, 2016—ERRANDS AND GRANITE

Penny and I went to the Home Depot and Target. We also stopped at Ferguson for information about granite. I spoke to Rayla who recommended we call Chisel Granite and Marble. In the afternoon, Penny and I walked in the neighborhood for forty minutes.

FRIDAY, DECEMBER 23, 2016—AIR DUCT CLEANING

At 8:00 a.m. Jim from Efficiency Mechanical Air Duct Cleaning Service cleaned all of our air ducts and a dryer vent. Since we were Efficiency Mechanical's customer, we received a 10% discount on the Air Duct Cleaning,

SATURDAY, DECEMBER 24, 2016—POTATO LATKAS

Jan Aver and Penny made potato latkes for our Chanukah party.

SUNDAY, DECEMBER 25, 2016—WAFFLES AND CHINESE FOOD

I made waffles with caramelized bananas and turkey sausage for breakfast. For dinner, Jan was staying at the Bluhms so we ordered Chinese food from Joyful Chinese Cuisine with Jan, Rich, Jeffrey, Susan and Jacqui Schesnol and a friend of Jan with her friend.

MONDAY, DECEMBER 26, 2016—US EGG AND A MOVIE

Penny and I ate breakfast at US Egg on Shea Blvd. Harriet and Jay Weintraub arrived in Peoria and were staying with Dan & Annie Murphy. After breakfast we went shopping at Steinmart and Nordstrom where I bought some clothes. I had purchased a brand-new DVD copy of the musical *Singin In The Rain* at the Scottsdale Library *so* Penny and I watched the movie and the documentary that came with it.

TUESDAY, DECEMBER 27—FIREWOOD AND CHANUKAH

Harriet and Jay Weintraub are in Peoria and staying with Dan & Annie

Murphy. Penny and I drove to Berry Brothers and I paid $27.50 for firewood, then we stopped at Target on the way back to the condo. We had a Chanukah party at Becky Bluhm's house off of Indian Bend with Jay and Harriet, Dan and Annie Murphy, Jan and Rich Aver and Penny and Alan. Becky was in Chicago and Jan was dog sitting at Becky's house.

WEDNESDAY, DECEMBER 28, 2016—COZY CORNER

At 12:00 noon Penny, me, Jay, Harriet, Dan and Annie Murphy met Fran and Mike Stricker for lunch at the Cozy Corner Cafe in Mesa. Fran had a doctor's appointment so it was convenient location.

THURSDAY, DECEMBER 29, 2016—THEE PITTS AGAIN

After breakfast, Penny and I bought a $100.00 Fox restaurant gift certificate for Jan and Rich Aver for taking care of our condo while we're in Northbrook. At 4:45 p.m. I picked up Jan and Rich and we drove to Glendale to Thee Pitts Again BBQ restaurant for a 5:30 p.m. dinner reservation where we met Jay and Harriet, Dan and Annie Murphy.

FRIDAY, DECEMBER 30, 2016—GOLF AT LEGENDS

At 9:20 a.m. Jay Weintraub, Dan Murphy and I had a tee time at the Legend at Arrowhead Golf Club and we were through by 2:45 p.m. For dinner that evening, Penny and I went to Goldman's Deli.

SATURDAY, DECEMBER 31, 2016—GRANITE AND NEW YEAR'S

In the morning, Penny and I drove to The Stone Collection in Phoenix to look at granite for our new kitchen counters and Lisa Harrow helped us choose some samples. In the afternoon, I ordered two Spinato's take and bake pizzas for our New Year's party. I picked them up at 4:00 p.m. and put them in our refrigerator. The Avers picked up Penny and me at 7:30 p.m. for the New Year's Eve Party at the Schesnols. For the first time, I used the selfie stick Bennett had given me for Chanukah and took photos. Jacqui Schesnol's friend, Phil Voyce also attended.

SUNDAY, JANUARY 1, 2017—NEW YEAR'S DAY

Penny and I slept late and stayed in all day chilling out from the night before.

TUESDAY, JANUARY 3—A MOVIE AND LUNCH AT BLUE 32

At 9:45 a.m. Penny and I picked up Rich Aver and saw *Manchester By The Sea* at the Cine Capri Theater located at the 101 and E. Mayo Blvd. then we had lunch right by the theater at Blue 32 Sports Grill 7000 E Mayo Blvd Phoenix. After dropping off Rich, we drove to the Claim Jumper restaurant by I-17 and the 101 and bought two chocolate cakes, one for the Avers anniversary that night and the other we froze for a later time. At 7:00 p.m. Jan and Rich drove to our condo to celebrate their anniversary and eat some chocolate cake.

WEDNESDAY, JANUARY 4, 2017—MARGIE AND CONCERT

Today is Jan and & Rich Aver's 47th Anniversary. Margie Hayes came to our condo to help us choose granite for our new kitchen and bathroom. We also drove back to The Stone Collection in Phoenix to look for more granite with Margie. We found two pieces of granite that will work well in our condo. After looking for granite, we went to lunch at Chelsea's Kitchen on 40th Street just north of Camelback Road. On the way home we stopped at New York Bagel & Bialys. At

7:30 p.m. Penny and I saw Dennis Rowland, Diana Lee, Greg Warner and a jazz concert at the ASU Kerr Institute. We sat in section A, row 2, seats 5 & 6.

FRIDAY, JANUARY 6, 2017—EAGLE DESIGN SOLUTIONS

Penny and I were told Eagle Design Solutions located at 447 W. Watkins Road #5 in Phoenix, a wholesale distribution store, would sell discounted sinks to contractors but also to the public. They were very helpful and we found a Schock beige-color granite composite German-made kitchen sink and two-bathroom sinks but were not sure if we should buy them. They were loaded into our car and we took them back to our condo. After dropping off the sinks at our condo, we went grocery shopping at Sprouts.

SATURDAY, JANUARY 7, 2017—COUSIN GERT AND BELINKYS

At 11:15 a.m. Penny and I drove to Sun City to pay my 101-year-old Cousin Gert Phillips a visit and had lunch at Coco's Restaurant. We bought an apple pie there. After my cousin's visit, Penny went to Sprouts and got salmon and sweet potatoes for dinner with the Belinkys. Around 7:15 p.m. Herb and Linda Belinky arrived in Scottsdale. Penny had food for them.

SUNDAY, JANUARY 8, 2017—BELINKYS AND GOLDEN GLOBES

Herb and Linda Belinky stayed in our condo for the next few days. During the day, we watched the HBO documentary on Carrie Fisher and Debbie Reynolds. And in the evening, we watched the Golden Globe Awards.

TUESDAY, JANUARY 10—ANASAZI AND EDEN'S GRILL

Herb and Linda Belinky accompanied Penny and me to Anasazi Stone where we bought sand and black river rocks for the front of our condo door for $53.00. I used the dolly to bring the stones back to our condo. I made 6:15 p.m. dinner reservations at the Eden Grill with Herb and Lynda Belinky. Three of us had catfish dinners and Lynda had chicken kabobs.

WEDNESDAY, JANUARY 11—PINNACLE AND DINNER

After breakfast, we took Herb and Lynda to Pinnacle Peak Park and then drove to Fountain Hills. For dinner we ate at George and Son's Asian Restaurant.

THURSDAY, JANUARY 12, 2017—BELINKYS LEAVE

After breakfast, at 10:30 a.m. Herb and Linda Belinky left Scottsdale and drove back to Los Angeles.

FRIDAY, JANUARY 13, 2017—EAGLE DESIGN SINK

Aaron Aver was in Scottsdale so at 10:30 a.m. Penny and I ate breakfast at the Hash Kitchen where we met Jan and Rich and Aaron Aver. After breakfast, Penny and I went back to Eagle Design Solutions and bought the two-bathroom sinks and the new Schock kitchen sink for the wholesale price of $297.56. When we got home, we saw that the kitchen sink had a black mark on it so we decided to return it for another sink we had seen there. They were loaded the sinks into our car and we took them back to our condo. At 7:30 p.m. we attended the Or Adam Service Shabbat Service with speaker Gert Schuster, a holocaust survivor and comedienne. Gert was a real character and told many jokes.

SATURDAY, JANUARY 14, 2017—SUNNYSLOPE & KARL'S

After breakfast, Penny and I took a ride to the Sunnyslope area of Phoenix and went to Karl's Bakery where we bought some delicious desserts. I also went to Steinmart and bought some fishing shirts and a London Fog jacket. For dinner we ordered vegetable Pad Thai from Thai House located at 6949 E. Shea Blvd.

MONDAY, JANUARY 16, 2017—EAGLE DESIGN AND CONCERT

Today is Martin Luther King's birthday, a national holiday. Today is also Steve Klein's birthday and we called to wish him a happy birthday. Penny and I returned the Schock sink we purchased at Eagle Design Solutions and exchanged it for one that did not have a mark on the bottom. We also bought a stopper for the new kitchen sink. Afterwards, we went on a twenty-two-minute walk and then went shopping at Fry's.

At 7:00 p.m. Penny and I attended Ladysmith Black Mambazo at the Musical Instrument Museum in row M seats 2 and 3. Penny bought a Ladysmith Black Mambazo T-shirt.

WEDNESDAY, JANUARY 18, 2017—BARRETT JACKSON

I left the house at 7:30 a.m. so I could be at the parking lot by 8:00 a.m. for the Barrett Jackson Auto Auction-shuttle that took me to Westworld.

THURSDAY, JANUARY 19, 2017—HAIRCUT AND PLUMBER

In the morning, I got a haircut at Angelo's Hair Styling with Vito. After my haircut, Mark Booher from Master Plumbers came to our condo and gave us an estimate of the plumbing work that had to be done on our kitchen and bathroom. Penny put together oatmeal cookies and put them in the freezer. Later in the day, Penny and I saw the movie *Jackie* at the Harkins Cine-Capri at the 101 and Mayo.

FRIDAY, JANUARY 20, 2017—SALMONS LUNCH AND CORKY

Today is Alan Appelbaum, Remey Rubin and Ted Jass birthdays. At 12:15 p.m., we met Jeff and Michaele Salmon in the parking lot and went to lunch at Noci Café at the corner of Hayden and Mountain View. In the evening, we met cousin Corky Weily and Natalie Kane for dinner at the Village Tavern.

SATURDAY, JANUARY 21, 2017—SYMPHONY IN EVENING

We didn't do much during the day. Penny watched ice-skating on television. In the evening, we picked up Jan and Rich Aver and I drove into Phoenix to Ace Regency garage and parked the car. We walked across the street to Symphony Hall, sat in the balcony and listened to the Phoenix Symphony Orchestra play *A Night of Leonard Bernstein*. Suzy Ernst sang in the chorus and we ran into her husband Tim who was sitting in our same row.

MONDAY, JANUARY 23, 2017—ROBERTO AND TEMPLATE

After breakfast, Roberto from Chisel Marble & Granite, came to our condo to make a template for the cutting of the granite we chose at the Stone Collection in Phoenix. Using balsa wood strips, he measured and constructed templates for the kitchen countertops and for both bathrooms. Penny and I went to lunch at True Food at the Scottsdale Quarter, then went to Whole Foods and in the afternoon, we went to the Harkins Theater to see the movie *Hidden Figures*. The film was fantastic.

TUESDAY, JANUARY 24, 2017—CHISEL AND GRANITE

The granite we chose from The Stone Collection was delivered to Chisel

Marble & Granite so in the afternoon, we had an appointment at Chisel Marble & Granite to show us how the granite would be cut based on the templates Roberto made on Monday, January 23rd. Using a forklift, each piece of granite was pulled from storage and Penny and I were shown exactly how the granite would be cut by laying out the master templates on each piece of granite.

FRIDAY, JANUARY 27, 2017—GOLF AND CONCERT

Dan Murphy and I played golf at the Arizona Grand Resort and Golf Course. We made up the foursome with husband-and-wife Melissa and Tim Hitson from Grand Rapids, Michigan. After the game, we took a photo of the four of us. At 7:30 p.m. Penny and I went to see pianist and resident artist Ang Li we went to the Kerr Institute and sat in section A, row 2, seats 5 & 6.

SATURDAY, JANUARY 28, 2017—PHOENIX THEATER

After breakfast, Penny got ambitious and made Marni's turkey meatballs and froze them for the future. At 2:00 p.m. Penny and I went to a play at the Phoenix Theater and saw *Sherlock Holmes Hounds of the Baskerville* and met Susan and Jeffrey Schesnol there. After the show we went for dinner at Little Cleo's Seafood Legend. The restaurant gave Penny a special dessert in honor of her upcoming birthday. It was a piece of cheesecake with raspberries on top and whipped cream on top and on the two sides.

SUNDAY, JANUARY 29, 2017—A WALK AND SUNDAY A'FAIR

After breakfast, Penny and I walked the path behind our condo. From 2:00 to 4:00 p.m. Penny and I went to Sunday A'Fair at the Scottsdale Center for the Performing Arts where Jan Sandwich and Friends were performing. Nicole Pesce was on keyboards and Felix Saint was on the bass. Renee Patrick also performed. For dinner, Penny and I went to Basil and Garlic and had pizza.

MONDAY, JANUARY 30—MOVIE AND PENNY'S BIRTHDAY

In the morning, I ordered a Trinsic single handle Delta kitchen faucet with a pull-down handle with magic docking from Amazon for $339.99. We went to Harkin's Theater to see the film *Lion*. Today is also Talia's tenth birthday as well as Penny's birthday. In the afternoon, Penny and I celebrated her birthday with a Happy Hour at the Grand Blue restaurant. The restaurant served a special birthday chocolate gluten-free molten chocolate cake.

TUESDAY, JANUARY 31, 2017—SNOOZE AND FAUCETS

For breakfast, Penny and I went to Snooze in Kierland. I also ordered two Delta 551-SS-DST stainless bathroom faucets for the new bathroom granite tops for $536.00. We also stopped at Sur La Table and Loft for Penny to buy clothes.

WEDNESDAY, FEBRUARY 1, 2017—THE FIVE DIVAS

In the afternoon, we went to Lowes and bought two patio chairs for the condo. I bought online tickets to Modern Phoenix and the Willo Historic District house tour on February 12th. Before the show at the Kerr, Penny and had dinner at Wildflower restaurant. At 7:30 pm. we saw *The Five Divas* at the ASU Kerr Institute section E, row 10, seats 5 & 6. Camela Ramirez, Renee Patrick, Blaise Lantana, Sherry Roberson and Delphine Cortez were the divas. The show was very entertaining.

SATURDAY, FEBRUARY 4, 2017—TUCSON TRIP

After breakfast, Penny and I drove to Oro Valley to meet Fran and Mike at the Golden Goose Thrift Shop. I bought four-dozen used golf balls for $5.00 and Penny purchased earrings. Afterwards, Penny and I met Steve Klein and Melissa and Matt Landau for lunch at Truland Burgers & Greens. After lunch we drove to the Landau home. Before heading back to Scottsdale, I bought gas at Quiktrip.

SUNDAY, FEBRUARY 5, 2017—SUPER BOWL SUNDAY

Penny stopped at Home Goods for a few items, and then she opened her birthday presents at Jan and Rich Aver's condo. Rich and I stopped at Papa Murphy's to pick up a pizza for our mini–Super Bowl Party. Jeffrey Schesnol, Rich and I watched the Super Bowl in the afternoon and into the evening in the Aver's condo and we took a silly photo of the three of us; I had my hand over my mouth, Jeffrey put two hands over his ears and Rich put two hands over his eyes.

MONDAY, FEBRUARY 6, 2017—MAGITS AND THE BERNSTEINS

The Magits and Bernsteins arrived in Scottsdale. Penny and I had lunch at Wildflower. After lunch, we went to Sprouts for groceries. I also went to Home Depot to pick up some plastic drop cloths to put in our cabinets to protect the dust when our new countertops are being installed tomorrow morning. Mark Booher from Master Plumbers came to disconnect all of the plumbing underneath each sink so the granite installation could be installed. For dinner we went to Pita Jungle.

TUESDAY, FEBRUARY 7, 2017—GRANITE COUNTERTOPS

The installation of our new granite countertops took place today. A trailer with the cut granite pieces was backed into an open space in our condo's parking lot. Alejandro and Roberto from Chisel Marble & Granite unloaded the granite pieces and bought each piece to our condo for installation.

The guys first removed the old countertops and took them to their trailer. They placed plywood on top of the cabinets in the same shape as the template. After the plywood was installed, the new granite tops were installed on top of the plywood. The final payment of $2,708.65 was made for the granite countertops.

WEDNESDAY, FEBRUARY 8, 2017—PLUMBER INSTALLS

Mark Booher our plumber from Master Plumbers came to our condo and reattached all of the plumbing to the kitchen and in both bathrooms. Mark also installed new shut-off valves underneath the kitchen cabinets and under the guest and master bathroom sinks. He removed the garbage disposal and said we didn't have enough room to install it.

THURSDAY, FEBRUARY 9—DINNER AND DESSERT

Penny and I went to AJ's Fine Foods to buy sugar-free cookies for Alan Magit. I picked up Jan and Rich Aver and Penny and I met Jerry and Linda Bernstein and Alan and Ellen Magit for dinner at Jalapeno's Inferno located at 23587 N. Scottsdale Road. After dinner, everyone came back to our condo for dessert.

FRIDAY, FEBRUARY 10, 2017—GATEWAY TRAIL AND DINNER

It's President's Day Weekend. Penny and I went for a walk at The Gateway Trailhead just north of Bell Road in Scottsdale. After our walk, I got a pedicure with Pam at Pauline's Luxury Nails. We had dinner at Ajo Al's Mexican Café with

Jeff Stein and his friend Rich Mullen. Jeff was in Scottsdale looking around to possibly buy a place.

SATURDAY, FEBRUARY 11, 2017—BARLEENS LUNCH SHOW

At 10:00 a.m. I picked up Jan and Rich Aver and drove to Apache Junction at the Arizona Opry. We had a luncheon show reservation for the Barleens show. The lunch and show were from 11:15 a.m. to 3:45 p.m. Barleens AZ Opry is located at 2275 E. Old West Highway in Apache Junction. We met Dan and Annie Murphy, Alan and Ellen Magit and Jerry and Linda Bernsteins there. The Murphys, Spencers, Avers and Susan and Jeffry Schesnol sat at one table and the Magits and Bernsteins sat at another table close by. We sat in the center row, table 38, and seats 1-8. After the show we drove to a restaurant and sat outside at a table while Penny opened birthday presents from the Weintraubs and the Murphys.

SUNDAY, FEBRUARY 12, 2017—WILO TOUR AND CONCERT

In the morning, Penny and I picked up Jan Aver and we went on the Willo Historic District Home and Street Fair Tour. The tour was from 10:00 a.m. until 4:00 p.m. The Wilo district neighborhood is in between 3rd and 5th Avenues around 2400 north and 500 west. We saw ten homes built in the 1930s, 1940s and 1950s. At 7:30 p.m. Penny and I drove to the Scottsdale Center for the Performing Arts in the Virginia G. Piper Theater to see a concert with Branford Marsalis with Special Guest Kurt Elling. The cost of the concert was $104.00 and we sat in row G, seats 21 & 23.

WEDNESDAY, FEBRUARY 15—BIRNBAUMS IN ARIZONA

Sam and Gay Birnbaum along with their family were staying in a rental house in Fountain Hills. Penny and I went grocery shopping at Sprouts.

THURSDAY, FEBRUARY 16—RECORDING, FOUNTAIN HILLS, THEN FRIEND'S DINNER

After breakfast, I had a 10:00 a.m., Chicago Time, recording session for the 2017 IHA *gia* Awards voice-over narration at the WG audio studio. I was able to listen in on the phone to the session and interact with the recording session. After the recording session, we went grocery shopping at Safeway and Fry's.

Later in the day, we drove to Fountain Hills for the mini art fair where Penny bought earrings and a necklace at Jewelry with Pizzazz. In the evening, we picked up Jan and Rich Aver and met Susan and Jeffery Schesnol and Susie Flax and Jimmy Stavish at LaCucina Bistro & Wine Bar for dinner.

FRIDAY, FEBRUARY 17, 2017—MESA FLEA MARKET

We picked up Jan and Rich Aver and headed to the Mesa Flea Market off of Signal Butte Road. Before we got to the flea market, we stopped in Gilbert and ate outrageous and decadent marshmallow s'mores desserts at Fluff-it. Can you believe we ate marshmallow s'mores before lunch? At the flea market, Penny and I bought two walking sticks and a few kitchen items. After the flea market we had a late lunch sitting on the outdoors patio at Mesa's Macayo's Kitchen.

SUNDAY, FEBRUARY 19, 2017—THE BIRNBAUMS IN ARIZONA

Penny and I attended a BBQ with Sam and Gay Birnbaum and his family at their rental house in Fountain Hills. We had a great time and I took photos of Sam and his family. Bonny and Ron Gimple also attended.

MONDAY, FEBRUARY 20, 2017—JEWISH FILM FESTIVAL

At 7:00 p.m. Penny and I picked up Jan and Rich Aver and went to the Jewish Film Festival at the Shea 14 to see Phillip Roth's movie *Indignation*.

FRIDAY, FEBRUARY 24, 2017—TRIP TO BREA, CALIFORNIA

Today is Brooke's 9th birthday. Penny and I drove to Brea, California. On the way, we stopped at Flying J for gasoline and to use the restroom facilities. We ate lunch at TKB Bakery & Deli located at 44911 Golf Center Parkway in Indio, California. Penny ate a Cobb sandwich and I ate a turkey sandwich on sweet wheat & cranberry spice bread. We also bought two huge loaves of homemade bread. The lunch was delicious. We arrived at the Jass home in time for dinner at Alza Osteria with the entire Jass family.

SATURDAY, FEBRUARY 25, 2017—JANET EVANS COMPLEX

For breakfast, I drove to Starbucks and bought two coffees. Linda had bagels, so Penny and I ate them for breakfast. We drove to the Janet Evans Swim Complex to see Lexi swimming practice for the Special Olympics. After swimming, we went to a not very good craft show at This & That Arts & Craft Show where Penny bought a Jaffa discontinued lipstick. For lunch we went to Kimmie's Coffee Cup. After lunch, Penny bought masks at Albertson's and we went to Sprouts to buy cranberry almond toasties. For dinner, we ordered Chinese food at the Magic Wok and Ted and I went to pick it up.

SUNDAY, FEBRUARY 26, 2017—JUNK IN THE TRUNK

For breakfast, I drove to Starbucks for two coffees and Penny and I ate bagels. After breakfast Ted drove us to Pomona for the Junk in the Trunk Vintage Market. We paid the $16.00 entrance fee and bought a $7.00 ice tray. We took a photo in front of the Junk in the Trunk sign. For lunch we all ate grilled cheese sandwiches from a Greenz on Wheetz food truck. For dinner, I paid for Tony's Little Italy Pizza and in the late afternoon we watched the Academy Awards.

MONDAY, FEBRUARY 27, 2017—DRIVE TO SCOTTSDALE

For breakfast, I drove to Starbucks for two coffees and ate bagels that Linda had in her freezer. After breakfast, Penny and I headed back to Scottsdale. We stopped for lunch at TKB Bakery & Deli in Indio, California and at Flying J for gasoline in Ehrenberg, Arizona. We arrived at our condo in late afternoon.

TUESDAY, FEBRUARY 28, 2017—THE APPELBAUMS ARRIVE

At 12:44 p.m. Penny and I drove to Sky Harbor Airport and picked up Alan and Marilyn Appelbaum who arrived in Phoenix on American Airlines. We went to Goldman's for lunch and afterwards took Alan and Marilyn to pick up their rental car at Scottsdale's Doubletree Hotel on N. Scottsdale Road.

THURSDAY, MARCH 2, 2017—HISTORIC TEMPE

Penny and I drove to Tempe and took a driving tour of the Mitchell Park neighborhood. Beautifully decorated and very colorful mosaics dot the entire neighborhood. We also took a driving tour around the Maple Ash neighborhood. After the tours, we had a late lunch at Tempe's Salut Kitchen Bar and ordered our favorite Salut sampler with Parmesan fries, Mac N Cheese balls, hummus nachos and capese. After our driving tours, we went for a short visit to the Phoenix Botanical Garden. Penny bought some clothes at Hot Petunias Boutique and we went to Yogurtology for dessert.

FRIDAY, MARCH 3, 2017—SPRING TRAINING GAME

At 10:30 p.m. I picked up Alan Appelbaum and we drove to Mesa's Sloan Park for a 1:05 p.m. start of a spring training game between the Chicago Cubs and the Cincinnati Reds. We took a selfie outside the ballpark before the game. We sat in our usual section 117 in row 10 and seats 21 & 22.

Meanwhile Penny, Jan Aver and Marilyn Appelbaum went to the Fountain Hills Artist Studio Tour. The Fountain Hills Art League sponsored the event. Penny bought some earrings at Jewels with Pizazz and the two women ate lunch at the All-American Sports Grill in Fountain Hills. Penny also purchased artwork from Desert Vista Fiber Art.

SATURDAY, MARCH 4, 2017—OPERA PREMIERE

For breakfast, Penny and I went to US Egg. After breakfast we drove to Costco. In the evening, at 7:30, Penny and I drove to the Phoenix Symphony Hall located at 75 N. 2nd Street to see the World Premiere of the Arizona Opera's production of *Riders of the Purple Sage*. Before the show started, the opera's composer, Craig Bohmler spoke to the audience. After Mr. Bohmler spoke, the librettist, Steven Mark Kohn, gave a brief audience talk. The paintings of Arizona artist Ed Mell provided the scenic design of the stage set as it was projected on a large screen. The opera is based on a famous Zane Grey novel set in Arizona. This opera, sung in English, was an amazing experience and one that Penny and I thoroughly enjoyed.

SUNDAY, MARCH 5—*SINGIN IN THE RAIN* PARTY

Today is Spencer's 6th birthday. A few weeks ago, I purchased a brand-new unopened DVD of *Singin in the Rain* at the Mustang Library. Penny and I saw the film and we decided to have a *Singin in the Rain* party at our condo. Jeffrey and Susan Schesnol, Annie and Dan Murphy, Jan and Rich Aver attended the party. The musical film is a classic and the evening was a lot of fun.

TUESDAY, MARCH 7, 2017—PICNIC AND TEMPLERS

At 12:00 noon, Penny and I met Jeff and Michaele Salmon in the parking lot for a picnic lunch. We walked on a path near Mountain View and ate lunch on a park bench. In the evening, we met Jackie and Stu Templer for dinner at Eest Asian Bistro located in Avondale. This is a modern Chinese restaurant serving Mandarin and Cantonese style cooking and the food was very good.

WEDNESDAY, MARCH 8—MUSEUM AND JUDY ROBERTS

Penny and I drove to Scottsdale's Museum of the West to hear Nicole Bonilla's presentation. Her grandfather, Buss Carson, started a Wild West show in the 1930s and involved his family in the venture. Nicole grew up performing various rope tricks and riding her horse Majestic as part of the show. Nicole's talk, along with slides was very entertaining and interesting.

Penny and I ate dinner with Alan and Marilyn Appelbaum at Wildflower restaurant before the evening show. At 7:30 p.m. we drove to the ASU Kerr Institute at Rose Street and Scottsdale Road to see and hear Judy Roberts on the piano along with Bob Lashier on bass, Tony Vacca on saxophone and Sheila Hurley on drums. We sat in section A, row 2, seats 5 & 6 and the Appelbaums sat next to us. For the second set, Danny Long played the piano while Judy Roberts was on the electric keyboards. Delphine Cortez sang a few songs and Danny Long's daughter sang one song.

THURSDAY, MARCH 9, 2017—EISENDRATH HOME TOUR

With the Appelbaums, we went on a guided tour of the Eisendrath House located at 1400 N. College Street in Tempe. After the extensive renovation, the house is now a Tempe city office. I'll describe a little background on how this tour came about: on Saturday, March 28, 2015, Penny and I drove by the Eisendrath house for an outside look as it was being rehabbed and under construction by the Rio Salado Foundation and the city of Tempe. I previously wrote about the history of this remarkable house on March 28. 2015 but I wanted to mention it again because of the story behind this significant adobe house is fascinating.

AN FASCINATING STORY ABOUT THE EISENDRATH HOUSE

Early in 1930, Ruth Eisendrath, a Jewish woman from Chicago, whose late husband was in the glove business, had spent winters in Arizona. On April 23, 1930 she acquired a forty-four-acre parcel in the hills above the Salt River in North Tempe. Mrs. Eisendrath had been refused accommodations at a Phoenix valley resort because of her religion. So, she decided to build a house on nine-acres of pristine Sonoran Desert that sits on top of a hill. She commissioned famed Arizona architect, Robert Thomas Evans to design this adobe revival house. The house can be rented for weddings and other special event gatherings.

FRIDAY, MARCH 10, 2017—PEORIA SPRING TRAINING

I picked up Alan Appelbaum t 10:30 a.m. and we drove to the Peoria Sports Complex. At 1:10 p.m. we saw the Chicago Cubs play the Seattle Mariners. We sat in section 307, row 2, seat 7 and 8. In the meanwhile, Penny went with Marilyn Appelbaum to Two Plates Full.

SATURDAY, MARCH 11, 2017—IHA TRIP TO CHICAGO

I wanted to spend as much time in Arizona, so I decided to take a midnight flight back to Chicago for a client meeting. I got the rental car washed and put gas in the rental car for Penny while I was in Chicago. Penny drove me to Sky Harbor Airport around 9:30 p.m. My non-stop United Airlines flight left Phoenix at 11:43 p.m. and I arrived in Chicago at 5:08 a.m. Sunday morning.

SUNDAY, MARCH 12, 2017—BACK TO CHICAGO FOR A CLIENT

I arrived at 5:08 a.m. at Chicago O'Hare Airport. Uri picked me up at the airport and drove me to Northbrook. I went to Panera Bread for breakfast, then to Mariano's for groceries. Ronna invited me for dinner in Buffalo Grove so later in the day I drove to the Belinky home.

WEDNESDAY, MARCH 15, 2017—REVIEW AND HAIRCUT

I took a Metra train to Chicago for my 10:00 a.m. Program Review of the International Housewares Association's Exhibitor Innovation Awards slides at

WG's office. My clients Perry Reynolds, Connie Chantos, Derek Miller, M.C. Dan Gately, Art Director, Tony Sanchez and I were at the meeting.

At 10:30 a.m. we had a program review of the modules and an IHA Review of all *gia* graphics and Discover Design. At 3:00 p.m. I walked to my haircut appointment with Otto Bodner and took a taxi to the Metra train ride back to Glencoe, then drove back to Northbrook from the train station.

THURSDAY, MARCH 16, 2017—DINNER AT BELINKYS

Today is my birthday but I didn't do much. Ronna invited me to spend my birthday with her family.

SATURDAY, MARCH 18—LOAD-IN, REHEARSAL AND SHOW
SUNDAY, MARCH 19, 2017—FLIGHT BACK TO PHOENIX

Uri picked me up at 6:00 a.m. for a 7:30 a.m. departure from Chicago O'Hare to Phoenix. I had breakfast at Starbucks at the airport. My non-stop United Airlines flight arrived at Phoenix Sky Harbor Airport at 9:17 a.m. Penny picked me up and we drove back to our condo. Penny and I ate dinner at Pita Jungle.

MONDAY, MARCH 20, 2017—BASEBALL AND ANNUAL MEETING

I picked up Alan Appelbaum at 10:30 a.m. for a 1:10 p.m. spring training game between the Chicago Cubs and the Colorado Rockies at Salt River Field. We sat in section 207, row 11, seat 2 and 3. Penny went to Soul Café for lunch with Marilyn Appelbaum. At 6:00 p.m. Penny and I attended our condo's annual meeting of Mission de los Arroyos at Scottsdale Mustang Library.

TUESDAY, MARCH 21, 2017—MY SISTER LINDA ARRIVES

At 9:45 a.m. my sister Linda arrived in Phoenix on a Southwest Airlines flight. Penny and I picked her up at Sky Harbor Airport and drove back to our condo. Meanwhile, in the afternoon, the Appelbaums left Phoenix for Chicago.

WEDNESDAY, MARCH 22, 2017—SPRING TRAINING

In the morning, Penny went to Old Navy and bought clothing. Penny, Linda and I drove to Salt River Fields for a 1:10 p.m. spring training baseball game between the Cleveland Indians and the Colorado Rockies. We sat in section 216, row 9, and seats 1, 2 & 3. The Indians were losing so we left in the seventh inning.

THURSDAY, MARCH 23, 2017— ALISON HAYES BREAKFAST

Alison, Marin and Birk Hoette were visiting Alison's mother, Margie Hayes, who lives in Scottsdale. They invited us to join them for breakfast at First Watch. At 9:30 a.m., Linda, Penny and I drove to First Watch restaurant and met Alison, her two children and Margie Hayes for breakfast. Charlie, Alison's oldest child, did not make the trip to Phoenix. After breakfast, Penny, Linda and I walked the path next to our condo. After our walk, Linda and Penny went to the pool. For dinner, we ate Penny's defrosted and delicious eggplant Parmesan.

FRIDAY, MARCH 24, 2017—WRIGLEY TOUR AND LUNCH

Linda, Penny and I went to the Wrigley Mansion for lunch and a tour of the home. The meal was fine and the tour was very interesting.

SATURDAY, MARCH 25, 2017—PHOENIX THEATER PLAY

I picked up Jan and Rich Aver to see a 7:30 p.m. *Bullets Over Broadway* at the Phoenix Theater. Linda saw the play in Cleveland so she didn't go with us.

SUNDAY, MARCH 26, 2017—SALT RIVER FIELD

At 1:10 p.m. Linda and I saw the Cleveland Indians play the Arizona Diamondbacks at Salt River Fields. We sat in section 216, row 7, seat 5 and seat 6.

MONDAY, MARCH 27, 2017—TRIP TO JEROME AND LUNCH

After breakfast, Linda, Penny and I drove to Jerome for lunch at the Mile High Grill. We stopped at Nelly Bly II and bought a few items. Penny also bought a Christy Fisher creation. We stopped for ice cream at the Ice Cream Shop, and then drove back to Scottsdale in the late afternoon.

For dinner Penny, Linda and I went to George & Son Asian Cuisine and ordered our favorite green spinach fried rice and a few other dishes.

TUESDAY, MARCH 28—LINDA LEAVES, MOVIE CLASS

Today is Rich Aver's 72[h] birthday. At 7:30 a.m. I drove Linda to Sky Harbor Airport for her 10:15 a.m. non-stop Southwest Airlines flight to Cleveland. She arrived in Cleveland on time at 5:00 p.m.

At 10:00 a.m. Penny and I had our Tuesday morning Movie Group with Ed Everroad at the Mustang Library. Later in the day I had a haircut appointment with Vito at Angelo's Hair Styling on 90th Street.

WEDNESDAY, MARCH 29, 2017—ENCANTO PARK AND LUNCH

After breakfast, Penny and I drove to Encanto Park on North 15th Avenue in Phoenix. We paid for a train ride around the amusement park and I did some fishing in the park lake. After Encanto, we had lunch at Cherry Blossom Noodle Café located just east of 12th Street at 914 E. Camelback Road in Phoenix. In 2019, this restaurant was listed in *New Times* magazine as one of the ten best Japanese restaurants in metro Phoenix. They feature mouth-watering noodle dishes from all over the world. Penny and I ordered Ramen noodles in a miso base soup with salmon slices. The noodles were the best Ramen noodles we had ever eaten.

FRIDAY, MARCH 31, 2017—PRESCOTT TRIP WITH THE AVERS

After breakfast, I picked up Jan and Rich Aver and we drove to Prescott, Arizona. We ate lunch at El Gato Azul located at 316 W. Goodwin Street. It was 48 degrees in Prescott and I wore my hoodie under my leather jacket. We couldn't sit outside because of the cool temperature, so we sat inside. This is a terrific restaurant and the food is very tasty. After lunch we went to Van Gogh's Ear located at 156 S. Montezuma Street where we bought a large ceramic cooking dish for eggplant Parmesan.

The girls were still shopping at Van Gogh's Ear so Rich and I decided to leave. Not far from the store where the girls were shopping, I parked the car in a mufti-story garage. Rich and I went to Wild Iris Coffee House located at 124 S. Granite Street. I ordered a black coffee and Rich drank a hot chocolate. We both ate pastry for a snack. At the coffee house, I started talking to John Lutes who was wearing custom-made shoes he had purchased at Van Gogh's Ear.

SATURDAY, APRIL 1—McCORMICK RANCH CATFISH

After breakfast, I went fishing at McCormick Ranch Lake near my favorite fishing spot and had a very productive day. I saw two men fishing in a small boat near me. I caught a blue gill on a rattletrap and a largemouth bass also on a rattletrap. I caught a large four lb. catfish on a Mepps spinner.

While I was fishing, Jan Aver picked up Penny and they met Jacqui and Susan Schesnol at Panera Bread for breakfast.

SUNDAY, APRIL 2, 2017—PARADISE GARDENS TOUR

Penny and I went on a Modern Phoenix Driving Tour of Paradise Gardens and Encanto Vista Homes. Architect Al Beadle designed some of the tour homes. The tour was from 1:00 to 6:00 p.m. and took place on N. 34th and N. 35th Streets, Gold Dust Avenue, E. Mountain View, E. Turquoise Avenue, West Vernon Avenue and N. Encanto Drive locate the neighborhoods. These homes were spectacular and I made a slide show of the eleven homes we toured. The homes were decorated with impeccable taste. After the home tour, Penny and I ate dinner at The Parlor located at 1916 E. Camelback Road in Phoenix not far from the end of the driving tour.

MONDAY, APRIL 3, 2017—THE MIM AND THE DRAGON GUITARS

Penny and I went to the Musical Instrument Museum and saw the dragons and vines exhibit of inlaid guitar masterpieces. These beautifully designed guitars were on display and we especially wanted to see them because of our grandson Danny's musical talents. Larry Sifel was a pioneer who radically changed the guitar inlay industry. In 1979, Paul Reed Smith built a guitar with a small dragon inlaid on its body. This amazing exhibit showed many beautifully inlaid guitars and provided a history of the leaders in this industry. In the MIM gift shop, we bought Danny a book on the exhibit, a guitar birthday card and guitar wrapping paper.

WEDNESDAY, APRIL 5, 2017—HAYDEN LIBRARY

Penny and I drove to Tempe, parked the car and walked to the Hayden Library on the campus of Arizona State University. There was a very interesting exhibit on the Thunderbird School of Global Management, a unit of the university. In 1946, the management school was founded on the grounds of a deactivated airbase [Thunderbird Field No. 1]. Derek Miller, a client of mine at the International Housewares Association, received a master's degree from the Thunderbird School of Global Management.

After our tour of the Hayden Library, we drove to the Tempe Center for the Arts to look around. This architecturally beautiful building is a performing arts center. The theater is magnificent but we have never been here for a show. There is a view of Tempe Town Lake from inside the building.

There was a gallery inside the building with an exhibit of Western Pop Art. We saw Arizona artist, Ed Mell's artwork in the exhibit. Ed provided his paintings as backdrop to the *Riders of the Purple Sage* opera we had seen in March 2017. Afterwards, we ate lunch at Pita Jungle located at 4 E. University Drive in Tempe.

THURSDAY, APRIL 6, 2017—FLYING TO CHICAGO

Penny and I drove to the Phoenix Sky Harbor Airport at 11:00 a.m. for our non-stop United Airlines flight to Chicago. Before our flight, we ate lunch inside terminal 2 at Paradise Café. Our plane left Phoenix at 2:15 p.m. and we arrived in Chicago at 7:37 p.m. Uri picked us up at O'Hare Airport and drove us home.

CHAPTER THIRTY
Columbus, Indiana Trip and Other Travels

INDIANAPOLIS AND COLUMBUS, INDIANA TRIP
MONDAY AUGUST 7, 2017—FIRST STOP, INDIANAPOLIS

Penny and I left early in the morning for our road trip to Indianapolis and Columbus, Indiana. Our first stop was the Indianapolis Motor Speedway Museum. We checked in at the registration desk for the museum's self-guided tour that cost $10.00 per person. The speedway was the brainchild of Carl Fisher and first constructed in 1909. This museum showed the history of the racetrack through the different owners over the years. A large display room houses many winning race cars from various 500-mile races. The oldest race car was a 1908 Mercedes, driven to victory by Otto Salzer. Another old race car on display was the 1911 six-cylinder Marmon "Wasp" driven by famous auto racer, Ray Harroun. We were also able to see the Borg Warner trophy awarded to the winner of each 500-mile race. You could not go to the grandstand but we were able to see part of the grandstand from a museum parking lot. After the museum tour, Penny and I ate lunch at a Subway in Speedway, Indiana.

COLUMBUS, INDIANA OUR NEXT STOP

After lunch, we drove to Columbus crossing over the famous Robert N. Stewart designed J Muller International Bridge that took us into Columbus. The city is noted for the various buildings designed by famous architects. We first stopped at the Columbus Visitor's Center located at 506 5th Street and got a map of the famous buildings and landmarks. Artist Paul Rand designed the sign outside the center and there was a Dale Chilhuly chandelier hanging inside.

Next door to the visitor center is the 1969 I.M. Pei designed Bartholomew County Library located at 536 5th Street. Penny and I went into the library for a quick tour. In front of the library was a Henry Moore sculpture from 1971. Directly across the street from the library located at 531 5th Street, was the First Christian Church, designed by Eliel Saarinen in 1942. We also saw St. Peter's Lutheran Church and School at 719 5th Street was designed by Gunnar Birkerts in 1988. We drove by the Bartholomew County Memorial for Veterans. We checked into the Sleep Inn & Suites, and then ate dinner at the Garage Pub & Grill. After dinner we ate ice cream at Zaharakos old-fashioned ice cream parlor opened in 1909.

TUESDAY AUGUST 8, 2017—COLUMBUS
INN AT IRWIN GARDENS AND MILLER HOME TOUR

Penny and I went on a driving tour of Columbus. We checked out the 2006 Eos-Dessa Kirk designed sculpture located at 5th and Lindsey Streets. We also saw the temporary installation next to the old post office and the 1970 Kevin Roche & John Dinkeloo designed Columbus Post Office at 450 Jackson Street.

We drove by the 2005 Kevin Kennon designed principal of the Kohn Petersen Fox Learning Center located at 4555 Central Avenue in Columbus. Inside of the building was a spectacular Dale Chilhuly designed Sun Garden Panels in a

Suspended Circle on the ceiling and we took a selfie with the panels in the background. Part of the Learning Center Campus was Indiana University and Purdue University. Near this campus was a 2010 designed Howard Meehan Indiana University-Purdue University sculpture located at 4601 Central Avenue. Dedicated in 2007, an unusual rotating discovery fountain was nearby and I took a video of the fountain.

We ate lunch at Puccini's pizza and pasta restaurant before our 1:00 p.m. tour of the Inn at Irwin Gardens located at 608 5th Street. This old house is also a bed and breakfast. The house and the formal gardens were amazing and I took many photos of the property. After lunch, we walked to the visitor's center for our next tour where we boarded a shuttle bus for the 3:00 p.m. Miller house tour. The shuttle dropped us off by the house's carport. Famous architect Eero Saarinen designed The Miller home and the interior furnishing were designed by Alexander Girard. This modern looking home had a sunken living room conversation area and a custom round dining room table among other unusual built-in cabinets and spaces. Landscape architect Dan Kiley designed the backyard and gardens.

At 5:15 p.m. Penny and I checked into the Ruddick-Nugent House, our bed and breakfast residence built in 1884. We were greeted by the owner, signed the register and stayed in Martha's room on the second floor. The cost of the room and breakfast was $150.08. The room was very nice with a sink and shower, a queen-size bed, several chairs, a small desk and small sofa and a fireplace. The kitchen looked like it had been updated and a large chandelier hung from the ceiling of the living room. The owners had been in the Peace Corp during the 1960s and the home was filled with Ethiopian artifacts.

We drove to the Upland Pump House for dinner. This restaurant is located at 148 Lindsey Street and was previously used as a pump house by the city. Penny ordered a salad and I ate a turkey sandwich

WEDNESDAY, AUGUST 9, 2017—DRIVE TO NORTHBROOK

Penny and I got up early and had breakfast served in the dining room. We checked out of the house and were on our way around 10:30 a.m. making a stop in Spencer, Indiana, Home of the Patriots, as the sign stated. Of course, I took a photo of the sign leading into town. In Spencer, Indiana we stopped for lunch the Birdhouse restaurant inside the McCormick Creek Canyon Inn located in McCormick State Park.

After lunch before headed to Bloomington stopping first at the Tippecanoe Battlefield Museum but unfortunately it was closed. We got out of our car and walked around the actual battlefield that had an open fence saying the battle of Tippecanoe, November 7, 1811. A sign said, "here, on this site, military forces commanded by General Williams Henry Harrison, engaged in battle with the Indians of the Wabash country led by The Prophet, brother of the great Indian leader, Tecumseh. This battle destroyed forever the hope of Tecumseh for a complete Indian Confederacy, launched Harrison toward the Presidency of the United States twenty-nine years later, and is considered one of the primary events leading to the conflict between the United States and Great Britain in the War of

1812." We drove to Bloomington and through the Indiana University campus, had a Dairy Queen and arrived back in Northbrook just as it was getting dark. This trip was terrific, fun and educational.

FRIDAY, SEPTEMBER 22, 2017—FLY TO NEW YORK
FOR MARSHALL HERMAN'S BAR MITZVAH

Uri picked up Penny and me at 8:00 a.m. for our 10:57 a.m. non-stop United Airlines flight to New York's LaGuardia Airport. We left on time and arrived in New York at 2:09 p.m. Arleen and Michael Gomshay picked us up at the airport and we went back to their home for lunch.

SATURDAY, SEPTEMBER 23—MARSHALL HERMAN'S
NEW JERSEY BAR MITZVAH

Michael Gomshay drove to Harding, New Jersey, the site of the Bar Mitzvah at Lauri and Michael Herman's home. Shelly Pressler's grandson, Marshall Herman, was having his Bar Mitzvah this morning. Lauri Herman is Shelly and Carol Pressler's daughter and my first cousin, once removed. We arrived well before the bar mitzvah ceremony had a chance to speak with first cousin Shelly, his son Lee and his wife Amy and their two daughters, Julia and Muriel and their son Michael. We shared old photos of the family with them. The theme of the bar mitzvah was magic. Marshall is very much into magic and the invitation and many elements of the bar mitzvah were themed around magic. In fact, after the bar mitzvah, Marshall performed several magic tricks.

My cousin Shelly was recently diagnosed with lung cancer that spread to his brain and Lauri was so moved that we would fly to see Shelly and attend her son's bar mitzvah. It was sad to hear about Shelly's health and he passed away on Saturday, December 23, 2017 at age 87. In the evening, we drove back to Roslyn Heights.

SUNDAY, SEPTEMBER 24, 2017—FLIGHT TO CHICAGO

Arleen and Michael Gomshay dropped off Penny and me at the La Guardia Airport for our 3:44 p.m. non-stop United Airlines flight to Chicago's O'Hare Airport. We arrive in Chicago at 5:28 p.m. and Uri took us back to Northbrook.

FRIDAY, NOVEMBER 10, 2017—MADISON FAMILY TRIP

We had a surprise in the morning before we left Northbrook for Madison, Wisconsin. It snowed one and one-half inches. Ronna and her family drove separately from Penny and me. We arrived in Madison in time for dinner meeting Ronna and family at the Great Dane Pub & Brewery located at 123 Doty Street. After dinner, we took a little walk on State Street and then we checked into the Hampton Inn and Suites at the East Towne Mall located in Madison.

SATURDAY, NOVEMBER 11—FOOTBALL-UW VS. IOWA

We all met in the hotel lobby for breakfast. After breakfast, Ted and I parked our cars in an alley near Camp Randall Stadium. We walked from the corner of Orchard and Spring Streets to the University Bookstore and took a selfie on the way. Ronna did some shopping at the store, then after the bookstore we walked to the south student union for the "Badger Bash" where we ate pizza and ice cream. Outside of the student center, we listened to the University of Wisconsin Marching

Band play before the game. After listening to the band, we walked to Camp Randall Stadium and part of band was right next to us.

Our seats were in the corner, on an angle near the end zone. It was very cold. Ted and Spencer left early but Ronna, Talia, Penny and I stayed for the Fifth Quarter where the band marches and plays after the game. Penny was dressed in her nutria fur coat with a hood and looked like the wicked witch of the west. Ronna and Talia were laughing at how Penny looked. We walked to the car and drove to our hotel.

FRIDAY, DECEMBER 1, 2017—SANDI'S 75TH BIRTHDAY

Doug and Mara planned a surprise party for Sandi Fishman's 75th birthday. Penny and I plus Lois and Roy decided to go for this special event. At 7:30 a.m. Uri picked up Penny and me for our non-stop United Airlines flight to Tampa/St. Petersburg, Florida. Before our flight, Penny and I ate breakfast at the airport Starbuck. Our flight left Chicago O'Hare at 10:57 a.m. and we arrived in Tampa at 11:32 a.m. I made reservations for us and Roy and Lois at Springhill Suites located at 3485 Ulmerton Road in Clearwater. After our arrival in Tampa, I rented an Avis car at the Tampa Airport. We waited for Lois and Roy to arrive from Boston and drove them to our hotel. After checking into the hotel, we ate lunch nearby at Taziki's Mediterranean Café.

At 5:25 p.m., a shuttle picked up Roy, Lois, Penny and me at the Springhill Suites and brought us to Doug and Biddy home on S. Track Street. We arrived around 6:15 p.m. and Sandi showed up at the Fishman home for the surprise at 6:30 p.m. At 7:15 p.m. the shuttle took everyone to Platt Street Borough Bar and Eatery for dinner where we had a private room. After dinner, the shuttle took everyone back to his or her hotel.

SATURDAY, DECEMBER 2, 2017—SANDI LUNCH AND PARTY

I drove Lois, Roy and Penny to Sandi's condo, about twenty minutes from our hotel. We visited with Sandi and I got to rub Sandi's French bulldog, Bailey, on the couch. We gave Sandi a pillow with Bailey's photo on the front. After visiting with Sandi, we drove to Big Jim's Tavern & Tap for lunch. Janice Cannazaro, Marcia Turek and Linda Zipp joined us for lunch. After lunch we drove back to our hotel and dressed for the evening.

At 7:00 p.m. we drove to Mara and Mike's home located at 10614 Park Place Drive in Largo, Florida for cocktails and heavy hor d'ourves. Mara and Mike's home is about fifteen to twenty minutes from our hotel. The catered food was outstanding and plentiful. Many of Sandi's friends were there including her first cousins, Elaine Smith, Linda Zipp and Janice Cannazaro and niece, Marcia Turek. Sandi's grandchildren, Christian, Samantha and LJ were also at the party.

SUNDAY, DECEMBER 3—TAMPA TRIP TO CHICAGO

Penny and I met Lois and Roy for breakfast is the hotel. After breakfast we all drove to the Carillon Walking Path for a short walk along the nature trail. I took some photos of us. We saw a duckbill heron, egrets, other beautiful birds and much wildlife in this beautiful park. And of course, I took a selfie of the four of us.

In the early afternoon, I drove us to Doug and Biddy's home for lunch before taking Lois and Roy to the Tampa Airport for our flights. Our non-stop United Airlines flight to Chicago O'Hare Airport left at 4:20 p.m. and arrived in Chicago at 6:12 p.m. Uri picked us up at O'Hare and drove us home.

TUESDAY, DECEMBER 5, 2017—TRIP TO SCOTTSDALE

Uri pick up Penny and me at 6:30 a.m. and we arrived at the airport a little after 7:00 a.m. for our departure from Chicago O'Hare Airport to Phoenix Sky Harbor Airport. Our non-stop United Airlines flight left at 9:02 a.m. and arrived in Phoenix at 11:59 a.m. By the time we got our luggage it was 12:35 p.m.

Rich Aver picked us up and we drove to Goldman's Deli for our traditional "Welcome to Scottsdale" lunch. Rich then drove us to our condo so we could unload our luggage. After unloading, Rich drove Penny and me to pick up our Avis rental car located at 7125 E. Shea Blvd. Suite 101 a 2018 Toyota Camry SE for a one-hundred- and twelve-day rental.

WEDNESDAY, DECEMBER 6, 2017—US EGG AND SHOPPING

The *Arizona Republic* newspaper was supposed to start delivery but I had to call to get it started. Barb and Jim Hayes, our newspaper delivery people, delivered two papers the next day. At 9:30 a.m. Penny and I had breakfast at U.S. Egg Shea & Scottsdale Road. After breakfast, Penny and I went to Fry's for grocery shopping and Sprouts in the afternoon.

THURSDAY, DECEMBER 7, 2017—PENNY LUNCH AND FISHING

At 12:00 p.m. Penny had lunch with Jan Aver and Susan Schesnol at The Gladly Restaurant located at 2201 E. Camelback Road in Phoenix. Meanwhile, I went fishing at McCormick Ranch and the Evelyn Hallman pond in Tempe and got skunked with not a bite.

FRIDAY, DECEMBER 8, 2017—EFFICIENCY MECHANICAL

From 8:00 to 10:00 a.m. Efficiency Mechanical came to our condo to inspect heat pump and air conditioning. The charge was $209.00 for two visits a year. In the afternoon Penny and I went to Bed, Bath & Beyond for a few items and also to JC Penney for three long-sleeve polo shirts for me and to Costco for grocery items.

SATURDAY, DECEMBER 9, 2017—Z'TEJAS DINNER

At 5:15 p.m. Reservations at Z'Tejas and after dinner went to Yogurtology.

SUNDAY, DECEMBER 10, 2017—RE-SET MODEM AND DINNER

Bennett had to come to our Northbrook home to re-set the modem so we could see our Ring doorbell and control Nest thermostat from Arizona. I went to Fry's for some last-minute items while Penny stayed at the condo. At 6:00 p.m. Jan and Rich Aver invited Penny and me to dinner for cabbage soup and to see the movie *We're No Angels* featuring Humphrey Bogart, Peter Ustinov and Aldo Ray.

MONDAY, DECEMBER 11, 2017—CONFERENCE CALL

At 9:30 am, I had a conference call with one of our financial advisors, Joe Smith from Northwestern Mutual Investments. After my conference call, I steam cleaned the condo floors, then we went for a forty-minute walk on the path by our condo..

FRIDAY, DECEMBER 15, 2017—MESA FLEA MARKET

At 9:00 a.m. we picked up Jan and Rich Aver and drove to Mesa, exiting route

60 at Signal Butte Road and we ate lunch at Panera Bread on Signal Butte Road. After lunch, we drove around the corner to the Mesa Flea Market on Baseline Road and I brought my black Perfect belt with me because it had a scratch in it. I had a faulty belt buckle and had it replaced by Chris. I also bought a $20.00 brown perfect belt and buckle and I found a locking clamp to hold my iPhone in the car. Rich and I met Whitney who was selling tickets to the Barleens show and we took a selfie with her. We also took a selfie with all four of us at the flea market.

From 5:30 p.m. to 8:15 p.m. we attended a Christmas Party at Mission de los Arroyos Club house. We sat with Jeff and Michaele Salmon.

TUESDAY, DECEMBER 19, 2017—YOGA FOR PENNY

After breakfast, at 10:30 a.m., Penny went to yoga at Yoga Village located at 8241 E. Evans Road in Scottsdale. After yoga, we ate lunch and I made guacamole in the afternoon. Penny made a quiche for dinner and we ate around 6:30 p.m. After dinner we celebrated the last night of Chanukah by lighting the menorah with all candles blazing.

MONDAY, DECEMBER 25, 2017—CHINESE FOOD

Penny and I didn't do much in the morning or afternoon. For dinner, we placed an order Chinese food at Joyful Chinese Dining in Scottsdale. Rich Aver and I picked up the food at 5:45, Jeffrey, Susan and Jacqui Schesnol and Avers came to our condo for dinner.

TUESDAY, DECEMBER 26, 2017—WASHER AND DRYER

Jay and Harriet Weintraub left Northbrook for Scottsdale. Penny and I went to Spencer's TV and Appliances to look at and order another washer & dryer because the Lowes washer and dryer did not fit into our space. The dryer we bought at Spencer's had a flat back and was able to nicely fit into our laundry area in our pantry.

THURSDAY, DECEMBER 28, 2017—LUNCH AND A HAIRCUT

Harriet and Jay Weintraub arrived in Scottsdale. At 3:30 p.m. Penny and I drove to Chelsea's Kitchen for a late lunch. At 5:30 p.m. I drove Penny to Mane Attraction for her haircut appointment with Chris Knudsen. While Penny was getting her hair cut, I went to the Apple Store to have a few minor technical issues resolved.

FRIDAY, DECEMBER 29, 2017—WASHER, DRYER DELIVERED & DINNER WITH WEINTRAUBS

At 11:00 a.m. I got gas for our 2018 Toyota Camry SE rental car and a $100 gift card for Chris Knudsen at Flower Child. At 1:30 p.m. our new GE washer and dryer from Spencer's TV and Appliances were delivered and installed. Harriet and Jay Weintraub picked us up for a 6:00 p.m. dinner reservation at Basil and Garlic and we were able to sit on the patio because the weather was fantastic.

SUNDAY, DECEMBER 31, 2017— SCHESNOLS NEW YEAR'S

At 7: 40 p.m. Penny and I picked up Suzy Flax and Jim Stavish at 14550 N. 106th Place and drove to Jeffrey and Susan Schesnol's home for a New Year's party. We met Jan and Rich Aver there. Aaron Aver and his fiancé Stacey Gorman flew in from Los Angeles for the party. Jacqui's friend Vanessa from Tucson and Phil

Voyce were also at the party. We got home early in the morning of January 1, 2018.

MONDAY, JANUARY 1, 2018—BENNETT AND RONNA CALL

Penny and I slept in and called Bennett and Ronna to wish them a Happy New Year. I watched some college bowl games and we just relaxed.

TUESDAY, JANUARY 2, 2018—SALMONS AND SUPER MOON

Jay Weintraub left for his Florida show. Jeff and Michaele Salmon and Penny and I ate lunch at Sweet Basil restaurant and Gourmetware & Cooking School located on Scottsdale Road. The weather was pleasant so we sat outside. Afterwards we went to CVS and bought a few items. There was a Super Moon tonight and we drove to Fountain Hills to see it. We parked in a parking lot and I took a photo of it. After we returned, I took a photo of the Super Moon from outside our condo.

WEDNESDAY, JANUARY 3, 2018—DR. ROBERTS

The thumb on my right hand got infected, turned red and it was evident that I needed to see the doctor about it. I made a 2:00 p.m. appointment to see Dr. Abby Roberts about my thumb on Thursday.

THURSDAY, JANUARY 4, 2018—ANNIVERSITY DINNER

Today is Jan and & Rich Aver's 48th Anniversary. We decided to celebrate the Avers anniversary by going to the Barrio Queen restaurant in Desert Ridge. It was crowded, so we had to sit on a bench waiting for an open table. We finally got a table and ate dinner. After dinner we invited Jan and Rich to our condo to celebrate their anniversary with dessert.

FRIDAY, JANUARY 5, 2018— D'ALIESIO'S AND TEMPLERS

We went to see Vince and Cheryl d'Aliesio's new home in Carefree and we met Jackie and Stu Templer there. Unbeknownst to the D'Aliesio's, before they bought the house, their home was the first house built in Carefree. Part of a rock is built into the house. Black Mountain can be clearly seen from the back of their home. I took a photo of Cheryl, Vince, Noah, Sophie and Matthew.

Since Jay was in Florida, Harriet Weintraub and Penny and I went to dinner at Takeda Thai by Moulay in the same shopping center as Two Plates Full off of Shea Blvd. After dinner, we went to Dairy Queen for dessert.

SATURDAY, JANUARY 6, 2018—GERT AND MUSEUM

At 11:15 a.m. Penny and I drove to Sun City to visit with my 102-year-old Cousin Gert Phillips and had lunch at Coco's Restaurant. We bought an apple pie. After lunch we went to the Scottsdale Museum of the West and heard a lecture from Charlie LeSueur on the movies of John Ford. After the lecture, we saw the Rennard Strickland collection of Western Film History with many old and rare movie posters. The oldest movie poster on display was from Denton's Moving Pictures from 1898. You entered the Christine and Ted Mollring Sculpture Garden through a door in the museum. Since Jay Weintraub was working at an Orlando trade show, we invited Harriet Weintraub to join Penny and me for dinner at Takeda Thai restaurant in the same shopping center as Two Plate Full on Scottsdale Road and Shea Blvd.

SUNDAY, JANUARY 7, 2018—GOLDEN GLOBE AWARDS

Penny and I were invited to watch the Golden Globes at Jan and Rich Aver's condo. Jay's cousins, Barry and Nancy Slavin, were also at the party.

MONDAY, JANUARY 8, 2018—PEDICURE AND HAIRCUT

After breakfast, Penny got a pedicure at Shona Nails N Spa. In the afternoon, Penny had a haircut appointment with Chris Knudsen at Mane Attractions in Phoenix.

WEDNESDAY, JANUARY 10, 2018—A MOVIE AND DINNER

Penny and I went to see the movie, *Three Billboards in Ebbing Missouri* at the Harkins Theater. We also had dinner at The Village Tavern with cousin Corky Weily and Natalie Kane.

FRIDAY, JANUARY 12, 2018—JEWELRY AND SHABBAT

Penny bought jewelry at Practical Art and the Purple Lizard. At 12:00 noon, Rich Aver picked me up and we had lunch at Breakfast Kitchen Bar in the Scottsdale Quarter. We sat outside and had a terrific lunch. At 7:30 p.m. Penny and I drove to the Aver's condo and I gave Rich a lesson on how to trim the beard he had grown. After the lesson, I drove everyone to an Or Adam Service Shabbat Service with guest of honor speaker Gert Schuster, a holocaust survivor and comedienne.

SATURDAY, JANUARY 13, 2018—CARDS AND & CHINESE FOOD

In the morning, Penny and I went to Rose's Hallmark to buy greeting cards. Later in the day, I picked up Jan and Rich Aver and we had dinner at Nee House in Phoenix. After Chinese food, we went to Yogurtology for dessert.

SUNDAY, JANUARY 14, 2018—GATEWAY TRAILHEAD

After breakfast and at 11:00 a.m., Penny and I drove to Gateway Trailhead off of Thompson Peak Road and just north of Bell Road for a hike. For the hike, I brought the two walking sticks we had purchased at the Mesa Flea Market. On the way back from the hike, we stopped at the Green Bee Farmer's Market so look around but did not buy anything. After the hike we went grocery shopping at Fry's.

MONDAY, JANUARY 15, 2018—BARRETT JACKSON

Today is Martin Luther King's birthday, a national holiday. I got up early, ate breakfast and by 8:00 a.m. I drove to the Barrett Jackson Auto Auction and spent most of the day there. While I was at the auto auction, Penny cleaned the condo.

WEDNESDAY, JANUARY 17, 2018—GOLF, GUIDO'S DELI

I played golf with Dan Murphy, Jay Weintraub and Mike Stricker. Mike was in Scottsdale with his wife Fran so we were able to play together. After playing at Silverado, Mike, Fran, Rich and Jan Aver, Jay and Harriet and Penny and me had dinner at Guido's Italian Deli on North Scottsdale Road. Meanwhile, I paid Harriet $118.00 for tickets to the upcoming Phoenix *Dancing With The Stars* tour show.

THURSDAY, JANUARY 18, 2018—ERMA BOMBECK

In the morning, Penny bought clothes at The Gap. In the early afternoon, Penny and I spent a short time at the condo pool and I took a selfie.

SATURDAY, JANUARY 20, 2018—BISTRO & CONCERT

Penny and I had lunch at the VU Bistro restaurant with Jay and Harriet

Weintraub, Jan and Rich Aver. This restaurant has a spectacular view of Fountain Hills. After lunch, Rich went back to his condo and we drove Jan Aver to the Fountain Hills Theater to see a performance of Erma Bombeck. It was a one-woman show that was very entertaining and full of humor. At 8:00 p.m. Penny and I saw guitarist Tommy Emmanuel at the Scottsdale Center for the Performing Arts in the Virginia Piper Theater in seats H-9 and H-11. The concert was fantastic.

FRIDAY, JANUARY 26, 2018—RONNA AND FAMILY ARRIVE

Ronna, Ted, Talia and Spencer arrived for a Scottsdale visit. Upon their arrival, Talia and Spencer went in our condo's swimming pool. For dinner, Penny had previously made eggplant Parmesan. After dinner, Ronna made S'Mores in our fireplace and Spencer sat on the floor with Ronna while she was making S'Mores. We all enjoyed some sticky S'Mores.

SATURDAY, JANUARY 27, 2018—PAPAGO PARK

After breakfast, we drove the Belinky's to the Hole In The Rock in Papago Park and we all hiked up to the top and took photos. Around 12:15 p.m. we met Faith, Maddy and Tyler Beall at Sweet Tomatoes for lunch and I took a photo of the group. After lunch, the entire group came back to our condo and the kids along with Ronna and Ted went into our condo pool.

SUNDAY, JANUARY 28, 2018—RIVERVIEW AND SLOAN PARK

In the morning, we drove to Tempe's Riverview Park to have fun on the playground. Ted and Spencer played catch on the open field. After the playground, we went to Sloan Park and took some photos in front of the park entrance. After Sloan Park, we went to In-Out-Burger for lunch and took the food back to our condo. Grandma Penny got a cheeseburger.

MONDAY, JANUARY 29, 2018—MIM AND CRACKER JAX

After breakfast, we all went to the Musical Instrument Museum. We went through the United States and Canada sections and ate lunch at the Café Allegro inside the museum. I took videos of Spencer playing the Theremin and drums, Talia playing the xylophone, Ted pounding the drums and Penny playing the rain pipe. Spencer played the bells and Grandma and Talia played the large drum. Spencer and Ted played guitars. A video of the nickelodeon was also taken. After the Musical Instrument Museum, Ted, Talia and Spencer went to our condo pool.

The Belinkys went to Cracker Jax to ride the go-karts. Talia drove her own go-kart and Ted and Spencer went in the other go-kart. Then each of the Belinkys went on their own boats and played miniature golf. For dinner, we ate Brie En Croute for an appetizer and I went to the Thai House and ordered Thai food.

TUESDAY, JANUARY 30, 2018—TWO BIRTHDAYS

Today is Talia and Penny's birthday. We all celebrated Talia's 11th birthday by reading birthday cards and opening gifts, After opening cards and presents, we ate an ice cream pie that Penny made.

WEDNESDAY, JANUARY 31, 2018—THE BELINKYS LEAVE
THURSDAY, FEBRUARY 1, 2018—GOLF IN SUN CITY

Dan Murphy picked up Jay Weintraub and me and we drove to Sun City and played golf at Riverview Golf Course. We were teamed up with Rodney Marks, retired from the U.S. Air Force, but working with the Air Force as a civilian. Penny went to Fountain Hills and bought some jewelry from Charles Skiera. For dinner, Penny and I ate at Guido's Chicago Deli with the Jay and Harriet Weintraub, Fran and Mike Stricker, Jan and Rich Aver.

FRIDAY, FEBRUARY 2, 2018—LADYSMITH CONCERT

In the morning, I got a pedicure at Shona Nails N Spa and afterwards I took in our winter comforter to Continental Cleaners. Then we bought some wine at Total Wine. At 8:00 p.m. Penny and I went to a concert at the Scottsdale Center for the Performing Arts in the Virginia Piper Theater and saw Ladysmith Black Mambazo. We sat in row E, seats 6 & 8. Before the performance, Penny bought a few gifts at the Scottsdale Center shop. We thoroughly enjoyed this amazing group of entertainers. After the show, a few of the ensemble were in the lobby signing autographs and taking photos with audience members.

SATURDAY, FEBRUARY 3, 2018— MURPHYS LUNCH

After breakfast, Penny and I went on a thirty-five-minute walk in our neighborhood. Jay and Harriet Weintraub, Jan and Rich Aver and us were invited to Dan and Annie Murphy's home in Peoria for lunch. We had a delicious lunch and saw their new dog, Deeter.

SUNDAY, FEBRUARY 4, 2018—PENNY'S LUNCH & JAN

Penny had lunch at White Chocolate Grill with Jan Aver. Later in the day, Penny and I met Sherry and Harvey Amend, Jay and Harriet Weintraub, Jan and Rich Aver and Jeffrey and Susan Schesnol for dinner at dinner at George & Son,

MONDAY, FEBRUARY 5, 2018—SOUL CAFÉ BREAKFAST

At 10:00 a.m. the Avers and Spencers had breakfast at Soul Café. Afterwards we went to the Vitamin Shoppe for a few supplements and shopped at Sprouts.

WEDNESDAY, FEBRUARY 7, 2018—NICOLE PESCE AND THE DAVE BRUBECK CONCERT

Before our concert at the ASU Kerr Institute, we went to dinner at Wildflower on Indian Bend. At 7:30 p.m. Penny and I saw one of our favorite Arizona entertainers, Nicole Pesce playing *A Tribute to Dave Brubeck a*nd his music. The trio played with Jimmy D'Amato on the saxophone and I don't remember who played the drums. Nicole Pesce is an amazing pianist and performer and we thoroughly enjoyed the evening.

FRIDAY, FEBRUARY 9, 2018—HASHKNIFE PONY EXPRESS

Penny and I ate breakfast at US Egg. After breakfast, we drove to the Scottsdale Museum of the West to see the arrival of the Hashknife Pony Express mail delivery. The street in front of the museum was blocked off and many people were gathered to see the arrival of about twenty-three horseback riders. A small stage was constructed in front of the museum with a country band playing and couples dancing the two-step in front of the stage. There were people dressed in period costumes. I took videos of the Hashknife Pony Express riders as they approached the museum. This special occasion marked the sixty-year anniversary (from 1958 to 2018) of this special mail delivery. After watching this event, Penny and I ate lunch and a dessert at Super Chunk.

SATURDAY, FEBRUARY 10, 2018—DOOWOP PROJECT

After breakfast, Penny and I drove to Chaparral Park and walked around the lake. After our walk, we stopped at Barnes and Noble to buy Brooke a birthday present and got gas for our rental car at Circle K.

In the evening, we picked up Jan and Rich Aver and Harriet and drove to the Arizona Musicfest at the Highlands Church where we saw *The DooWop Project*. The subtitle of the show was "From Bop to Pop, the Evolution of a Sound." It was a fantastic evening with a six-piece band to back up the four singers.

SUNDAY, FEBRUARY 11, 2018—DRIVE TO TUCSON

After breakfast at our condo, Penny and I drove to Tucson to have lunch with Melissa and Matt Landau and Steve Klein. We arrived at Steve's apartment around 11:30 a.m. and Steve drove us to the Blue Willow restaurant & gift shop located at 2616 N. Campbell Avenue. Melissa and Matt Landau met us there. We had a delicious lunch and caught up and I took two selfies. After lunch, Steve drove us back to his apartment. Before we left Tucson, we stopped at Fresh Produce located at 7113 N. Oracle Road where Penny bought a blouse and pants. Right next door we ate gelato outside at Frost Gelato Shoppe.

TUESDAY, FEBRUARY 13, 2018—YOGA, BASIL AND GARLIC

Penny went to one-half restorative and one-half stretching yoga and said it was great when she returned. After lunch, Penny baked Lois's lemon pound cake. Penny and I had dinner at Basil and Garlic with Jay and Harriet Weintraub and Rich and Jan Aver. After dinner, we went back to Jan and Rich's condo and had the lemon cake. We left around 10:30 p.m.

WEDNESDAY, FEBRUARY 14, 2018—SENIOR EXPO

After breakfast, Penny and I went to the Scottsdale Center for the Performing Arts and Senior Expo. This event is given each year with many vendors offering seniors different services. They give away cloth bags with different goodies inside. We have a collection of the bags and giveaway items. We thought this expo was not as good as past ones.

THURSDAY, FEBRUARY 15, 2018—PEDICURE, ARCADIA FARMS
LUNCH AND MUSEUM OF THE WEST

After breakfast, Penny had a pedicure at Shona Nails N Spa. While Penny was having her pedicure, I mailed Brooke's birthday present at the Post Office. We had an 11:30 a.m. lunch reservation at Arcadia Farms before going to a 1:00 p.m. lecture. After lunch, Penny and I went to a 1:00 p.m. lecture at the Scottsdale Museum of the West to hear Dr. Tricia Loscher talk about *From Calamity Jane to Johnny Guitar: Cowgirl Women in Western Movie Posters*. This lecture was based on the Rennard Strickland poster collection we had seen earlier. After the lecture, we looked at an exhibit featuring the art of Joe Beeler: A Western Original. There were sculptures and paintings created by Joe Beeler. In 1965, Joe Beeler co-founded the Cowboy Artists of America. Today, the Cowboy Artists of America is recognized as one of the most influential artists groups in the nation's history. Their visual arts in many mediums convey the spirit of the west and keep it alive.

SATURDAY, FEBRUARY 17, 2018—ART AND TAKEDA THAI
Penny picked up Harriet Weintraub and they went to the Scottsdale Ranch Art Show benefit for the Virginia Piper Cancer Institute. She said they had some interesting jewelry and paintings. She bought a few handmade cards of Arizona photos. Before our 6:00 p.m. dinner reservation, we saw a beautiful sunset from the restaurant parking lot and had dinner at Takeda Thai with Jay and Harriet Weintraub. We ordered pad Thai with tofu, fried rice with pineapple and eggplant and sweet & sour chicken. After dinner, we went to The Baked Bear for ice cream.

SUNDAY, FEBRUARY 18, 2018—SUNDAY A'FAIR
After breakfast, Penny and I drove to the Scottsdale Mall in front of the Performing Arts Center to see a Sunday A'Fair. An all-women Mariachi Pasion was playing. There were four violins, two flutes, one trumpet and three guitars playing. I took several videos of the group. There was also a fourteen-year-old singer that performed. The Villalobos Brothers performed after the Mariachi Pasion.

After Sunday A'Fair we had dinner at The Coronado restaurant at the corner of Monte Vista and 7th Street in Phoenix. Penny and I sat outside and ordered fried guacamole, garlic & Parmesan French fries and a beet burger. Everything was delicious and we would come back to this restaurant.

TUESDAY, FEBRUARY 20, 2018—LUNCH WITH SALMONS AND DINNER WITH YOUNGSTOWN FRIENDS
Today is Brooke's 10th birthday and we left a happy birthday message for her. Penny and I had lunch with Jeff and Michaele Salmon at the Phoenix Whole Foods at the corner of Tatum and Shea Blvd.

In the evening, Penny and I ate dinner with Jim and Bobby Pazol and Ron and Bonny Gimple at the Pinnacle Grille in North Scottsdale. It's always a fun evening with the Youngstown group.

THURSDAY, FEBRUARY 22, 2018—APPELBAUMS ARRIVE
At 11:43 a.m. Alan and Marilyn Appelbaum arrived in Phoenix on an American Airlines flight from Chicago and Penny and I picked them up on the south side of Terminal 4 at Sky Harbor Airport. We went to Goldman's Deli for lunch. After lunch I dropped them off to pick up their rental car at the Doubletree Hotel on N. Scottsdale Road.

FRIDAY, FEBRUARY 23, 2018—NEIGHBORHOOD WALK
Today is cousin Norman's 77th Birthday. After breakfast, Penny and I took a neighborhood walk. It was cold today and Penny wore two layers of clothes for our walk. In the afternoon, Penny made two tins of Jan Aver's bark. I made a fire in our condo chimney because of the chilly weather. After dinner, Penny made S'Mores in our fireplace.

SATURDAY, FEBRUARY 24, 2018—THE SIMON'S BRUNCH
Carol and John Simon were staying with Jay and Harriet Weintraub at their Scottsdale rental condo. The Avers and we were invited for an 11:00 a.m. brunch at Jay and Harriet's condo to see and visit with the Simons. Penny brought fruit and the bark she made. Of course, I took a selfie of the group after brunch.

After brunch and later in the afternoon, Stu and Jackie Templer drove to our condo from Sun City Grand and I drove everyone to the Canal Convergence at the Scottsdale waterfront. I took videos of the waterfront decorations. There was a band playing and we walked on the Soleri Pedestrian Bridge & Plaza. After attending the Canal Convergence, the Templers and us went to Z'Tejas for dinner.

SUNDAY, FEBRUARY 25, 2018—CUBS VS. GIANTS

I picked up Alan Appelbaum at his hotel and we drove to the Scottsdale Stadium and paid $5.00 to park in a free lot close to the stadium. We arrived in plenty of time for the 1:05 p.m. start of the Chicago Cubs playing the San Francisco Giants. We sat in section 309, row 8, seats 9 & 10. I had a pizza for lunch. Meanwhile, Penny and Marilyn Appelbaum had lunch at Eggstacy, then went to Beall's Outlet and bought some miscellaneous household items. At 5:00 p.m. we went to Basil & Garlic for dinner.

MONDAY, FEBRUARY 26, 2018—SOUL CAFÉ LUNCH

Penny and I went for a walk in our neighborhood and after our walk she sat in the sun and read a book. Jay Weintraub, Rich Aver and I had lunch at Soul Café in North Scottsdale. Penny went to the Paper Source in the Scottsdale Quarter to buy birthday cards.

TUESDAY, FEBRUARY 27, 2018—CUBS VS. WHITE SOX

In the morning, I picked up Alan Appelbaum and we drove to Sloan Park for the 1:05 p.m. start of the spring training baseball game between the Chicago Cubs vs. Chicago White Sox. We sat in section 104, row 18 and seats 1 & 2. Jon Lester was pitching. While Alan and I were at the spring training game, Penny had lunch with Betty Koppelman, Beverly Semans and Bonny Gimple at Arcadia Farms for a delicious lunch. Penny introduced the women to the Scottsdale Museum of the West and docent gave them a tour. For dinner, Penny made blintzes.

WEDNESDAY, FEBRUARY 28, 2018—EAGLE MOUNTAIN GOLF

Jay Weintraub and I played golf at the Eagle Mountain Golf Club in Fountain Hills with Mike Stricker, Joe Rauch, and Mark Johnson. The course was difficult with lots of hills and expensive at $104.54. After golf, for dinner, Fran and Mike Stricker, Harriet and Jay and me ate at Basil and Garlic. After dinner, the Strickers drove back to Tucson. In the meantime, Penny had dinner plans at Bandera with Betty Koppelman, Beverly Semans and Bonny Gimple.

THURSDAY, MARCH 1, 2018—HAIRCUT AND CHASE BANK TOUR

In the afternoon, Penny had a haircut appointment at Mane Attractions with Chris Knudsen. After her haircut, we got a gelato at the Gelato Spot, and then decided to check out the usual Chase Bank on 44th Street. Penny and I have passed this unique Chase Bank at the corner of 44th Street and Camelback Road many times, so we decided to stop, park in the bank lot and look around. This bank is definitely distinctive. It was originally built in 1968 as the Valley National Bank. The architecture firm of Weaver and Drover designed this award-winning building. The individual designer was Frank Henry who worked for the firm for thirty years and teaches at Taliesin West.

The outside architecture is surprising because the building is round. It has various pieces of large colored stone built into the wall and the stone piece surrounds the entire building. Covered concrete structures dot the outside and look like giant mushrooms. On the bank's inside, two large mushroom structures support the ceiling. Several female sculptures are included in a garden setting surrounded by flowers, plants and shrubs. Every time we pass this bank, we think of our close-up look at the place.

FRIDAY, MARCH 2, 2018—THE BARLEENS SHOW

Penny bought jewelry at Artworks by Judith, by George Originals and Marcia McClellan Art. I went to the post office and mailed Spencer's birthday gift.

At 4:00 p.m. I picked up Jan and Rich Aver and we drove to Apache Junction. Jay and Harriet Weintraub and Dan and Annie Murphy drove separately and we all met in front of the theater. The door opened at 5:15 p.m. and the show ended at 9:45 p.m. The Barleens AZ Opry *Rock N Roll Through The Ages* is located at 2275 E. Old West Highway in Apache Junction. Our seats were in the center row, table 38, seats 1-8 and our table sat Dan and Annie Murphy, Jan and Rich Aver, Harriet and Jay Weintraub and Penny and Alan. This is always an enjoyable entertainment experience. The show is full of great music and lots of humor.

SATURDAY, MARCH 3, 2018—WESTERN LECTURE, STAR DANCING

After breakfast, at 10:00 a.m., Jay and Harriet Weintraub picked up Penny and me and drove us to the Scottsdale Museum of the West to hear Charles LeSueur give an 11:00 a.m. talk on the *Spaghetti Westerns*. After the lecture, we went to Super Chunk for lunch. I had a turkey sandwich on wheat bread.

After lunch we drove to Comerica Theater in Phoenix and parked in the garage across the street from the theater. The 4:00 p.m. show was *Dancing with the Stars Live! light up the night*. We checked in and took our seats and a selfie. I took some videos but the show was somewhat disappointing because we were seated far away from the stage; however, it was a good experience to see this show once.

After the show, Jan and Rich Aver joined us for dinner at The Parlor located at 1916 E. Camelback Road in Phoenix. Some of us ordered pizza and Rich ordered a sandwich and fries. We bought dessert at Pomo Cucina & Pi.

SUNDAY, MARCH 4, 2018— STARFIRE BRUNCH AND OSCARS

Alan and Marilyn Appelbaum raved about the Sunday brunch at the Starfire Golf Club on N. Hayden. Alan made a 10:00 a.m. reservation and we picked them up at their hotel around 9:45 a.m. The Sunday brunch is from10:00 until 1:00 p.m. There was a wide variety of food from lox and bagels to hot entrees plus dessert. The cost of the brunch was $45.75 for both of us. We will definitely go back in the future. In the evening, we picked up Jan and Rich Aver and met Susie Flax in Chompie's parking lot and we all drove to Jeffrey and Susan Schesnol's home for an Oscar Party. Others attending were Phil Voyce, Karen Melnick, Jacqui Schesnol and her male friend from Washington DC.

MONDAY, MARCH 5, 2018—SPRING TRAINING GAME

Today is Spencer's 7th birthday. Alan and Ellen Magit arrived in Phoenix and will stay until Monday, March 26. Penny took me to the Holiday Inn where Alan and Marilyn Appelbaum were staying and Alan and I took a $5.00 hotel shuttle to Salt River Fields to see the Chicago Cubs play the Colorado Rockies. We sat in section 215, row 16, seats 1 & 2. Meanwhile, while I was at a spring training game, Penny and Marilyn went to Kohl's and bought clothes then went to Two Plates Full and purchased gifts and cards.

THURSDAY, MARCH 8, 2018—CHIP IN WINDSHIELD AND DINNER IN OLD SCOTTSDALE

Earlier in the day, I had a chip repaired on the windshield of the rental car for $30.00. An auto glass guy from the Genie Carwash fixed the chip. Later in the day, Jay and Harriet, Weintraub, Alan and Ellen Magit and Penny and me went to dinner at the Forte Café located at 7032 E. Main Street in Old Scottsdale.

SATURDAY, MARCH 10, 2018—APPELBAUMS HOME AND PIZZA

Late in the day, Alan and Marilyn Appelbaum left Scottsdale for Chicago. Penny had lunch at Wildflower with Margie from our complex. For dinner, Jan and Rich Aver took Penny and me to IL Bosco Pizza located at 7120 E. Becker Lane in Scottsdale. The restaurant serves artisanal wood-fired pizzas with a patio and simple décor. The meal was delicious and we will go back there again.

SUNDAY, MARCH 11, 2018—WINDSOR SQUARE TOUR

After breakfast, I picked up Jan Aver and we drove to the Windsor Square registration area, parked the car and walked to check in at the corner of Medlock Drive and N. 2nd Street for the Windsor Square Historic District Home Tour. Three large tents were set up with an Ollie The Trolley Stop near the tents. The first home on the tour was at 510 East Pasadena Avenue and a slide show was created for the tour. We toured a total of eleven homes. At a booth during our tour, we bought two muffins and two bottles of filtered water from Lilly B. Gourmet Muffins. A twelfth home was seen on the 2016 Windsor Square Home Tour, so we didn't see it again; however, it was included in the 2018 slide show.

TUESDAY, MARCH 13, 2018—GERT BREAKS HIP

During the winter months in Scottsdale and on many occasions, Penny and I would visit my first cousin once-removed Gert Phillips who lived in Brookstone in Sun City, an assisted living apartment about thirty-five miles from our condo. My sister Linda also went with us when she was visiting.

In February 2018, we left several messages on Gert's home phone wanting to visit her but she did not return our calls. Apparently in early March, Gert fell and broke her hip. Her son and my second cousin, Ron Spritzer, was visiting his mother in rehab in Peoria, Arizona. When he was at his mother's apartment, he heard our several messages on his mother's home phone so he called informing us that his mother had broken her hip and was in rehab.

On Tuesday March 13, 2018, Penny and I went to visit Gert in rehab and Ron was there too. She seemed to be in good spirits at the time but was in a lot of pain. After visiting Gert, Ron, Penny and I went to dinner to catch up on family news at Firebirds Wood Fired Grill in North Peoria. We had the server take our photo at the table. Ron called us later in the month saying his mother was in too much pain and gave up living. She died on March 29, 2018 at the age of 102 and was "with it" until she broke her hip.

FRIDAY, MARCH 16—SPRING TRAINING WITH FRIENDS

Today is my 77th birthday. Penny and I drove to Camelback Ranch at 10710 W Camelback Road in Glendale to see a spring training game between the Chicago Cubs and the Chicago White Sox. Karen and David Hudachko bought $28.00 tickets and the following Chicago friends were at the game: Mike and Fran Stricker, Jay and Harriet Weintraub, Alan and Ellen Magit and Penny and me attended. Unfortunately, David and Karen Hudachko were unable to be there because of some family obligations. After the game, the Chicago gang met at The Pitts Again BBQ located at 5558 W. Bell Road in Glendale for dinner. Jan and Rich Aver met us there and we had the server take a photo of our table.

SUNDAY, MARCH 18, 2018—PENNY--A GLASS TRAY CLASS

After breakfast I went to Target and bought new Panasonic phones for the condo. The old Radio Shack phones finally died. After target I drove to Costco to buy Kleenex. Penny went to a glass tray making class at Nancy's in Fountain Hills. She said the class was different from the Phoenix Art Center class.

WEDNESDAY, MARCH 21, 2018—BREA, CALIFORNIA TRIP

Penny and I made a bagel run to New York Bagel 'N Bialys on Scottsdale Road for Linda and Ted Jass. It was our first stop on our way for our overnight stay in Lake Havasu. We drove on I-10 and headed north Arizona route 95 and stopped for lunch at the Crossroads Cafe in Parker, Arizona. The sign outside the restaurant said, "home-style cooking."

STOPT AT LAKE HAVASU, ARIZONA

After lunch, we continued north on Arizona route 95 and we arrived in Lake Havasu later in the afternoon. The first thing we saw was Gateway to the English Village and walked around. We could see London Bridge in the background. There was a large fountain in the village. We took a drive and saw Lake Havasu State Park and a national wildlife refuge. We stopped by one of the many boat launches on the lake and watch a man in a Ram truck launch is bass boat. I took a photo of London Bridge just before sunset. The sunset over the lake was beautiful. After taking a driving tour of the area, we checked into the Quality Inn & Suites and unloaded our carry-ons. Our television didn't work so we got a 20% discount on the room price.

Penny and I drove over London Bridge and ate dinner at Shugrue's Restaurant & Lounge that was in a small shopping center called Island Mall. Penny had a glass of white wine and I drank an Arnold Palmer. I don't remember what we ate. After dinner, we stopped at Bass Tackle Master and bought new line for one of my reels. We drove around and saw the beautiful sunset. I was excited to rent a Hobie Kayak the next day.

THURSDAY, MARCH 22, 2018—FISHING AND BREA, CALIFORNA

On our walk in the village on Wednesday, I noticed a store, Southwest Kayaks that rented Hobie Kayaks by the hour. I couldn't resist, so this morning, after breakfast, I rented a Hobie Kayak. Ben, a heavily bearded man, helped me get into the Hobie. It seemed like rain, so I put my rain jacket around my waist and put on a life jacket. My fishing rods and other fishing equipment were put in the kayak and I was all set for my Hobie adventure. Ben gave me some instructions before I shoved off. Penny took video of me as I peddled around Lake Havasu under and near London Bridge. I took a video of me peddling from my vantage point in the boat. Although the lake is known as one of the best bass lakes in the United States, I tried fishing but I had no luck, not even a bite. I took a Lake Havasu selfie with London Bridge in the background. I was in the kayak for two hours and it was fantastic.

We had lunch at Panera Bread and left to Brea, California. Penny drove for two hours and we arrived in Brea, California around 6:00 p.m. We ate dinner in Brea's Fish California Grill because Linda Jass had a nutrition class until 8:00 p.m. After dinner, we went to the Jass home and waited for Linda to come home from her class.

FRIDAY, MARCH 23, 2018—FULLERTON AND LEO FENDER

For breakfast, I stopped at Starbucks around the corner from the Jass home to buy coffee. Ted drove to Fullerton and we took a selfie by a mosaic sculpture. We ate lunch at Brownstone Café and took a photo with the owner, Chef Glen and his wife Kim. We ate delicious and healthy veggie burgers. After lunch, Ted and I went to the Leo Fender Museum. Fender was an early innovator of electric guitars, basses and amplifiers. The Fender Stratocaster, an electric guitar that revolutionized the music world. Fender won a Technical Grammy Award in 2009. I thought of grandson Danny while going through this museum. Meanwhile, Linda and Penny went shopping at The Loft. In the evening, we watched *The Florida Project* movie that we thought was not very good.

SATURDAY, MARCH 24, 2018—LEXI'I SWIM AND SHOPPING

For breakfast, I stopped at Starbucks around the corner from the Jass home to buy coffee. Linda drove Ted, Penny and me to Santa Margarita Catholic High School to see Lexi Houghton's swim meet in Rancho Santa Margarita, California. Lexi and Kyle took a photo at the outside Special Olympics swim meet and she got an award at the end of the meet. After the swim meet, we drove to the Outlets at San Clemente and ate lunch at Panera Bread. I bought a pair of Columbia fishing pants and a pair of Asics shoes. Penny bought some clothes at the Daisy Shoppe. While walking, we saw an Orange County Theater group performing a routine. We went to Slater Brothers super market and bought a box of matzos.

SUNDAY, MARCH 25, 2018—A MOVIE AND DINNER

Ted, Linda, Penny and I had breakfast at Kimmie's Coffee Cup. After breakfast, we saw a fabulous movie, *Black Panther,* at the Edwards Cinemas. After the movie, we ate dinner at Elbows Mac N' Cheese.

MONDAY, MARCH 26, 2018—DRIVE TO SCOTTSDALE

For breakfast, I stopped at Starbucks around the corner from the Jass home to buy coffee. On our drive back to Scottsdale, we stopped a TKB Bakery & Deli to buy sandwiches and to take a bathroom break. We stopped at Flying J in Ehrenberg, Arizona for gas and a picnic lunch. At 6:00 p.m. our condo association's annual meeting was held at Mustang Library

WEDNESDAY, MARCH 28, 2018—GOLDMAN'S LUNCH

Today is Rich Aver's 73[h] birthday. Penny and I had lunch at Goldman's Deli and bought two pieces of gefilte fish for Passover.

THURSDAY, MARCH 29, 2018—PASSOVER DINNER

After breakfast, Penny made hard boiled eggs for Passover. In preparation for a Passover dinner, Penny was cooking all day. She made soup and charoset.

SUNDAY, APRIL 1, 2018—MET GOMSHAYS AND A MOVIE

After breakfast, we walked to Desert Cove Street. Later in the day, Penny and I drove to the Four Seasons Resort in Troon and met Arleen and Michael Gomshay and Justin and Dylan Paley who were on a Tauck Tour of the Grand Canyon, Zion and Brice National Parks. The grandchildren were swimming in the hotel's pool when we got there.

TUESDAY, APRIL 3, 2018—HAIRCUT, DINNER AND CONCERT

After breakfast, Penny and I went on a thirty-five-minute walk in our neighborhood on the walking path next to our condo to Gary and 96th Street and back on Cholla. In the afternoon, Penny had a haircut appointment at Mane Attractions. After her haircut, we had dinner next door at Twisted Grove Parlor & Bar. We sat outside on the patio and were the only ones there. We each had a glass of wine and had a fantastic meal. We ate grilled Brussels sprouts in a jar and on a piece of wood plus bruschetta: goat cheese, dates, candied pecans, honey & arugula, avocado, pickled onion, cilantro & garlic aioli and jamming spicy tomato arugula & sea salt. Wow!! Delicious. In the evening, we had a Jeffrey Siegel Keyboard Conversations concert at the Scottsdale Center for the Performing Arts.

ROAD TRIP TO JEROME, CLARKDALE AND COTTONWOOD
WEDNESDAY, APRIL 4, 2018—JEROME, THEN CLARKDALE

Penny and I drove to Jerome, Arizona and stopped by Jerome Artists Cooperative Gallery. The gallery is housed in the old Hotel Jerome. We went there specifically to see Christy Fisher so Penny could get video instructions on how to wear a convertible wrap she had purchased in Christy's store the year before. Christy was working in this coop store, so I took several videos of Christy demonstrating how to tie and wear the wrap. Penny also bought some clothes that Christy had on display. After seeing Christy, we ate lunch at the Mine Café.

After leaving Jerome, Penny and I drove to Dead Horse Ranch State Park. There was a $7.00 entrance fee to enter the park and there were three ponds where fishing was permitted. I tried fishing in pond #3 but had no luck. After fishing, we enjoyed a Dairy Queen and then we checked into the Clarkdale Lodge. Our overnight hotel was built in 1912 and is located at 23 N. 11th Street #870. The hotel lobby was quaint and we stayed in room 105 with a queen-size bed and a small chair. A view of the mountains in the distance was seen from the hotel.

In the evening, Christy Fisher's band, *Catty Wampus*, was playing at a free outdoor concert in the Mabery Pavilion at Clarkdale's Yavapai College from 6:30 to 8:30 and Penny and I decided to attend. The community college campus is virtually brand new with very impressive buildings. There is an outdoor stage with plenty of seating. The eleven-piece band played for two hours with a twenty-minute break. I took a few videos of parts of the concert.

THURSDAY, APRIL 5, 2018—CLARKDALE AND FISHING

Before breakfast, we took a brief driving tour of Clarkdale's Historic District. A sign read, Arizona's First Company Town. The town was founded in 1912, the same year Arizona became a state and incorporated in 1957. Another sign said Historic Clarkdale welcomes you with arrows pointing to the Town Hall, Clark Memorial Clubhouse, Museums, Train Depot and Tuzigoot National Monument.

Violette's Bakery Café located at 900 Main Street was recommended for breakfast so we decided to try it. The bakery is inside an old railroad caboose and is famous for their $8.99 Le Belgian Waffle Royale. So of course, Penny and I ordered two different waffles. Penny ordered a chocolate hazelnut waffle with whipped cream and a cut strawberry on top and I ordered a cinnamon waffle with strawberries and whipped cream on top. Wow! The waffles were delicious along with black coffee. We sat outside at a round wire table with a large blue umbrella sticking in a hole in the middle of the table. A man with a white pit bull was leaving the bakery so Penny had to stop and take a photo with his gentle pit bull.

After breakfast, we checked out of the hotel and drove to the Tuzigoot River Access Point where I went fishing underneath the Tuzigoot Bridge over the Verde River. The moving water was fun to fish but I caught nothing; however, I did take video where I was fishing. I also went to another Verde River location at the Tapco River Access Point and I fished at the lower Tapco Access Point on the Verde River. After fishing, Penny started looking for sticks to wrap with yarn and I took photos of Penny looking for sticks. The mountains along our drive were beautiful.

COTTONWOOD, ARIZONA AND DRIVE TO SCOTTSDALE

We stopped in nearby Cottonwood for lunch at the Crema Craft Kitchen + Bar located at 917 Main Street. We sat outside and split an arugula & quinoa salad and a side of fresh fruit skewer. The restaurant made a bar out of an old Hapag-Lloyd shipping container with padded stool-like seating in front of the container, something we had never seen before.

After lunch we started talking to two women artists, Debbie Gallagher and Vada Lovato, eating outside the Crema Craft restaurant and they told us about their works were for sale at Hart of AZ. We stopped by the artist filled shop and Penny bought a whistle and cards there. We drove back to Scottsdale late in the day stopped at Sunset Point on I-17 for a bathroom break and enough time to take a selfie with the mountains in the background.

FRIDAY, APRIL 6, 2018—TWO PEDICURES, MANICURE

After breakfast, Penny had a mani-pedi with Ben, the owner at Shona Nails N Spa. Hannah gave me a pedicure. Later in the day, we drove to Faith and Matt Beall's house in Chandler. The Jass family was there in anticipation for Maddy's Bat Mitzvah the next day. Ronna, Talia and Spencer, Linda Jass, Faith Beall, Lexi and Kyle Houghton and Penny were in a photo I took before dinner was served.

SATURDAY APRIL 7, 2018—MADDY'S BAT MITZVAH

Maddy Beall's Bat Mitzvah was scheduled for 10:00 a.m. at Tempe's Temple Emanuel at 5801 S. Rural Road. Maddy did a great job and after the service, many

438

people who attended headed to Gilbert's Joe's Real BBQ located at 301 N. Gilbert Road for lunch. The restaurant is inside the Heritage District's Tone Building and in 1918 Timmons Garage was located on this site. The original garage was torn down in 1924 and the building with the current restaurant was built in 1929. The place had a long line so someone told us about a side window where you could quickly order, so we went to the window and ordered our lunch. A large group of the Jass and Beall family guests sat on long tables inside the restaurant. We ordered turkey sandwiches and the food was delicious. In the evening, at 8:00, a reception and party for Maddy was held in the Seville Gold and Country Club located at 6683 S. Clubhouse Drive in Gilbert, Arizona.

MONDAY, APRIL 9, 2018—BREAKFAST KITCHEN BAR

Penny and I had breakfast at the Breakfast Kitchen Bar in the Scottsdale Quarter. We sat in the outside patio in the beautiful weather.

TUESDAY, APRIL 10—PAZOLS AND GIMPLES DINNER

Penny and I drove to Al Hamra Pakistani/Indian Restaurant in north Scottsdale at Pinnacle Peak and Pima Roads and met the Jim and Bobby Pazol and Ron and Bonny Gimple for dinner. The dinner was very good and not spicy with very few people eating in the restaurant.

THURSDAY, APRIL 12, 2018—CORKY AND NATALIE

For dinner, Penny and I met my cousin Corky Weily and Natalie Kane at the Village Tavern.

SATURDAY, APRIL 14, 2018— KONA GRILL DINNER

In the afternoon, Penny read on our patio. Later in the day, we picked up Jan and Rich Aver and drove to the Kona Grill on High Street right near the Desert Ridge Shopping Center. We sat in a large booth for dinner with Annie and Dan Murphy, Jan and Rich and Penny and me. After dinner, the Avers and Spencers went to Yogurtology for dessert.

MONDAY, APRIL 16, 2108—DESERT BOTANICAL GARDEN

Penny and I wanted to visit the Desert Botanical Garden before heading back to Chicago. There was a Jun Kaneko sculpture exhibit in the garden. Giant "head" sculptures were placed throughout the garden as well as other animal sculptures. Penny took a picture of me standing next to a large polka-dotted bear with an orange head.

After our walk in the Desert Botanical Garden, we drove to Tempe's Salut Kitchen Bar for lunch. We ordered our usual meal consisting of a Salut sampler: caprese salad, hummus nachos, Quinoa fritters, Mac N Cheese bites and Salut fries. We had lunch on the patio and the food was delicious. We were leaving Scottsdale for our trip back to Chicago so before we left, I took photos of the beautiful and colorful blooming bushes and trees near our condo and put them into my "show."

TUESDAY APRIL 17, 2018—FLYING TO CHICAGO

At 8:00 a.m. Penny and I left for Phoenix Sky Harbor Airport to drop off our luggage at curb side and I returned our rental car to the Transportation Center. Our non-stop United Airlines flight left on time at 11:27 a.m. and arrived at Chicago O'Hare at 4:50 p.m. Uri picked us up at the airport and drove us to Northbrook.

FRIDAY, APRIL 27, 2018—KENOSHA AND SPENCER

Penny and I had a desire to drive to Kenosha, Wisconsin and have breakfast at Frank's Diner located at 508 58th Street in Kenosha. After breakfast, we drove to Pleasant Prairie to the Outlet Mall. I bought new dress shoes at GH Bass and Penny bought a black light weight jacket there too. I bought Hanes underwear to leave in Scottsdale and we bought a gift for Bennett.

Penny and I were concerned when Ronna called to say Spencer was diagnosed with Nephritic Syndrome. It is a kidney disease involving inflammation. In general, the treatment is to reduce the inflammation by various methods. Spencer is taking a variety of drugs for the condition.

SUNDAY, APRIL 29, 2018—SKOKIE LIBRARY CONCERT

Alan and Marilyn Appelbaum suggested going to the Skokie Library for a free concert, so at 1:00 p.m. Penny and I drove to the Skokie Library's Auditorium and saw the vocal stylings of the Petra Van Nuis Jazz Quartet. Andy Brown, Petra's husband played the guitar along with Joe Policastro on bass and Jon Deitemyer on drums. The concert was entertaining with many songs from the 1940s.

MONDAY, APRIL 30, 2018—CHIROPRACTIC AND DR. FAUSONE

Penny went to see Dennis Molloy for her back and to Dr. Fausone for her annual exam. It was a beautiful day so we also walked at the Chicago Botanic Gardens. It was crowded there. Penny made a kale salad and blintzes for dinner.

WEDNESDAY, MAY 2, 2018—MT. PROSPECT GOLF

I picked up Jay Weintraub and we played golf at Mt. Prospect Golf Course with the Wednesday golf group.

SATURDAY, MAY 5, 2018—WALK & BLACK ENSEMBLE

In the morning, Penny and I drove to Elawa Farms in Lake Forest and walked in the Savannah. It was warm this day at 80 degrees. We bought tickets to Chicago's Black Ensemble Theater located at 4450 N. Clark Street for $98.50 to see *A New Attitude: In Tribute To Patti LaBelle* on Friday, May 18, 2018.

SUNDAY, MAY 13, 2018—MOTHER'S DAY
AND FEED MY STARVING CHILDREN

We had a very nice Mother's Day brunch at the Spencer home. After brunch, Bennett, Marni, Danny, Brooke, Penny and I went to Feed My Starving Children in a warehouse located at 742 E. Park Avenue in Libertyville, Illinois. The place had many families volunteering and was extremely organized. We volunteered to pack food in sealed bags for children in Peru. We had to wash our hands and wear hairnets before doing any work. Marni poured grain into a funnel and Bennett collected it in a container. Penny weighted rice. Brooke helped Bennett with loading bags. I sealed the bags using a special machine that heated the plastic bags shut.

After packing for one-hour, we sat on benches and heard the results of our efforts. During our one-hour session, the entire group packed ninety-seven boxes of food, 20,952 meals and fifty-seven kids would be fed for one year for a total cost of $4,609.44. At the end of the event, there was a raffle. Danny and Brooke entered Penny's name in the raffle and she won a basket of prizes.

PLAN ROAD TRIP TO MICHIGAN'S UPPER PENINSULA

For some time, I wanted to plan a road trip to Michigan's upper peninsula so I started planning this trip for this coming August. The first thing I did today was go online and started searching for information, I found a website sponsored by the tourist bureau and ordered upper peninsula information to be sent to me. I wanted to spend at least an overnight stay on Mackinac Island. I read many reviews of bed and breakfast inns on the island and decided to book the Market Street Inn for our Tuesday, August 7th overnight stay there and I emailed a deposit of $109.20.

STAINING & PAINTING INTERIOR ROOMS

Our neighbor, Raul Dilig, introduced me to Francisco Juarez, a painter Raul had used for this new home in Wildbrooke. I talked to Francisco and negotiated a price for the staining of the exterior of our Northbrook home plus painting three interior rooms. Francisco emailed me a contract and his insurance company emailed me his workmen's comp and liability insurance policy information. After reviewing the documents, I signed the contract on Saturday, May 12 and emailed it back to Francisco. Francisco signed the contract on Sunday, May 13 and emailed it back to me. We were all set with the work to begin by the end of May.

MONDAY, MAY 14, 2018—NEW SUMP PUMP INSTALLED AND POWER WASHED THE HOUSE

In the morning, Bill Swanson from Glenbrook Plumbing came to our Northbrook home to install a new sump pump in the laundry room. First, Bill took out our old Barnes sump pump, and then installed the new one.

In the afternoon, Francisco Juarez came to our house to power wash the outside in preparation of staining our home at a future date. Francisco meticulously power washed the cedar around the entire property. Meanwhile, Penny went to Convito Café & Market and bought a gift for Jill and Michael Maremont. The next day, we were planning on visiting the Maremonts in Michigan City, Indiana.

TUESDAY, MAY 15, 2018—MAREMONTS AND THE BIRNBAUMS

Hilton Head, South Carolina residents and my friend since elementary school, Sam Birnbaum and his wife Gay, were visiting their daughter Jill and her husband Michael Maremont. A few years ago, Jill and Michael moved from their Chicago condo to Michigan City, Indiana. Sam invited Penny and me to see them and the Maremont's home. After breakfast, Penny and I left for Michigan City by the Indiana Skyway and east on I-94. The Maremonts live in a picturesque two-story A-frame house in a secluded wooded area just inside the Michigan border. When we arrived around 11:15 a.m. and we got a tour of the home. Jill, an interior designer by occupation, beautifully decorated the place. During our visit, their Doberman Pincher, Oscar, kept close to Penny and I included several photos of Oscar and Penny in my sideshow. I know Sam since 6th grade in Youngstown. He lived on the south side of Youngstown and we used to take him to the old Bryson Street Jewish Center on Youngstown's north side.

Sam drove us to Three Oaks, Michigan for lunch, a short distance from the Maremont's home. We ate at Froehlich's located at 26 N. Elm Street in Three Oaks. The sandwiches were delicious. After lunch we walked around the town but no one was there because the "season" hadn't yet begun. We went into 3 Trilogy Antiques & Design and that was about it. We headed back to the Maremonts and said goodbye to everyone around 4:30 p.m. heading back to Northbrook.

FRIDAY, MAY 18, 2018—COFFEE TABLE AND THEATER

Penny and I went to Dania Furniture and picked out a glass coffee table and put down a $75.00 deposit. The coffee table will be sent to Dania and delivered to our house sometime in the next few months. At 4:45 p.m. I picked up Marcy and David Levinson and we drove to Anna Maria Pasteria before going to the Black Ensemble Theater to see A *New Attitude: In Tribute To Patti LaBelle*. The show was very entertaining as usual. After the show, I drove back to Northbrook and dropped off the Levinsons at their home.

TUESDAY, MAY 22, 2018—BENNETT'S BIRTHDAY

Today is Bennett's 46th birthday. The entire Spencer family is going downtown Chicago to spend the day and will see a U2 concert in the evening. Penny went to yoga in Evanston with instructor Rhoda Miriam and I stayed home.

WEDNESDAY, MAY 23, 2018—GOLF AT CHEVY CHASE

I played golf at Chevy Chase Golf Course with my Wednesday group. In the meantime, Penny was in the mood to bread eggplant so she could make eggplant Parmesan tomorrow. In doing so, she messed up her back. She picked up Marcy Levinson and met Jill Cole for lunch at Georgie Vs in Northbrook. Marcy fell and hurt her knee.

THURSDAY, MAY 24, 2018—LUNCH WITH ARNIE

I had lunch with Arnie Grauer at Butterfield's in Northbrook. I hadn't seen Arnie since last November before we left for Arizona.

TUESDAY, MAY 29, 2018—STAINS NORTHBROOK HOME

Around 8:00 a.m., Francisco Juarez and two of his workers arrived to put two coats of red stain on our cedar wood. I made a "show" of the staining process. They replaced a rotted board in the front of the carport and used Sherman Williams WoodScapes stain. The home looks great.

WEDNESDAY, MAY 30, 2018—PAINTED THREE ROOMS

Two of Francisco Juarez's men arrived in the morning to paint the master bedroom, Ronna's old room and the living room. The total cost of the outside staining and the painting of the living room, master bedroom and the middle bedroom was $4,600.00 made payable to Francisco The Painter. He did a great job and he was reasonably priced.

THURSDAY, MAY 31, 2018—*DOORS* CONCERT AND DANNY

Danny, almost age 13, was playing in a *Doors* tribute concert at the venue 210 in Highwood, Illinois. Penny and I drove to see and hear Danny and the School of Rock band in the concert. The bar and restaurant have a stage at one end. Danny had several guitar solos, played the keyboards, added some vocals on "Touch Me Babe" and played the drums. It was a fantastic concert.

SATURDAY, JUNE 2, 2018—BROOKE'S DANCE RECITAL

Penny and I drove to Waukegan to see Brooke's Dance Recital at the Genesee Theater located at 203 N. Genesee Street. The marquee said Welcome Releve

Dance Recital. Brooke, age 10, was in three different dances and I took videos of her dancing. There was Core Icons hip-hop, jazz and another one I don't know.

WEDNESDAY, JUNE 6, 2018—WEINTRAUBS DINNER

In honor of Danny's upcoming Bar Mitzvah, Penny and I sent in a contribution to the BJBE Music Fund. In the evening, Penny and I went to dinner with Jay and Harriet Weintraub at Dengeos in Buffalo Grove.

WEDNESDAY, JUNE 13, 2018—MILLER PARK, MILWAUKEE

At 10:15 a.m. Alan Appelbaum picked me up with Lou Bluestein and Alan Freeman in the car and we drove to the Deerfield Hyatt to meet Joel Probisky who would drive us to Milwaukee. We arrived in plenty of time to get lunch and the game started at 1:10 p.m. Harriet and Jay Weintraub just happened to be at the same game and I walked to where they were sitting and we took a selfie.

After the game, we lost Lou. He was walking behind me and when I turned around, he was gone. It took us thirty minutes of walking around but we finally found him standing by one of the doors. Joel, Alan and I decided this would be the last game with Lou and Al Freeman. Both Lou and Al are 93 years old. A person in the row in front of us took a photo of the five of us.

FRIDAY, JUNE 15, 2018—BEFORE DANNY'S BAR MITZVAH

Lois, Roy, Aaron, Leah and Josh Eaker arrived in the late morning and they rented a car and drove to our house for lunch. At 6:00 p.m. our family gathered at B'Nai Jehoshua Beth Elohim (BJBE) for an early service before Danny's Bar Mitzvah the next day. Danny was on the bimah for a short time during the service. There was an Oneg after the service in honor of Danny.

After services, the family gathered at Deerfield's El Tradicional restaurant on Lake Cook Road for dinner. Danny's grandparents from Philadelphia, Alan and Jill Miller were there as well as Marni's sister Abbey and her husband and children. Lois, Roy, Aaron, Leah and Josh Eaker were also in attendance. It was a fun evening and it was a nice get together.

SATURDAY, JUNE 16, 2018—DANNY'S BAR MITZVAH
AND OUR 50TH ANNIVERSARY

After breakfast, Penny and I drove to B'Nai Jehoshua Beth Elohim (BJBE) for Danny's 11:00 a.m. Bar Mitzvah. Danny did an amazing job on the service and gave a great speech. Following the ceremony, there was a luncheon at Wheeling's Saranello's restaurant for the family and a few friends. The first course was a Caesar Salad and I had delicious salmon Vesuvio for my entrée. Since it was our 50th wedding anniversary, a special cake was brought out in our honor.

After lunch, there was a sweet table set up with a variety of desserts served. Mascarpone Tiramisu, mocha and framboise macaroons, lemon cake, chocolate mousse, key lime pie and chef's fruit was on the sweet table. Others in attendance were cousin Norman and Sheila Lockshin, Todd and Jacob Waldman, my sister Linda Waldman, Lois Camberg, Roy, Aaron Cramer and Leah and her husband Josh Eaker, Michael and Arleen Gomshay. David and Marcy Levinson, Jill and Jeffrey Cole and Remey and Julie Rubin were three of our friends who attended.

SUNDAY, JUNE 17, 2018—GUESTS LEFT FOR HOME
Todd and Jacob and Norman and Sheila were at Bennett and Marni's house on Sunday. All the out-of-town guests went home later in the day.

TUESDAY, JUNE 19, 2018—SPEECH AND 50TH DINNER
After breakfast, Alan Appelbaum picked me up and we drove to the Patty Turner Center located at 375 Elm Street in Deerfield to hear a speech by retired NFL referee Jerry Markbreit. The speech was part of a men's club meeting and was very interesting. The meeting room was packed with older guys our age.

In the evening, David and Marcy Levinson and Jeffrey and Jill Cole treated Penny and me to dinner at L Woods Tap & Pine Lodge located at 7110 Lincoln Avenue in Lincolnwood to celebrate our 50th anniversary. The restaurant gave us a small dessert with ice cream and a candle in the middle.

WEDESDAY, JUNE 20, 2018—FOX RIVER AND BANGS LAKE
After breakfast, I drove northwest to the Fox River Preserve to try my luck at fishing in the Fox River. The docks were empty and I was able to fish on all five of them. I decided to buy worms at Walmart and caught some small bluegill on a night crawler using a bobber. After trying Fox River, I drove back to Bangs Lake and fished off the covered dock. I caught a baby northern pike on a number 2 Mepps spinner and a few bass as well.

SATURDAY, JUNE 23, 2018—50TH ANNIVERSARY DINNER
In the early afternoon, Penny and I went to the AMC Theater at Northbrook Court to see the documentary film, RBG about Supreme Court Justice Ruth Bader Ginsburg. Later in the day, as a treat, Jay and Harriet picked up Penny and me and treated us to dinner at Lake Forest's MLG restaurant to celebrate our 50th anniversary. The weather was beautiful and we sat outside on a patio. The restaurant gave us an anniversary chocolate cake but we also ended the meal with the most amazing bread pudding. We vowed to return next summer to celebrate Jay and Harriet's 50th anniversary and to order the bread pudding for dessert. Skip ahead to August 2019. We came back to MLG

TUESDAY, JUNE 26, 2018—BANGS LAKE FISHING
After breakfast, I drove to Bangs Lake and had a good time catching a small perch and some other fish. I also went to the Bass Pro Shops to buy Thermacell mosquito holster and replacement repellent canisters for our upcoming August trip to the Upper Peninsula of Michigan.

THURSDAY, JUNE 28, 2018—NIPPERSINK FOREST PRESERVE ROUND LAKE AND BANGS LAKE
I caught a bluegill at Nippersink Forest Preserve and a bass, a baby walleye and a rock bass at Bangs Lake. All catch and release.

FRIDAY, JUNE 29, 2018—RISE AND DINE AND PORTILLO'S
Penny and I had breakfast at Rise and Dine Pancake Café located at 102 S. Milwaukee Avenue in Wheeling. For dinner, we took Talia and Spencer to Portillo's in Vernon Hills and dessert at Sweet in Wheeling.

SUNDAY, JULY 1, 2018—MURPHYS IN NORTHBROOK
Dan and Annie Murphy were in Chicago for their family cooking competition.

Jay and Harriet invited Penny and me and Dan and Annie to their house for a BBQ.

WEDNESDAY, JULY 4, 2018—FOURTH OF JULY FIREWORKS

Penny and I drove to the Crate & Barrel parking lot and watched the Northbrook fireworks.

FRIDAY, JULY 6, 2018—SANDI FISHMAN PASSES AWAY

Doug Fishman texted us that his mother, Sandi Fishman had passed away in Clearwater, Florida and that a Celebration of Life would be held in her memory on Saturday, July 21, 2018 in Tampa. Upon hearing the sad news, Penny and I decided to fly to Tampa for the event. Lois Camberg, Roy, and Aaron Cramer and, Leah Cramer Eaker also decided to attend.

I bought a hibiscus plant from the Sunset Ridge house and planted it a few weeks ago and the first hibiscus flower bloomed today.

SUNDAY, JULY 8—TEMPLERS, LEVINSONS AND COLES

Jackie and Stu Templer were in Chicago visiting so Marcy and David Levinson invited Jackie and Stu, Jill and Jeffrey Cole and Penny and me to their house for a barbecue. Marni Levinson was also there and took a photo of our group. Then I took a photo of all of the women. It was a fun evening and we did a lot of catching up with everyone.

MONDAY, JULY 9, 2018—RONNA'S 43RD BIRTHDAY

For dinner, we celebrated Ronna's birthday at Saranello's restaurant on Milwaukee Avenue in Wheeling. After dinner, we all went back to the Belinky home for an ice cream cake and I took a photo of the Belinky family.

TUESDAY, JULY 10, 2018—FISHING AND MAGITS DINNER

After breakfast, I drove to Jerry Bernstein's house in Highland Park and he drove to Lake Marie, part of the chain of lakes, where we met Mike Stricker and Neal London at Barnacle Bob's Boats, Bait and Tackle. We rented a pontoon boat and had a great time fishing. The guys were only using "live" bait and catching small blue gills and some bass. I was using all artificial bait and had no luck.

In the evening, Alan and Ellen Magit invited Mike and Fran Stricker, Jerry and Linda Bernstein, Jay and Harriet Weintraub and Penny and me to their home for a barbecue dinner. The food was plentiful and delicious and we all had a great time. Of course, I had to take a selfie of our group.

TRIP TO TAMPA, FLORIDA
SATURDAY, JULY 21—SANDI'S CELEBRATION OF LIFE

Uri picked up Penny and me at 6:00 a.m. for our non-stop United Airlines flight to Tampa, Florida for Sandi Fishman's Celebration of Life. We boarded the plane at 7:25 a.m. The plane took off on time but was diverted to Orlando International Airport because of Tampa's bad weather. We sat on the plane at the Orlando Airport for over two hours until the Tampa weather cleared. Upon arriving at Tampa International Airport, I rented an intermediate car from Enterprise Rent-A-Car through Costco for $53.20 We drove to and checked into the Springhill Suites located at 3485 Ulmerton Road in Clearwater, FL 33762 for a suite with 1 King size bed. We met the Cramer/Cambergs in the lobby of the hotel.

The Celebration of Life was scheduled for 6:00 p.m. at Mara and Mike Knapp's home located in Largo. Many of Sandi's friends were at the event. A group photo was taken with Doug, Biddy, Mara, Mike, Lois, Roy, Leah Cramer Eaker, Penny and me. After the event, Doug and Aaron went to a bar for a nightcap. Afterwards, Doug brought back Aaron to the hotel.

SUNDAY, July 22, 2018—TRIP TO CHICAGO

At 10:00 a.m. I dropped off our rental car at Tampa International Airport for our United Airlines flight to Chicago. We departed on time at 12:40 p.m. and our two-hour arrived in Chicago O'Hare Airport at 2:27 p.m. Uri picked us up from the airport and drove us home to Northbrook. It was another great but sad trip.

CHAPTER THIRTY-ONE
Michigan's Upper Peninsula Road Trip

FRIDAY, AUGUST 3, 2018—GREEN BAY, WISCONSIN

Penny and I left Northbrook to our first overnight stop at Florence, Wisconsin (Distance 294.1 miles 4 hours 27 minutes) on I-43 north, then routes 41/141. Our first stop was Green Bay, Wisconsin and an outside look at Lambeau Field, the home of the Green Bay Packers. We drove around the parking lot and I took photos. We ate lunch at Green Bay's Erbert and Gerbert's Sandwich Shop. You order sandwiches at a counter and your order is delivered to the table. After lunch I stopped at Mills Fleet Farm to pick up a few fishing lures before driving to Florence. On the way to Florence, we stopped at The Ice Cream Station for some Key Lime ice cream.

FLORENCE, WISCONSIN—BED AND BREAKFAST

We arrived at Doll's Bed & Breakfast around 2:30 p.m. located at 509 Furnace Street in Florence, Wisconsin. A set of old golf clubs sat in the corner of our golf themed queen-size bedroom on the 2nd floor. The cost of the bed and breakfast was $95.00 a night plus tax for a total of $100.23. The room had a chair, a wall unit with a television and a large window looking out the front of the house. The home was located on Fisher Lake and the two-story B & B had a covered porch wrapping around the second floor. I had a chance to fish off of the pontoon boat and catch several bluegills with my fly rod using a wooly bugger.

I made 6:15 p.m. dinner reservations at Maxsells Restaurant located on 209 Central Avenue in Florence, a short walk from our B & B. The original 3-story Prairie school home was built in 1899. A large sign in front of the house said it is called the Fulmer-Sells home and on Fisher Lake. The house was listed on the Wisconsin register August 23, 2013 and also listed on the National Historic Register on May 5, 2014. There were two wood sculptures on the porch as you entered the front door. We were seated in a table for two inside the restaurant.

To begin our meal, Penny ordered a glass of Sauvignon Blanc and I had a glass of Pinot Noir. Our server took a photo of us sitting at our table. We ordered a delicious onion and mushroom flatbread as an appetizer and a fantastic pan-seared northern pike on top of faro for a shared entrée. The food was absolutely delicious. They have a large outdoor patio overlooking Fisher Lake.

Directly across the street from Maxsells located at 200 Central Avenue was Queen Anne Victorian Webb Judge House built in 1883. A sign in front explained the history of the home. After dinner, we walked back to our B & B and went to sleep, as we were tired from the drive.

SATURDAY, AUGUST 4, 2018—FLORENCE TO HOUGTON

Before our breakfast, I went fishing on a pontoon boat in Fisher Lake and caught two perch. After fishing, Penny and I ate breakfast in the dining room around 7:30 a.m. Around 9:30 a.m. we headed toward Copper Harbor, Michigan by the way of Eagle River. (The distance from Florence to Copper Harbor, Michigan was 144.5 miles or 2 hrs. 46 minutes). We stopped for lunch at Fitzgerald's Restaurant inside the Eagle River Inn overlooking Lake Superior. I ordered a hummus trio, featuring peanut butter, roasted red pepper & black beans with carrots, celery and pita bread. Penny ordered a Pitmaster pie with smoked brisket, pork, carrots, peas & cauliflower baked in a red wine sauce and topped with mashed potatoes. For dessert, we ordered key lime pie. After lunch, someone took a photo of Penny and me with Lake Superior in the background.

After lunch we were on our way to Copper Harbor and Houghton, we stopped at the Jam Pot Bakery, Jams and Jellies, run by monks. The store was 47 miles or 1 hour 3 minutes from our lunch stop. The two monks behind the counter had long black beards. There was a long line, so we decided not to wait or buy anything there. After the Jam Pot, we took a short walk to look at Jacobs Falls and someone took a photo of us in front of the falls. There was a sign near the falls that read Welcome to Eagle Harbor Township.

After leaving the Jam Pot Bakery's parking lot, we drove to Brockway Mountain on the Keweenaw Coastal wildlife corridor on top of the Brockway Mountain Drive. I took a video from the top of the mountain with Lake Superior and Copper Harbor in the distance as the strong wind was blowing. We also stopped at another spot-on top of the Brockway Mountain Drive observation area and took photos looking down at Cooper Harbor below. We also stopped at Copper Harbor State Harbor and a boat launch into Lake Superior.

On our way to our overnight stay in Houghton from Copper Harbor, we passed Temple Jacob located at 301 Front Street in Hancock, Michigan. We pulled in the temple's parking lot and took photos of the building. We stopped at the Holiday Inn Express [Keweenaw Peninsula] located at 1110 Century Way in Houghton, Michigan. The cost of our hotel room was $225.63.

SUNDAY, AUGUST 5, 2018—ROAD TO MARQUETTE

Penny and I ate breakfast in the hotel then headed toward Marquette, Michigan. The distance from Houghton, Michigan to Marquette, Michigan was 100 miles or 1 hr. 52 min. Upon arriving in Marquette, we ate lunch at the Iron Bay Restaurant & Drinkery located at 105 E. Washington Street. After lunch we took a walk along the lakeshore. We also drove around Northern Michigan University's campus and around Presque Isle Park. After our drive, we checked into the Hampton Inn Marquette/Waterfront Hotel located at 461 South Lakeshore Boulevard. We had a king-size bed with an AARP discount for a total of $233.02 per night including tax. Our hotel room was very spacious with a beautiful view overlooking Lake Superior. We saw two people practicing scuba diving outside of our window.

From our hotel, we walked to dinner at Sol Azteca Mexican Restaurant located at 105 E. Washington Street. We ate delicious guacamole & cheese rice dish with homemade chips. It rained while eating but after our dinner there was a rainbow in the sky that I captured in a photo. In the background of the photo was a "pocket dock" that remains. By in the day when iron ore was mined, the old docks were used to transfer iron ore from trains to ships. During dinner, I asked one of the servers if there was a good place to fish in Marquette and he suggested the Dead River and told me where to go. After dinner, I went fishing in the Dead River and caught my first smallmouth bass on a flyrod downstream from a bridge on the Marquette's Dead River. Penny sat in the car while I went fishing in the river. After fishing, we drove back to our hotel and fell asleep.

MONDAY, AUGUST 6, 2018—ROAD TO MANISTIQUE

Penny and I ate breakfast in the hotel and afterwards, I took a video from the hotel's patio. We packed our car and started on our drive from Marquette, Michigan to Manistique, Michigan, a distance of 90.6 miles or 1 hr. 33 min. On the way to Manistique, we passed the Grand Island National Recreation Area, part of the Hiawatha National Forest. We didn't stop because you had to take a ferryboat to the island. This rustic island was mainly for camping.

We arrived in Manistique in the afternoon and checked into the Comfort Inn located at 617 E. Lakeshore Drive in Manistique, Michigan. The cost of hotel room was $147.14 that included breakfast. In front of the hotel was a large moose painted wearing a tuxedo. Across the street from our hotel was Lake Michigan. Carol Randall recommended seeing Kitch-iti-kipi, an Ojibwa word for Big Spring so we drove to it and parked our car. Penny sat in the car while I took a walk to see why Carol wanted us to see it. There was a long line of people waiting to get on a glass bottom boat to see crystal clear water. Instead of waiting in line, I took several photos and you could see large fish swimming under the boat. There was also a billboard with a map showing many of the locations of Michigan State Parks. We went to Indian Lake State Park and I tried to fish but the water was too shallow.

TUESDAY, AUGUST 7, 2018—MACKINAC ISLAND

Penny and I ate breakfast at the hotel and drove from Manistique, Michigan to Mackinaw City, Michigan, a distance of 95.5 Miles or 1 hr. 43 minutes. On the way to Mackinaw City, we stopped in St. Ignace at a Big Boy restaurant and ordered a strawberry pie, then sat in the parking lot and ate the pie.

We crossed the Mackinac Bridge from Michigan's Upper Peninsula to the Lower Peninsula, arrived in Mackinaw City before 9:00 a.m. We had reservations on the Starline Ferry located at 801 S. Huron Street Mackinaw City, Michigan. The cost of the Starline Ferry to Mackinac Island was $24.00 each round trip or $48.00 and the cost of parking our car in a secured parking lot was $5.00 per day.

Upon our arrival, I drove to the parking area of the Mackinac Island Ferry Dock #1. I dropped off Penny near the dock with our luggage and drove our car to a remote and secure parking lot and parked our car. A shuttle took me back to the dock where I met Penny and our luggage. We got in line for our Starline Ferry [our boat name was Marquette II] to Mackinac Island. Our luggage was tagged and put on a cart and loaded onto the ferryboat. The ferry passed the Mackinac Island Bridge and arrived in Mackinac Island around 9:30 a.m.

Our goal was to visit the Island, see as much as possible in a short amount of time and have fun. After we landed on the island, picked up our luggage from the cart and walked a short distance on Main Street to our Bed & Breakfast, the Market Street Inn located at 7237 Market Street. Since we were early, we placed our luggage in a storage space in the Inn's lobby until check-in time at 3:00 p.m. The total cost of our Bed and Breakfast room was $218.40. On Monday May 14, 2018, I had prepaid for half of the room of $109.20.

After we deposited our suitcase at the B & B, we walked a short distance back to Main Street and bought two tickets at the official Mackinac Island Carriage Tours for an 11:25 a.m. tour of the island. We walked around for a short time before our tour started. We got into the carriage and the driver took a photo of us in the carriage before our tour got underway. Our carriage tour took us around the perimeter of the island and past the historic and famous Grand Hotel.

After our island tour carriage ride, we stopped at The Grand Hotel located at 286 Grand Avenue for an inside self-guided walking tour. The cost of our self-guided tour was $20.00. We walked on the world's longest porch and took a selfie sitting in chairs with the sun in our eyes. I took several photos from the front porch. We then walked inside the hotel to the lobby and living room. The dining room was being set for dinner. We took an elevator to the top floor and took photos out the window at the grounds below and Lake Huron. One photo was the Hydra Jet Ferry on its way to the island.

Penny and I were hungry after our self-guided tour of The Grand Hotel so we decided to eat lunch in a tented area inside The Jockey Club near hotel. After lunch we walked to the Market Street Inn at 3:45 p.m. and checked in. I took photos of our room that was very quaint having two windows that faced Market Street. After checking in, we took a walk on Main Street and several other streets. We stopped at Murdicks Fudge located at 190 S. Huron Street and bought some fudge. This store was an original since 1887. At 6:30 p.m., we ate dinner at The Pink Pony Bar and Grill located at 7221 Main Street. After dinner we walked around and went back to our room ready for a good night's sleep.

WEDNESDAY, AUGUST 8, 2018—MACKINAC ISLAND
TO SAULT STE MARIE, ONTARIO

Penny and I were the only ones eating breakfast in the lobby of the Market Street Inn. After breakfast we packed our suitcase and put it in a storage area in the lobby. We spent the entire day on the Island walking around to different street we hadn't seen. We passed by Cindy's Riding Stable located on Market Street and saw twelve horseback riders starting on a ride through the streets of the island. You could rent horses at this place and I took video of the riders. We walked by the Biddle House located at 7406 Market Street. The sign in front said in part, "This house is probably the oldest on the island. Parts of it date back to 1780." At 9:15 a.m. we walked by the Mackinac Island Public Library. Next to the library is a marker

"The Round Island Lighthouse, seen south of this site, was completed in 1895." We went back to the Market Inn and picked up our suitcase and walked to the dock for our trip back to the mainland.

We left on the 10:00 a.m. Starline Ferryboat to Mackinaw City. When we arrived on shore, we picked up our luggage from the cart. Penny stayed by the dock with our suitcase while I took a shuttle to the secure parking lot and drove the car to near the boat and put our suitcase in the car.

Traveling north on I-75, Penny and I drove from Mackinaw City, Michigan to Sault Ste. Marie, Ontario, a distance of sixty miles that took one hour and five minutes. The toll on the Mackinac Island Bridge from the Lower Peninsula to the Upper Peninsula was $4.00. There was a long line of cars entering Canada so we had to wait awhile. The toll on the International Bridge from the Lower Peninsula Michigan to Sault Ste. Marie Ontario, Canada was $3.50 US or $4.40 in Canadian money. There was a long line of cars entering Canada

We arrived at the Delta Hotel Sault Ste. Marie Waterfront located at 208 St. Mary's River Drive in Sault Ste. Marie, Ontario Canada. Our stay was from Wednesday, August 8 to Thursday, August 9. The cost of the hotel room was $144.00 plus $23.60 tax =$167.60 [converted to US (about $199.16). We had a very spacious room with two queen-size beds overlooking the St. Mary's River and you could see the International Bridge in the background. Inside the hotel, we ate lunch in The View restaurant with a scenic window view of the St. Mary's River's waterfront. I ordered a kale & broccoli salad with apple slices, red cabbage, raisins and sunflower seeds. Penny ordered a kale & spinach salad with sliced apples, red peppers, sliced almonds and raisins. Both salads were delicious. During lunch with our scenic view, we watched the Soo Locks Boat Tours boat travel on the St. Mary's River.

After lunch we asked a man behind the registration desk where we could go that would give us a taste of the area. He suggested taking a drive north along a beautiful stretch of Lake Superior to Pancake Bay, a distance of about fifty miles. We took the man's advice and travelled on a beautiful drive to Pancake Bay. Along the way, we stopped to go to the bathroom at a wood carving store and a Canadian Carver store that sold handmade crafts. The drive we experienced was part of the Lake Superior water trail. If we would have continued all around Lake Superior, ending in Duluth, Minnesota, a distance of seven-hundred fifty miles. We headed back to Sault Ste. Marie and decided to eat dinner at Giovanni's Italian Restaurant located at 516 Great Northern Road Sault Ste. Marie. We had a delicious dinner and afterwards headed back to our hotel for a good night's sleep because tomorrow would be a big day.

THURSDAY, AUGUST 9, 2018—HARBOR SPRINGS

Penny and I checked out of the Delta Hotel around 8:00 a.m. and went to breakfast at The Breakfast Pig located at 265 Bruce Street. This restaurant was quite a place, very laid back and sparsely decorated serving breakfast all day. When you walked into the eatery, there was a menu board that had the history of the restaurant and a little about the owner, Angela Caputo who opened the place on June 27, 2015. The Breakfast Pig coffee cup had written below the name, Badass Eatery. The breakfast cost $30.52 and was delicious.

Before leaving Sault Ste. Marie, Ontario for Michigan's Lower Peninsula, we stopped at an Esso station to fill our car with gas, then we were on our way to Harbor Springs and Petoskey, Michigan. The toll on the International Bridge from Sault Ste. Marie Ontario, Canada to the Upper Peninsula in Michigan was $3.50 US or $4.40 Canadian money. Then the toll on the Mackinac Island Bridge from the Upper Peninsula to the Lower Peninsula was $4.00, a distance from Sault Ste. Marie, Ontario to Petoskey, Michigan of 152.4 Kilometers or one hour forty-seven minutes.

On the way to Harbor Springs we drove through the "Tunnel of Trees" to Cross Village, Michigan. Once we got to Cross Village, we saw The Legs Inn. The sign in front of this place read in part "The Legs Inn, named for the stove legs that trim the roofline, is one of Michigan's most exuberant and unusual landmarks. The building reflects Stanley Smolak's creativity and craftsmanship of local Odawa (Ottawa) Indians. A Polish immigrant, Smolak came to the United States in 1912 and settled in Cross Village in 1921." The building is very unusual in design and is a mixture of stone and wood. The same family has owned The Legs Inn for the past eighty years and part of the property is a monument to nature and is listed as a State of Michigan Historic Landmark.

After leaving Cross Village, we arrived in Harbor Springs. The first place we stopped was the Harbor Springs Marina Public Bathrooms located at 250 East Bay Street. Penny and I walked along the marina and to Yummies Ice Cream Shop on Main Street for ice cream. We also walked by the Harbor Springs Library located at 206 S. Spring Street. The library is in a building built in 1908. We arrived at the Comfort Inn located at 1314 US 31 N. in Petoskey and checked into our room. The lobby had a moose head hanging on the wall near the registration desk.

PETOSKEY, MICHIGAN

We ate a late dinner at the City Park Grill located at 432 E. Lake Street in Petoskey. City Park Grill, one of Petoskey's oldest buildings, was originally constructed in 1875. McCarty Hall, as it was then known, was a males-only billiard parlor that offered cigars and "intoxicating beverages." The storied history includes tales of prohibition and underground tunnels, of young Ernest Hemingway, and ghost sightings. Visit City Park Grill in Petoskey to make a little history of your own. From the 1910s – 1920s, Ernest Hemingway made northern Michigan his home. The story goes that Hemingway sat in the second chair by the bar.

In 1997, Bob and Mary Keedy, Dick and Laura Dinon, Chef John Norman, and Patrick Faylor purchased the Park Garden Café, changing the name to City Park Grill. The menu was changed as well to reflect the scratch kitchen focus with daily and seasonal specials. Since, the restaurant has been restored to the glory days of the past, serving and entertaining a wide array of guests from around the world. Penny and I shared garlic and pistachio covered whitefish with green beans and mashed potatoes. For dessert, we shared a mango/strawberry crisp with ice cream. The meal was delicious.

After dinner, we walked around Petoskey. Penny went into Pappagallo store and bought a cute outfit on sale for one-half off the regular price. What a deal and I took a photo of Penny standing in front of the store. Our Petoskey walk also took us past the Public Library and the Old Petoskey Carnegie Library Building where a plaque in front read, "Hemingway's Michigan, When living in Petoskey in 1919, the library was a favorite haunt of Hemingway's and, in December, wearing his Italian cape and Red Cross uniform, he spoke here to the Ladies Aid Society about his World War I experience. At this event he met the Connable family who led to his connections with the Toronto Star newspaper and his employment as its European correspondent." The Department of the Interior placed this building on the National Register of Historic Places. We walked to a park after dinner, sat on a park bench facing Lake Michigan and the boats in the marina and took a selfie.

FRIDAY, AUGUST 10, 2018—CHARLEVOIX AND ELK RAPIDS

After eating breakfast at the hotel, we drove from Petoskey to Charlevoix, Michigan, a distance of seventeen miles or twenty-three minutes. The first place we visited was the Charlevoix Chamber of Commerce & Visitors Bureau. They told us about all of the mushroom houses in the area and recommended we see them. They gave us a map and before seeing them drove by the Charlevoix Harbor and stopped to read a sign put up by the Charlevoix Historical Society that showed a photo of the Harsha House Museum and other historical places to visit.

Then we drove by seven mushroom houses ending at the Charlevoix Public Library located at 220 Clinton Street. It was an impressive and beautiful building built in 1927 to originally serve as the Charlevoix High School. In 2006, it became the Charlevoix Public Library with the interior that looked like Frank Lloyd Wright had designed it in the arts and craft style. After a brief self-guided tour of the library, we walked on Charlevoix's main street and walked past Central Drugs, a Rexall store located at 301 Bridge Street. This drugstore has been serving the communities of Charlevoix and Beaver Island since 1897. We were quite surprised to see the name Rexall on the sign in front of the pharmacy.

ELK RAPIDS, MICHIGAN AND COUSINS

After Charlevoix, we drove to Elk Rapids, Michigan to meet my second cousin Ron Spritzer and his wife Carol at a local restaurant for lunch. The distance from Charlevoix to Elk Rapids, Michigan was thirty-three miles or a forty-minute drive. After lunch, we saw some river otters swimming nearby and we also stopped at the Elk Rapids District Library and went inside.

After the library we followed the Spritzers to Farmer White, a small white building along a road where we bought some cherry jam and other goodies. After Farmer White, we went to the Spritzer's home in Rapid City. We got a tour of their home and I went fishing on their lake. Penny, Ron and Carol were standing on their lawn when I caught a bass but it jumped off so nobody saw the fish. After spending time with the Spritzers, we drove to Mount Pleasant, Michigan, a distance of one-hundred fifteen miles or one hour and fifty-seven minutes via US 131 north. On our way to Mount Pleasant, I took a photo of Kalkaska County Public Library

MOUNT PLEASANT, MICHIGAN

We arrived in Mount Pleasant in the late afternoon at the Fairfield Inn & Suites located at 2525 South University Park Drive. I used 15,000 Marriott Rewards Points for a free night. We had a spacious room with a divided wall with a couch. After checking in, we went for a tour of the Central Michigan University campus. There is a brand-new Park Library has a unique architecture and the only building I recognized was Warriner Hall. The city of Mount Pleasant and the CMU campus and buildings have totally changed since I got my Master's degree in June 1966. The main street, Mission Street, was a two-lane street and now it is four lanes. The Embers restaurant, an upscale restaurant, no longer exists and there were only a few restaurants on Mission Street. Now there are four lanes and many franchise restaurants.

I wanted to check out a local bar Steve Klein and I frequented when we were in graduate school. I went inside The Bird Bar and Grill located at 2223 S. Main Street because Steve and I used to play pool in the back room on one pool table. This brick building remains virtually the same as it was in the 1960s except now there are two pool tables in the back room. I met Ben Bridenstein, the third-generation owner of The Bird and a photo was taken of us. The Bird visit was very nostalgic. After going to The Bird, we decided to eat dinner at Red Lobster.

SATURDAY, AUGUST 11, 2018—SOUTH HAVEN
AND DRIVE HOME TO NORTHBROOK

After breakfast, we filled up our car with gas and headed to South Haven on Michigan's route 127 south to Michigan route 46 and turned west to US route 131. We drove through Grand Rapids to I-196 south. We got off the main highway and stopped in Fennville and Cranes Pie Pantry and Restaurant. We bought fresh picked peaches and a few baked goods and stopped by the Fennville Public Library to take a photo.

We arrived in South Haven around `11:30 a.m. in time for lunch at the home of Remey and Julie Rubin located at 622 North Shore at Webster Street. Remey's daughter, Karry happened to be there and was staying with the Rubins. The distance from Mount Pleasant, Michigan to South Haven was one hundred forty-eight miles and it took two hours and thirty-eight minutes. We had a very nice lunch and visit. After lunch and before we headed back to Northbrook, Penny and I stopped at Sherman's Dairy Bar for ice cream. I had a single scoop of Mackinac Island fudge and Penny ordered chocolate ice cream. After eating the delicious ice cream, I filled up our gas tank and started our drive to Northbrook. The distance from South Haven, Michigan to Northbrook, Illinois was one hundred fifty-six miles or two hours and twenty-seven minutes. We arrived home in the afternoon after a fantastic trip to Michigan's upper and lower peninsula and a little of Canada.

THURSDAY, AUGUST 23, 2018—MARCIA BALL

In the evening, Penny and I went to Space located 1245 Chicago Avenue in Evanston, Illinois for a Marcia Ball concert. She was accompanied with a four-piece band and her performance was outstanding and very entertaining. Marcia crosses her legs while playing the piano, a unique style.

SATURDAY, AUGUST 27, 2018—BLACK ENSEMBLE

Penny and I picked up Jay and Harriet and we drove to Chicago's Black Ensemble Theater located at 4450 N. Clark Street for a show. I got a parking space right in front of the theater. The show was *Rick Stone Blues Man*. The stage was set like a nightclub called Ricky's Place. The five-piece band was set up on the main stage. The band is usually up above the stage. Rick Stone's performance was fantastic and we thoroughly enjoyed the evening.

TUESDAY, SEPTEMBER 4, 2018—MILLER PARK

After breakfast, Alan Appelbaum had purchased tickets to the Chicago Cubs vs the Milwaukee Brewers but couldn't go because he was recuperating from a heart operation that went wrong. I drove to the Deerfield Hyatt and met Joel Probisky in the parking lot. Joel drove to Miller Park and we watched the Milwaukee Brewers defeat the Chicago Cubs 11 to 2. The best part of the game was the sausage race in between one of the late innings.

FRIDAY, OCTOBER 5, 2018—TED'S BIRTHDAY

Carol Randall came to our home in Northbrook and gave Penny and me a massage. I took a photo of Penny on the massage table. In the evening, we celebrated Ted's birthday at their home. Ronna bought an ice cream pie for the occasion.

SATURDAY, OCTOBER 6, 2018—HAIRCUTS AND LATE LUNCH

After breakfast, Penny and I drove downtown for our haircuts. I got dropped off at the Hyatt Regency Chicago a little before 10:00 a.m. and Penny took the car to J Gordon Design for her 11:30 a.m. haircut appointment with Cheryl. After my haircut with Otto Bodner, I walked to Dearborn Street and took the number 22 Clark Street bus to Starbucks at the corner of Clark Street and Deming Place. When Penny was done with her haircut, I walked to J Gordon and met her.

We decided to drive north to Pauline's Breakfast & Lunch located at 1554 W. Balmoral Avenue in Chicago for a late lunch. I would describe the restaurant as American comfort food served in a country-diner setting. There were red and white checked tablecloths. After lunch, we drove home.

SUNDAY, OCTOBER 7, 2018—GOLDSHOLL EXHIBIT

After breakfast, Penny and I drove to the Mary and Leigh Block Museum of Art on the campus of Northwestern University. The Mort and Millie Goldsholl Exhibit was on display with the *Up Is Down-Mid-Century Experiments in Advertising and Film* at the Goldsholl Studio. The Chicago based Goldsholl Design Associates was founded in 1954 and was a leading design firm in the United States. The exhibit was very interesting. Many years ago, I went to the Goldsholl Studio in Northfield and met Mort.

THURSDAY, OCTOBER 11, 2018—A NORTHLIGHT PLAY

In the evening, we had tickets to see Mike Nusbaum perform in *Curve of Departure* at the Northlight Theater. Mike is a famous Chicago actor who was 94 years old and still acting in the theater. Penny and I enjoyed the four-person play, especially Mike Nusbaum's performance. We stayed for a panel discussion held after the play with three of the actors.

SATURDAY, OCTOBER 13, 2018—COLVIN HOUSE TOUR

Every year, the Chicago Architecture Foundation holds Open House all over Chicagoland so people can tour various places for free that are not normally available or charged admission. In October 2017, Chicago's Colvin House located at 5940 N. Sheridan Road was part of an open house tour during a Chicago Architecture Foundation Open House. The owner, Angela Valavanis, gave a tour when she first purchased the house for 1.15 million dollars and Penny and I saw the house when it was in total disrepair and neglected with water damage. In 1909, architect George W. Maher designed The Edwin Colvin House and is one of the last remaining large-scale residences to survive along Sheridan Road. The house was designated a Chicago Landmark on October 5, 1994. Today, after breakfast, Penny and I drove to Chicago's Colvin House to see the newly renovated open house tour. Ms. Valavanis gave the tour today. She put in over a million dollars to renovate the property and today we saw the completed project. The house is spectacular and is restored to its original. It now has several rental offices.

EDGEWATER BEACH APARTMENTS TOUR

Our final stop on the Open House tours was the Edgewater Beach Apartments located at 5555 N. Sheridan Road. We parked the car on a side street and walked through the entrance to the beautiful lobby of the apartment building. There is also a swimming pool in the building. The apartment building is located in the Bryn Mawr Historic District.

SUNDAY, OCTOBER 14, 2018—GENEALOGICAL SOCIETY

I hadn't been to a meeting of the Jewish Genealogical Society of Illinois meeting in several years. But I wanted to go today to hear Scott Meyer make a presentation on finding his grandfather's store. After the meeting I had a chance to see some old friends and to speak with Scott.

FRIDAY, OCTOBER 19, 2018—WISCONSIN FOOTBALL

Penny did not want to go with me this trip to Wisconsin to watch a football game because last year, the weather was very cold and she did not enjoy the experience. After breakfast I headed north to Wisconsin to do some fishing before going to Madison to meet Ronna and family. I stopped at the Mount Vernon Creek Fishery Area on the upper Sugar River but couldn't find an actual spot to fish. I then went to Lake Stewart in Mount Horeb and fished for a short time with no luck. After that, I drove to Madison and fished in Lake Mendota. The lake was beautiful and calm but didn't have a bite.

At 3:30 p.m. I checked into Tru by Hilton Madison West located at 8102 Watts Road in Madison. A big mural of the Madison capital building, Bucky Badger and the convention center was in the hotel's lobby. I drove to downtown Madison and parked across from Dotty Dumpling's Dowry restaurant located at 317 N. Frances Street and ate a late lunch by myself. Afterwards, I waited for Ronna and family and Katie to arrive at the Colectivo coffee bar so we could attend the Homecoming Parade. While waiting for Ronna and family, I ordered a black coffee. When Ronna and Katie arrived, we walked to West Gilman Street to watch the Homecoming parade with Katie. During the parade I took a selfie with Talia. I also took a video of Wisconsin's Premiere Dance Team and videos of music, Bucky Badger, cheerleaders and of course the University of Wisconsin Marching Band. After the homecoming parade, we ate pizza at a nearby restaurant. I drove back to the hotel and parked my car until tomorrow, after the football game. I will leave my car in the hotel's parking lot and take an Uber to the Prep Rally.

SATURDAY, OCTOBER 20, 2018—WISCONSIN VS. ILLINOIS

I met Ronna and family for breakfast at the hotel. After breakfast, I took an

Uber to Madison and met Ronna and family at the South Student Union to the Badger Bash and Pep Rally before the 11:00 a.m. football game. We listened to the band and walked to Camp Randall Stadium to watch the football game. It was chilly and we wore our winter jackets. During the game, it started snowing. Spencer was not happy so Ted and Spencer went back to the student union to hang out. Toward the end of the game, the band did a jump on the field. After the jump, Ronna, Talia and I walked to the Sky Box. Katie had invited us to watch part of the game from there. Ronna, Talia and I watched the last part of the football game and the Fifth Quarter from the Sky Box. We also met Katie's cousin Laura and Cindy Kennedy. The final score of the game was Wisconsin 49, Illinois 20. After the game we met up with Ted and Spencer near the University Bookstore. I took an Uber back to the hotel to pick up my car and motored home to Northbrook.

FRIDAY, OCTOBER 26, 2018—MECUM AUTO AUCTION

Bennett invited me to attend the Chicago Mecum Auto Auction held at the Schaumburg Renaissance Center. Bennett picked me up around 8:30 a.m. and we drove to Schaumburg and parked the car in a remote lot. We had to wait in line to get a shuttle bus to the convention center. We met Dave Nusbaum and his father.

SATURDAY, OCTOBER 27, 2018—BACKSTROM'S GARAGE

A neighbor on Gregg Road, Bob Backstrom, collects and restores old Jeeps as a hobby. I pass his house all the time but today I decided to pay him a visit because he had his 1948 Knoxville, Illinois Jeep fire truck sitting in the driveway. Inside his garage he is restoring a 1946 Willy's Jeep. He let me sit in the Jeep and took a photo of me. He also gave me a short ride down Midway in his 1948 Willy's fire truck ride. It was a "kick" riding in that old open air Jeep fire truck.

SUNDAY, NOVEMBER 4, 2018—BLACK ENSEMBLE

Penny and I went to a 3:00 p.m. matinee of *Women of Soul* at the Black Ensemble Theater located at 4450 N Clark Street. Afterwards we went to DiPescara for dinner.

WEDNESDAY, NOVEMBER 13, 2018—TALIA'S CONCERT

At 6:00 p.m. we drove to Twin Grove School for Talia's Orchestra Concert.

SATURDAY, NOVEMBER 17, 2018—OUR FIRST SNOW

Penny and I couldn't believe it but we had our first snow today.

MONDAY, NOVEMBER 26, 2018—OUR SECOND SNOW DEEP

The snowfall was much deeper than on November 17th. I had to shovel because our snow removal service does not start until December 1st.

THURSDAY, NOVEMBER 29, 2018—THIRD SNOW DEEPER

The snowfall was much deeper than on November 26th. I had to shovel because our snow removal service does not start until December 1st.

FRIDAY, NOVEMBER 30, 2018—BOXES TO ARIZONA

After breakfast, I went to UPS and shipped five boxes to Jan and Rich Aver's condo.

SATURDAY, DECEMBER 1, 2018—MOLLOY CHIROPRACTIC

After breakfast, Penny and I went to see Dr. Dennis Molloy at Molloy Chiropractic. I had a manipulation and ultrasound on my knee from a problem that developed when I stood up at the Black Ensemble Theater last October. Penny had a manipulation performed.

SUNDAY, DECEMBER 2, 2018—CHANUKAH PARTY

After breakfast, around 10:30 a.m., Penny and I started preparing the potatoes for making potato latkes at Ronna and Ted's home in the afternoon. At 2:30 p.m. Penny and I drove to the Belinky's home and Penny started making potato pancakes. At 5:00 p.m. our family Chanukkah party started at Ronna and Ted's home. Ronna had quite a layout of appetizers with hummus, olives, carrots and peapods and an eggplant dip. After dinner, Talia, Spencer lit the menorah and Bennett, Marni, Danny, Brooke, Penny and me opened our presents.

MONDAY, DECEMBER 3, 2018—WALKER BROTHERS BEFORE OUR PHOENIX TRIP

Penny and I decided to go to Walker Bros. Original Pancake House for breakfast before our Phoenix trip. We shared an apple pancake. I got the Subaru washed at Splash Car Wash and put a full tank of gas in the Subaru as well as filling up the Chevy Malibu at the Mobil station. I put a trickle charge on each car.

TUESDAY, DECEMBER 4, 2018—FLIGHT TO PHOENIX

Uri picked up Penny and me at 6:45 a.m. and we arrived at Chicago O'Hare Airport a little after 7:10 a.m. Our non-stop United Airlines flight left on time from O'Hare Airport at 10:08 a.m. and we arrived in Phoenix at 12:58 p.m. Rich Aver picked us up at Sky Harbor Airport and we drove to Goldman's Deli for our traditional arrival lunch. Rich then drove us to our condo to unload our luggage. After unloading, Rich drove Penny and me to pick up our Avis car rental [112-day rental with unlimited miles] located at 7125 E. Shea Blvd. Suite 101 in Scottsdale. In June 2018, I ordered the rental car through Costco through Chris Frieh, owner of the Avis franchise. After we settled in, we went to Fry's for our first grocery shopping and started cleaning the condo.

FRIDAY, DECEMBER 7, 2018—EFFICIENCY MECHANICAL

At 9:00 a.m. Rob with Efficiency Mechanical was at condo to inspect heat pump and air conditioning. We did not pay because we paid $209.00 in December 2017 for two visits. At 9:50 a.m. after Rob left, Penny went to Target to buy some miscellaneous items. At 11:45 a.m. Penny and I met Jeff and Michaele Salmon in the parking lot for lunch at Goldman's Deli at the corner of Indian Bend and Hayden. We also bought three blintzes that Penny will make at another meal.

SATURDAY, DECEMBER 8, 2018—ART FAIR & LUNCH

After breakfast, Jan picked up Penny and they went to the Stagecoach art show. I picked up Rich at 12:15 and we went to lunch at NCounter restaurant located at 7000 E. Mayo in Scottsdale at 12:30 p.m. I also went to Walmart and bought Hewlett Packard ink for the condo printer.

SUNDAY, DECEMBER 9, 2018—NFL FOOTBALL WITH DAN

Back in Northbrook, I invited Dan Murphy to go with me to State Farm Stadium located at 1 Cardinals Drive in Glendale to see an NFL game, the Arizona Cardinals vs the Detroit Lions. The tickets were through Central Michigan University. I picked up Dan Murphy at his rental house at 12:30 p.m. and we drove to stadium by 1:15 p.m. We sat in the Terrace Level, section 448, row 18, seats 7 & 8. The game started at 2:25 p.m. I parked in the Preferred Black parking lot. I made the reservation ahead of time online. Dan and I left the game in the 4th quarter. The Lions defeated the Cardinals 17 to 3. I was back at the condo by 6:06 p.m. to watch the Bears played the LA Rams (Bears beat the Rams 15 to 6).

MONDAY, DECEMBER 10, 2018—CONDO HOLIDAY PARTY

From 5:30 p.m. to 8:15 p.m. Christmas Party at Mission de los Arroyos Club house. We sat with Jeff and Michaele Salmon and talked to several owners.

TUESDAY, DECEMBER 11, 2018—YOGA AND CONCERT

At 10:00 a.m. Penny left for yoga at the Yoga Village on Evans. From 10:30 a.m. to 11:45 a.m. Penny was at Yoga. In the afternoon, we shopped at Trader Joe's. We left for old Scottsdale at 6:30 p.m. for 7:30 p.m. and Jeffrey Siegel's *Keyboard Conversations*. The program was *The Joyous Music of Beethoven* at the Scottsdale Center for the Performing Arts in seats E-17 & E-19. There is always a Question-and-Answer session after Jeffrey Siegel's concerts.

WEDNESDAY, DECEMBER 12, 2018—ROBERT CRAY IN MESA

From 10:00 to 10:30 a.m. Penny and I went for a walk in the neighborhood. At 7:30 p.m. Penny and I drove to the Mesa Center for the Performing Arts located at 1 East Main Street to see The Robert Cray Band concert. We sat in the parterre section, row V, seats 307 & 308. Our excellent seats were right behind the audio console and a great view of the stage.

SATURDAY, DECEMBER 15, 2018— WEINTRAUB'S DINNER

In the afternoon, I steam cleaned our condo floors, cleaned the patio and vacuumed the living room. Jay and Harriet Weintraub left Tucson and arrived in Scottsdale. Penny and I met them for dinner at Chompie's.

SUNDAY, DECEMBER 16, 2018—94TH WAY & A HAWK

After breakfast, Penny and I went for a walk in the neighborhood and saw a hawk in a tree on 94th way. At 5:30 p.m. we were invited for dinner at Jay and Harriet Weintraub's condo.

MONDAY, DECEMBER 17—NEW VACUUM CLEANER

After breakfast Penny and I drove to Bed, Bath and Beyond at the corner of Tatum and Shea Blvd. and bought a Shark Navigator upright vacuum cleaner for carpet and hard floors. It has a lift-away handheld HEPA filter and anti-static seal and is lavender in color. Across the street, we went to Whole Foods and bought needed groceries. We also went to Macy's and bought my sister Linda a $75.00 gift card for her upcoming 75th birthday. We ate dinner at condo. After dinner, we picked up Jan and Rich at 7:20 p.m. because we were invited for dessert at the Weintraubs. We picked up Jan and Rich at 7:20 p.m. I picked up Rich and Jan Aver at 7:20 p.m. for dessert at the Weintraubs condo.

THURSDAY, DECEMBER 20, 2018—CONDO POOL

The weather was very warm so Penny and I went to the condo pool. Penny read her book and I sat in the hot tub. In the afternoon, I went to Home Depot to buy a Water Dog Detector. The water detector was placed on the floor next to our hot water heater to detect any water or moisture leaking from it.

FRIDAY, DECEMBER 21, 2018—GOLF AND MIM CONCERT

Today is my sister Linda's 75th birthday. Dan Murphy picked up Jay Weintraub, Rich Aver and me and we drove to the Cave Creek Golf Course in Phoenix. The cost was $42.75. After golf the four of us ate lunch at Good Fellas Grill, a middle-eastern restaurant located at 15414 N. 19th Avenue in Phoenix, not too far from the golf course. At 7:00 p.m. I picked up Jay and Harriet and we drove to Cafe Zupas in Desert Ridge before going to the Musical Instrument Museum to see *The Manhattan Transfer*. Annie and Dan Murphy met us at the Museum for the concert. Three of the four original members are with the group including Janis Siegel.

SUNDAY, DECEMBER 23, 2018—FOOTBALL AND OPA CAFE

Rich Aver picked me up at 1:15 p.m. and Jay Weintraub and Jeffrey Schesnol met us at Scottsdale's Tavern Grille to watch the Chicago Bears play the San Francisco 49ers. In the evening at 5:30 p.m. Penny and I drove to the Opa Life Greek Café located at 227 E. Baseline Road in Tempe for dinner and a show. Nicole Pesce was playing the keyboards, Suzanne Lansford was on the violin and singer, Renee Patrick were performing here. We met Larry and Patty and sat at their table. Carmela Ramirez also sang a song.

TUESDAY, DECEMBER 25, 2018—CHINESE FOOD

For a 2:10 p.m. showtime, Jay and Harriet Weintraub picked us up and we went to see *The Favourite* at the Roadhouse Cinema. Penny and I liked the film but Jay and Harriet did not care for it. After the movie, we also ordered Chinese food at Scottsdale's Joyful Chinese Dining located at Hayden and Mountain View in Scottsdale. Rich Aver and I picked up the food at 5:45 p.m. The Avers and Weintraubs were at our condo for the evening.

SATURDAY, DECEMBER 29—MOVIE AND GUIDO DINNER

Jan and Rich Aver picked up Penny and me and we went to see *On The Basis of Sex* at the Harkins Theater in Fashion Square. After the film, we went to dinner at Scottsdale's Guido's Chicago Meat and Deli on Scottsdale Road and met Jay and Harriet Weintraub there.

SUNDAY, DECEMBER 30, 2018—BEARS FOOTBALL

At 11:00 a.m. Rich Aver picked me up and we drove to the 92nd Street Café at the corner of 92nd Street and Shea Blvd. to watch the Chicago Bears defeat the Minnesota Vikings 24 to 10. I also bought two more tickets to a spring training game. After the game, I went shopping at Sprouts.

MONDAY, DECEMBER 31, 2018—NEW YEAR'S PARTY

For the 2:10 afternoon show, Jan, Penny and I went to the Roadhouse Cinema to see *Mary Poppins Returns* but Rich was not interested in going, so he stayed home. At 7:40 p.m. Penny and I picked up Jan and Rich Aver and we drove to Jeffrey and Susan Schesnols for a New Year's party. We had lots of different appetizers and desserts Penny made cucumber topped with cream cheese and lox. There was also toast topped with eggplant dip and hummus. Jacqui Schesnol made baked cream cheese with jam. For dessert, Jan made a crisp and there were cupcakes, cookies, apple pie and banana bread. We took lots of photos wearing 2019 decorations props and I used my selfie stick to take a group photo. Phil Voyce wasn't at this party because he wasn't feeling well.

Jacqui Schesnol made a fun game and I captured some of it on video. She wrapped Saran Wrap around various items and made it into a gigantic ball. The object was to roll the dice and unwrap the Saran Wrap blob to find the objects placed hidden inside. The person next to you throws two dice and when you get doubles, the unwrapping goes to the next person then, played the dictionary game.

TUESDAY, JANUARY 1, 2019—HAPPY NEW YEAR!

Penny and I awakened at 9:25 a.m. and didn't do much the entire day. I had recorded many episodes of *The Twilight Zone* so Penny and I watched several episodes during the day. Penny baked some cookies.

FRIDAY, JANUARY 4, 2019—JUDY ROBERTS SHOW

Today is Jan and & Rich Aver's 49th Anniversary. At 5:00 p.m. we went to Opa Café in Tempe to see Judy Roberts and Greg Fishman perform. We talked to Judy and Greg at different times between sets. I took videos of their performance.

SATURDAY, JANUARY 5, 2019—MUSEUM AND CORKY

At 10:15 a.m. Jan and Rich Aver picked up Penny and me and we drove to the Scottsdale Museum of the West for an 11:00 a.m. lecture by Charlie LeSueur, Arizona's Official Western Film Historian, who spoke on the subject of Is *Star Wars Really A Cowboy Movie?* Harriet and Jay Weintraub met us at the museum for the lecture. There was a new exhibit at the museum, *New Beginnings, An American Story of Romantics and Modernists in the West* and we toured it briefly before the lecture started. After the program, all of us went to lunch at the Alo Café located at 6960 E. 1sr Street at the corner of Goldwater in Scottsdale. The small inside café is located in an old garage with outdoor seating for the six of us. I ordered a Torilla Espanola. The food is delicious and reasonably priced. In the afternoon, Penny went to Old Navy and bought some clothes.

At 7:00 p.m. I made a dinner reservation at Basil and Garlic with Natalie Kane and Corky Weily. After dinner, we invited them to our condo for coffee and cookies.

SUNDAY, JANUARY 6, 2019—PENNY AND PHOENIX SHOW

Penny picked up Jan Aver and drove to the Palette Restaurant in the Phoenix Art Museum for lunch with Susan and Jacqui Schesnol. After lunch the group went to the Phoenix Theater next to the restaurant to watch a Second City show.

In the evening we picked up Jan and Rich and drove to Harriet and Jay Weintraub's condo to watch the Golden Globe Awards on television.

WEDNESDAY, JANUARY 9, 2019—SALMONS LUNCH
AND DINNER WITH YOUNGSTOWN FRIENDS

At 12:00 p.m. Penny and I met Jeff and Michelle Salmon in the parking lot and we went to Goldman's Deli for lunch. At 5:30 p.m. Penny and I met Bonny and Ron Gimple and Bobby and Jim Pazol for dinner at Soi 4 Bangkok Eatery at Gainey Ranch shopping center. The food was very good.

THURSDAY, JANUARY 10, 2019—SCOTTSDALE MUSEUM

At 10:30 a.m. Penny and I drove to Faith's house to drop off a present for Ted

Jass who was celebrating his 70th birthday in California. The Beall family was driving to Brea, California to be with Ted to celebrate his birthday so we wanted our gift to be delivered to him. From 1:00 to 2:00 p.m. we went to the Scottsdale Museum of the West to hear, Curator of the C.M. Russell Museum, Emily Watson, give a lecture on *Of Fantasy to Fiction: C.M. Russell and The Female Form*. The talk was an exploration of C.M. Russell's artistic influences, depictions of women and connections with some of the women in his life. We also looked at the Barry Goldwater Photography Collection. After the museum program, Penny and I went for a late lunch at Panera Bread on Indian School.

At 3:15 p.m. I had an appointment with Dr. Abby Roberts regarding my knee problem that I developed while standing up at the Black Ensemble Theater last October. The doctor recommended physical therapy to help with the knee pain and a CVS prescription of diclofenac Sodium Topical gel to rub on my knee.

FRIDAY, JANUARY 11, 2019—WEINTRAUBS AND STRICKERS

In the afternoon, Penny and I took a drive up north not too far from where the Gimples live. At 6:00 p.m. Jay and Harriet Weintraub picked us up to go to Wally's Bistro and Pub located at 7704 E. Doubletree Ranch Road in Scottsdale for dinner with Fran and Mike Stricker who were in Scottsdale for the day.

SATURDAY, JANUARY 12, 2019—STARFIRE GOLF CLUB

At 7:58 a.m. Dan Murphy picked up Jay Weintraub, Rich Aver and me and we played golf at Scottsdale's Starfire Golf Club at 11500 N. Hayden Blvd. Meanwhile, Penny and Harriet went to Beall's on Bell Road, Ross, and then had lunch at the 32nd Street Café.

SUNDAY, JANUARY 13, 2019—BREAKFAST, MESA MARKET

At 10:15 a.m. Penny and I picked up Harriet and Jay and we ate breakfast at The Breakfast Joynt on Bell Road. At 12:30 p.m. I drove to the Mesa Flea Market with Harriet and Jay and bought some kitchen utensils and a $2.00 rug to place our shoes by our condo's front door. At 5:00 p.m. Penny and I drove to Opa's Restaurant to see Judy Roberts perform but Greg Fishman was not there.

MONDAY, JANUARY 14, 2019—MOVIE AND DICK VAN DYKE

From 9:30 to 10:35 a.m. I had my first rehab session with physical therapist Angela Barroso at Foothills Sports Medicine located at 9332 N. 95th Way Road Suite 105 in Scottsdale for my aching right knee. At 12:15 p.m. Jan and Rich picked us up to see *Vice* at the Roadhouse Cinema that started at 1:00 p.m. After the film, we went back to the Aver condo to watch several Dick Van Dyke programs and have dinner.

TUESDAY, JANUARY 15, 2019—YOGA AND A MOVIE

Penny went to Yoga in the morning. After Penny returned, we ate lunch in the condo and at 1:30 p.m. drove to the Mustang Library and saw the movie *Crazy Rich Asians*. At 5:15 p.m. Jay and Harriet Weintraub picked us up and we went to The Twisted Grove for dinner before the Jeffrey Siegel show. At 7:30 p.m. we went to see Jeffrey Siegel's *Keyboard Conversations* Debussy and Rachmaninoff at the Scottsdale Center for the Performing Arts located at 7380 E. 2nd Street in the Virginia G. Piper Theater Seating G-13 & G-15.

WEDNESDAY, JANUARY 16, 2019—BARRETT JACKSON

Today is Steve Klein's actual birthday (we called Steve and wished him a happy birthday). I left at 7:30 a.m. to park and board the shuttle bus at 8:00 a.m. to go to the Barrett Jackson Auto Auction for an all-day ticket cost of $18.73. Meanwhile, Penny washed some windows and vacuumed the living room and bedrooms and took a walk in the neighborhood. At 6:15 p.m. Penny made salmon, kale salad and a quinoa for dinner and we watched *This Is Us* and *Finding Your Roots* on television

TUCSON TRIP FOR STEVE KLEIN'S 75TH BIRTHDAY
FRIDAY, JANUARY 18, 2019—TUCSON & AIR & SPACE

At 7:00 a.m. Penny and I drove to Tucson. Along the way, we stopped at a rest stop to go to the bathroom. There was a sign in front of the rest stop about the Gadsden Purchase. The sign said in part "The Gila River north of this site marked the international border of the United States and Mexico from 1848 to 1854. James Gadsden negotiated to purchase 38,000 square miles of "Wild Country" for $15 million in gold. Amended to $10 million for 29,640 square miles. Today the Gadsden Purchase comprises 24 per cent of Arizona's total land area." There was also another sign that read in part "Gila River Indian Reservation established in 1859. Here the first government Indian school was established for Pimas and Maricopas in 1871, with Reverend Charles H. Cook as teacher."

Our goat today was to visit the Pima Air and Space Museum located at 6000 E. Valencia Road. We took a tram ride tour around the outside area and then while Penny went back to the visitor's center while I walked to the B-17 Fighting Fortress hanger that was the 390th Memorial Museum. I also walked around outside for a short time. I also went to Hanger #3 that housed a restored B-24 World War II bomber. The main museum was inside and housed many planes. I took lots of photos that I put into a slide show and we ate lunch in the museum's restaurant. The cost to enter the museum was $27.50 and the cost of the tram tour was $12.00. After leaving the Pima Air and Space Museum, Penny and I drove to the Sonoran Desert Museum, paid a $33.90 entrance fee, walked around and went into the humming birdcage and that was really cool. We also stopped at Phoebe's Coffee Bar and ordered a black coffee.

For dinner, we went to Sushi Ten located at 4500 Speedway Blvd. I used to take my crew to this sushi restaurant when I did shows in Tucson. We spent the night in Tucson at the Comfort Inn and Suites Sabino Canyon located at 7007 E. Tanque Verde for $107.50.

SATURDAY, JANUARY 19—STEVE KLEIN'S BIRTHDAY

We had breakfast at the hotel and before the birthday party we bought some bread at Bookman's. From 1:00 to 4:00 p.m. we went to Steve Klein's 75th Birthday Party at the home of Matt and Melissa Landau located at 6522 N, Sun Bluff Drive in Tucson. Steve's sister Ellen and her husband Jack flew in from Detroit for the celebration. We saw Matt's mother, Brenda and also met Steve's two nieces, one of them being, Michelle. Steve's cousins David and Sherry from Palo Alto, California was also at the party and we had a chance to speak with them for quite a while. For many years, David was a PBS documentary producer at WGBH in Boston. The lunch was catered by a friend of Melissa and was delicious with lots of vegetarian options. We left the party around 5:00 p.m. and drove back to Scottsdale.

SUNDAY, JANUARY 20, 2019—SUNDAY A'FAIR & JUDY ROBERTS & GREG FISHMAN PERFORMANCE

Today is Alan Appelbaum, Remey Rubin and Ted Jass birthday. After breakfast, Penny and left for the 12:00 noon beginning of Sunday A'Fair at the Scottsdale Center for the Performing Arts outdoor stage. The theme was *Motown: The Sound That Changed America.* We saw Gina Fletcher and Friends along with Sandra Bassett. Singer Dennis Rowland also joined in on several songs. The Soul Power Band ended the program. At 5:30 p.m. we drove to Fountain Hills for dinner at The Hills Pizza to hear Judy Roberts and Greg Fishman play. It is a small restaurant with a few people eating there. We ate pizza and listened to Judy and Greg perform.

WEDNESDAY, JANUARY 23, 2019—TWO FISHING PLACES

At 10:00 a.m. I had another physical therapy session for my left knee. After lunch, I went fishing at Chaparral Park Lake and caught a rainbow trout. A woman happened to walk by as I landed the fish and took a short video and photo of me with the rainbow trout. After Chaparral, I drove to McCormick Ranch Lake to fish but had no luck. Penny went to lunch with Harriet Weintraub at Hash Kitchen and bought some clothes at Turnstyle.

Meanwhile back in Northbrook, there was a snowstorm and the men removed the snow from our driveway, front walk and back patio. My Ring doorbell captured the storm and snow removal and I inserted the images into my slide show

FRIDAY, JANUARY 25, 2019—DINNER AND CONCERT

After breakfast I got the rental car washed at Genie Wash and bought groceries at Safeway. At 5:00 p.m. Penny and I picked up Jan and Rich Aver and met our friends at Scottsdale's PNPK restaurant located at 23335 N. Scottsdale Road for sliders before the show. The Great Eight were at the restaurant (Weintraubs, Murphys, Spencers & Jan and Rich Aver). Rich Aver did not go to this show with the group.

At 7:30 p.m. our group went to see *Human Nature* at the Highlands Church located at 9050 E. Pinnacle Peak Road in Scottsdale. Regular Price Per The *Human Nature* ticket cost was $42.95 per ticket x 2 tickets for a total of $85.90 with the Weintraubs, Murphys, Spencers & Jan Aver.

SUNDAY, JANUARY 27, 2019—STU AND JACKIE TEMPLER

Stu and Jackie Templer drove to Scottsdale and I met them in our parking lot. I drove to the Scottsdale Museum of the West because the Templers had not been there. We saw the Barry Goldwater photography collection, the sculpture garden and the Abe Hayes Family Spirit of the West collection and the Native American pottery collection. After spending time in the museum and the sculpture garden, we walked on E. Main Street in Old Town Scottsdale. We bought a book for Annie at the Arizona West Galleries located at 7149 E. Main Street. After spending some time in Old Scottsdale, we ate dinner at Stu's favorite Scottsdale restaurant, The Village Tavern located at 8787 N. Scottsdale Road in Gainey Village.

MONDAY, JANUARY 28, 2019—SNOWSTORM IN NORTHBROOK AND A WALK IN THE DESERT

It was a beautiful day in Scottsdale so Penny and I decided to take a walk in the desert at The Gateway Trailhead just north of Bell Road. On our walk, I used the two walking sticks we had purchased at the Mesa Flea Market. We also went to Costco. Meanwhile, there was more snow in Northbrook, more plowing and snow removal and it was captured on my Ring doorbell.

WEDNESDAY, JANUARY 30, 2019—PENNY'S BIRTHDAY

Today is Talia's 12th birthday and Penny's 75th birthday. Penny and I had lunch at Sugar Jam with Jan and Rich Aver and Harriet and Jay Weintraub. That evening Penny and I celebrated her 75th birthday at Scottsdale's The Twisted Grove. For dessert, we went to Yogurtology.

FRIDAY, FEBRUARY 1, 2019—SOUL CAFÉ AND A CONCERT

Today, Harvey and Sherry Amend arrived in Phoenix and will be here for the entire month of February. Before our show at the Highlands Church, the great eight had dinner on the patio at Soul Café in North Scottsdale. At 7:30 p.m. we all met at *Big Bad Voodoo Daddy* at the Highlands Church located at 9050 E. Pinnacle Peak Road in Scottsdale.

SATURDAY, FEBRUARY 2, 2019—MUSEUM OF THE WEST

At 11:00 a.m. Rich and I went to the Scottsdale Museum of the West and heard host Charles LeSueur lead a discussion of the Top 10 Westerns. After the presentation Rich and I had lunch at Biscuits. I ordered a four-egg omelette with mushrooms, green peppers, onions with hash brown potatoes and two biscuits. Meanwhile Penny went to Two Plates Full and had lunch with Jan and Harriet at the House of Tricks.

SUNDAY, FEBRUARY 3, 2019—SUPER BOWL FIFTY-THREE

Jan Aver picked up Penny and went to the National Council of Jewish Women luncheon from 10:30 until 4:00 p.m. There were four speakers presenting about women's reproductive rights. I did some shopping at Sprouts. From 4:00 p.m. to 8:00 p.m. I watched the Super Bowl with Rich Aver, Jay Weintraub and Jeffrey Schesnol at our condo. The Patriots beat the Rams 13 to 3.

TUESDAY, FEBRUARY 5, 2019—*VIOLINS OF HOPE*

After breakfast, I cleaned the guest closet. In the evening, Penny and I drove to the Arizona Jewish Historical Society located at 122 E. Culver Street in Phoenix and saw a film on the *Violins of Hope*. Susie Ernst introduced the film. Daniel Levin, the photographer whose photographs were on display, spoke at the event. *Violins of Hope* was a project of the Jewish Federation of Greater Phoenix. Amnon Weinstein, a master violinmaker and the man behind the music, was featured in the film and was part of the photographic exhibit. Our friend, Jeffrey Schesnol, assistant director of the society, put together the exhibit. It was also a pleasure getting a chance to meet photographer Daniel Levin.

WEDNESDAY, FEBRUARY 6, 2019—FILM GROUP AND LUNCH

From 10:30 to 11:45 a.m. Penny and I were at our film discussion group at the Mustang Library. After film class, we went to lunch with Jay and Harriet at

Chompie's. After lunch Penny and I went to Ginny's Laundromat to wash rags and rugs. At 3:00 p.m. I had a follow-up appointment with Dr. Roberts about my knee. For dinner, Penny and I went to Joyful Chinese and ordered hot and sour soup.

FRIDAY, FEBRUARY 8, 2019—CHICAGO FRIENDS DINNER
Jerry and Linda Bernstein arrived in Scottsdale for two week and Jerry Schecter and his wife also arrived in Phoenix staying at the Desert Ridge Marriott condos for two weeks. In the morning, I got a haircut with Vito at Angelo's Hairstyling. For dinner Penny and I went to dinner at the Eden Grill with Jerry and Linda Bernstein and Jay and Harriet Weintraub. Penny and I ordered the catfish.

SATURDAY, FEBRUARY 9, 2019—EVENING CONCERT
At 7:30 p.m. we saw *The Hitmen* at the Highlands Church located at 9050 E. Pinnacle Peak Road in Scottsdale.

SUNDAY, FEBRUARY 10, 2019—WILO HOME TOUR
Penny and I picked up Jerry and Linda Bernstein and we went on the Wilo House Tour. The Bernsteins really enjoyed the day and appreciated us asking them to join us.

MONDAY, FEBRUARY 11, 2019—ORANGE TREE GOLF
At 10:10 a.m. Rich Aver picked me up for golf at Orange Tree and an 11:00 a.m. tee time. There were eight golfers including Jerry Schecter, Jerry Bernstein, Jay Weintraub, Mike Stricker, Rich Aver, Harvey Amend and me. Mike Dyer from Calgary, Alberta also played with us. After golf, we were all invited for dinner at the Weintraub's condo.

TUESDAY, FEBRUARY 12, 2019—JEFFREY SIEGEL CONCERT
At 7:30 p.m. Penny and I saw a Jeffrey Siegel concert: *The Romantic Connection Music of Chopin, Schumann & Liszt* at the Scottsdale Center for the Performing Arts, Virginia G. Piper Theater located at 7380 E. 2nd Street in Scottsdale. Our seats were in row E-17 & E-19.

AZ FAMILY REUNION WITH LOIS, ROY, LYNNE AND CLAIRE
WEDNESDAY, FEBRUARY 13, 2019—EVERYONE ARRIVES
Before Lois and Roy arrived in Phoenix, I went to the Scottsdale Avis location at 14880 N. Northsight in Suite 105 very close to Costco and rented a 2019 Dodge mini-van for the weekend. Penny and I picked up Lois and Roy from Sky Harbor Airport when they arrived at 5:00 p.m. on American Airlines flight #105. Lynn & Claire also arrived in Phoenix and met up with Lois and Roy. After we picked everyone up from the airport, we drove to the Wildflower for dinner located at 6428 S. McClintock Drive in Tempe. After dinner we dropped off Lynne and Claire at their hotel, Motel 6, located at 1612 N. Scottsdale Road in northern Tempe and drove back to our condo with Lois and Roy.

THURSDAY, FEBRUARY 14, 2019—MUSEUM OF THE WEST
Today is Valentine's Day. Lois, Roy, Penny and I drove to Motel 6 and picked up Lynne and Claire. Then, we all drove to the Scottsdale Museum of the West and spent several hours looking at the Barry & Peggy Goldwater Foundation photography exhibit as well as going to the sculpture garden.

For dinner at our condo, Penny made eggplant Parmesan and mostaccioli.

Before dinner, we took a selfie. After dinner, I drove Claire crazy rinsing the dishes and she couldn't stop laughing. Roy and I drove Lynne and Claire back to their hotel on N. Scottsdale Road.

FRIDAY, FEBRUARY 15, 2019—GATEWAY TRAILHEAD
AND FOUNTAIN HILLS

After breakfast, Roy and I picked up Lynne and Claire at their hotel, Motel 6 located at 1612 N. Scottsdale Road and we all went for a short walk at Gateway Trailhead in the desert. Before our walk, someone near the entrance took our photo. We took the easy walking path with all of the educational markers along the trail. After the desert walk, we drove to Fountain Hills to see the fountain erupt at 3:00 p.m. Then, everyone went into the Artists Gallery but no one bought anything.

After Fountain Hills, I drove everyone to Cave Creek and went inside the Rare Earth Gallery to check out all of the unusual gems and rocks. This place is absolutely amazing with all of the rare gems, petrified wood, crystals, geodes, rocks, boulders, fossils and other rare colorful objects. We came back to our condo and ate leftovers.

SATURDAY, FEBRUARY 16, 2019—HOLE IN THE ROCK
AND THE PUEBLO GRANDE MUSEUM IN PHOENIX

After breakfast, we picked up Lynne and Claire at Motel 6 and took everyone to the Evelyn Hallman Pond to show them where I go fishing. Then we drove to Papago Park and hiked to the top of the Hole in the Rock. We took lots of great photos and videos of us walking down the mountain toward the car.

Then we drove to Pueblo Grande Museum located at 4619 E. Washington Street in Phoenix and spent time exploring the inside and the outside of the museum. For dinner, we all went to Scottsdale's Twisted Grove Parlor & Bar located at 8220 N. Hayden Road. We ate a delicious meal and had our picture taken by our server.

SUNDAY, FEBRUARY 17, 2019—COUSIN'S FAREWELL

As we left for the airport, Lois took a photo of Penny and me. We dropped off Lois and Roy at the Phoenix Sky Harbor Airport and they left on American Airlines flight at 10:05 a.m. We also picked up Lynn & Claire at their hotel and took them to Sky Harbor Airport for their Southwest flight to Portland, Oregon. Meanwhile back in Northbrook, it snowed during the day and in the evening, our snowplow service was at it again, clearing our driveway, front walk and patio from the snow. For dinner, Penny and I went to Nee House located on Tatum and Thunderbird in Phoenix.

MONDAY, FEBRUARY 18, 2019—ORANGE TREE GOLF

It's President's Day Weekend. Jay Weintraub picked up Jerry Bernstein and me and we played golf at Orange Tree. Jerry Schecter, Mike Dyer from Calgary, Alberta and his brother-in-law Danny also played. It rained and hailed and then there was sunshine at 52 degrees. We took a group photo at the end of our game. Meanwhile it snowed overnight in Northbrook and once again our snowplow service got rid of the snow in our driveway, front walk and back patio. Penny and I went to dinner at IL Bosco pizza.

TUESDAY, FEBRUARY 19, 2019—PENNY'S EYE AND HAIRCUT

At 10:00 a.m. Penny went to yoga. At 1:45 p.m. she had an eye doctor appointment with Dr. Kessler. We left Dr. Kessler's office and we drove her for a haircut at Mane Attractions while I went to Starbucks in Macy's and drank coffee and used my iPad. Later in the day, Penny and I met Jan and Rich at Lush Burger on Thompson Peak Road for dinner.

WEDNESDAY, FEBRUARY 20, 2019—FRIENDS DINNER

Today is Brooke's 11th birthday. At 10:00 a.m. we attended our film class at the Mustang Library. *The Favourite* was the film we discussed. For dinner, the Great Eight came to our condo to celebrate Annie Murphy's birthday with Dan Murphy, Jay and Harriet Weintraub, Jan and Rich Aver and Penny and me. Penny served eggplant Parmesan and we celebrated Annie's birthday and I made a fire. I think Jan made a chocolate Bundt cake and Penny put a candle on top.

THURSDAY, FEBRUARY 21, 2019—BREA, CALIFORNIA TRIP

After eating breakfast, Penny and I made a stop at New York Bagel N Bialys for the Jass family before driving to Brea, California. We stopped for gasoline at a Flying J gas station in Ehrenberg, Arizona to fill up with gas and go to the bathroom. We also took a bathroom break at Bouse Wash Rest Stop in California. We stopped for lunch at TKB Bakery & Deli located at 44911 Golf Center Parkway in Indio, California and ordered sandwiches. We arrived in the afternoon in time for dinner. On our way to dinner, we saw snow-capped mountains in the distance. After dinner, Penny and I sat with Coco, the Jass family dog.

FRIDAY, FEBRUARY 22, 2019—FULLERTON AND A MOVIE

Today is Norman's 78th birthday. I drove to Starbucks and got two black coffees and brought them back to the Jass home for breakfast. After breakfast, Linda drove Penny and me to Fullerton, a neighboring suburb, where we stopped at The Brick Basement store and looked around but bought nothing. We had lunch at the Brownstone Café located at 305 N. Harbor Blvd Suite 117 in Fullerton. I ordered an egg white omelette with tomato, onion, spinach and avocado. Penny ordered a cup of tomato basil soup and a Mediterranean sandwich. We took a group photo with the chef/owner Chef Glen and his wife Kim.

For dinner, Ted, Linda, Penny and I drove to the Wood Ranch BBQ & Grill located at 8022 E. Santa Ana Canyon Road in Anaheim. After dinner we went to the Edward's Theater located at 155 W. Birch Street in Brea and saw the film *Black Klansman*. It was a very interesting and entertaining film. After the movie, we went back to the Jass home.

SATURDAY, FEBRUARY 23, 2019—BRUNCH AND JUNK TRUNK

In the morning, I went to Starbucks for black coffee. After breakfast we drove to the Original Pancake House for brunch. Kyle Houghton came with us. After brunch we drove to the "Junk In The Trunk" Vintage Market in Pomona. While driving to Pomona, we saw snow on top of the mountains in the distance. Penny also went to The Loft and bought some clothes. For dinner we went to Pick Up Stix for Chinese food and watched a film on a DVD, *The Wife* starring Glen Close and Jonathan Pryce. Penny sat with Coco, the Jass family dog.

SUNDAY, FEBRUARY 24, 2019—BRUNCH WITH MARILYN AND LARRY LEVY AND THE OSCARS IN THE EVENING

Penny and I drove to Santa Monica and had brunch with cousins Marilyn and Larry Levy at their apartment. We had a terrific visit and a delicious brunch. Before leaving Santa Monica on the recommendation of Larry, we stopped at N.Y. Bagel & Deli located at 2216 Wilshire Blvd. in Santa Monica and bought a variety of bagels and bialys. We stayed at the Jass home and watched the Academy Awards with their dog Coco on the couch.

MONDAY, FEBRUARY 25, 2019—TRIP TO SCOTTSDALE

I went to Starbucks for our black coffee and Penny and I left Brea for Scottsdale after breakfast. We stopped for lunch at TKB Bakery & Deli located at 44911 Golf Center Parkway in Indio, California. We also stopped at an Arizona rest stop for a bathroom break. We arrived back in Scottsdale before dark and our trip was lots of fun.

WEDNESDAY, FEBRUARY 27, 2019—AMENDS AND TEMPLERS

From 10:30 to 11:45 a.m. Penny and I went to our film class at the Mustang Library. The film we discussed was *Stan & Ollie*. After the class we ate lunch with Sherry and Harvey Amend at Chompie's. Later, Stu and Jackie Templer drove to our condo and I met them in the parking lot. We decided to drive to Old Town Scottsdale and walk up and down Main Street and Marshall Way. After spending several hours, we ate dinner at Ajo Al's Mexican Café near our condo.

THURSDAY, FEBRUARY 28, 2019—FOUNTAIN HILLS

After breakfast, Penny and I drove to Fountain Hills to see Charles Skiera, the custom jewelry guy. I took a photo of Charles Skiera hugging Penny. On the way back, we stopped at CVS and Sprouts for some groceries. We also picked up Harriet and went to the Cine-Capri Harkins Theater to watch the film *They Shall Not Grow Old* for our next film class.

For dinner, I cooked turkey burgers on the outdoor grill near our condo. After dinner we picked up Harriet and went to the Cine-Capri Harkins Theater to see the 7:20 p.m. film, *They Shall Not Grow Old*, the subject for next week's film class. Jay was working in Orlando.

SATURDAY, MARCH 2, 2019—ORANGE TREE GOLF

Rich Aver picked me up and we drove to Orange Tree to play golf for $85.79 and Al Magit met us there. After golf, Rich and I went to Biscuits for lunch. I ordered an omelet with hash brown potatoes and two biscuits but Al did not join us. Meanwhile, Penny, Ann Dyer from Calgary, Jan Aver, Harriet Weintraub and Ellen Magit went to lunch at Vu Restaurant located at 14815 E. Shea Blvd. in Fountain Hills. After lunch, Penny and the group went to the Tour D'Artist and she bought three watercolors from Christine Ehmann for $30.00.

SUNDAY, MARCH 3, 2019—THREE PLACES FISHING

After breakfast, I first went fishing at Chaparral Lake, then drove to Evelyn Hallman Park, and then my third spot was McCormick Ranch Lake. I had no luck at either place but enjoyed myself anyway. The landscapers started cutting down the bushes in our complex getting ready for the summer months and I took photos and videos to include in my "shows." Penny and I ate dinner on the patio at the Pita Jungle located at 7366 E. Shea Blvd. in Scottsdale.

MONDAY, MARCH 4—3 HISTORIC NEIGHBORHOODS

Penny and I took a very interesting driving tour of four historic Phoenix neighborhoods we had not previously seen. The historic Phoenix neighborhoods are Yaple Park, Pierson Place, Medlock Place and Woodlea Historic District. I took photos of each neighborhood in a separate "show." Our lunch was at The Coronado Restaurant. We ordered a beet burger, garlic fries and fried guacamole.

TUESDAY, MARCH 5, 2019—SPENCER'S BIRTHDAY

Today is Spencer's 8th birthday. We went to Costco to fill us on gas for our rental car and also to The Vitamin Shoppe for supplement refills. We also went to the post office to mail Roy Cramer's birthday card and package.

WEDNESDAY, MARCH 6, 2019—LAST CINEMA CLASS

From 10:30 until 11:45 a.m. Penny, Harriet and I had our last contemporary cinema class with Ed Everroad and Melanie Gazele. The film reviewed in class was *They Shall Not Grow Old*, a documentary about British soldiers in World War I. Using state-of-the-art technology from BBC interviews and Imperial War Museum materials filmmaker Peter Jackson put together an amazing story. After the cinema class Harriet, Penny and I met Jan and Rich Aver and Ellen and Al Magit at the Paris Café for lunch. This restaurant is a delicious place to eat.

THURSDAY, MARCH 7, 2019—SLOAN PARK GAME

After breakfast, Penny and I headed to Sloan Park for a 1:05 p.m. start to a spring training baseball game. Penny and I met Al and Ellen Magit and Harriet Weintraub to see the Chicago Cubs play the Colorado Rockies. We had great seats in section 108, row 22 and seats 15 & 16. Penny and I ate lunch at the ballpark. A photo was taken of the five of us. Jay was still in Orlando on a show.

FRIDAY, MARCH 8, 2019—*VIOLINS OF HOPE* AT THE AJHS

Rich Aver and I went to a very interesting exhibit at the Arizona Jewish Historical Society. We saw a film about The Violins of Hope and a photographic exhibition by Daniel Levin of Amnon Weinstein, The Man Behind the Music. This exhibit was a project of the Jewish Federation of Greater Phoenix. After the exhibit, we had lunch at Angels Trumpet Ale House with Jeffrey Schesnol. I ordered a two egg, mozzarella, Brussel sprouts, pecorino Romano flatbread that was delicious. Rich ordered a brisket sandwich with French fries.

SATURDAY, MARCH 9, 2019—THREE PLACES FISHING

After breakfast, I drove to my first fishing stop at Roadrunner Park located at 3502 E. Cactus Road in Phoenix. There is a large pond in this park and I walked around it fishing but had no luck. Then I drove to Encanto Park located at 2605 N. 15th Avenue in Phoenix. I took a few selfies and also caught nothing.

My third and final stop was at Papago Park and the farthest pond where I caught a largemouth bass on a Mepps spinner. I also hooked onto a large catfish but couldn't bring it to the shore. I got it close to shore but the line snapped. A man and his son were standing next to me and I gave him my cell phone and asked him if he could take a video of me trying to land the catfish.

For dinner this evening, we picked up the Avers, Anne Dyer, Jay and Harriet Weintraub and Al and Ellen Magit who met us at the Eden Grill. I ordered three catfish dinners ahead of time with jasmine rice, raisins and two skews of vegetables. We enjoyed good company and the delicious food.

SUNDAY, MARCH 10, 2019—A WALK AND FISHING

In the morning, Penny and I took a walk down Cholla. Since I had a lot of luck the day before at Papago Park Pond, so we went back to Papago Park but had no luck catching any fish this time.

MONDAY, MARCH 11, 2019—GOLF AT ORANGE TREE

Jay Weintraub picked me up and we played golf with Al Magit and we got teamed up with a guy named Alex.

TUESDAY, MARCH 12, 2019—THE SIMONS ARRIVE

Carol and John Simon arrived in Phoenix and will be staying with Jay and Harriet Weintraub for a few days.

WEDNESDAY, MARCH 13, 2019—WICKENBURG, ARIZONA TRIP

Al and Ellen Magit picked up Penny and me at our condo and we drove to Wickenburg for the day. Our first stop was the Desert Caballeros Western Museum (Arizona's Most Western Museum) that cost a $20.00 entrance fee. Harriet and Jay Weintraub had condo guests, John and Carol Simon, so they drove separately and met us at the museum where we took a group photo. We toured the museum for several hours and saw a variety of interesting items reflecting the history of Wickenburg, founded by Henry Wickenburg. His 1880s photo was displayed near the entrance. There were many artifacts, paintings, memorabilia and sculptures depicting the old west. On the lower level, early Wickenburg scenes were constructed. The general store had a hologram of a man behind the counter talking about the town.

After spending several hours in the museum, we decided to have lunch around the corner at Nana's Sandwich Shop and Bakery. After lunch, we went into a second museum building and saw more interesting items on display. Outside of the second museum building was a large statue of a cowboy and his horse created by artist Joe Beeler. We also stopped the Antiques Artisans Emporium and inside Cactus Maddy's store. Penny and I went to The Twisted Grove for dinner.

THURSDAY, MARCH 14, 2019—SOUL CAFÉ WITH FRIENDS

Jay and Harriet Weintraub, John and Carol Simon and Penny and me ate breakfast at the Soul Café located at 7615 E. Pinnacle Peak Road in North Scottsdale. Our server took a group photo of our table. After breakfast, we drove separately to Fountain Hills. John, Jay and I sat on a bench while the women talked to Charles Skiera, the jewelry guy. On our way back, Penny and I stopped at the Fountain Hills Botanical Garden, a very small piece of land originally part of the P-Bar Ranch. In 1968, Robert McCulloch, the developer of Lake Havasu City, purchased 12,000 acres in the Fountain Hills area that included the garden area and part of the ranch. When we got back to our condo, we stopped at Fry's for a few items and Penny read in the sun outside.

FRIDAY, MARCH 15, 2019— FRIENDS AND CUBS VS. SOX

Karen Hudachko got group tickets to a spring training baseball game at Camelback Ranch located at 10710 W Camelback Rd in Glendale. The game was between the Chicago Cubs and the Chicago White Sox. At 10: 30 a.m., I picked up Gerri Menn and her friend Lori Hershman at Gerri's condo across the street from our condo. The game started at 1:10 p.m. and we sat in section 104, row 28 and seats 17 & 18. Fran and Mike Stricker drove to the stadium from Tucson. Jay and Harriet Weintraub, Dave and Karen Hudachko, Al and Ellen Magit, John and Carol Simon and Penny and I were at the game. After the game we all met, sat at two different tables and ate dinner at Glendale's Thee Pitts Again on W. Bell Road.

SATURDAY, MARCH 16, 2019—DINNER AT PASTA BRIONI

Today is my 78th birthday. Aaron Aver was in Scottsdale, so we had a happy birthday breakfast at the Aver's condo. To celebrate my birthday, Penny and I went to Pasta Brioni.

SUNDAY, MARCH 17, 2019—ST. PATRICK'S DAY PARTY

From 1:00 to 2:00 p.m. we went to the Scottsdale Museum of the West located at 3830 N. Marshall Way to see a film, *American Indians in Hollywood* in the museum's theater. The Magits, the Murphys, the Hudachkos, the Avers and the Spencers celebrated St. Patrick's Day at Jay and Harriet's condo. Harriet served many delicious appetizers.

TUESDAY, MARCH 19, 2019—GOLF AND LINDA ARRIVES

Jay Weintraub picked up Al Magit, Michael Menn and me and we headed to the Aguila Golf Course in Phoenix. I took a selfie of our foursome. Later in the day, Linda arrived in Phoenix on Southwest Airlines flight and Penny and I picked her up at Sky Harbor Airport.

WEDNESDAY, MARCH 20, 2019—ROSSON HOUSE TOUR

After breakfast, I drove Linda and Penny for a guided tour of the Rosson House at Heritage Square located at 113 N. 6th Street in downtown Phoenix. We parked the car in the garage across the street from the house is Science Park. Dr. Roland T. Rosson, an Army doctor at Fort McDowell and the mayor of Phoenix, had the house built in 1895. The house is absolutely amazing and has been placed on the Phoenix Historic Property Register and National Register of Historic Places. I created a slide show of the tour.

After the guided tour, we walked around the corner from the Rosson House to Pizzeria Bianco to eat lunch. The restaurant is in the original Baird Machine Shop built in 1929. We sat outside and ate lunch. After lunch we walked around Heritage Square and went inside Stevens-Haustgen house, a bungalow built in 1901 that houses a gift shop today.

SCOTTSDALE STADIUM—INDIANS VS. GIANTS

Linda and I drove to the Scottsdale Library's parking garage and walked up the steps for our 7:05 p.m. spring training baseball game at Scottsdale Stadium between the San Francisco Giants and the Cleveland Indians. We had great seats in section 309, row 7 and seats 12 and 13. The Indians had a very bad day and lost the game by a wide margin. The Indians had 4 hits and 0 runs, the Giants had 15 hits and 13 runs but Linda and I had fun anyway. The Scottsdale Stadium is one of the oldest Arizona ballparks and is small compared to other area spring training facilities.

THURSDAY, MARCH 21, 2019—FOUNTAIN HILLS LUNCH

On the way to Fountain Hills, Linda, Penny and I had lunch at the Vu Bistro located at 14815 E. Shea Blvd. and sat outside on the patio overlooking Fountain Hills. After lunch Penny bought some earrings from Charles Skiera for $70.85 and the women stopped at Bealls Outlet where Penny bought some items.

For dinner we ate Penny's eggplant Parmesan and mostaccioli.

FRIDAY, MARCH 22, 2019—MUSEUM AND TONTO LUNCH

After breakfast, Linda, Penny and I drove to Cave Creek and the relatively new (1968) Cave Creek Museum. The museum covers the early days of Cave Creek founded in 1870. A sign inside the museum said "For 20 years after 1870, Cave Creek was on the old military wagon road used by the troops at Ft. McDowell in obtaining supplies from and communicating with headquarters at Ft. Whipple." Fort Whipple was a U.S. army post that served as Arizona's Territory's capital prior to the founding of Prescott, Arizona." The old black mountain community church is part of the museum. There was also a tubercular cabin built in 1920 on the museum property and is placed on the National Register of Historic Places. Mining was done near Cave Creek at the Golden Reef Mine, a 10-stamp mill and tramway tower located 5.2 miles northeast of the Cave Creek Museum.

After the museum tour, we ate a delicious lunch at the Tonto Bar & Grill located at 5736 E. Rancho Manana Blvd. The restaurant is part of the Rancho Manana Resort and Golf Club. We sat in a table near the golf course. At 7:00 p.m. we met Corky Weily and Natalie Kane for dinner at Jade Palace located at 9160 E. Shea Blvd in Scottsdale for delicious Chinese food.

SATURDAY, MARCH 23, 2019—GOODYEAR AND DINNER WITH CORKY WEILY AND NATALIE KANE

Linda and I drove to Goodyear Ballpark at 1933 S. Ballpark Way to see the Cleveland Indians play the Cincinnati Reds so Linda wanted to buy Indian's fanwear. It's a fifty-mile ride from our condo to the Goodyear Ballpark

SUNDAY, MARCH 24, 2019—MODERN PHOENIX TOUR

Before the Modern Phoenix home tour, we went to the Scottsdale Center for the Performing Arts and saw the *Violins for Hope* exhibit. Before the self-guided Modern Phoenix home tour, we had lunch at Zoes Kitchen in Phoenix next to the tour's registration building.

My sister Linda, Penny and me registered for the tour of 10 Robert Haver homes and buildings from the 1950s. The cost was $45.00 per ticket. There were three sections to this tour. Part A is called uptown Phoenix. This area is bordered by Bethany Home Road on the south to Northern Avenue on the north and 15th Avenue on the west to the 51 on the east. Part B is called Arcadia Lite and it borders on McDowell Road to the south and Camelback Road to the north, 36th Street on the west and 44th Street to the east. Part C is call Dreamy Draw and borders on Shea Blvd to the south and Cholla Street to the north, the 51 on the west and east of 36th Street to the east.

The check-in for the tour started at 1701 E. Camelback Road at the current home of Copenhagen Imports, a building originally designed by Robert Haver and built in 1953. The building was the former Lou Regester Furniture. The actual start was in the Rancho Ventura neighborhood on Coronado Road. Neat aspects of the tour were the 1950s and early 1960s automobiles parked in many of the home's driveways. The 8th home was the only one designed and built in 1949.

MONDAY, MARCH 25, 2019—LINDA LEAVES PHOENIX
CATTLE TRACK ARTS COMPOUND

We ate breakfast at The Breakfast Kitchen Bar before taking Linda to Sky Harbor Airport for her Southwest Airlines flight back to Cleveland. Her flight left Phoenix at 2:25 p.m. After we dropped Linda at the airport, Penny and I drove to the Cattle Track Compound and Artist Haven located at 6105 N. Cattle Track Road in Scottsdale. Penny read about this place in the *Arizona Republic* newspaper and we wanted to check it out. We met Chance Phillips who does felt and fiber art and she gave us a quick tour of the place. We saw a man painting in a large room. There is a theater where magic shows are sometimes performed. We saw color pencil drawings on wood created by Mark McDowell displayed on the wall. We checked out Santo Press and the studio of Brent Bond and met Timothy Chapman who invented natural history. He also builds furniture and shares space with a jewelry maker. Mark McDowell gave us a quick tour and explanation of his colored pencil on wood technique. We met photographer Mark Hendrickson and saw some of his portraits on the wall. Mark had photographed Danica Patrick and her portrait was hanging in his space. On our way back to the condo, we stopped at Sweet Provisions and bought dessert.

At 6:00 p.m. we had our Mission de los Arroyos Annual Meeting held at the Mustang Library on 90th Street. We sat near Jeff and Michaele Salmon.

THURSDAY, MARCH 28, 2019—LUNCH AND ROOT & SOUL

Today is Rich Aver's 73h birthday. Rich and I ate lunch at the Canton Dragon. For dinner to celebrate Rich Aver's 73rd birthday, the "Great Eight" ate dinner at The Root and Soul restaurant and we took a group photo.

SATURDAY, MARCH 30, 2019—LINDA JASS AND THE GREAT EIGHT

Linda Jass was in Phoenix to watch her granddaughter Maddy play in a baseball game. Penny and I drove to the west side to have lunch with Linda, Faith, Maddy and Tyler at Souper Salad located at 10005 N. Metro Parkway in Phoenix. The place has a gigantic salad bar. In the evening, the Avers, Weintraubs and us were invited for dinner by Dan and Annie Murphy to their rental house. The Murphy's daughter, Karry was there with her husband Tim and their dog, Deeter, the Doberman Pincher. I took a selfie of the group sitting at the table.

SUNDAY, MARCH 31, 2019—DESERT AND MISSION EXHIBIT

Alan and Ellen Magit left Scottsdale on their way back to Chicago. After breakfast, Penny and I went for a walk in the desert at The Gateway to the McDowell Sonoran Preserve just north of Bell Road on Thompson Peak Road. After our walk, we drove to Old Scottsdale and went to the Scottsdale Artists League Exhibit at The Mission. The building is the old adobe mission and has been placed on the National Register of Historic Places by the United States Department of the Interior. I took some photos of the inside of the church and a few photos outside at the art exhibit. Across the street from The Mission is a garden with a Native American statue. Then we went inside the Scottsdale Center for the Performing Arts to see the exhibit, *All That You Can't Leave Behind,* suitcases packed during the Holocaust of few precious items packed for their journey to concentration camps. After the exhibit, we met Charles Skiera outside the Scottsdale Performing Arts Center at his tent. After dinner, we were invited to see the Kirk Douglas documentary at Jeffery and Susan Schesnol's home.

TUESDAY, APRIL 2, 2019—HOTEL TOUR AND PAUL MARTIN'S

After breakfast, Penny and I decided to take a mini driving tour to downtown Phoenix and our first stop was at the famous Westward Ho Hotel built in 1928. The old hotel is located at 618 North Central Avenue at Fillmore Street in Phoenix. Once inside the hotel there is a registration desk to the left. To the left of the entrance is a large room and a colorful decorated ceiling design. In another room there are giant columns and large chandeliers hang from the textured ceiling. Stain-glass murals of various scenes are scattered throughout the lobby. One such scene was an old miner with a mule walking in the desert. Another scene pictured three Native Americans sitting around a campfire. A third stain-glass scene featured a bird flying over a saguaro and prickly pear cactus. A fourth scene showed a mountain with what appears to be dwellings built into a mountain. Across the street from the Westward Ho Hotel is the light rail on Central Avenue.

We then decided to take a drive to Camelback Road and motor up Camelback Mountain to find Copenhaver Castle. Penny took video of the drive-up Camelback Mountain and also driving down the mountain. In the evening for dinner, we met Jay and Harriet Weintraub and the Murphys at Paul Martin's American Grill located at 6186 N. Scottsdale Road just north of Lincoln Avenue.

WEDNESDAY, APRIL 3—MURPHY'S AND LITTLE MISS BBQ

I picked up Jan and Rich Aver and we met Jay and Harriet Weintraub at Dan and Annie's new #29 home almost complete. The kitchen appliances had not arrived, the floors were covered with paper, no landscaping had been done and the pool would be put in during the summer.

After our visit to the Murphy's new home, we all drove to the Phoenix Little Miss BBQ located at 8901 N. 7th Street in Sunnyslope. We were told to go there early, so we arrived around 3:20 p.m. for the opening of the doors at 4:00 p.m. We were the second in line and customers quickly formed after our arrival. The owner Scott Holmes gave a little speech before the doors opened. Once you come through the door, you place an order with the people behind the counter. The person carves the brisket or turkey in front of your eyes and you move down the line for the side dishes. There is a large outdoor patio with picnic benches but our group decided to eat inside at a long table. We had someone take a group photo of the "Great Eight."

After Little Miss BBQ, Penny and I told everyone about Karl's Bakery located at 111 E. Dunlap Avenue Suite #13 very close to Little Miss BBQ. All of us enjoyed looking at all of the delicious and low calorie (ha ha) desserts in the refrigerated cases. Penny and I bought a few items for dessert. After this experience we took the Avers back to their condo and Penny and I went home.

THURSDAY, APRIL 4—FOUNTAIN HILLS PICNIC

After breakfast, I got a pedicure at Shona Nails N Spa and then got gas at Costco for the rental car. For lunch, Penny and I drove Jeff and Michaele Salmon to Fountain Hills. Our first stop was Fountain Park where we had a picnic in an outdoor pavilion. I took a selfie of the Salmons and us. After our picnic lunch, we walked by the Fountain Hills Community Garden, and then the Fountain Hills Public Library and the River of Time Museum. Standing in front of the museum was a statue of a boy with a newspaper in his hand along with several other statues of Native Americans. A plaque of Keith McMahan, "Mr. Fountain Hills" was also commemorated in front of the museum. Inside the museum was an 1890's doctor's buggy parked by the entrance. After the museum, we all went back to our condo.

FRIDAY, APRIL 5, 2019—SHEMER AND PA'LA DINNER

Penny had a haircut appointment at Mane Attractions located at 32nd Street and Camelback Road in Phoenix. After her haircut appointment, Penny and I took a drive to the Shemer Art Center located at 5005 E. Camelback Road in Phoenix for a look inside. On the outside of the building were statues overlooking Camelback Mountain in the background. Mini tiles were on a wall as you entered the building. Various sculptures were around the outside of the property. A plaque on the wall inside the entrance read "Martha Evvard Shemer purchased this historic home built in 1919 on a three-acre lot, then donated it to the City of Phoenix. She had two dreams: to preserve the property, and to provide an arts education facility and community center for the citizens of Phoenix. In 1984, the City dedicated the facility as the Shemer Art Center and Museum." There was a self-guided tour of New Art Arizona from March 26 to April 25, 2019 created by scholarship recipients. Beautiful pieces of artwork were displayed.

After the Shemer Art Center, we drove to Pa'La Wood-Fired Cooking located at 2107 N. 24th Street in Phoenix. We met Jay and Harriet and Jan and Rich Aver at the restaurant for dinner. We ordered a hummus and flatbread appetizer and ate outside on a picnic table with comfortable chairs. After dinner we decided to go to Scoop and Joy Lounge for ice cream located at 9397 E. Shea Blvd in Scottsdale. The place featured Lappert's Ice Cream.

SATURDAY, APRIL 6, 2019—TODD WALDMAN IN SCOTTSDALE

Penny and I picked up our nephew Todd Waldman who was staying at the Westin Kierland Resort and Spa located at 6902 Greenway Parkway in Scottsdale. He happened to accompany his wife Jessica Ciralsky who was attending a medical conference there. We drove to Biscuits for breakfast located at 15600 N. Hayden Road in Scottsdale. We sat on the patio but there was a motorcycle get together right across the street at the Harley Davidson dealership so the noise was a little overwhelming; however, the breakfast was delicious. After breakfast we drove Todd to The Gateway Trailhead just north of Bell Road on Thompson Peak and took a nice walk in the desert. After our walk, Jessica was through with her conference so we met her back at the Westin Kierland Resort and hung out for about thirty minutes. Penny and I had dinner at Hiro Sushi on 90th Street. Later in the day, Jessica and Todd went hiking at the same place and saw a rattlesnake.

SUNDAY, APRIL 7, 2019—MESA FLEA AND SINGH MEADOWS

I picked up Jan Aver and we drove to the Mesa Market Place Swap Meet. We call this place the Flea Market. I bought a green man purse exactly like my black purse and I'll leave it at the condo. I also bought a man's Sunday Charter hat with a stiff brim that I can wear to play golf and also can leave it in Scottsdale. Penny bought two seat belt cushions and a steering wheel cover, another black step stool and some kitchen items.

After the Flea Market we drove to Singh Meadows for lunch located at 1490 E. Weber Drive in Tempe. This was one amazing place with the restaurant and main building housed in the former clubhouse of the defunct Tempe Golf Course. The sign in front says home grown and good. The restaurant is known for its organic menu and fresh vegetables of every kind. The beautifully landscaped grounds are all grass-covered with a small pond and you would not think you were in Arizona. You order food at a counter and we waited for our food sitting at a picnic table outside of the restaurant.

I ordered beet toast on a crusty grilled country loaf from Noble Bread with a braised beet and cream cheese mixture helped with glistening gold and ruby red beets, some shaved, some pickled & some curled into flowers, almond slices & avocados for $10.00. Penny ordered an egg salad sandwich with a side salad of buttered brown bread, Munster, shaved fennel, pickles, simple greens for $12.00. Jan ordered a grilled sweet potato and cooked carrot bowl, basmati rice, avocado, herbs & green lentils bowl for $11.00. This place was terrific.

WEDNESDAY, APRIL 10—DINNER AND MESA CONCERT

After breakfast, Penny and I headed to Ginny's Laundromat to wash throw rugs and rags. After the laundromat we went back to our condo for lunch. After lunch, Penny sat outside in the sun and read her book.

Later in the day we drove to the Scottsdale Museum of the West and paid our yearly membership of $60.00. After the museum, we ate dinner at Salut Kitchen & Bar located at 1435 E. University Drive in Tempe. We ordered our favorite meal there; the Salut sampler of caprese salad, hummus nachos, Mac N Cheese bites & Salut fries. After dinner we drove to the Mesa Center for the Performing Arts to see the Kenny Wayne Shepherd Band and blues singer Beth Hart. We sat in the mezzanine level seats with a railing in front of us and won't sit on these seats again, although we could see fine. We had a real treat because Kenny Wayne Shepherd's Band was fantastic and didn't know they were on the same bill as Beth Hart.

THURSDAY, APRIL 11, 2019—LIGHT FIX AND EXHIBIT

The ballast on our overhead kitchen florescent light burned out so we had to call a repairman named Will from Bolt Electric to replace the worn-out ballast. The cost of the new ballast was $138.00. After the kitchen light was fixed, I got a haircut at Angelo's Hair Styling and Penny got a pedicure at Shona Nails N Spa.

After dinner, Penny and I drove to the Arizona Jewish Historical Society in

Phoenix to see and hear a presentation on The Liberators of the Concentration Camps during World War II. Oskar Knoblach, a Holocaust survivor, spoke at the event. Robert Sutz, an artist, who was also at the event, created a life mask of one of the liberators.

FRIDAY, APRIL 12, 2019—BOXES AND PHOENIX THEATER

After breakfast, I took four cardboard boxes to the UPS Store located at 8776 E. Shea Boulevard to be sent to Northbrook. And then we went to the Desert Botanical Garden for a walk to see all of the different cactus and flowers in full bloom. We also went inside the butterfly exhibit and I took a video inside the building. We drove to the Phoenix Palette restaurant at 1625 N. Central Avenue next to the Phoenix Theater and Art Museum and ate a delicious dinner. I can't remember what we ate for dinner but Penny and I shared a salted Carmel gelato for dessert. The play started at 7:30 p.m. and the title, *Sisters in Law*, was based on a conversation between Sandra Day O'Connor and Ruth Bader Ginsburg. The play was thoughtful and entertaining.

MONDAY, APRIL 15, 2019—OUR FAREWELL LUNCH

We met Jan and Rich Aver at 18 Degrees, a restaurant located at 9375 E. Bell Road in Scottsdale where we sat outside to say goodbye before our trip to Northbrook. After lunch Penny and I went to Old Town Scottsdale and the Outrageous Olive Oil Store to buy two bottles of olive oil to ship to Northbrook as a Mother's Day present for Ronna and Marni. We also bought a bottle of olive oil for us. In the evening, we saw our last sunset before we left Scottsdale for our trip back to Northbrook for the summer and fall.

TUESDAY, APRIL 16, 2019—FLIGHT TO CHICAGO

We left our condo at 10:30 a.m. and dropped off our luggage at curb side in Terminal 2 of Sky Harbor Airport. I left Penny inside the airport while I returned our rental car to the Airport Transportation Center. After dropping off the rental car, I took the shuttle bus back to the airport to meet Penny. Before our flight, we had a bite to eat at Paradise Café that's still going strong in Terminal 2. Our United Airlines flight departed Sky Harbor Airport at 2:55 p.m. and arrived at Chicago O'Hare at 8:25 p.m. Uri picked us up at the airport and drove us to our Northbrook home. We had such a great winter in Scottsdale and Phoenix.

FRIDAY, APRIL 19, 2019—PASSOVER DINNER

Penny and I went shopping for groceries at Mariano's. After Mariano's I went to Nutritional Concepts to buy supplements. Around 5:00 p.m. Penny and I were invited to Bennett and Marni's home to celebrate Passover. Ronna and family went to services at BJBE so they didn't attend the dinner.

FRIDAY, MAY 3, 2019—RIDE RAUL'S PORSCHE 911S

Our next-door neighbor, Raul Dilig, brought his 2013 Porsche 911 Carrera S to our driveway so we could take a drive and go the Porsche dealership for a cup of coffee while they washed his car. I also had a chance to drive the car. It is so fast. At 5:30 the evening, the Appelbaums picked us up and we went to dinner at Max's Deli in Highland Park.

WEDNESDAY, MAY 8, 2019—BROOKE'S CONCERT

Penny went to A.M. Jewelers to replace the battery in her watch and bought some shoes at Lori's. Penny and I went to hear Brooke play the cello in her orchestra concert at Alan Shepard Middle School in Deerfield.

THURSDAY, MAY 9, 2019—TALIA'S CONCERT

At 7:00 p.m. Penny and I went to hear Talia play the cello in her orchestra concert at Twin Groves Middle School n Buffalo Grove.

SUNDAY, MAY 12, 2019—MOTHER'S DAY

Penny and I hosted Mother's Day at our home this year. We made lox and cream cheese on cucumbers and a bought a Happy Mother's Day cake at Mariano's.

SUNDAY, MAY 19, 2019—ROLLING STONES CONCERT

Penny and I were excited to see our grandson Danny play in a *Rolling Stones* concert at Evanston Rocks.com located at 1012 Church Street in Evanston. Ronna also was at the concert. Danny played the guitar on *Brown Sugar* and *19th Nervous Breakdown* and the drums, the bass guitar on one song and keyboards on *Time On My Side* and played a solo on the last song. The concert was terrific and Danny's playing was spectacular. Penny and I thoroughly enjoyed seeing and hearing Danny.

MONDAY, MAY 20, 2019—MY COLONOSCOPY

It was my turn to have a colonoscopy and I was scheduled for one at Lake Forest Hospital located at 1000 N. Westmoreland Road. Penny and I arrived at the hospital at 7:30 a.m. The procedure went smoothly and there were no signs of any polyps. I had Penny take a photo of me with two thumbs up before the colonoscopy.

WEDNESDAY, MAY 22, 2019—OLD SCHOOL LAKE

After breakfast I went fishing at Old School Lake part of the Lake County Forest Preserves. It is a small lake and I caught a huge bullfrog on a white artificial lure with two tails. After fishing for about one hour, I drove to Wright Woods, another Lake County lake but caught no fish.

SATURDAY, JUNE 1, 2019—BROOKE'S DANCE RECITAL

Penny and I drove to the Genoese Theater located at 203 N. Genesee Street in Waukegan for our granddaughter Brooke's dance recital. Brooke did a great performance of dancing in several numbers. For dinner this evening, we picked up Jay and Harriet Weintraub and went to dinner at Ewa's Pierogi located at 976 Harlem Avenue in Glenview.

THURSDAY, JUNE 6, 2019—CANTIGNY TOUR

After breakfast, I bought a pair of size 9 ½ Asics gel-nimbus shoes at Dick's Sporting Goods. It was the most expensive walking shoe I ever bought at $164.60.

For several years Penny and I had been talking about driving to Cantigny located at 1 S. 151 Winfield Road in Wheaton and we finally had a chance to do it today. June 6th happened to be the 74th anniversary of D-Day. This place was amazing and the spacious home of Robert McCormick. Robert was a member of the Chicago McCormick family who was a lawyer, distinguished Army officer in World War I and eventually the owner and publisher of the *Chicago Tribune*, started by his grandfather.

Our navigation system brought us in the backway to the park and grounds, so we didn't have to pay. We parked our car in the lot and walked to the visitor's center. In order to get to the home and museum, we walked through the extensive garden and entered the home through the back entrance. As we entered the home, there were portraits of Joseph Medill who helped Abraham Lincoln become president and Robert McCormick's grandfather hanging over the mantle and fireplace. Penny and I walked around to the front of the home, sat on the bench and took a selfie on the huge front porch. I also took many photos of the home and I put them into a "show." Once we left the home, we saw a huge sand sculpture with the heading First Division Omaha Beach in honor of D-Day. There were several U.S. Army tanks on the grounds. One of them was an M1 Abrams tank used in Operation Desert Storm. A sign next to the tank said it was the Army's longest serving tank and entered service in 1980. There were two boys playing on another nearby tank. Overall, it was a great afternoon.

FRIDAY, JUNE 7, 2019—WALKING PATH AND KITCHEN SINK LEAK

Penny and I took a thirty five-minute walk on our neighborhood bike path. Plumber Bill Swanson from Glenbrook Plumbing came to our house because we had a water leak underneath our kitchen sink. Penny and I thought it might be from the dishwasher but Bill told us we needed a new kitchen faucet. He suggested going to Banner Plumbing to buy a new faucet. For dinner this evening, Marcy and David Levinson picked up Penny and me for dinner and drove us to Arlington Heights at Bistro Chen located at 10 E. Miner Street.

SATURDAY, JUNE 8, 2019—SPENCER'S BASEBALL

Penny and I drove to Buffalo Grove to watch Spencer play baseball at Emmerich East Park. I took a video of Spencer batting. It is always fun to see how much progress Spencer has made with baseball's fundamentals. At 5:30 p.m. Penny and I had dinner with Ray Pershing and Carol Einhorn at Bonta Pizzeria & Restaurant located at 430 Milwaukee Avenue in Lincolnshire.

MONDAY, JUNE 10, 2019—PLUMBING & BROOKE'S TALENT

In the morning, Penny and I drove to Buffalo Grove and bought a Delta faucet for our kitchen sink. The faucet is the exact model of the one we have in our Scottsdale condo. Penny and I didn't get a chance to actually see Brooke perform her dance routine at the Kipling School Talent Show but Marni texted us a video of her performance and I incorporated it into my slide show. For dinner this evening, Penny and Harriet Weintraub went to Max & Benny's.

TUESDAY, JUNE 11, 2019—NEW KITCHEN FAUCET
AND THE CHICAGO BOTANIC GARDEN

We called Glenbrook Plumbing and Reggie came to the house to install a new Delta kitchen faucet. Reggie had to remove the kitchen sink in order to install the new faucet. He removed the old Grohe kitchen faucet and replaced it with our new more modern one. We picked up Spencer and took him to the Chicago Botanic Gardens Model Railroad Garden. There were different parts of the United States represented at the model railroad. I took videos of the trains and Spencer. We took a selfie and had a good time watching all of the trains. We even saw Mount St. Helens volcano erupt. We dropped off Spencer at his house and went to dinner at Uncle Julio's located at 20423 N. Rand Road in Kildeer, Illinois.

FRIDAY, JUNE 14, 2019—ALAN AND PENNY HAIRCUTS

Penny and I drove downtown for our haircuts. I was dropped off at the Hyatt Regency Hotel for my haircut with Otto Bodner and Penny drove the car to J Gordon Design and parked. After my haircut I walked to the CBIC Theater located at 18 W. Monroe Street where *Hamilton* was playing a bought four tickets to the August 21st matinee performance of *Hamilton*.

SUNDAY, JUNE 16, 2019—FATHER'S DAY

Today was a relaxing day. Penny made a fruit bowl with watermelon to Marcy Levinson. We had dinner and Marni brought a Queen Anne cake to our house to celebrate our 51st wedding anniversary.

SATURDAY, JUNE 22, 2019—SPENCER'S BASEBALL GAME

Penny and I went to see Spencer play baseball on his Orioles team at Emmerich East Park located at 150 Raupp Blvd. in Buffalo Grove. I took a video of Spencer getting a hit. We saw Lori Margolis and Spencer's friends Jack and Max who were there to support him. After the game, we picked up pizza at Lou Malnati's located at in Buffalo Grove and went back to the Belinky home for dinner.

SUNDAY, JUNE 23, 2019—BLACK ENSEMBLE THEATER

Jay and Harriet picked up Penny and me and drove us to the 3:00 p.m. matinee performance of *Style & Grace: A Musical Tribute to Lena Horne & Nancy Wilson* at Chicago's Black Ensemble Theater located at 4400 N. Clark Street. After the show we ate dinner at Reza's restaurant located at 5255 North Clark Street.

WEDNESDAY, JUNE 26, 2019—DR. HAHR & EMA DINNER

Penny had an afternoon doctor's appointment with Dr. Alison Hahr in Galter at Northwestern Medicine and parked in the Northwestern Hospital parking lot at 21 W. Ohio Street. After her appointment, we parked our car and walked to Ema located at 74 W. Illinois Street where we had a fantastic dinner.

CHAPTER THIRTY-TWO
A Crazy Boston Trip—Take Two

SATURDAY, JUNE 29, 2019—TRIP TO BOSTON: TAKE ONE
DIDN'T MAKE IT TODAY

Roy Cramer was having a retirement and 70th birthday party on Sunday, June 30th and Penny and I were excited to be flying to Boston to help celebrate the occasion. We tried to make the party but didn't. The following is what happened.

Next is a letter I wrote to United Airlines about our Boston trip.

I am a loyal customer of United Airlines (Mileage Plus Number listed) and yesterday (Saturday, June 29, 2019) was the worst travel day I have ever experienced on United Airlines. My wife, Marylin and I were booked on a non-stop United flight #301 leaving from Chicago's O'Hare Airport from Gate 10 scheduled for an 11:40 a.m. departure to Boston's Logan International Airport. We arrived at O'Hare at 9:00 a.m. for this flight and checked our two pieces of luggage outside.

I received a 9:28 a.m. text message from United saying my 11:40 a.m. flight from Chicago to Boston is delayed because an earlier delay impacted your plan's arrival. United Text Message: Gate Change: Now the plane is leaving from Gate B7. UA301 now departs at 1:30 p.m.

United Text Message: Your inbound plane is arriving late because of a plane change in Chicago this morning caused by engine maintenance. It's now expected to arrive from Baltimore at 1:07 p.m. We know this isn't part of your plans, and we greatly appreciate your patience.

At 11:43 a.m. I received the following United text message. Your inbound plane is now on its way from Baltimore and is expected to arrive at 1:11 p.m. Thank you for your continued patience.

United Text Message: Reminder: Flight UA301 from Chicago to Boston departs at 1:46 p.m. on June 29.

United Text Message: Delay Update: Your 11:40 a.m. flight from Chicago to Boston is delayed further. UA301 now departs at 1:50 p.m. on June 29. We're sorry for the extra delay and are working to get you on your way.

United Text Message: We're now boarding flight UA301 to Boston. We look forward to seeing you on board soon. Around 1:45 p.m. we start to board the plane. The plane is full of passengers and we pull away from the gate and are taxing for over 1 ½ hours when around 4:00 or 4:15 p.m. the pilot asks everyone to get off the plane and take all of your carry-ons with you. Then I get another United text.

United Text Message: Delay Update: Your 11:40 a.m. flight from Chicago to Boston is delayed further because air traffic control reduced the number of planes allowed to land each hour until weather conditions and/or air traffic improves. UA301 now will depart at 5:00 p.m. We're sorry for the extra delay and are working to get you on your way.

We're sorry for returning to the gate. Severe thunderstorms in the Boston area have reduced the number of planes allowed to land per hour. We apologize for this inconvenience and we appreciate your patience. Meanwhile all of the passengers are off the plane.

United Text Message: Gate change: Flight UA301 from Chicago to Boston now departs from Gate B2 at 5:00 p.m. on June 29.

United Text Message: Delay update: UA301 now departs at 5:30 p.m. We're sorry for the extra delay and are working to get you on your way.

United Text Message: Delay update: UA301 from Chicago to Boston is delayed further now departs at 6:00 p.m. on June 29. We're sorry for the extra delay and are working to get you on your way.

Around 6:00 p.m. I get another text. **Canceled**: Your UA301 from Chicago to Boston is canceled because of severe weather conditions on the way to your destination. We're sorry for the cancellation and are working to get you on your way. You can view other flight options and check here with the listing of a website.

United Text Message: We're sorry to let you know your **flight UA 301 from Chicago to Boston has been canceled** because of prolonged schedule disruptions caused by thunderstorms in Boston. Check out your options on the United app or united.com under saved reservations. You can also contact 1 (800) UNITED-1. By the way, a later scheduled plane for Boston left at 3:30 p.m.

At this point, the loud speaker also told all of the passengers to go to the Customer Service desk for rebooking, so all of the passengers started walking from Gate B2 to the Customer Service desk by the large dinosaur. The line was very long. While waiting in line, a United staff person was handing out slips of paper with the phone number 1- (877) 437-2998. I called the number and after 15 minutes or so I got a United agent. I was on the phone for 1 hour and 5 minutes with a United person. She said all flights to Boston were booked for Saturday and Sunday, so the first flight we could get was on Monday morning, July 1st with UA flight 301 to Boston leaving at 11:40 a.m. We also changed our return flight to July 5th instead of July 4th.

Now the challenge really began as I tried to get our checked luggage back. I first went to Customer Service in the baggage claim area. With a long line of people also trying to get their luggage, I finally met with a United agent who said it could take 2 to 3 hours to get our luggage. She marked 7:08 p.m. on my two luggage receipts and told me to check back in an hour and I did. No luggage. I went to another agent who told me to go home and I wouldn't be getting my luggage because it was still on the plane and it would be transferred to Boston on a future flight. I told them I wanted my luggage back tonight.

And finally, at 10:15 p.m. I got both of our checked suitcases. They were found and brought back to claim area 7 after waiting for over three hours.

I left the airport around 10:20 p.m. and I'm not sure if any other person got their luggage from UA 301. A persistent United agent kept calling someone who finally retrieved my two pieces of luggage from either the plane or a holding area. No one knew exactly where the UA 301 luggage was. If our plane had not been delayed in the first place, with having to wait for a plane from Baltimore, we would have made it to Boston in the first place. We missed a retirement party for our brother-in-law that took place on Sunday, June 30, 2019.

We are now flying to Boston on Monday, July 1 on the same flight as the one from Saturday. There is no reason why United had me wait over three hours to get our luggage from a canceled flight. It cost me over $90.00 because I had to pay for two rides to the airport; one ride on Saturday, June 29 and one ride on Monday, July 1. We were lucky our son could pick us up on Saturday night to take us back to our home in Northbrook.

There were so many passengers upset with the way United handled the flight delays and the last plane from Baltimore and also trying to get their luggage after the flight was canceled. I am retired and as part of my profession I flew on United Airlines and never had any type of problem that occurred as described. I was not happy with United Airlines on Saturday, June 29, 2019. It was the worst travel day of my life.

MONDAY, JULY 1, 2019—OUR BOSTON TRIP—TAKE TWO

Uri picked up Penny and me at 8:30 a.m. and we arrived at Chicago O'Hare Airport at 9:00 a.m. for our 11:40 a.m. non-stop United Airlines flight#301 to Boston and we were scheduled to arrive in Boston at 3:00 p.m. This time Penny and I did not check our luggage but consolidated all of our belongings into two carry-ons. We bought two coffees, a muffin and two scones at Starbucks and ate breakfast while waiting for our flight to depart. After eating, I took a photo of Penny sitting in the airport waiting for our flight but she was not looking too happy. A short time later we both received a United Airlines text message: "We appreciate your patience while our maintenance team finished their work and required paperwork. We're making our final preparations for departure, and you can expect to be on your way shortly." So, we boarded the plane and the main flight attendant made a safety check announcement, but we had to get off the plane waiting for maintenance. And then we got back on the plane and the flight attendant made a second safety check announcement. There was a late passenger arriving on the flight so the flight attendant had to make a third safety check announcement but this time he announced it really fast and I was able to take a video of the last part when everyone cheered at the end. Our United flight finally arrived in Boston at 5:45 p.m. and Lois and Roy picked us up at the airport. Lois took a photo of us just before dinner.

TUESDAY, JULY 2, 2019—THE NEEDHAM RESERVOIR

After breakfast, Roy, Lois, Penny and I drove to the Needham Reservoir so Roy and I could go fishing. Roy and I fished off of the Roland Johnson Fishing Pier but neither Roy nor I had a bite. Meanwhile, Sally Weitzen showed up and she spoke with Penny and Lois while Roy and I fished. We saw a giant blue heron in the beautiful surroundings of the Needham Accessible Reservoir Trail. Penny spent time with Luna, the Cramberg's dog.

Back at Lois and Roy's home, I feel asleep on their couch and two photos were taken of me sound asleep on their sofa. Meanwhile, after lunch Penny took an afternoon nap outside on a chaise lounge chair as well as Roy sleeping in a chair. For dinner that night we had leftovers from the party we missed on Sunday. After dinner, we drove to Wellesley and ate ice cream at Truly Yogurt, Ice Cream & More. We took a selfie sitting on a bench with our ice in a cup and cone. After our ice cream we walked to Wellesley Books, a huge bookstore a few blocks away.

WEDNESDAY, JULY 3, 2019—EUSTIS ESTATES, SEAFOOD AND EVENING ENTERTAINMENT

After breakfast, Lois drove us to the Eustis Estate Museum, a huge home and part of historic New England, located at 1424 Canton Avenue in Milton, Massachusetts. There are many locations of different historic New England properties that are part of this program and Lois and Roy are members. If you are member, entrance fees to these historic places are free. The visitor's center was a separate building. We went inside. signed the register and it was a short walk to the three-story home. Just outside of the home's entrance was a very large copper beach tree planted in 1879. The outside of the home had beautiful stones in different shapes and bricks in multi-colors of browns. There were also brick arches.

Roy held open the large wood door and we walked inside. Once inside we took a self-guided tour of the first and second floors and of course I made a slide show of the inside and outside. To the immediate right was an ornately covered wood fireplace. The home had many spacious rooms with inlay wood flooring, one room with Spanish tile and an amazing wood staircase leading to the second floor with two landings. There was a seat halfway on one of the stair landings. There was also many stain glass windows.

After the Eustis Estate home tour, we drove to Quincy, Massachusetts and ate lunch at The Original Clam Box located at 789 Quincy Shore Drive, home of the famous fried clams, serving quality seafood since 1968. We ordered food at the counter and when it was ready Roy brought a tray of two lobster rolls with French fries and fried clams strips with a cup of clam chowder. The lunch was delicious. After lunch Penny and I sat on a bench overlooking Boston Bay. Lois took a photo of us turned around and I took a photo of Roy turned around.

In the evening, we drove into Boston for a free concert at Boston's Fine Arts Museum located at 465 Huntington Avenue. We parked on the street a few blocks away and schlepped lawn chairs to the venue. The outside concert was packed with people. I took several videos of the crowd and the entertainment. The first act was a woman from Madagascar backed up by a guitar player and drums. She got the crowd to participate on several of her songs. The second act was called EFE, a strange group with a percussionist and drummer, a bongo player, a keyboard player and a woman standing and making weird sounds into the microphone. Another woman was dressed in a strange and colorful outfit with her head covered dancing to weird music with no melody.

THURSDAY, JULY 4, 2019—NEEDHAM'S HOLIDAY PARADE

Lois, Roy, Penny and I took lawn chairs to downtown Needham and parked ourselves on the side of the street that was not in the sun so we could see the Fourth of July Parade. The parade started with a Needham policeman on a motorcycle, followed by several fire trucks of various types, a police car and five marching policemen carrying an American flag and a flag of Massachusetts. World

War II Army veterans riding in a U.S. Army Jeep followed with marching veterans carrying flags. People were lined up on both sides of the street watching the parade. Five men on horseback and a group of men playing fifes and drums and wearing Revolutionary uniforms and carrying old muskets followed the procession. Other parade participants were a steel drum band on the back of a truck, a Dixie-land band on the back of a 1940s fire truck, a rock n roll band, The Reminisants, playing sloopy was on the back of a modern truck.

After the parade, we returned to Lois and Roy's home where niece Leah and her husband Josh Eaker arrived with their miniature Doberman, Dexter. Later, nephew Aaron Cramer and his girlfriend Jess Ferguson came to the home. Leah, Josh, Aaron and Jess were in the swimming pool. Penny, Lois, Roy and I relaxed outside enjoying the warm weather. Josh put on hot dogs and hamburgers on the grill. Penny sat with Luna and Dexter on a lounge chair inside the house.

FRIDAY, JULY 5, 2019—BUCKMASTER POND AND CHICAGO

Roy and I went to Needham's Bagel's Best and I bought bagels and cream cheese for breakfast. After breakfast, Lois drove us to Westwood, Massachusetts and Buckmaster Pond. We tried fishing in this terrific lake but had no luck. The girls watched as Roy and I tried out best to get a bite.

After fishing, we drove to Wellesley and to the Wellesley Bakery Café located at 542 Washington Street #1 and bought several sandwiches for lunch. Back at Lois and Roy's home, we ate lunch and relaxed before our later 7:30 p.m. non-stop United Airlines flight to Chicago. Later in the afternoon, Lois and Roy drove us to Logan International Airport. While going through the TSA line, Penny was stopped and searched by a TSA officer with a wand. I guess the TSA agent was taking no chances with Penny to make sure she was not a spy or terrorist. We departed Boston at 7:30 p.m. and arrived in Chicago's O'Hare Airport at 9:05 p.m. I called Uri and he had one of his drivers pick us up and take us home to Northbrook.

TUESDAY, JULY 9, 2019—RONNA'S BIRTHDAY

Penny went to lunch with Harriet Weintraub at Northbrook's Trattoria Oliveri restaurant located at 1358 Shermer Road. Penny and I met Ronna, Talia and Spencer at Lincolnshire's Wildfire restaurant located at 235 Parkway Drive to help her celebrate her 44th birthday. Ted was out of town for the occasion. We also bought gas at Woodman's for the 2016 Chevrolet Malibu.

SUNDAY, JULY 13, 2019—BREAKFAST ON OUR PATIO

Penny and I decided to have breakfast on our back patio. Alison Hayes Hoette was visiting Ronna, so we drove to Ronna's home and had a very nice visit with Alison. I took a selfie of Alison, Penny, Ronna and me. In the evening, for dinner, we joined Mike and Fran Stricker and Harriet and Jay Weintraub at Northbrook's Grill House restaurant for a fun evening of conversation.

TUESDAY, JULY 16, 2019—INDEPENDENCE GROVE

Penny and I drove to Independence Grove located at 16400 Buckley Road on Illinois route 137 in Libertyville and took our foldable chairs out of the car for an outdoor concert in the Plaza. The concert featured the blues band *Mississippi Heat* featuring Pierre Lacocque on the harmonica and Ms. Inetta Visor on vocals.

Mississippi Heat was fantastic and the weather was perfect with the sun setting in the background over the water toward the end of the concert.

THURSDAY, JULY 18, 2019—RONNA AND BRIAN PATTI

Penny and I met Ronna for lunch at the Purple Sprout Café & Juice Bar located at 341 E. Dundee Road in Wheeling, Illinois at the corner of Milwaukee Avenue. We took a selfie after lunch. After dinner, Penny and I drove to Niles, Illinois to the White Eagle restaurant at 6839 N. Milwaukee Avenue in Niles, Illinois to hear the Brian Patti Orchestra. Brian's father taught choir at Cleveland Heights High School when Penny was attending high school and in the choir. Penny saw Brian Patti's name in the newspaper and had to see if it was the same name she knew from high school and it was. They played old standards and people were dancing to the music.

SATURDAY, JULY 20, 2019—HAIRCUTS, LUNCH AT SBK

After breakfast, I dropped off Penny on North Clark Street so she could get her haircut at J Gordon Designs and I drove to the Hyatt Regency Chicago for my haircut with Otto Bodner. I parked the car in the Hyatt garage and took the escalator to the first floor and the escalator down to Otto on the lower level of the hotel. After my haircut, I drove the 2016 Chevrolet Malibu to 2326 N. Clark Street, parked the car in front and waited for Penny. We drove to SBK Sauce and Bread Kitchen located at 6338 N. Clark Street for lunch. Penny ordered a Cubana sandwich and I ordered a smoked trout sandwich with cream cheese, homemade bread, capers & kimchi that was a bit spicy for me.

MONDAY, JULY 22, 2019—CAROL RANDALL MASSAGES

I was at Ronna's home when Spencer came home from camp. Carol Randall was at Ronna's for Penny and my massages. Carol told us about a chiropractor she has used on herself named Dr. John Nikitow whose office was located at 207 Park Avenue in Libertyville. He uses KST technique without cracking any bones. After Carol left, we ordered Thai food from Siam Siam located on Deerfield Parkway and on the way home we stopped at Dairy Queen for dessert.

CHAPTER THIRTY-THREE
My Surprise Hospital Visit

THURSDAY, JULY 25, 2019—BENNETT GOLF & CHICAGO

At 6:30 a.m. I picked up Bennett and we drove to Deerfield Golf Course and played golf. Bennett had some fantastic drives and handily had a better score than me. At 3:45 p.m. we picked up Alan and Marilyn Appelbaum and drove to Paul Mesnick's apartment building located at 1530 N. Dearborn Parkway. Paul met us at the door and I parked our Subaru Outback inside his garage building. We spent some time in Paul's condo, then walked two and one-half blocks to Mario's Table casual Italian restaurant for a 6:15 p.m. reservation. Our server took a photo of our table and we had a terrific meal. After dinner, we walked back to Paul's condo and we said goodbye. I dropped off the Appelbaums at their Wilmette home and we drove home.

FRIDAY, JULY 26, 2019—HOSPITAL EMERGENCY ROOM

I woke up in the morning with a severe pain in my right groin area. I was fine the day before having played golf with Bennett plus walking back and forth from Mario's restaurant in Chicago. During the day, I went on Northwestern's my chart website and asked to see Dr. Goldstein as soon as possible. I got an immediate response and I could see Dr. Goldstein at 12:30 p.m. on July 29th.

As the day wore on, the pain got worse and around 9:00 p.m. I couldn't stand it any longer so Penny drove me to Highland Park Hospital's Emergency. They ran a few tests and gave me some pain medication.

SATURDAY, JULY 27, 2019—HIGHLAND PARK PHARMACY

After midnight leaving Highland Park Hospital Emergency, we stopped at CVS Pharmacy and picked up a prescription for pain. Later in the day, we ordered pizza for dinner at Lou Malnati's in Northbrook.

MONDAY, JULY 29, 2019—DR. DAN, NIKITOW AND ACCIDENT

Penny drove me for my 12:30 p.m. appointment with Dr. Goldstein because the pain in my groin was too painful and I couldn't get comfortable. Dr. Daniel Goldstein examined me for my groin pull and said I should have a back X-ray on the first floor. So, after my appointment, I went to the first floor and had an X-ray of my back. After my appointment I went to CVS to get a prescription. Dr. Goldstein also gave me a referral for physical therapy but I did not realize I should contact them immediately and to start therapy.

In the meantime, Penny contacted Carol Randall who recommended I see a chiropractor named Dr. John Nikitow located at 207 Park Avenue in Libertyville who did a different kind of chiropractic practice using KST, a gentile instrument on various parts of the body. Carol has seen him in the past for some of her ailments. On Carol's recommendation, I made an appointment to see Dr. Nikitow.

At 2:00 p.m. I had an appointment with Dr. Nikitow. The initial visit cost $105.00 because Dr. Nikitow does not accept any type of medical insurance so I paid him with my debit card.

On our way back from Dr. Nikitow's appointment, we decided to stop at

Mariano's to buy some groceries. Penny was driving and as we were looking for a parking spot at 4:30 p.m., a 2005 Toyota Camry backed into the passenger side door of our 2016 Chevrolet Malibu. The accident was not that much but it dented the passenger door and part of the wheel well.

We called the Northbrook Police who came to Mariano's parking lot and wrote up a report. The police report number was number 19-12572 at 15:41 p.m. The boy who hit us, Joseph Kruse, was age seventeen and worked at Mariano's. The accident was totally Kruse's fault and he admitted he caused the accident to the Northbrook Police officer. He had an American Family Insurance policy so we called the insurance company agent to get the ball rolling with fixing the Chevy.

MONDAY, AUGUST 1, 2019—NIKITOW AND HOSPITAL

My next appointment with Dr Nikitow was at 11:00 a.m. today. During his examination I became very light-headed, dizzy and my blood pressure dropped. I could hardly stand up and Dr. Nikitow suggested I lay down on his bench. He told me I should go to a hospital emergency room. Penny and I decided to drive to Lake Forest Hospital's parking lot and I called Dr. Goldstein's office and explain the situation. Dr. Goldstein told me I should be admitted to Lake Forest Hospital Emergency. I think I was dehydrated. I hadn't eaten much for breakfast this morning nor had I drunk any amount of water.

At 12:45 p.m. I was admitted to Lake Forest Hospital for testing and evaluation. The emergency room staff initially thought I could have had a mini stroke but after doing some preliminary tests with moving my arms and legs, a mini stroke was totally ruled out. Not to take any chances, I was admitted for more testing and was wheeled to a private room ECDU7 1551. An IV was put in my arm and I connected me to a monitor machine. I was smiling when Penny took a photo of me in the hospital bed. During my overnight stay, I underwent a variety of tests including X-rays, an electro-cardiogram and an MRI of my brain. Although an MRI makes lots of noise, I actually feel asleep during the procedure.

TUESDAY, AUGUST 2, 2019— DISMISSED FROM HOSPITAL

Penny came to Lake Forest Hospital to see me. Earlier in the day a woman from the hospital's physical therapy staff came to visit me and gave me some tips on what to do about my groin pain. Later in the day I was dismissed and Penny drove me home. Later in the day, I took the Chevrolet Malibu to Bojan's Auto Body to get an estimate to fix the smashed passenger side door and wheel well.

I had a tough time sitting for any length of time because the pain had gone from my groin to my thigh. For several weeks after returning from the hospital, I had to stand to eat because the pain was too severe to sit for any length of time.

TUESDAY, AUGUST 6, 2019—PENNY'S MAMMOGRAM

Penny drove into Chicago and parked the car in the Huron St. Clair parking garage across the street from Northwestern Hospital where she had a mammogram. I stayed home because I was in no shape to sit in the car while Penny drove into Chicago for her appointment.

WEDNESDAY, AUGUST 7, 2019—PHYSCIAL THERAPY

It was time to start physical therapy. Penny's friend Ellyn Greenbaum had been going to a physical therapist at Just Be Fit located at 420 Lake Cook Road Suite 101 in Deerfield and was very happy with her therapist. I called Just Be Fit and made my first physical therapy appointment at 9:00 a.m. on Monday, August 12, 2019 with Kinesiotherapist Marianne Vuckovich.

MONDAY, AUGUST 12, 2019—PHYSICAL THERAPY

At 9:00 a.m. I had my first physical therapy session with Kinesiotherapist Marianne Vuckovich from Just Be Fit. Penny drove me to the session and was with me during my first session. She also took some photos of me lying on a table face down with a cushion by both feet. Marianne worked on my right thigh and used a machine to massage the spot. At the end of the session, Marianne put some CBD ointment on my back to aid in the healing. She also printed exercises for me to do on my own at home. At 3:45 p.m. I had another appointment with Dr. Nikitow in Libertyville.

WEDNESDAY, AUGUST 21, 2019—*HAMILTON* IN CHICAGO

At 8:00 a.m. I had a physical therapy session with Marianne Vuckovich and I was worried that I wouldn't be able to sit during *Hamilton*. After breakfast, Jay and Harriet Weintraub picked up Penny and me and we drove downtown. Jay parked in a garage about one block east of the CIBC Theater located at 18 W. Monroe. We had great seats on the orchestra level C, row S, seats 111, 112, 113 & 115 on the aisle for Jay. The total cost per ticket was $185.50 that I had pre-paid. I had no problem sitting during the 1:30 p.m. performance of *Hamilton*. After the show, Jay drove us to Chicago's La Scarola Restaurant located at 721 W. Grand Avenue at Halstead Street where we ate a wonderful dinner.

SATURDAY, AUGUST 24, 2019—WEINTRAUB CELEBRATION

In August 2018, Jay and Harriet had treated Penny and me to MLG Restaurant located at 181 Laurel Avenue in Lake Forest to celebrate our 50th wedding anniversary. We enjoyed the restaurant so much, especially the bread pudding for dessert, we made a date for 2019 to celebrate the Weintraub's 50th anniversary. So tonight, we picked up Jay and Harriet and we drove to Lake Forest and ate dinner at MLG Restaurant in Lake Forest.

THURSDAY, AUGUST 29, 2019—BOTANIC GARDENS

At 9:00 a.m. I had a physical therapy session with Marianne Vuckovich at Just Be Fit. After my physical therapy session, Penny and I went for a walk in the Chicago Botanic Gardens. We saw two women standing in the water near the water lilies, pulling out weeds and cleaning the area near the water lilies. Penny sat on a bench and read a little of a book.

SATURDAY, AUGUST 31, 2019—DANNY'S CONCERT
TRIBUTE TO SOUTHERN ROCK

Penny and I drove to 28 Mile Vodka located at 454 Sheridan Road in Highwood to see and hear our grandson, Danny, play in a School of Rock band featuring a tribute to Southern Rock. He played keyboards, drums and guitar on a number of songs. One of the last songs he played a long guitar solo on Lynyrd

Skynyrd's song *Freebird*. After the concert Penny and I walked up and down Sheridan Road because it was *Nashwood, Highwood Meets Nashville on Labor Day Weekend*. We decided to eat an early dinner at Maria's Bakery and Café. I ordered eggplant Parmesan and Penny ordered fettuccini with broccoli & scallops.

SUNDAY, SEPTEMBER 1, 2019—SPENCER'S BASEBALL GAME

Penny and I drove to Mundelein Park District to watch Spencer play baseball. Penny went to the game while I went fishing in a pond next to the ballpark but didn't get a bite. I joined the game after thirty minutes of fishing.

WEDNESDAY, SEPTEMBER 4, 2019—NEW PRINTER

At 10:00 a.m., I had a physical therapy session at Just Be Fit with Marianne Vuckovich. After physical therapy, I was on the phone with a technician from Hewlett Packard because I had bought new ink cartridges at Office Depot for my Northbrook HP printer/scanner and they wouldn't work after installation. After many minutes, it was determined there was a problem with my HP printer and it couldn't be fixed so I had to order a new HP printer/scanner for $235.36.

THURSDAY, SEPTEMBER 5, 2019—JUDY ROBERTS CONCERT

Penny and I went to a free 7:00 p.m. concert at the Northbrook Library to see and hear Judy Roberts and her husband Greg Fishman concert. Judy played the piano and sang and Greg played the saxophone, clarinet and flute. It is always a great concert with these two performers.

SUNDAY, SEPTEMBER 8, 2019—MILLER PARK BASEBALL

At 10:00 a.m. I was picked up by Alan Appelbaum and driven to the Hyatt Regency Deerfield where we met Joel Probisky. Joel drove Alan and me to Milwaukee, Wisconsin and Miller Park to see the Chicago Cubs play the Milwaukee Brewers for a 1:10 p.m. start. We had great seats in family section 217, row 9 and seats 5, 6 & 7. Upon entering the ballpark, we stopped at TGI Friday's. Joel and Alan ate lunch there before the game started. I preferred to wait and eat veggie tacos for lunch and later a giant pretzel at the ballpark.

Before the game started, we went through The Selig Experience at Miller Park. It is a show about Bud Selig who brought the Brewers to Milwaukee. We walked through the exhibit that consisted of many photos and memorabilia. It was an interesting presentation.

FRIDAY, SEPTEMBER 13, 2919—BOJAN'S AND RENTAL CAR

I brought our 2016 Chevrolet Malibu to Bojan's Auto Body to get the passenger door and wheel well dent repaired. American Family Insurance paid for the repairs. I also picked up a rental car at Enterprise located on Waukegan Road in Glenview. At 2:30 p.m. I had an appointment with Dr. Nikitow in Libertyville but before going, we stopped at Rocky Mountain Chocolate Factory for a frozen banana and shared it on a bench before my appointment. I also took another photo of the hibiscus plant in our front yard.

SUNDAY, SEPTEMBER 15, 2019—WALK ALONG BIKE PATH

After breakfast Penny and I took a walk along the bicycle path near our Northbrook home. Penny picked up different wild flowers, weeds and got mosquito bites too. For dinner, we were invited at Ronna's home.

TUESDAY, SEPTEMBER 17, 2019—PETER NOLAN SPEECH

After dinner, Penny and I drove to the Glenview Public Library located at 1930 Glenview Road to hear a speech by former Chicago news anchor Peter Nolan. Peter spoke about the book he wrote about his days broadcasting Chicago television news. I had to meet him because he once worked with my father at Youngstown's Woodrow Wilson High School. To supplement his income, he was a substitute teacher when he was a reporter and anchor on Youngstown's CBS affiliate, WKBN TV Channel 27.

Penny and I arrived well before the 7:00 p.m. start of Peter's talk in hopes of meeting him before his presentation. I saw him enter the library, approached him and introduced myself. I showed him a photo of my father and he remembered him. In 1969, I remember my father telling me Peter Nolan was moving to Chicago and that if I saw him, I was supposed to say hello from my father. It only took me fifty years for me to say hello.

FRIDAY, SEPTEMBER 20, 2019—PICKED UP CHEVY

I received a call early in the morning saying the 2016 Chevrolet Malibu had been repaired and I could pick it up anytime. After breakfast, I walked to Bojan's Auto Body, looked over the repairs and drove it home. Later, Penny and I returned the rental car back to Enterprise in Glenview.

MONDAY, SEPTEMBER 23, 2019—LEVINSONS AND JILL COLE

Before I had to pick up Spencer, I took my fly rods to Green Lake near the Belinky home and did some fly-fishing and I caught a few bluegills. I was able to leave a little early from sitting with Spencer and Talia. After I came home, David and Marcy Levinson picked up Penny and me and we went to dinner at Yummy Bowl located at 1908 Sheridan Road in Highland Park.

WEDNESDAY, SEPTEMBER 25, 2019—DINNER WITH DILIGS

We drove to our next-door neighbor's other Northbrook home located at 3610 Palm Canyon Drive in Charlemagne. Raul and Anne Dilig invited Penny and me to dinner and drove us to San Soo Kab San Korean BBQ & Sushi located at 7901 Golf Road in Niles. The Dilig's son, Kyle, joined us. Raul kept on ordering different appetizers like seafood pancakes, shrimp cooked at the table, soup, various vegetables. Raul cooked pork bellies on a grill at the table. Raul also ordered a whole corvina fish including the head for me. There was so much food but our table seemed to eat a lot. We left at 8:15 p.m.

After dinner we drove to Tous les Jours located at 1685 Milwaukee Avenue in Glenview and picked up two different desserts, then went back to the Dilig's home for dessert and coffee.

FRIDAY, SEPTEMBER 27, 2019—WOMEN'S LUNCHEON

Penny went to a luncheon at Harriet Weintraub's home. Harriet was giving this lunch for some of her female friends. She made a Cowboy Cao salad and other goodies and Penny took a photo of the table and I included the food spread. I had a 1:00 p.m. physical therapy session at Just Be Fit with Marianne Vuckovich and a 4:00 p.m. appointment with Dr. Nikitow in Libertyville.

SUNDAY, SEPTEMBER 29, 2019—ROSH HASHANAH DINNER

At 5:00 p.m. Bennett, Marni, Danny and Brooke came to our home to have Rosh Hashanah dinner. Ronna and her family went to services so they weren't able to join us for dinner.

MONDAY, SEPTEMBER 30, 2019—DINNER AT THE COHANS

In the evening, we were invited to Todd and Carrie Cohans for a second night of Rosh Hashanah dinner in Buffalo Grove. Charles Schuster and Sharon Krivitzky were there along with Ronna, Ted, Talia and Spencer. Carrie's cousin Randi was also there and she is a good friend of Fran Meyer who is married to Scott Meyer, my former assistant editor of *Search*.

WEDNESDAY, OCTOBER 2, 2109—TED'S BIRTHDAY

Penny and I met Ronna, Ted, Talia and Spencer at Saranello's to celebrate Ted's 50th birthday.

THURSDAY, OCTOBER 3, 2019—DINNER WITH THE DILIGS

Penny and I have been talking about going to a Northbrook Coin Laundry for a long time so, we finally made it there to wash large rugs that have been sitting in the garage. The Diligs invited us to go to dinner at Siam's House on Milwaukee Avenue in Niles. Once again, Raul ordered all kinds of food. We had vegetable spring rolls in a delicious sauce, vegetable pad Thai, a whole red snapper with the head, beef curry sauce, a large egg pancake and other dishes too numerous to mention. The food was very good and the company was too.

MONDAY, OCTOBER 7, 2019— PHYSICAL THERAPY

At 1:00 p.m. I had a physical therapy session at Just Be Fit with Marianne Vuckovich. At 3:00 p.m. I picked up Spencer from Prairie School and took Talia and Spencer to the orthodontist for a 4:20 p.m. appointment.

WEDNESDAY, OCTOBER 9, 2019—BREAK THE FAST

Penny and I went to the 12:00 p.m. family Yom Kippur service at B'Nai Jehoshua Beth Elohim in Deerfield. After the service we drove home, then went to Ronna's around 2:30 p.m. because she was at a temple service wouldn't be home until 5:30. We were able to turn on the oven to cook the kugel. Bennett, Marni, Danny and Brooke arrived around 5:45 p.m. and we had a "Break the Fast" meal. Ted came home at 7:00 p.m. after attending the evening yizkor and final service.

THURSDAY, OCTOBER 10, 2019—JUDY ROBERTS CONCERT

Penny and I went to the Skokie Theater and met Remey and Julie Rubin there for a 7:30 p.m. concert to see and hear Judy Roberts and her husband Greg Fishman. Judy played the piano and sang and Greg played the saxophone, clarinet and flute. It is always a great concert with these two performers. We sat in the first row of the raised level and caught up on news.

SATURDAY, OCTOBER 12, 2019—RAY AND CAROLE DINNER

At 5:30 p.m. we met Ray Pershing and Carole Einhorn for dinner at the Happ Inn and Grill in Northfield. After dinner, we went to our home and had dessert.

SUNDAY, OCTOBER 13, 2019—DINNER WITH THE SCHESNOLS

Talia had makeup done as a test for her Bat Mitzvah and Ronna took a photo of her. She looked so grown up in the photo. For dinner this evening, Jeffrey and

Susan Schesnol were in town visiting their daughter and grandchildren so we had dinner with them at Players Restaurant in Highland Park.

MONDAY, OCTOBER 14, 2019—BLOOD TESTS AND THERAPY

At 9:00 a.m. Penny and I went to Northwestern Medicine at 350 S. Waukegan Road in Deerfield to have our blood tests in anticipation of our annual physical exam on Wednesday October 16th. At 12:00 p.m. I had a physical therapy session at Just Be Fit with Marianne Vuckovich.

WEDNESDAY, OCTOBER 16, 2019—PHYSICAL EXAMS

At 10:00 a.m. Penny had her annual physical exam with Dr. Dan Goldstein at Deerfield's Northwestern Medicine office. My annual physical exam was scheduled for 10:45 a.m. with Dr. Goldstein. Arnie Grauer picked me up and we ate lunch at Panera Bread in Northbrook.

THURSDAY, OCTOBER 17, 2019—RONNA GOES TO LOS ANGELES

Ronna visited Los Angeles and was able to go to the filming of *Will & Grace* and to see some of the people she worked with on the show. She sent us two photos taken during the filming. The first photo was with her and Megan Mullaly and Nick Opperman and the other was with the cast of *Will & Grace*. At 1:00 p.m. I had a physical therapy session at Just Be Fit with Marianne Vuckovich.

SATURDAY, OCTOBER 19, 2019—CHARLES SHUSTER RE-HAB VISIT

Ronna flew back from Los Angeles. Charles Shuster had an episode after our Rosh Hashanah dinner on September 30th at the Cohan's home and ended up in the hospital emergency room. We visited him and Sharon Krivitzky at the Lincolnshire rehab facility, Radford Green. Charles is doing great. They thought he had a minor stroke but fully recovered. We brought him Russian tea biscuits as a treat. After seeing Charles and Sharon, Penny and I ate dinner at Lincolnshire's Bonta Pizzeria.

OCTOBER 20, 2019—MARNI'S BIRTHDAY AND ELAWA FARM

Today is Marni Spencer's 37th birthday and Penny and I texted her birthday wishes. After breakfast, we drove to Elawa Farm in Lake Forest and walked in the savannah area-walking path for about forty-five minutes.

MONDAY, OCTOBER 21, 2019—BENNETT AND MARNI'S 19TH ANNIVERSARY

Penny and I called them to offer our good wishes on this special day.

FRIDAY, OCTOBER 25, 2019—BELINKYS IN CHICAGO

Herb and Lynda Belinky flew into Chicago from Los Angeles and are staying with Ted and Ronna. The leaves were falling off our front crab-apple tree.

SATURDAY, OCTOBER 26, 2019—DANNY'S SLEEPOVER

Bennett and Marni held their annual Halloween party this evening so our grandson Danny slept overnight at our home. Danny had plans with a friend but his plans fell through so he decided to stay at our home instead. Brooke had an overnight sleepover at a friend's house.

At 7:00 p.m. Penny and I picked up Danny at the School of Rock in Highwood because he had a band rehearsal there for his January 24, 2010 Beatles concert. We ordered a Domino's pizza near door to the School and brought it back to our home and ate dinner together. After dinner, Danny played some guitar songs for us. He also brought a Rolling Stones Monopoly game and we played until 11:00 p.m. Danny beat Penny and me and we had a great time. The Spencer's party was a success and Bennett texted a photo of their costume.

SUNDAY, OCTOBER 27, 2019—DANNY PICK UP
For breakfast, I made waffles for Danny, then Bennett and Marni picked up Danny from our home.

MONDAY, OCTOBER 28, 2019—HERB'S BIRTHDAY DINNER
At 3:00 p.m. I picked up Spencer from school. I drove Herb and Lynda Belinky to Mi Mexico on Milwaukee Avenue in Buffalo Grove and we met Ronna at the restaurant. Ted was out of town. At the end of dinner, the restaurant staff brought out a flaming dessert and sang Happy Birthday in Spanish and English to Herb and gave him a Mexican sombrero to wear and keep.

TUESDAY, OCTOBER 29, 2019—BROOKE'S CONCERT
Penny and I drove to Alan Shepard Middle School in Deerfield to see and hear Brooke's 7:00 p.m. orchestra concert. Brooke plays the cello and we enjoyed the concert.

THURSDAY, OCTOBER 31, 2019—FIRST SNOWSTORM
We couldn't believe it snowed on Halloween because it usually rains and is damp. It was a huge surprise to see snow on our front tree. Of course, I took photos and incorporated them into my slide show.

FRIDAY, NOVEMBER 1, 2019—MICKEY HOFFMAN
After breakfast, Penny and I decided to drive to Northbrook Court and started walking inside. After walking for a little while, Penny was a little behind me. I heard a voice and I thought some man was trying to ask Penny for money so I didn't pay any attention or even turn around to look. It was Mickey Hoffman talking to Penny. He noticed us walking and we had a great conversation and got caught up on what he's been doing. Someone took a photo of us and I included it in my show. At 11:30 a.m. Penny drove to M Henry restaurant located at 5707 N. Clark Street in Chicago and ate lunch with Jill Cole.

SUNDAY, NOVEMBER 3, 2019— JAY AND HARRIET DINNER
After breakfast, I did a dry run of putting a suitcase in the back of the Subaru and testing how two suitcases would fit in the back for our December Arizona trip. At 5:45 p.m. Penny and I picked up Jay and Harriet Weintraub and we drove to D'Agostino's Pizzeria in Glenview and ate dinner together.

THURSDAY, NOVEMBER 7, 2019—*LINDIWE* MUSICAL
Penny and I left at 5:00 p.m. and drove to Chicago and parked in a garage about three blocks from The Steppenwolf Theater located at 1650 N. Halsted Street to see the 7:30 p.m. performance of the musical *Lindiwe*. Before the play we had a snack and coffee at the restaurant inside the theater. The play featured Ladysmith Black Mamboso throughout. We enjoyed the play because we love Ladysmith. Seated in back of the theater was the playwright and Director Eric Simonson with several staff taking notes and I took a photo of them.

FRIDAY, NOVEMBER 8, 2019—DR. NIKITOW AND SHABBAT

Penny and I had lunch with Ronna and I had a 3:00 p.m. appointment with Dr. Nikitow in Libertyville. Penny and I attended a Shabbat service at BJBE where it was Artists-In-Residence Weekend featuring Feliza Bascara-Zohar and Rabbi Or Zohar from Israel. Ronna, Ted, Talia and Spencer also attended. My mother's name was mentioned during the memorial part of the service.

SUNDAY, NOVEMBER 10, 2019—FRAN AND SCOTT MEYER

At 5:30 p.m. Penny and I finally had a chance to make dinner plans with Scott and Fran Meyer at Montira Thai and Sushi restaurant located at1845 Tower Drive in Glenview. For ten years, Scott and I worked on *Search, The International Journal on Jewish Genealogy* and we lost touch. It was through Carrie Cohan's cousin Randi that we were able to re-connect. Randi is friends with Fran Meyer.

WEDESDAY, NOVEMBER 13, 2019—TALIA'S CONCERT

At 10:00 a.m. I had a physical therapy session at Just Be Fit with Marianne Vuckovich. Penny picked up Spencer at 3:00 p.m. and took him to Hebrew School. I picked up Talia at BJBE and took her to Twin Groves Middle School located at 2600 N. Buffalo Grove Road by 6:15 p.m. for her 7:00 p.m. orchestra concert. Talia plays the cello in the orchestra.

SUNDAY, NOVEMBER 17, 2019—THE MAGIT'S DINNER

At 5:20 p.m. I picked up Al and Ellen Magit at their new Northbrook condo located at 1125 Lake Cook Road and I drove us to dinner at El Traditional Mexican Restaurant & Cantina located at 649 Lake Cook Road in Deerfield. After dinner, we drove back to their apartment and they gave us a tour. After dinner, I watched the Chicago Bears play the LA Rams on NBC.

MONDAY, NOVEMBER 18, 2019—MARIANNE PHOTO

I wanted to remember my kinesiotherapist, Marianne Vuckovich, so we had two selfie photos taken before I left for Arizona. For dinner David and Marcy Levinson picked us up and we went to Yummy Bowl in Highland Park. Jill Cole was grandchild sitting nearby so she was able to join us for Chinese food at Yummy Bowl.

THURSDAY, NOVEMBER 21, 2019—THE BELINKYS IN MEXICO
SITTING FOR TALIA AND SPENCER

Ronna and Ted flew to Cancun, Mexico for a mini vacation so Penny and I were at the Belinky home at 6:00 a.m. before they left on their trip. I took Spencer to Prairie Elementary School at 8:15 a.m.

FRIDAY, NOVEMBER 22, 2019—TALIA AND SPENCER

I took Spencer to school a little early today at 7:20 a.m. because he had choir rehearsal.

SATURDAY, NOVEMBER 23, 2019—TALIA AND SPENCER

I drove Talia to Highland Park and the Original Pancake House to meet up with some friends because she was going to a B'Nai Mitzvah in Chicago and sleeping over a friend's house. For dinner, we ordered sushi at AO Sushi located at 1178 McHenry Road in Buffalo Grove for Spencer, Penny and me. Talia was at a B'Nai Mitzvah and had a sleepover at her friend's house.

SUNDAY, NOVEMBER 24, 2019—TALIA IN HIGHLAND PARK
At 11:30 a.m. I drove to Highland Park and picked up Talia at her friend Rennie's house after her sleepover.

WEDNESDAY, NOVEMBER 27, 2019—LEONARD'S BAKERY
At 6:55 a.m. I went to Leonard's Bakery and bought four-day-old challahs so Penny could make her mother's stuffing for Thanksgiving. Right before Thanksgiving, there was no school so Ronna brought Spencer to our home and Penny and I watched him the entire day. We went to lunch at Calzone & Macaroni Co. located at 260 Hawthorn Village Commons in Vernon Hills.

THURSDAY, NOVEMBER 28, 2019—FAMILY THANKSGIVING
I helped Penny make stuffing and we brought it to Bennett and Marni's home for a very nice and delicious Thanksgiving Day buffet meal. For appetizers, Marni prepared a variety of different foods including carrots and dip, stuffed mushrooms, cranberry goat cheese with crackers, vegetable dips and hummus. Ronna made her famous baked Brie and Granny Smith Apple platter. The buffet was set up in the kitchen with turkey, roasted Brussels sprouts, cooked carrots, cranberry sauce, a corn scuffle and Penny's stuffing. For dessert there was pumpkin pie and an apple pie. Marni also made chocolate covered strawberries and chocolate apricots. After dinner we opened Chanukah gifts.

SATURDAY, NOVEMBER 30, 2019—TWO HAIRCUT DAY
Before our road trip to Arizona, I had a 10:00 a.m. haircut appointment with Otto Bodner at the Hyatt Regency Chicago. After dropping me off at the hotel, Penny took the car and drove to J Gordon Design for her 11:00 a.m. appointment with Cheryl. We were invited for dinner at Todd and Carrie Cohan's home for an after-Thanksgiving dinner.

MONDAY, DECEMBER 2, 2019—SENT BOX TO ARIZONA
After breakfast I brought the cardboard box to UPS Customer Center and had it sent to the Avers. On the way back, I stopped at Sunset Foods to buy egg and tuna salad for sandwiches for our road trip to Arizona, and then I packed the car.

CHAPTER THIRTY- FOUR
Road Trip To Arizona

TUESDAY, DECEMBER 3, 2019—DRIVING TO SCOTTSDALE

Penny and I backed out of the driveway at 6:12 a.m. headed to St. Louis on I-294 the Tri-State. Our first stop was at 7:38 a.m. at the Limestone rest area in Coal City or 71.8 miles from Northbrook. Our second bathroom break stop was at Funks Grove at 9:11 a.m. and 113.1 miles from Northbrook. We stopped a third time at 10:35 a.m. at Coalfield Rest Area 240.6 miles from Northbrook.

We approached St. Louis at 12:00 noon and 300 miles from home and stopped for gas at 12:07 p.m. at Webster Groves BP just past downtown St. Louis. The mileage was 316.9 miles from home. Penny and I took another bathroom break at 12:50 p.m. and 362.1 miles from Northbrook. After our bathroom break, Penny took over driving and drove for about two hours. Our next stop was at 3:07 p.m. at Exit 88 on I-44 and the mileage was 507.0 and I took over driving.

We arrived at the Hampton Inn Miami at 5:02 p.m. and 614.7 miles from Northbrook. The hotel is located at 115 Deacon Turner Road Miami, Oklahoma. Upon arrival, I checked in, we unpacked a bit and went to dinner at Zack's Café in Miami. Penny and I were tired so we went to sleep at 8:30 p.m.

WEDNESDAY, DECEMBER 4, 2019—MIAMI, OKLAHOMA
TO SANTA ROSA, NEW MEXICO

Penny and I awakened at 5:22 a.m. got dressed and ate breakfast at 6:00 a.m. After packing our overnight suitcases, we left Miami at 7:02 a.m. at 6:20.7 miles from Northbrook. We stopped at 9:02 a.m. and 755 miles from Northbrook at a Loves gas station to go to the bathroom. Penny took over driving and we stopped again at 9:05 a.m. in Oklahoma City, 178 miles from Miami.

We stopped again at 10:45 a.m. and 236.7 miles from Miami and 857.5 miles from Northbrook for a bathroom break and to buy gas. We left Loves at 10:58 a.m. heading west. Our next stop at a Loves gas station was at 11:55 a.m. and 297.1 miles from Miami and 917.9 miles from Northbrook. We decided to park our car at a Super 8 motel's parking lot and eat lunch.

After lunch, we left at 12:20 p.m. and 918.3 miles from Northbrook and stopped at 1:35 p.m., 384.2 miles from Miami and 1,005 miles from Northbrook. At 1:50 p.m. we started back on the road and Penny took over driving until we got to a rest stop near Amarillo in Alan Reed, Texas. The mileage was 1,062.5 miles from Northbrook and 446.7 miles from Miami, Oklahoma. We stopped again in Amarillo and went to a very dirty bathroom in a Speedway gas station and got a Dairy Queen at 2:55 p.m. in Amarillo, Texas. We left Amarillo and the Dairy Queen at 3:10 p.m. We stopped for gas at 3:45 p.m., 479.4 miles from Miami and 1,100.2 miles from Northbrook. As we entered New Mexico, the clouds got very dark and it started to drizzle. We reached Santa Rosa, New Mexico and the Best Western motel located at 2491 Historic Route 66 in Santa Rosa.

At 4:35 p.m., 610.9 miles from Miami and 1,231.7 miles from Northbrook. Jay Weintraub recommended The Best Western motel over the Hampton Inn because it had recently been renovated and updated so we decided to take his advice. The motel was very nice and our room was spacious. We were able to park directly outside of our room 102 and unloading our overnight suitcases was very easy. The cost of the room was $99.98 plus $13.00 tax for a total $112.98. The registration person recommended eating at the Santa Fe Grille but the dinner was not very good. Penny ordered spaghetti with marinara sauce and I ordered veggie tacos but forgot to tell them to leave out the peppers and it was too hot and virtually inedible. After dinner we drove back to the motel and went to sleep.

THURSDAY, DECEMBER 5, 2019—SCOTTSDALE

Penny and I awaken at 5:18 a.m., got dressed, and walked across the parking lot to breakfast at 6:00 a.m. After breakfast, we packed the car and left Santa Rosa, New Mexico at 6:47 a.m. We stopped for gas at a Loves at 8:35 a.m. and 126.0 miles from Santa Rosa and 1,360.5 miles from Northbrook. Penny took over driving at 8:50 a.m. and stopped driving at 10:42 a.m., near Gallup, New Mexico, 251.9 miles from Santa Rosa and 1,486.4 miles from Northbrook.

We entered Arizona at 11:46 a.m. 308.3 miles from Santa Rosa and 1,542.8 miles from Northbrook and took a bathroom break. We reached Winslow, Arizona and stopped at La Posada at 12:52 p.m. 379.3 miles from Santa Rosa and a total of 1,613.9 miles from Northbrook. We had a very delicious lunch in the Turquoise Room at La Posada. Penny ordered a black bean and corn soup and a Caesar Salad and I ordered a turkey and Swiss cheese sandwich on toasted sourdough bread and a garden salad. We had bread pudding for dessert.

After lunch at 2:10 p.m. we left Winslow headed to Payson and the final leg of our journey. We arrived in Payson at 4:10 p.m. 467.3 miles from Santa Rosa and 1,701.8 miles from Northbrook. In Payson, we stopped at a Walmart, went to the bathroom and Penny bought a few items. We got gas in Payson and left for Scottsdale at 4:25 p.m. arriving at our condo at 11333 N. 92nd Street Unit. 1031, Building 4 at 5:25 p.m. 468.6 miles from Santa Rosa and 1,774.4 miles from Northbrook. It was a long ride.

SATURDAY, DECEMBER 7, 2019—CMU AND CHINESE FOOD

The *Arizona Republic* started delivery today. After breakfast I went to Cold Beers & Cheeseburgers on Shea just east of the 101 and at 10:50 a.m. was the first one in the place to watch the Mid-American Championship Game between Central Michigan University and Miami University. Dale Wernette and his wife Karen, Jason from Watervliet, Michigan and Sam were the only ones watching the game besides me. I left at half time. The final score was Miami Redhawks 26 and Central Michigan Chippewas 21. I came back to the condo and ate lunch. Penny and I continued to unpack and settling in.

For dinner, Jan was dog sitting at a condo off of 90th Street so in the late afternoon we ordered Chinese food from Chef J at 9030 E. Via Linda in Scottsdale. Then we picked up Rich and went to Chef J to get our order and took it to the condo where Jan was dog sitting and ate dinner there. I took a photo of Penny with the dog Barkley sitting on her lap.

MONDAY, DECEMBER 9—EFFICIENCY MECHANICAL

Around 9:15 a.m. Matt and Javier from Efficiency Mechanical came to be our condo to inspect heat pump and air conditioning and put in a new filter. We met Jeffrey and Susan Schesnol for dinner at Nori Sushi & Asian Dining in the Desert Ridge Shopping Center Phoenix. We ordered a variety of sushi rolls that were on the Happy Hour menu and split the order.

TUESDAY, DECEMBER 10, 2019—IRWIN FURNITURE

Penny and I ate breakfast at US Egg in Scottsdale. I had my usual protein pancake and Penny ordered scrambled eggs, well-done hash brown potatoes and crisp bacon. After breakfast, we went back to the condo and then I drove to Irwin Furniture Restoration at 2922 N. 35th Avenue in Phoenix and brought in our three sofa pillows to get restuffed with new foam.

WEDNESDAY, DECEMBER 11, 2019—PENNY AND DOCTOR

Penny had a 10:30 a.m. doctor appointment with Dr. Abby Roberts. After the appointment we went to CVS Pharmacy to pick up a prescription for Nystatin Acetonide ointment. We also went to Costco and took a twenty-minute walk in our neighborhood.

FRIDAY, DECEMBER 13, 2019—PICKED UP RESTUFFED SOFA CUSHIONS AND CONDO WATER LEAK

Before breakfast, we got a call from Irwin's Furniture Restoration saying our sofa cushions were ready to be picked up. So, Penny and I drove back to 35th Avenue and picked up our re-stuffed sofa cushions. After lunch, we took a twenty-five-minute walk in the neighborhood.

Penny noticed water dripping from the ceiling in the master bathroom and some drywall that was bubbling near the showerhead. She put a bucket on the side of the bathtub to catch the water and also noticed water on the floor so she put down a towel to absorb the water. We immediately called our upstairs neighbor Hillary who said her bathtub was having a drainage problem and perhaps that was the cause of the leak. She called the condo's owner and was waiting for the owner to get back to her.

In the evening for dinner, we picked up Rich and Jan Aver and I drove to the Cien Agaves Tacos & Tequila next to the Harkins 101 Theater. Dan and Annie Murphy were already waiting for us in a large booth. I ordered grilled maxi mahi tacos with refried beans and rice and Penny and Jan split shrimp fajitas with guacamole, beans and sour cream. Rich had cheese enchiladas. The food was very good and we might go back there. It was the first time we saw the Murphys since our return to Arizona.

SUNDAY, DECEMBER 15, 2019—PANCAKES AND DA BEARS

I made blueberry pancakes for breakfast. At 11:00 a.m. the Chicago Bears played the Green Bay Packers and I watched part of the game but the Bears lost. We watched several episodes of The Twilight Zone and CBS Sunday Morning.

MONDAY, DECEMBER 16—CONDO HOLIDAY PARTY

Jay and Harriet Weintraub left Northbrook for Scottsdale. Penny and I bought some brownies at Fry's for the Christmas Party that evening. From 5:30 p.m. to

8:15 p.m. Penny and I were at the Christmas Party at the Mission de los Arroyos Club house. We sat with Mary Ellen and her invited guest, Margie and another woman.

WEDNESDAY, DECEMBER 18, 2019—LEAK FIXED

Penny went to yoga at 11:00 a.m. Plumber Curtis Stratman from Affordable Plumbing came to our condo to fix the leak from the upstairs condo. First, he put a plastic drop cloth down and taped it to the wall to catch any debris falling from the ceiling. He went upstairs and saw that the tub spout was leaking and that could be the cause of the water leak. Then he cut a square out of the drywall in the ceiling to see where the water was dripping. I went upstairs to Hilliary Ryan's unit and ran the water so Curtis could see the dripping. After cutting out a square from the ceiling, Curtis removed the water-damaged drywall. He went upstairs and replaced the tub spout with a new one and cleaned up our master bathroom.

Jay and Harriet Weintraub arrived in Scottsdale around 4:00 p.m. At 6:30 p.m. we picked up Jan and Rich Aver and met Jay and Harriet and Gerri and Michael Menn at Chompie's for dinner.

FRIDAY, DECEMBER 20, 2019—THREE SPOTS FISHING

After breakfast, I went fishing at three different locations. I started out at Chaparral Lake and didn't get a bite. Then I drove to McCormick Ranch Lake and went to my favorite spot and still not a bite. Then I drove to Evelyn Hallman Pond in Tempe for my third location and didn't get a bite. There was not a person fishing in either location.

SATURDAY, DECEMBER 21, 2019—NEW MEXICO BOWL

Today is Linda's 76th birthday. Penny and I called her in New York and left a message to wish her a happy birthday. I watched a little of the Central Michigan University playing the San Diego State University in the New Mexico Bowl in Albuquerque. Central Michigan lost 48 to 11.

I picked up Jan and Rich and we drove to Dan and Annie Murphy's new home. Jay and Harriet had already arrived by the time we got there. We celebrated Chanukah with the "Great Eight." The women were wearing the same tops so I took a photo of them. For appetizers, Annie had cheese and crackers, nuts and whitefish salad she bought at Chompie's. Harriet made brisket and I bought two kinds of turkey at Fry's, oven roasted and honey maple. Jan made potato latkes, egg salad and applesauce. Penny made brownies and Annie provided cookies and ruggala for dessert. I took some photos of Penny with Deeter, the Doberman. After dropping off Jan and Rich Aver, we got back to our condo around 11:00 p.m.

SUNDAY, DECEMBER 22, 2019—NEIGHBORHOOD WALK

Penny and I woke up at 9:02 a.m. and ate breakfast at 10:00 a.m. After breakfast we walked for thirty minutes. After lunch we watched *CBS Sunday Morning* I had previously recorded. We walked in the neighborhood for 30 minutes. At 6:15 pm. I watched a little of the Chicago Bears vs. Kansas City and gave up after they were losing.

MONDAY, DECEMBER 23, 2019—POWER WASHING

We woke up at 7:03 a.m. and after breakfast I went to Einstein Bagels and

Fry's. We walked for forty minutes down Cholla for 1.25 miles. Advanced Painting started power washing Building 4 so I started taking photos and videos of the process.

TUESDAY, DECEMBER 24, 2019—DRYWALL REPAIRED

Penny and I got up at 7:30 a.m. took showers and ate breakfast. At 10:10 a.m. Sabah and Amir Sasan came to our condo to repair the drywall in our master bathroom. First, a plastic sheet was put up on the wall to catch all of the dust and debris. Then they scraped the spots and filled in the spots that had water damage.

They put small pieces of two by fours in the hole and cut a piece of drywall to fit the hole. Then they finished repairing by caulking and putting drywall joint compound into the wall. Texture was then added to blend into the ceiling. Sabah and Amir Sasan completed the work at 12:00 noon. They will be back to paint the ceiling after it dries. I picked up Jan Aver around 6:15 pm. and we drove to Jay and Harriet Weintraub's condo where we saw the Weintraub's daughter, Mandy, son-in-law Paul and their children, Charlie and Emma who had driven in from Chicago a day before. Dan and Annie Murphy and Gerri and Michael Menn were there. Harriet put out dessert and we had a nice chat. Rich was dog sitting and not there.

WEDNESDAY, DECEMBER 25, 2019—CHINESE FOOD

At 11:00 a.m. Rich ordered Chinese food at Canton Dragon in Scottsdale. Rich Aver, Michael Genender and I picked up the food at 6:45 p.m. and went back to the Avers condo to eat the Chinese food. Jeffrey, Susan and Jacqui Schesnol had already arrived. Penny and I talked to Jacqui about watching her in action during a trial and she told us she'd be doing a preliminary hearing the next day. We told Jacqui we would be there to observe and she gave us the instructions of where to park and the details of where to see her.

THURSDAY, DECEMBER 26, 2019—FEDERAL COURTHOUSE

After breakfast at 10:15 a.m., Penny and I drove to Phoenix and parked on the third floor in the garage across from the Sandra Day O'Connor United States Court House to see Jacqui Schesnol at a hearing in room 304 for Judge Deborah Fine. After going through security, we took the elevator to the third floor and walked into courtroom 304 and waited until about 11:20 when Jacqui appeared. Jacqui came over to where we were seated and said hello. The judge came into the courtroom at 11:30 and Jacqui went into action. Unfortunately, the hearing had to be on recess until 1:15 p.m. so Penny and I left. We drove to Pita Jungle located at 5505 N. 7th Street and ate lunch. Upon returning to our condo, I ordered a stainless-steel kitchen sink grid for the bottom of our kitchen sink from Amazon.

SUNDAY, DECEMBER 29, 2019—PENNY GOES TO HIGH TEA

For breakfast, I had a toasted bagel and two fried eggs while Penny had cereal. After breakfast I tried to turn on the television but no signal again. I had unplugged the power cable to the Blu-Ray DVD player. Still no signal so I watched some of the Green Bay vs. Detroit football game on the bedroom television. Jeffrey Schesnol dropped off his wife Susan at Jan and Rich Aver's condo. I ate a peanut butter and banana sandwich for lunch.

At 2:00 p.m. Jan Aver and Susan picked up Penny drove to The Phoenician for High Tea where Jacqui Schesnol met them. Meanwhile, Jeffrey and Rich picked me up and we drove to the 92ⁿᵈ Street Café. While eating we watched the Arizona Cardinals vs. Los Angeles Rams football game and a few other football games. The women were through around 4:30 p.m. and we left the 92ⁿᵈ Café round 4:45 p.m. and Jeffrey drove me back to our condo. Penny arrived home about twenty-five minutes after me. Penny sautéed mushrooms and made spaghetti for dinner and I watched most of the San Francisco 49ers vs. the Seattle Seahawks football game on my iPad because our television still did not have a signal.

MONDAY, DECEMBER 30, 2019—CEILING REPAIR

At 3:00 p.m., Sasan arrived to paint the master bathroom ceiling that was repaired on December 24. He left at 5:15 p.m. with the painting done and drying.

TUESDAY, DECEMBER 31, 2019—NEW YEAR'S PARTY

After breakfast I went to Chompie's to buy bagels for tomorrow's breakfast. At 7:45 p.m. I picked up Jan Aver and we drove to Jeffrey and Susan Schesnols for our annual New Year's party. We arrived around 8:15 p.m. and unloaded the turkey meatballs Penny made the day before and the cheesecake dessert we bought at Costco. Rich Aver was dog sitting in north Scottsdale so he drove separately to the party. Phil Voyce, Jacqui Schesnol's friend was also at the party. There were many varieties of hors oeuvres including Jan Aver's cheese ball, Jacqui Schesnol's baked cream cheese, mini quiches, spinach dip, carrots, pita chips and crackers, turkey meatballs, nuts and ginger cookies. We took lots of photos including the annual selfies of ourselves.

We played the "Saran Wrap" game before midnight. This year, Penny and Jan Aver put together a ball full of "Saran Wrap" with various prizes inside. The idea was to unwrap as much of the ball until the next person rolled doubles with the dice. After midnight, we played the dictionary game and left the Schesnols around 1:30 a.m. We dropped off Jan at her place and finally got in bed around 2:50 a.m.

A FINAL COMMENT

It took me fifteen years to write, edit and publish my memoir/journal but I finally did it. I hope you've enjoyed reading about my interesting life so far, and hopefully the best is yet to come.

A POST SCRIPT

This part memoir/part journal concludes at the end of 2019. Unexpectedly a deadly COVID-19 pandemic occurred in 2020. That year and everything that happened to us may possibly be written in another book.

PHOTO ALBUM

68 Morrison Street Struthers, Ohio—My First Home

1942-Mom and Dad and 1942 Dad and Alan
Struthers, Ohio

1944-Alan Brooklyn, NY

1945—Summer--Sister Linda and Alan
Loch Sheldrake, New York

1946—Alan (Almost 6 Years Old)

1946—Dad and Mom—Brooklyn-
Dad back From World War II

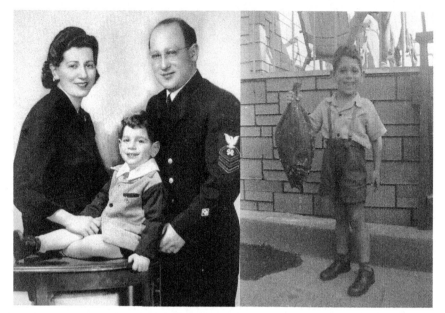

1943---Mom and Dad in Navy uniform just before leaving for Guam during WWII.

1945---Alan with flounder caught cousin Shelly in Sheepshead Bay

1945---Alan, Brooklyn, New York.

1950---Alan, northside pool Youngstown, Ohio

1950—store with original sign located at 2633 Market Street Youngstown, Ohio

1952---Expanded store with new sign and 1952 Nash Rambler station wagon

October 29, 1939—Dad and Mom's
Wedding in Brooklyn, New York

1946—Mom and Dad
right after returning from WWII
stationed in Guam

1976—Mom and Dad
Youngstown, Ohio

1979—Mom and Dad
Youngtown, Ohio

1963--Alan at the controls of WBBW-AM 1240 on
the dial in Youngstown, Ohio

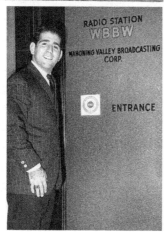

Summer 1963--WBBW was a rock n' roll
radio station and Alan Gerald was an all-night
disc jockey, calling himself WBBW's
"Night Watchman."

In the fall of 1963, WBBW radio switched
to beautiful music

ALAN G. SPENCER

1965—Alan (center) performing as Speedy Valenti in the Youngstown Playhouse
production of *Wonderful Town*---Youngstown, Ohio—

Alan with New York
Director Ella Gerber
dressed as a 65-year old
garbage man in *Wonderful
Town*

1965—Alan performing in a scene from the
production of *Wonderful Town* at the Youngstown
Playhouse, Youngstown, Ohio

510

December 1967—Alan and
Penny Camberg
during our engagement
photo taken by
Lake Michigan

1970—Alan and Penny Spencer in their W. Briar Place apartment, Chicago

1975—Alan, Penny, Bennett & Ronna   1984---Alan, Bennett, Penny and
Chicago, Illinois   Ronna—Cleveland, Ohio

1982—Alan, Ronna, Penny and Bennett Spencer—Northbrook, Illinois

1970—Alan Spencer with Hosts Bob Kennedy and Jenny Crimm
Interview about the film, *Turn Off Pollution*
on *Kennedy and Company* WLS-TV Channel 7 in Chicago

1972—Producer Alan Spencer, Albert Weisman and host Bob Hale
Sunday In Chicago—WMAQ-TV—Channel 5 NBC in Chicago—
Interview about the documentary *Old Glory Marching Society*

1977—Producer Alan Spencer, Cameraman Larry Bloodworth, Director Guy Guilbert and actress Terri Kreeger for Chicagoland Job Mart TV commercial produced by The Spot Shop in Chicago, Illinois

1978—Producer Alan Spencer and Music Director Guy Guilbert mixing an original musical commercial, created and orchestrated by Guy. Produced by The Spot Shop

December 19, 1978—"WMAQ Is Going To Make Me Rich"
TV commercial—Talent Gil Pearson--Produced by The Spot Shop

February 4, 1980—Producer Alan Spencer, Director Guy Guilbert and
Cinematographer Andy Costikyan—Headlite TV commercial
produced by The Spot Shop in Chicago, Illinois

1972—Alan editing 16mm film on his KEM editing machine

1979—Director Guy Guilbert and Producer Alan Spencer working on a
Sportmart television commercial

Saturday, May 25, 1985—Bennett's Bar Mitzvah-Temple Jeremiah Northfield, IL
Ronna, Penny, Alan and Bennet

Saturday, May 28, 1988— Ronna's Bat Mitzvah Temple Jeremiah Northfield
Ronna, Bennett, Penny and Alan

August 22, 2008—Lake Galena—Largest Walleye Alan Ever Caught

July 21, 2012—Silver Lake, Wisconsin—Alan caught al 27" northern pike

Friday, August 1, 2014—Chesapeake Bay fishing for rockfish
Left to right: Arnie Grauer, Norman Lockshin, Alan Spencer and Ben Lockshin

Friday, July 28, 2017—Chesapeake Bay fishing for rockfish
Left to right: Steve Exelbert, Bennett Spencer, Norman Lockshin and
Ben Lockshin

March 31, 1973—Penny and Alan Spencer in Chicago

March 23, 2014—Penny and Alan Spencer at a Tucson, Arizona wedding

Family Photograph—Thanksgiving 2018
Seated: Brooke Spencer and Spencer Belinky
Kneeling: Danny Spencer, Penny and Alan Spencer & Talia Belinky (next to Alan)
Back Row: Bennett and Marni Spencer, Ted and Ronna Belinky

A B O U T   T H E   A U T H O R

Alan G. Spencer has been an elementary teacher, radio announcer, filmmaker, radio and television commercial producer, genealogist, founder and editor of *Search: International Journal for Researchers of Jewish Genealogy*, has authored and edited chapters two and three of *The Encyclopedia of Jewish Genealogy* and was an event and entertainment producer for corporations and associations. Alan is retired after thirty-six years from his third career. Alan is an alumnus of Ohio University with a BS in Education degree and Central Michigan University with a Master's Degree in Elementary Education.

Alan lives with Penny, his wife of almost 53 years, dividing their time between a home in Northbrook, Illinois and a condo in Scottsdale, Arizona. Alan and Penny have two children, Bennett and his wife Marni and Ronna and her husband Ted. Alan and Penny have four grandchildren, Bennett's Danny and Brooke and Ronna's Talia and Spencer.

Made in the USA
Monee, IL
12 May 2021